The Copyright/Trademark Interface

Information Law Series (INFO)

VOLUME 44

Editor

Prof. P. Bernt Hugenholtz, Institute for Information Law, University of Amsterdam.

Objective & Readership

Publications in the Information Law Series focus on current legal issues of information law and are aimed at scholars, practitioners, and policy makers who are active in the rapidly expanding area of information law and policy.

Introduction & Contents

The advent of the information society has put the field of information law squarely on the map. Information law is the law relating to the production, marketing, distribution, and use of information goods and services. The field of information law therefore cuts across traditional legal boundaries, and encompasses a wide set of legal issues at the crossroads of intellectual property, media law, telecommunications law, freedom of expression, and right to privacy. Recent volumes in the Information Law Series deal with copyright enforcement on the Internet, interoperability among computer programs, harmonization of copyright at the European level, intellectual property and human rights, public broadcasting in Europe, the future of the public domain, conditional access in digital broadcasting, and the "three-step test" in copyright.

The titles published in this series are listed at the back of this volume.

The Copyright/Trademark Interface

How the Expansion of Trademark Protection
Is Stifling Cultural Creativity

Martin Senftleben

Wolters Kluwer

Published by:
Kluwer Law International B.V.
PO Box 316
2400 AH Alphen aan den Rijn
The Netherlands
E-mail: international-sales@wolterskluwer.com
Website: lrus.wolterskluwer.com

Sold and distributed by:
Wolters Kluwer Legal & Regulatory U.S.
7201 McKinney Circle
Frederick, MD 21704
United States of America
Email: customer.service@wolterskluwer.com

ISBN 978-94-035-2370-5

e-Book: ISBN 978-94-035-2371-2
web-PDF: ISBN 978-94-035-2372-9

To E.

Table of Contents

Preface and Acknowledgements

This book is the end point of a long journey that started in 2008 with my inaugural lecture 'The Cultural Imperative in Intellectual Property Law' at the VU University Amsterdam, the Netherlands, and subsequent publications on preconditions for the proper functioning of copyright law (Senftleben 2010a), the continuous expansion of trademark rights (2011b) and tools to prevent overprotection as a result of protection overlaps (2011c). Via the 'Study on Misappropriation of Signs' which I coordinated for WIPO (2012b), this research interest finally led to more specific publications on the tension between indefinitely renewable trademark rights and the need to preserve and cultivate the public domain of cultural expressions (2013a, 2013c, 2017b, 2018).

The journey took so long because I had a book in mind that would go beyond the intricacies of legal-doctrinal questions arising from overlapping copyright and trademark protection. I set out to develop a universal template for the prevention of problems and imbalances caused by protection overlaps in intellectual property law. From this perspective, the following analysis of the copyright/trademark interface is only one individual case study that serves the purpose of bringing overarching solution mechanisms to light. The discussion of this specific overlap scenario with the described broader ambition required the exploration of various roads and several detours before I finally found the right avenue leading to the completion of the book.

In addition, I aimed at a discussion of copyright/trademark overlaps that reflects a broader societal phenomenon, namely the continuous subordination of societal subsystems, including the field of literary and artistic production, to commercial commodification interests. Viewed through this lens, copyright and trademark law are of particular interest because they represent the field of literature and art on the one hand and the field of trade and commerce on the other. The clash of the two protection regimes can be perceived as a repercussion of societal tensions between cultural and commercial interests. Cumulative copyright and trademark protection for icons of contemporary mainstream culture, such as Mickey Mouse, and signs belonging to mankind's universal cultural heritage, such as the Mona Lisa, raises the question of whether our society lends sufficient weight to concerns about cultural follow-on innovation – an issue that can be studied from a comparative perspective when considering the far-reaching measures that are taken willingly to shield follow-on innovation in the (more important?) field of technology from potential corrosive effects of trademark protection.

It is for the reader to decide whether the following analysis yields an adequate general recipe for regulatory responses to protection overlaps in intellectual property law and a convincing answer to the dynamics between culture and commerce in society.

In any case, the long journey leading to this book would not have been possible without support from many peers who took the time to debate the questions and solutions I had in mind. I would like to thank all colleagues who commented on my plans, including Richard Arnold, Barton Beebe, Lionel Bently, Robert Brauneis, Irene Calboli, Vincenzo Di Cataldo, Margaret Chon, Tobias Cohen Jehoram, Jorge Contreras, Bill Cornish, Carys Craig, Jennifer Davis, Estelle Derclaye, Graeme Dinwoodie, Thomas Dreier, Rochelle Dreyfuss, Séverine Dusollier, Christine Farley, Susy Frankel, Jeanne Fromer, Dev Gangjee, Christophe Geiger, Charles Gielen, Jane Ginsburg, Jonathan Griffiths, Willem Grosheide, Michael Handler, Paul Heald, Laura Heymann, Marcus Höpperger, Bernt Hugenholtz, Justin Hughes, Robin Jacob, Sabine Jacques, Jan Kabel, Philipp von Kapff, Annette Kur, Marshall Leaffer, Xiuqin Lin, Glynn Lunney, Wee Loon Ng-Loy, Ansgar Ohly, Justyna Ożegalska-Trybalska, Sean Pager, Alexander Peukert, Antoon Quaedvlieg, Lisa Ramsey, Marco Ricolfi, Ole-Andreas Rognstad, Thomas Sambuc, Maximiliano Santa Cruz, Jens Schovsbo, Ilanah Simon Fhima, Jaap Spoor, Sybilla Stanisławska-Kloc, Katherine Strandburg, Haochen Sun, Madhavi Sunder, Anna Tischner, Elżbieta Traple, Rebecca Tushnet, Dirk Visser, Jacques de Werra, Tomas Westenbroek, Peter Yu and Łukasz Żelechowski.

I would also like to thank the organizers and participants of conferences and roundtables that offered me the opportunity to test ideas, including the 2009 Conference of the Trademark Law Institute 'Trademark Law and the Public Interest in Keeping Signs Available' held at the University of Leiden, the 2013 'Intellectual Property Scholars Roundtable' at Drake University, the 2017 Roundtable 'International Intellectual Property' at New York University, the 2016 Roundtable 'Social Science Approaches to Copyright Law' at the Goethe University Frankfurt, the 2017 Roundtable 'The Protection of Non-Traditional Marks: Critical Perspectives' at Singapore Management University, the 2018 Workshop 'Trademark Law – Work in Progress' at American University, the 2018 Seminar 'Intellectual Property Work in Progress' at the University College London, the 2019 Conference '3D

Trademarks and Other Non-Traditional Trademarks' at the University of Geneva, the 2019 Colloquium 'Limiting Trademark Rights in the Age of Character Merchandising and Cultural Heritage Grabbing' at the Jagiellonian University, and the 2019 Conference 'Limitations on Trademark Rights from Comparative and Interdisciplinary Perspectives' held at Hong Kong University.

My special thanks go to Annette Kur for in-depth discussions of my approach during our work on 'European Trade Mark Law – A Commentary' (Kur/Senftleben 2017), Graeme Dinwoodie, Dev Gangjee and the Oxford Intellectual Property Research Centre for a very inspiring research stay in 2014 and to Barton Beebe, Rochelle Dreyfuss, Jeanne Fromer, Katherine Standburg, the Engelberg Center on Innovation Law & Policy and my Hauser Program co-fellow Séverine Dusollier for many fruitful discussions of the topic during my sabbatical at NYU Law School in 2017.

Most of all, I would like to thank Stephanie Steinmetz for all patience and encouragement during all these years. Apart from advice on systems theory and cultural sociology, she offered endless support and inexhaustible interest in all thoughts and theories I developed over the years. She also did not hesitate to pose critical questions when I ended up in a meandering lane or simply got on the wrong track. Without her, my research would not have resulted in this book, nor would the writing periods have been as happy and meaningful as they actually were. Looking back, I guess I should apologize to her for lengthy monologues about carelessness in respect of cultural concerns in intellectual property law (and society).

I am very grateful for the excellent research assistance provided by Lotte Anemaet, Laurens Buijtelaar and Hein Scholtens, the patience and support which the editors, Christine Robben and Simon Bellamy, offered at Wolters Kluwer, and the diligent copy-editing carried out by Pritha Nirmalraj, Srinivasan R. and Stellamary A. at Newgen.

Finally, I want to mention the teams of *Stadscafé De Boterwaag* in The Hague and *Le Kiosque Saint-François* in Lausanne who master the art of creating a perfect mix of diffuse background noise, discreet jazz music and good coffee and tea to facilitate the writing process. Thanks so much!

The Hague, 14 October 2020
Martin Senftleben

List of Abbreviations

AMI	Tijdschrift voor auteurs-, media- en informatierecht
BC	Berne Convention for the Protection of Literary and Artistic Works of September 9, 1886, lastly revised at Paris on July 24, 1971, and amended on September 28, 1979
CDR	Council Regulation (EC) No. 6/2002 of 12 December 2001 on Community Designs (*OJ* 2002 L 3, p. 1)
CFR	Charter of Fundamental Rights of the European Union (*OJ* 2000 C 364, p. 1)
CJEU	Court of Justice of the European Union
CTMR 2009	Council Regulation (EC) No. 207/2009 of 26 February 2009 on the Community Trade Mark (codified version) (*OJ* 2009 L 78, p. 1)
DD	Directive 98/71/EC of the European Parliament and of the Council of 13 October 1998 on the Legal Protection of Designs (*OJ* 1998 L 289, p. 28)
DSMD/DSM Directive	Directive (EU) 2019/790 of the European Parliament and of the Council of 17 April 2019 on Copyright and Related Rights in the Digital Single Market and Amending Directives 96/9/EC and 2001/29/EC (*OJ* 2019 L 130, p. 92)
ECHR	European Convention on Human Rights
ECtHR	European Court of Human Rights
EFTA	European Free Trade Association
EIPR	European Intellectual Property Review
EU	European Union

EUIPO	European Union Intellectual Property Office (formerly known as OHIM)
EUTM	European Union Trade Mark
EUTMR	Regulation (EU) 2017/1001 of the European Parliament and of the Council of 14 June 2017 on the European Union Trade Mark (codification) (*OJ* 2017 L 154, p. 1)
F.2d	Federal Reporter, second series
F.3d	Federal Reporter, third series
F.Supp	Federal Report, supplement
GCEU	General Court of the European Union
GRUR	Gewerblicher Rechtsschutz und Urheberrecht
GRUR Int.	Gewerblicher Rechtsschutz und Urheberrecht – Internationaler Teil
IIC	International Review of Intellectual Property and Competition Law
ISD/Information Society Directive	Directive 2001/29/EC of the European Parliament and of the Council of 22 May 2001 on the Harmonisation of Certain Aspects of Copyright and Related Rights in the Information Society (*OJ* 2001 L 167, p. 10)
IP	Intellectual Property
JR WKM	WIPO Joint Recommendation Concerning the Protection of Well-Known Trademarks, adopted by the Assembly of the Paris Union for the Protection of Industrial Property and the General Assembly of the World Intellectual Property Organization (WIPO) at the Thirty-Fourth Series of Meetings of the Assemblies of the Member States of WIPO September 20 to 29, 1999, WIPO publication No. 833, Geneva: WIPO 2000
MCAD	Directive 2006/114/EC of the European Parliament and of the Council of 12 December 2006 Concerning Misleading and Comparative Advertising (codified version) (*OJ* 2006 L 376, p. 21)
NJ	Nederlandse Jurisprudentie
NJW	Neue Juristische Wochenschrift
OHIM	Office for Harmonisation in the Internal Market
OJ	Official Journal of the European Communities
PC	Paris Convention for the Protection of Industrial Property of March 20, 1883, lastly revised at Stockholm on July 14, 1967, and amended on September 28, 1979
RIDA	Revue internationale du droit d'auteur

STLT	Singapore Treaty on the Law of Trademarks, done at Singapore on 27 March 2006
TD	Directive 2006/116/EC of the European Parliament and of the Council of 12 December 2006 on the Term of Protection of Copyright and Certain Related Rights (codified version) (*OJ* 2006 L 372, p. 12)
TLT	Trademark Law Treaty, done at Geneva on October 27, 1994
TMD 2008	Directive 2008/95/EC of the European Parliament and of the Council of October 22, 2008, to approximate the laws of the Member States relating to trade marks (codified version) (*OJ* 2008 L 299, p. 25), which entered into force on November 28, 2008, and repealed the earlier Directive 89/104/EEC of the Council of December 21, 1988
TMD	Directive (EU) 2015/2436 of the European Parliament and of the Council of 16 December 2015 to approximate the laws of the Member States relating to trade marks (*OJ* 2015 L 336, p. 1)
TRIPS	Agreement on Trade-Related Aspects of Intellectual Property Rights, Annex 1C of the Marrakesh Agreement Establishing the World Trade Organization, signed on 15 April 1994, *ILM* 33 (1994), p. 1197
UN	United Nations
UNESCO	United Nations Educational, Scientific and Cultural Organization
UPCA	Agreement on a Unified Patent Court, concluded at Brussels on 19 February 2013 (*OJ* 2013 C 175, p. 1)
USPTO	United States Patent and Trademark Office
WCT	WIPO Copyright Treaty, adopted in Geneva on 20 December 1996
WIPO	World Intellectual Property Organization
WTO	World Trade Organization

Chapter 1
Introduction

In intellectual property law, overlaps of exclusive rights stemming from different protection regimes raise particular problems. The protection available in one intellectual property system may undermine policy choices and corresponding checks and balances in other intellectual property systems.[1] An amalgam of protection may offer the rights owner the opportunity to strengthen her private legal position at the expense of public interests. In *Dastar/Twentieth Century Fox*, the U.S. Supreme Court pointed out that overlaps between trademark rights and copyright or patent protection could have a corrosive effect on the 'carefully crafted bargain' under which, once the patent or copyright monopoly has expired, the public may use technical know-how and literary and artistic creations at will.[2] The CJEU expressed similar concerns in *Hauck/Stokke* where it explained that the functionality doctrine in trademark law served the purpose of preventing the exclusive and permanent right which a trademark confers 'from serving to extend indefinitely the life of other rights which the EU legislature has sought to make subject to limited periods'.[3]

Despite the awareness of the potential corrosive effect of protection overlaps on both sides of the Atlantic, however, the intellectual property system fails to draw clear boundary lines between individual protection regimes. Industrial designs may attract cumulative sui generis, copyright and

---

1. Cf. Dreyfuss 2020, 322-323; Samuelson 2017, 1512-1516; Calboli 2014a, 30-31; Beckerman-Rodau 2011, 73-89; Moffat 2004, 1476; Hugenholtz 2000b, 240-242.
2. U.S. Supreme Court, 2 June 2003, Dastar/Twentieth Century Fox, 539 U.S. 23, 33-34 (2003).
3. CJEU, 18 September 2014, case C-205/13, Hauck/Stokke, paras 19-20.

trademark protection.[4] Software may be eligible for copyright and patent protection.[5] Overlap scenarios and mixed intellectual property portfolios are not exceptional. In consequence, the question arises whether owners of intellectual property rights stemming from two different protection regimes should have the chance of enjoying the 'best of both worlds' or, on the contrary, face a reduction of the scope of protection to the smallest common denominator.[6]

Exploring this spectrum of regulatory reactions, the following analysis brings an area of overlapping protection into focus where the 'best of both worlds' approach has traditionally prevailed to a large extent: cumulative copyright and trademark protection is often deemed unproblematic.[7] With the commercial success of character merchandising, the combination of copyright and trademark claims has become a standard protection strategy in the field of contemporary cultural symbols that evolve from literary and artistic mainstream productions.[8] In the case of Mickey Mouse, for example, not only the name[9] but also several drawings are registered as trademarks in respect of a wide variety of goods and services.[10] The registrations are not confined to goods and services that are unrelated to the primary information products. They encompass audiovisual recordings and players, including CDs and DVDs, printed publications, including books and comic strips, and the production, presentation, distribution and rental of films.[11]

4. CJEU, 23 April 2020, case C-237/19, Gömböc, paras 51-54. Cf. Dinwoodie 2002, 504-505. For an overview of the different approaches to the regulation of cumulative copyright and industrial design protection, see the various contributions to Derclaye 2018. As to the position in the EU, see CJEU, 12 September 2019, case C-683/17, Cofemel, para. 31 and 35-48 and 52-55. As to shape marks, cf. Kur 2018, 89. See CJEU, 12 February 2004, case C-218/01, Henkel/DPMA, para. 49; CJEU, 8 April 2003, cases C-53/01 to C-55/01, Linde and others, para. 48.
5. For a discussion of this protection overlap, see Samuelson 2019, 291-301; Li 2019, 823; Dane 2018a, 1; Dane 2018b, 5; Sterckx/Cockbain 2010, 366; Ballardini 2008, 563; Leistner 2008, 188; Ghidini/Arezzo 2005, 166; Hilty/Geiger 2005, 615; Burk/Lemley 2005, 81; Weyand/Haase 2005, 647; Cohen/Lemley 2001, 41; Caron 2000, 3.
6. Cf. Verkade 1998, 72-73. For an overview of the existing spectrum of regulatory responses, see the in-depth analysis offered by Derclaye/Leistner 2011.
7. GCEU, 30 June 2009, case T-435/05, Danjaq/OHIM (Mission Productions), para. 26. Cf. Stieper 2012, 1090-1091; Peukert 2012, 111-113.
8. Cf. Curtin 2018, 971; Ginsburg 2016, 53-54; Köklü/Nérisson 2016, 568-569; Dusollier 2015, 160-161; Calboli 2014a, 29-30; Liu 2013, 1433-1438; Mende/Isaac 2012, 157; Assaf 2008, 19-21.
9. IR no. 983421, MICKEY; EUTMs no. 002827426 and 005240668, MICKEY MOUSE. See also Disney's registration of the word mark MICKEY in France, no. 1567169 and 1128324, and Germany, no. 39716409. For the particulars of the registrations, see www.tmdn.org/tmview/.
10. IR no. 135377 and 296478; EUTMs no. 003335981 and 003332913.
11. IR no. 296478; EUTMs no. 003335981 and 003332913.

Mickey Mouse, however, is not a singular case. Minnie,[12] Goofy,[13] Pluto,[14] Donald Duck,[15] Alice,[16] 101 Dalmatians,[17] Pinocchio[18] and Snow White[19] are further examples of characters which Disney converted into trademarks. Competitors in the market for animation films and comic books follow similar registration strategies. Marvel, for instance, registered various drawings of its characters as trademarks.[20] Registrations of Peter Rabbit,[21] Miffy,[22] Lucky Luke and the Daltons,[23] Asterix and Obelix,[24] Suske and Wiske,[25] Tintin and Snowy,[26] the Smurfs and Gargamel,[27] Snoopy, Charly Brown, Linus and Lucy[28] corroborate the finding that the cumulation of copyright and trademark protection has become a widespread exploitation strategy in the area of fictional characters. As in the case of Mickey Mouse, trademark registrations often cover not only merchandising articles but also goods and services that are directly related to the underlying primary literary and artistic productions.

During the term of copyright, the burden which these protection conglomerates place on literary and artistic creativity remains under the radar unless the rights owner makes excessive use of the parallel entitlement to trademark protection and invokes trademark rights to suppress use of the protected sign in the cultural domain.[29] Otherwise, the additional layer of trademark protection may go unnoticed as long as copyright protection exists. The societal costs – in the sense of an impediment of free artistic expression and cultural follow-on innovation[30] – may easily be overlooked.

12. EUTM no. 003332921.
13. EUTM no. 003334042.
14. EUTM no. 003332772.
15. IR no. 135376, particulars available at www.wipo.int/madrid/en/search/. See also French registration no. 1421670; German registration no. 100880.
16. EUTM no. 003332806.
17. EUTM no. 003332897.
18. EUTM no. 003332855.
19. EUTM no. 003332848.
20. For instance, see EUTMs no. 003466638, 003466638, 003466513, 003466562, 003466596, 003466621, 003466604, 003466653, 008197394. German registration no. DD643100.
21. Cf. U.S. District Court for the Southern District of New York, 19 December 1979, Frederick Warne/Book Sales, 481 F. Supp. 1191, 1193 (S.D.N.Y. 1979). Cf. Ginsburg 2016, 58-59; Dusollier 2015, 160-161.
22. Benelux registration no. 0653451.
23. EUTMs no. 002826212, 002730620 and 002903847.
24. EUTMs no. 000016089 and 000016121.
25. Benelux registrations no. 0381971 and 000016121.
26. EUTMs no. 000145151, 000145243, 001962638, 001962646. Cf. Jacques 2016, 471.
27. EUTM no. 000686527 and Benelux registration no. 0390273.
28. EUTMs no. 009695222, 008947781, 000423178, 008947715, 008748386, 008947772, 008947814.
29. For a more detailed analysis of this point, see Chapter 6 and, in particular, section 6.3.
30. Frosio 2014, 380-385.

After copyright expiry, however, the corrosive effect of indefinitely renewable trademark rights clearly comes to the fore: these rights survive the end of copyright protection. Hence, the cultural expression at issue does not enter the public domain in its entirety. To the extent to which trademark rights subsist, the literary and artistic work does not become freely available for follow-on innovation in the cultural domain.

As character merchandising has only become a mainstream exploitation strategy in recent decades, it is not surprising that these inroads into the public domain have not raised serious concerns and much opposition yet. Mickey Mouse and other animation film stars still enjoy copyright protection.[31] Therefore, it does not appear unusual that one individual player has the right to control the communication surrounding the literary and artistic work. As indicated, the impact of coexisting trademark protection will be felt, however, once copyright expires. As trademark rights persist, they provide a basis for preventing cultural remix and reuse which, otherwise, would not have given rise to the question of intellectual property infringement at all. The discourse concerning affected literary and artistic creations is not opened up completely.[32] Instead of giving up definition power, the former copyright holder remains a centre of gravity in the communication process. Zombie trademark rights afford the opportunity to challenge unauthorized use which does not comply with the owner's own vision of the right meaning and interpretation of the cultural expression at stake. Hence, current copyright holders who seek additional trademark protection leave less in common for future generations of authors. Popular cultural symbols of our time will not become resources for new literary and artistic productions that are available as unrestrictedly as cultural heritage material that entered the public domain before copyright/trademark protection overlaps became a mass phenomenon.

The cumulation of copyright and trademark protection in the area of fictional characters, however, is only one side of the coin. In principle, it is also possible to acquire trademark rights to cultural heritage symbols that are in the public domain.[33] In *Vigeland*, the EFTA Court dealt with an attempt to

---

31. As to extensions of the term of copyright protection that delay the transition of protected material to the public domain, see U.S. Supreme Court, 15 January 2003, Eldred/Ashcroft, 537 U.S. 186, 202 (2003).
32. As to corresponding concerns about a deterrent effect on cultural follow-on innovation, see Ramsey 2018, 427; Schovsbo 2018, 562; Adler 2016, 566; Köklü/Nérisson 2016, 572; Cramer 2015; McGeveran 2015, 739-742; Aufderheide/Jaszi/Bello et al. 2014, 5; Frosio 2014, 378-380; Calboli 2014a, 31-32; Lemley/McKenna 2010, 418-422 and 443; Banerjee 2012, 564; Sakulin 2010, 292-293; McGeveran 2008, 1206-1207 and 1224-1225; Morrison 2008, 131-136; Hofrichter 2007, 1926; Gibson 2007, 913; Cohen 2006, 156; Aufderheide/Jaszi 2004, 29-30; Lessig 2004, 185-188; Amabile 1996, 115-120 and 231-232.
33. Vanovermeire 2009, 182. For examples ranging from Raphael Putti to Michelangelo's 'Creation of Adam' and a Rembrandt self-portrait, see Bugdahl 2010, 372-373; Ohly 2008, 205 and 208-210.

register various artworks of the famous Norwegian sculptor Gustav Vigeland as trademarks.[34] The reason for the initiative to acquire trademark rights was the expiry of the term of copyright protection. The trademark applicant – the Municipality of Oslo – sought to preserve exclusive rights to the artworks even though they had already become freely available public domain material.[35] Following the guidance which the EFTA Court provided, the Norwegian Board of Appeal for Industrial Property Rights finally refused the trademark application.[36] This final decision in a Norwegian case, however, does not mean that attempts to register cultural heritage material as trademarks can never have success. Another iconic piece of Norwegian art – Edvard Munch's famous painting 'Scream' ('Skrik') – has been registered as a trademark at the international level with legal effect in the EU, Japan and the U.S.[37] In France, Vermeer's famous 'Milkmaid' ('Het Melkmeisje') has been used for the marketing of dairy products to such an extent that it seems safe to assume that the registered cultural icon has become a well-known mark.[38] In Germany, the State of Saxony-Anhalt managed to acquire EU trademark rights in the ancient Nebra Sky Disk that was found on its territory.[39] The Higher Court of Appeals of Dresden had to deal with the registration of the name and portrait of Johann Sebastian Bach as trademarks for a broad range of goods and services.[40] As the trademark registration had been obtained in 1999, it seems to have been the trademark owner's intention to exploit Bach's name and portrait during the anniversary year 2000 (Bach

34. EFTA Court, 6 April 2017, case E-5/16, Municipality of Oslo ('Vigeland'), paras 20-26. Cf. ECS 2017, 457. 13 November 2017, cases 16/00148, 16/00149, 16/00150, 16/00151, 16/00153 and 16/00154, 'Vigeland'.
35. EFTA Court, *ibid.*, para. 20. Gustav Vigeland died on 12 March 1943. As to the reasons underlying the registration initiative, see Report for the Hearing, Judge-Rapporteur Baudenbacher, 5 October 2016, case E-5/16, Municipality of Oslo ('Vigeland'), para. 32 and 36.
36. Norwegian Board of Appeal for Industrial Property Rights, 13 November 2017, cases 16/00148, 16/00149, 16/00150, 16/00151, 16/00153 and 16/00154, 'Vigeland', para. 14 and 23-24.
37. IR no. 1179290 concerning beers, mineral waters and other alcoholic and non-alcoholic beverages.
38. EUTM no. 002998334 concerning, among other goods, dietetic foodstuffs and baby food; vegetables, fruits, meat, poultry, game, fish and seafood; milk products; coffee, tea, cocoa and chocolate products; bakery products, snack foods, breakfast cereals and ice cream. Cf. Bianchi 2017.
39. EUTM no. 009763475. As to the previous controversy about the grant of the trademark right in Germany, see Regional Court of Magdeburg, 16 October 2003, case 7 O 847/03, 'Himmelsscheibe von Nebra', *GRUR* 2004, 672. Cf. Stieper 2012, 1090-1091; Ohly 2008, 209-211.
40. Higher Court of Appeals of Dresden, 4 April 2000, case 14 U 3611/99, 'Johann Sebastian Bach', *NJW* 2001, 615 (616).

died on 28 July 1750).[41] Despite a finding of lack of distinctive character at Benelux level,[42] the EUIPO registered the original Dutch titles of Anne Frank's famous books – 'Het achterhuis' ('The Secret Annex') and 'Het dagboek van Anne Frank' ('The Diary of Anne Frank') – in respect of books, films, theatre productions and guided tours.[43] In contrast to the Court of Appeals of Brussels,[44] the EUIPO deemed these titles distinctive and granted trademark rights in areas of literary and artistic creativity where the books play a crucial role.[45] Similarly, the verdict of insufficient distinctive character in the Benelux[46] could not prevent the EUIPO from granting EU-wide trademark rights to Rembrandt's famous painting 'The Night Watch' ('De Nachtwacht').[47]

In *Neuschwanstein*, the CJEU further encouraged cultural heritage branding by holding that frequent use on souvenir items was irrelevant for the purpose of assessing the descriptive character of the name of the famous castle in Bavaria. According to the Court, the fact that the name 'Neuschwanstein' transformed regular goods into souvenir articles could not be deemed an essential descriptive characteristic of the goods concerned. The memory evoked in the minds of consumers was not sufficient to qualify the name as an indication of a product quality or an essential product characteristic.[48] If this line of reasoning is applied mutatis mutandis to souvenir and merchandising articles bearing famous artworks, it will inevitably deprive trademark offices of the possibility to deny the grant of exclusive rights on the grounds that the artwork is descriptive or decorative. It may also pose an obstacle to a finding of aesthetic functionality. Prior to the CJEU decision, the EUIPO already granted trademark rights in a prominent cultural heritage

41. Cf. Götting 2001, 615. In addition to the Johann Sebastian Bach registration, the trademark proprietor had also registered signs relating to Michelangelo, Leonardo da Vinci, Paul Gauguin and Paul Cézanne.
42. Court of Appeals of Brussels, 3 October 2013, cases 2013/7132 and 2013/7133, Anne Frank Foundation/Benelux Office for Intellectual Property, para. 8.
43. See EUTM no. 012451787 (HET ACHTERHUIS) and EUTM no. 012452281 (HET DAGBOEK VAN ANNE FRANK) which cover various goods and services in classes 9, 16 and 41.
44. As the CJEU, 6 September 2018, case C-488/16P, Bundesverband Souvenir - Geschenke – Ehrenpreise ('Neuschwanstein'), para. 72, pointed out, the EU trademark system is 'an autonomous system with its own set of objectives and rules peculiar to it; it applies independently of any national system'. Hence, the EUIPO was not bound to follow the decision on distinctiveness taken by the Court of Appeals of Brussels on the basis of the harmonized Benelux trademark system.
45. For the particulars of EUTMs no. 012451787 and 012452281, see https://euipo.europa.eu/eSearch/.
46. Court of Appeals of The Hague, 29 August 2017, case 200.205.771/01, ECLI:NL:GHDHA:2017:2446, Chiever/Benelux-Organisatie voor de Intellectuele Eigendom ('Nachtwacht'), para. 12.
47. EUTM no. 016613903 concerning the chemical element strontium.
48. CJEU, 6 September 2018, case C-488/16P, Bundesverband Souvenir - Geschenke – Ehrenpreise ('Neuschwanstein'), paras 44-46.

sign – the ancient Nebra Sky Disk – in respect of souvenir and merchandising articles.[49] The *Neuschwanstein* ruling is likely to increase this tendency to burden more and more cultural signs with trademark rights.

Surveying these developments, it is not surprising that in *Vigeland*, the EFTA Court saw a need for 'protecting creations of the mind from commercial greed' and 'ensuring the freedom of the arts'.[50] The Court did not hesitate to point out that we live in a 'greedy' era where trademark law is employed strategically to withhold or remove cultural symbols from the public domain. In the Mickey Mouse scenario (fictional characters), trademark registrations prevent literary and artistic creations from *entering* the public domain. In the Mona Lisa scenario (cultural heritage material), trademark rights prevent literary and artistic creations from *staying* in the public domain. In both cases, the acquisition of trademark rights reduces the reservoir of freely available source material for cultural follow-on innovation. Offering the option of indefinitely renewable protection, trademark law and practice have lost sight of the quid pro quo underlying the grant of copyright: the acceptance of the expiry of protection and the enrichment of the public domain are the price to be paid for the enjoyment of exclusive rights during the limited term of copyright protection.[51]

Interestingly, the situation in the copyright/trademark arena differs markedly from the status quo reached in the area of patent/trademark overlaps. At the intersection of these latter protection regimes, the trademark doctrine of utilitarian functionality thwarts the cumulation of exclusive rights.[52] After the expiry of patent rights in Lego brick functionality, for instance, courts around the globe had little difficulty in excluding trademark rights categorically on the ground that the brick design fulfilled an important technical function and had to be kept free to safeguard freedom of competition.[53] Invoking the functionality doctrine, it was possible to prevent

49. EUTM no. 009763475. As to the previous debate about the trademark right in Germany, see Regional Court of Magdeburg, 16 October 2003, case 7 O 847/03, 'Himmelsscheibe von Nebra', *GRUR* 2004, 672. Cf. Stieper 2012, 1090-1091, and Ohly 2008, 209-211, whose counterarguments based on the assumption that the Nebra Sky Disk would only be perceived as a descriptive or decorative element seem difficult to maintain after the CJEU decision in *Neuschwanstein*.
50. EFTA Court, *ibid.*, para. 65.
51. Cf. U.S. Supreme Court, 2 June 2003, Dastar/Twentieth Century Fox, 539 U.S. 23, 33-34 (2003); German Federal Constitutional Court, 31 May 2016, case 1 BvR 1585/13, 'Sampling', *GRUR* 2016, 690, para. 87; EFTA Court, 6 April 2017, case E-5/16, Municipality of Oslo ('Vigeland'), para. 66. Cf. Vanovermeire 2009, 180.
52. CJEU, 18 June 2002, case C-299/99, Philips/Remington, para. 82; U.S. Supreme Court, 20 March 2001, TrafFix Devices/Marketing Displays, 532 U.S. 23, 33-34 (2001).
53. CJEU, 14 September 2010, case C-48/09 P, Lego/Mega Brands, para. 45 and 53-58; Supreme Court of Canada, 17 November 2005, Kirkbi AG/Ritvik Holdings Inc., [2005] 3 S.C.R. 302, 2005 SCC 65, para. 46.

an artificial perpetuation of patent protection[54] – even if the technical solution at issue had acquired distinctiveness during the limited term of the monopoly right.[55] The firmness with which courts banned trademark rights to technical know-how creates a sharp contrast with the elasticity in the field of copyright/trademark overlaps. It gives rise to a broader societal question. Undoubtedly, the Lego brick design is brilliant and of crucial importance to every childhood. But it hardly constitutes a pioneering technical solution. How come that there is so much agreement on the outright exclusion of trademark rights to inventions (even if they are not technical milestones) and so little agreement on comparable resoluteness when it comes to literary and artistic works (even if they belong to mankind's universal cultural heritage)?[56] Does this imbalance in intellectual property law reflect a deeper societal problem of carelessness vis-à-vis cultural concerns? Do we care more about freedom to build upon Lego brick functionality than we care about freedom to remix Mickey Mouse and the Mona Lisa? Is follow-on innovation in the field of technology really more important than follow-on innovation in the literary and artistic domain?

Against the background of these overarching questions, the following analysis will first shed light on the main branches of the current intellectual property system, the problem of growing overlaps between these branches and the risk of undermining central features of individual protection regimes ('imperatives') that ensure the proper functioning of intellectual property protection in the domains of culture, technology and trade (following Chapter 2). An examination of the exposure of the copyright regime to protection overlaps will yield the insight that, in the absence of a registration requirement and a clear delineation of the domain of literary and artistic creativity, copyright law has become a melting pot of rights accumulation, including growing overlaps between copyright and trademark protection. Accordingly, the identification of central preconditions for the proper functioning of the copyright system in the cultural domain and society at large – the guarantee of intergenerational equity and the recognition of the public domain (Chapter 3) – offers an important reference point for a detailed analysis of problems arising from protection overlaps.

A discussion of potential interferences of trademark protection with intergenerational equity and public domain recognition in copyright law will show that the registration of literary and artistic works as trademarks creates a high risk of impeding creative processes in the cultural domain. While both copyright and patent law seek to support cyclic processes of follow-on innovation, trademark law aims at a stable distribution of intellectual

54. CJEU, 18 June 2002, case C-299/99, Philips/Remington, para. 82; CJEU, 18 September 2014, case C-205/13, Hauck/Stokke, paras 19-20.
55. CJEU, 14 September 2010, case C-48/09 P, Lego/Mega Brands, para. 40.
56. Opinion of Advocate General Colomer, 3 April 2003, case C-283/01, Shield Mark/Kist, para. 52.

resources – signs used as identifiers of commercial source – in the domain of trade (Chapter 4). Before embarking on a more detailed analysis of the corrosive effect of trademark protection, however, it is necessary to obtain clarity about the spectrum of signs that have particular relevance to cultural follow-on innovation and should be available for cyclic innovation processes in the artistic domain ('cultural signs'). The survey of candidates for cultural sign status in Chapter 5 covers signs ranging from famous artworks in the public domain, traditional cultural expressions, fictional characters and other contemporary mainstream creations to work titles and iconic trademarks that symbolize a particular lifestyle or attitude. The discussion will address the criteria for identifying signs with cultural significance in these categories.

Shedding light on the extravagant proportions of trademark protection in advanced trademark systems, such as EU trademark law, the subsequent risk assessment will confirm that indefinitely renewable trademark rights have the potential to frustrate cultural remix and reuse activities that are indispensable for cultural follow-on innovation (Chapter 6). More concretely, trademark protection allows copyright holders to perpetuate intellectual property protection artificially after the expiry of copyright (encroachment upon intergenerational equity, Chapter 7). Furthermore, it removes cultural expressions from the public domain and reduces the reservoir of source material that is freely available for new literary and artistic productions (encroachment upon public domain recognition, Chapter 8).

To reduce the risks arising from cumulative copyright and trademark protection, literary and artistic creations may categorically be excluded from trademark protection. Less draconic countermeasures concern the recalibration of the infringement analysis. Seeking to stop infringement actions against artistic use at an early stage, owners of trademark rights to cultural signs may be obliged to justify their claim by demonstrating that use of the protected sign in a cultural setting has trademark relevance at all (introduction of a strict gatekeeper requirement of 'use as a mark'). Trademark law may also develop robust defences to enable artists to escape the verdict of infringement. Chapter 9 discusses the conceptual contours and practical implementation of these risk reduction tools.

The final Chapter 10 provides a summary of results and sheds light on general guidelines for the regulation of protection overlaps in intellectual property law that can be deduced from the detailed discussion of copyright/trademark overlaps. It will lead to the conclusion that dysfunctional protection overlaps can only be avoided by weaving values of one protection regime, such as intergenerational equity and public domain recognition in the case of copyright law, into the fabric of another, overlapping protection regime, such as trademark law. The owner of intellectual property rights stemming from different domains of protection should have not only double rights but also double obligations. The rights owner must ensure that both protection regimes remain fully intact: the protection overlap must not interfere with the proper functioning of affected protection regimes in their respective societal domains. Considering the spectrum of regulatory responses ranging from the opportunity to enjoy the best of both worlds to the diminution of cumulative protection to the smallest common denominator, the following analysis will thus support a cautious approach that brings the reaction of the intellectual property system closer to the pole of the smallest common denominator. In this way, intellectual property law can make rights cumulation strategies less attractive and avoid the loss of inner consistency and social legitimacy.

Chapter 2
Overlap Dilemma

Intellectual property law offers protection for creations of the mind and seeks to reconcile resulting exclusive entitlements with competing social, cultural and economic needs.[57] *Traditionally, the field of intellectual property is divided into two main branches: copyright and neighbouring rights relating to literary and artistic works on the one hand, and rights to industrial property, such as technical inventions and distinctive signs, on the other hand. The architecture of international intellectual property law reflects this distinction. It rests on the Berne Convention for the Protection of Literary and Artistic Works and the Paris Convention for the Protection of Industrial Property.*[58] *For the purposes of the following analysis, however, it is important to note that the three major protection regimes in intellectual property law – copyright, patent and trademark law – have evolved in different domains of society.*[59] *Copyright law has its roots in the domain of culture.*[60] *Patent law concerns the field of*

57. Cf. Articles 7 and 8 TRIPS. See the analysis by Yu 2009, 1000-1014. As to the need for balance in different intellectual property protection systems, see Senftleben 2011c, 143-145, 161-162 and 171-175.
58. See the various references to the Paris Convention and the Berne Convention in the TRIPS Agreement, and in particular Articles 2(2) and 9(1) TRIPS which confirm that these international treaties are the cornerstones of the worldwide intellectual property system to this day.
59. Hugenholtz 2000b, 240-242.
60. The preamble of the Berne Convention refers to '[t]he countries of the [Berne] Union, being equally animated by the desire to protect, in as effective and uniform a manner as possible, the rights of authors in their literary and artistic works'. As to the strong link of copyright protection with the field of art, see also Cooper 2018, 1-6, 20-22, 257-261; Heymann 2013, 243; Sherman/Bently 1999, 119-125.

technology.[61] *Trademark law has been distilled from practices of trade.*[62] *As a result of this evolution in different domains, copyright, patent and trademark law have distinct features. In particular, the limits set to exclusive rights in these areas of intellectual property are tailored to the specific needs in the corresponding domains, i.e. the domains of culture, technology and trade (following section 2.1). Growing overlaps of protection, however, blur the conceptual contours of individual protection regimes and endanger the proper functioning of intellectual property rights in affected domains (section 2.2). Against this background, the question arises whether the intellectual property system is capable of diminishing potential corrosive effects of cumulative protection (section 2.3).*

2.1 INDIVIDUAL IMPERATIVES OF INTELLECTUAL PROPERTY REGIMES

Seeking to promote the creation of literary and artistic works, copyright protection does not extend to ideas, methods or concepts as such. This raw material of cultural expression remains free as a universal basis of future creativity in accordance with the idea/expression dichotomy in copyright law.[63] The recognition of a right of quotation[64] and exemptions for parody and other forms of 'transformative' use[65] offer additional support for the use of pre-existing source material for the creation of new literary and artistic works. Moreover, copyright law permits the exemption of use that serves the dissemination and preservation of cultural expressions. It allows the introduction of limitations for libraries, archives and educational institutions, and

61. See Article 27 TRIPS which confirms that 'patents shall be available for any inventions, whether products or processes, in *all fields of technology*, provided that they are new, involve an inventive step and are capable of industrial application' (emphasis added). Cf. Pessers 2016, 23-49, 59-62, 90-93; Sherman/Bently 1999, 101-110.
62. Cf. Bently 2008a, 16-41; Fezer 2003, 457-462; Sherman/Bently 1999, 166-172.
63. Article 9(2) TRIPS; Article 2 WCT. Cf. Dutch Supreme Court, 29 March 2013, case LJN BY8661, Broeren/Duijsens, para. 3.5.
64. Article 10(1) BC; Article 5(3)(d) ISD. For a discussion of the scope of this international recognition of the quotation right, see Aplin/Bently 2020, 156-222; Bently/Aplin 2019, 28-31. As to the development at the national level, see Senftleben 2012a, 359.
65. Article 5(3)(k) ISD. As to the conceptual contours of quotation and parody privileges in EU copyright law, see CJEU, 1 December 2011, case C-145/10, Painer, para. 132-134; CJEU, 3 September 2014, case C-201/13, Deckmyn, paras 25-27. Cf. Jacques 2019, 91-133; Jongsma 2019, 203-213; De Cock Buning/Van Lingen 2014, 191; De Zwaan 2014, 195-196; Senftleben 2012a, 374-381. As to the notion of transformative use in U.S. copyright law, see U.S. Supreme Court, 7 March 1994, Campbell/Acuff-Rose, 510 U.S. 569, 579 (1994). Cf. Sag 2012, 47; Samuelson 2009, 2537; Beebe 2008, 156; Leval 1990, 1105; Litman 1997, 588; Nimmer 2003, 263.

for the purpose of private study.[66] After a limited period of protection, copyrighted works enter the public domain and may be used freely.[67]

Patent law, similarly, seeks to support the production, exchange and further development of creations of the mind. Its focus, however, is on the enhancement of knowledge in the field of technology. The inventor is obliged to fully disclose the invention when applying for registration.[68] Protection is awarded only to new and inventive solutions that enlarge the pre-existing state of the art. The exclusive rights of patent owners can be limited to enable scientific experimentation already during the term of the patent.[69] Furthermore, a compulsory licence may be granted for the exploitation of dependent inventions that involve an important technical advance.[70] As copyrighted material, patented inventions fall into the public domain after a limited term of protection.[71]

Trademark law, finally, contributes to fair competition, consumer protection and the proper functioning of markets by safeguarding market transparency with regard to signs used by enterprises to distinguish their goods and services from those of competitors. In this context, functional product features, descriptive signs that designate product characteristics, and signs that have become customary in trade practices are kept free for use by all traders.[72] The exclusive rights of trademark owners only govern use in trade.[73] Moreover, the protection of trademarks against use liable to cause confusion is limited to specific goods and services. For protection going

66. For example, see Articles 5(2)(a), (b) and (c) and 5(3)(a) and (n) ISD; Articles 3(1), 5(1) and 6 DSMD. Cf. Senftleben 2010c, 68.
67. Article 7(1) BC; Article 1(1) TD. Cf. CJEU, 27 January 2011, case C-168/09, Flos, paras 39-40. As to the term extension in the U.S., see U.S. Supreme Court, 15 January 2003, Eldred/Ashcroft, 537 U.S. 186, 202 (2003). Cf. Austin 2003, 163. As to the public domain dimension of the limited term of protection, see German Federal Constitutional Court, 31 May 2016, case 1 BvR 1585/13, 'Sampling', *GRUR* 2016, 690, para. 87; EFTA Court, 6 April 2017, case E-5/16, Municipality of Oslo ('Vigeland'), para. 66.
68. Article 29(1) TRIPS.
69. Article 30 TRIPS. Cf. WTO Panel, 17 March 2000, WTO Document WT/DS114/R, Canada – Patent Protection of Pharmaceutical Products, para. 7.664. For a restrictive approach, see U.S. Court of Appeals, Federal Circuit, 3 October 2002, Madey/Duke University, 307 F.3d 1351 (Fed. Cir. 2002). For a flexible approach, see German Federal Court of Justice, 11 July 1995, case X ZR 99/92, 'Klinische Versuche I', *GRUR* 1996, 109 (113). Cf. Senftleben 2011c, 163-165.
70. Article 31(l) TRIPS.
71. Article 33 TRIPS.
72. Article 6quinquies(B) PC. Cf. CJEU, 4 May 1999, cases C-108/97 and C-109/97, Windsurfing Chiemsee, paras 35-37; CJEU, 6 May 2003, case C-104/01, Libertel, para. 55; CJEU, 18 September 2014, case C-205/13, Hauck/Stokke, para. 18; CJEU, 18 June 2002, case C-299/99, Philips/Remington, para. 78; CJEU, 14 September 2010, case C-48/09 P, Lego/Mega Brands, para. 43. Cf. Senftleben 2013a, 797-802; Peukert 2012, 26-27; Phillips 2005, 389; Sambuc 1997, 403.
73. Article 16(1) TRIPS.

beyond this principle of speciality, a particular reputation is required.[74] Besides these conceptual limits that are inherent in trademark rights, the use of a protected trademark may be permitted without the authorization of the trademark proprietor, for instance, where this is necessary for the purposes of indicating the intended purpose of goods or services, comparing different offers in the marketplace and criticizing the trademark owner's behaviour and policies.[75]

These examples illustrate individual checks and balances of intellectual property protection in the domains of culture, technology and trade. For intellectual property law to have beneficial effects in these fields, it must exclude certain subject matter from protection, establish appropriate eligibility criteria for the acquisition of protection, delineate the scope of rights and exempt certain forms of unauthorized use that serve important economic, social and cultural interests. Like two sides of a coin, rights and limitations complement each other to provide an appropriate level of protection.[76] Hence, there is a delicate balance between rights and freedoms in copyright, patent and trademark law. The individual preconditions for the proper functioning of intellectual property protection in the domains of culture, technology and trade can be qualified as inalienable *imperatives* of the configuration of the respective protection systems. Three of these fundamental imperatives can be identified on the basis of the foregoing outline of core features of copyright, patent and trademark law: the imperative of cultural follow-on innovation that can be derived from checks and balances in copyright law, the imperative of technological follow-on innovation resulting from the configuration of patent law, and the imperative of market transparency that is inherent in trademark law.

From the bird's-eye perspective of human rights, the delicate balance between rights and limitations in individual systems of intellectual property protection can be regarded as a specific configuration of fundamental rights and freedoms.[77] The grant of exclusive rights in literary and artistic works,

---

74. Article 16(3) TRIPS. As to different standards of reputation in domestic legislation, see Senftleben 2009a, 50-55; Beebe 2006, 1157.

75. Article 17 TRIPS; Article 14(1)(b) and (c) EUTMR; Article 14(1)(b) and (c) TMD. As to comparative advertising, see also Article 9(3)(f) EUTMR and Article 10(3)(f) TMD. Cf. WTO Panel, 15 March 2005, WTO Document WT/DS174/R, European Communities – Protection of Trademarks and Geographical Indications for Agricultural Products and Foodstuffs, para. 7.671; CJEU, 23 February 1999, case C-63/97, BMW/Deenik, para. 62; CJEU, 17 March 2005, case C-228/03, Gillette/LA-Laboratories, para. 29; CJEU, 12 June 2008, case C-533/06, O2/Hutchison, para. 45; CJEU, 18 June 2009, case C-487/07, L'Oréal/Bellure, para. 54. For a broader overview, see Kur/Senftleben 2017, para. 6.16-6.70.

76. For a comparison of the mechanisms applied in copyright and trademark law, see O'Rourke 2000, 1184-1198.

77. As to the influence of freedom of expression on copyright protection, cf. Geiger/Izyumenko 2020, 292-298; Jongsma 2019, 195-222; Geiger/Izyumenko 2019, 133-136; Hugenholtz 2016, 242; Geiger/Izyumenko 2016, 43; Geiger/Izyumenko 2014, 316;

inventions and trademarks rests on the fundamental guarantee of property, including intellectual property.[78] The grant of protection to rights owners, however, impacts fundamental rights and freedoms of users, particularly freedom of expression and freedom of competition.[79] Imposing certain limits on protection, the lawmaker seeks to reconcile the guarantee of intellectual property with competing rights and freedoms. Acts of excluding and limiting protection can be understood to define the coastline of islands of copyright, patent and trademark protection in a sea of freedom of expression and freedom of competition.[80]

Against this background, the central problem arising from protection overlaps comes to light. In recent decades, the individual protection regimes of intellectual property have grown continuously. The insatiable appetite for increasing commodification of intellectual creations can be traced back to a broader trend in society to subordinate more and more subsystems with individual values, such as the field of art and the field of science, to the prevailing market logic of exchange value.[81] Due to the openness of the notions of 'work', 'invention' and 'trademark', this process had a deep impact on intellectual property law.[82] New subject matter of protection could easily be included in copyright, patent and trademark law. As a result, areas of overlap between these distinct types of intellectual property have been broadened substantially. Nowadays, generous bridges and submarine tunnel systems connect the islands of copyright, patent and trademark protection with each other, and enable lively traffic.[83] In advanced intellectual property systems, a creation of the mind is not unlikely to enjoy cumulative protection in different regimes.

Netanel 2008; Geiger 2006, 371; Strowel/Tulkens/Voorhoof 2006; Hugenholtz 2002, 239; Macciacchini 2000; Benkler 1999, 354; Netanel 1996, 283. With regard to the debate on how to reconcile trademark protection with freedom of expression, see the dissertation by Sakulin 2010. See also Bohaczewski 2020, 856; Żelechowski 2018, 115-135; Senftleben 2015, 354; Ramsey/Schovsbo 2013, 671; Simon Fhima 2013, 293; Geiger 2010a, 163; Burrell/Gangjee 2010, 544; Nasser 2009, 188; Bently 2008, 1205; Dreyfuss 2008, 261; Geiger 2007, 317; Ramsey 2010a, 405; Weckström 2007, 671; Gulasekaram 2005, 887; Leval 2004, 187; Timbers/Huston 2003, 1278; Aoki 1997, 523; Dreyfuss 1990, 415-418.

78. Article 17(2) CFR. Jongsma 2019, 163-168; J. Griffiths/McDonagh 2013, 75-93; Geiger 2009, 113-117.
79. CJEU, 24 November 2011, case C-70/10, Scarlet/Sabam, paras 48-53; CJEU, 16 February 2012, case C-360/10, Sabam/Netlog, paras 46-51.
80. As to the allegoric play with islands and oceans in the debate on limits of protection, see Kur 2009, 292-293.
81. For a discussion of this broader trend in the light of Karl Polanyi's concept of fictitious commodities, see Peukert 2019, 1178-1179 and 1185-1188. Cf. also Gangjee 2013, 56-59; Coombe 2005, 47-52.
82. Peukert 2019, 1166-1169.
83. Heymann 2013, 242-247; Ohly 2008, 203; Dinwoodie 2002, 499-501; Kur 2002, 594-595; Spoor 1990, 41-60; Lange 1981, 147.

2.2 GROWING AREAS OF CUMULATIVE COPYRIGHT AND TRADEMARK PROTECTION

The copyright/trademark interface can serve as an example. Complementary developments in copyright and trademark law led to far-reaching extensions of the area of overlap. The conceptual contours of protected subject matter are drawn flexibly in copyright law. The Berne Convention confirms that the term 'literary and artistic work' comprises 'every production in the literary, scientific and artistic domain, whatever may be the mode or form of its expression' and provides an illustrative list of subject matter ranging from 'books, pamphlets and other writings' to 'works relative to geography, topography, architecture or science'.[84] At the national level, elastic tests of 'originality' are applied to identify the subject matter of protection.[85] The CJEU asks whether a creation for which copyright protection is sought constitutes 'an author's own intellectual creation'.[86] Applying this flexible formula, the Court could not rule out copyright protection for a text fragment of not more than 11 words and a standard portrait photograph taken routinely of pupils at school.[87] In EU Member States, the relaxed originality test at EU level prompted national courts to abandon more restrictive tests that had evolved in their domestic systems, such as the requirement of an enhanced degree of artistic merit in the case of industrial design.[88]

The elasticity of the originality test, however, is not the only factor that led to widespread availability of copyright protection. In addition, evidence of a literary and artistic nature is not required. The reference to 'the literary, scientific and artistic domain' in Article 2(1) BC is not understood as a separate threshold requirement. Although protection is awarded for 'literary and artistic works',[89] there is no symmetry between this subject matter of protection and the protection requirements: the domain of copyright is not confined to creations that fall within the province of well-established categories of literature and art.[90] In *Levola Hengelo*, for instance, the CJEU refrained from categorically denying copyright protection for a mass-produced cream cheese. The Court did not put an end to the copyright claim

84. Article 2(1) BC.
85. For an early study of European copyright systems yielding this insight, see Dietz 1978, 62-63.
86. CJEU, 16 July 2009, case C-5/08, Infopaq/DDF, para. 37.
87. CJEU, *ibid.*, para. 45; CJEU, 1 December 2011, case C-145/10, Painer, para. 89.
88. Cf. German Federal Court of Justice, 16 June 2016, case I ZR 222/14, 'Geburtstagskarawane', *GRUR* 2016, 1291, para. 44. As to the traditional German requirement of a higher degree of artistic merit, see Geier 2015, 203-206; Derclaye/Leistner 2011, 239; Ohly 2008, 215. In CJEU, 12 September 2019, case C-683/17, Cofemel, para. 31 and 35-48 and 52-55, the CJEU explicitly rejected assessment criteria based on a specific aesthetic effect in the field of industrial design protection.
89. Articles 1 and 2(1) BC.
90. Dinwoodie 2002, 501-502.

by stating that the taste of cheese[91] was a priori ineligible for protection because it did not belong to the domain of literature and art. Instead, the Court elaborated that:

> for there to be a 'work' […], the subject matter protected by copyright must be expressed in a manner which makes it identifiable with sufficient precision and objectivity, even though that expression is not necessarily in permanent form.[92]

Obviously, the Court did not have the ambition to introduce an upfront 'literature and art' test. Instead, the decision focused on the practical need to 'identify, clearly and precisely, the subject matter so protected'.[93] While the Court deemed it possible to determine 'a precise and objective form of expression' in the case of literary, pictorial, cinematographic or musical creations, the taste of a food product could not be pinned down with precision and objectivity. Taste sensations and experiences were 'subjective and variable'.[94] In the Court's view, they depend on factors that are particular to the person tasting the product concerned, such as age, food preferences and consumption habits. The environment or context in which the product is consumed also impacts the product's taste.[95]

Hence, there is no precondition of belonging to the realm of literature and art that functions as a separate gatekeeper requirement capable of precluding copyright protection from the outset. A creation of the mind need not display standard features of literature and art to be eligible for copyright protection. In literature, Willem Grosheide espoused the introduction of a two-stage test procedure to determine a creation's eligibility for copyright protection. To achieve an external delimitation of the domain of copyright (in relation to other domains of intellectual property), the enquiry should first address the question of whether an intellectual creation falls within the province of literature and art.[96] Seeking to sharpen the conceptual contours of this gatekeeper criterion,[97] he proposed an alternative formula focusing on 'cultural information brought into communication'.[98] As a second step, the originality test should be applied to also delimit the domain of copyrighted creations internally – within the field of literary and artistic production.[99]

91. See the description in CJEU, 13 November 2018, case C-310/17, Levola Hengelo, para. 14.
92. CJEU, *ibid.*, para. 40.
93. CJEU, *ibid.*, para. 41. Cf. Van Gompel 2019, 11-12.
94. CJEU, *ibid.*, para. 42. For critical comments on these assessment criteria, see Van Gompel 2019, 13-14.
95. CJEU, *ibid.*, para. 42.
96. Grosheide 1986, 193-195. Cf. Hugenholtz 1989, 19; Dietz 1978, 60.
97. As to the difficulty of distinguishing cultural products from technical and industrial products, see Grosheide 2015, 208-209; Grosheide 1986, 262-263.
98. Grosheide 2015, 208; Grosheide 1994, 232; Grosheide 1986, 296. Cf. Spoor/Verkade/Visser 2019, 99.
99. Grosheide 1986, 193-195.

Grosheide's proposal of a two-tiered approach can be traced back to earlier proposals in German literature.[100] Gernot Schulze, for instance, had developed a threshold criterion focusing on the 'intellectual and aesthetic' or 'intellectually stimulating' effect of literature and art.[101] Alois Troller sought to draw a line between the domain of copyright and other fields of intellectual property by focusing on the objectifiable 'existence in sensually perceivable form' of literary and artistic works.[102]

As explained, an upfront enquiry into the literary and artistic nature of creations for which copyright protection is sought – in the sense of a gatekeeper criterion preceding the originality test – has not made its way into EU copyright law.[103] In line with CJEU jurisprudence, it is not decisive whether subject matter for which protection is sought qualifies as a genuine cultural production that has been created to enrich mankind's treasury of literature and art. Instead, the CJEU only requires subject matter to be 'identifiable with sufficient precision and objectivity'.[104] While this criterion resembles Alois Troller's concept of an objectifiable 'existence in sensually perceivable form',[105] it does not pose an obstacle to the cumulation of copyright and trademark protection. EU trademark law also requires a 'clear and precise' identification of the subject matter which an applicant seeks to register as a trademark.[106] Therefore, the *Levola Hengelo* test of identifying literary and artistic works 'clearly and precisely'[107] does not place an additional hurdle. Trademarks routinely pass the test of a clear and precise identification of protected subject matter.

As a result, the doors to an amalgamation of copyright and trademark protection are wide open. In the absence of a strict originality test and a clear delineation of the domain of literature and art, many trademarks are capable of passing the threshold for copyright protection. Rather unimaginative word marks and simple logos may be held to constitute literary and artistic works under the described EU standards.[108] Trademark norms, such as Article 60(2)(c) EUTMR and Article 5(4)(b) TMD, openly recognize an earlier

---

100. Cf. Hugenholtz 1989, 18; Dietz 1978, 60.
101. Schulze 1983, 123-130; Dreier/Schulze 2018, 76-77 (§1, para. 5) and 85 (§2, para. 12).
102. Troller 1983, 350-351 and 358-360.
103. Cf. Van Gompel 2019, 11; Grosheide 2015, 208-209; Spoor 2006, para. 19; Hugenholtz 2006, 822-823.
104. CJEU, 13 November 2018, case C-310/17, Levola Hengelo, para. 40.
105. Troller 1983, 350-351 and 358-360.
106. Article 3(b) and Recital 13 TMD; Article 4(b) and Recital 10 EUTMR. Cf. CJEU, 12 December 2002, case C-273/00, Sieckmann, paras 50-55. A line with the trademark criteria is also drawn by Spoor/Verkade/Visser 2019, 70-71; Van Gompel 2019, 12.
107. CJEU, *ibid.*, para. 41. Cf. Van Gompel 2019, 11-12.
108. See the low threshold for acquiring copyright protection for word combinations in CJEU, 16 July 2009, case C-5/08, Infopaq/DDF, para. 45, on the one hand, and the elastic criteria for granting trademark protection for advertising slogans in CJEU, 21 January 2010, case C-398/08P, Audi/OHIM ('Vorsprung durch Technik'), paras 56-57, on the other hand. Cf. Ohly 2019, 331-332.

third-party copyright as a relative ground for invalidating the rights of the trademark proprietor.[109]

Similar tendencies come to the fore in U.S. copyright law. As Barton Beebe explains, the 1903 *Bleistein* decision of the U.S. Supreme Court[110] paved the way for a copyright tradition which, instead of insisting on aesthetic merit and strictly confining protection to the domain of literature and art, focuses on commercial value and refrains from setting a high originality threshold requirement.[111] In *Bleistein/Donaldson Lithographic Co.*, the U.S. Supreme Court had to decide on copyright protection for three posters that had been produced to advertise a travelling circus: the Great Wallace Shows.[112] Confronted with an infringement claim because of unauthorized reproductions, Donaldson Lithographing argued that the posters – depicting circus acts, such as the bicycle act of the 'Renowned Stirk Family' and the 'Grand Spectacular Ballet' – did not enjoy copyright protection because a sufficient 'connection with fine arts', as required under statutory American copyright law at the time, was missing.[113] The Court, however, dismissed these defence arguments and granted protection.[114]

Considering the outlined debate on an upfront domain test in European literature – seeking to confine copyright to creations that fall within the province of literature and art[115] – it is of particular interest that American copyright law, as in force at the time of the *Bleistein* ruling, explicitly set forth a requirement of 'pictorial illustrations or works connected with the fine arts'.[116] The requirement of a 'connection with the fine arts' could have offered a statutory basis for a strict domain test that would have made copyright unattainable for banal creations lacking a high degree of aesthetic merit, such as the advertising posters that were at issue in *Bleistein*.[117] A strict fine arts test could also have excluded other creations that are made for marketing purposes, such as logos designed to serve as trademarks. In this way, the risk of copyright/trademark overlaps could have been minimized from the outset. Delivering the opinion of the U.S. Supreme Court, however, Justice Holmes refrained from establishing a strict fine arts test:

109. Cf. Kur/Senftleben 2017, para. 4.422-4.424.
110. U.S. Supreme Court, 2 February 1903, Bleistein/Donaldson Lithographic Co., 188 U.S. 239 (1903).
111. U.S. Supreme Court, *ibid.*, 250-252. Cf. Beebe 2017, 328-329 and 373-374; Parchomovsky/Siegelman 2002, 1497-1498.
112. U.S. Supreme Court, *ibid.*, 248-249. Cf. Beebe 2017, 348-349.
113. Beebe 2017, 349. As to the establishment of statutory protection for 'works connected with the fine arts' in the 1874 amendment to the Copyright Act of 1870, see Beebe, *ibid.*, 356.
114. U.S. Supreme Court, *ibid.*, 251-252.
115. Cf. Grosheide 1986, 193-195; Hugenholtz 1989, 19-20; Dietz 1978, 60.
116. Beebe 2017, 356 and 362.
117. For a description of case law with this tendency at the time, see Beebe 2017, 355-357.

> Certainly works are not the less connected with the fine arts because their pictorial quality attracts the crowd, and therefore gives them a real use – if use means to increase trade and to help to make money. A picture is nonetheless a picture, and nonetheless a subject of copyright, that it is used for an advertisement.[118]

Instead of categorically excluding 'prints or labels designed to be used for any other articles of manufacture',[119] Holmes thus relaxed the fine arts requirement and gave advertising posters and other marketing creations access to the realm of copyright. In addition to this relaxation of the upfront domain test, he set a low threshold for assuming originality. Justice Holmes held that an author's work:

> is the personal reaction of an individual upon nature. Personality always contains something unique. It expresses its singularity even in handwriting, and a very modest grade of art has in it something irreducible which is one man's alone. That something he may copyright unless there is a restriction in the words of the act.[120]

As Barton Beebe points out, the reference to 'personality' left room for requiring a work to contain the author's personality.[121] This personality requirement could have been aligned with a concept of aesthetic progress (in the sense of 'if personality, then progress')[122] to satisfy the overarching objective of the U.S. Constitution to 'promote the Progress of Science and useful Arts, by securing for limited Times to Authors and Inventors the exclusive Right to their respective Writings and Discoveries'.[123] Instead, however, subsequent court decisions applied a simplified version of the *Bleistein* test and confined the enquiry to the question of whether an expression had not been copied from another author and contained economic value.[124] As Beebe concludes, the 'more easily digestible economistic rhetoric of commercial value'[125] supplanted the 'more abstruse humanistic rhetoric of personality'.[126] *Bleistein* thus came to stand 'for the proposition simply that uncopied commercial value could meet the originality requirement'.[127] To this day, the *Bleistein* decision is understood in this sense: as a decision that calls for judicial aesthetic neutrality[128] and sets a very low originality requirement – 'so low that nearly any uncopied work should be

118. U.S. Supreme Court, *ibid.*, 251. Cf. Beebe 2017, 362-363.
119. U.S. Supreme Court, *ibid.*, 251.
120. U.S. Supreme Court, *ibid.*, 250.
121. Beebe 2017, 378. Cf. U.S. Supreme Court, *ibid.*, 249-250.
122. Beebe 2017, 374-375.
123. Article I, Section 8 of the U.S. Constitution. Cf. Beebe 2017, 371-373 and 378.
124. Beebe 2017, 377-380. Cf. U.S. Supreme Court, *ibid.*, 251-252.
125. Beebe 2017, 380.
126. Beebe 2017, 380.
127. Beebe 2017, 378.
128. U.S. Supreme Court, *ibid.*, 251-252.

able to meet it'.[129] In both EU and U.S. law, the domain of copyright, thus, has no clear borders. The reference to 'literary and artistic works'[130] is not understood as an inherent restriction of protection to creations in the domain of literature and fine art. Moreover, the originality test is elastic.

The openness of the copyright system, however, is only one side of the medal. To explain the substantial growth of copyright/trademark overlaps in recent decades, developments in trademark law must be factored into the equation as well. With its protection requirements of distinctiveness[131] and a sufficiently clear and precise representation of signs on the register,[132] trademark law also offers a flexible framework. As Irene Calboli has pointed out, the understanding of distinctiveness in trademark law has gradually shifted: from a strict interpretation focusing on a sign's capacity to identify goods or services in the marketplace to a looser concept that means 'little more than "recognizable" by the human senses': a concept that easily covers product features that are characteristic, typical, appealing, 'or just interesting to see'.[133] The recognition of non-traditional types of marks reflects the elasticity of these protection requirements and strengthens the trend towards cumulative copyright and trademark protection.[134] Three-dimensional objects may serve as shape marks.[135] A short melody may constitute a sound mark.[136] A computer animation may qualify as a motion mark or be part of a multimedia mark.[137] Even single colours – raw material of artistic creativity – are registrable.[138] With this broader range of signs qualifying as

129. Beebe 2017, 350. Cf. Fromer/McKenna 2018, 132-133; Bracha 2008, 265.
130. Articles 1 and 2(1) BC.
131. Article 15(1) TRIPS.
132. Article 3(b) and Recital 13 TMD; Article 4(b) and Recital 10 EUTMR. Cf. CJEU, 12 December 2002, case C-273/00, Sieckmann, paras 50-55.
133. Calboli 2018, 294. Cf. McGeveran 2015, 714-715.
134. Calboli 2018, 296-304; Kur 2002, 595-596. For a critical discussion of the worldwide trend to recognize non-traditional types of marks, see the various contributions to Calboli/Senftleben 2018. As to the discussion during the evolution of non-traditional marks in the EU, see Lewalter/Schrader 2005, 476; Hauck 2005, 363; Kur 2004, 755; Bouvel 2004, 863; Arnet 2004, 829; Pagenberg 2004, 831; Bölling 2004, 384; Bingener 2004, 377; Firth/Gredley/Maniatis 2001, 86.
135. CJEU, 12 February 2004, case C-218/01, Henkel/DPMA, para. 49; CJEU, 8 April 2003, cases C-53/01 to C-55/01, Linde and others, para. 48. As to the possibility of registering design elements as position marks, see German registration no. 302010059754 (Steiff button in ear); German registration no. 30142541, 39504594; Italian registration no. 00011748533 (Lloyd Shoes red stripe).
136. CJEU, 27 November 2003, case C-283/01, Shield Mark/Kist, para. 64. For instance, see the Norwegian registration no. 226092.
137. EUTM registration no. 3429909, 017279712, 017279704, 017350901; Finnish registration no. 229446. As to hologram marks, see EUTM registration no. 017579491.
138. CJEU, 6 May 2003, case C-104/01, Libertel, para. 41 and 68. For example, see EUTM registration no. 000031336 (Milka lilac); EUTM registration no. 000212787 (Deutsche Telekom magenta); EUTM registration no. 000962076 (UPS brown). As to colour combinations, see CJEU, 24 June 2004, case C-49/02, Heidelberger Bauchemie, para. 35; CJEU, 29 July 2019, case C-124/18P, Red Bull/EUIPO, paras 65-66.

trademarks, new areas of overlap emerge with regard to traditional categories of literary and artistic works, in particular sculpture and plastic art, musical compositions and audiovisual creations.

Surveying the evolution of copyright/trademark overlaps, it must finally be considered that copyright protection follows from the very act of creation. Registration is not required.[139] Thus, copyright law generates protection overlaps automatically because no specific procedural steps are necessary to acquire exclusive rights. The cumulation of rights may even occur accidentally – without a strategic decision to maximize protection titles. Hence, it is the recognition of new subject matter in trademark law that, together with an elastic originality test and the absence of registration requirements in copyright law, substantially broadened the area of overlap between the two protection regimes.[140] The option of cumulating copyright and trademark protection has encouraged marketing and rights acquisition strategies that rely on overlapping copyright and trademark protection. As pointed out in Chapter 1, character merchandising leads to cumulative copyright and trademark protection of contemporary cultural symbols. In principle, it is also possible to acquire trademark rights to cultural heritage symbols once distinctive character has been acquired through use in trade.

2.3 SELF-HEALING FORCES OF INTELLECTUAL PROPERTY LAW

The overlap between intellectual property rights, such as cumulative copyright and trademark protection, thwarts the conceptual differences between the individual protection regimes involved. In particular, the delicate balance inherent in copyright and trademark law may be sacrificed on the altar of enhanced possibilities of intellectual property *forum shopping*. Where it becomes possible to invoke coexisting protection under different regimes, the individual balance between rights and freedoms in one protection regime is in danger of being superseded by parallel protection in another regime.[141] As the delicate balance in copyright and trademark law is tailored to specific needs in the domains of culture and trade, the problem of overlapping protection must not be underestimated. It constitutes a serious threat to the inner consistency of the intellectual property system and its efficient functioning in different sectors.

---

139. Article 5(2) BC prohibits formalities with regard to 'the enjoyment and the exercise' of copyright. Cf. Van Gompel 2011, 194-199.
140. Kur 2001, 44.
141. Cf. Dreyfuss 2020, 322-323; Samuelson 2017, 1512-1516; Calboli 2014a, 30-31; Beckerman-Rodau 2011, 73-89; Moffat 2004, 1476; Hugenholtz 2000b, 240-242.

At the core of the overlap problem lies the continuous expansion of intellectual property protection during the last decades.[142] This expansion has given rise to serious concerns about overprotection. In academic literature, external balancing tools have been proposed as remedies. Important research has been undertaken to explore the potential of fundamental rights to serve as a yardstick for the recalibration of the intellectual property system.[143] By the same token, it has been examined whether competition law could be employed to keep intellectual property protection within reasonable limits.[144] Without neglecting or questioning the merits of these approaches, it is the central hypothesis of the present enquiry that *the answer to the alarming growth of the system is in the system.*[145] By identifying the requirements for the proper functioning of intellectual property protection in the domains of culture and trade, and strictly aligning the regulation of copyright/trademark overlaps with these functional preconditions, it will be possible to bring the intellectual property system back into shape.

Based on this premise, the following analysis contrasts central functional parameters of the copyright system – the copyright imperative of cultural follow-on innovation (Chapter 3) – with the market transparency imperative that underlies trademark law (Chapter 4). Comparing preconditions for the proper functioning of copyright and trademark law, it will become apparent that the checks and balances of the copyright system are presently at risk. With growing areas of coexisting trademark protection, central characteristics of copyright law, such as the limited term of protection

142. Cf. Coombe 2003, 1173-1174.

143. Cf. Geiger 2008b, 111; Helfer 2007, 977; Yu 2007a, 1041; Yu 2007b, 711; Marceau 2002, 756. As to the influence of freedom of expression on copyright protection, cf. Geiger/Izyumenko 2020, 292-298; Jongsma 2019, 195-222; Geiger/Izyumenko 2019, 133-136; Hugenholtz 2016, 242; Geiger/Izyumenko 2016, 43; Geiger/Izyumenko 2014, 316; Netanel 2008; Geiger 2006, 371; Strowel/Tulkens/Voorhoof 2006; Hugenholtz 2002, 239; Macciacchini 2000; Benkler 1999, 354; Netanel 1996, 283. With regard to the debate on how to reconcile trademark protection with freedom of expression, see Bohaczewski 2020, 856; Żelechowski 2018, 115-135; Senftleben 2015, 354; Ramsey/Schovsbo 2013, 671; Simon Fhima 2013, 293; Sakulin 2010; Geiger 2010a, 163; Burrell/Gangjee 2010, 544; Nasser 2009, 188; Bently 2008, 1205; Dreyfuss 2008, 261; Geiger 2007, 317; Ramsey 2010a, 405; Weckström 2007, 671; Gulasekaram 2005, 887; Leval 2004, 187; Timbers/Huston 2003, 1278; Aoki 1997, 523; Dreyfuss 1990, 415-418.

144. Cf. Podszun 2019, 720-745; Ghidini 2018, 50-63, 331-390; Podszun 2017, 786-805; Senftleben 2017d, 257-278; Lamping 2015, 121-145; Farrar 2014, 373; Drexl 2013; Cheng 2013, 385; Lemley/McKenna 2012, 2055; Hovenkamp 2012, 2133; Hou 2012, 251; Maggiolino 2011; Podszun 2010, 57-76, Hilty 2009a, 633-644; Conde Gallego 2006, 16-28; Heinemann 2006, 705-713; Drexl 2004, 788-808; Ullrich 2004, 401-430; Dreier 2001b, 51-81; and the contributions to Drexl 2008.

145. The focus, therefore, is on the exploration of internal legal instruments – within the system of protection requirements, exclusive rights and limitations of individual protection regimes – that may be capable of reducing the corrosive effect of protection overlaps. As to the discussion on internal or external (based on a direct invocation of higher-ranking fundamental rights) balancing of interests in intellectual property law, see Geiger 2006, 371; Voorhoof 2002, 639-640; Dreier 2001a, 295.

and the exemption of transformative use, may be undermined. To activate the self-healing forces of intellectual property law and shield copyright law against the corrosive effect of coexisting trademark protection, the cultural imperative in copyright law must be brought into focus. Otherwise, overlapping trademark protection may impede central societal functions of the copyright system and undermine the credibility of copyright law as an engine of autonomous cultural productions.

Hence, it is submitted here that preconditions for the proper functioning of copyright law are central to the elimination of deficiencies of the current, increasingly inconsistent interplay between copyright and trademark protection. As it is the foremost task of intellectual property law to ensure the proper functioning of its individual protection subsystems, the internal self-healing forces of the intellectual property system can be demonstrated by identifying the preconditions for the proper functioning of copyright law and aligning the regulatory response to copyright/trademark overlaps with this functional essence of the copyright regime. Once the inalienable core of copyright law has been brought to light, it is clear which functional parameters of copyright protection must remain intact when overlapping trademark rights are acquired.

Chapter 3
Cultural Imperative in Copyright Law

As explained in the preceding chapter, the cultural imperative represents the inalienable core of copyright law. It can be described as the functional essence of the protection regime that is indispensable for the maintenance of a proper balance between rights and freedoms in the cultural domain. Tracing the conceptual contours of the cultural imperative in copyright law, the following section 3.1 identifies two central elements: the guarantee of intergenerational equity and the recognition of the public domain. The principle of intergenerational equity is indispensable because it supports autonomous literary and artistic productions. Public domain recognition ensures the availability of alternative visions of society that are expressed in works of art. These two core elements of the cultural imperative play a central role in both legal traditions of copyright law (section 3.2). Moreover, they have particular societal relevance (section 3.3). In line with an approach that seeks to activate the self-healing forces of the intellectual property system (preceding section 2.3), the identification of these core elements of the cultural imperative paves the way for the use of this essence of copyright law as an elixir to cure the disease of overlapping copyright and trademark protection. The cultural imperative offers guidance for the calibration of the copyright/trademark interface. It shows which rights and freedoms are inalienable from a copyright perspective. Hence, it also shows which rights and freedoms must be preserved when copyright/trademark overlaps arise (section 3.4).

3.1 INTERGENERATIONAL EQUITY AND PUBLIC DOMAIN RECOGNITION

On its merits, copyright law is an inspiration system. It is the core function of copyright law to further the incessant process of the creation of fresh, original human expression on the basis of pre-existing sources of inspiration. The author's essential trait is her ability to find new ways of individual expression in a given cultural environment. As Jessica Litman pointed out:

> the very act of authorship in any medium is more akin to translation and recombination than it is to creating Aphrodite from the foam of the sea. Composers recombine sounds they have heard before; playwrights base their characters on bits and pieces drawn from real human beings and other playwrights' characters; novelists draw their plots from lives and other plots within their experience; software writers use the logic they find in other software; lawyers transform old arguments to fit new facts; cinematographers, actors, choreographers, architects, and sculptors all engage in the process of adapting, transforming, and recombining what is already 'out there' in some other form. This is not parasitism: it is the essence of authorship.[146]

Similarly, Julie Cohen emphasized that the creative process 'is one of active engagement with and reinterpretation of [pre-existing cultural] artifacts'.[147] References and allusions to already existing literary and artistic works are a feature of cultural productions that runs all the way through the different epochs of intellectual creation.[148] For the purpose of creation, authors extract building blocks and sources of inspiration from existing expressions, forms and traditions, and add their own ingenuity to arrive at new and fresh cultural material.[149] Rewarding this contribution to the maintenance of the cultural innovation cycle, copyright law recognizes exclusive rights in literary and artistic works that result from the author's labour. These rights, however, expire after a limited period of time. The works which the author created on the basis of available material ultimately enter the public domain where they serve as a basis for new creations. Copyright law, therefore, ultimately seeks to *safeguard the cultural innovation cycle*. This is the core function of the copyright system. To safeguard this core function, copyright law imposes the obligation on authors acquiring copyright to acquiesce in a limited term of protection. The international

146. Litman 1990, 966-967.
147. Cohen 2006, 152. Cf. Peukert 2019, 1181.
148. Frosio 2018, 15-68; Frosio 2014, 345-376; Cohen 2006, 144-146. Cf. Buccafusco/Bechtold/Sprigman 2017, 42-43, stating in the light of consumer preferences that '[c]reativity, in this context, does not mean doing something entirely new, but rather doing something old in a new way'.
149. See the analysis of research on the social psychology of creativity by Cohen 2006, 154-155. Cf. Dusollier 2018, 180-183; Craig 2011, 52-56; Cohen 2006, 144-152.

minimum term of copyright protection amounts to 50 years *post mortem auctoris*.[150] Many national laws offer a more generous term of 70 years after the author's death.[151]

Moreover, the idea/expression dichotomy in copyright law excludes mere ideas, concepts and styles from copyright protection to prevent the monopolization of basic source materials for cultural follow-on innovation. Copyright concerns the individual expression in which an idea is presented in a literary and artistic work. It does not extend to ideas, procedures, methods or concepts as such.[152] As a result of the exclusion of copyright protection, the ideas underlying a literary or artistic work remain freely available. Later authors may base their own individual expression on this raw material without having to seek permission. The rationale underlying the idea/expression dichotomy clearly comes to the fore in case law. In *Broeren/Duijsens*, for example, the Dutch Supreme Court explained that copyright law:

> gives no exclusive right to someone working in accordance with a characteristic style. At the core of this jurisprudence lies the consideration that copyright protection of abstractions, such as style characteristics, would amount to an impermissible limitation of the freedom of creation and, consequently, constitute an impediment of cultural development.[153]

Hence, the idea/expression dichotomy seeks to keep basic building blocks of cultural follow-on innovation free. Ideas, concepts and styles must be available for all authors. Copyright law would dry out the very sources of cultural creativity if it granted exclusive rights to these abstract features of literary and artistic works. The cultural innovation cycle would come to a standstill if ideas, concepts and styles could be monopolized.

The *Broeren/Duijsens* case is of particular interest with regard to copyright/trademark overlaps because it required the Dutch Supreme Court to weigh the free availability of ideas, concepts and styles against a potential risk of consumer confusion and unfair freeriding. The painter Gerdine Duijsens had filed the lawsuit because she was confronted with imitations of her characteristic way of painting overweight people at fancy cocktail receptions. Applying very similar style elements, Theo Broeren had created paintings that could hardly be distinguished from Duijsens' works. Seeking to put an end to this imitation practice, Duijsens argued that copyright infringement followed not only from the copying of individual paintings but also from Broeren's imitation of her way of painting people as such. On its

150. Article 7(1) BC.
151. Article 1(1) TD. Cf. CJEU, 27 January 2011, case C-168/09, Flos, paras 39-40. As to the term extension in the U.S., see U.S. Supreme Court, 15 January 2003, Eldred/Ashcroft, 537 U.S. 186, 202 (2003). Cf. Austin 2003, 163.
152. Article 9(2) TRIPS; Article 2 WCT.
153. Dutch Supreme Court, 29 March 2013, case LJN BY8661, Broeren/Duijsens, para. 3.5.

merits, she sought protection for an archetypical theme and characteristic style element of her paintings.[154]

Given the high degree of similarity between the original paintings and Broeren's later imitations, Duijsens had success with this claim in lower instances. The Court of Appeals of Den Bos found copyright infringement with regard to five individual works.[155] In addition, the Court was of the opinion that the idea/expression dichotomy in copyright law did not preclude the invocation of more general unfair competition law. Accordingly, the Court saw room for protection against slavish imitation, at least in cases where the second author exploits the reputation of the original works and is likely to cause confusion:

> With his imitations, Broeren can profit from the commercial potential which Duijsens' works have. This can lead to confusion among the public. A work by Broeren may easily be regarded as a painting by Duijsens. [... T]he Court is of the opinion that, as a result of the imitation of Duijsens' style, confusion among the public is to be feared.[156]

According to this approach, the objective to guarantee market transparency would thus prevail over the freedom of ideas, concepts and style in copyright law. Protection against slavish imitation could serve as a vehicle to achieve style protection through the backdoor and undermine the distinction between protected expression and free ideas. In the light of this risk, the Dutch Supreme Court unequivocally rejected the approach taken by the Court of Appeals and posited that the law left no room for supplementary protection of an author against slavish imitation in respect of a style or style characteristics. A different conclusion would thwart the objective to keep ideas, concepts and style free for cultural development.[157] While not completely ruling out the possibility of style protection against slavish imitation under exceptional circumstances, the Dutch Supreme Court expressly stated that consumer confusion was not sufficient to justify such protection.[158] Hence, the idea/expression dichotomy in copyright law prevailed. Protection against slavish imitation was unavailable as an alternative avenue to arrive at the protection of ideas, concepts or style – even though the style imitation at issue caused consumer confusion.

---

154. Court of Appeals of Den Bos, 15 November 2011, case LJN BU4770, Duijsens/Broeren, para. 4.10.3.
155. Court of Appeals of Den Bos, ibid., para. 4.11.11.
156. Court of Appeals of Den Bos, *ibid.*, para. 4.12.5.
157. Dutch Supreme Court, 29 March 2013, case LJN BY8661, Broeren/Duijsens, para. 3.6.
158. Dutch Supreme Court, *ibid.*, para. 3.6. As pointed out by Pinckaers 2013, 117, it is hard to imagine which exceptional circumstances could still justify protection against slavish imitation in the case of style imitations. Potentially, the intention to deceive the public or the intention to damage the original author's reputation could serve as examples.

In copyright law, not only the freedom to use ideas, concepts and styles but also the freedom to make unauthorized use of an author's individual, protected expression is central to the promotion of a continuous cycle of new creations on the basis of pre-existing cultural material.[159] This freedom becomes crucial, for example, in the case of authors who need to quote existing cultural material to express their own view and authors seeking to criticize existing material in the guise of parody. The fundamental importance of use privileges for these transformative purposes is widely recognized in copyright law. At the international level, the exemption of quotations in the Berne Convention constitutes the sole mandatory limitation of copyright. According to Article 10(1) BC, '[i]t shall be permissible to make quotations from a work which has already been lawfully made available to the public … '. The prevailing French text[160] reads '[s]ont licites les citations tirées d'une œuvre … '. The Berne Convention, therefore, postulates that there is room for quotations in copyright law. It does not offer Berne Union members a choice in this respect.[161] If the adoption of a copyright limitation is optional, the Convention uses different wording, such as the formula '[i]t shall be a matter for legislation in the countries of the Union … '.[162] Arguably, parody falls within the scope of the mandatory right of quotation recognized in Article 10(1) BC. As Antoon Quaedvlieg has shown, parodies can be qualified as permissible quotations.[163] They constitute a specific form of quotation aiming at a critical comment in the guise of a mockery. As Quaedvlieg points out, the confrontation of the original work with the parodist's artistic reaction is comparable with the confrontation of the original work with the rationalist reaction of the polemist who may rely on quotations taken from the original work.[164]

Seeking an explanation for the elevated status of copyright limitations for transformative use, such as quotations and parodies, the guarantee of freedom of expression enters the picture. In national decisions on the right of quotation and the exemption of parody, freedom of expression plays a central role as a counterweight to copyright protection. The fair use doctrine enshrined in Section 107 of the U.S. Copyright Act, for instance, may be invoked to defend unauthorized use for purposes 'such as criticism, comment, news reporting, teaching […], scholarship, or research'. The words 'such as' indicate that the expressly mentioned purposes merely serve as examples. U.S. courts enjoy the freedom of identifying additional purposes and new forms of fair use. The Senate and House Committee Reports that accompanied the codification of the fair use doctrine leave no

159. For an argument in favour of broad support for 'aesthetic practice' based on protected pre-existing works as raw material, see Beebe 2017, 390-393.
160. Article 37(1)(c) BC.
161. Aplin/Bently 2020, 72-84.
162. Articles 2bis(2), 9(2), 10(2), 10bis(1) and (2) BC.
163. Quaedvlieg 1987, p. 279.
164. Quaedvlieg, *ibid.*, p. 285.

doubt about the intention to preserve the flexibility of the doctrine following from its evolution in case law:

> since the doctrine is an equitable rule of reason, no generally applicable definition is possible, and each case raising the question must be decided on its own facts ... The bill endorses the purpose and general scope of the judicial doctrine of fair use [...] but there is no disposition to freeze the doctrine in the statute ... Beyond a very broad statutory explanation of what fair use is and some of the criteria applicable to it, the courts must be free to adapt the doctrine to particular situations on a case-by-case basis.[165]

When it comes to an analysis of unauthorized use in the light of the fair use factors set forth in Section 107 of the U.S. Copyright Act, the transformative nature of the use in question is a decisive factor capable of tipping the scales in favour of a finding of fair use.[166] With regard to the conditions for a successful invocation of the freedom of transformative use in the U.S., Pierre Leval explains that:

> [t]he use must be productive and must employ the quoted matter in a different manner or for a different purpose from the original. A quotation of copyrighted material that merely repackages or republishes the original is unlikely to pass the test; [...] If, on the other hand, the secondary use adds value to the original – if the quoted matter is used as raw material, transformed in the creation of new information, new aesthetics, new insights and understandings – this is the very type of activity that the fair use doctrine intends to protect for the enrichment of society.[167]

In its famous decision in *Campbell/Acuff-Rose*, the U.S. Supreme Court applied this standard to a rap version of Roy Orbison's and William Dees' song 'Oh, Pretty Woman' which the rap group 2 Live Crew had composed to satirize the naive, intact world built up in the original. The Court explained that it was the central purpose of the fair use investigation to see:

> whether the new work merely supersedes the objects of the original creation [...] or instead adds something new, with a further purpose or different character, altering the first with new expression, meaning, or

165. Seltzer 1978, 19-20. As to the application and importance of the fair use doctrine in practice, see Sag 2012, 47; Samuelson 2009, 2537; Beebe 2008, 156; Leval 1990, 1105; Litman 1997, 588. For critical comments on the predictability and consistency of U.S. fair use decisions, see Nimmer 2003, 263; Förster 2008, 197-201.
166. Sag 2012, 55-58, 76-77, 79-81. While the empirical analysis conducted by Beebe 2008, 603-606, did not find evidence that transformativeness is addressed in almost every fair use analysis, it confirmed a major impact in those cases where the issue played a role. See Beebe, *ibid.*, 605, referring to 'nearly dispositive force'.
167. Leval 1990, 1111.

> message; it asks, in other words, whether and to what extent the new work is 'transformative'.[168]

Applying this standard, the Court clarified that parody using parts of the original work to make the target of its mockery identifiable could constitute fair use, even if the critique expressed in the guise of parody killed the demand for the original work. It was the role of the courts to distinguish between biting criticism that merely suppressed demand for the original work and copyright infringement which usurped it.[169] At the core of this ruling lies the insight that the parodist depends on the use of protected, pre-existing material to be able to express herself:

> Parody's humor, or in any event its comment, necessarily springs from recognizable allusion to its object through distorted imitation. Its art lies in the tension between a known original and its parodic twin. When parody takes aim at a particular original work, the parody must be able to 'conjure up' at least enough of that original to make the object of its critical wit recognizable.[170]

Hence, the central function of the fair use analysis in parody cases clearly comes to the fore. As a defence supporting the transformative remix of copyrighted works, the U.S. fair use doctrine shields the creative activities of second authors against infringement claims based on copyright to protected source material. In this way, copyright protection is balanced against freedom of expression and prevented from becoming an obstacle to new cultural productions. Second authors can express themselves freely on the basis of existing cultural material. In this vein, the U.S. Supreme Court characterizes the open-ended fair use defence in the U.S. Copyright Act as a 'built-in' safeguard that allows judges to reconcile the protection interests of copyright owners with free expression interests of unauthorized users.[171]

A close connection between freedom of expression and use privileges for the transformative remix of copyrighted works has also been recognized in EU copyright law. The EU Information Society Directive and the DSM Directive provide for specific statutory limitations relating to 'quotations for purposes such as criticism or review'[172] and 'use for the purpose of caricature, parody or pastiche'.[173] Relying on freedom of expression as a counterbalance to copyright protection, the CJEU created a substantial degree of flexibility in this area. In *Painer*, the Court underlined the need for

168. U.S. Supreme Court, 7 March 1994, Campbell/Acuff-Rose, 510 U.S. 569, 579 (1994).
169. U.S. Supreme Court, *ibid.*, 591-592.
170. U.S. Supreme Court, *ibid.*, 588.
171. U.S. Supreme Court, 15 January 2003, Eldred/Ashcroft, 537 U.S. 186 (2003), 219; U.S. Supreme Court, 20 May 1985, Harper & Row/Nation Enterprises, 471 U.S. 539 (1985), 560. Cf. Samuelson 2009, 2546-2547.
172. Article 5(3)(d) ISD; Article 17(7) DSMD.
173. Article 5(3)(k) ISD; Article 17(7) DSMD. Cf. Senftleben 2019, 485-490.

an interpretation of the right of quotation set forth in Article 5(3)(d) ISD that enables the effectiveness of the copyright limitation and safeguards its purpose.[174] More specifically, the Court clarified that Article 5(3)(d) ISD was:

> intended to strike a fair balance between the right of freedom of expression of users of a work or other protected subject-matter and the reproduction right conferred on authors.[175]

In its further decision in *Deckmyn*, the CJEU followed the same path with regard to the parody exemption in Article 5(3)(k) ISD. As in *Painer*, the Court underlined the need to ensure the effectiveness of the parody exemption[176] as a means to reconcile copyright protection with freedom of expression.[177] Instead of adopting strict criteria, the Court rejected several conditions that had been proposed by the Court of Appeals of Brussels when asking prejudicial questions about the scope of the use privilege. In particular, the CJEU dismissed the view that for being permissible, a parody:

- should display an original character of its own, other than that of displaying noticeable differences with respect to the original parodied work;
- could reasonably be attributed to a person other than the author of the original work itself;
- should relate to the original work itself or mention the source of the parodied work.[178]

As these examples demonstrate, the fundamental guarantee of freedom of expression plays a crucial role. Invoking Article 11 CFR and Article 10 ECHR, the CJEU could interpret the quotation right and the parody exemption less strictly than limitations without a comparably strong transformative use component. In its earlier *Infopaq* decision, the Court had adhered to the traditional continental-European dogma of a strict interpretation of copyright limitations. Scrutinizing the mandatory exemption of transient copies in Article 5(1) ISD, the Court pointed out that for the interpretation of each of the cumulative conditions of the limitation, it should be borne in mind that:

> according to settled case-law, the provisions of a directive which derogate from a general principle established by that directive must be interpreted strictly […]. This holds true for the exemption provided for in Article 5(1) of Directive 2001/29, which is a derogation from the general principle established by that directive, namely the requirement

174. CJEU, 1 December 2011, case C-145/10, Painer, para. 132-133.
175. CJEU, *ibid.*, para. 134.
176. CJEU, 3 September 2014, case C-201/13, Deckmyn, paras 22-23.
177. CJEU, *ibid.*, paras 25-27.
178. CJEU, *ibid.*, para. 21.

of authorisation from the rightholder for any reproduction of a protected work.[179]

According to the Court:

> [t]his is all the more so given that the exemption must be interpreted in the light of Article 5(5) of Directive 2001/29, under which that exemption is to be applied only in certain special cases which do not conflict with a normal exploitation of the work or other subject-matter and do not unreasonably prejudice the legitimate interests of the rightholder.[180]

The CJEU thus established the rule that copyright limitations had to be construed narrowly. Both the *Painer* and the *Deckmyn* decision create a remarkable contrast with this general position. Instead of confirming the rule of strict interpretation, the Court emphasized in *Painer* and *Deckmyn* the need to achieve a 'fair balance' between, in particular, 'the rights and interests of authors on the one hand, and the rights of users of protected subject-matter on the other'.[181] The Court thus referred to quotations and parodies as user 'rights' rather than mere user 'interests'.[182] In the light of freedom of expression, a user engaged in transformative remix activities thus meets the copyright owner at eye level. Her legal position is not a priori weaker than the protection status which the copyright owner enjoys by virtue of copyright law. In *Funke Medien* and *Spiegel Online*, the CJEU explicitly confirmed the status of user rights by pointing out that, 'although Article 5 [ISD] is expressly entitled "Exceptions and limitations", it should be noted that those exceptions or limitations do themselves confer rights on the users of works or of other subject matter'.[183]

National case law in the EU also sheds light on the strong human rights dimension of quotation and parody cases. In its *Germania 3* decision, the German Federal Constitutional Court had to decide on comprehensive takings from works by Bertolt Brecht that Heiner Müller had included in his play 'Germania 3 Gespenster am toten Mann'. Contending that Müller had overstepped the limits of the quotation right recognized in German copyright law,[184] the holders of the rights in Brecht's works sued for copyright

179. CJEU, 16 July 2009, case C-5/08, Infopaq International/Danske Dagblades Forening, paras 56-57.
180. CJEU, *ibid.*, para. 58.
181. CJEU, 1 December 2011, case C-145/10, Eva Maria Painer/Standard VerlagsGmbH, para. 132; CJEU, 3 September 2014, case C-201/13, Deckmyn, para. 26.
182. For an analysis of this development in EU copyright law, see Griffiths/Geiger/Senftleben/Xalabarder/Bently 2015, 127.
183. CJEU, 29 July 2019, case C-516/17, Spiegel Online, para. 54; CJEU, 29 July 2019, case C-469/17, Funke Medien NRW, para. 70. For a more detailed discussion of this point, see Aplin/Bently 2020, 75-84; Geiger/Izyumenko 2020, 292-298.
184. § 51 No. 2 German Copyright Act (Urheberrechtsgesetz). As to the continuous broadening of the quotation right in German copyright law, see Förster 2008, 85-96.

infringement. Müller's widow and the play's publisher, by contrast, invoked Müller's freedom of artistic expression as a defence. They asserted that the quotations were indispensable for the discussion of Brecht's political position, as intended by Müller.[185] The Court, thus, had to decide whether Brecht's copyright inhibited Müller from freely expressing himself artistically. To strike a proper balance, it emphasized that copyright limitations had to be construed in the light of the freedom of artistic expression, as guaranteed in German constitutional law.[186] The Court maintained that at least when the possible economic harm flowing from a quotation could not be deemed significant, the second author's interest in using a pre-existing work prevailed over the exploitation interests of the first author.[187]

As the rulings of the CJEU, the *Germania 3* decision in Germany highlights the fundamental rights guarantee underlying transformative use defences in copyright law. The artistic freedom of expression of second authors imposes limits on the intellectual property of the original author. The fundamental right to property, including intellectual property, is to be balanced against the fundamental guarantee of freedom of expression.[188] As in the U.S., breathing space for transformative use, thus, results from the need to reconcile the grant of copyright with the necessity to preserve areas of freedom for cultural follow-on innovation.

In sum, a survey of checks and balances in copyright law yields the insight that the overarching objective of the protection system – to serve as an inspiration system that ensures the constant renewal of the cultural landscape on the basis of pre-existing source material ('cultural innovation cycle') – requires not only the grant of exclusive rights but also the introduction of a limited term of protection, the recognition of the freedom of ideas, concepts and styles, and the creation of breathing space for transformative use. At a higher level of abstraction, these central preconditions for the proper functioning of copyright law can be regarded as exponents of two core principles that form the cultural imperative in copyright law:

---

185. German Federal Constitutional Court, 29 June 2000, case 1 BvR 825/98, 'Germania 3', Zeitschrift für Urheber- und Medienrecht 2000, 868.
186. Article 5(3) of the German Basic Law (Grundgesetz). See German Federal Constitutional Court, *ibid.*, 869: 'Dem Interesse der Urheberrechtsinhaber vor Ausbeutung ihrer Werke ohne Genehmigung zu fremden kommerziellen Zwecken steht das durch die Kunstfreiheit geschützte Interesse anderer Künstler gegenüber, ohne die Gefahr von Eingriffen finanzieller oder inhaltlicher Art in einen künstlerischen Dialog und Schaffensprozess zu vorhandenen Werken treten zu können.' Cf. von Becker 2000, 864-865.
187. German Federal Constitutional Court, *ibid.*, 869. Cf. Metzger 2000, 925.
188. As to the influence of freedom of expression on the scope and enforcement of copyright, cf. Geiger/Izyumenko 2019, 133-136; Jongsma 2019, 123-243; Hugenholtz 2016, 242; Geiger/Izyumenko 2016, 43; Geiger/Izyumenko 2014, 316; Netanel 2008; Geiger 2006, 371; Strowel/Tulkens/Voorhoof 2006; Hugenholtz 2002, 239; Macciacchini 2000; Benkler 1999, 354; Netanel 1996, 283.

- on the one hand, it is imperative that authors enjoying copyright protection be obliged to allow later authors to use protected material as a source and basis for their subsequent creations. Later authors should be free to ground their own creative activities in the creations of their predecessors. This first element of the cultural imperative is the *guarantee of intergenerational equity*. The efforts made in copyright law to offer room for transformative use reflect this first principle. Moreover, the limitation of the term of protection supports intergenerational equity;
- on the other hand, it is imperative that the need to preserve a rich and robust public domain be recognized. Public domain material can serve as a source of inspiration and basis of new acts of creation. The second element of the cultural imperative, therefore, is the *recognition of the public domain*. The idea/expression dichotomy reflects this second principle. The limited term of protection ensures that the public domain is constantly enriched with fresh cultural expressions.

3.2 RECOGNITION IN BOTH LEGAL TRADITIONS OF COPYRIGHT LAW

An analysis of the theoretical groundwork for the protection of literary and artistic works in copyright's legal traditions confirms the central importance of these elements of the cultural imperative. The utilitarian line of argument in Anglo-American countries emphasizes benefits which society can derive from cultural follow-on innovation. It recognizes the crucial role of intergenerational equity and a robust public domain in the incessant creation of new cultural productions that enhance the overall welfare of society (3.2.1). The natural law approach in continental Europe invokes Locke's labour theory to explain the author's entitlement to exclusive rights in literary and artistic works. The author – regarded as a labourer in the abundant world of ideas and cultural expressions – mixes her own creative effort with available raw material, thereby enriching the stock of cultural creations with new expression and acquiring a property right to her creation. As a precondition for the acquisition of this property right, however, the author is obliged to leave sufficient resources for later creators. The guarantee of intergenerational equity and the recognition of the public domain thus also constitute central elements of continental-European copyright systems (3.2.2).

3.2.1 *Utilitarian Argument*

Utilitarian copyright theory focuses on considerations of social utility to explain the grant of exclusive rights in copyright law.[189] It does not recognize an inherent right of authors to their creations.[190] Focusing on benefits for society instead, it sees copyright as a vehicle to spur the creation of socially valuable works. The resulting system of copyright protection mirrors the reliance on the motivating power of economic incentives. The promise of monetary rewards is offered to authors as a bait to encourage their intellectual productivity.[191] A marketable right is conferred to ensure a sufficient supply of disseminated knowledge and information.

These utilitarian arguments imply the existence of a community. Utilitarian theory conceives of property as a conventionally recognized stability of possession. The convention thereby arises out of the perception of men that individual advantage can be derived from mutual forbearance to interfere with the possessions of others. Any security of possessions stems from the belief that the establishment of a lasting association will be impossible as long as members of the envisioned community trespass against one another.[192] In the course of development towards a permanently ordained association, the evolving practice of mutual forbearance is fortified through an established set of rules. Private property is therefore rooted in the historical evolution of the customary acceptance of certain rules.[193]

In this framework of ingrained habits, a high level of productivity depends on arrangements which assure to every labourer a predictable amount of the fruits of his labour. It is assumed that the time and effort necessary to create a new product will not be spent unless generally accepted rules secure that the labourer is permitted to enjoy a substantial share of the product.[194] This explains the reliance of utilitarian copyright systems on the motivating power of the grant of exclusive rights. As these rights afford an author the control of the use and enjoyment of her intellectual work, they offer the possibility of deriving economic profit from a work's creation. Copyright protection, thus, provides an incentive to create. The legal assurance that exclusive rights in works of the intellect will be conferred on every author is offered to encourage intellectual productivity. This theoretical model underlies, for instance, the U.S. Constitution which seeks to:

---

189. Strowel 1994, 235; Fisher 1988, 1686-1692.
190. Weinreb 1998, 1211 and 1214-1215; Calandrillo 1998, 310; Michelman 1967, 1208-1213.
191. Michelman 1967, 1211; Calandrillo 1998, 310-312; Geller 1994, 159 and 164-166.
192. See the description of utilitarian theories given by Michelman 1967, 1208-1209, who bases his analysis on Hume and Bentham.
193. Michelman 1967, 1209-1210.
194. Michelman 1967, 1211-1212.

promote the Progress of Science and useful Arts, by securing for limited Times to Authors and Inventors the exclusive Right to their respective Writings and Discoveries.[195]

The outlined incentive mechanism, however, is neutral with regard to the level of protection. The objective to spur intellectual creation does not automatically lead to the maximization of protection. As the overall welfare of society constitutes the centre of gravity, exclusive rights can only be justified and are only to be conceded insofar as this can be deemed beneficial for society as a whole. This conception leads to the understanding that there is a dualism inherent in the grant of exclusive rights.

On the one hand, copyright must provide the economic incentives necessary to achieve the desired production and dissemination of literary and artistic works. At the core of this incentive rationale lies the economic insight that literary and artistic works constitute 'public goods'. Because of non-rivalry in consumption[196] and non-excludability in use,[197] they are unlikely to be created in sufficient quantities in the absence of appropriate incentives.[198] On the other hand, the grant of exclusive rights as part of a strategy to ensure the required incentives involves considerable costs in terms of access to information and cultural follow-on innovation. Once copyright holders obtain exclusive rights, consumers may be inhibited from access to copyrighted works and future creators may be inhibited from building new creations on the basis of pre-existing ones. The incentive scheme intended to spur the creation and dissemination of works inevitably becomes a burden on the creation and dissemination of secondary works.[199] To achieve optimal results for society as a whole, copyright law thus requires a constant effort to strike a proper balance between costs and benefits. As summarized by Guy Pessach, the conceptual contours of protection are to be drawn:

> in a manner that concurrently maximizes the incentive for investing resources in the production and dissemination of diversified, socially valued creative works; and to minimize the costs and burdens that copyright imposes on the public and on other creators.[200]

The U.S. Constitution, for instance, is understood to grant monopoly rights to authors not only to enrich the common store of information. The dissemination of literary and artistic works is also qualified as an integral part

---

195. Article I, Section 8 of the U.S. Constitution.
196. Use by one actor does not restrict the ability of another actor to benefit as well.
197. Unauthorized parties ('free riders') cannot be prevented from use.
198. Fisher 1988, 1700; Landes/Posner 1989, 326; Netanel 2008, 84-85. The grant of property rights is only one strategy for providing these incentives. A system of public subsidies could solve the problem as well. Cf. Posner 2005, 58-59; Calandrillo 1998, 301.
199. Posner 2005, 57; Pessach 2003, 1077; Benkler 1999, 392-393.
200. Pessach 2003, 1077.

of the overarching objective to foster the welfare of the public.[201] Hence it follows that, besides the beneficial effect of copyright which consists of the incentive for authors, the detriment to the users of literary and artistic works who have to pay monopoly prices if they want to enjoy or modify a copyrighted work must be factored into the equation as well.[202] The dialectic inscribed in copyright law clearly comes to the fore in Thomas Macaulay's famous statement that the grant of exclusive rights imposes a 'tax on readers for the purpose of giving a bounty to writers'.[203]

The closer analysis of the utilitarian approach to copyright, therefore, confirms the need for a proper balance between rights and freedoms. Both sides of the coin – the benefit for authors and the detriment to users – must be taken into account when conferring copyright.[204] Taking this insight as a starting point, the aforementioned elements of the cultural imperative – intergenerational equity and public domain recognition – can easily be located in the theoretical texture of utilitarian copyright law:

- *intergenerational equity*: to maximize the overall welfare of society, the protection enjoyed by authors of existing literary and artistic works must not thwart the creative efforts of later authors wishing to build upon pre-existing, protected material. Otherwise, the protection of works created in the past would become an obstacle to the making of works in the future. The overarching objective to incentivize the creation of fresh cultural expression would be compromised if the protection of existing works became too heavy a burden for the creation of new works. The first element of the cultural imperative – the guarantee of intergenerational equity in the sense of an obligation of authors enjoying protection to allow later authors to explore and use protected material as a source and basis for subsequent creations – thus follows directly from the objectives underlying utilitarian copyright systems;
- *recognition of the public domain*: this second element of the cultural imperative is also inherent in utilitarian copyright law. The protection of literary and artistic works does not constitute an end in itself. It serves the purpose of furthering the public good by ensuring a sufficient supply of cultural productions. The ultimate goal of utilitarian copyright law does not lie in the grant of protection but in the constant enrichment of the common store of information. Society accepts the temporary burden of exclusive rights in light of the

201. Weinreb 1998, 1232; Calandrillo 1998, 310.

202. Weinreb 1998, 1231; Calandrillo 1998, 304. See in respect of the 'deadweight loss' that results from the grant of exclusive rights Fisher 1988, 1700-1702.

203. See the statement by Thomas Babington Macaulay, First Speech on Copyright (5 February 1841), as quoted by Weinreb 1998, 1231.

204. Cf. Moffat 2004, 1488, 1508 and 1517; Nimmer/Brown/Frischling 1999, 76; Elkin-Koren 1997, 113; Ginsburg 1997, 4.

prospect of unrestricted access and use of literary and artistic works once protection expires. Viewed from this perspective, it is the very purpose of utilitarian copyright law to provide a rich and robust public domain of cultural expressions that can serve as a starting point for new acts of creation.

Not surprisingly, the debate on how to strike a proper balance between rights and freedoms in utilitarian copyright systems sheds light on various parameters that determine the degree of intergenerational equity and public domain recognition. The economic analysis of copyright law, for instance, highlights the risk of over-rewarding copyright holders and unnecessarily restricting access by applying a long and uniform term of protection to all kinds of literary and artistic works.[205] It warns of prohibitive transaction costs that would frustrate a work's use for the purposes of parody, criticism and review, and the enormous transaction costs that would result from the appropriation of ideas. Discussing the risk of market failure in these latter areas, Richard Posner concludes that authors themselves may prefer the limitation of their rights to enable reviews of their works that can serve as a credible form of advertising, and the free use of ideas, concepts and styles as raw materials of new cultural expressions.[206]

As explained above, the debate on a proper balance between rights and freedoms in utilitarian copyright systems also addresses copyright's impact on freedom of expression. In *Harper & Row/Nation Enterprises*, the U.S. Supreme Court referred to copyright as the 'engine of free expression'.[207] It went on to elaborate that 'by establishing a marketable right to the use of one's expression, copyright supplies the economic incentive to create and disseminate ideas'.[208] This line of reasoning can be traced back to the age of enlightenment when the grant of copyright protection replaced traditional systems of censorship.[209] By offering authors the opportunity to derive economic profit from their works, copyright protection ensured them independence from any kind of patronage potentially seeking to restrict their freedom of expression.[210] The users of copyrighted material, in turn, could enjoy works that had been created in the absence of manipulation and

205. Posner 2005, 59-61. However, Posner also expresses the view that long copyright terms can have economic benefits, namely the prevention of congestion, boredom and a net reduction in market value, and continued expenditures on advertising and promotion (*ibid.*, 61).
206. Posner 2005, 63 and 65.
207. U.S. Supreme Court, 20 May 1985, Harper & Row v. Nation Enterprises, 471 U.S. 539 (1985), III B.
208. U.S. Supreme Court, *ibid.*, 558. Cf. Hugenholtz 1989, 150-151.
209. For a historical analysis of the joint origin of freedom of expression and copyright, see Dommering 2000, 431-439; Netanel 1996, 353-358.
210. Netanel 1996, 288: 'Copyright supports a sector of creative and communicative activity that is relatively free from reliance on state subsidy, elite patronage, and cultural hierarchy.'

censorship. From this historical perspective, copyright promotes a free and independent intellectual debate.[211] Considering the described dualism inherent in the grant of exclusive rights, however, it must not be overlooked that with the introduction of copyright, authors also obtained a position which allows them to control the use and enjoyment of protected works.[212] In principle, the author is free to (mis)use copyright to impede or even prevent access, thereby barring others from freely speaking or freely receiving information.[213]

Considering these free speech burdens, Neil Netanel adds several nuances to the utilitarian incentive argument. In his view, modern copyright still fulfils an important production function with regard to 'sustained works of authorship' that require a 'material commitment of time and money to create'.[214] Even though myriad works are nowadays created and disseminated in the online environment without any expectation of monetary reward, copyright still generates 'incremental free speech benefits' by enabling commercial productions of mass media and freelance creators that complement the works offered for free.[215] Against this background, copyright does not constitute 'the' engine of free expression. However, it can be characterized as one of several engines that contribute to 'a lively interplay among copyright-supported speakers and a wide array of nonmarket and quasi-market speakers, ranging from bloggers to publicly funded broadcasters'.[216] A copyright law aligned with free speech values, then:

> must navigate between the shoals of proprietary lockup and digital anarchy. It must be tailored to minimize copyright's speech burdens – even beyond what might be required by First Amendment doctrine. Yet it must simultaneously serve copyright's continuing 'engine of free expression' role.[217]

To allow copyright law to fulfil this complex task, Netanel proposes, among other measures, a considerable broadening of the breathing space available for the productive reuse of existing protected material: the exemption of 'creative appropriations' covering modifications and adaptations of single works as well as samplings, remixes and mash-ups of fragments taken from different works.[218] Refining an earlier concept developed by Jed Rubenfeld,[219] he argues for complete freedom of second authors

211. Grosheide 1986, 139-141; Netanel 1996, 288; Hugenholtz 1989, 151.
212. Grosheide 1986, 139-143; Dommering 2000, 452-455.
213. Netanel 2008, 111-121 and 144-153; Hugenholtz 2000b, 483.
214. Netanel 2008, 88, referring to Ginsburg 1995, 1499. In the same sense already Netanel 1996, 347.
215. Netanel 2008, 86-88 and 93-95.
216. Netanel 2008, 107-108.
217. Netanel 2008, 195.
218. Netanel 2008, 196-197.
219. Rubenfeld 2002, 1.

to create derivative works through modifications and reformulations of existing ones. Second authors would be obliged, however, to notify the copyright holder of the intent to produce a derivative work. They would also be obliged to pay a licence fee reflecting the profits attributable to the use of the original work. The appropriateness of a licence fee offered by the copyright holder, however, would be subject to scrutiny by the courts.[220] Seeking to balance free speech costs and benefits, Netanel thus argues for more freedom of future authors to use protected works as building blocks for new creations. In the terminology used here, it may be said that he sees a need to strengthen the first element of the cultural imperative: second authors should obtain a stronger position vis-à-vis copyright holders to enhance intergenerational equity.

Arguably, this need to strengthen the guarantee of intergenerational equity becomes even more pressing when copyright's contribution to freedom of expression is assessed less favourably. As described, Netanel assumes that modern copyright contributes substantially to a rich and diverse information production by fostering the creation of works requiring a considerable investment of time and money. From this perspective, copyright is 'an' engine of free expression.[221] Yochai Benkler, however, has argued that large commercial media companies owning big information inventories are likely to benefit most from continuous expansions of copyright protection, whereas non-commercial and amateur creators will be most adversely affected by this trend.[222] As large media companies may moreover merge to consolidate their information inventories and maximize profits, he concludes that copyright overprotection will not only silence small, independent creators but also concentrate production in the hands of a small number of commercial organizations which tend to prefer inoffensive mainstream works to attract the attention of broad audiences.[223]

From this alternative perspective, copyright protection appears as an obstacle to, rather than an engine of, 'diverse and antagonistic information sources in society'.[224] In comparison with Netanel's assessment of the situation, the analysis of free speech costs and benefits conducted by Benkler is much less in favour of copyright protection. However, even Netanel sees a need to substantially broaden the freedom of second authors to adapt and

---

220. Netanel 2008, 198-199. Cf. Geiger 2018b, 443-454 and 450-451; Geiger 2017, 308-318; Geiger 2010b, 541-544, who proposes a remunerated statutory limitation for commercial creative uses, administrated by an independent regulation authority which could solve *ex post* disputes between original and derivative creators on the price to be paid for the transformative use via mediation. See also Senftleben 2019, 486-487; Hilty/Senftleben 2015, 328-329, for a proposal pointing in the same direction in the area of user-generated content.
221. Netanel 2008, 88 and 107-108.
222. Benkler 1999, 400-408.
223. Benkler 1999, 407 and 410-411.
224. Benkler 1999, 412.

remix protected works.[225] Arguably, this need for more freedom of second authors (and thus a higher degree of intergenerational equity) becomes even stronger with Benkler's less positive assessment of copyright's role in securing information diversity. If the contribution of copyright protection to free speech is doubtful, there is even more reason to incorporate safety valves for transformative use and ensure that protected material enters the public domain. Utilitarian copyright theory thus offers ample room for the inclusion of intergenerational equity as a core principle of copyright law and policy. With its focus on a proper balance between rights and freedoms, it requires the consideration of both the benefit for authors enjoying copyright protection and the detriment to authors who depend on the use of protected works as a basis of new creations.

Utilitarian copyright theory also attaches importance to the second element of the cultural imperative: the recognition of the public domain. Reflections on the importance of the public domain as a counterbalance for the grant of protection[226] have led to the insight that the public domain – a reservoir of cultural resources freely available for all – deserves positive legal recognition. Discussing ongoing expansions of publicity rights and protection instruments against dilution and unfair competition in the 1960s and 1970s, David Lange criticized the 'metastasizing' of intellectual property protection and the recognition of exclusive rights in the absence of legitimate claims.[227] Having diagnosed uncontrolled growth of intellectual property 'to the point of recklessness',[228] he posited that the recognition of new intellectual property interests should be counterbalanced by the recognition of corresponding public domain rights:

> What I would suppose, then, is not that intellectual property is undeserving of protection, but rather that such protection as it gets ought to reflect its unique susceptibility to conceptual imprecision and to infinite replication. These attributes seem to me to require the recognition of two fundamental principles. One is that intellectual property theory must always accept something akin to a 'noman's land' at the boundaries; doubtful cases of infringement ought always to be resolved in favor of the defendant. The other is that no exclusive interest should ever have affirmative recognition unless its conceptual opposite is also recognized. Each right ought to be marked off clearly against the public domain.[229]

In this early analysis of the need for affirmative recognition of the public domain, Lange did not focus on copyright because he felt that a

225. Netanel 2008, 198-199.
226. See the overview provided by Boyle 2003a, 3-28; Samuelson 2006a, 145-154.
227. Lange 1981, 153.
228. Lange 1981, 147.
229. Lange 1981, 150.

'substantial and fairly satisfactory set of accords' within the protection system would allow an appropriate preservation of the public domain in spite of certain 'doubtful premises' and 'conceptual complexities'.[230] Revisiting the public domain question in the new millennium, however, Lange conceded that this assessment had become erroneous.[231] In light of expansionist tendencies in the area of copyright, he stressed the need to give the public domain 'an affirmative existence of its own'.[232] Considering the necessity to allow creativity in the cultural sector to survive the continuous expansion of protection, Lange then proposed to conceive of the public domain as 'a status that arises from the exercise of the creative imagination, thus to confer entitlements, privileges and immunities in the service of that exercise'.[233] With this proposal, he sought to give the public domain a legal position that would secure freedom 'to think and to imagine, to remember and appropriate, to play and to create'.[234] In spite of copyright protection, the resources required for basic activities that lie at the core of cultural creativity should thus be preserved as part of the public domain.

In this line of reasoning, it is the very purpose of public domain recognition to safeguard the cultural innovation cycle. To prevent copyright protection from drying up the sources of creativity, it is necessary to confer 'entitlements, privileges and immunities' that guarantee the freedom to use cultural expressions that have entered the public domain. In this way, it becomes possible to maintain a rich and robust public domain of cultural expressions that can serve as a source of inspiration and basis of new acts of creation. As the grant of exclusive rights, the recognition of the public domain constitutes an integral element of the copyright system. It is an indispensable counterpart of exclusive rights that keeps utilitarian copyright systems in balance. Not surprisingly, Lange's work became the starting point[235] of a rich debate on the conceptual contours of the public domain in copyright law – a debate which attests to the particular importance that is attached to the recognition of the public domain in utilitarian copyright theory.[236]

230. Lange 1981, 157.
231. Lange 2003, 468.
232. Lange 2003, 473. Cf. Dusollier 2015, 167-168. For an application of this concept in respect of attempts to reprivatize elements of the public domain of cultural expressions, see Curtin 2018, 965.
233. Lange 2003, 474.
234. Lange 2003, 483.
235. Boyle 2003b, 59; Cohen 2006, 132.
236. For an overview of different public domain conceptions, see Boyle 2003a, 3-28; Samuelson 2006a, 145-154. As to problems in tracing the conceptual contours of the public domain, see Samuelson 2006b, 13-17.

3.2.2 *Natural Law Argument*

In contrast to utilitarian approaches, the natural law argument for copyright protection is not primarily concerned with the social desirability of access to and reuse of literary and artistic works. The natural law argument focuses on the author. As the author spends time and effort on the creation of a work, it is deemed right and just to afford her the opportunity of reaping the fruit of this labour.[237] Accordingly, it is posited that the author acquires a property right in her work by virtue of the mere act of creation.[238] A copyright law awarding authors exclusive rights, therefore, merely recognizes formally what has already occurred in the course of the act of creation. The labourer's property right in her work is regarded as an unalterable result of her creative activity – a natural consequence that is inherent in the 'very nature of things'.[239] Hence, the central element of the natural law argument is that an intellectual property right accrues directly from creative labour.

To explain this central feature, advocates of the natural law approach follow the lines of Locke's elaboration of a natural right to property in his Second Treatise on Government. Locke envisions an unrestricted supply of resources in a world of abundance and for individuals born free to enjoy the 'rightful liberty to use the earth's plenty'.[240] In this world, so runs Locke's argument, whenever one mixes his effort with the raw stuff of the world, he has joined to it:

> something that is his own, and thereby makes it his Property. It being by him removed from the common state Nature placed it in, it hath by this labour something annexed to it that excludes the common right of other Men.[241]

A certain degree of correspondence between Locke's world of abundance and the realm of literary and artistic works can hardly be denied. As pointed out above, intellectual creations are public goods characterized by non-rivalry in consumption.[242] Use by one actor does not restrict the ability of another actor to benefit as well. Literary and artistic works, in other words, can be used and enjoyed without being exhausted. Later authors can ground their own creative activities in the creations of their predecessors without diminishing the intellectual world's supply of ideas and individual expression.[243]

Nevertheless, certain deviations from Locke's theoretical example must not be concealed. At first, it is to be noted that the world of cultural

237. Cf. Grosheide 1986, 128 (argument B).
238. Cf. Desbois 1978, 538; Hubmann 1988, 5.
239. Cf. Ricketson 1987, 5-6; Ulmer 1980, 105-106.
240. Cf. Weinreb 1998, 1223; Gordon 1993, 1553; Strowel 1993, 184.
241. Locke 1698, book II chapter 5 § 27. Cf. Michelman 1967, 1204; Strowel 1993, 183.
242. Fisher 1988, 1700; Landes/Posner 1989, 326; Netanel 2008, 84-85.
243. Weinreb 1998, 1224; Fisher 1988, 1700.

expressions cannot be qualified as a world of abundance without a public domain offering an immeasurable supply of readily accessible ideas and individual forms of expression.[244] The second element of the cultural imperative – the recognition of the public domain – is crucial to the whole line of argument. This public domain, however, does not come into existence with the grant of exclusive rights and the establishment of high standards of protection. As pointed out by Wendy Gordon, Locke's labourer does not need to pay before turning to her creative labour.[245] By contrast, it is due to the limits set to copyright that the realm of literary and artistic expressions resembles a world of abundance. The idea/expression dichotomy frees the myriad of ideas underlying cultural productions from the control of individual authors. The expiry of copyright protection secures that, after a certain period of time, the individual expression embodied in a work becomes part of the public domain. The guarantee of intergenerational equity enters the picture as well. During the limited period for which protection is granted, the exemption of transformative use from the author's control ensures that not only public domain material contributes to the intellectual world of abundance but also new and fresh material that still enjoys protection. A further proviso of Locke confirms the indispensability of the limited term of protection, the idea/expression dichotomy and breathing space for transformative use:

> Labour being the unquestionable Property of the Labourer, no Man but he can have a right to what that is once joined to, at least where there is enough and as good left in common for others.[246]

Obviously, Locke did not intend to encourage the plundering of his world of abundance. As necessitated by the cultural imperative, the public domain has to be preserved and cultivated instead. The natural right to property, accordingly, can only be acquired on the condition that other labourers will find a world of abundance as well. With regard to this further condition of Locke's labour theory, the limits set to copyright become central again. By excluding ideas, procedures, methods and concepts from copyright protection, the idea/expression dichotomy ensures that the common stock of ideas is left untouched and remains freely available for use by all labourers in the world of cultural expression. The obligation to leave 'enough and as good' in common, however, also concerns an author's own individual expression. Obviously, an essential feature of the world of cultural expression is the fact that fresh ideas and new forms of expression constantly strengthen the already existing stock of creations. It is not advisable to

244. In this context, the public domain is understood to comprise not only works that are not or no longer protected by copyright law but also the range of privileged uses that are exempted from the authors' control by copyright limitations.
245. Gordon 1993, 1557-1558.
246. Locke 1698, book II chapter 5 § 27. Cf. Gordon 1993, 1562-1564.

exclude the public domain of cultural expression from this process of constant renewal. Otherwise, the intellectual world of abundance would gradually become impoverished and outdated. An antiquated monolith of ideas and expression of ancient times, however, bears little resemblance to the intellectual world of abundance upon which contemporary authors build their creations.[247]

As copyright expires after a limited period of time, new material is constantly added to the public domain and becomes freely available for creative activities. Moreover, the exemption of transformative use allows contemporary authors to use individual expression of their colleagues that still enjoys copyright protection. Undoubtedly, there is a strong interest of later authors to relate their own creative efforts not only to individual expression that is no longer protected but also to creations that still fall under a colleague's copyright monopoly. It appears safe to assume that all generations of authors have shared this strong interest in freedom to use copyrighted material insofar as necessary for expressing themselves.[248]

Locke's proviso that no man but the labourer 'can have a right to what that is once joined to, at least where there is enough and as good left in common for others'[249] thus introduces considerations of intergenerational equity into natural law copyright theory: later creators should be as free to use incessantly renewed intellectual resources as their predecessors were.[250] The first element of the cultural imperative – the guarantee of intergenerational equity – follows from Locke's labour theory just like the acquisition of property rights. The author is obliged to allow second creators to use and enjoy the fruit of her labour in the same way as she was permitted to access and use pre-existing works.

The moment the work of an author enters the cultural landscape, it thus has to be made subject to the cultural innovation cycle: the process of renewal in the world of ideas and expression. Like their predecessors, contemporary authors must accept the idea/expression dichotomy, a limited term of protection, and the exemption of transformative use of protected works, if they want to leave 'enough and as good' in common for later authors. It is only then that an author can fulfil the condition put forward by Locke and acquire a natural right to her cultural creation. The acceptance of intergenerational equity and copyright's public domain principle, in other words, are preconditions and the price to be paid for the acquisition of copyright protection. Both elements of the cultural imperative play a crucial

247. Cf. Cohen 2006, 159-160, who underlines the importance of contemporary mass commercial culture as a source and basis of new creations.
248. As discussed by Cohen 2006, 154-155, research in the social psychology of creativity confirms the dependence of authors on access to works of predecessors and peers to arrive at new associations, experiments and cultural productions that 'play' with pre-existing material.
249. See Locke 1698, book II chapter 5 § 27.
250. Gordon 1993, 1557-1558.

role in the natural law approach underlying continental-European copyright systems.

3.3 FUNDAMENTAL INTEREST OF SOCIETY

An analysis of Anglo-American and continental-European copyright theory, thus, confirms the importance of intergenerational equity and a rich and robust public domain for society. Besides this evidence following from copyright's legal traditions, however, broader sociological and aesthetic theories also shed light on the crucial societal importance of these elements of the cultural imperative. On the basis of Pierre Bourdieu's sociological analysis of the field of literary and artistic production, it can be demonstrated that the recognition of intergenerational equity is a precondition for an autonomous system of art and culture within society and that the constant evolution of new trends and movements in the literary and artistic community depends on this autonomy (section 3.3.1). Friedrich Schiller's, Theodor Adorno's and Peter Osborne's aesthetic theories about the contribution of works of art to societal changes demonstrate the importance of the recognition of the public domain: the need to preserve cultural productions as genuine, independent forms of expression that provide indispensable impulses for the artistic discourse and the development and improvement of society (section 3.3.2).

3.3.1 *Supporting the Autonomy of the Cultural Field*

From the perspective of cultural sociology, it can be said that the guarantee of intergenerational equity ensures that the copyright system remains neutral in the ongoing struggle between autonomous, independent artists and profit-oriented mainstream artists for power to set quality standards and dictate the internal discourse in the literary and artistic domain. According to Pierre Bourdieu, the autonomy of the field of literary and artistic production requires independence from economic and political powers. From this perspective, the grant of exploitation rights and the focus on pecuniary incentives in copyright law is problematic. The prospect of monetary rewards may entice autonomous artists away from the independent *l'art pour l'art* logic of the literary and artistic field (section 3.3.1.1). The offer of copyright appears not only as a bait to spur creativity but also as an attempt to persuade autonomous artists to spend time and effort on the production of economically successful mainstream works (section 3.3.1.2). This, however, does not mean that copyright law has nothing to offer for authors with an independent *l'art pour l'art* orientation. As Bourdieu explains, the constant evolution of fresh, autonomous avant-garde productions depends on mechanisms that allow new generations of autonomous authors to legitimize their unorthodox, new rules by criticizing the dogmata of the presently predominant school of thought. The principle of intergenerational equity in copyright law supports this constant process of renewal within the group of autonomous artists by guaranteeing freedom of transformative use (section 3.3.1.3).

3.3.1.1 Bourdieu's Sociological Analysis

Refining Niklas Luhmann's concept of relatively closed social systems with a distinct identity and a boundary between them and their environment,[251] Pierre Bourdieu developed the concept of 'fields' in society. Although constituting an autonomous social space with individual rules, dominance structures and an established set of opinions, a field is not isolated from other social spaces and processes surrounding it. According to Bourdieu, the structure of a field results from constant internal fights of competing players for predominance and leadership.[252] A field's degree of autonomy, then, depends on the extent to which external players can influence these internal fights. External factors may have a deep impact on a field's constitution.[253] Given the continuous change of power relations, the structure of a social field is not static and fixed. By contrast, a field has its own history reflecting different stages of development – from the field's genesis as a result of the attainment of far-reaching autonomy to the potential loss of this autonomous position as a result of powerful external influences.[254] For the analysis of a given field, it is thus necessary to examine its relationship with the social environment in which it is embedded at a given point in time.

Applying this theoretical model to the field of literary and artistic production, Bourdieu assumes that the field's autonomy rests on the rejection of the capitalism of the bourgeoisie. The field of literature and art militates against the bourgeois logic of profit maximization by developing its own, independent logic. This specific 'nomos' of the literary and artistic field lies in the independence from economic and political powers.[255] Instead of striving for business, an autonomous literary or artistic production aims at internal recognition within the field. It emancipates itself from the focus on monetary success and honours awarded by the bourgeois society.[256] As a result of this nomos, the consecration mechanisms in the literary and artistic field – the power to set quality standards and dominate the internal discourse – become self-referential: *l'art pour l'art*. The field of literature and art becomes a universe countering the profit logic that impregnates the economic and political discourse in society.[257] The break with the ruling powers

251. Luhmann 1984, 31 and 35-70.
252. Bourdieu 1996, 134-135; Bourdieu 1992/1999, 253-255 and 368.
253. Bourdieu/Chartier/Darnton 1985, 28.
254. Bourdieu 1996, 134; Jurt 2008, 91-92.
255. Bourdieu 1992/1999, 103-105.
256. Bourdieu 1992/1999, 344.
257. Cf. Peukert 2019, 1178-1179.

constitutes the basis of an artist's independent, autonomous existence.[258] Autonomous literature and art is a provocation. It challenges the pervasive 'economism' in society.[259]

It follows from this configuration of the field of literary and artistic production that an artist seeking to attain recognition in this field must not align her work with the tastes of the masses and produce mainstream works in the hope of commercial success. This decision would be perceived as a concession to the predominant profit orientation of society.[260] By contrast, it is the renunciation of any commercial interest and the focus on the internal quality standards within the literary and artistic field that attest to an artist's genuinely literary and artistic orientation. In consequence, the field generates a peculiar reverse economy. An artist can only win recognition in the field of literature and art by losing on the territory of monetary rewards: the one who loses (in economic terms), wins (in artistic terms).[261]

This reverse economy also determines the structure of the field of literature and art. As long as the field is autonomous, the highest positions will be held by those artists turning their back on the bourgeois economy and the prospect of commercial gains. The degree of the field's autonomy, in other words, depends on whether independent artists striving for recognition within the field (limited production for other independent artists), or dependent artists striving for recognition outside the field (mainstream production for the masses), hold the highest hierarchical positions.[262] Accordingly, the fight for predominance and leadership in the literary and artistic field is a fight between autonomous/independent and bourgeois/dependent artists for the power to set quality standards and dictate the internal discourse.[263] The stronger the position of dependent, profit-oriented artists in this power struggle, the bigger is the influence of external economic and political players on the structure of the literary and artistic field, and the lower is the field's autonomy.[264]

---

258. Bourdieu 1992/1999, 105.
259. Bourdieu 1992/1999, 342.
260. See Fromer 2010, 1479-1480, with regard to consumers' preference for limited newness in the area of literary and artistic works; Buccafusco/Bechtold/Sprigman 2017, 41-43, for a discussion of consumers' preference for established, known forms of literary and artistic expression, and the impact of this preference on innovation in the cultural domain.
261. Bourdieu 1992/1999, 136 and 344-345. See also Klamer 1996, 7-8, who confirms this 'reverse economy' in the art world. Cf. Fromer 2012, 1745, who discusses different motivations leading to expressive works.
262. Bourdieu 1992/1999, 344-345.
263. Bourdieu 1992/1999, 198-203. Within the group of autonomous, independent artists, Bourdieu, *ibid.*, 198, 253-255 and 379-380, also describes a further fight between established artists presently holding the consecration and discourse power, and upcoming avant-garde artists challenging this established position.
264. Bourdieu 1992/1999, 344.

On the basis of this analysis of the power relations in the literary and artistic field, Bourdieu paints an alarming picture of the field's current degree of autonomy. In the light of reduced state subsidies for cultural productions and the rise of culture sponsoring by enterprises, he warns of an increasing mutual penetration of the world of art and the world of money: more and more literary and artistic productions become subject to entrepreneurial marketing strategies and commercial pressures.[265] With the growing influence of external commercial players and profit rationales, the distinction between autonomous, independent productions and bourgeois, dependent productions is increasingly blurred. To a growing extent, the profit logic of commercial productions prevails even in avant-garde works.[266] Therefore, the autonomy of the field of literature and art is currently at risk.[267]

3.3.1.2 Critique of Copyright

Against the background of Bourdieu's analysis, the role of copyright law in the field of literary and artistic production seems ambiguous. As explained in section 3.2.1, utilitarian copyright theory regards copyright as a vehicle to encourage the creation of literary and artistic works by providing an economic stimulus: the promise of monetary rewards is offered to authors as an incentive to create new works. From the perspective of Bourdieu's analysis, this utilitarian incentive rationale is questionable. It will primarily enhance the productivity of dependent artists who share the profit orientation of the bourgeois society. Artists following the specific *l'art pour l'art* nomos of the literary and artistic field, by contrast, will focus on the establishment of a reputation within the artistic community. The commercialization of their works will be more difficult and is less likely to generate substantial royalty revenue. The prospect of a solid income, however, may entice autonomous artists away from the independent *l'art pour l'art* logic of the literary and artistic field. The offer of copyright appears not only as a bait to spur creativity but also as an attempt to persuade autonomous artists to spend time and effort on the production of economically successful mainstream works. Copyright law may thus even be seen as a risk factor. It may corrupt independent artists instead of supporting their efforts to create autonomous works.[268]

265. Bourdieu 1992/1999, 530.
266. Bourdieu 1992/1999, 531.
267. Bourdieu 1992/1999, 533.
268. Cf. Peukert 2019, 1187. For an approach that seeks to reconcile commercial trade interests and a focus on mainstream consumption patterns with the interest in the cultivation and enrichment of national culture and identity, see Pager 2011, 65-74 and 109-113. Pager's example of the 'Korean Wave', however, does not dispel the general concern about the corrosive effect of an alignment of the field of literary and artistic productions with the maxim of profit maximization.

A less critical picture can be drawn on the basis of the natural law argument. As elaborated in section 3.2.2, this copyright theory posits that the author acquires a property right in her work by virtue of the mere act of creation. As the author spends time and effort on the creation of a work, it is deemed right and just to afford her the opportunity to reap the fruit of this creative labour. Copyright law merely recognizes formally what has already occurred in the course of the act of creation. This approach is less directly linked with an incentive scheme. Continental-European *droit d'auteur* systems following the natural law approach do provide not only strong economic rights but also strong moral rights allowing an author to safeguard the unbreakable bond with her work as a materialization of her personality.[269] Nonetheless, the idea of recognizing copyright as a reward for creative labour leads to a comparable dilemma. It implies that the author derives financial benefits from the exclusive entitlement to exploit a work. As the utilitarian incentive approach, this reward mechanism is tailored to the interests of profit-oriented, dependent artists. Autonomous authors following the *l'art pour l'art* rationale aim primarily at recognition among other independent artists. As they do not strive for commercial success and are less likely to create commercially successful works, the exploitation opportunity secured by copyright law offers much less support for their creative efforts. A focus on reputational rewards would be more appropriate.

Hence, it seems difficult to reconcile the rationales of copyright protection with the maxim of *l'art pour l'art* in the field of literary and artistic production.[270] By definition, copyright seeks to provide the opportunity to commercially exploit literary and artistic works. For autonomous authors striving for recognition among other independent authors, this core mechanism of copyright law seems to have little importance. Instead of supporting independent creations, the prospect of exclusive exploitation rights furthers profit-oriented mainstream productions that may undermine the autonomy of the literary and artistic field.

3.3.1.3 Importance of Intergenerational Equity

In assessing copyright law through the lens of Bourdieu's analysis, however, it must not be overlooked that the grant of exclusive exploitation rights, even though constituting a central element, is not the only feature of the protection system. Moreover, copyright law can hardly be expected to take a position in the fight between autonomous/independent and bourgeois/dependent authors for predominance, leadership and consecration power in the literary and

269. As to continental-European moral rights theory, see Geller 1994, 169-170; Strowel 1994, 236-237; Edelman 1994, 82-87; Ulmer 1980, 110-111. See Desbois 1978, 538: 'L'auteur est protégé comme tel, en qualité de créateur, parce qu'un lien l'unit à l'objet de sa création.'

270. For a more detailed analysis of this point, see Senftleben 2017a, 28-32.

artistic field. As long as copyright law remains neutral in the sense that it offers support for the specific modes of production of both competing groups, it does not alter the rules of the power struggle and does not favour one camp over the other.

Against this background, the question arises whether other features of copyright law offer support for autonomous artists following the *l'art pour l'art* nomos of the literary and artistic field. The grant of exclusive exploitation rights has already been identified as an element of the system that is aligned with the profit orientation of dependent mainstream artists. It may even entice independent artists to abandon their autonomous orientation and turn to commercial productions instead. This, however, does not exclude the possibility of copyright law supporting autonomous productions in other ways. The aforementioned moral rights of authors, including the right of attribution and the right to prevent derogatory actions,[271] can serve as an example of rules that may be of particular importance to autonomous authors seeking to preserve the integrity of their artistic creations. Commercially oriented authors may have less difficulty to accept modifications of their works as long as these modifications increase exploitation revenues.

Searching for further copyright rules that offer support for autonomous productions, Bourdieu's description of fights for power and predominance at a different level of the field of literary and artistic production is of particular importance. Apart from the competition between autonomous and bourgeois artists that defines the level of autonomy of the literary and artistic field as a whole, Bourdieu describes internal fights within the group of autonomous artists. In the community of independent artists, newcomers can only establish a new school of thought by rebelling against the teachings of the generation of autonomous artists that is presently in power. The new generation must necessarily challenge existing, established convictions to obtain the power to set quality standards and dictate the discourse. It must degrade the reigning avant-garde to an arrière-garde. Otherwise, there is no room for new directions in the creation of autonomous literature and art. Once a new school has taken over the consecration power, it faces the same internal challenges and will finally also be superseded by a new avant-garde movement.[272] The constant evolution of fresh, autonomous avant-garde productions thus depends on mechanisms that allow new generations of autonomous authors to legitimize their unorthodox, new rules by criticizing the dogmata of the presently predominant school of thought.

Interestingly, Bourdieu's analysis of this internal power struggle within the group of autonomous artists leads to the insight that the room for possible new positions in the creation of independent art – the range of options available for the establishment of a new avant-garde movement – depends on

271. See the international recognition of moral rights in Article 6*bis* BC. As to the recognition of these rights in Anglo-American countries, see Dworkin 1995, 229.
272. Bourdieu 1992/1999, 253-255.

the positions that have already been taken by previous artists.[273] For a new generation of autonomous artists to challenge the leading avant-garde, it must detect the structural gaps within the texture of already known aesthetic positions. It must formulate an alternative artistic position in the light of the weaknesses and contradictions of the present state of the art.[274] From this perspective, the positions that have already been taken in the literary and artistic field constitute potential lines of development and starting points for a revolution within the group of independent, autonomous artists.

Copyright law can support this constant process of renewal within the group of autonomous artists by guaranteeing user freedoms. To be capable of challenging established positions, an autonomous artist must be free to dissociate herself from the dogmata set forth by her predecessors. Copyright law can thus enable a new generation of artists to destruct an established order and erect a new one by exempting the use of protected, pre-existing works for the formulation of new aesthetic positions. The idea/expression dichotomy ensures that the ideas and concepts underlying literary and artistic works remain free for this purpose. The freedom to refer to earlier creations, for example in quotations and parodies,[275] allows a new generation to criticize the currently prevailing school of thought. In this way, new autonomous artists can demarcate their new position from previous ones. They can lay the foundations for a new avant-garde movement by defining their own position in relation to pre-existing works.

Apart from the freedom to use and criticize pre-existing works in the process of defining and demarcating a new aesthetic position, Bourdieu's analysis highlights a further freedom of use that is crucial to the process of constant renewal in the area of autonomous *l'art pour l'art* productions. To enable a new generation of autonomous authors to formulate a new aesthetic position, these newcomers must first learn of the positions that have already been taken by previous independent artists.[276] Unless they master the history of their particular art and know the heritage of former generations of artists, they are inhibited from detecting structural gaps that allow them to take a legitimate and plausible next step in the evolution of literary and artistic productions.[277] Therefore, the guarantee of freedom to use pre-existing material for the creation of new avant-garde creations is only one way in which copyright law can support the process of aesthetic renewal in the area of autonomous productions. In addition, copyright law can support the foundation of a new avant-garde movement by exempting the use of existing works for educational purposes and private study: measures that allow new

273. Bourdieu 1992/1999, 370.
274. Bourdieu 1992/1999, 372.
275. For a discussion of the scope of this right in the light of the meaning of 'quotation' in different areas of artistic creativity, see Aplin/Bently 2020, 156-222; Bently/Aplin 2019, 28-31.
276. Cf. Peukert 2019, 1180.
277. Bourdieu 1992/1999, 385.

generations of autonomous artists to explore the cultural landscape and find starting points for the formulation of new positions to challenge and supersede established convictions.[278]

In sum, Bourdieu's analysis of the preconditions for a constant renewal of autonomous literary and artistic productions, thus, confirms the importance of intergenerational equity. It is imperative that there be an obligation on authors enjoying copyright protection to allow later authors to use this protected material as a source and basis for subsequent creations. Later authors should be free to learn of the history of their art and ground their own creative activities in the creations of their predecessors. While the grant of exclusive exploitation rights in copyright law is central to profit-oriented, dependent authors, freedom to learn of pre-existing works and freedom to use and criticize them for the purpose of establishing a new avant-garde movement is of particular importance to authors with an autonomous, independent orientation. For copyright law to remain neutral in the ongoing fight between bourgeois and autonomous artists for the power to set quality standards and dictate the discourse in the field of literary and artistic production, it must therefore find a proper balance between rights and freedoms. As the guarantee of intergenerational equity constitutes a precondition for the constant evolution of new avant-garde movements, it plays a crucial role in this context and contributes substantially to copyright's neutrality in the power struggle between bourgeois and autonomous artists. By offering exploitation rights on the one hand and guaranteeing the freedom to explore the cultural landscape and base new creations on pre-existing works on the other, copyright law supports both bourgeois and autonomous productions, and enhances diversity in the literary and artistic field.[279]

3.3.2 *Generating and Preserving Alternative Visions of Society*

With regard to the second element of the cultural imperative – the preservation of the public domain – Friedrich Schiller's and Theodor Adorno's aesthetic theories offer important insights. While Schiller sees works of art as catalysts paving the way for an ethical and free society (following section 3.3.2.1), Adorno describes the task of art to challenge reality and suggest necessary societal changes (section 3.3.2.2). The underlying insight is relevant to this day: contemporary art and aesthetic play are central to the evocation of alternative visions of society and the improvement of social and political conditions (section 3.3.2.3). Copyright law can support this societal function by preserving the cultural dimension of artworks.

278. In this sense also Cohen 2006, 154-155.

279. Cf. Netanel 2008, 88 and 107-108, as discussed in section 3.2.1. In the context of the present analysis based on Bourdieu, however, 'rich and diverse information production' would have to be understood in the sense of richness and diversity arising from support for both autonomous and bourgeois authors alike.

Emphasizing the need to preserve the public domain of cultural expressions, the cultural imperative secures an artwork's potential to serve as a reference point for an open discourse in the artistic domain that can lead to changes of social and political conditions (section 3.3.2.4).

3.3.2.1 Schiller's Aesthetic Theory

Disillusioned by the French Revolution which had culminated in chaos and violence instead of leading to a free and equal society, Schiller wrote his letters about mankind's aesthetic education to explore the possibility of a transition from an absolutist, authoritarian state to a purified, ethical state that is founded on human reason.[280] As a precondition for this transition, Schiller emphasizes the need to harmonize human desires with the rules of reason. As it is not the destiny of mankind to renounce its natural senses in favour of moral laws,[281] support for an ethical, reasonable state must come from the totality of human dispositions: desire and reason alike. Individuals should not only feel an obligation to follow the rules of reason but also feel a desire to do so. If human desires are brought in line with the postulates of reason, a revolution will no longer end in chaos and violence. It will lead to the establishment of a moral state instead.[282]

To align human desires with the rules of reason, a catalyst is required that brings moral laws not only to people's heads but also to their hearts. Schiller solves this problem by positing that art can serve as such a catalyst. Even though being incapable of changing mankind directly, art can point the way to a change for the better by focusing people's thoughts on the 'necessary and eternal', and make them strive for this ideal.[283] Art is predestined to accomplish this task because it satisfies the desire to play and enjoy. Instead of openly criticizing people's actions and attitudes, art can improve society in a subtle way by making visions of ethical behaviour part of people's play and pleasure:

> In vain will you combat their maxims, in vain will you condemn their actions; but you can try your moulding hand on their leisure. Drive away caprice, frivolity, and coarseness, from their pleasures, and you will banish them imperceptibly from their acts, and length from their feelings. Everywhere that you meet them, surround them with great, noble, and ingenious forms; multiply around them the symbols of perfection, till appearance triumphs over reality, and art over nature.[284]

280. Schiller 1794-1795, 11-14 (Letter 3).
281. Schiller 1794-1795, 28 (Letter 6).
282. Schiller 1794-1795, 120-121 (Letter 27).
283. Schiller 1794-1795, 36 (Letter 9).
284. Schiller 1794-1795, 35 (Letter 9).

Schiller thus relies on art as a vehicle to let people experience an ideal balance between desire and reason until they finally orient their actions by moral laws instead of following mere physical necessities.[285] A person succumbing to a temptation while knowing that it is against the rules of reason feels overpowered by nature. A person fulfilling a moral obligation in spite of inner resistance feels forced by reason. The aesthetic play, however, reconciles reason with desire, neutralizes physical and moral constraints and, in consequence, allows mankind to enjoy full freedom.[286] It enables the individual to experience a state of perfection in which neither the power of nature nor the postulates of reason restrict possible courses of action: in the aesthetic play, mankind experiences humanity in its entirety.[287]

A true work of art is capable of evoking this equilibrium between reason and desire, and this freedom of the mind through appearances of beauty that neither reflect nor require reality.[288] To accomplish this task, the artist must not be a protégé of her time. She must leave the realm of reality behind and employ the techniques of art to depict a vision of the ultimate ideal.[289] In Schiller's view, the experience and enjoyment of this ultimate perfection can pave the way for the establishment of a moral society in which individual freedom no longer follows from the restriction of the freedom of others but from a consensus on ethical norms that corresponds with people's desires – as refined in the aesthetic play.[290] An individual driven by physical necessity must first experience beauty – the aesthetical balance between desire and rules of reason – before he can actively and freely opt for moral norms and moral actions.[291] It is thus the task of art to prepare mankind for the transition from the physical state of desire to the moral state of reason.[292]

3.3.2.2 Adorno's Aesthetic Theory

In his aesthetic theory, Theodor Adorno also underlines the societal relevance of art. Against the background of the alienation which the individual faces in a fully rationalized, efficiency-driven world, he warns of the affirmative nature of art. An artwork bringing a conciliatory reflection of enchantment into the disenchanted, empirical reality offers comfort in the rationalized world and supports the unbearable status quo.[293] In the light of the

285. As to the political dimension of this educational effect of art, see Beebe 2017, 336-337, who describes the belief of 'early-republic Americans' that the progress of the fine arts promises to promote the 'overall progress of civic virtue and good government'.
286. Schiller 1794-1795, 57-58 (Letter 14).
287. Schiller 1794-1795, 60-64 (Letter 15) and 105-106 (Letter 25).
288. Schiller 1794-1795, 111-112 (Letter 26).
289. Schiller 1794-1795, 34-35 (Letter 9).
290. Schiller 1794-1795, 120-121 (Letter 27).
291. Schiller 1794-1795, 90-91 (Letter 23).
292. Schiller 1794-1795, 92 (Letter 23).
293. Adorno 1970, 10 and 34.

inhumanity of the real world, art would make itself an accomplice of present and coming disasters if it sustained positive visions of society and obscured the defects and poorness of reality.[294] With the prospect of a better world which, as an ultimate truth,[295] shimmers through each genuine artwork,[296] art may falsely pretend that existing societal conditions are acceptable. Therefore, art is constantly at risk of becoming guilty of supporting the inhuman status quo and fortifying present ideologies.[297]

On the other hand, art must not be condemned altogether because true artworks are capable of unmasking the negativity of present societal conditions. Showing visions of a better, happier life, art can rouse opposition against the existing reality and contribute to necessary societal changes.[298] Autonomous art can play a decisive role in society because it generates utopian views of a better life that may become drivers of a change for the better. This role of authentic art defines its social character: art is the 'social antithesis' of society.[299] Given this delicate position in the social fabric of modern societies, there is a fine line to be walked: the artist must relentlessly expose the inhumanity of reality without offering any prospect of reconciliation. In doing so, the artist creates genuine works which, by their very nature, offer shining visions of a better life and a better society in spite of the hopelessness reflected in the artworks themselves.[300] As an antithesis of the total disaster in the real world, art becomes the messenger of an ideal, utopian world.[301]

There is thus an inescapable dualism in contemporary authentic art: the sadness of presenting a happier life as a goal that remains unattainable under present societal conditions.[302] To accomplish this task, art must seek to escape tendencies to undermine and neutralize its critical and irrational impetus, such as the efforts of the cultural industry to commercialize and canonize even the most rebellious and resistant works.[303] Reacting to the growing demand for enchantment in the disenchanted, rationalized reality,[304] the cultural industry offers artworks as consumer goods: abstract objects that function as a *tabula rasa* into which the bourgeois purchaser can project her own feelings and aspirations.[305] As a result, an artwork becomes an echo and confirmation of the viewer's own hopes and attitudes. It becomes an escape

294. Adorno 1970, 28 and 503.
295. Adorno 1970, 128 and 196-197.
296. Adorno 1970, 199-200.
297. Adorno 1970, 203.
298. Adorno 1970, 25-26 and 56.
299. Adorno 1970, 9-10, 19 and 53.
300. Adorno 1970, 127 and 199.
301. Adorno 1970, 55-56.
302. Adorno 1970, 204-205.
303. Adorno 1970, 32.
304. Adorno 1970, 34.
305. Adorno 1970, 33.

from the unbearable real world. This, however, leads to the 'disartification' of art. Once it is consumed as an object of pleasure that offers comfort in an inhuman world, its critical impetus – the exposure of the ugliness of reality as an impulse for societal changes – is negated. The purchaser who only projects her own aspirations into the artwork can no longer experience the underlying truth. Instead of assimilating oneself to the artwork and exploring its genuine meaning,[306] a person consuming a work of art as an object for the projection of her own emotions only seeks to ignore the shameful difference between the utopia shimmering through the artwork and the poorness of her own life.[307] Instead of seeing the artwork as a subject and disappearing in the utopian vision of a radical change of society offered by the artwork,[308] the art consumer simply annexes the artwork to other objects of possession and deprives it of its genuine meaning by replacing the unpleasant critique of the empirical reality with her own projections. The cultural industry initiates and exploits this process leading to the neutralization of art.[309]

To escape this threat of disqualification, art must insist on its difference and autonomy by refusing claims for rule obedience and resisting the temptation to fulfil societal expectations. It must preserve its opposition and dissonance by producing works of a non-identical and fragmentary nature that negate the unity of traditional productions, fall outside aesthetical categories and bring chaos in the established order.[310] To mirror the ugliness and futility of present society in an authentic way, artworks must become ugly and futile themselves. The world of art must become a closed counter universe: the last refuge of humanity in an inhuman world that is disfigured by deal and profit maxims.[311] Remaining alien to the world, true art, by definition, is puzzling and gives rise to conflicting interpretations based on internal tension in the work or its connection to conflicts in society.[312] For the final resolution of these tensions and conflicts, society as a whole would have to be transformed. It would have to decipher the contradictions reflected in authentic works of art and extrapolate the underlying ultimate truth that is expressed by simultaneously challenging reality and suggesting improvements.[313]

3.3.2.3 Relevance to Contemporary Art

By no means do these two aesthetic theories exhaust the possibilities of describing the role of literary and artistic works in society. Nonetheless, the

306. Adorno 1970, 27-28.
307. Adorno 1970, 32.
308. Adorno 1970, 27.
309. Adorno 1970, 33.
310. Adorno 1970, 41.
311. Adorno 1970, 337-338.
312. Adorno 1970, 197-198.
313. Adorno 1970, 55 and 193-196.

two examples of an assessment of art's societal relevance already show that by presenting alternative visions of society, art can play a crucial role in the improvement of social and political conditions.[314] From this perspective, the cultivation of the public domain of cultural expressions – in line with the cultural imperative in copyright law – is an important contribution to societal change. Offering a rich and constantly updated reservoir of freely available public domain material, copyright law provides source material for the artistic discourse and supports cultural follow-on innovation that leads to new artworks and new reflections of societal conditions.

As Schiller's Letters date back to the Age of Enlightenment and Adorno developed his aesthetic theory in the second half of the last century, however, the question arises whether it is still appropriate to rely on this theoretical framework today. In his recent discussion of aesthetic progress in the light of the progress clause of the U.S. Constitution,[315] Barton Beebe resorts to John Dewey's and Richard Shusterman's concept of 'pragmatist aesthetics'[316] for a discussion of copyright's contribution to aesthetic progress.[317] Pragmatist aesthetics focuses on everyday events as a gateway to aesthetic experience and practice:

> In order to understand the meaning of artistic products, we have to forget them for a time, to turn aside from them and have recourse to the ordinary forces and conditions of experience that we do not usually regard as esthetic. We must arrive at the theory of art by means of a detour.[318]

Providing examples, Dewey refers to 'sights that hold the crowd',[319] such as a fire engine rushing by, machines that excavate enormous holes in the earth, men 'perched high in air on girders, throwing and catching red-hot bolts'.[320]

Building on pragmatist aesthetics, Beebe departs from the focus on autonomous aesthetic objects in the Kantian tradition of aesthetic theory[321] – the predominant tradition in the Age of Enlightenment which also served as a reference point for Schiller's Letters on the Aesthetic Education of Man.[322] In Beebe's analysis, a critique of the focus on 'mummified museum art'[323] serves as a vehicle to arrive at a new progress paradigm for U.S. copyright

314. Cf. van den Braembussche 1996, 41-42, who arrives at a similar conclusion on the basis of the philosophical discourse about 'the sublime'.
315. Article I, Section 8. Cf. Beebe 2017, 371-373 and 378.
316. Dewey 1934, 5-10; Shusterman 2000, 143 and 208.
317. Beebe 2017, 342-348.
318. Dewey 1934, 4.
319. Dewey 1934, 5.
320. Dewey 1934, 5; Beebe 2017, 344.
321. Beebe 2017, 344.
322. Schiller 1794-1795, as discussed in section 3.3.2.1. As to the impact of the Kantian school of thought on Schiller, see Osborne 2013, 42-44.
323. Beebe 2017, 343.

law. Beebe seeks to overcome the traditional accumulationist approach (the more works, the more progress) and replace it with a focus on the encouragement of aesthetic practice.[324] He relies on pragmatist aesthetics because they offer a vision of aesthetic progress that focuses 'not on the stockpiling over time of fixed, archivable works but rather on the quality of ephemeral aesthetic experience in the present'.[325] This preference for pragmatist aesthetics, however, does not imply a rejection of the idea that art can play an important role in the improvement of societal conditions. Beebe explicitly confirms the positive social and political side effects of aesthetic experience and aesthetic play:

> Aesthetic play has intrinsic value – as a source of pleasure, of moral and political cultivation, of imaginative freedom and self-actualization – even when it does not ultimately result in the production of an aesthetic work.[326]

As explained in section 3.3.2.1, Schiller's aesthetic theory rests on similar considerations. The experience of a balance between desire and rules of reason in the aesthetic play enables the individual to opt actively and freely for moral norms and moral actions.[327] In the context of Beebe's discussion of the role of copyright law, the focus on aesthetic practice, moreover, leads back to the question of freedom to use pre-existing aesthetic objects as raw materials for aesthetic play. Beebe emphasizes:

> the importance to the everyday individual of aesthetic engagement, aesthetic practice, and aesthetic play, in the form of the active assimilation, appropriation, and creative recombination of aesthetic expression.[328]

Beebe's reliance on pragmatist aesthetics, thus, does not indicate that Schiller's aesthetic theory has lost its relevance. By contrast, his analysis merely shifts the focus from the production of aesthetic works to the encouragement of aesthetic play. While the stimulation of new artistic productions may have been regarded as copyright's primary policy goal in the past, Beebe considers it more important nowadays to facilitate the creative remix of protected works in the context of aesthetic play.[329] Instead of dismissing the idea that art is capable of providing impulses for desirable social and political changes, Beebe returns to Schiller's aesthetic theory and its focus on aesthetic experience in his concluding remarks.[330]

324. Beebe 2017, 347, 373-374 and 384-385.
325. Beebe 2017, 346.
326. Beebe 2017, 346-347.
327. Schiller 1794-1795, 90-91 (Letter 23) and 120-121 (Letter 27).
328. Beebe 2017, 347.
329. Beebe 2017, 390-391.
330. Beebe 2017, 395-396.

Besides references to aesthetic theory in legal literature, developments in aesthetic theory itself confirm that artworks, including works of contemporary art, are still seen as critical reflections of social and political conditions and manifestations of alternative visions of society. In his 'Philosophy of Contemporary Art', Peter Osborne refers to Adorno's Aesthetic Theory as a text that 'towers above all other twentieth-century philosophical texts about art'.[331] His own description of the role of art in today's society is embedded in the discussion of the subjective temporality of works of contemporary art and – in line with Augustine's contraction of the temporal dimensions of present/past/future into the subjective orientations of attention/memory/expectation – the question of 'what modes of *attention*, *memory* and *expectation* contemporary art produces and requires as conditions of its experience'.[332]

With regard to the adequate mode of expectation, Osborne employs the concept of 'horizon of expectation' as a point of departure: horizon of expectation in the sense of Edmund Husserl's elaboration of a boundary concept that refers to an indeterminateness which, while being determinable as an obscure, misty phenomenon, never becomes fully determinable because the horizon is infinitely receding.[333] With increasing knowledge, the horizon of expectation is moved and expanded as well:

> As a spatial *image*, horizon points towards a beyond, something existent but out of sight, and hence unknown – and yet in principle knowable once you travel there. The horizon will move, but what was beyond the horizon can come to be within it, if you travel; hence the inherent hopefulness of travel.[334]

Despite the elasticity of the horizon metaphor, the concept of 'horizon of expectation' has inherent limitations. In particular, it remains impossible to 'break through the ultimate indeterminateness of the horizon of expectation as such'.[335] Otherwise, it would no longer be justified to speak of a horizon of expectation. This inherent limitation of the concept has become problematic as a result of the abandonment of the Christian doctrine of the Last Days in modernity. Instead of a predetermined expectation of the apocalypse, the individual in modern times is exposed to 'the hazards of an open but "progressive" future'.[336] The moment the future is open and known to bring something new, we paradoxically come to expect the unexpected. Instead of accepting the horizontal predelineation of the world of experience, we project the penetration of the horizon of expectation.[337]

331. Osborne 2013, 10.
332. Osborne 2013, 175 (emphasis in the original text).
333. Osborne 2013, 203.
334. Osborne 2013, 203-204 (emphasis in the original text).
335. Osborne 2013, 204.
336. Osborne 2013, 206-207.
337. Osborne 2013, 207.

Against this background, Osborne criticizes Reinhart Koselleck's reliance on the horizon concept and emphasis on the disjunction between experience and expectation as a constituent characteristic of modernity.[338] Nonetheless, he agrees that only the unexpected has the 'power to surprise'[339] and create new experiences. It is 'the *unexpected* that we come to *expect* and also to value'.[340] Osborne describes the sensation of the unexpected as follows:

> *In the unexpected, meaning is produced (in so far as it is produced) through dialectical negation – not further determination – of the expected.* It is true, of course, that we may come to expect such negations – and 'revolution' did, of course, become established as a horizon of expectation in the 200-year period from 1789 to 1989.[341]

The reference to the French Revolution and the fall of the Berlin Wall indicates that the paradoxical penetration of the horizon of expectation (following from the expectation of the unexpected that creates new meaning through negation) has a particular societal value. It enables the individual to include fundamental transformations of society in the spectrum of valid, determinable expectations for the future: even unexpected events can be deemed plausible projections of developments to come. In this regard, however, Osborne points out that alternative visions of society – capable of heightening expectations of the unexpected – have become scarce. In his view, the collapse of historical communism did not broaden the spectrum of horizons for further social and political development. While the concrete end of communist regimes at a particular point in time may have been unexpected, the inviability of non-capitalist systems did not come as a surprise.[342] Instead of opening up new horizons, the collapse of communism entailed the loss of two historical horizons, namely those of communism and revolution.[343] At the same time, the inviability of communist systems confirmed and reinforced the victorious horizon of 'capitalism' – in the sense of 'the renewed development and planetary universalization of capital accumulation as the basis of social development'.[344]

The current predominance of capitalism does not exclude unexpected events. Instead of opening new avenues for social and political changes, however, these unexpected events tend to remain within the prevailing capitalist paradigm. China's adherence to the WTO and corresponding

338. Osborne 2013, 207-208. Cf. Koselleck 1985, 276.
339. Osborne 2013, 207, referring to Koselleck 1985, 275.
340. Osborne 2013, 207 (emphasis in the original text).
341. Osborne 2013, 208 (emphasis in the original text).
342. Osborne 2013, 208-209.
343. Osborne 2013, 209. As to repercussions on policymaking in intellectual property law, see Peukert 2019, 1199-1200, who recommends to ensure that 'market-based transactions coexist with non-market modes of accessing and sharing information ... '.
344. Osborne 2013, 209.

reforms of land ownership and capital regulation, for instance, opened up a new horizon for the global economic system. New prospects of business development in China, however, only brought 'a new horizon of expectation within capitalism'.[345] According to Osborne, even the 9/11 terrorist attack was nothing more than 'a symbolic harbinger of a new, religiously-coded geopolitical antagonism' that remained emblematic and merely darkened the capitalist Western horizon of expectation.[346] For the creation of truly alternative visions of society – expectations of the 'genuinely *un*expected'[347] – it is necessary to commit to experimental practices of negation: practices that are capable of producing new meaning through the negation of established expectations.[348] In this regard, contemporary art plays a crucial role:

> At its best, contemporary art models experimental practices of negation that puncture horizons of expectation.[349]

Osborne's analysis of the role of contemporary art, thus, confirms the conclusion that has been drawn above on the basis of Schiller's and Adorno's aesthetic theories: art can provide important impulses for social and political changes by modelling experimental practices that open up new horizons for the development of society.[350] Hence, the description of art's societal impact in Schiller's and Adorno's theories is not outdated. The emphasis on moral and political cultivation in Beebe's analysis relying on pragmatist aesthetics[351] and the importance which Osborne attaches to experimental artistic practices of negation in his 'Philosophy of Contemporary Art'[352] confirm that by providing raw material for the aesthetic play and puncturing predominant horizons of expectation, art can play a crucial role in the improvement of social and political conditions.

3.3.2.4 Importance of a Robust Public Domain

The foray into aesthetic theory in the preceding sections offers answers to questions that go beyond Bourdieu's sociological description of the field of literary and artistic production. With the outlined aesthetic theories, Bourdieu's analysis can be supplemented with an assessment of the value and importance of artworks for society as a whole: what would be lost if the field of literary and artistic production was no longer autonomous? If it were

345. Osborne 2013, 210.
346. Osborne 2013, 210.
347. Osborne 2013, 208 (emphasis in the original text).
348. Osborne 2013, 208.
349. Osborne 2013, 211.
350. Cf. Cramer 2019, 15, who also draws a line between Adorno's critical theory and Osborne's focus on experimental practices of negation.
351. Beebe 2017, 346-347.
352. Osborne 2013, 211.

dominated by commercial considerations? If literature and art did no longer follow its own, independent logic – its 'nomos' of self-referential *l'art pour l'art*?

Considering Schiller's and Adorno's theories, the answer to these questions lies in the potential of art to mirror shortcomings of present society and raise a desire for changes for the better. As an independent, autonomous observer, the artist is capable of depicting alternatives to an insufficient and inacceptable reality. An artwork can unmask defects of existing societal conditions and prepare society for the transition to a better community. Once the field of literary and artistic production loses its autonomy, this constant challenge of reality and indispensable training for a better world would be lost. Society would remain in a lamentable state of imperfection without the impulses necessary to improve the situation. Given this fundamental importance of literary and artistic productions, it is safe to assume that particular importance must be attached to the preservation of the genuine, cultural meaning of artworks as a basis for dialogue and discussion in the artistic domain ('artistic discourse potential').[353] Once a work of art is created, society should seek not to interfere with the artistic discourse potential which the respective literary and artistic creation offers. Otherwise, an important impulse for the required social and political changes may be lost.

Bourdieu's sociological analysis confirms this assumption by stressing the need for a new generation of artists to define its position in respect of the reservoir of pre-existing cultural expressions.[354] If the potential of pre-existing literary and artistic works for dialogic communication in the artistic community is lost, parts of this reservoir are rendered useless. They are no longer available for the formulation of new artistic positions and the creation of new works that can provide new impulses for societal changes. Schiller directly points out the merit of preserving the genuine, cultural meaning of works of art as a basis for ongoing dialogue in the literary and artistic domain and impulses for societal change. As artworks reflect human dignity, they can serve as prototypes for the restoration of an ethical order whenever the principles of morality and reason are lost:

> Humanity has lost its dignity, but art has saved it, and preserves it in marbles full of meaning; truth continues to live in illusion, and the copy will serve to reestablish the model.[355]

From this perspective, the preservation of an artwork's potential for dialogic communication in the artistic domain is an act of preserving expressions of human dignity as templates for desirable improvements of

353. For a more detailed discussion of the dialogic process underlying acts of creation, see Gervais 2019, 22-23; Dusollier 2018, 180-183; Frosio 2018, 15-68; Frosio 2014, 345-376; Craig 2011, 52-56; Cohen 2006, 144-152.
354. Bourdieu 1992/1999, 370-372.
355. Schiller 1794-1795, 35 (Letter 9).

social and political conditions. The recognition of the public domain in copyright law supports this preservation of the cultural discourse potential of literary and artistic works in line with Bourdieu's and Schiller's theories. Once again, it becomes apparent that the various aspects of the cultural imperative – in the sense of efforts made in copyright law to provide source material for open, dialogic communication in the artistic domain – are of utmost importance to society.[356]

At the same time, the described sociological and aesthetic theories allow a first estimate of the impact of overlapping trademark protection. The grant of trademark rights in artworks is likely to have a corrosive effect on the communication process in the artistic domain. The grant of trademark rights gives one individual speaker – the trademark proprietor – more communication power than other participants in the debate. Even if trademark claims finally have no success, the mere fact that the trademark owner can bring a lawsuit because of her exclusive rights to the sign can change 'the nature of the social conversation about things'.[357] As trademark rights offer the trademark owner an exclusive position, the definition power is higher than the degree of control resulting from other forms of commercial use, such as mere use in advertising without trademark rights. As Alexander Peukert points out in his critique of the continuous expansion of intellectual property protection[358] in the light of Karl Polanyi's concept of fictitious commodities:[359]

> [t]he more information is covered by IPRs [intellectual property rights], the less communication of technical teachings, expressions of various sorts, and brand images can occur spontaneously and without regard to exclusive rights of others. Taken to the extreme, the interruptions caused by IPRs would bring communication and, thus, societal exchange effectively to a halt or reconfigure today's society to a nightmarish system where only those are allowed to speak and act who can afford it[360] (explanation within brackets added).

As a result of the authorization requirement that comes along with trademark protection,[361] the debate on affected artworks is no longer as open and free as it was before. If trademark rights are acquired after an artwork entered the public domain, the resulting climate change is self-evident.[362]

---

356. Cf. Peukert 2019, 1185-188; Dusollier 2018, 180-183; Assaf 2008, 4-5; Coombe 1998, 52-55. See also Dusollier 2015, 167-168, including an entitlement of each member of the public to 'use, modify, exploit, reproduce and create new works from public domain material' in her concept of *res communis*.
357. Lemley/McKenna 2010, 443.
358. Peukert 2019, 1166-1169.
359. Peukert 2019, 1174-1176.
360. Peukert 2019, 1188.
361. Peukert 2019, 1169. Cf. Frosio 2014, 390-391.
362. Peukert 2019, 1178-1179; Senftleben 2017b, 688.

Unlimited freedom of use is sacrificed in favour of a scenario where all speakers, including artists in the cultural domain, must ensure that their contributions to the debate do not amount to trademark infringement. Intentionally or unintentionally, the trademark proprietor will bring trademark claims against those forms of artistic use which, from her point of view, interfere with her own strategy for the development of the message and meaning of the sign. Moreover, the grant of stable, indefinitely renewable trademark rights substantially enhances the risk of impregnating the artwork with commercial messages that dilute the sign's cultural meaning[363] and create a substantial risk of devaluing the sign as a reference point in the artistic discourse. Adorno explicitly warns of the risk of artworks losing their subversive character through efforts to submerge their critical meaning and popularize them in commercial products.[364] Once art is consumed and enjoyed, it inevitably loses its value as a mirror of defects in society and a provocation that is capable of triggering necessary changes. Instead, it becomes a means of pretending that the present situation is sufficient and acceptable.[365] From this perspective, it seems necessary to shield artworks from the corrosive effect of use in product marketing to safeguard the potential of art to expose flaws in society (for a more detailed discussion of this point, see section 8.2.3.3).

Therefore, the recognition of the need to preserve a rich and robust public domain of cultural expression – understood in the sense of efforts to preserve an artwork's potential for dialogic communication in the artistic domain – is of particular importance to society. It ensures that alternative visions of society that are evoked in literary and artistic works remain intact – visions that may provide impulses for artistic follow-on innovation and societal reforms. A public domain of genuine, cultural expressions serves as a source of inspiration and basis of new acts of creation. These new creative efforts will lead to fresh cultural productions that, as the pre-existing works on which they are built, mirror shortcomings of reality and offer the prospect of a better society. An analysis of the second element of the cultural imperative – the recognition of the public domain – in the light of Schiller's and Adorno's aesthetic theories thus confirms the importance of public domain preservation for society as a whole. In particular, it shows that this preservation task must focus on the artistic discourse potential of works of art.

Case law reflects the need for measures to safeguard the incessant process of cultural renewal on the basis of an open artistic discourse. The German Federal Constitutional Court explicitly recognized that, in the process of cultural renewal, a literary and artistic work becomes an independent factor influencing the cultural and intellectual perception of its

363. Assaf 2008, 21-23.
364. Adorno 1970, 33-34.
365. Adorno 1970, 32. Cf. van den Braembussche 1996, 41-42.

age which increasingly evaporates in the process of its communication until the time of protection finally expires:

> once a work is published it is no longer at its owner's sole disposal, but enters the social sphere, just as it was intended to do, and can thereby become an independent factor that helps define the cultural and intellectual scene of its era. As over time, the work is no longer only subject to disposal under private law and becomes common intellectual and cultural property, the author must accept that it will increasingly serve as a link to an artistic dialogue.[366]

Similarly, the EFTA Court stressed that the public domain status of cultural expressions is a corollary of the process of communicating literary and artistic works:

> [o]nce communicated, creative content belongs, as a matter of principle, to the public domain. In other words, the fact that works are part of the public domain is not a consequence of the lapse of copyright protection. Rather, protection is the exception to the rule that creative content becomes part of the public domain once communicated.[367]

From this perspective, the cultivation of the public domain of cultural expressions is a societal task of outstanding importance. It ensures the constant renewal of the cultural landscape on the basis of a rich reservoir of pre-existing works that serve as reference points for open, dialogic communication in the artistic domain.

3.4 CONCLUSION

The cultural imperative consists of two elements that ensure the constant evolution of fresh cultural expressions on the basis of pre-existing source material. On the one hand, it is imperative to guarantee intergenerational equity. Later authors should be free to learn of the history of their art and ground their own creative activities in the creations of their predecessors. On the other hand, it is imperative to preserve and cultivate the public domain of cultural expressions as a reservoir of source material for new literary and artistic productions. Copyright law achieves these goals by limiting the term of protection, keeping ideas, concepts and styles free, and exempting transformative use from the control of copyright owners.

---

366. German Federal Constitutional Court, 31 May 2016, case 1 BvR 1585/13, 'Sampling', *GRUR* 2016, 690, para. 87. English translation available at: https://www.bundesverfassungsgericht.de/e/rs20160531_1bvr158513en.html. Cf. Peukert 2019, 1180-1181; Cohen 2006, 154-155; Kreile 1993, 257-258; Kirchhof 1988, 34-35.
367. EFTA Court, 6 April 2017, case E-5/16, Municipality of Oslo ('Vigeland'), para. 66.

A closer analysis of the cultural imperative in the light of theoretical foundations of copyright law shows that the guarantee of intergenerational equity and the recognition of the public domain are central to the proper functioning of the copyright system from the perspective of both legal traditions of copyright law. Taking a utilitarian approach, intergenerational equity is indispensable to prevent the grant of copyright protection from becoming an obstacle to the creation of new works inspired by, or based upon, pre-existing protected material. The recognition of the public domain is necessary to preserve an area of freedom that makes cultural expressions available for future creativity and cultural follow-on innovation. Following the natural law approach, the recognition of the public domain constitutes a precondition for the acquisition of copyright. Without a rich public domain of freely available cultural expressions, there would be no world of abundance in which an author could acquire copyright through the mere act of creation. Moreover, acceptance of intergenerational equity is the price to be paid for the acquisition of copyright. An author can only fulfil her obligation to leave the abundant world of cultural expressions intact by offering later generations of authors freedom to use protected works as a source of inspiration and basis for the creation of new works.

In addition, the foregoing analysis demonstrates that the cultural imperative has societal relevance that goes far beyond the objective to secure the proper functioning of copyright law. In the field of literary and artistic production, the guarantee of intergenerational equity ensures that the copyright system remains neutral in the ongoing struggle between different groups of authors for power to set quality standards and dictate the internal discourse. Based on Pierre Bourdieu's sociological analysis, it can be said that the autonomy of the field of literary and artistic production requires independence from economic and political powers. From this perspective, the grant of exploitation rights and the focus on pecuniary incentives in copyright law is problematic. The prospect of monetary rewards may entice autonomous artists away from the independent *l'art pour l'art* logic of the literary and artistic field. The offer of copyright appears not only as a bait to spur creativity but also as an attempt to persuade autonomous artists to spend time and effort on the production of economically successful mainstream works. This, however, does not mean that copyright law has nothing to offer for authors with an independent *l'art pour l'art* orientation. As Bourdieu explains, the constant evolution of fresh, autonomous avant-garde productions depends on mechanisms that allow new generations of autonomous authors to legitimize their unorthodox, new rules by criticizing the dogmata of the presently predominant school of thought. Copyright law can support this constant process of renewal within the group of autonomous artists by guaranteeing user freedoms. It can enable a new generation of artists to destruct an established order and erect a new one by exempting the use of protected, pre-existing works for the formulation of new aesthetic positions. The guarantee of intergenerational equity ensures this freedom. It ensures that copyright law does support not only the creative efforts of profit-oriented authors but also the work of independent, autonomous authors.

The second aspect of the cultural imperative – the recognition of the public domain – has particular societal relevance as well. It ensures that artworks remain freely available resources for dialogic communication in the literary and artistic domain. The freedom of remixing pre-existing cultural expressions is pointless in the absence of appropriate efforts to preserve the 'artistic discourse potential' of public domain material: after copyright expiry, works of art must constitute free sources of inspiration that are made available as building blocks for new acts of creation in an open communication process that is not dominated by an individual speaker, such as the owner of exclusive rights stemming from trademark law. In the light of Friedrich Schiller's, Theodor Adorno's and Peter Osborne's aesthetic theories, it becomes apparent that this contribution to an open artistic discourse supports literary and artistic productions that can offer important impulses for the improvement of societal conditions by identifying defects in social and political systems and providing alternative visions of a better society.

Chapter 4

Market Transparency Imperative in Trademark Law

As indicated above, the cultural imperative – understood as the inalienable core of copyright law that ensures the proper functioning of the protection system – is only one 'imperative' in intellectual property law. Other protection systems, such as patent and trademark law, also rest on fundamental considerations and have functional parameters that are indispensable for the attainment of underlying societal goals and the proper functioning of the respective intellectual property regime (section 2.1). By extracting this inalienable functional core not only from copyright law but also from other intellectual property regimes, it becomes possible to establish a systems theory in intellectual property law – in the sense of a functional analysis of central objectives and features of individual intellectual property regimes that makes it possible to identify parallels and incompatibilities between different protection systems, and group intellectual property regimes in accordance with their predominant functional tasks.

To prepare the later analysis of concrete legal problems arising from protection overlaps, the present chapter is dedicated to this theoretical exercise of tracing the outlines of a systems theory in intellectual property law. For this purpose, it will be asked to which extent the proper functioning of patent and trademark law depends on a functional disposition that is comparable to the one prevailing in copyright law. As the cultural imperative, comprising the guarantee of intergenerational equity and the recognition of the public domain (Chapter 3), reflects the preconditions for the proper functioning of copyright law, this examination raises the question of whether comparable principles play an important role in patent and trademark law. Taking this question as a starting point, the following analysis will show a convergence of principles in the relationship between copyright and patent law (section 4.1), and a divergence of principles in the relationship between copyright and trademark law (section 4.2). Already at this theoretical level, it will become obvious that copyright/trademark overlaps give rise to particularly delicate legal questions that merit closer inspection.

4.1 CONVERGENT PRINCIPLES IN COPYRIGHT AND PATENT LAW

When the core elements of the cultural imperative in copyright law – the guarantee of intergenerational equity and the recognition of the public domain – are placed in the context of patent law, several parallels between the protection systems come to the fore. In the case of copyright, these core elements support the *cultural innovation cycle*. The central function of patent law lies in safeguarding the *technical innovation cycle*. In several respects, the preconditions for the proper functioning of patent law are thus similar to those identified in the area of copyright. Intergenerational equity and public domain recognition play a fundamental role in patent law as well (4.1.1).

With regard to the assessment of copyright/trademark overlaps, these functional parallels offer an important reference point. As copyright and patent law share functional elements and both seek to safeguard cyclic follow-on innovation, it can be asked whether the intellectual property system as a whole should attach the same importance to the maintenance of the cultural innovation cycle as it attaches to the maintenance of the technical innovation cycle when coexisting trademark protection could endanger the proper functioning of the respective innovation system. Hence, the identification of functional parallels between copyright and patent law gives rise to the question of whether the need to shield copyright law from potential corrosive effects of trademark protection is as strong as the necessity to preclude interferences of trademark protection with the proper functioning of patent law. Is the cultural innovation cycle as vulnerable as its technical counterpart (4.1.2)?

4.1.1 *Parallel of Intellectual Creation Cycles*

The notion of intellectual creation cycles does not only feature prominently in copyright law. For an invention to enjoy patent protection, it must be new, involve an inventive step and be capable of industrial application.[368] These protection requirements reveal a functional set-up similar to copyright law. It is an essential trait of the inventor to be capable of developing new technical solutions on the basis of the pre-existing state of the art. As a reward for the disclosure of this contribution to the enhancement of know-how, patent law confers exclusive rights for a limited period of time.[369] The restriction of the term of protection ensures that the invention, ultimately, enters the public domain where it can serve as a source of knowledge for further technical innovation. The exemption of experimental use during the term of protection also serves the purpose of facilitating technical progress.[370] As the copyright system, patent law thus seeks to support an intellectual creation cycle.[371] In the domain of technology, it fulfils a function similar to copyright's role in the domain of culture.[372] To allow patent law to accomplish this task, inventors must be free to use the technical solutions of their predecessors as a source of knowledge and basis for new inventions.

In copyright law, it is recognized that the fundamental guarantee of freedom of expression supports the exemption of transformative use, such as use for the purposes of quotation and parody, during the term of copyright protection. Given the link with constitutional freedoms, use privileges for transformative remix activities rest on a solid basis that is capable of justifying the inroads made into the exclusive rights of copyright owners (section 3.1).[373] Similar conclusions can be drawn with regard to the exemption of experimental use in patent law. In the WTO Panel report *Canada – Patent Protection of Pharmaceutical Products*, the Panel explained in the context of Article 30 TRIPS that the requirement in patent law that the nature of the invention be disclosed to the public would partly be

368. Article 27(1) TRIPS.
369. See Article 29(1) TRIPS as to the disclosure rationale and Article 33 TRIPS as to the international minimum term of protection of 20 years.
370. The need for breathing space in the area of experimental use is particularly underlined in restrictive national systems, such as the U.S. patent system. Cf. Dreyfuss 2004, 457; Strandburg 2004, 81; Mohr 2004, 671; Mueller 2001, 1. However, see also the critical comments by Devlin 2009, 599.
371. O'Rourke 2000, 1183.
372. The function is only similar – not identical – because of differences in the type of progress that may be deemed desirable from a societal perspective. As Beebe 2017, 345-346, has argued, the technical innovation cycle can focus on superseding, refining and supplementing previously available technical knowledge. The cultural innovation cycle, by contrast, should not simply strive for the 'stockpiling over time of fixed, archivable works' (Beebe, *ibid.*, 346). Instead, it should focus on 'the quality of ephemeral aesthetic experience in the present' and measure aesthetic progress 'largely by the extent of popular, democratic participation in aesthetic practice' (Beebe, *ibid.*, 346). See also Fromer 2010, 1444-1445, for an analysis of differences with regard to the focus on problem-solving in patent law and problem-finding in copyright law. These differences, however, do not concern the functional disposition of copyright and patent law that is central to the current analysis.
373. Cf. Geiger 2018a, 11-12; Geiger 2004b, 268.

frustrated if the patent owner could prevent experimental use during the term of the patent. Both society and the scientist had a legitimate interest in using the patent disclosure to support the advance of science and technology.[374] In this line of reasoning, the exemption of experimental use is a corollary of the disclosure rationale underlying the grant of patent protection.[375] As transformative use in copyright law, experimental use is supported by a fundamental principle of patent law that lies at the heart of the protection system. From this perspective, the exemption of experimental use in patent law constitutes a functional parallel corresponding to the exemption of transformative use in copyright law.[376] The exemption of the productive reuse of existing source material is central to both protection regimes because they share the objective to promote cyclic innovation processes.

Admittedly, the scope of the experimental use defence may differ from country to country. A restrictive approach often prevails when research has a commercial dimension, such as regulatory approval for marketing purposes.[377] In the U.S., even indirect commercial benefits may frustrate the invocation of the use privilege. Following the traditional distinction between unjustified commercial and exempted non-commercial use, the U.S. Court of Appeals for the Third Circuit held in *Madey/Duke* that the use of Madey's patents by the Duke University went beyond the scope of the experimental use defence because it furthered Duke's overall business objectives, including educating and enlightening students and faculty. The research also benefited Duke's reputation. The Court concluded that:

> regardless of whether a particular institution or entity is engaged in an endeavor for commercial gain, so long as the act is in furtherance of the alleged infringer's legitimate business and is not solely for amusement, to satisfy idle curiosity, or for strictly philosophical inquiry, the act does not qualify for the very narrow and strictly limited experimental use

374. WTO Panel, 17 March 2000, WTO Document WT/DS114/R, Canada – Patent Protection of Pharmaceutical Products, para. 7.69.
375. In international patent law, Article 29(1) TRIPS reflects the objective of fully disclosing technical knowledge in the framework of patent registrations.
376. This line between transformative use in the field of copyright law and a patent fair use defence that would offer more breathing space for experimental use is also drawn, for instance, by Mueller 2004, 976.
377. See U.S. Court of Appeals for the Federal Circuit, 733 F.2d 858 (Fed. Cir. 1984), Roche Products vs. Bolar Pharmaceutical; Dutch Supreme Court (Hoge Raad), December 18, 1992, *GRUR Int.* 1993, p. 887, ICI/Medicopharma ('Atenolol'). Cf. Schutjens, 827. In both countries, a specific exception for the use of patented material to obtain marketing approval has been introduced in the meantime. See § 271(e) of the U.S. Patent Act and Article 53(4) of the Dutch Patent Act. With regard to this statutory solution, see Strandburg 2006, 112-115.

defense. Moreover, the profit or non-profit status of the user is not determinative.[378]

Given the broad notion of commercial use applied in this case, and the increasing number of collaborative research involving universities and private companies, this approach jeopardizes the effectiveness of the experimental use defence.[379] Nonetheless, it would be wrong to infer from this national approach that the experimental use defence has lost its central role in the patent system. More flexible approaches have evolved in other countries. The decisions *Clinical Trials I* and *Clinical Trials II* of the German Federal Court of Justice can serve as examples. In Germany, § 11 No. 2 of the German Patent Act exempts 'acts done for experimental purposes relating to the subject matter of the patented invention'.[380] The *Clinical Trials I* decision concerned the use of patented material for the identification of new medical indications. In this context, the German Federal Court of Justice clarified that all kinds of experimental use were exempted to the extent to which the use served the purpose of obtaining knowledge and, therefore, concerned scientific research on the subject matter of the patented invention, including its application. In particular, it was not decisive whether the experiments were undertaken merely to review the particulars of the patent specification. The experimental use defence covered use for the purpose of obtaining new research results irrespective of whether the user had further intentions, such as use of the results for commercial purposes.[381] In *Clinical Trials II*, the Court confirmed that the defence applied to all experimental acts that related to the subject matter of the invention, regardless of whether the tests produced purely scientific or industrially exploitable results. The defence could be invoked as long as the research did not specifically aim at impeding or frustrating the sale of the original product.[382]

This German approach clearly reflects the described objective to create breathing space for the productive reuse of patented knowledge and technical follow-on innovation by exempting research that is carried out to understand and improve a protected invention, and explore new fields for its application – even when the experiments, ultimately, aim at the commercial exploitation of research results.[383] In consequence, the experimental use defence is rendered capable of supporting the advance of science and technology in line

378. U.S. Court of Appeals, Federal Circuit, 3 October 2002, Madey/Duke University, 307 F.3d 1351 (Fed. Cir. 2002).
379. Cf. Pulsinelli 2006, 393; Owens 2005, 453; Sewell 2005, 759; Garde 2004, 241.
380. Like corresponding provisions in many other European countries, this provision has been modelled on Article 27(b) of the Community Patent Convention. Cf. Cornish 1998, 735-736.
381. German Federal Court of Justice, 11 July 1995, case X ZR 99/92, 'Klinische Versuche I', *GRUR* 1996, 109 (113).
382. German Federal Court of Justice, 17 April 1997, case X ZR 68/94, 'Klinische Versuche II', *NJW* 1997, 3092.
383. Cf. O'Rourke 2000, 1199; Merwe 2000, 388; Hieber 1996, 447.

with the aforementioned statement made by the WTO Panel in *Canada – Patent Protection of Pharmaceutical Products*. If the defence covers research for commercial purposes, judges hearing an infringement case have the opportunity to weigh the detriment to the patentee against the benefits accruing from enhanced technical knowledge that can be expected from the more flexible regulation of reuse in the area of technology. The more substantial the technical advance to be expected from research, the more clearly the regulation of experimental use can weigh in favour of the exemption of research use.[384] To facilitate the task of establishing a proportionate relation between the detriment to the patentee and the benefits for the researcher and the public, it may even be an option to provide, where necessary, for the payment of equitable remuneration.[385] In this way, an additional balancing tool is provided that allows the courts to reduce the harm to the patentee to reasonable limits when extensive experimental use is undertaken with a profit motive.[386]

The flexible regulation of experimental use in patent law can have particular importance in areas of technology where the high number of patents creates an 'anti-commons': rights are held by so many different owners that the costs of accumulating all required licences for an envisaged production become prohibitively high. This problem has been identified, for instance, in the field of biotechnology.[387] With a flexible limitation infrastructure extending the scope of the experimental use defence to commercially motivated activities, research use can be exempted that is undertaken to find ways of inventing around the patent for the purpose of enabling a production for which the necessary licence is unavailable. If a developer has already amassed the majority of the required licences to market a product, this freedom may serve as a catalyst inducing the patentee of the remaining technology to enter into a licensing agreement.[388]

384. Cf. O'Rourke 2000, 1203. For proposals of patent fair use factors to be applied in this context, see O'Rourke 2000, 1230-1235; Mueller 2001, 973-979.

385. The copyright three-step test laid down in Article 13 TRIPS has traditionally been understood to recognize the possibility of providing for the payment of equitable remuneration to enhance flexibility in the outlined sense. In the context of the third test, an unreasonable prejudice to legitimate interests can be reduced to a permissible, reasonable level by securing the payment of equitable remuneration. See Senftleben 2004, 127-133. Arguably, the same breathing space is available under the patent three-step test enshrined in Article 30 TRIPS. See Senftleben 2006, 139 and 165-166.

386. As to beneficial effects of an equitable remuneration option on the software sector, see O'Rourke 2000, 1235.

387. See O'Rourke 2000, 1236-1237; Heller/ Eisenberg 1998, 698. However, see also Hamme Ramirez 2004, 359; Epstein/Kuhlik 2004, 54, calling doubt upon the assumption of an anticommons in the field of biotechnology.

388. Cf. O'Rourke 2000, 1238, who envisages a system in which a court 'might allow the infringement to proceed and award a royalty while the infringement continues'. This proposal goes beyond the solution developed here which focuses on designing around

Besides room for experimental use activities during the term of patent protection, the patent system also seeks to promote follow-on innovation in the field of technology by cultivating the public domain. A rich and robust public domain of technical knowledge serves as a basis of further research and development.[389] It is central to incessant technical innovation. Patent law satisfies this need by encouraging inventors to fully disclose their technical advances.[390] Without the offer of protection, know-how is likely to be kept secret. It is the prospect of patent protection that prompts inventors to make fresh technical knowledge available. Once protection expires, this knowledge becomes part of the public domain. Hence, the disclosure rationale in patent law does not only provide a strong underpinning for the introduction of experimental use privileges. It also forges a link between the grant of protection and the ultimate goal of enriching the public domain.

The recognition of the public domain does not only constitute a key element of the cultural imperative in copyright law. It is also of paramount importance to the technical imperative inherent in patent law. In *Graham/John Deere*, the U.S. Supreme Court expressly recognized the need to preserve the public domain in the context of patent law:

> The Congress in the exercise of the patent power may not overreach the restraints imposed by the stated constitutional purpose. Nor may it enlarge the patent monopoly without regard to the innovation, advancement or social benefit gained thereby. Moreover, Congress may not authorize the issuance of patents whose effects are to remove existent knowledge from the public domain, or to restrict free access to materials already available.[391]

In *Bonito Boats/Thunder Craft Boats*, the same Court, moreover, warned of the corrosive effect which inroads into the public domain could have on the advancement of technology:

> Reverse engineering of chemical and mechanical articles in the public domain often leads to significant advances in technology. If Florida may prohibit this particular method of study and recomposition of an unpatented article, we fail to see the principle that would prohibit a State from banning the use of chromatography in the reconstitution of

the patented technology. It would have to be clarified whether this broader approach complies with the restrictive Article 31 TRIPS.

389. Cf. Dinwoodie/Dreyfuss 2006, 191.

390. See the disclosure requirement reflected in Article 29(1) TRIPS.

391. U.S. Supreme Court, 21 February 1966, Graham/John Deere Co., 383 U.S. 1, 5-6 (1966). For a discussion of the underlying anti-monopolist criticisms in the evolution of intellectual property law in the U.S., see Boyle 2003b, 53-58.

unpatented chemical compounds, or the use of robotics in the duplication of machinery in the public domain.[392]

As in copyright law, it may thus be posited that considerations of intergenerational equity play an important role: later inventors should be free to ground their own innovative activities in the know-how produced by their predecessors.[393] Research on the sociology of creative practices confirms this parallel between the domains of culture and technology. Exploring the social psychology of creative processes, Julie Cohen encountered several correspondences between artistic and scientific creativity which confirm the similarity of the preconditions for innovation in the respective domains. According to her analysis, open exchange models within scientific communities translate surprisingly well to creative communities. Authors and inventors alike need room to share and discuss their creative work. Norms of sharing are integral to the creative process.[394] Major advances are not unlikely to be the result of intense collaboration and exchange among members of artistic or scientific communities.[395] Dealing with the use of pre-existing material for the purpose of making new creations, Cohen concludes that:

> a relational account of creative practice must acknowledge the role of preexisting cultural artifacts as constituent elements of the network. [...] Within both the study of art and the study of science and technology, there is considerable agreement on this point but much disagreement about exactly how to frame it.[396]

Intergenerational equity in the sense of freedom for later creators to use pre-existing material as a source of inspiration and basis for new creations is thus not only relevant to creativity in the field of art. It also constitutes a central element of creative processes in the area of science and technology.[397] Acceptance of a limited term of patent protection and the imposition of certain limits on exclusive patent rights, particularly in favour of scientific experimentation, are indispensable to ensure a proper balance between rights and freedoms not only in copyright law but also in patent law. As in copyright law, the limitations imposed on exclusive patent rights, such as the limitation of the term of protection and the exemption of experimental use during the period of protection, constitute the price to be paid for the acquisition of patent rights.

392. U.S. Supreme Court, 21 February 1989, Bonito Boats/Thunder Craft Boats, 489 U.S. 141, 160 (1989).
393. Lemley 1997, 997-998.
394. Cohen 2006, 151.
395. Cohen 2006, 151.
396. Cohen 2006, 152.
397. Cf. Peukert 2019, 1180-1182; Gervais 2019, 22-23.

Hence, there is a *convergence of principles*. The cultural imperative in copyright law and the technical imperative in patent law seek to safeguard similar preconditions for the proper functioning of intellectual property protection in the respective domains of culture and technology.[398] This convergence of principles can reduce incompatibilities when copyright and patent protection overlap, although the general comparability of functional preconditions must not be confused with a carte blanche for the accumulation of rights. As the scenario arising from software patents shows, conflicts between the protection systems may arise with regard to exclusions from protection and incongruent catalogues of exceptions.[399] Moreover, the term of protection differs markedly.[400] Nonetheless, it is important to note with regard to the question of coexisting trademark protection that copyright and patent law rest on comparable functional pillars. The guarantee of intergenerational equity and the recognition of the public domain are central to the configuration of both protection systems.

4.1.2 *Need for Comparable Preservation Efforts*

The functional parallels between copyright and patent law may have important repercussions on the regulation of overlaps with other regimes of intellectual property, in particular trademark law. The fact that both copyright and patent law regulate processes of cyclic innovation may imply that the same effort must be made to safeguard the respective cyclic innovation processes when it comes to overlaps with trademark protection that can be renewed indefinitely.[401] The U.S. Supreme Court emphasized in *Dastar/ Twentieth Century Fox* that it was necessary to shield the quid pro quo underlying both – copyright and patent law – from the corrosive effect of protection regimes with potentially indefinite rights:

> The rights of a patentee or copyright holder are part of a 'carefully crafted bargain,' under which, once the patent or copyright monopoly has expired, the public may use the invention or work at will and without

398. Cf. the analysis conducted by O'Rourke 2000, 1184-1198, providing an overview of the interplay of threshold requirements and exemptions from exclusive rights in copyright and patent law.

399. For a discussion of this protection overlap and the need for limitations supporting derivative innovation in this area, see Samuelson 2019, 291-301; Li 2019, 823-859; Dane 2018a, 1-16; Dane 2018b, 5-15; Sterckx/Cockbain 2010, 366-402; Ballardini 2008, 563-575; Leistner 2008, 188; Ghidini/Arezzo 2005, 166; Hilty/Geiger 2005, 615; Burk/Lemley 2005, 81-100; Weyand/Haase 2005, 647; Cohen/Lemley 2001, 41-42; Caron 2000, 3. As to the denial of copyright protection for functional elements of software, see CJEU, 2 May 2012, case C-406/10, SAS Institute, paras 39-41.

400. See Article 33 TRIPS (international minimum of 20 years of patent protection) on the one hand and Article 7 BC (international minimum of life of the author and 50 years *post mortem* of copyright protection) on the other hand.

401. Article 18 TRIPS.

> attribution. Thus, in construing the Lanham Act, we have been 'careful to caution against misuse or over-extension' of trademark and related protections into areas traditionally occupied by patent or copyright.[402]

However, the argument of a need to safeguard the cultural innovation cycle (copyright law) to the same extent as the technical innovation cycle (patent law) rests on the assumption that the respective processes of cyclic innovation are vulnerable to a comparable degree. This raises the question of whether coexisting protection under another regime, such as trademark law, is likely to harm the cyclic evolution of new cultural productions to the same extent as it would harm the cyclic evolution of new technical knowledge.

4.1.3 *Rejection of Substitutability Argument*

The answer to this question seems to be influenced by general perceptions of the domain of technology on the one hand and the domain of culture on the other. While technical knowledge is seen as the result of exact, objective science, cultural productions are often portrayed as the result of subjective, intuitive imagination.[403] This fundamental difference – the *objective* domain of technology and the *subjective* domain of culture – may be understood to justify the further assumption that there is also a fundamental difference with regard to the substitutability of intellectual creations stemming from these distinct domains. Whereas it is often readily accepted that a technical problem can only be solved by applying one particular patent, the same assumption may appear less plausible when it comes to literary and artistic works. If a particular literary or artistic work is not available even though copyright protection has already expired, the view may be held that it can easily be replaced with a comparable work that also fits in the envisaged cultural production.

Hence, the exact, objective nature of technical know-how and the subjective, imaginative nature of artworks may predetermine our assessment of the need to ensure the availability of intellectual resources in the respective domains of technology and culture when it comes to overlaps with protection regimes offering indefinitely renewable protection, such as trademark law. Whereas technical knowledge may be regarded as non-substitutable to an extent that justifies strong measures to keep it freely available for technical follow-on innovation, the existence of alternatives for a literary or artistic work is often readily assumed without considering a potential corrosive effect on the evolution of new cultural productions. In the context of assessing the vulnerability of processes of technical and cultural innovation, this may lead to the conclusion that technical innovation will

402. U.S. Supreme Court, 2 June 2003, Dastar/Twentieth Century Fox, 539 U.S. 23 (2003), 33-34.
403. Quaedvlieg 1987, 21-22.

inevitably be frustrated if a particular technical solution is not available because of coexisting trademark protection. Cultural innovation, by contrast, will continue even if a particular work is not available.

For several reasons, however, this line of argument must fail. First, the argument that literary and artistic works can easily be substituted is doubtful even at the consumption level: a museum seeking to show a particular line of development in art history may depend on a particular work that played a central role in the process. This unique work may constitute a non-substitutable part of the planned exhibition. A concert programme may make much less sense when one musical work must be replaced with another that does not have the same connection or does not create the same contrast with other pieces on the programme. Therefore, the situation is not much different from the dilemma in the technical field. In some cases, a particular technical solution may be unique and non-substitutable. In other cases, it may be possible to invent around technical know-how, as it may be possible to include a different musical work in a concert programme. Nonetheless, the result of using another technical solution or another musical work may be less satisfactory and far from offering a true alternative. The substitutability argument, therefore, is doubtful already at the consumption level.

The argument becomes even more doubtful, however, when the production level is taken into account. The constant production of new intellectual creations in the domains of culture and technology is central to the present analysis. Instead of the conditions of consumption that often occupy centre stage in the substitutability debate, the present analysis deals with the conditions for the use of pre-existing material in the production of new intellectual creations. Against this background, an argument based on substitutes for the consumption of a particular literary and artistic work misses the point because it does not focus on the needs of authors seeking to use pre-existing literary and artistic productions for the purpose of creating new works. It is not the vulnerability of the process of consumption but the vulnerability of the process of production that must be considered when assessing the potential corrosive effect of protection overlaps, such as overlaps with trademark law, on the cyclic innovation systems which copyright and patent law seek to support. This production dimension constitutes the core of cyclic innovation in the fields of culture and technology and the focus of the present analysis. Accordingly, the impact of protection overlaps on the availability of resources for the productive reuse leading to new intellectual creations must be the central yardstick for assessing the validity of the substitutability argument.

With regard to this production perspective, Bourdieu's sociological analysis of the field of literary and artistic production, again, offers important insights. According to Bourdieu, it is naïve to assume substitutability of literary and artistic works in the context of the production of new works. As explained in section 3.3.1.3, his analysis shows that the room for the evolution of new directions in the creation of independent art depends on the range of options that is available in the light of the positions that have already been taken by previous artists.[404] For a new generation of autonomous artists to challenge the leading avant-garde, it must detect the structural gaps within the texture of already known aesthetic positions. It must formulate an alternative artistic position in the light of the weaknesses and contradictions of the present state of the art.[405] The positions that have already been taken in the literary and artistic field determine the room for new artistic positions and new impulses for the creation of literary and artistic works. In other words, they predetermine the room available for cultural follow-on innovation.[406]

For an artist seeking to formulate a new artistic position in the light of an aesthetic position reflected in a particular pre-existing work, this has far-reaching consequences. If the work is not available for this purpose, the envisaged cultural innovation step will simply not take place. In other words, every pre-existing aesthetic position that is not freely available for cultural follow-on innovation reduces the range of options which later generations of artists have at their disposal to find and formulate new aesthetic positions.[407] Every literary and artistic work that does not enter the public domain after the expiry of copyright protection reduces the resources available for cultural follow-on innovation.

From the production perspective, this copyright scenario is thus not much different from the situation in the field of technology. It may be argued that it is an exaggeration to assume that each and every literary and artistic work is relevant to cultural follow-on innovation. However, the same may be said about technical solutions. Undoubtedly, not each and every patented invention represents a pioneering technical step. And not each and every patented invention still has relevance after the expiry of patent protection. Moreover, it will be possible in many cases to invent around patented know-how or use alternative ways to solve a technical problem. Therefore, it is also an exaggeration to assume non-substitutability with regard to each and every patented invention. Admittedly, there are pioneering and unique technical solutions that are non-substitutable. With regard to these pioneering and unique technical solutions, freedom of use must be guaranteed and preserved after the expiry of patent protection in order not to frustrate technical follow-on innovation. However, the same may be said about certain literary and artistic works. There are non-substitutable masterpieces in the realm of literary and artistic works that must be kept free after the expiry of copyright protection. Otherwise, cultural follow-on innovation would be

404. Bourdieu 1992/1999, 370.
405. Bourdieu 1992/1999, 372 and 379-380.
406. For examples in the field of literature and music, see Bourdieu 1992/1999, 379-384.
407. For a corresponding line of argument addressing the marketing of cultural productions and competitive necessities arising from non-substitutability of cultural signs, see Curtin 2018, 1005-1008.

frustrated. Hence, it is wrong to assume that the substitutability argument has more weight in the domain of technology than it has in the domain of culture.

At this point, however, the fundamental difference between the two domains must be factored into the equation again: the objectivity of the technological domain on the one hand and the subjectivity of the cultural domain on the other. This difference does not imply that the cultural innovation cycle is less vulnerable than the technical innovation cycle. Nor does it imply that literary and artistic works are substitutable to a larger extent. By contrast, it simply means that the *assessment of non-substitutability* is objective in the case of technical solutions, whereas it is subjective in the case of literary and artistic works. For determining whether a given technical solution is unique, pioneering and non-substitutable, an objective assessment can be made. Persons skilled in the respective field of technology can be expected to reach agreement on non-substitutability on the basis of objective criteria. This, however, is fundamentally different in the field of culture. As the creation of new literary and artistic works is subjective, the assessment of pre-existing 'masterpieces' that are indispensable (and thus non-substitutable) for follow-on creativity is subjective as well. Every artist will make her own, subjective assessment of pre-existing aesthetic positions and identify those that are relevant to her own creativity on the basis of this subjective assessment. In contrast to specialists in a particular field of technology who can rely on objective assessment criteria, artists specializing in a particular field of art, thus, do not have shared objective criteria at their disposal because of the subjectivity of the domain of culture and creativity. In consequence, artists are unlikely to generally agree on the non-substitutability of a given literary and artistic work. A cultural expression that may be non-substitutable for one artist may appear unimportant and substitutable for another.

4.1.4 *Inclusion of a Wide Range of Literary and Artistic Works*

In terms of vulnerability of innovation processes in the domains of culture and technology, this insight does not permit the conclusion that cultural follow-on innovation need not be shielded from potential corrosive effects of indefinitely renewable trademark protection to the same extent as technical follow-on innovation. By contrast, even broader measures are necessary to safeguard cultural follow-on innovation because it is not foreseeable which aesthetic positions reflected in a literary or artistic work will be non-substitutable from the perspective of later generations of artists. As it is possible to identify unique, non-substitutable technical solutions on the basis of objective criteria, efforts to inhibit protection overlaps from interfering with technical follow-on innovation, at least theoretically, could be confined to these unique, non-substitutable solutions.[408] However, as it is not possible to reach agreement on a list of unique, non-substitutable cultural expressions on the basis of the subjective assessment inherent in production processes in the cultural field, efforts to prevent protection overlaps from interfering with cultural follow-on innovation, a priori, cannot be confined to specific literary and artistic works. In principle, each aesthetic position may become indispensable for the creation of a new work because it is not foreseeable to which pre-existing aesthetic position a later generation of artists will attach fundamental importance on the basis of its subjective assessment of pre-existing works.[409]

Therefore, it is wrong to assume that the cultural innovation cycle is less vulnerable than the technical innovation cycle when it comes to protection overlaps that may restrict the intellectual resources available for follow-on creativity. In both domains, certain intellectual creations are unimportant or substitutable, while others are unique and non-substitutable. While these unique and non-substitutable creations can be identified clearly on the basis of objective criteria in the domain of technology, it is not foreseeable which creations are indispensable for cultural follow-on innovation because the decision depends on the subjective assessment of later generations of artists seeking to find and formulate new aesthetic positions. Hence, there is reason to undertake even broader efforts to shield the cultural innovation cycle from the potential corrosive effect of protection overlaps. While, in the case of the technical innovation cycle, these efforts could theoretically be confined to those inventions that are non-substitutable from an objective, technical perspective, such confinement is inconceivable in the case of literary and artistic works because an objective assessment of the needs of future generations of authors is not possible. In the subjective domain of culture, non-substitutability – and thus the need to guarantee freedom of use for the purpose of creating a new work – depends on the subjective assessment of the individual artist. As an objective assessment that could be generalized is not possible, it is advisable to include a wide range of literary and artistic

408. However, see Quaedvlieg 1987, 40-45, who describes the profound problems arising from this approach focusing on non-substitutability in a strict sense.

409. It would be cynical to take the opposite view and argue that, because of the subjectivity of the assessment of non-substitutability in the cultural domain, it does not matter which literary and artistic works remain available for later generations of authors because – whatever work is left – there will always be some artist who is still capable of taking this work as a point of departure for follow-on creativity. Under this cynical view, measures to ensure the availability of literary and artistic works for the creative work of later generations of authors could be restricted to a minimum. At the same time, however, the reservoir of works available for follow-on innovation in the cultural domain would be confined to a minimum. The cultural diversity resulting from the efforts of the few authors who are still capable of generating new works on the basis of this minimum reservoir, accordingly, is also likely to remain minimal. Cf. Cohen 2006, 155-156.

works in initiatives to shield cultural follow-on innovation from the potential negative impact of cumulative trademark protection.[410]

4.2 DIVERGENT PRINCIPLES IN TRADEMARK LAW

In the preceding section, it has already been indicated that trademark law has certain features, such as the rule of indefinite renewal, that differ markedly from the configuration of copyright and patent law. The reason for this fundamental difference lies in a different focus of the protection system: while copyright and patent law seek to support processes of cyclic innovation in the domains of culture and technology, it is the central task of trademark law to ensure market transparency. Instead of cyclic protection that becomes available whenever a new creation evolves in the ongoing process of cultural and technical innovation, trademark protection must be static. The goal of market transparency can only be attained with a stable distribution of intellectual resources among market participants (following section 4.2.1). Irrespective of this fundamentally different objective and focus of the protection system, certain traces of intergenerational equity and public domain recognition can be identified in trademark law (4.2.2). These traces, however, are not sufficient to conclude that there is a convergence of protection principles when the cultural imperative in copyright law is taken into account. By contrast, the configuration of trademark law is incompatible with the cultural imperative inherent in copyright law (4.2.3).

4.2.1 *Static Instead of Cyclic Protection*

The notion of an intellectual creation cycle is alien to trademark law. Instead of seeking to support the creative reuse of pre-existing material and the constant enrichment of the public domain, trademark law aims at a rather static assignment of exclusive entitlements to right owners.[411] The reason for this deviation from the configuration of copyright and patent law lies in protection needs to be satisfied in the sector of trade. It is the core function of trademark law to ensure *market transparency*. In a transparent market where distinctive signs are exclusively linked with the goods or services stemming from one individual commercial source, an enterprise can clearly identify its offer in the marketplace, and consumers can easily individualize

410. This conclusion is supported by previous studies that have highlighted the importance of keeping a reservoir of cultural expressions for cultural follow-on innovation as rich as possible. For instance, see Cohen 2006, 154: 'The centrality of borrowing, reworking, and cross-fertilization to creative practice suggests that creative practice will thrive under conditions that allow a substantial degree of unplanned, fortuitous access to and use of a variety of cultural goods.' Cf. Frosio 2018, 15-68; Frosio 2014, 345-376.
411. Cf. Dinwoodie/Janis 2007a, 1613.

different offers and express their preference by selecting one specific product or service.[412] This, in turn, will help the public's preferred suppliers, products and services to prevail in the marketplace. Contributing to the regulation of supply and demand in this way, trademark law supports the proper functioning of markets. In the field of trade, the guarantee of market transparency through trademark protection thus ensures fair competition, consumer protection and the efficient functioning of markets. These objectives constitute the different elements of the trade imperative that is inherent in trademark law.[413]

Trademark law could not realize these objectives if the term of protection was strictly limited. A temporal limitation would have the effect that all market participants could freely use the trademark after the expiry of protection. In consequence, consumers could no longer rely on the trademark as an indicator of commercial source. The trademark could no longer contribute to market transparency and fair competition. It would lose its identifying function and the capacity to support the proper functioning of the market. For this reason, the trademark owner can renew the registration of the trademark indefinitely.[414] The rule of indefinite renewal allows an enterprise to uphold the exclusive link with its trademarks as long as it keeps using them in trade.[415] The distinctiveness of trademarks used in the market can thus be preserved, and consumers and the public at large are not misled.

The preconditions for the proper functioning of trademark law thus differ markedly from those shaping copyright and patent law (and the corresponding cultural and technical imperatives discussed above). A limited term of protection would cut the exclusive link between a trademark and the goods or services of its owner after a certain period of time. In a transparency-centred framework, this removal of established links is undesirable. In contrast to copyright and patent law, the trademark system thus provides for the possibility of indefinite renewal of protection. Trademark law also refrains from encouraging the reuse of signs. As long as a sign refers to an individual commercial source, use as a trademark by another market participant would be misleading and undesirable. Hence, there is a tension between the core objective of trademark law to ensure market transparency and the cultural imperative seeking to safeguard intergenerational equity and recognizing the need to preserve the public domain. Instead of striving for

412. Kur/Senftleben 2017, para. 1.06-1.09. With regard to the economic search costs argument that is related to this function of trademarks, see A. Griffiths 2008, 241; Strasser 2000, 379-382. With regard to search cost questions arising in the digital environment, see Dogan/Lemley 2004, 777.

413. Cf. Heymann 2013, 248; McKenna 2009a, 880-881.

414. Article 18 TRIPS.

415. As Article 19 TRIPS indicates, use may be required to maintain a trademark's registration. The registration may be cancelled after an uninterrupted period of at least three years of non-use, unless valid reasons based on the existence of obstacles to such use are shown by the trademark owner.

the productive reuse of pre-existing intellectual creations and the cultivation of the public domain, trademark law merely contains certain instruments that aim at the economical use of existing intellectual resources.

4.2.2 *Traces of Intergenerational Equity and Public Domain Recognition*

According to the principle of speciality, the acquisition of trademark rights in a given sign is limited to specific goods and services. In unrelated market segments, the sign remains available as long as it has not acquired the status of a well-known mark that allows the trademark owner to bring an action against use in non-competitive situations.[416] The maintenance of trademark rights, moreover, requires use of the sign with regard to the goods and services for which protection is claimed. After a period of uninterrupted non-use, a trademark registration may be cancelled.[417] Hence, trademark law contains certain safeguards against the use of a trademark registration as a means to artificially withhold a sign from other market participants. At the registration stage, trademark law also contains grounds for refusal that allow the denial of trademark protection for certain types of signs, such as functional, non-distinctive, descriptive and generic signs.[418] Trademark law may contain additional rules on the exclusion of mere concepts from trademark protection.[419]

These features of trademark law can be regarded as traces of intergenerational equity among traders. They may also be seen as a recognition of the public domain. A reservoir of signs free to common use offers traders equal access to communication tools that can be used to inform consumers about product characteristics and compete for market shares. Freedom to use non-distinctive, descriptive and generic signs ensures that traders can easily convey information about their goods or services.[420] A commons of

---

416. As to the scope of protection of well-known marks, see Article 16(3) TRIPS and the provisions in the JR WKM. For a discussion of anti-dilution protection in different national systems, see Swann 2013, 721; Handler 2007, 307; Senftleben 2009a, 50-55; Beebe 2006, 1157; McCarthy 2004, 1163.
417. Cf. Article 19(1) TRIPS. As to the implementation of the use requirement in EU trademark law and the requirement of finding an outlet for goods or services, see CJEU, 11 March 2003, case C-40/01, Ajax/Ansul, para. 36 and 43. Cf. Kur/Senftleben 2017, para. 6.154.
418. These categories of signs ineligible for trademark protection are reflected in the absolute grounds for refusal of many countries. For an overview, see the contributions to Senftleben 2012b. See also the international regulation of *telle quelle* protection in Article 6quinquies(B) No. 2 and 6quinquies(A)(1) PC. Cf. Pflüger 2011, 235-241; Kunz-Hallstein 2006, 487; Beier 1992, 243; Ladas 1975, 1211-1240; Bodenhausen 1969, 113-119.
419. CJEU, 25 January 2007, case C-321/03, Dyson, para. 38.
420. Cf. Peukert 2012, 26-27; Sambuc 1997, 403. For a critical comment on the need to keep free in trademark law, see Phillips 2005, 389.

functional signs enhances competition by supporting the development of product alternatives.[421]

Besides this focus on free and fair competition, it can be argued that trademark law must satisfy speech interests of the general public. As copyright law, trademark law is not immune to the fundamental guarantee of freedom of expression.[422] The richness of associations and meanings attached to a trademark is often the result of a joint effort of trademark owners and consumers. It is the consuming public that frequently imbues trademarks with connotations distinct from and sometimes unrelated to the advertising messages conveyed by the trademark owner.[423] From this perspective, the public's entitlement to the use of trademarks in social and cultural discourse is a corollary of the public's contribution to the creation of trade symbols with complex meanings and connotations. Accordingly, consumers should be free to refer to trademarks as symbols of a particular lifestyle or attitude. Commentators should be free to use trademarks as a basis for criticizing an enterprise's policies. Artists should be able to include trademarks in their creative productions.

The impact of considerations of this nature on the architecture of the trademark system, however, must not be overestimated. In contrast to copyright law, intergenerational equity and public domain recognition do not lie at the core of trademark law. As pointed out above, the objective to ensure market transparency occupies centre stage. Not surprisingly, the aforementioned options to exclude mere concepts from trademark protection (4.2.2.1), keep certain types of signs free for use by other traders (4.2.2.2), and cancel trademark registrations because of a lack of genuine use (4.2.2.3) are aligned with this trade imperative. These features of the trademark system may contribute to intergenerational equity among traders and avoid encroachments upon the public domain. However, they are subject to thorough scrutiny in the light of trademark law's overarching objective to ensure market transparency.

421. CJEU, 18 June 2002, case C-299/99, Philips/Remington, para. 78.

422. With regard to the debate on how to reconcile trademark protection with free speech interests, see Bohaczewski 2020, 856; Żelechowski 2018, 115-135; Senftleben 2015, 354; Ramsey/Schovsbo 2013, 671; Simon Fhima 2013, 293; Sakulin 2010; Geiger 2010a, 163; Burrell/Gangjee 2010, 544; Nasser 2009, 188; Bently 2008, 1205; Dreyfuss 2008, 261; Geiger 2007, 317; Ramsey 2010a, 405; Weckström 2007, 671; Gulasekaram 2005, 887; Leval 2004, 187; Timbers/Huston 2003, 1278; Aoki 1997, 523; Dreyfuss 1990, 415-418.

423. Litman 1999, 1732-1733. Cf. Peukert 2019, 1181-1182; Gangjee 2013, 51-56; Tan 2013, 225; Gerhardt 2010, 101; Heymann 2009, 651; Wilf 1999, 4-5; Kozinski 1993, 960; Ramsey 2010b, 851; Dreyfuss 1990, 415 and 424. However, see also the critical comments on the limitation of trademark rights made by Richardson 2004, 193.

4.2.2.1 Exclusion of Concepts from Trademark Protection

From the perspective of intergenerational equity and public domain recognition, it is of particular interest that trademark law offers room for the exclusion of mere concepts from protection. As explained above, the idea/expression dichotomy plays a central role in copyright law (section 3.1). The freedom of ideas, concepts and styles is a well-established principle. As the analysis of the *Broeren/Duijsens* ruling of the Dutch Supreme Court showed,[424] it is acceptable from a copyright perspective to run the risk of consumer confusion in order to safeguard the idea/expression dichotomy. This gives rise to the question of whether judges hearing a trademark case are also prepared to sacrifice market transparency for the freedom of ideas, concepts and styles. Interestingly, the CJEU came close to this position in *Dyson*.[425] The case concerned Dyson's attempt to register, as a trademark, 'a transparent bin or collection chamber forming part of the external surface of a vacuum cleaner'. The description was accompanied by pictures showing different versions of Dyson vacuum cleaners with the relevant transparent features.[426] In the proceedings, the European Commission pointed out that acceptance of unspecific signs of this kind would lead to an extension of trademark protection to mere concepts. It argued that the registration sought by Dyson did not concern a sign eligible for protection because it related to:

> a concept, in this case, the concept of a transparent collecting bin for a vacuum cleaner, irrespective of shape. Since a concept is not capable of being perceived by one of the five senses and appeals only to the imagination, it is not a 'sign' within the meaning of Article 2 of the Directive.[427]

The Court shared the view that the Dyson application concerned too unspecific a subject matter to qualify as a 'sign' in the sense of trademark law. The holder of a trademark relating to such unspecific subject matter – a transparent external element of a vacuum cleaner:

> would obtain an unfair competitive advantage, contrary to the purpose pursued by Article 2 of the Directive, since it would be entitled to prevent its competitors from marketing vacuum cleaners having any kind of transparent collecting bin on their external surface, irrespective of its shape.[428]

---

424. Dutch Supreme Court, 29 March 2013, case LJN BY8661, Broeren/Duijsens, para. 3.5.
425. Cf. Derclaye/Leistner 2011, 49-50, who also mention the recognition of the need to keep colours and colour combinations available in this context. Cf. CJEU, 24 June 2004, case C-49/02, Heidelberger Bauchemie, paras 41-42; CJEU, 6 May 2003, case C-104/01, Libertel, paras 52-56.
426. CJEU, 25 January 2007, case C-321/03, Dyson, para. 10.
427. CJEU, *ibid.*, para. 29.
428. CJEU, *ibid.*, para. 39.

Viewed through the prism of intergenerational equity, this decision appears as a victory for the freedom of ideas, concepts and styles. Instead of focusing on market transparency, the Court referred to the need to ensure the availability of concepts for other traders wishing to enter into meaningful competition. Nonetheless, the *Dyson* decision must not be equated with general freedom of ideas, concepts and styles in trademark law. It does not impose a general ban on the registration of conceptual signs as trademarks. This became apparent in the subsequent CJEU decision in *Apple* where the Court dealt with a request for the registration of the minimalistic design of Apple flagship stores as a trademark. In the trademark application, Apple had included a picture showing the store design in stylized form and the explanation that the registration concerned 'the distinctive design and layout of a retail store'.[429]

Arguably, a minimalistic store design with a couple of wooden tables is a rather conceptual subject matter of trademark protection as well. However, Apple was wise enough to provide a concrete representation of the flagship store design showing the arrangement of tables and other design elements in the room. Against this background, the CJEU saw no reason to draw conclusions similar to its ruling in *Dyson*. Instead, the Court held that:

> a representation [...] which depicts the layout of a retail store by means of an integral collection of lines, curves and shapes, may constitute a trade mark provided that it is capable of distinguishing the products or services of one undertaking from those of other undertakings.[430]

The Court added that distinctiveness was conceivable if the store design departed significantly from the norm in the sector.[431] In any case, the conceptual nature of the representation provided in the trademark application did not form an insuperable obstacle. The CJEU was willing to qualify the store design as subject matter eligible for trademark protection 'without it being necessary [...] to attribute any relevance to the fact that the design does not contain any indication as to the size and proportions of the retail store that it depicts ... '.[432]

The difference between the decisions in *Dyson* and *Apple* lies in the fact that Apple had chosen a concrete representation of its store design concept. This was sufficient to eclipse the freedom of ideas, concepts and styles and allow trademark law's market transparency rationale to prevail. Although the registration remained confined to a concrete depiction of the Apple store design, the impact on the freedom of competitors to develop minimalistic retail store concepts with wooden elements may be considerable. Trademark law offers protection not only against identical copying but also against

429. CJEU, 10 July 2014, case C-421/13, Apple, para. 9.
430. CJEU, *ibid.*, para. 19.
431. CJEU, *ibid.*, para. 20.
432. CJEU, *ibid.*, para. 19.

similar design concepts that may cause consumer confusion.[433] A comparison between the exclusion of unspecific concepts in *Dyson* and the general denial of style protection in the copyright decision of the Dutch Supreme Court in *Broeren/Duijsens* (section 3.1) sheds light on the difference between the approach in trademark law and the well-established idea/expression dichotomy in copyright law. If Duijsens had followed in Apple's footsteps and registered one concrete representation of her overweight people at cocktail receptions as a trademark, she could have acquired trademark rights strong enough to prevent the use of similar design elements by Broeren. After all, it had been established in *Broeren/Duijsens* that Broeren's depictions of overweight people at fancy parties were confusingly similar to the design elements chosen by Duijsens.[434]

In the *Dyson* decision of the CJEU, a trace of intergenerational equity – the need to ensure the freedom of concepts for other traders – comes to light in trademark law. However, this trace of intergenerational equity is not comparable with the focus on follow-on innovation that has led to the recognition of the idea/expression dichotomy in copyright law. The moment a trademark applicant limits the request for trademark rights to a concrete representation of a distinctive design concept, the overarching trademark rationale to ensure market transparency prevails. A potentially perpetual monopoly on concrete representations of style elements is not excluded.[435] Style branding strategies in the fashion industry attest to the use of trademark law as a vehicle to set the protection of distinctive design features in stone.[436] Hence, the *Dyson* ruling only offers a glimpse of intergenerational equity. It must not distract from the fact that, in contrast to copyright law, trademark law does not seek to support processes of cyclic remix and reuse of intellectual resources.

4.2.2.2 Need to Keep Free

Apart from the exclusion of unspecific concepts in *Dyson*,[437] it is noteworthy that trademark law offers room for the exclusion of non-distinctive, descriptive, generic and functional signs from protection.[438] To explain these exclusions, it can be argued that there is a need to keep signs of this nature

433. Article 16(1) TRIPS; Article 9(2)(b) EUTMR; Article 10(2)(b) TMD.
434. Court of Appeals of Den Bos, 15 November 2011, case LJN BU4770, Duijsens/Broeren, para. 4.12.5.
435. Calboli 2018, 305.
436. See the analysis of this trend and its problematic results by Calboli 2018, 293-307.
437. CJEU, 25 January 2007, case C-321/03, Dyson, para. 39.
438. As pointed out above, this is reflected in the international regulation of *telle quelle* protection in Article 6quinquies(B) No. 2 and 3, and Article 6quinquies(A)(1) PC. The functionality doctrine in trademark law is a subcategory of a refusal based on public order or morality. Cf. Kur 2011, 20; Kur 2017, 1086. For an example of grounds of refusal in national law, see Article 7(1) EUTMR; Article 4(1) TMD.

free for other traders (intergenerational equity) and the public at large (public domain recognition).[439] However, a closer look at the regulation of these exclusions reveals that, in many cases, the reason for the denial of trademark protection is a lack of distinctive character. The public does not perceive non-distinctive, descriptive or generic signs as indications of commercial source. Signs of this nature simply do not function as trademarks. Once distinctive character is acquired through use in trade, this changes the equation. The grant of trademark rights may then be deemed necessary to safeguard market transparency.[440]

In the EU, for instance, non-distinctive, descriptive and generic signs become eligible for trademark protection once distinctive character is acquired in consequence of use in trade.[441] The exclusion from protection can thus be overcome through advertising that educates consumers to perceive the sign as a source identifier. If distinctiveness is acquired in this way, the overarching objective to ensure market transparency forces considerations of intergenerational equity and public domain recognition onto the sidelines. It may even be argued that, by offering the prospect of obtaining trademark protection as a result of use in trade, trademark law provides an incentive for merchants to invest in advertising that adds distinctive character to non-distinctive, descriptive and generic signs. In this line of reasoning, trademark law paves the way for the removal of these signs from the public domain.[442] With regard to descriptive marks, Lisa Ramsey expressed this concern as follows:

> circular reasoning underlies the argument that confusing use of a descriptive term as a mark is misleading and can therefore be restricted to protect consumers. By granting and enforcing exclusive rights in descriptive marks, the government helps to make those marks source-identifying, which leads to the possibility of consumer confusion in the first place.[443]

---

439. This need to keep free has been recognized, for instance, in CJEU, 4 May 1999, cases C-108/97 and C-109/97, Windsurfing Chiemsee, paras 35-37; CJEU, 6 May 2003, case C-104/01, Libertel, para. 55; CJEU, 18 September 2014, case C-205/13, Hauck/Stokke, para. 18; CJEU, 18 June 2002, case C-299/99, Philips/Remington, para. 78; CJEU, 14 September 2010, case C-48/09 P, Lego/Mega Brands, para. 43. Cf. Senftleben 2013a, 797-802; Peukert 2012, 26-27; Phillips 2005, 389; Sambuc 1997, 403.
440. As pointed out in Article 15(1) TRIPS, '[w]here signs are not inherently capable of distinguishing the relevant goods or services, Members may make registrability depend on distinctiveness acquired through use'. In other words: once distinctiveness is acquired through use in trade, it becomes legitimate (or even necessary) to grant trademark rights.
441. Article 7(3) EUTMR; Article 4(4) TMD.
442. Curtin 2018, 965 and 988-992.
443. Ramsey 2003, 1150. Cf. also Denicola 1982, 170; McKenna 2007, 1899; Assaf 2008, 82-83; Lemley/McKenna 2010, 440; Senftleben 2013a, 812-813; Anemaet 2020, 188-189 and 211-212.

The circular protection reflex following from the acquisition of distinctiveness through use clearly comes to the fore in the area of non-traditional types of marks. While trademark courts may unequivocally refer to considerations of intergenerational equity in this context – relating to other traders' freedom of competition – the rationale to ensure market transparency prevails once the trademark owner can demonstrate that distinctive character has been obtained after continuous use in trade. In *Libertel*, for instance, the CJEU articulated concerns about the curtailment of freedom of competition that are quite similar to those expressed in the *Dyson* decision which was discussed in the preceding section. *Libertel* concerned the question of whether an orange colour could be registered – in abstracto – as a trademark for telecommunications goods and services.[444] The Court pointed out that, as the number of colours actually available was limited, it had to be feared that a small number of trademark registrations for certain goods or services could exhaust the entire range of colours available. The Court deemed such an extensive monopoly 'incompatible with a system of undistorted competition, in particular because it could have the effect of creating an unjustified competitive advantage for a single trader'.[445] Against this background, the Court stated that there was:

> a public interest in not unduly restricting the availability of colours for the other operators who offer for sale goods or services of the same type as those in respect of which registration is sought.[446]

Despite these concerns, however, the Court finally paved the way for trademark rights to abstract colour marks. It acknowledged that abstract colour signs, normally, could not be deemed inherently capable of distinguishing the goods of a particular undertaking. Without any prior use, inherent distinctiveness was conceivable only in exceptional circumstances, for instance, where the number of goods or services was very restricted and the relevant market very specific.[447] In normal circumstances, inherent distinctiveness could not be assumed. However, the required distinctive character could be acquired through use in trade:

> However, even if a colour per se does not initially have any distinctive character within the meaning of Article 3(1)(b) of the Directive, it may acquire such character in relation to the goods or services claimed following the use made of it, pursuant to Article 3(3) of the Directive. That distinctive character may be acquired, inter alia, after the normal process of familiarising the relevant public has taken place.[448]

---

444. CJEU, 6 May 2003, case C-104/01, Libertel, para. 14.
445. CJEU, *ibid.*, para. 54.
446. CJEU, *ibid.*, para. 55.
447. CJEU, *ibid.*, para. 66.
448. CJEU, *ibid.*, para. 67.

This ruling attests to the elasticity of trademark law with regard to the identification of the subject matter of protection. With the focus on consumer perception, a flexible, changeable factor enters the picture.[449] While, according to the Court, colour per se is not inherently distinctive, use in trade can change this verdict and lead to the acquisition of trademark rights. On its merits, the decision confirms that substantial investment in the education of the public will be rewarded with trademark rights to the colour concerned. The moment a trader succeeds in establishing the necessary link between the abstract colour sign and her enterprise in the minds of consumers, she will acquire exclusive trademark rights to the colour per se. Once this point is reached, the need to ensure market transparency, thus, outstrips concerns about colour depletion and insufficient room for other traders – concerns that may be qualified as traces of intergenerational equity in trademark law. Offering the prospect of trademark rights, the *Libertel* decision may even encourage marketing campaigns based on a specific colour.[450] Enterprises may perceive the decision as an incentive to reserve 'their' individual colour in a particular market segment.

With regard to traces of intergenerational equity in trademark law, the analysis, therefore, yields mixed results. On the one hand, the exclusion of non-distinctive, descriptive and generic signs from trademark protection follows from the recognition of the need to keep signs of this nature free for other traders. In the trade-centred environment in which trademark law operates, this may be seen as a trace of intergenerational equity among traders. On the other hand, this trace of intergenerational equity is not a prevailing principle. Once distinctive character is acquired in consequence of use in trade, the overarching trademark rationale to ensure market transparency reigns supreme. This is only different when it comes to functional product characteristics. As the more detailed analysis in sections 7.1.1 and 7.2.1 will show, functional product features are categorically excluded from trademark protection to safeguard the freedom of other traders to enter into meaningful competition – even if a functional product element has acquired distinctiveness as a result of use in trade.[451] On balance, traces of intergenerational equity can thus be found in the area of grounds for refusing

449. Cf. McKenna 2007, 1899: 'Loosed from its natural rights moorings and bounded only by consumer expectations, modern trademark law essentially instantiates a one-way ratchet to broader trademark rights. As courts in the early twentieth century broadened trademark owner's rights, consumers grew to expect that trademark owners had increasingly broad control over their marks. Those changed consumer expectations then became the basis for even broader trademark rights, which then in turn created even greater expectations. And on it has spiraled, with the help of marketers, who specialize in influencing consumer expectations.'

450. Ramsey 2003, 1150. Cf. Denicola 1982, 170; McKenna 2007, 1899; Lemley/McKenna 2010, 440; Senftleben 2013a, 812-813; Anemaet 2020, 188-189 and 211-212.

451. As to the categorical, unconditional character of this exclusion from trademark protection, see CJEU, 18 June 2002, case C-299/99, Philips/Remington, para. 57 and 75; CJEU, 16 September 2015, case C-215/14, Nestlé/Cadbury ('Kit Kat'), paras 38-39;

trademark protection. As in the *Dyson* scenario discussed in the preceding section, however, concerns about intergenerational equity are regularly pushed aside when this seems necessary to ensure market transparency.

4.2.2.3 Requirement of Genuine Use

The maintenance of trademark rights depends on use of the protected sign in the marketplace. International law reflects this standard feature of trademark law. The TRIPS Agreement clarifies that the registration of a trademark that is no longer used may be cancelled after an uninterrupted period of at least three years of inexcusable non-use.[452] As a result, the sign concerned becomes available anew for other market participants – at least to the extent that national law allows other market participants to adopt it after cancellation. The cancellation action will normally be brought by a competitor who wishes to use an identical or similar sign.[453] It may thus be said that the requirement of genuine use contributes to intergenerational equity in the domain of trade.

From the perspective of public domain recognition, however, the analysis is less favourable. As the cancellation action will normally be brought by a competitor wishing to use the sign herself, the cancellation of a trademark registration based on non-use does not ensure that the sign returns to the public domain and becomes freely available. In practice, the cancellation action is likely to be only a vehicle to clarify whether the owner of a senior trademark right is still entitled to prevent a junior user from use even though no use has been made of the protected sign for a considerable period of time. In other words: the requirement of genuine use is a means of clarifying the ownership situation and enhancing market transparency. The enrichment of the public domain is not its primary purpose.

4.2.3 *Remaining Incompatibility*

On balance, a *divergence of principles* comes to the fore when comparing the cultural imperative inherent in copyright law and the trade imperative underlying trademark law. To ensure market transparency, trademark law seeks to achieve a stable distribution of available intellectual resources among traders. This trade imperative focussing on stability is incompatible with the notion of incessant cycles of creation and constant changes in the allocation of rights in reused and rearranged material that underlies the

---

CJEU, 11 May 2017, case C-421/15 P, Yoshida Metal Industry/EUIPO, para. 35. Cf. also U.S. Supreme Court, 20 March 2001, TrafFix Devices/Marketing Displays, 532 U.S. 23, 33 (2001).

452. Article 19 TRIPS.

453. For instance, see the situation underlying CJEU, 11 March 2003, case C-40/01, Ajax/Ansul.

cultural imperative in copyright law. The static market transparency model that shapes the trademark system is an antipode of the copyright model that seeks to support a constant flow of intellectual resources.[454]

Trademark protection, therefore, is likely to interfere with intergenerational equity and public domain recognition in copyright law. In the case of coexisting copyright and trademark rights, attempts may be made to constantly renew trademark protection to escape the obligation of freeing cultural expression to the public domain after the expiry of copyright protection.[455] The maintenance of trademark rights may encroach upon both the objective of cultivating the public domain (because material is withheld from it), and the guarantee of intergenerational equity (because second authors are not entirely free to use material as they wish). The public domain of cultural expression may also be impoverished when parts of the cultural heritage that already belong to the public domain are reappropriated through use or registration as trademarks.[456] In this case, important cultural material is removed from the public domain to the extent to which trademark law offers protection – material that, otherwise, would entirely be free and available for cultural follow-on innovation.[457] Considering this functional incompatibility between the cyclic cultural imperative of intergenerational equity and public domain recognition on the one hand and the static trade imperative of market transparency on the other hand, it is necessary to analyse the potential corrosive effect of trademark rights in cultural expressions in more detail.

4.3 CONCLUSION

A comparison of the configuration of copyright and patent law brings to light several functional parallels. As copyright law, patent law can be understood to support a process of cyclic innovation. While copyright law seeks to safeguard cyclic cultural innovation, patent law seeks to stimulate cyclic technical innovation. It confers exclusive rights to provide an incentive for the development of new technical solutions on the basis of pre-existing technical knowledge. Accordingly, patent protection expires after a limited period of time. In this way, the protection system makes protected know-how freely available for future generations of inventors. As in copyright law, the guarantee of intergenerational equity and the recognition of a need to preserve the public domain are of crucial importance in patent law. Hence, a convergence of principles comes to the fore: both intellectual property

454. Cf. the problem analysis by Wilf 1999, 1-5.
455. Cf. CJEU, 18 September 2014, case C-205/13, Hauck/Stokke, paras 19-20; U.S. Supreme Court, 2 June 2003, Dastar/Twentieth Century Fox, 539 U.S. 23, 33-34 (2003).
456. Cf. EFTA Court, 6 April 2017, case E-5/16, Municipality of Oslo ('Vigeland'), para. 65.
457. Senftleben 2017b, 688.

systems aim to foster an incessant process of follow-on innovation. Protection under these systems is cyclic in the sense that it is awarded whenever a new creation evolves in the constant process of innovation in the respective field, and it is taken away after a limited period of time to prevent an impediment of the cyclic innovation process that lies at the core of both protection systems.

A discussion of trademark law, however, reveals that core ingredients of cyclic intellectual property protection systems – the guarantee of intergenerational equity and the recognition of the public domain – do not have much weight. By contrast, the objective to ensure market transparency occupies centre stage. To achieve market transparency, trademark law must offer static protection that guarantees a stable distribution of available intellectual resources. Instead of seeking to support the productive reuse of distinctive signs, trademark law aims at stability once a certain sign is linked with a particular trader. Protection is not a reward for the creation of something new on the basis of pre-existing source and inspiration material. By contrast, it is a means of solidifying the ownership situation with regard to a particular intellectual resource that plays a central role in the distinction of goods and services in the marketplace. Accordingly, trademark protection must continue as long as this is necessary to secure market transparency. If the trademark owner does not cease making genuine use of the protected sign in the marketplace, she can renew trademark protection indefinitely. Comparing this trade imperative with the cultural imperative inherent in copyright law, the conclusion is inescapable that there is a divergence of principles. Certain traces of intergenerational equity and public domain recognition may be found in trademark law. The possibility to exclude signs from protection, the principle of speciality and the requirement of genuine use are relevant in this regard. However, a closer inspection of these elements of the trademark protection system shows that they are subordinated to the overarching objective to ensure market transparency. In contrast to copyright law, intergenerational equity and public domain recognition are not essential, constituent parts of trademark law.

When protection overlaps arise, the incompatibility between the cultural imperative in copyright law and the trademark imperative of market transparency will inevitably pose major difficulties, including the risk of an encroachment upon the cultural innovation cycle which copyright law seeks to support. While copyright protection is limited in time, trademark protection is not. While copyright law stimulates the creative remix of pre-existing intellectual resources, trademark law does not. With regard to this incompatibility, the foregoing analysis has also shown that it would be wrong to assume that the technical innovation cycle is less vulnerable than its cultural counterpart. By contrast, even more extensive measures are required to shield the cultural innovation cycle from potential corrosive effects of coexisting trademark protection. In the domain of technology, it is possible to rely on objective criteria to identify non-substitutable technical solutions which must be kept free to safeguard the technical innovation cycle. At least theoretically, efforts to keep technical know-how available in the case of protection overlaps can thus be confined to these indispensable solutions. In the domain of culture, by contrast, it is impossible to identify non-substitutable literary and artistic works on the basis of objective criteria. Cultural creativity depends on how an artist embarking on the creation of a new work assesses the relevance of pre-existing literary and artistic resources for this envisaged creative work. The assessment criteria are thus subjective. They are likely to differ from artist to artist. Accordingly, it is not foreseeable which literary and artistic works will be indispensable for future generations of authors to arrive at new cultural productions and keep the cultural innovation cycle intact. Therefore, efforts to prevent potential encroachments of coexisting trademark protection upon the cultural innovation cycle should cover a wide range of cultural signs that are relevant to the constant evolution of new literary and artistic works in the cultural domain. A distinction between substitutable and non-substitutable cultural material is not possible.

Chapter 5
Cultural Signs

Before embarking on a more detailed analysis of legal challenges evolving from cumulative copyright and trademark protection, it is important to clarify the notion of 'cultural sign' that underlies the following examination. The discussion in the preceding chapter led to the insight that a wide range of cultural signs should be kept available for cultural follow-on innovation (section 4.1.4). But which signs precisely? Which signs stemming from the cultural domain need to be shielded from potentially corrosive trademark protection in order to avoid an impediment of cyclic cultural innovation processes? Must all signs that are eligible for copyright protection, as a matter of principle, be qualified as 'cultural signs'? Or is it possible to trace more specific conceptual contours? As several aesthetic and sociological theories support initiatives to safeguard the cultural imperative in copyright law (section 3.3), it is consistent to rely on these theories as signposts for the identification of signs that should be included in initiatives to prevent trademark protection from interfering with cultural follow-on innovation (following section 5.1). For practical purposes, however, assessment factors are required that enable trademark examiners and judges to identify relevant cultural signs. Can trademark offices and courts be expected to assess the artistic merit of literary and artistic works for which trademark protection is sought? Will examiners and judges have to distinguish between important works of art that are relevant to cultural follow-on innovation and less important creations? If so, which criteria should inform the analysis? Is there any definition of cultural significance that can be applied consistently in practice (section 5.2)?

Turning to the development of appropriate guidelines for the identification of cultural signs, it is important to note at the outset that the following conceptual considerations merely aim at a clarification of the notion of 'cultural sign' to lay groundwork for the detailed analysis of potential interferences of trademark protection with intergenerational equity (Chapter 7) and public domain recognition (Chapter 8). Hence, the purpose of the enquiry is a proper understanding of the type of signs which, if encumbered by trademark rights, raise concerns about an impediment of cultural follow-on innovation. The following enquiry does not concern a final decision on whether measures to safeguard cyclic cultural innovation are necessary with regard to a given cultural sign. It must not be misunderstood as a general statement that, by definition, all signs falling within the scope of the concept of 'cultural sign' are to be kept free from trademark protection. By contrast, the spectrum of regulatory responses to safeguard the cultural innovation cycle will be discussed in Chapter 9, including a discussion of practical implementation options in section 9.1.2.5.

5.1 OPERATIONALIZATION OF AESTHETIC AND SOCIOLOGICAL THEORIES

At first sight, the aesthetic and sociological theories discussed in section 3.3 seem to require the identification of cultural signs on the basis of a value judgment.[458] In line with Schiller's, Adorno's and Osborne's aesthetic theories, works of art can be regarded as catalysts for processes leading to an improvement of societal conditions. Relying on Bourdieu's sociological analysis, it can be said that copyright law should foster autonomous artistic expression as a propelling force for the constant renewal of the cultural landscape. Against this background, one may assume that the cultural imperative in copyright law only requires measures against trademark rights in cultural signs if a literary and artistic work is likely to offer important impulses for cultural follow-on innovation, such as a point of departure for a new avant-garde movement. In this vein, the denial of trademark rights or the limitation of the scope of trademark protection could only be justified in the case of cultural signs contributing to cultural follow-on innovation in the strict sense of paving the way for a new artistic movement and new critical reflections of societal conditions.

In his analysis of avant-garde movements of the last century, Peter Bürger, for instance, refers to the central goal of several avant-garde

458. For a discussion of the traditional resistance of copyright judges to embark on an assessment of aesthetic merit, see Beebe 2017, 332-334.

movements to organize a new life practice on the basis of art.[459] Avantgardists sought to overcome the isolation of art as a societal institution for the preservation of values that had no place in the modern, rationalized world, such as humanity, happiness, truthfulness and solidarity. Criticizing the detachment of art from everyday life, they strove for the integration of art in the societal mainstream to transform the inhuman, rationalized world by providing models for a new, better practice of life.[460] According to Bürger, these avant-garde movements failed: art has not become a transforming factor changing daily life for the better. Instead, a false integration of art occurred. Everyday products have become more aesthetical, but only as a result of industry efforts to make consumer goods and mainstream entertainment more appealing. This aestheticization of daily life, however, enhances the pressure of consumerism and materialism. It intensifies the subjection of the individual to the dictates of the market. Life does not become more human, truthful, solidary and happier. By contrast, the pressure of the rationalized world is further increased. Instead of helping the individual to emancipate herself from the pressure of consumerism and materialism, aesthetical consumer goods are a driving force and stabilizing factor behind the rationalization of daily life. They encourage mainstream consumption patterns. At the same time, they mask the exertion of pressure in the form of enhanced consumerism and materialism by lending mainstream consumption patterns the air of extravagance.[461]

Bürger's analysis can easily be placed in the context of Schiller's and Adorno's aesthetic theories about works of art showing visions of a better, happier life that can rouse opposition against the existing reality and contribute to necessary societal changes.[462] Considering the ambition of historical avant-garde movements to change life for the better on the one hand and the risk of aesthetical consumer goods intensifying and obscuring the inhumanity of the status quo on the other hand, it becomes possible to draw a distinction between 'true' art capable of fulfilling the societal functions envisaged in aesthetic theories, namely to provide a stimulus for societal change, and 'false art' making consumer goods and mainstream entertainment more appealing – art which stabilizes the modern, rationalized world and does not provide impulses for societal change. Based on this distinction, it could be assumed that for socially desirable follow-on innovation in the cultural sector, it is sufficient to take measures to shield literary and artistic works falling in the 'true art' category from the corrosive effect of trademark protection. Works falling in the category of 'false art', by contrast, could be registered and protected as trademarks.

459. Bürger 1974, 28-29 and 67.
460. Bürger 1974, 67-68.
461. Bürger 1974, 72-73.
462. Section 3.3.2. Bürger 1974, 60-63 and 81-85, himself refers to Schiller's and Adorno's aesthetic theories in the context of his analysis.

Obviously, such a distinction would be impracticable. Trademark offices and courts can hardly be expected to become referees of art and specialists in art theory. Moreover, it is questionable whether trademark protection of literary and artistic works used for consumer goods and mainstream entertainment can really be deemed unproblematic from the perspective of socially desirable follow-on innovation. Should trademark rights to Mickey Mouse readily be granted for the sole reason that the drawing itself is a figurehead of mainstream entertainment? Pierre Bourdieu's sociological analysis of literary and artistic productivity suggests otherwise. As explained in section 3.3.1.3, Bourdieu points out that the room for possible new positions in the creation of art depends on the positions that have already been taken by previous artists.[463] For a new generation of autonomous artists to challenge the leading avant-garde, it must detect the structural gaps within the texture of already known aesthetic positions. It must formulate an alternative artistic position in the light of the weaknesses and contradictions of the present state of the art.[464] The positions that have already been taken in the literary and artistic field constitute potential lines of development and starting points for new works.

Against this background, it has already been pointed out in section 4.1.4 that broad measures are necessary to safeguard cultural follow-on innovation because it is not foreseeable which aesthetic positions reflected in a literary or artistic work will be non-substitutable from the perspective of later generations of artists seeking to formulate a new artistic position. As it is not possible to reach general agreement on the non-substitutability of cultural expressions because of the subjectivity of the assessment made by each individual artist, efforts to prevent protection overlaps from interfering with cultural follow-on innovation, a priori, cannot be confined to a small circle of literary and artistic works. In principle, each aesthetic position may become indispensable for the creation of a new work because it is not foreseeable to which pre-existing aesthetic position a later generation of artists will attach importance on the basis of its subjective assessment of pre-existing works.[465] Even though it is a mainstream entertainment creation, Mickey Mouse may be an important point of departure for the creation of 'true' works of art.[466] In the ongoing struggle between avant-garde and profit-oriented authors described by Bourdieu,[467] the drawing may play a central role as a symbol of mainstream culture and prime target of criticism seeking to encourage a critical reflection on mainstream consumption patterns and societal conditions.

463. Bourdieu 1992/1999, 370.
464. Bourdieu 1992/1999, 372.
465. Cf. Cohen 2006, 155-156.
466. See Cohen 2006, 159-160, who underlines the importance of contemporary mass commercial culture as a source and basis of new creations. Cf. Frosio 2014, 380-385.
467. Section 3.3.1.1.

In other words, Bourdieu's analysis makes it plausible that works belonging to the realm of consumer goods and mainstream entertainment aesthetics, while not constituting 'true' art in the sense of avant-garde theories themselves, may nonetheless constitute important objects and reference points for the creation of such genuine art.[468] From this perspective, it is wrong to impede access to this potential source of socially desirable creativity by awarding trademark protection. By contrast, Bourdieu's analysis confirms a conclusion that has already been drawn above in the context of non-substitutability of literary and artistic creations: a wide range of literary and artistic works must be included in initiatives to shield cultural follow-on innovation from the potential negative impact of protection overlaps.[469] Besides avant-garde artworks, mainstream productions enter the picture because they may constitute important reference points for artists seeking to mirror current societal conditions. Hence, both Mickey Mouse and the Mona Lisa constitute artistic expressions that fall within the concept of 'cultural sign'. Both types of signs – artworks and mainstream cultural symbols – should be included in initiatives to prevent trademark protection from interfering with cultural follow-on innovation.

A further guideline for the identification of cultural signs can be derived from the discussion of non-substitutability in section 4.1.4. As it is not foreseeable which aesthetic positions reflected in a literary or artistic work will be non-substitutable from the perspective of later generations of artists seeking to formulate a new artistic position, the concept of 'cultural sign' must be broad enough to cover not only current needs of artists but also potential future needs for source material. To factor this future need into the equation, it is advisable to follow an approach which the CJEU adopted in *Windsurfing Chiemsee* with regard to geographical names. The Court explained that it was in the public interest that geographical names remained available – not least because they may indicate quality and product characteristics and influence consumer tastes by forging a link between products and 'a place that may give rise to a favourable response'.[470] On this basis, the Court held that, for justifying the exclusion of geographical names from trademark protection, it was not necessary to give evidence of a real, current need to leave the indication free. By contrast, it was sufficient that the name may be used as an indication of geographical origin with regard to a certain category of goods or services in the future.[471] Accordingly, the

468. The decision of the French Supreme Court in *Klasen/Malka* illustrates this point. The case concerned the inclusion of three photographs taken from an Italian fashion magazine in paintings. The appropriation artist, Peter Klasen, used the photographs as symbols of consumerism to provoke reflection on excessive consumption patterns. See the discussion of the facts underlying the case in French Supreme Court, 15 May 2015, case 13-27391, ECLI:FR:CCASS:2015:C100519, Klasen/Malka. Cf. Geiger 2018a, 6-7.
469. Section 4.1.4. Cf. Cohen 2006, 154.
470. CJEU, 4 May 1999, cases C-108/97 and C-109/97, Windsurfing Chiemsee, para. 26.
471. CJEU, *ibid.*, paras 35-37.

resulting test comprises current as well as potential future needs. It asks whether a geographical name:

> designates a place which is currently associated in the mind of the relevant class of persons with the category of goods concerned, or whether it is reasonable to assume that such an association may be established in the future.[472]

Applying this line of reasoning to cultural signs by analogy, it can be posited that the notion of 'cultural sign' should cover not only signs that are currently used as source material for remix and reuse in the cultural domain but also signs in respect of which it is reasonable to assume that they may serve as such source material in the future. Obviously, a bias in favour of current source materials and against future sources is highly problematic from the perspective of cultural follow-on innovation. As in the case of descriptive signs, such as the geographical name discussed in *Windsurfing Chiemsee*, the assessment of a need to keep free or a need to set limits to trademark protection should not be confined to use necessities that have already materialized. Otherwise, measures seeking to minimize the corrosive effect of trademark protection on cultural remix will focus on current building blocks of derivative works and lose sight of potential future sources of inspiration. These future sources, however, are particularly relevant. They may pave the way for new, currently underexplored artistic positions.

Hence, the theoretical groundwork laid in previous chapters yields two important insights. First, the concept of 'cultural sign' must cover both signs derived from works of art and signs derived from mainstream productions. Second, the status of 'cultural sign' must not depend on whether a given sign currently serves as a reference point for remix and reuse in the cultural domain. By contrast, a prospective analysis is necessary that asks whether a sign can reasonably be expected to serve as source material for the creation of new works in the future.

5.2 IDENTIFICATION OF CULTURAL SIGNS

In practice, the identification of cultural signs based on these guidelines need not always pose particular difficulties. In many cases, trademark examiners and judges will be able to recognize cultural signs because they are widely known. An enterprise seeking to register a cultural sign as a trademark is likely to select a work that has considerable resonance as a result of its evolution in the cultural domain. Choosing a widely recognized cultural icon, the enterprise can benefit from the spectrum of positive associations which the sign triggers in the minds of consumers.[473] Not surprisingly, cases raising

472. CJEU, *ibid.*, para. 31.
473. Senftleben 2017b, 697.

trademark disputes often concern famous artworks, such as signs belonging to mankind's universal cultural heritage (Mona Lisa scenario, following section 5.2.1). Going beyond widely known pieces of art in mankind's cultural treasury, it must not be overlooked that the branding of culture may also affect traditional cultural expressions of indigenous peoples. In this regard, a specific scenario arises in the light of the desires and interests of indigenous communities that may reject not only the use of traditional cultural expressions in product marketing but also the use in the framework of remix activities in the literary and artistic domain (section 5.2.2).

As already pointed out in Chapter 1, cumulative copyright and trademark protection, moreover, plays an important role in the field of contemporary mainstream culture. To address this mass phenomenon in line with the guidelines developed in the preceding section, symbols of contemporary mainstream culture must be qualified as cultural signs and included in the subsequent analysis as well (Mickey Mouse scenario, section 5.2.3). At the same time, it is important to recognize an additional category of cultural signs. Even though stemming from the domain of commerce and trade, trademarks and other industrial objects may acquire the status of iconic lifestyle symbols. This symbolic value can be of particular importance to the artistic discourse. Like symbols of cultural mainstream productions, such as Mickey Mouse, iconic trade symbols may constitute important reference points for artists seeking to mirror current societal conditions. For this reason, it makes sense to include not only symbols of contemporary mainstream culture but also iconic trade symbols in measures to safeguard the cultural innovation cycle. Their cultural dimension may justify the recalibration of the scope of trademark protection in a way that allows sufficient room for unauthorized use in the literary and artistic domain (Coca Cola scenario, section 5.2.5). Finally, the question of recognition as a cultural sign arises with regard to work titles. While not necessarily constituting literary and artistic works themselves, work titles are so closely linked to literary and artistic productions that they share the same status. As the literary and artistic works they signify, they can be qualified as cultural signs for the purposes of preventing impediments of cultural follow-on innovation (Winnetou scenario, section 5.2.4).

5.2.1 *Mona Lisa and Other Works of Art*

The Mona Lisa scenario concerns a situation where an attempt is made to obtain a trademark registration of a work of art that is recognized as an important literary or artistic expression in the cultural domain. While a trademark office or court can hardly be expected to know all works of art in this category and assess the potential of individual pieces to serve as a source of inspiration for new literary and artistic creations, case law indicates that specialist knowledge in the field of art will not always be necessary. In *Shield*

Mark/Kist, for example, the CJEU had to decide on the right mode of representing the first nine notes of Ludwig van Beethoven's piano piece 'Für Elise' graphically on the trademark register.[474] The *Johann Sebastian Bach* case of the Higher Court of Appeals of Dresden was about the registration of the name and portrait of the composer as a trademark for various goods and services, including glassware, porcelain and crockery.[475] In the *Anne Frank* cases between the Swiss Anne Frank Foundation and the Benelux Office for Intellectual Property, the Court of Appeals of Brussels had to decide on the registration of the signs 'Het dagboek van Anne Frank' ('The Diary of Anne Frank') and 'Het achterhuis' ('The Secret Annex') in respect of books, films and guided tours.[476] In *Nachtwacht* (Night Watch), the Court of Appeals of The Hague was called upon to determine whether the masterpiece of Rembrandt van Rijn could be registered as a trademark for the marketing of the chemical element strontium.[477] In *Vigeland*, the EFTA Court had to assess an attempt to register several artworks of the eminent Norwegian sculptor Gustav Vigeland. Among other works, the application concerned Vigeland's 'Monolith' (*Monolitten*) and 'Angry Boy' (*Sinnataggen*) – popular works that feature prominently in the Vigeland Installation in the centre of Oslo's Frogner Park.[478] Finally, the *Mona Lisa* decision of the German Federal Patent Court concerned the registration of the famous Leonardo da Vinci painting as a trademark.[479] Arguably, the importance of these signs for cultural remix and reuse is self-evident. A trademark office or court will have little difficulty to identify these signs as important cultural creations that may provide impulses for new, derivative literary and artistic works. In general, it should not be an insurmountable hurdle for trademark examiners and judges to detect, on their own initiative, signs belonging to mankind's universal cultural heritage and signs that form central elements of the cultural landscape of their own country. Gustav Vigeland's sculptures, for instance, will hardly escape scrutiny by trademark tribunals in Norway. The titles of Anne Frank's writings are unlikely to remain unnoticed at the Benelux Office for Intellectual Property.

However, the range of artworks that currently serve as reference points for cultural remix, or have the potential of fulfilling this function in the future, is broader than these easy cases of widely known works of literature

474. CJEU, 27 November 2003, case C-283/01, Shield Mark/Kist, para. 64.
475. Higher Court of Appeals of Dresden, 4 April 2000, case 14 U 3611/99, 'Johann Sebastian Bach', *NJW* 2001, 615 (616).
476. Court of Appeals of Brussels, 3 October 2013, cases 2013/7132 and 2013/7133, Anne Frank Foundation/Benelux Office for Intellectual Property, para. 1.
477. Court of Appeals of The Hague, 29 August 2017, case 200.205.771/01, ECLI:NL:GHDHA:2017:2446, Chiever/Benelux-Organisatie voor de Intellectuele Eigendom ('Nachtwacht'), para. 12.
478. EFTA Court, 6 April 2017, case E-5/16, Municipality of Oslo ('Vigeland'), paras 20-26.
479. German Federal Patent Court, 25 November 1997, case 24 W (pat) 188/96, Mona Lisa, *GRUR* 1998, 1021 (1023).

and art. In *Medusa*, for instance, the German Federal Court of Justice had to deal with the 'Medusa Rondanini' – a Roman marble copy of the head of Medusa which king Ludwig of Bavaria purchased from the heirs of marquis Rondanini. Nowadays, the 'Medusa Rondanini' is exhibited in the Glyptothek in Munich.[480] Undoubtedly, museums and archives offer a wide variety of examples of relatively unknown artworks that may sooner or later become important sources of inspiration. Besides cultural signs from the past, contemporary works of art broaden the range of cultural signs that are less prominent than classical masterpieces and cornerstones of a country's treasury of cultural expressions. Following the guidelines developed in section 5.1, these less known works of art should enter the picture as well. Hence, the question arises whether general assessment criteria are available that allow the identification of signs with cultural significance even if they are not widely known.

Arguably, trademark offices and courts can apply an amalgam of different factors to appreciate a sign's cultural significance. The CJEU confirmed this approach in *Gömböc*. With regard to technical subject matter, the Court underlined that the assessment had to be based on 'objective and reliable information'.[481] The Court listed factors ranging from product descriptions and patent data to expert opinions and 'scientific publications, catalogues and websites'.[482] Without specifying factors, the CJEU confirmed that an assessment of aesthetic characteristics also required 'objective and reliable evidence'.[483] In the light of this CJEU jurisprudence, it becomes possible to identify assessment factors that could satisfy the requirement of objectivity and reliability when the cultural significance of a sign is at issue. First, the fact that a sign is exhibited as an artwork in a museum or gallery indicates quite clearly that it constitutes a cultural sign.[484] In the case of a musical work, the same conclusion may be derived from the fact that the work is recorded and performed in concerts. If a trademark examiner or judge has evidence of this museum or concert status, this factor weighs heavily in favour of a finding of cultural significance. Large music libraries are available online. Institutions in the visual arts sector – museums, galleries, auction houses – are increasingly digitizing their collections.[485] Hence, relevant information on cultural signs in this segment may be available on the Internet. It is also conceivable that the museum or concert status comes to the fore in opposition or infringement proceedings. In

480. German Federal Court of Justice, 24 November 2011, case I ZR 175/09, 'Medusa', para. 5.
481. CJEU, 23 April 2020, case C-237/19, Gömböc, para. 34.
482. CJEU, *ibid.*, para. 34.
483. CJEU, *ibid.*, para. 41.
484. As to the impact of this factor on the copyright assessment, see Kummer 1968, 75 and 103; Cherpillod 1985, 125; Kehrli 1989, 128-130; Dreier/Schulze 2018, 84, 100-101 and 130.
485. For example, see https://www.rijksmuseum.nl/en/rijksstudio.

Medusa, for instance, the defendant drew the Court's attention to the Medusa heads in the Glyptothek to establish that his marble mosaics had been modelled on this museum item instead of constituting a copy of the Versace logo which also depicts a Medusa head.[486]

Second, online search tools may offer information on past and current remix and reuse practices. An image search concerning the Mona Lisa, for instance, yields not only digital reproductions of the artwork itself but also examples of parodies and other mash-ups: evidence of the use of the painting as a basis for new creations. In her analysis of the Cinderella tale, Rebecca Curtin had little difficulty to demonstrate that the famous character resurfaced in various cultural productions over the centuries.[487] Similar indications of past and current use in the context of cultural remix activities may be available with regard to less known literary and artistic works for which trademark protection is sought.[488] Again, these remix and reuse activities may also be brought to the attention of trademark examiners and judges in the framework of opposition or infringement proceedings.

Third, trademark offices can develop art identification tools themselves. The trademark law of New Zealand, for instance, contains a specific provision prohibiting the registration of marks 'likely to offend a significant section of the community, including Māori'.[489] One of the difficulties posed by this provision is the identification of signs in trademark applications that contain Māori words and imagery. Accordingly, the Intellectual Property Office of New Zealand established practice guidelines to provide signposts for the detection of aspects of Māori culture. As Susy Frankel explains, these guidelines indicate details of certain features that identify Māori words and imagery. They also provide a summary of Māori customary concepts and references to relevant resources.[490] Similar efforts could be made with regard to classical and contemporary styles of art. Pointing out typical style features, offering examples of representative artworks, summarizing underlying concepts and providing references to resources with further examples and explanations, a trademark office can create useful reference material for the identification of signs with cultural significance.

Fourth, it seems plausible that trademark examiners and judges have a basic understanding of the domain of literature and art. Even if they are not experts, the artistic nature of a sign in a trademark application need not escape their attention. For a trademark examiner or judge to be capable of identifying the 'Medusa Rondanini' as a cultural sign, he need not be an expert in late Hellenistic or Augustan Roman art. The question is, however,

486. German Federal Court of Justice, *ibid.*, para. 5.

487. Curtin 2018, 974-981.

488. For example, see Curtin 2018, 1010-1011, with regard to productions inspired by the story of Wyatt Earp.

489. Section 17(1)(c) of the 2002 Trade Marks Act of New Zealand. Cf. Handler 2012, 242; Frankel 2008, 455-456; Frankel 2005, 83-86 and 90-91; Morgan 2004, 62-75.

490. Frankel 2005, 93.

how this basic understanding of the domain of literature and art can be translated into consistent office or court practice. In this respect, the illustrative list of well-established categories of literary and artistic works in Article 2(1) BC can serve as a first reference point. If a sign for which trademark protection is sought falls under one of the categories listed in Article 2(1) BC, this is a preliminary indication of its cultural character. Conversely, however, the fact that a creation cannot readily be assigned to one of the prototypes in Article 2(1) BC should not be seen as a clear indication that the sign falls outside the realm of literature and art. Otherwise, the examination may disregard avant-garde works that transcend the boundaries of traditional work categories.[491] After a preliminary assessment based on the work categories in Article 2(1) BC, copyright's originality test may have an important role to play in the final determination of a sign's cultural character. Trademark offices and courts are already used to the application of the requirement of distinctiveness in trademark cases.[492] The assessment of distinctiveness requires the evaluation of flexible and complex factors, such as the relation between the sign and the goods and services for which protection is sought, the need to keep free because of public policy reasons and the influence of use in the course of trade on the sign's degree of distinctiveness.[493] Arguably, the assessment of originality in the light of copyright criteria does not pose fundamentally different challenges. Both tests are flexible and elastic.[494] As in the case of distinctiveness, trademark examiners and judges could rely on court decisions illustrating the application of the test and its central criteria, in particular the requirement of free, creative choices.[495] The application of the originality test is thus unlikely to be an unfeasible task. Using the threshold criterion of originality as a common denominator, it seems possible to channel the basic understanding of literature and art which trademark examiners and judges have at their disposal and prevent the evolution of highly individualistic artistic relevance tests that are detached from the standard applied in copyright law itself.

Nonetheless, doubts about the appropriateness of this approach may arise from the fact that, as already indicated in section 2.2, the originality test in copyright law is not aligned with the conceptual contours of the domain

---

491. Cf. Dreier/Schulze 2018, 130-131.
492. The test of distinctiveness is a shared standard worldwide. At the international level, the criterion is clearly reflected in Article 15(1) TRIPS.
493. Kur/Senftleben 2017, para. 4.50-4.74.
494. For a comparative analysis highlighting the elasticity of eligibility criteria in trademark as well as copyright law, see Spoor 1990, 15-16 and 20-23. As to convergence of the criteria applied in copyright and trademark law, see also Grosheide 1998, 121.
495. With regard to the EU, see in particular CJEU, 16 July 2009, case C-5/08, Infopaq/DDF, para. 45, stating that '[i]t is only through the choice, sequence and combination of those words that the author may express his creativity in an original manner and achieve a result which is an intellectual creation'; CJEU, 1 December 2011, case C-145/10, Painer, para. 89, asking whether '[t]he author was able to express his creative abilities in the production of the work by making free and creative choices'.

of literature and art in a strict sense. Originality can hardly be equated with artistic value. The doors to copyright protection are wide open. The copyright system has become a vehicle to obtain intellectual property protection for subject matter which, strictly speaking, falls outside the category of literature and art. Under the elastic test of originality that is currently applied, more and more industrial creations have become eligible for copyright protection, such as slogans, drawings, logos and designs made for industrial rather than artistic purposes.[496] As copyright's originality test is not congruent with the limits of the domain of literature and art, the fact that a given creation satisfies the test of originality can hardly inform the final decision on the cultural significance of a sign for which trademark protection is sought. It may even seem paradoxical to extend measures seeking to safeguard follow-on innovation in the literary and artistic domain to creations which, strictly speaking, constitute non-literature and non-art.[497]

To solve this dilemma, it is advisable to make certain adjustments. Instead of asking whether a given sign reflects the low degree of creative input necessary to attract copyright protection at all, trademark offices and courts should examine whether a sign *clearly* meets the originality test. More concretely, they should ask whether a sign displays a high degree of free, creative choices.[498] In this way, it becomes possible to filter out problematic cases at the lower end of the spectrum of creations that are eligible for copyright protection. If a trademark examiner or judge has doubts about a sufficient degree of free, creative choices, this adjustment allows a fast decision against cultural significance. If in doubt about a sufficient degree of originality, a trademark examiner or judge need not embark on an appreciation of all traces of free, creative features of the sign at issue. He can simply assume that the sign does not constitute a cultural sign. Instead of complicating matters, the application of this adjusted originality test can thus

---

496. Geier 2015, 203-206; Derclaye/Leistner 2011, 48-49; Kur 2002, 596; Kur 2001, 44; Spoor 1990, 20-23. As to court decisions increasing this tendency, see German Federal Court of Justice, 16 June 2016, case I ZR 222/14, 'Geburtstagskarawane', *GRUR* 2016, 1291, para. 44; CJEU, 12 September 2019, case C-683/17, Cofemel, para. 31, 35-48 and 52-55. For a case discussing copyright protection for Diesel's coin pocket label, see District Court of The Hague, 22 May 2019, case ECLI:NL:RBDHA:2019:5189, Diesel/Calvin Klein Europe, para. 4.15.

497. Cf. Coombe 2003, 1172-1173.

498. In the EU, the CJEU, 12 September 2019, case C-683/17, Cofemel, para. 31 and 35-48 and 52-55, rejected assessment criteria based on a specific aesthetic effect in the field of industrial design protection. Accordingly, national systems which traditionally applied a threshold criterion of a higher degree of artistic merit in cases of industrial design have abandoned these specific criteria. Cf. German Federal Court of Justice, 16 June 2016, case I ZR 222/14, 'Geburtstagskarawane', *GRUR* 2016, 1291, para. 44. This development concerning the regulation of copyright/design protection overlaps, however, need not preclude an assessment based on a high degree of free, creative choices (a reflection of enhanced artistic merit) for the purpose of identifying cultural signs in a trademark context.

lead to a focus on situations where a sign's cultural nature is clear – easy cases where a sign reflects a high degree of free, creative choices.

A further assessment factor comes to the fore when cultural signs are viewed through the prism of experiences with consumer perception. In trademark law, the basic requirement of distinctiveness plays a central role. For a sign to enjoy trademark protection, it must be capable of distinguishing goods or services in the marketplace.[499] Hence, it is essential that consumers perceive the sign as an identifier of commercial source. In the case of cultural signs, compliance with this threshold criterion may be doubtful because consumers often regard relevant signs as mere descriptive or decorative elements. A photograph of the actress Marlene Dietrich on a book or CD cover, for example, is likely to be understood as an indication of the contents of the information product at issue.[500] The reproduction of a Mark Rothko painting on a T-shirt will most probably be perceived as an embellishment.[501] Given these experiences with the perception of cultural signs, it seems possible to identify signs with cultural significance by placing them in these hypothetical contexts. Trademark examiners and judges should ask whether a sign could theoretically serve as an embellishment to improve the outward appearance of a product, or whether it would describe the contents of a product when applied to goods or services in the cultural domain. If, in these hypothetical scenarios, consumers would be likely to perceive the sign as a mere product decoration or a description of the contents of cultural goods or services, this finding indicates that the sign has a cultural character. In *Nachtwacht*, for instance, the Court of Appeals of The Hague had to decide on the registration of Rembrandt's 'Night Watch' as a trademark for the marketing of the chemical element strontium.[502] While the trademark test of distinctiveness requires an examination whether the painting is distinctive in respect of this specific good, the described cultural significance test would rest on the hypothetical scenario where the Night Watch is placed prominently on a T-shirt or merchandising article. It also asks whether consumers would perceive the Night Watch as a descriptive indication when applied to goods or services in the cultural domain. The difference is obvious: while it may be difficult to deny distinctiveness (in the sense of trademark law) when

499. Cf. Article 15(1) TRIPS which reflects this threshold criterion for the acquisition of trademark rights.
500. German Federal Court of Justice, 24 April 2008, case I ZB 21/06, Marlene-Dietrich-Bildnis, paras 12-15.
501. Cf. a similar scenario discussed in Court of Appeals of The Hague, 29 August 2017, case 200.205.771/01, ECLI:NL:GHDHA:2017:2446, Chiever/Benelux-Organisatie voor de Intellectuele Eigendom ('Nachtwacht'), para. 12. See also CJEU, 23 October 2003, case C-408/01, Adidas/Fitnessworld, paras 39-41, where the Court discusses the fact that design features of a product may be perceived as mere embellishment.
502. Court of Appeals of The Hague, *ibid.*, para. 1.4.

the Night Watch is attached to strontium containers,[503] a finding of cultural significance is inescapable when assessing the impression given by the Night Watch on a T-shirt (decorative) or art book cover (descriptive).

Revisiting the 'Medusa Rondanini' in the light of these factors, there can be little doubt that the Medusa head constitutes a cultural sign. It satisfies the first test because it is exhibited in the Glyptothek in Munich. An image search on the Internet reveals that depictions of Medusa may serve as a basis for derivative works. Medusa parodies and mash-ups can easily be found. Considering the interest in the sujet, it cannot be ruled out that the 'Medusa Rondanini' has already served, or may serve in the future, as source material for new cultural creations. The second test is thus fulfilled as well. If the trademark office assessing the sign has established practice guidelines including examples of Hellenistic and Roman art, factor three will also weigh in favour of a finding of cultural significance. The 'Medusa Rondanini' – when examined in the light of copyright's originality test – meets the fourth test because it reflects various free, creative choices. Finally, the 'Medusa Rondanini' could theoretically serve as a T-shirt decoration or an indication of the contents of books or films dealing with a Medusa myth. It is a cultural sign.[504]

While, in the case of the 'Medusa Rondanini', all assessment factors support the qualification of the sign as a cultural sign, the application of the proposed multifactor test will not always yield such clear-cut results. In some cases, individual factors may be decisive. Avant-garde creations, for instance, do not necessarily satisfy the originality test in copyright law. Even though they are exhibited in museums and sold in art galleries, it is doubtful whether a 'work' and 'originality' in the traditional sense of copyright law would be found in the case of avant-garde works, the creation of which is left to aleatoric or automatic processes; works consisting of a single geometric

503. In fact, the Court of Appeals of The Hague, *ibid.*, para. 12, denied distinctive character even though use of the painting in relation to the sale of strontium seems quite exotic.

504. In the *Medusa* case of the German Federal Court of Justice, 24 November 2011, case I ZR 175/09, 'Medusa', para. 5, the defendant referred to the 'Medusa Rondanini' to rebut infringement arguments of Versace. If the Medusa depicted on the Versace logo is qualified as a stylized version of the 'Medusa Rondanini' or other Medusa heads stemming from the late Hellenistic or Augustan Roman period, the qualification of the 'Medusa Rondanini' as a cultural sign implies that the Versace logo constitutes a (derivative) cultural sign as well. This finding, however, need not automatically put an end to the protection of Versace's logo as a trademark. As also indicated above, the multifactor test for detecting cultural signs serves the purpose of drawing the attention of offices and courts to a sign's cultural dimension. Once they are alert to a sign's cultural significance, the question of appropriate measures to safeguard the cultural innovation cycle arises. These measures, however, may range from the denial and invalidation of trademark protection to limitations of the scope of protection (Chapter 9). If the Versace logo has specifically been made to serve as a trademark, Versace would also have the option of signing a declaration of non-use in a cultural context to safeguard trademark rights. See section 9.1.2.5.

form, such as Kazimir Malevitch's 1915 'Black Square'; ready-mades based on mass articles, such as Marcel Duchamp's 1917 'Fountain'; works consisting of *objets trouvés*, such as several of Joseph Beuys' objects; landscape explorations based on instructions for the creation of 'Sculptures by Walking', such as Richard Long's works. Advanced forms of conceptual art may thus fail to meet copyright's originality standard.[505] Nonetheless, certain elements of the proposed multifactor test will reveal their cultural dimension. A sign's exhibition in museums, sale in art galleries, prominent position in descriptions of art movements are factors that can tip the scales in favour of a finding of cultural significance even if an artwork falls outside traditional categories.

Hence, the fact that avant-garde creations may yield mixed results does not automatically discredit the proposed multifactor test. As explained, the test is intended to alert trademark examiners and judges to a sign's potential cultural significance. It must not be misunderstood as a bright-line rule for the categorical exclusion of signs from trademark protection. Duchamp's use of an ordinary manufactured urinal for the creation of 'Fountain', for example, must not be misinterpreted as an instruction to mechanically deny trademark rights whenever protection is sought with regard to some kind of urinal shape. By contrast, the multifactor test indicates clearly that the museum context and the work's impact on the discourse about art are decisive. In the case of a trademark application that concerns the specific contrast created by Duchamp – the transformation of a standard urinal into a work of art – countermeasures to prevent an encroachment upon cultural follow-on innovation may be necessary. If a trademark application does not evoke this particular contrast, no cultural dimension comes to the fore and no specific measures to safeguard cultural remix activities seem necessary (section 9.1.2.5). Therefore, it is consistent that the proposed multifactor test does not generate one definite answer. Instead of jumping to conclusions, examiners and judges should carefully evaluate whether the trademark application addresses the museum context and the underlying discourse about art in such a way that the qualification as a cultural sign seems appropriate (see also the discussion of the Coca Cola scenario in section 5.2.5).

As already indicated, opposition and infringement procedures can also yield insights into a sign's cultural dimension. In the case of infringement procedures, this is obvious. If measures to safeguard the cultural innovation cycle make its way into the trademark system, a defendant who is confronted with an infringement claim will seek to use these tools – invalidation and defence arguments – in his favour. Hence, he will try to substantiate that the sign at issue falls within the category of cultural signs to be kept free from trademark protection and seek to produce evidence of the sign's cultural significance for this purpose. Opposition proceedings are less likely to have

505. Cf. Dreier/Schulze 2018, 130-131.

the same effect. If the party filing an opposition has prior trademark rights, evidence that reveals the cultural nature of the contested sign may also affect the sign of the opposing party. Seeking to avoid exposure to measures that aim at safeguarding cultural follow-on innovation, such as the invalidation of the earlier trademark right or the limitation of the range of goods and services, the opposing party will refrain from invoking arguments based on cultural significance. Instead, it will simply rely on the risk of confusion. This is different in trademark systems where a prior copyright constitutes a ground for opposition.[506] Inevitably, an opposing party that asserts copyright will draw the attention of the office to the question of originality and a sufficient degree of free, creative choices. As the opposing party must demonstrate that the sign in the trademark application copies original features of its literary and artistic work, it will embark on a detailed discussion of these cultural aspects.

In addition to the recognition of earlier copyright as a ground for opposition, it is possible to enhance the potential of opposition proceedings to provide information on cultural aspects of signs for which trademark protection is sought by giving cultural heritage institutions and associations in the field of literature and art standing in opposition procedures. It is even conceivable to establish and support specific associations with the mission to safeguard cyclic cultural innovation. As part of their activities, these associations could bring oppositions against trademark applications that concern signs with cultural significance, including cultural heritage signs in the public domain. Besides the development of a multifactor test for the identification of cultural signs, it is thus possible to support the work of trademark examiners by establishing advisory bodies with expertise in literature and art.[507]

Therefore, the identification of cultural signs in the Mona Lisa category – works of art that are recognized as important literary or artistic expressions in the cultural domain – need not pose insuperable difficulties. To meet the *Gömböc* requirement of 'objective and reliable' evidence or information,[508] such as descriptions and data, experts opinions and 'publications, catalogues and websites',[509] trademark offices and courts can develop a multifactor test to detect this type of cultural signs in cases where cultural significance is not self-evident anyway because the sign at issue belongs to mankind's universal cultural heritage or a country's most prominent works of art. Relevant factors may include the exhibition or sale of the sign as an artwork, search results showing existing remix practices, conformity with typical style features of classical or contemporary art (described in reference material compiled for the purpose of identifying cultural signs), a high degree of free, creative

506. Cf. Bercovitz 2001, 612-613.
507. Cf. Geier 2015, 191.
508. CJEU, 23 April 2020, case C-237/19, Gömböc, para. 34 and 41.
509. CJEU, *ibid.*, para. 34.

choices that provides clear evidence of the sign's originality and copyrightability, and the potential to serve as a decorative or descriptive element when applied to a literary or artistic good or service. Moreover, measures to safeguard cultural follow-on innovation can include the establishment of an advisory body with expertise knowledge in the field of literature and art. Seeking to strengthen the informatory function of opposition procedures, it is advisable to recognize copyright protection as a ground for opposition and afford cultural institutions and associations the opportunity to bring oppositions, including oppositions based on hypothetical copyright protection which cultural heritage material in the public domain would enjoy if created today.

5.2.2 *Māori Imagery and Other Traditional Cultural Expressions*

In the context of cultural heritage signs, it is important to devote particular attention to the debate on traditional knowledge and, more specifically, traditional cultural expressions. They constitute a specific category of cultural signs that may appear as a subcategory of the cultural heritage signs discussed in the preceding section. The work of WIPO's Intergovernmental Committee on Intellectual Property and Genetic Resources, Traditional Knowledge and Folklore has led to the following draft definition of the term 'traditional cultural expression':

> Traditional Cultural Expressions are any forms in which traditional culture practices and knowledge are expressed, [appear or are manifested] [the result of intellectual activity, experiences, or insights] by indigenous [peoples], local communities and/or [other beneficiaries] in or from a traditional context, and may be dynamic and evolving and comprise verbal forms[510], musical forms[511], expressions by movement[512], tangible[513] or intangible forms of expression, or combinations thereof[514] (brackets and footnotes in the original text).

Considering the reference to a broad spectrum of literary and artistic forms of expression,[515] it is not difficult to draw a parallel with the problem statement that has been developed above. As in the case of signs belonging

510. [Such as stories, epics, legends, popular stories, poetry, riddles and other narratives; words, signs, names and symbols.]
511. [Such as songs, rhythms, and instrumental music, the songs which are the expression of rituals.]
512. [Such as dance, works of mas, plays, ceremonies, rituals, rituals in sacred places and peregrinations, games and traditional sports/sports and traditional games, puppet performances, and other performances, whether fixed or unfixed.]
513. [Such as material expressions of art, handicrafts, ceremonial masks or dress, handmade carpets, architecture, and tangible spiritual forms, and sacred places.]
514. WIPO 2019, Article 1.
515. Cf. Hilty 2009b, 884.

to mankind's universal cultural heritage, a strong interest in preventing use for marketing purposes may require measures to avoid the acquisition of trademark rights to traditional cultural expressions. As Antony Taubman observed:

> it has often been argued that IP is inherently a form of commodification, that, in operation, takes a rich cultural intellectual tradition, captures its commercial value – extracts and isolates from their original context the easily exploited expressions of a tradition of ancient wisdom, culture, and spirituality – and crudely turns them into a commodity, owned and controlled by others, to be traded on global markets.[516]

Taubman adds an important nuance to this line of argument by pointing out that:

> [i]n its most fundamental conception, the essential legal character of an IP 'right' is not, at its core, an entitlement to enter the market and to trade with the protected material as a commodity. Rather, its central characteristic is that it empowers its holder to object to another's 'commodification' of what properly is held by the right holder – recognised elements of knowledge, cultural works, or distinctive signs or symbols.[517]

While this is a correct and important response to an oversimplified critique of the intellectual property system, it can hardly be overlooked that this preventive, negative aspect of intellectual property protection – the right to object to modes of use that conflict with the desires and interests of the right holder, such as use seeking to trivialize traditional cultural expressions in connection with product marketing[518] – is only one side of the medal. With its requirement of genuine use for the purpose of finding an outlet for goods or services,[519] the trademark system imposes an obligation on the trademark proprietor to place a protected sign in the context of product marketing sooner or later. Inevitably, the grant of trademark rights implies not only passive use to prevent others from undesirable misappropriation but also active use in a marketing context by the trademark proprietor himself.

516. Taubman 2019, 384. Cf. Frankel 2012, 269-270; Coombe 2003, 1177-1181.

517. Taubman 2019, 386.

518. Cf. Taubman 2019, 386-387. As to the debate on negative and positive use of trademark rights, see Kur/Senftleben 2017, para. 5.03-5.08; J. Griffiths 2015, 343; Davison/Emerton, 2014, 505; Frankel/Gervais 2013, 1149; Bonadio 2012, 599; Davison 2012, 81; Maniatis/Kamperman Sanders 1997, 237; Kur 1996b, 198; Castren 1995, 87; Bernitz 1990, 137.

519. Cf. Article 19(1) TRIPS. As to the implementation of the use requirement in EU trademark law and the requirement of finding an outlet for goods or services, see CJEU, 11 March 2003, case C-40/01, Ajax/Ansul, para. 36 and 43. Cf. Kur/Senftleben 2017, para. 6.154.

This active use of traditional cultural expressions for marketing purposes may play a central role when indigenous communities themselves opt for the development of commercial relationships to exploit their traditional knowledge, hoping to improve their economic and cultural situation.[520] The protection and use of distinctive symbols and traditional names as badges of origin may offer a gateway to channels of trade in this scenario.[521] However, Susy Frankel rightly emphasizes that:

> [t]he challenge with branding traditional knowledge as a way of protecting cultural identity is to ensure that the brand does not overtake the culture and that the brand is used to support cultural outputs, rather than become the driving force in and of itself.[522]

Given this need to walk a fine line when taking branding initiatives, it is not surprising that developments in trademark law rather reflect the necessity to allow indigenous peoples to object to the use of traditional cultural expressions as trademarks and, more specifically, to enable them, as guardians of traditional cultural expressions, to bring their concerns about corrosive effects of trademark protection to the attention of trademark offices.[523] As already indicated in the preceding section, a specific Māori Trade Marks Advisory Committee has been established in New Zealand to facilitate the task of identifying signs in trademark applications, the registration of which may be offensive to Māori.[524] The Advisory Committee under the 2002 Trade Marks Act consists of members with specific knowledge of the world view, protocol and culture of Māori. They are appointed by the Commissioner of Trade Marks.[525] As the advice of the Committee on Māori text and imagery is not binding, it does not predetermine the office decision on the grant of trademark rights. However, it provides guidance and functions as a compass for the trademark office.[526]

With regard to measures to prevent the misappropriation of traditional cultural expressions, it seems justified to draw a parallel with the interest in keeping cultural heritage signs free from trademark protection (section 3.3.2.4) and qualify traditional cultural expressions as cultural signs in the sense of the Mona Lisa scenario described in the preceding section 5.2.1. Accordingly, the findings and recommendations which the following analysis will yield with regard to the prevention of trademark rights to cultural

520. Frankel 2012, 254-255; Hilty 2009b, 907-908.
521. Taubman 2019, 394.
522. Frankel 2012, 260.
523. See WIPO 2019, Article 2, which reflects the aim to prevent unauthorized use, the erroneous grant of intellectual property rights, and the misappropriation of signs. Cf. Ubertazzi 2017, 563; Hilty 2009b, 892-893 and 901-902, for a discussion of concerns about misappropriation of intangible cultural heritage.
524. Taubman 2019, 393-394; Frankel 2008, 455-456; Morgan 2004, 62-75.
525. Frankel 2005, 90-91; Morgan 2004, 73-75.
526. Frankel 2008, 455-456; Frankel 2005, 93.

heritage signs apply mutatis mutandis to traditional cultural expressions. Whenever conclusions are drawn with regard to the need to keep signs in the Mona Lisa category free from trademark protection, these conclusions can be extended to traditional cultural expressions insofar as the interest of indigenous peoples in preventing the misappropriation of traditional cultural expressions by third parties is concerned.

It is to be conceded, however, that other premises underlying the following analysis may fail to address the specific interests and concerns in the traditional knowledge arena, including traditional cultural expressions. For instance, it is doubtful whether the objective to preserve the public domain status of cultural heritage signs – in the sense of freedom of remix in the literary and artistic domain – should fully apply to traditional cultural expressions. Discussing wishes and values in traditional knowledge communities, Taubman refers to concerns 'about their intellectual and cultural heritage being exploited to yield IP held by others or simply transferred to the public domain against their wishes'.[527] Hence, indigenous peoples may object not only to the grant of trademark rights to their traditional cultural expressions (in this regard, the following recommendations apply mutatis mutandis) but also to the qualification of their cultural signs as elements of the public domain[528] (in this regard, the emphasis on unrestricted freedom of artistic remix in the following chapters may appear inadequate from the perspective of the traditional knowledge debate).

Hence, it is necessary to bear in mind that there is a general category of cultural heritage signs (in the sense of the Mona Lisa scenario, section 5.2.1) and a specific subcategory of traditional cultural expressions. This necessity follows from the fact that in the case of traditional cultural expressions, it may be possible to identify an indigenous community that can legitimately claim to fulfil an important guardianship function when defining appropriate and inappropriate modes of use and seeking to preserve the traditional meaning and connotations of traditional signs in accordance with the customary law and cultural context of indigenous artistic creativity.[529] In the case of signs in the general cultural heritage category that never enjoyed, or no longer enjoy, copyright protection (such as the Mona Lisa), this type of guardianship arguments can easily be unmasked as a mere pretence to justify the artificial creation of exclusive intellectual property rights on the basis of

527. Taubman 2019, 387. For a practical example of misappropriation in the industrial design area, see Osei-Tutu 2017, 1053-1054.

528. Cf. Osei-Tutu 2017, 1065.

529. Cf. Taubman 2019, 393-395; WIPO 2019, Article 2. As to the recognition of the customary law of indigenous peoples in the context of intellectual property disputes concerning traditional knowledge, see Federal Court of Australia, 13 December 1994, Milpurrurru/Indofurn Pty Limited [1994] 30 IPR 209, paras 11-21, 127-129. For an example of national legislation regulating the use of traditional symbols, see Osei-Tutu 2017, 1058-1059.

trademark law.[530] In the case of traditional cultural expressions, by contrast, the legitimacy of guardianship arguments – as a basis of definition and consecration power in the discourse surrounding relevant traditional symbols – follows from international legal instruments, such as the UN Declaration on the Rights of Indigenous Peoples which explicitly recognizes a collective right of indigenous communities to 'maintain, control, protect and develop their intellectual property over [their] cultural heritage, traditional knowledge and traditional cultural expressions'.[531] Therefore, the range of legal impact factors goes beyond the parameters of the debate on overlapping copyright and trademark protection. With regard to the aim to preserve the public domain – in the sense of unbridled freedom to use cultural heritage material as a basis for new literary and artistic creations – it could thus be problematic to readily follow recommendations concerning unrestricted freedom to remix cultural heritage signs.[532] The recommendations given in the following chapters in this regard should not be extended to traditional cultural expressions without ascertaining in each individual case whether the recommended solution also satisfies the specific interests and complies with the specific use protocols of indigenous peoples that have been recognized as legitimate guardians.[533]

5.2.3 *Mickey Mouse and Other Icons of Mainstream Culture*

The Mickey Mouse scenario concerns a situation where an attempt is made to register a cultural sign stemming from a contemporary mainstream production as a trademark. Arguably, the criteria for identifying Mickey Mouse and other signs that evolve from cultural mainstream productions are similar to those developed in section 5.2.1 with regard to the Mona Lisa scenario. In many cases, the cultural nature of signs in the Mickey Mouse category will be self-evident. As in the case of signs belonging to mankind's universal cultural heritage or signs that constitute core elements of a country's individual cultural treasury, trademark offices and courts will have little difficulty to detect well-known icons of mainstream culture, such as fictional characters that feature prominently in successful (animated) films,

---

530. See section 8.2.3.2. Cf. EFTA Court, 6 April 2017, case E-5/16, Municipality of Oslo ('Vigeland'), para. 66; Senftleben 2017b, 688-689.
531. Article 31 UN Declaration on the Rights of Indigenous Peoples, General Assembly Resolution 61/295, dated 2 October 2007, UN Document A/Res/61/295, available at https://undocs.org/a/res/61/295. Cf. Taubman 2019, 385; Frankel 2012, 254-255.
532. Cf. Coombe 2003, 1184-1186.
533. Cf. WIPO 2019, Article 5, which refers to the principle of 'prior informed consent'. See Hilty 2009b, 909-910; Coombe 2005, 47-52; Coombe 2003, 1180-1181; Oguamanam 2004, 137, who warns against neglecting 'indigenous episteme' when applying Western intellectual property standards to traditional knowledge and cultural expressions. With regard to the question of ownership, see Federal Court of Australia, 3 September 1998, Bulun Bulun/R&T Textiles Pty Limited [1998] 41 IPR 513.

and musical works that reach top positions in the charts. Given their high popularity and widespread recognition, cultural signs derived from blockbusters and chart hits are unlikely to escape the attention of examiners and judges.

In respect of less known literary and artistic works in the Mickey Mouse category, it is possible to conduct a multifactor analysis that applies the criteria known from the Mona Lisa scenario mutatis mutandis. The relevant questions are as follows:

- does the sign feature in a mainstream cultural production, such as a film or concert? Can it be found in online music libraries or collections of popular visual works that are available on the Internet? (factor one);
- does an online search reveal that the sign has already served as a basis for parodies, remixes or other forms of mash-up? (factor two);
- does the sign display typical style features known from other mainstream creations which the trademark office has included in reference material for the identification of signs with cultural significance? (factor three);
- does the sign fall under one of the work categories listed in Article 2(1) BC? Does it clearly meet copyright's originality test due to a high degree of free, creative choices? (factor four);
- could the sign theoretically serve as an embellishment to improve the outward appearance of a product, or would it describe the contents of a good or service when it was applied to goods or services in the cultural domain? Would consumers perceive the sign as a descriptive or decorative element in a hypothetical scenario where the sign features prominently on a product or where it is used in relation to goods or services in the cultural domain? (factor five).

5.2.4 *Winnetou and Other Work Titles*

Strictly speaking, the freedom to refer to titles of pre-existing works in the context of remix and reuse activities in the cultural domain is not an issue of copyright/trademark protection overlaps. A work title satisfying the originality test in copyright law is the exception rather than the rule.[534] As long as a work title does not enjoy copyright protection, the problem of incongruent copyright and trademark norms does not arise. Moreover, the particular problem resulting from continued protection of work titles after copyright expiry does not lie in the maintenance of exclusive rights to the cultural substance of a literary and artistic creation. Work titles and names of

534. Ohly 2008, 211; Mende/Isaac 2012, 138-145. For a critique of copyright protection for work titles, see Derclaye/Leistner 2011, 322.

personages are only signifiers of literary and artistic productions. They do not comprise the contents of these productions. While a trademark registration of the Mickey Mouse drawing concerns the copyrighted, cultural expression as such, the registration of the word mark MICKEY MOUSE only concerns the name of the copyrighted, cultural expression. It constitutes a reference to the Mickey Mouse drawing but not the artistic work.

Second authors embarking on remix and reuse activities, however, may have to play not only with the contents and substance of a pre-existing work but also with the title of the work and the names of main personages to make their point and convey their message to the public.[535] Hence, the problem is that the work title and the names of protagonists are indispensable signifiers of the cultural creation concerned. They are focal points of the communication surrounding a literary and artistic work. A second author seeking to build upon a pre-existing cultural production may have difficulty to clearly inform the public about her derivative work if she must refrain from use of the title of the original work.[536]

As relevant register entries and court decisions show, obstacles to the use of work titles in the context of derivative works may follow from trademark protection. Work titles that are actively used for marketing purposes, such as 'James Bond' and '007', or 'Harry Potter' and 'Harry Potter and the Half-Blood Prince', constitute trademarks registered in respect of primary information products, such as films and books, and related services, including book publishing and film production and distribution.[537] Names of other characters featuring in these productions, such as 'Dr. No' and 'Lord Voldemort', may be registered as trademarks in respect of merchandising articles and other goods and services that are not directly

535. As to the recognition of a need to use the name of fictional characters for marketing purposes, see U.S. District Court for the Central District of California, 14 November 2012, Fleischer Studios/A.V.E.L.A., 925 F. Supp. 2d 1067, 1074-1075 (C.D. Cal. 2012), 'Betty Boop'.

536. See the discussion of use of the name 'Tanja Grotter' to market a derivative work based on 'Harry Potter and the Sorcerer's Stone' in Court of Appeals of Amsterdam, 6 November 2003, case ECLI:NL:GHAMS:2003:AN7646, Rowling/Byblos, para. 4.9 and 4.10. Cf. Senftleben 2012a, 364; Frosio 2014, 381-382. As to the comparable dilemma that arises after the exhaustion of trademark rights and the advertising of the resale of genuine products, see CJEU, 4 November 1997, case C-337/95, Dior/Evora, para. 38.

537. For example, see the list of goods and services included in the registration of JAMES BOND, EUTM 017010984, JAMES BOND 007, EUTM 002461150, HARRY POTTER, EUTM 000935593, and HARRY POTTER AND THE HALF-BLOOD PRINCE, EUTM 003276862. See also the various other title registrations relating to Harry Potter books: EUTMs 001729557, 003121911, 003141231, 003426533, 003426558, 003426831, 005587951, 005956561 and 010110195. As to the impact of this protection in practice, see Court of Appeals of Amsterdam, 6 November 2003, case ECLI:NL:GHAMS:2003:AN7646, Rowling/Byblos, para. 4.10.

related to underlying information products. With regard to primary information products, they may acquire distinctiveness as a result of use in trade.[538] In addition, examples of names of famous artists on the EUIPO trademark register range from Beethoven to Warhol.[539] The same can be said about the broad spectrum of names of fictional characters that are registered as trademarks.[540]

If trademarked titles and names are included in derivative works, the exclusive rights following from the grant of trademark protection may raise concerns about an impediment of cultural follow-on innovation that correspond to those articulated in the preceding sections with regard to cultural heritage signs, such as the Mona Lisa (section 5.2.1) and symbols of cultural mainstream productions, such as Mickey Mouse (section 5.2.3).[541] In *ERB/Beukenoord*, for instance, the Court of Appeals of Amsterdam assumed that the mark TARZAN was a valid identifier of commercial source in respect of films and books in the 'Tarzan' series.[542] On this basis, the intellectual property holding of Edgar Rice Burroughs (ERB Inc.) had success in prohibiting use of the title 'Tarzan of the Apes' for the marketing of an unauthorized animation film.[543] While the copyright to the story 'Tarzan of the Apes' – originally published in the U.S. and the UK in a 1912

538. See the registrations of DR. NO, EUTM 004810438, and LORD VOLDEMORT, EUTM 001423193. Cf. GCEU, 30 June 2009, case T-435/05, Danjaq/OHIM (Mission Productions), paras 25-27.
539. For example, see EUTM 001081314, BEETHOVEN; EUTM 000945774, DESCARTES; EUTM 001593128, ALBERT EINSTEIN; EUTM 003805942, GOETHE; IR 0858800, HENRIK IBSEN; EUTM 001358621, VINCENT VAN GOGH; EUTM 005468996, MONA LISA; EUTM 000021071 MOZART; EUTM 001334036, PICASSO; EUTM 000119354, REMBRANDT; EUTM 004278214, SHAKESPEARE; EUTM 003877354, GIUSEPPE VERDI; EUTM 000047365, VERMEER; EUTM 000996199, LEONARDO DA VINCI; EUTM 003437811, ANDY WARHOL.
540. For example, see EUTM 000559674, ANAKIN SKYWALKER; EUTMs 000016147 and 002794162, ASTERIX; EUTM 005238118, CINDERELLA; EUTMs 003494325, 004354551 and 014484571, DARTH VADER; EUTMs 002828341, 005240271 and 008939381, DONALD DUCK; EUTMs 000174946, 002025773, 002362408, 006455257, 006455273, 006455281, 006455927, 006455943, 016608291 and 016914087, GANDALF; EUTM 005238449, GOOFY; EUTMs 000935593, 001301688 and 001433952 HARRY POTTER; EUTMs 000251918, 001205137, 012210936 and 017010984, JAMES BOND; EUTM 002658821, MACBETH; IR 983421, MICKEY; EUTMs 002827426 and 005240668, MICKEY MOUSE; EUTM 013876628, MIFFY; EUTM 000016154 and 002793545, OBELIX; EUTM 001087303, POCAHONTAS; EUTMs 001263342, 001622539 and 006758569 SHERLOCK HOLMES; EUTMs 000408591 and 008735003, SNOOPY; EUTM 011571511, SNOWWHITE; EUTM 001335884, SPONGEBOB; EUTM 002973675, SUPERMAN; EUTM 002735017, WINNETOU; EUTMs 003031630, 005399787, 013696811 and 014321657, ZORRO. See also Benelux registration no. 0578407, NIJNTJE (Miffy).
541. Cf. Derclaye/Leistner 2011, 253-254; Ohly 2008, 214.
542. Court of Appeals of Amsterdam, 26 juli 2001, ERB/Beukenoord, *AMI* 2002, 12, para. 2.17-2.19.
543. Court of Appeals of Amsterdam, *ibid.*, para. 2.14 and 2.22. Cf. Visser 2002, 15-16.

issue of the journal 'The All-Story' – had expired in the U.S. in 1987, the application of the rule of simultaneous publication in a Berne Union country (Article 3(1)(b) BC with regard to publication in the UK) led to the result that, besides the trademark right, ERB could still invoke copyright in the Netherlands.[544] In *Rowling/Byblos*, the Court of Appeals of Amsterdam accepted Time Warner's argument that the name HARRY POTTER constituted a valid mark for books and films in the Harry Potter series. In this case, the Court prohibited the marketing of the derivative work 'Tanja Grotter and the Magical Contrabass' written by the Russian author Dimitri Yemets.[545] Even if an infringement claim, finally, has no success, the registration of work titles and names of fictional characters offers the trademark proprietor additional ammunition to threaten second authors not only with copyright claims but also with allegations of trademark infringement.[546] After copyright expiry, trademark rights in work titles and names of protagonists constitute stumbling blocks for the marketing of derivative works that refer to the original literary and artistic production.[547]

In addition to trademark protection, authors of derivate works must take into account specific protection regimes for work titles, such as the sui generis protection available in Germany.[548] In *Winnetous Rückkehr*, the German Federal Court of Justice pointed out that, after the expiry of copyright protection, these specific work title rights could not be invoked to prevent the use of a protected title for the publication and dissemination of reprints of the work that had entered the public domain. However, work title rights could be asserted against the use of the title in respect of new, different works.[549] Specific protection regimes for work titles can thus pose an additional obstacle to the remix of literary and artistic works. In *Winnetous Rückkehr*, the German Federal Court of Justice solved this problem by assuming that the degree of distinctiveness of the work title 'Winnetou' was low. The protection of the title under the specific German sui generis protection regime was justified because consumers perceived the name of the famous Apache chief as an identifier of Karl May's works. However, the name also had a descriptive character with regard to the contents of the

544. Court of Appeals of Amsterdam, *ibid.*, para. 2.2-2.10. Cf. Visser 2002, 15.
545. Court of Appeals of Amsterdam, 6 November 2003, case ECLI:NL:GHAMS:2003:AN7646, Rowling/Byblos, para. 4.10.
546. Cf. Court of Appeals of Amsterdam, 30 januari 2003, Van Toor/Phanta Vision, *AMI* 2003, 94, para. 4.17-4.20, discussing several unfounded allegations of trademark infringement based on the registration of the names of fictional characters – BASSIE & ADRIAAN and CLOWN BASSIE – as trademarks.
547. Visser 2002, 17; Vanovermeire 2009, 185-186. For a less critical statement seeking to limit trademark rights instead of abandoning them altogether, see Reeskamp 2010, 36.
548. This specific protection regime of work title rights rests on §§ 5(1) and (3), 15 of the German Trademark Law (Markengesetz).
549. German Federal Court of Justice, 23 January 2003, case I ZR 171/00, 'Winnetous Rückkehr', p. 11-12.

Winnetou novels.[550] For this reason, consumers were likely to pay particular attention to additional indications, such as the numbering 'I', 'II', 'III', etc. of the original novels. In the case of a derivative work, it was thus sufficient to add an element to the title that eliminates the risk of confusion vis-à-vis the protected titles of the original works. Against this background, the Court was satisfied that the title 'Winnetous Rückkehr' ('Winnetou's Return') did not infringe sui generis rights to the titles of the novels written by Karl May.[551]

While these tailor-made solutions in the area of specific protection regimes for work titles may help to reduce the corrosive effect on cultural follow-on innovation, the problem of an additional obstacle to the publication and dissemination of derivative works remains.[552] Therefore, it seems advisable to avoid further inroads into the freedom of using public domain works as reference points for the creation of new cultural material. Not surprisingly, the German Federal Court of Justice used a different yardstick to assess the distinctive character of the sign 'Winnetou' in the context of trademark law. In the decision *Winnetou* which preceded the judgment in *Winnetous Rückkehr*, the Court stated that the sign lacked the degree of distinctiveness necessary to obtain trademark protection. Consumers would understand the sign 'Winnetou' as a mere synonym of Karl May's fictional character. The name of the Apache chief was descriptive in respect of books, films and related services.[553] In the context of trademark law, the fact that the sign describes the contents of Karl May's novels was thus sufficient to deny the acquisition of rights. More specific protection under the German sui generis protection regime for work titles, by contrast, remains possible. According to the German Federal Court of Justice, this result is not contradictory. While consumers would expect trademarks not to be descriptive, they were accustomed to the use of descriptive indications as titles of literary and artistic works. Therefore, the assessment had to be different and protection under the German sui generis regime for work titles could not be excluded from the outset.[554]

While this result implies that, in Germany, work titles do not become freely available after copyright expiry (they remain eligible for sui generis work title protection), it is noteworthy that the German Federal Court of Justice is prepared to make an effort to prevent the acquisition of trademark rights on the basis of the protection requirement of sufficient distinctive character. However, this strategy is likely to fail in cases where a character's name – constituting a work title or an element of a work title – is used

550. German Federal Court of Justice, *ibid.*, p. 9-10 and 13.
551. German Federal Court of Justice, *ibid.*, p. 13-14. Cf. Derclaye/Leistner 2011, 252-253.
552. Ohly 2008, 211-213; Visser 2002, 17.
553. German Federal Court of Justice, 5 December 2002, case I ZB 19/00, Winnetou, p. 6.
554. German Federal Court of Justice, 23 January 2003, case I ZR 171/00, 'Winnetous Rückkehr', p. 10.

consistently as an indicator of commercial source.[555] The above examples of trademark registrations relating to 'James Bond', '007', 'Harry Potter' and 'Harry Potter and the Half-Blood Prince' attest to the grant of trademark rights at EU level. Authors of derivate works may thus be confronted with a bundle of rights: trademark protection and sui generis work title protection alike. While the establishment of a specific sui generis protection system reflects a deliberate decision of national lawmakers which judges can only attenuate but not ignore when remix activities take place in the cultural domain, the trademark system is not specifically designed to offer protection for work titles. Hence it makes sense to explore the room for measures to avoid an impediment of cultural follow-on innovation in trademark law.[556] With regard to decisions on (the scope of) trademark protection for work titles, this analysis can strengthen efforts to prevent interferences with cultural follow-on innovation.

In the subsequent analysis of risks arising from trademark protection and countermeasures that may reduce corrosive effects on cultural follow-on innovation, it is thus important to develop solutions that cover not only the artistic substance of a cultural creation but also its title. This goal does not require the introduction of work titles as a separate category of cultural signs besides the Mona Lisa and Mickey Mouse categories that have already been established above (sections 5.2.1 and 5.2.3). Considering the objective to avoid impediments of cultural follow-on innovation, work titles can be deemed direct accessories of the literary and artistic substance to which a second author may wish to refer.[557] Accordingly, the following findings and recommendations concerning the corrosive effect of trademark rights to literary and artistic works and the prevention of interferences with cultural remix activities apply mutatis mutandis to relevant work titles. Whenever conclusions are drawn with regard to the Mona Lisa category of cultural heritage signs (section 5.2.1), these conclusions can be understood to encompass the titles of cultural signs in this category. Conclusions concerning the Mickey Mouse category of contemporary mainstream productions (section 5.2.3) can be extended to the titles of cultural signs in this category. In this way, it is possible to ensure that artists basing their new creations on pre-existing cultural expressions are free to use not only the substance of prior literary and artistic works but also the signifiers which make these pre-existing works identifiable for their audience.

555. Ohly 2008, 213-214.
556. Ohly 2008, 214.
557. Cf. Court of Appeals of Brussels, 3 October 2013, cases 2013/7132 and 2013/7133, Anne Frank Foundation/Benelux Office for Intellectual Property, para. 5.

5.2.5 Coca Cola and Other Trade Symbols

Besides the described categories of cultural signs and work titles – concerning creations that belong to the canon of fine art, such as the Mona Lisa, and creations stemming from mainstream productions, such as Mickey Mouse – there is a further category of signs with particular relevance to the discussion on measures to safeguard the cultural innovation cycle. The identification of different forms of cultural signs in the preceding sections implies that there are also signs which fall outside this category: genuine identifiers of commercial source and other industrial objects that have evolved in the domain of trade and commerce. A boundary line between these industrial trade symbols and the signs described as cultural signs in the preceding sections has already been drawn in case law. In *Vigeland* – where public domain preservation and grounds for refusing trademark rights to cultural heritage signs occupied centre stage – the EFTA Court explained that:

> there would be no threat to the need to safeguard the public domain resulting from works that were primarily created to serve as signs to be registered as trade marks. The protection afforded to such signs under copyright law is merely incidental. In such circumstances, the purpose behind the sign's creation is to indicate commercial origin only. The same may be true in cases where the rights to a work were sold for the mere purpose of serving as a trademark.[558]

Hence, it can be said that genuine trade symbols are to be distinguished from cultural signs in the sense of the categories developed above. Trade symbols share the characteristic that they are primarily created to serve as trademarks or industrial objects: their primary function is in the world of trade and commerce.

Nonetheless, it would be wrong to exclude trade symbols from the discussion of measures to safeguard cultural follow-on innovation. As explained when operationalizing aesthetic and sociological theories in section 5.1, a given sign may constitute an important reference point for critical reflection on current societal conditions in a work of art, even though it has a commercial background and does not offer an alternative vision of society itself. Trade symbols that have their origin and primary function in the domain of commerce and trade – trademarks and other industrial objects – may play an important role in the artistic discourse. As they reflect current societal conditions, such as materialism and consumerism,[559] they allow artists to make critical statements by employing them as symbols of a given

558. EFTA Court, 6 April 2017, case E-5/16, Municipality of Oslo ('Vigeland'), para. 97.
559. Assaf 2008, 2-3.

lifestyle, attitude, etc.[560] For an artist to make her point and criticize the societal status quo, she may have to include genuine trade symbols in her work.[561] Nadia Plesner's creations 'Simple Living' and 'Darfurnica', for example, constitute artworks that use famous trademarks as symbols of a current lifestyle and societal orientation which the artist seeks to criticize. Her paintings incorporate product design and trademarks as symbols of consumption and entertainment culture that distracts from human disasters which truly matter.[562] Against the backdrop of the use of trade symbols in artworks, it is advisable to extend the discussion of potential measures to safeguard the cultural innovation cycle to the category of trade symbols.

In addition to use of product design and trademarks as reference points for a critique of societal conditions, trade symbols may also serve as a means to comment on the societal role and function of art itself. Andy Warhol's use of Campbell's soup cans in his 1962 work '100 Campbell's Soup Cans' can serve as an example of the use of a pre-existing trade symbol for the purpose of making an artistic statement. The example also indicates that it is advisable to distinguish between the Mickey Mouse category of symbols derived from contemporary mainstream culture and the Coca Cola category of trade symbols stemming originally from the domain of trade and commerce. While signs in both categories are of a commercial nature, the fulfilment of a function in commerce and trade is the sole *raison d'être* of Campbell's soup can. The same can hardly be said about Mickey Mouse: if icons of contemporary mainstream culture are no longer employed as identifiers of commercial source, they still remain signs with an individual meaning and function in the cultural domain. If, by contrast, trademark protection of trade symbols is phased out and trademark proprietors stop using them as commercial badges of origin, this deprives affected trade symbols of their very function in commerce and trade. However, it also deprives them of their value for the artistic discourse. The particular contrast which Warhol evokes in his works – the contrast arising from the use of an everyday industrial object in the context of art – is only possible as long as the soup cans from Campbell's are clearly defined and perceived as industrial objects and not as artworks.[563] In principle, the same argument can be made with regard to any trademark or industrial object that belongs to the domain of commerce and trade. The famous Coca Cola logo may also feature

560. Cf. French Supreme Court, 15 May 2015, case 13-27391, ECLI:FR:CCASS:2015:C100519, Klasen/Malka. Cf. Geiger 2018a, 6. As to the process of attaching lifestyle messages to trademarks, see Senftleben 2009a, 48-49; Assaf 2008, 2-3.

561. District Court of The Hague, 4 May 2011, case LJN BQ3525, Nadia Plesner/Louis Vuitton, para. 2.1-2.8. Cf. Peukert 2016, 424.

562. Cf. District Court of The Hague, *ibid.*; Visser 2011, 740-742. See section 6.2.3.

563. As to this contrast between the realm of art and the world of consumer goods, see Bürger 1974, 82-85. For a discussion of consumer interest in the stability of the meaning of iconic trade symbols, see Hughes 1999, 1003-1007.

prominently in artworks as a symbol of the world of commerce and trade. But the contrast arising from the use of Coca Cola in an artistic context can only be produced as long as the sign constitutes a well-functioning trade symbol. The reason for this specific contrasting effect clearly comes to the fore when drawing a comparison with the use of an icon of contemporary mainstream culture (Mickey Mouse) in a work of fine art. While the inclusion of Mickey Mouse may concern a comment on the relationship between fine art and mainstream art within the artistic domain (contrast between two internal factors within the artistic field), the inclusion of a Coca Cola logo in an artwork concerns a reference to commerce and trade as a subsystem of society that is distinct from the artistic domain (contrast between an internal factor (artistic field) and an external factor (field of trade)). Declaring Campbell's soup can and the Coca Cola logo cultural signs would thus miss the point. Instead of including them in the category of cultural signs, it is necessary to establish a distinct category: the category of genuine trade symbols that have not evolved in the cultural domain. This distinction adds important nuances to the following discussion of measures to safeguard cultural follow-on innovation.

As to the identification of genuine trade symbols that may play an important role in literary and artistic productions, the aforementioned enquiry into the sign's *raison d'être* will often lead to unambiguous results. Nadia Plesner's works (section 6.2.3), for instance, show that artists tend to employ well-known trade symbols that are capable of representing a broader societal phenomenon or orientation. In these cases, the commercial nature and trade relevance will be self-evident to judges hearing a case about trademark infringement because they know the landscape of commerce and trade and are confronted with these trade symbols on a regular basis. Hence, the qualification of a given sign as a trade symbol with cultural significance need not be difficult. To confirm the intuitive identification of a sign as a trade symbol, a judge can ask whether the sign's function in commerce and trade is its sole *raison d'être*. The question can be answered in the affirmative if a hypothetical end of the symbol's use as a commercial source identifier would deprive the sign of its primary function. While this question would have to be answered in the affirmative in the case of the Coca Cola logo, the answer would be different when Mickey Mouse is assessed. The cultural meaning and function of Mickey Mouse gives the sign an independent significance that does not depend on trademark protection and continuous use in trade.

However, it is to be conceded that there may be difficult cases in the category of genuine trade symbols. While the logos of Coca Cola and Louis Vuitton, obviously, constitute trade symbols with a clearly commercial *raison d'être*, one may find the determination of a sign's nature less straightforward when trade symbols are at issue that resemble fictional characters or other cultural creations. Tony the Tiger – the advertising cartoon mascot for Kellogg's Frosties – can serve as an example. As other fictional characters, Tony the Tiger is eligible for copyright protection.

Viewing the drawing in isolation, the conclusion seems inescapable that this is a cultural creation in the Mickey Mouse category (section 5.2.3). Considering the advertising context in which the fictional character has evolved, however, it becomes clear that Kellogg's famous Tiger is a trade symbol. It may be less convincing than in the Coca Cola or Louis Vuitton scenario to state that commerce and trade is Tony's sole *raison d'être*. Nonetheless, a primary, or at least predominant, function in commerce and trade can hardly be denied.[564] Although the Tiger drawing attracts protection as a literary and artistic work, the fictional character falls within the category of trade symbols against the backdrop of its evolution as a marketing and advertising tool. In line with the above-cited distinction drawn by the EFTA Court in *Vigeland*,[565] it may be said that the purpose behind the sign's creation was the use in commerce and trade from the outset. The fictional character was always intended to identify Kellogg's as the commercial origin of breakfast cereal.[566]

The example of Tony the Tiger shows that the *raison d'être* test may require the consideration of the background to a sign's creation. To solve cases where a sign, such as Tony the Tiger, is not exclusively used as a trade symbol but, despite a predominant function in commerce and trade, also appears in cultural contexts, it is possible to apply an inverted version of the multifactor analysis which has been developed above with regard to the Mickey Mouse category (section 5.2.3):

- does the sign feature in a cultural production that has been made for marketing purposes, such as an advertising film or another activity that is part of an advertising campaign, such as a concert? (factor one);
- does an online search reveal that the sign, because of its use in commerce and trade, has already served as a basis for parodies, remixes or other forms of mash-up? (factor two);
- has the sign evolved from product marketing and advertising even though it displays typical style features of mainstream cultural creations which the trademark office has included in reference material for the identification of signs with cultural significance? (factor three);
- does the sign fall under one of the work categories listed in Article 2(1) BC? If so, does it stem from commercial and trade-related activities even though it reflects a high degree of free, creative choices and clearly meets copyright's originality test? (factor four);

564. Curtin 2018, 1027.
565. EFTA Court, 6 April 2017, case E-5/16, Municipality of Oslo ('Vigeland'), para. 97.
566. Cf. the background information on the sign's creation and later trademark controversies at https://en.m.wikipedia.org/wiki/Tony_the_Tiger.

– does the sign serve as an embellishment to improve the outward appearance of a product, or does it describe the contents of a product because it is a tool for the marketing of goods or services? (factor five).

If the answer to these questions is 'yes', then the sign under consideration belongs to the category of trade symbols. Hence, only the conclusions drawn in the subsequent analysis with regard to trade symbols are relevant to the sign. The use of Tony the Tiger, for instance, would have to be regulated in line with the following recommendations concerning trade symbols and not in accordance with the conclusions drawn with regard to the Mickey Mouse category of signs stemming from cultural mainstream productions.

5.3 CONCLUSION

To offer sufficient room for cultural follow-on innovation, it is important to include a wide range of literary and artistic works in efforts to shield remix activities in the cultural domain from the potential negative impact of trademark protection (section 4.1.4). Considering the aesthetic and sociological theories discussed in Chapter 3, the need for measures to prevent an impediment of cyclic cultural innovation arises in respect of works of fine art ranging from works in the public domain to modern creations that still enjoy copyright protection. Moreover, contemporary mainstream works, such as fictional characters, enter the picture because they may constitute important reference points for artists seeking to mirror current societal conditions. Hence, both Mickey Mouse and the Mona Lisa constitute artistic expressions that fall within the concept of 'cultural sign'. Both types of signs – genuine artworks and symbols of contemporary mainstream culture – should be part of initiatives to prevent trademark protection from interfering with cultural follow-on innovation. It is also advisable to include work titles in the concept of 'cultural sign'. Viewed in isolation, work titles will often fail to meet the originality test in copyright law. Strictly speaking, trademark protection of work titles is not a copyright/trademark issue. Nonetheless, the close connection with literary and artistic works justifies their inclusion in the concept of 'cultural sign'. It allows artists to clearly identify the source material which they employ for their contribution to cyclic cultural innovation.

With regard to literary and artistic works in the cultural heritage category, it is advisable to add a nuance in the light of the debate on traditional cultural expressions. Considering the interests of indigenous peoples, it seems safe to assume that legal mechanisms to prevent the acquisition of trademark rights may be welcome in many cases. The ultimate goal of these initiatives, however, is very specific. In the following analysis, the focus is on the prevention of trademark protection to allow unrestricted use of cultural resources for remix activities in the artistic domain. In the case of traditional cultural expressions, however, the prevention of trademark rights serves the purpose of safeguarding the interests of an indigenous community. Hence, the following recommendations can be deemed appropriate only insofar as they concern the development of legal instruments to ban trademark rights. The following recommendations may be less appropriate, however, when they seek to ensure unrestricted freedom of use in the context of cultural follow-on innovation. In the area of traditional cultural expressions, the specific customary rules of indigenous peoples may impact this freedom. Therefore, the recommendations evolving from the following analysis should not be applied to traditional cultural expressions without considering potential use restrictions that may arise from the customary law of indigenous peoples.

Finally, the discussion in this chapter has led to the insight that creations with a genuine commercial character – trademarks and other trade symbols – can play a central role in works of art. They may constitute important signifiers of a particular lifestyle or attitude. Iconic product design and trademarks provide reference points for a critique of societal conditions, such as consumerism and materialism. The contrast between artworks and commercial trade symbols may also serve as a means to comment on the societal role and function of art itself. Nonetheless, the appearance of trademarks and other trade symbols in works of art does not make them 'cultural signs'. The contrast arising from the use of an iconic trademark, such as Coca Cola, in an artistic context can only be produced as long as the sign constitutes a well-functioning trade symbol that is used in a commercial marketing context to evoke a certain lifestyle or attitude. Declaring the Coca Cola logo a cultural sign would thus miss the point. As an antipode of cultural signs, trademarks and other trade symbols must be kept separate in a distinct category of genuine commercial creations that have not evolved in the cultural domain. This qualification of trademarks and other trade symbols as a separate group of signs does not entail that the following analysis will not affect them. Even though they constitute commercial signs, it may be advisable to take measures to support their use in artworks seeking to comment on societal conditions.

In sum, the concept of 'cultural sign' must cover both signs derived from works of art and signs derived from cultural mainstream productions. The concept includes the titles of works in both categories. Insofar as measures to safeguard cyclic cultural innovation are compatible with the use protocols of indigenous peoples, the concept of 'cultural sign' also includes traditional cultural expressions. However, it does not encompass trademarks and other trade symbols, even if these commercial signs have acquired cultural significance as symbols of a particular lifestyle or attitude. To identify cultural signs in practice, trademark offices can use a multifactor test with the following factors:

- does the sign feature in a fine art creation or cultural mainstream production? Can it be found in an online library or collection of a cultural institution, ranging from museums to movie theatres? (factor one);
- does an online search reveal that the sign has already served as a basis for parodies, remixes or other forms of mash-up? (factor two);
- does the sign display typical style features known from other literary and artistic creations which the trademark office has included in reference material for the identification of signs with cultural significance? (factor three);
- does the sign fall under one of the work categories listed in Article 2(1) BC? Does it clearly meet copyright's originality test because of a high degree of free, creative choices? (factor four);
- could the sign theoretically serve as an embellishment to improve the outward appearance of a product, or would it describe the contents of goods or services when it was applied to goods or services in the cultural domain? Would consumers perceive the sign as a descriptive or decorative element in a hypothetical scenario where the sign features prominently on a product or where it is used in relation to goods or services in the cultural domain? (factor five).

In the assessment based on these factors, the status of 'cultural sign' must not exclusively depend on whether a given sign currently serves as a basis for remix activities in the cultural domain. If it does, this is a clear indication that it is relevant to cultural follow-on innovation. In addition, however, a prospective analysis is necessary that asks whether a sign can reasonably be expected to serve as source material for the creation of new literary and artistic works in the future. Hence, the assessment should not be confined to use necessities that have already materialized. Otherwise, measures seeking to minimize the corrosive effect of trademark protection on cultural remix would only focus on current building blocks of derivative works and lose sight of potential future sources of inspiration. These future sources, however, are particularly relevant. They may pave the way for new, underexplored artistic positions.

Chapter 6
Risk Assessment

The cyclic cultural imperative of intergenerational equity and public domain recognition differs fundamentally from the static trade imperative of market transparency (section 4.2.3). The mere fact that copyright and trademark protection are incompatible from this functional perspective, however, does not automatically allow the conclusion that, by definition, trademark rights to signs with cultural significance thwart the process of incessant renewal in the cultural domain. The nature and scope of trademark rights may differ from the exclusive rights granted in copyright law to such an extent that, in practice, the impact of trademark protection remains limited and concerns about an impediment of cyclic cultural innovation seem unfounded. Hence, the question arises whether trademark rights are so different in nature and scope that their corrosive effect on future creativity in the cultural domain appears negligible. Are trademark rights capable of impeding cultural follow-on innovation? Is it true that they may pose obstacles to the remix of protected signs in the cultural domain? Could they even serve as vehicles to artificially perpetuate the exclusive rights enjoyed under copyright law?

The discussion of these questions will show that at least in advanced trademark systems offering protection for brand development and brand-based communication, trademark rights can be qualified as exploitation instruments with a scope that comes close to the rights awarded in copyright law. Advanced trademark systems, such as trademark law in the EU, offer the trademark proprietor far-reaching control over the communication surrounding the protected sign (section 6.1). As general infringement requirements, such as use in the course of trade and use in relation to goods and services, no longer serve as reliable safeguards against infringement claims targeting use in the cultural domain, trademark protection against confusion and dilution may constrain the productive remix of protected signs in the context of cultural follow-on innovation. The fortification of defences against infringement claims is unlikely to eliminate the risks arising from trademark protection with these extravagant proportions (section 6.2). Therefore, the corrosive effect which trademark rights to signs with cultural significance may have on cultural follow-on innovation must not be underestimated (section 6.3).

6.1 NATURE OF TRADEMARK RIGHTS

In theory, there is a fundamental difference between the exclusive rights granted in copyright and trademark law. Copyright law serves the purpose of rewarding the creative work of the author and encouraging investment in information products (section 3.2). In consequence, copyright protects literary and artistic works *as such*. The author obtains exploitation rights and moral rights relating to the original literary and artistic expression embodied in the work. Trademark law, by contrast, aims at market transparency to ensure fair competition, consumer protection and the proper functioning of markets. Trademark rights concern the exclusive link which a trademark establishes between the trademark owner and the goods and services offered under the mark (section 4.2.1). Hence, trademark rights are not designed as exploitation rights. They have a rather defensive character. The trademark owner obtains a position that allows her to shield the trademark from encroachments upon the sign's proper functioning in trade. Whereas copyright law offers an exclusive position with regard to the exploitation of literary and artistic works, trademark law only grants an exclusive position with regard to *functions* which the mark fulfils in respect of goods and services.[567] In this vein, the German Federal Constitutional Court stated that, in contrast to copyright law which seeks to reserve the exploitation of literary and artistic works for the author:

> the protection of trademarks rests on a different consideration. In the framework of limiting boundless freedom of trade, the trademark is

567. For an overview of trademark functions, pointing out this traditional focus on identification and distinction functions and potential extensions with regard to communication, investment and advertising functions, see Keim 2009, 37-61.

intended to ensure transparency in respect of entrepreneurial achievements and unfold a mitigating effect on competition in this way.[568]

Given this different configuration, one might be tempted to assume that trademark rights are incapable of posing a serious obstacle to the remix and reuse of protected signs in the cultural domain. Whereas copyright protects the Mickey Mouse drawing as such, trademark rights only cover the functions which the drawing fulfils with regard to Disney as the commercial source of the goods and services offered under the Mickey Mouse trademark.[569] The cumulation of copyright and trademark protection may thus be deemed acceptable because trademark rights are not intended to protect a cultural creation as such, but only functions which the cultural creation fulfils as a distinctive sign in respect of goods and services to which it is attached.[570]

6.1.1 *Protection of Economic and Communication Value*

This line of argument, however, ignores the remarkable development of trademark rights in recent years. The EU trademark system can serve as an example. Gradually, trademark rights in the EU have been transformed into exploitation instruments that come close to the exploitation rights enjoyed by the copyright owner.[571] Taking traditional trademark theory as a starting point, the CJEU still refers to:

> the essential function of the trade mark, which is to guarantee the identity of the origin of the trade-marked product to the consumer or final user by enabling him to distinguish without any possibility of confusion between that product and products which have another origin.[572]

---

568. German Federal Constitutional Court, 22 May 1979, case 1 BvL 9/75, 'Schloßberg', BVerfGE 51, 193, *GRUR* 1979, 773 (778): 'Dagegen liegt dem Schutz des Warenzeichens eine andere Erwägung zugrunde. Im Rahmen der Begrenzung einer schrankenlosen Gewerbefreiheit soll das Warenzeichen der durchsichtigen Gestaltung der unternehmerischen Leistung dienen und damit im Wettbewerb eine ausgleichende Wirkung entfalten.'
569. Cf. Ohly 2019, 334; Mende/Isaac 2012, 138-144; Bercovitz 2001, 611-612.
570. Cf. Ohly 2019, 332; Ginsburg 2018b, 261-264; Stieper 2012, 1090-1091; Peukert 2012, 111-113; Mende/Isaac 2012, 144; McGuire 2011, 774; Derclaye/Leistner 2011, 314-315; Bercovitz 2001, 612.
571. Cf. Peukert 2016, 415-418; Gangjee 2013, 43-47; Senftleben 2013b, 146-156; Vanovermeire 2009, 187-188; Senftleben 2009a, 45; Moskin 2004, 842; Fezer 2003, 457; Pollaud-Dulian 2001, 43; Strasser 2000, 375; Hughes 1999, 1006; Brown 1999, 1619; Dreyfuss 1990, 397.
572. For an early use of this formula, see CJEU, 3 December 1981, case C-1/81, Pfizer/Eurim-Pharm, para. 8. As to the reappearance of the same formula in later judgments, see particularly CJEU, 12 November 2002, case C-206/01, Arsenal/Reed, para. 48. Cf. Simon Fhima 2005, 401.

This traditional protection against 'any possibility of confusion' gives trademark owners only limited control over communication concerning their marks – control that only covers the identification and distinction of the goods or services they offer in the marketplace. Protection against confusion can be understood to serve the rather defensive purpose of preventing competitors from use that would interfere with the basic communication of information about the commercial origin of goods and services offered by the trademark owner.[573] Accordingly, an impediment of cultural processes of creation seems unlikely as long as use of a trademarked cultural sign does not cause confusion about the commercial origin of goods and services involved.

However, this reassurance that the impact of trademark rights will remain limited to cases of origin confusion becomes more and more doubtful with every additional trademark function – and every additional basis for infringement claims – that is recognized in trademark law. The inclusion of additional trademark functions may follow from strategic use of basic protection against confusion. To allow trademarks to convey reliable information on the commercial origin of goods and services, it is indispensable to reserve use of the trademark exclusively for the trademark owner in all market segments where use of identical or similar signs could lead to confusion.[574] As a result, the trademark owner obtains an exclusive channel of communication in all areas of the market where she is active. In principle, only the enterprise holding trademark rights is entitled to convey information to consumers via the trademark in these protected areas.[575]

Investing in advertising, the trademark owner can use this exclusive communication channel to add messages that are unrelated to the underlying objective of ensuring accurate information about the commercial source of goods or services. In particular, an enterprise can launch advertising campaigns to educate consumers to associate a certain attitude or lifestyle

---

573. CJEU, 18 June 2009, case C-487/07, L'Oréal/Bellure, para. 59; CJEU, 11 November 1997, case C-251/95, Puma/Sabel, paras 16-26. For an alternative view, emphasizing the attention devoted to the trademark owner's interest in exploiting brand value in the context of protection against confusion, see Cohen Jehoram/Van Helden 2011, 111; Buydens 2011, 33; Quaedvlieg 2007, 275.

574. In the case of collective marks, this exclusive reservation of a sign concerns an association of enterprises which use the trademark in trade. The basic mechanism, however, remains unchanged. The information conveyed via the trademark, by contrast, will focus on certain product characteristics rather than one particular commercial origin. See Articles 74(1) and 83(1) EUTMR. Cf. CJEU, 8 June 2017, case C-689/15, Gözze Frottierweberei, para. 50.

575. As in other fields of intellectual property protection, it is indispensable to set certain limits to the exclusive rights of trademark owners. The principle of an exclusive communication channel, therefore, is limited in several respects. See the general limitations set forth in Article 6 TMD. With regard to comparative advertising, see CJEU, 12 June 2008, case C-533/06, O2/Hutchison, para. 45; CJEU, 18 June 2009, case C-487/07, L'Oréal/Bellure, para. 54.

with the trademark.[576] The moment a trademark 'speaks' to consumers about a particular image that can be associated with the trademarked product, consumers no longer simply purchase products from a particular commercial source. They also buy the respective 'trademark experience' and 'brand image'.[577]

Inevitably, the exclusive rights necessary to ensure protection against confusion, therefore, also protect the investment made in the creation of a favourable trademark image. Basic protection against confusion safeguards the exclusive link between an enterprise and its trademark. However, it also offers legal security for substantial investment in the evocation of brand-related associations in the minds of consumers. The WTO Panel dealing with EC protection for trademarks and geographical indications for agricultural products and foodstuffs described this protection reflex as follows:

> The function of trademarks can be understood by reference to Article 15.1 [TRIPS] as distinguishing goods and services of undertakings in the course of trade. Every trademark owner has a legitimate interest in preserving the distinctiveness, or capacity to distinguish, of its trademark so that it can perform that function. This includes its interest in using its own trademark in connection with the relevant goods and services of its own and authorized undertakings. Taking account of that legitimate interest will also take account of the trademark owner's interest in the economic value of its mark arising from the reputation that it enjoys and the quality that it denotes.[578]

In trademark law, the protection of the 'economic value' addressed by the WTO Panel – the brand image following from investment in complex advertising messages – need not remain a mere reflex of protection seeking to safeguard the essential function of indicating origin. By contrast, a trademark's economic and communication value may be elevated to an independent subject matter of protection. In *L'Oréal/Bellure*, the CJEU held that the circle of protected trademark functions was not limited to the basic function of indicating the commercial origin of goods or services. By contrast, these functions:

> include not only the essential function of the trade mark, which is to guarantee to consumers the origin of the goods or services, but also its other functions, in particular that of guaranteeing the quality of the

576. Cf. Assaf 2008, 13-14; Griffiths 2008, 255; Brown 1999, 1619-1620; Fezer 2003, 461-462; Casparie-Kerdel 2001, 185-186; Lehmann 1986, 14-17.
577. Peukert 2016, 412-414; Schroeder 2008, 161.
578. See WTO Panel, 15 March 2005, WTO Document WT/DS174/R, European Communities – Protection of Trademarks and Geographical Indications for Agricultural Products and Foodstuffs, para. 7.664, based on a complaint by the U.S. A second and almost identical report, WTO Document WT/DS290/R, deals with a parallel complaint by Australia. For a discussion of the reports, see Senftleben 2006, 407.

goods or services in question and those of communication, investment or advertising.[579]

Hence, the Court expressly recognized brand image protection as an independent objective of EU trademark law.[580] Communication, investment, and advertising functions are typically fulfilled by marks with a reputation – marks with a strong brand image capable of conveying lifestyle messages that are the result of substantial investment in advertising. Protection of a trademark's communication, investment, and advertising functions is thus protection of the investment in the creation of a favourable brand image and the brand communication based on this image. The extension of trademark protection to these functions transforms trademark rights into brand exploitation instruments.[581]

6.1.2 *Impact on Use for Cultural Purposes*

On its merits, however, the grant of brand image protection leads to protection of a trademark as an individual communication product.[582] The recognition of a trademark's economic and communication value in trademark law means that trademarks enjoy protection not only as identifiers of commercial source but also as communication tools. Communication, however, also lies at the core of cultural processes of reuse and remix. The extension of trademark protection to communication, investment and advertising functions is thus particularly worrisome when assessing potential risks for cultural follow-on innovation. Once the economic and communication value of a trademark is recognized as an independent subject matter of protection, it is no longer accurate to confine the analysis of a potential encroachment upon remix and reuse in the cultural domain to the question of a likelihood of confusion. In trademark systems, such as the EU system, that offer protection of a trademark's communication, investment and advertising functions, an unauthorized user of a protected sign cannot escape an

579. CJEU, 18 June 2009, case C-487/07, L'Oréal/Bellure, para. 58.

580. Kur/Senftleben 2017, para. 1.20-1.39. For a positive assessment of this development, see Sun 2014, 794-795; A. Griffiths 2013, 635-637; Machnicka 2012, 138-139. For critical comments, see Simon Fhima 2014, 161; Banerjee 2012, 555; Senftleben 2011, 383.

581. Cf. Peukert 2016, 421-422; Fezer 2001, 827, who expresses the view that the purpose underlying the protection of well-known marks is 'an intensive protection of commercial possibilities of exploiting the mark as an entrepreneurial achievement in the market'. Moskin 2004, 843-844, refers to 'the expansion of trademark rights from a tort-based theory preventing direct diversion of sales between competitors to a broader set of rights resting on a recognition that trademarks themselves possess economic value'.

582. Kur/Senftleben 2017, para. 1.29-1.39; Peukert 2016, 421-422; Ginsburg 2016, 75-77; Senftleben 2009a, 48-49; Bently 2008b, 15-41; Schroeder 2008, 161; Bone 2006, 549; Moskin 2004, 843-844; Dinwoodie 2002, 503-504; Fezer 2001, 827; Casparie-Kerdel 2001, 185-186; Lunney 1999, 437-439; Lemley 1999, 1694-1698; Brown 1999, 1619-1620; Dreyfuss 1990, 397-398; Lehmann 1986, 14-17.

infringement claim by simply arguing that her use in a cultural context would not mislead consumers into believing that there was a connection with the trademark owner. In addition, the trademark proprietor has the argument at her disposal that – even in the absence of origin confusion – the use amounts to infringement because it damages, or derives unfair benefits from, the economic and communication value of the trademark.[583] If a sign with cultural significance enjoys trademark protection that goes beyond the essential origin function and covers the mark's economic and communication value, an encroachment upon the incessant process of remix and reuse in the cultural domain cannot be ruled out. Even if use for cultural purposes is unlikely to cause confusion, the user may face an infringement claim based on a conflict with the investment and communication strategy of the trademark proprietor.

6.1.3 *Missing Rationale of Protection*

Before turning to the analysis of this enhanced scope of protection, it is important to make a comment on the recognition of communication, investment and advertising functions that has taken place in EU trademark law. To this day, the rationale underlying the extension of trademark protection to communication, investment and advertising functions is dubious. In particular, it is unclear why a trademark owner's marketing effort leading to a powerful brand image justifies an additional layer of protection that goes far beyond traditional trademark protection against confusion.[584] The problem with the protection of communication, investment and advertising functions is that the creation of a favourable brand image is a selfish endeavour of the trademark owner. In contrast to other intellectual property owners enjoying exploitation rights, such as inventors and authors, the brand owner cannot validly claim to have created intellectual property that furthers science or art. Brand protection is protection of investments that are made to improve an enterprise's market position. It is not evident that this investment also furthers the overall welfare of society to such an extent that it should be incentivized through the grant of broad trademark rights.[585]

Typical rationales underlying the grant of exploitation rights in intellectual property law, such as the incentive rationale and the reward rationale,

583. Cf. Jacques 2016, 473; McKenna 2009a, 883-884 and 895.
584. Cf. Kur/Senftleben 2017, para. 1.29-1.39.
585. Senftleben 2009a, 59-61. For a detailed analysis of potential justifications, see Sakulin 2010, 35-67, who also casts doubt upon the justificatory basis of protection against dilution. Proponents of brand image protection in the framework of trademark law particularly point to the effort and financial expenses made by the brand owner. For instance, Breitschaft 2009, 497 (499). Considering the costs for society involved in the grant of brand image protection – in particular restrictions of freedom of expression and freedom of competition – this fact alone, however, can hardly be deemed sufficient for the grant of broad exclusive rights.

are inapplicable in this context. It is not obvious that the prospect of acquiring brand exploitation rights is needed as an incentive to spur investment in brand creation. In fact, there is little evidence of any need for brand image creation in society that would justify the invocation of this rationale and an extra incentive for brand image creators.[586] It may even be argued that seductive lifestyle messages conveyed by a trademark distract from a product's genuine qualities, thereby rendering consumers' buying decisions less objective and depriving the trader with the objectively best offer of corresponding market success.[587] Potential economic arguments, such as the facilitation of competition in mature markets and the enhancement of product popularity, are outweighed by social and cultural concerns about the privatization of words and phrases.[588]

The reward argument hardly offers stronger support.[589] Admittedly, it is the trademark owner who spent time and money on the creation of a particular brand image. Feelings of rightness and justice, therefore, might suggest that the result of these efforts be due to her. Comparing brand image with other intellectual creations, however, it becomes doubtful whether the trademark owner deserves this reward. Whereas works and inventions contribute to mankind's treasury of cultural expression and technical knowledge once they become part of the public domain, a trademark carrying a particular brand image can be monopolized *ad infinitum* by the trademark owner by constantly renewing registration. As already pointed out, the investment in the creation of a brand image is an individual, selfish marketing decision for which the trademark owner cannot expect a reward from society as a whole.[590]

The insight that classical rationales of intellectual property protection are unavailable in the case of brand image protection adds an important nuance to the analysis of the impact of trademark rights on cultural follow-on innovation. As pointed out, the extension of trademark protection to a mark's economic and communication value is problematic. It offers trademark owners an alternative basis for infringement claims. Unauthorized use of a

586. See Scott/Oliver/Ley-Pineda 2008, 296-297, who consider product differentiation, facilitation of consumer choice and incentives to purchasing and, nevertheless, reject utilitarian arguments. Cf. Lemley 1999, 1694-1696; Brown 1999, 1622-1634.

587. See Brown 1999, 1635-1637, who points out that '[t]he classical economists who enthroned the consumer never dreamed that he would make his decisions under a bombardment of stupefying symbols'. However, see also the economic analysis conducted by van den Bergh/Lehmann 1992, 589-593.

588. See Strasser 2000, 389-390 and 412-414, on the one hand, and Lemley 1999, 1694-1698; Dreyfuss 1996, 128, on the other.

589. For an analysis of Lockean justification models, see Scott/Oliver/Ley-Pineda 2008, 297-305; Sakulin 2010, 63-66.

590. Cf. Beebe 2006, 1159, stating that a court 'should not grant antidilution protection to reward – i.e., to promote – spending on advertising, just as it should not grant such protection in recognition of something like the plaintiff's good faith in trying as hard as it can to make its mark famous'.

protected sign may be actionable even though it is unlikely to cause consumer confusion. As a result, trademark owners obtain substantially broader control over the communication surrounding a protected sign. A sound rationale for protecting communication, investment and advertising functions, however, is sought in vain. Weighing the individual interest in the protection of these trademark functions against the societal interest in the incessant renewal of the cultural landscape (section 3.3), the arguments in favour of brand image protection are thus weak. The arguments supporting measures to safeguard cultural follow-on innovation, by contrast, are strong. The interest in the protection of a mark's communication, investment and advertising functions does not carry much weight when compared with the societal interests underlying measures to keep the cultural innovation cycle intact.

6.2 SCOPE OF TRADEMARK RIGHTS

The analysis of the nature and expansion of trademark rights in the preceding section offers a reference point for a detailed analysis of the scope of trademark rights in cases involving cultural forms of use. The advanced system of trademark protection in the EU will serve as a basis for this analysis in the following sections. The recognition of a mark's communication, investment and advertising functions does not imply that an EU trademark owner can assert trademark rights against any unauthorized use in the cultural domain. A rights owner still must surmount several hurdles to obtain protection. Besides the obligation to satisfy the general protection requirements of use in the course of trade and use in relation to goods or services (section 6.2.1), the trademark proprietor must satisfy specific infringement requirements to successfully obtain protection against confusion (section 6.2.2) and invoke enhanced protection against dilution (section 6.2.3). Moreover, the rights of trademark owners are limited in several respects. The limitations of protection create breathing space for unauthorized use, including references to protected signs that are made for cultural purposes (section 6.2.4).

6.2.1 *General Infringement Criteria*

The exclusive rights granted in EU trademark law are confined to use 'in the course of trade'.[591] Therefore, use is only actionable where it occurs 'in the context of commercial activity with a view to economic advantage and not

591. Article 9(2) EUTMR and Article 10(2) TMD.

as a private matter'.[592] This formula developed by the CJEU leads to a distinction between private and commercial spheres. The condition of use in the course of trade draws an important boundary line between the private exclusive rights of the trademark proprietor on the one hand and the entitlement of the general public to freely use protected marks in non-commercial contexts on the other. It confines EU trademark rights to use that takes place in a commercial context. The use of a trademark for the purposes of private study, political debate, teaching or academic research is unlikely to constitute use in the course of trade as long as it does not have a commercial background. If use for cultural purposes, such as the creation of an artwork including elements enjoying trademark protection, does not enter the commercial sphere, an interference with cultural follow-on innovation is thus unlikely.[593]

Given the elasticity of the formula of use 'in the context of commercial activity with a view to economic advantage and not as a private matter',[594] however, the test of use in the course of trade constitutes a low threshold. Use of a trademark in a cultural context will be qualified as use in trade the moment it is combined with a commercial activity.[595] Case law concerning the marketing of T-shirts or postcards with critical statements on trademarked products or policies of the trademark proprietor can serve as examples.[596] The moment a cultural sign is placed in a commercial context, the assumption of use in the course of trade will be inescapable. Surveying similar developments in the U.S., Katya Assaf concludes that 'even types of speech traditionally considered non-commercial, such as magazines, books, movies and stand-up comedies, often become subject to scrutiny and restriction because of violation of trademark rights'.[597]

Cultural activities, however, require not only freedom to create new works on the basis of pre-existing material but also freedom to bring these new works to the attention of the public and create a market for them. In this vein, it is recognized in the context of the fundamental guarantee of freedom

---

592. CJEU, 23 March 2010, cases C-236/08 to 238/08, Google France and Google, para. 50; CJEU, 12 November 2002, case C-206/01, Arsenal/Reed, para. 40.
593. Żelechowski 2018, 118-119.
594. CJEU, C-236/08-238/08, Google France and Google, para. 50; CJEU, C-206/01, Arsenal v. Reed, para. 40.
595. For instance, see Higher Court of Appeals Dresden, 4 April 2000, case 14 U 3611/99, 'Johann Sebastian Bach', *NJW* 2001, 615 (616), where the Court could not rely on a strict application of the requirement of use in the course of trade because the allegedly infringing use concerned the production of porcelain showing a portrait of Johann Sebastian Bach. Cf. Żelechowski 2018, 119-120.
596. For instance, see German Federal Court of Justice, 3 February 2005, case I ZR 159/02, Lila Postkarte, *GRUR* 2005, 583; French Supreme Court, 8 April 2008, case 06-10961, Greenpeace/Esso; French Supreme Court, 8 April 2008, case 07-11251, Greenpeace/Areva. For commentary, see Kur/Senftleben 2017, para. 6.59-6.70; Jacques 2016, 471-472 and 479; Geiger 2007, 317.
597. Assaf 2008, 56.

of expression and freedom of art that sufficient room must be offered not only for art creation but also for art marketing. In Germany, for instance, it is established case law of the Federal Constitutional Court that the freedom of art:

> protects artistic activity itself (the 'work produced' ['Werkbereich']), but also the presentation and dissemination of the artwork, which are essential in order for the public to encounter the work (the 'effect produced' ['Wirkbereich'])[598] (original German words within brackets added).

Hence, it would be wrong to confine the debate on a potential impediment of cyclic cultural innovation to the creation of literary and artistic works. It is not sufficient that an artist enjoys the freedom of using trademarked material in her atelier or studio. By contrast, the guarantee of freedom of expression and freedom of art requires that the artist also be free to sell and promote the artwork.[599] This, in turn, implies that the boundary line between non-actionable private use and actionable use in the course of trade is not sufficient to dispel concerns about an encroachment upon cultural follow-on innovation. The basic infringement criterion of 'use in the course of trade' does not constitute a safeguard that is strong enough to declare trademark rights to cultural signs unproblematic.

In addition to the general infringement requirement of 'use in the course of trade', EU trademark law also requires use 'in relation to goods or services'.[600] In principle, this further prerequisite for protection could be understood to require 'use as a trademark'. It may be applied to confine the scope of trademark rights to instances where another's trademark is employed as an identifier of commercial source with regard to one's own goods or services.[601] Following this approach, access to trademark protection could be contained from the outset.[602] The gatekeeper requirement of 'use in relation to goods or services' – understood in the sense of 'use as a trademark' – would serve as a filter to exclude claims that are unrelated to the identification and distinction of goods and services.

598. German Federal Constitutional Court, 31 May 2016, case 1 BvR 1585/13, 'Sampling', para. 68. English translation available at: https://www.bundesverfassungsgericht.de/e/rs20160531_1bvr158513en.html. The same point is made in German Federal Constitutional Court, 13 June 2007, case 1 BvR 1783/05, 'Roman Esra', BVerfGE 119, 1 (21-22); German Federal Constitutional Court, 17 July 1984, case 1 BvR 816/82, 'Anachronistischer Zug', BVerfGE 67, 213 (224); German Federal Court of Justice, 21 February 2019, case I ZR 98/17, 'HHole (for Mannheim)', *GRUR* 2019, 609, para. 35.
599. Cf. Peukert 2016, 424-425. Even though aiming at a more positive assessment of the general infringement criteria in EU trademark law, Bohaczewski 2020, 861, must concede that art promotion may qualify as use in the course of trade.
600. Article 9(2) EUTMR and Article 10(2) TMD.
601. CJEU, 25 January 2007, case C-48/05, Opel/Autec, para. 24, pointed in this direction. The course adopted in this judgment, however, was not followed in further decisions.
602. Dinwoodie/Janis 2007a, 1599-1600; Dogan/Lemley 2004, 809-811.

When seeking to prevent trademark rights to cultural signs from posing an obstacle to remix activities in the cultural domain, this approach to the requirement of 'use in relation to goods or services' can play a crucial role (section 9.2.1). In a cultural context, the use of a sign takes place for the purpose of expressing thoughts and ideas. Normally, the public will not perceive individual artistic expression as an indication of commercial source aiming at the identification and distinction of goods and services. As the decision of the Higher Court of Appeals of Dresden in *Johann Sebastian Bach* shows, this line of reasoning – based on a strict requirement of 'use as a trademark' – allows courts to create considerable breathing space for the use of trademarked signs in a cultural context.

The case concerned the registration of the name and portrait of Johann Sebastian Bach as a trademark for various goods and services, including glassware, porcelain and crockery.[603] While the trademark proprietor had not commenced using the sign himself, he systematically asserted his trademark rights against users referring to Johann Sebastian Bach.[604] As the trademark registration had only been obtained in 1999, it seems to have been the trademark owner's intention to exploit Bach's name and portrait during the anniversary year 2000 (Bach died on 28 July 1750). In addition to the Johann Sebastian Bach registration, the trademark proprietor had also registered signs relating to Michelangelo, Leonardo da Vinci, Paul Gauguin and Paul Cézanne.[605] Given this portfolio of cultural signs, there were clear indications of an exploitation strategy based on 'cultural heritage grabbing'.

The case decided by the Higher Court of Appeals of Dresden, however, was not brought by the owner of the Johann Sebastian Bach trademarks. Instead, the Meissen porcelain manufactory sought a declaration that the trademark proprietor was not entitled to prevent it from using Bach's name and portrait as decorative elements on glassware, porcelain and crockery. Having received a cease-and-desist letter, the Meissen factory wanted clarity about the scope of the trademark rights that had been asserted against product lines referring to the famous composer. Considering the facts of the case, the Court saw clear indications that the signs concerning Johann Sebastian Bach had been registered for the sole purpose of using the legal position following from the grant of trademark rights to prevent others from use and forcing them to enter into licensing agreements – without any true intention of the trademark owner to use the signs as source identifiers himself.[606] Nonetheless, the Court felt that there was no room for assuming an abuse of rights. Regardless of clear indications that the Bach trademarks were owned by a

603. Higher Court of Appeals of Dresden, 4 April 2000, case 14 U 3611/99, 'Johann Sebastian Bach', *NJW* 2001, 615 (616).
604. Götting 2001, 615, refers to parallel cases where the plaintiff sought to prohibit the sale of a Johann Sebastian Bach anniversary champagne and Johann Sebastian Bach souvenir articles.
605. Götting 2001, 615.
606. Higher Court of Appeals of Dresden, *ibid.*, 617.

trademark 'troll', the fact remained that the German Patent and Trademark Office had registered the name and portrait of the composer and had granted trademark rights. As the registration had occurred in 1999 and the case was decided in 2000, an obligation to put the trademarks to genuine use had not arisen yet. Instead, the trademark proprietor could rely on the possibility of acquiring trademark rights in the EU on the basis of mere registration – with the requirement of genuine use becoming an issue only five years after completion of the registration procedure.[607] The fact that the trademark owner had not developed plans for the use of the Bach signs to create or preserve an 'outlet for the goods or services'[608] was thus insufficient to justify the verdict of abuse of rights. Instead, the Higher Court of Appeals of Dresden was bound by the registration decision taken by the German Patent and Trademark Office.[609]

Against this background, a solution of the case had to be based on the applicable infringement criteria. As already indicated, the general requirement of 'use in relation to goods or services' – understood in the sense of 'use as a trademark' – played a decisive role in this context. The Court held that, insofar as the Meissen porcelain manufactory dealt with the composer Johann Sebastian Bach in an artistic manner, the basic requirement of use as a trademark was not fulfilled and the use did not amount to infringement.[610] The Court based this conclusion on the assumption that use as a trademark required the attachment of Bach's name or portrait to goods for the purpose of distinguishing them from others with a different commercial origin. In the case of an artistic discussion of historical events or historical persons, however, the name or portrait would not be used – in the Court's view – to identify the commercial source of goods. Hence, the use would not serve the purpose of distinguishing them from other goods with a different origin and would not amount to actionable use as a trademark. By contrast, a risk of confusion could be ruled out. In an artistic context, the consuming public would not perceive the Bach name and portrait as trademarks used to distinguish goods or services.[611]

The Higher Court of Appeals of Dresden thus created room for the artistic use of trademarked cultural signs by relying on the traditional requirement of use as a trademark and interpreting this requirement strictly – in the sense of a requirement of use for the purpose of indicating the commercial origin of goods. The Court did not address other trademark functions which the CJEU recognized later.[612] As the decision in *Johann Sebastian Bach* dates back to the year 2000, it is not surprising that the

607. Article 15(1) EUTMR and Article 16(1) TMD.
608. CJEU, 11 March 2003, case C-40/01, Ansul v. Ajax, para. 37.
609. Higher Court of Appeals of Dresden, *ibid.*, 617-618.
610. Higher Court of Appeals of Dresden, *ibid.*, 616.
611. Higher Court of Appeals of Dresden, *ibid.*, 616.
612. CJEU, 18 June 2009, case C-487/07, L'Oréal/Bellure, para. 58.

Dresden Court did not include communication, investment and advertising functions in its assessment of 'use as a trademark'. Instead, the Court added normative considerations. It stated that trademark law should not be employed in an inconsistent manner to prevent an artistic discussion of the person of Johann Sebastian Bach who had become part of the universal cultural heritage because of his musical works. Moreover, the protection of trademarks should not lead to a 're-monopolization' of public domain works, such as the Bach portrait painted by Elias Gottlob Haussmann.[613]

However, the resoluteness of the Higher Court of Appeals of Dresden in *Johann Sebastian Bach* must not conceal that the traditional, strict interpretation of the requirement of use as a trademark – in the sense of use for the purpose of distinguishing goods of the alleged infringer from others with a different commercial origin – has not been confirmed in subsequent CJEU jurisprudence. Therefore, it would be wrong to conclude on the basis of the *Johann Sebastian Bach* decision that the basic infringement criterion of 'use as a trademark' eliminates the risk of an impediment of cultural follow-on innovation because use in an artistic context will hardly ever be qualified as actionable trademark use.

At the time of the *Johann Sebastian Bach* decision, the status and scope of the requirement of use as a trademark was unclear at EU level. With the adoption of the first Trade Mark Directive 89/104/EEC and the Community Trade Mark Regulation 40/94, EU trademark law had been harmonized. However, the CJEU had not been given the opportunity to draw the conceptual contours of 'use as a trademark' prior to the *Johann Sebastian Bach* judgment. Discussing this vacuum, the Higher Court of Appeals of Dresden mentioned that it was not entirely clear whether the traditional, strict understanding of use as a trademark in Germany (in the sense of use to distinguish goods and services of the alleged infringer) had to be abandoned under the harmonized rules of EU trademark law. Nonetheless, the Court was confident that, in principle, the traditional requirement of use as a trademark, as interpreted and applied in *Johann Sebastian Bach*, had survived the harmonization of trademark law.[614]

This assumption, however, was premature. EU trademark law does not explicitly state that for an infringement claim to be successful, the allegedly infringing use must constitute use for the purpose of distinguishing the alleged infringer's own goods. The CJEU could have deduced this strict trademark use requirement from the statutory criterion of 'use in relation to goods or services' laid down in Article 9(2) EUTMR and Article 10(2) TMD.[615] Arguably, the statutory criterion of use in relation to goods or services can be understood to require use of a conflicting sign for the purpose

613. Higher Court of Appeals of Dresden, *ibid.*, 616.

614. Higher Court of Appeals of Dresden, *ibid.*, 616.

615. The gatekeeper requirement of 'use in relation to goods and services' has remained unchanged since the adoption of the first harmonized trademark legislation in the EU.

of identifying and distinguishing the goods and services of the alleged infringer. Following this approach, the CJEU could have established a strict trademark use requirement which, as demonstrated in *Johann Sebastian Bach*, could have served as a safeguard against the assertion of trademark rights against use in an artistic context. At the same time, the development of a strict trademark use requirement would have led to a boundary line between trademark actions falling under harmonized trademark law and additional protection against 'use of a sign other than use for the purposes of distinguishing goods or services' which EU law leaves to the discretion of EU Member States in accordance with Article 10(6) TMD.[616]

Instead of drawing these boundary lines, however, the CJEU opted for a much more flexible application of the gatekeeper criterion of 'use in relation to goods or services'.[617] The Court refrained from sharpening the conceptual contours of 'use in relation to goods or services' in the described way. It did not establish a strict requirement of 'use as a trademark'. Instead, the CJEU constantly weakened this general protection requirement. Prior to the German *Johann Sebastian Bach* decision, the CJEU had already found in *BMW/Deenik* that use for the purpose of informing the public about repair and maintenance services offered with regard to trademarked products satisfied the criterion of 'use in relation to goods or services' – even though Deenik had not used the trademark BMW to pass off his second hand cars and repair services as offers stemming from BMW. Deenik had merely referred to BMW as the owner of the car brand that was central to his own activities.[618]

The CJEU also qualified use in comparative advertising as use in relation to goods or services on the ground that the advertiser made use of a competitor's trademark to distinguish her own products from those of the competitor.[619] Summarizing the notion of 'use in relation to goods or services', the Court held that for satisfying this precondition for an infringement action, it was sufficient that a link was established with goods

---

Cf. Article 9 CTMR 2009 and Article 5 TMD 2008 for the infringement provisions that existed prior to the trademark law reform that led to the current provisions.

616. Article 10(6) TMD. As to this boundary line between harmonized trademark law and room for national approaches, see CJEU, 21 November 2002, case C-23/01, Robelco, paras 30-31 and 34; CJEU, 16 November 2004, case C-245/02, Anheuser-Busch, para. 62 and 64. Cf. Kur/Senftleben 2017, para. 5.361-5.379; Henning-Bodewig 2008, 306-309.

617. Cf. Ohly 2019, 335. For an overview of developments in this area, see Kur 2008, 11.

618. See CJEU, 23 February 1999, case C-63/97, BMW/Deenik, para. 42. For an overview of the development of the trademark use requirement in CJEU jurisprudence, see Kur 2008, 1.

619. See CJEU, 12 June 2008, case C-533/06, O2/Hutchison, paras 35-36. As to keyword advertising on the basis of services offered by a search engine, use of a competitor's trademark as a keyword for a sponsored link with one's own advertising has been found to constitute trademark use on similar grounds. See CJEU, 23 March 2010, cases C-236/08-238/08, Google/Louis Vuitton et al., para. 71.

or services. This formula can be found in the *Céline* decision where the Court held with regard to the interface between trademark and trade name rights that once a link was established between the company, trade or shop name and the goods or services offered by the alleged infringer, trademark use in relation to goods or services could no longer be denied – even where the name was not affixed to marketed goods as such.[620] The formula of a link with goods or services, then, became established case law in later decisions dealing with keyword advertising. In *Google France and Google*, the CJEU confirmed that relevant use in relation to goods or services existed 'in any event' where a third party used a conflicting sign in such a way that a link was established between that sign and the goods or services offered by the third party.[621] In *L'Oréal/eBay*, the Court found that the criterion of a link was satisfied because eBay's advertisements created 'an obvious association between the trade-marked goods which are mentioned in the advertisements and the possibility of buying those goods through eBay'.[622] Besides the extension of the trademark use concept to referential use designating the goods or services of the trademark owner, the CJEU thus also adopted a low threshold requirement with regard to the connection with goods or service as such: a mere 'link' or 'association' is sufficient.[623]

As a result, the gatekeeper criterion of 'use in relation to goods or services' does not prevent a trademark claim against references to the trademark that are only made to identify goods or services as those of the trademark owner and are not perceived by the public as indications of commercial source. The strict test of trademark use which the Higher Court of Appeals of Dresden applied in *Johann Sebastian Bach* has not been confirmed at EU level. By contrast, the CJEU brought several forms of referential use – references to the trademark as being the distinctive sign of the trademark owner – within the scope of EU trademark rights.[624] In contrast to the approach taken in *Johann Sebastian Bach*, this elastic interpretation of the trademark use requirement at EU level can have a deep impact on use in a cultural context. If a mere link with goods or services is sufficient to bring unauthorized use within the scope of trademark rights, a clear boundary line between non-actionable use for cultural purposes and

620. CJEU, 11 September 2007, case C-17/06, Céline, para. 23.
621. CJEU, 23 March 2010, C-236/08-238/08, Google France and Google, para. 72; CJEU, 12 July 2011, case C-324/09, L'Oréal/eBay, para. 92; CJEU, 19 February 2009, C-62/08, UDV North America, paras 47-48.
622. CJEU, 12 July 2011, case C-324/09, L'Oréal/eBay, para. 93.
623. As to the debate on this development, see the summary in Knaak/Kur/von Mühlendahl 2011, para. 2.178. Against the background of French case law, Bohaczewski 2020, 864-867, tries to correct the systematic weakening and erosion of the trademark use requirement that occurred at EU level. As long as the CJEU does not change its course, however, this attempt will not have the desired results in practice and French courts will have to bring their jurisprudence in line with the approach taken by the CJEU. For a more detailed discussion, see section 9.2.1.
624. Cf. Ohly 2019, 335; Kur/Senftleben 2017, para. 5.50-5.54.

actionable use as a trademark is missing. This development can be placed in the context of the extension of EU trademark protection to a mark's economic and communication value.[625] As discussed in section 6.1.1, the CJEU explicitly recognized a trademark's communication, investment and advertising functions in *L'Oréal/Bellure*.[626] Once trademark law is employed as a vehicle to protect not only the traditional origin function but also these accessory functions, the broadening of the concept of use in relation to goods or services is almost inevitable. A mark's economic and communication value may be damaged in contexts not involving confusion about commercial source. A biting Mickey Mouse parody, for example, is unlikely to mislead the public into believing that it stems from Disney. Nonetheless, it may have a negative effect on the perception of the Mickey Mouse trademark and its brand value. Hence, the Court's elastic interpretation of the threshold requirement of use in relation to goods or services can be regarded as a corollary of the broad function theory recognizing communication, investment and advertising functions in addition to the traditional origin function.

In practice, the evolution of this elastic concept of use in relation to goods or services brings about a remarkable change of the climate surrounding the use of protected signs in a cultural context. In the absence of a strict requirement of use as a trademark – understood in the sense of use for the purpose of identifying and distinguishing the goods or services of the alleged infringer – the threshold criterion of use in relation to goods or services loses its gatekeeper function.[627] With jurisprudence encouraging the inclusion of mere references to protected signs, the CJEU has opened the doors to trademark protection wide. A trademark claim can no longer be excluded from the outset if reference is made to protected signs in an artistic context. The mere use of a trademark in some relation to goods or services can serve as a starting point for an infringement claim.[628] As already pointed out, however, the freedom of art – as part of freedom of expression – does concern not only the creation of literary and artistic works as such but also the marketing and dissemination of resulting cultural productions.[629] The

625. Cf. Gangjee 2013, 47-51.

626. CJEU, 18 June 2009, case C-487/07, L'Oréal/Bellure, para. 58.

627. Kur/Senftleben 2017, para. 5.14-5.15 and 5.49-5.56. As to the discussion on the cultivation of the requirement of 'use as a mark', see Peukert 2012, 96-107; Senftleben 2011a, 39; Yap 2009, 86-87; Kur 2008, 11; Dogan/Lemley 2008a, 542; Dinwoodie/Janis 2007a, 1657-1658; Davison/Di Giantomasso 2009, 443; McKenna 2009, 773; Simon Fhima 2005, 401; Loughlan 2000, 328. As to the potential of this approach in the context of cultural signs, see Ohly 2019, 334.

628. Cf. Derclaye/Leistner 2011, 328; Simon Fhima 2006, 321. The risk of creating an automatism of property claims ('Eigentumslogik') is also recognized by proponents of an elastic notion of trademark use. See Kur 2008, 12. For similar concerns expressed against the background of developments in the U.S., see Dogan/Lemley 2008b, 1345.

629. German Federal Constitutional Court, 31 May 2016, case 1 BvR 1585/13, 'Sampling', para. 68; German Federal Constitutional Court, 13 June 2007, case 1 BvR 1783/05, 'Roman Esra', BVerfGE 119, 1 (21-22); German Federal Constitutional Court, 17 July

advertising and dissemination of works requires commercial activities which, inevitably, establish a link with goods or services in the sense of CJEU jurisprudence.

The case *Lila Postkarte* of the German Federal Court of Justice illustrates the potential corrosive effect of the relaxation of the requirement of use in relation to goods or services on artistic creativity. The case concerned the marketing of postcards that alluded ironically to trademarks and advertising campaigns of the chocolate producer Milka. On purple background corresponding to Milka's abstract colour mark, the postcard sought to ridicule the nature idyll with cows and mountains that is evoked in Milka advertising. It showed the following poem attributed to 'Rainer Maria Milka':

> Über allen Wipfeln ist Ruh,
> irgendwo blökt eine Kuh.
> Muh![630]

Under a strict test of trademark use – requiring use to identify and distinguish the goods or services of the alleged infringer – this ironic play with Milka insignia could have escaped more thorough scrutiny in the light of trademark rights because consumers are unlikely to perceive the use of Milka trademarks as an indication that Milka is the commercial source of the postcards. The German Federal Court of Justice, however, was bound to apply the broad notion of trademark use following from the jurisprudence of the CJEU.[631] Accordingly, the fact that the postcard producer referred to Milka trademarks was sufficient to meet the threshold requirement of use as a trademark. The Court held that for trademark use in the sense of Article 10(2)(c) TMD, it was sufficient that the postcard called to mind the well-known Milka signs.[632] Even though being decorative, the use in question therefore gave rise to the question of trademark infringement. Accordingly, the German Federal Court of Justice embarked on a scrutiny of the trademark parody in the light of the infringement criteria of detriment to distinctive character or repute, and the taking of unfair advantage. Weighing Milka's concerns about a disparagement of the trademarks against the fundamental guarantee of the freedom of art, the Court finally concluded that

---

1984, case 1 BvR 816/82, 'Anachronistischer Zug', BVerfGE 67, 213 (224); German Federal Court of Justice, 21 February 2019, case I ZR 98/17, 'HHole (for Mannheim)', *GRUR* 2019, 609, para. 35.

630. 'It is calm above the tree tops, somewhere a cow is bellowing. Moo!' The attribution to 'Rainer Maria Rilke' is an allusion to the famous German writer Rainer Maria Rilke. See German Federal Court of Justice, 3 February 2005, case I ZR 159/02, Lila Postkarte, *GRUR* 2005, 583. Cf. Born 2006, 192.

631. See the reference to CJEU, 23 October 2003, case C-408/01, Adidas/Fitnessworld, para. 39, in the decision 'Lila Postkarte' of the German Federal Court of Justice, *ibid.*, 584. With regard to the qualification of decorative use as relevant trademark use, see also Kur 2008, 5-6.

632. German Federal Court of Justice, *ibid.*, 584.

the freedom of art had to prevail in the light of the ironic statement made with the postcard.[633] The use of Milka trademarks was found to have taken place with 'due cause' in the sense of Article 10(2)(c) TMD.[634]

Even though constituting use in an artistic context, the elastic concept of use as a trademark in CJEU jurisprudence thus prevented a judgment putting an end to the infringement action at an early stage by holding that the use did not constitute actionable trademark use in the first place. Instead, the parodist had to invoke the defence of due cause and argue the case in several instances until the German Federal Court of Justice took a final decision. Hence, use in a cultural context is not immune to the assertion of trademark rights under the CJEU's flexible approach to the requirement of use in relation to goods or services. In *Johann Sebastian Bach*, the Higher Court of Appeals of Dresden denied relevant use as a trademark because Bach's name and portrait had not been attached to Meissen porcelain to distinguish Meissen products from others with a different commercial origin.[635] In *Lila Postkarte*, the Milka trademarks had not been used as identifiers of commercial source either. Nonetheless, the ironic reference to Milka insignia was a sufficient basis for an infringement claim in line with the jurisprudence of the CJEU. The postcard artist, thus, faced a valid claim of prima facie infringement and had to invoke the defence of due cause to rebut Milka's infringement arguments.

In sum, the CJEU has deprived EU trademark law of a meaningful gatekeeper criterion. The statutory requirement of use in relation to goods or services could have served as a filter to exclude, from the outset, all instances where the trademark is not used in the traditional manner, i.e., to indicate the commercial source of the user's own goods or services.[636] The CJEU, however, did not establish this strict criterion of use as a trademark. As a result, an effective filter that is capable of excluding trademark claims from the outset is missing. In line with CJEU jurisprudence, a mere reference to the trademark[637] and a mere link with goods or services may be sufficient to trigger an infringement action. In the light of the elastic standard developed by the CJEU, even decorative use of a trademark may amount to actionable

633. German Federal Court of Justice, *ibid.*, 584-585. For a further case in which freedom of speech prevailed over trademark protection, see German Federal Court of Justice, 11 March 2008, case VI ZR 7/07, 'Gen-Milch', *NJW* 2008, 2110.
634. German Federal Court of Justice, 3 February 2005, case I ZR 159/02, *GRUR* 2005, 583 (585).
635. Higher Court of Appeals of Dresden, 4 April 2000, case 14 U 3611/99, 'Johann Sebastian Bach', *NJW* 2001, 615 (616).
636. This stricter test, however, was mentioned with regard to the traditional identification function of trademarks in CJEU, 25 January 2007, case C-48/05, Adam Opel/Autec, para. 24.
637. CJEU, 23 October 2003, case C-408/01, Adidas/Fitnessworld, para. 39; CJEU, 10 April 2008, case C-102/07, Adidas/Marca, para. 41.

trademark use.[638] Not only references in comparative and keyword advertising but also references for artistic purposes, such as the use of a trademark in a parody, may thus fall within the scope of the exclusive rights awarded in EU trademark law. In the absence of a strict test requiring use to distinguish the goods or services of the alleged infringer, the requirement of use in relation to goods or services does not offer relief when it comes to cases involving use in a cultural context. The outright rejection of trademark claims on the ground that the alleged infringer does not make use for the purpose of distinguishing goods or services is unavailable. In *Johann Sebastian Bach*, this strict test served as a vehicle to create room for artistic use. As the CJEU did not develop a comparable filtering mechanism, this preclusion of trademark actions is beyond reach in current EU trademark law. Instead, breathing space for use in a cultural context can only be derived from more specific infringement criteria that must be satisfied to obtain protection against confusion (section 6.2.2) or dilution (section 6.2.3).

6.2.2 *Protection Against Confusion*

Trademark protection against confusion concerns the risk that the public might be misled into believing that goods or services bearing a sign identical with, or similar to, the trademark come from the trademark proprietor or an economically linked undertaking.[639] Accordingly, the function of indicating the commercial origin of goods or services occupies centre stage. As the CJEU explained in *O2/Hutchison*, a finding of infringement requires use liable to affect the 'essential function of the trade mark, which is to guarantee to consumers the origin of the goods or services … '.[640] In *L'Oréal/Bellure*, the Court explained that in case of similarity between the mark and the sign, and between the goods or services, the likelihood of confusion constituted 'the specific condition for such protection'.[641] Given this focus on the origin function and the risk of confusion, it seems plausible to argue that the corrosive effect on cultural follow-on innovation is likely to remain limited.

---

638. See CJEU, 23 October 2003, case C-408/01, Adidas/Fitnessworld, paras 39-41, where the Court established an ambiguous test by holding that 'the fact that a sign is viewed as an embellishment by the relevant section of the public is not, in itself, an obstacle to the protection conferred by Article 5(2) of the Directive where the degree of similarity is none the less such that the relevant section of the public establishes a link between the sign and the mark'. For a national precursor of this development, see Court of Appeals of Amsterdam, 26 juli 2001, ERB/Beukenoord, *AMI* 2002, 12, para. 2.16-2.18. Cf. Visser 2002, 15-16.
639. As to international protection standards in the area of protection against confusion, see Article 16(1) TRIPS. With regard to EU trademark law, see CJEU, 22 June 1999, case C-342/97, Lloyd Schuhfabrik Meyer ('Lloyd/Loint's'), para. 17. For a comparative analysis of EU and U.S. law, see McCarthy 2004, 1163.
640. CJEU, 12 June 2008, case C-533/06, O2/Hutchison, para. 57.
641. CJEU, 18 June 2009, case C-487/07, L'Oréal/Bellure, para. 59.

Instead of protecting a cultural creation as such, trademark protection against confusion only concerns a specific function – the function of indicating commercial origin – which a cultural creation may fulfil with regard to goods or services stemming from the trademark proprietor.[642] As the infringement claim only concerns the specific mode of using cultural material as a badge of origin, use of the cultural expression in an artistic context seems to remain unaffected from the outset.

In addition, a sign's cultural significance can tip the scales against a finding of a likelihood of confusion. This became apparent in *Picasso/Picaro* where the CJEU had to decide on an opposition against Daimler's application for registration of the sign PICARO for vehicles. The opposition had been lodged by the Picasso estate arguing that PICARO was likely to cause confusion with the earlier word mark PICASSO which it had registered for various goods, including vehicles.[643] Discussing the criteria for a finding of a likelihood of confusion in this context, the CJEU confirmed the first instance decision that in this particular case conceptual differences between the PICASSO mark and the PICARO sign counteracted the low degree of visual and phonetic similarity.[644] Conceptual differences could have this mitigating effect in cases where the meaning of at least one of the two signs was 'clear and specific' so that the relevant public could grasp it immediately.[645] As to the meaning of the PICASSO mark, the CJEU recalled the factual assessment of the first instance court which had found that:

> confronted with the word sign PICASSO, the relevant public inevitably sees in it a reference to the painter and that, given the painter's renown with that public, that particularly rich conceptual reference is such as greatly to reduce the resonance with which, in this case, the sign is endowed as a mark, among others, of motor vehicles.[646]

Hence, the fact that the name 'Picasso' is well known as a reference to the famous painter does not imply that the trademark PICASSO is highly distinctive and enjoys broad protection against confusion.[647] The painter's fame cannot simply be transferred to the trademark as an identifier of commercial source. By contrast, the well-known cultural meaning of the sign reduces the risk of confusion because its immediate impact on the perception

642. For instance, see Court of Appeals of Amsterdam, 30 januari 2003, Van Toor/Phanta Vision, *AMI* 2003, 94, para. 4.19, where the Court denies relevant use as a badge of origin and sees no starting point for assuming a likelihood of confusion. The sign at issue ('Bassie III') was deemed insufficiently similar to the registered marks BASSIE & ADRIAAN and CLOWN BASSIE.
643. CJEU, 12 January 2006, case C-361/04P, 'Picasso/Picaro', paras 5-6.
644. CJEU, *ibid.*, para. 20.
645. CJEU, *ibid.*, para. 20.
646. CJEU, *ibid.*, para. 27.
647. As to the rejection of this counterargument advanced by the Picasso estate, see CJEU, *ibid.*, paras 11 and 32.

of the public may outweigh visual and/or aural similarities. A sign with a strong cultural connotation may thus constitute a weak trademark.[648] In such a case, the scope of trademark protection will remain limited until use of the sign as a trademark also becomes known to such an extent that the commercial function of indicating the origin of goods and services becomes strong enough to play an independent role besides the sign's original cultural meaning.[649]

Apart from the assumption of limitations due to the 'clear and specific' meaning of signs with strong cultural connotations, courts have also resisted attempts to broaden the concept of confusion about the 'origin' of goods or services in the case of cultural productions. In *Danjaq/OHIM (Mission Productions)*, the GCEU drew a clear distinction between indications of artistic origin on the one hand and indications of the commercial origin of goods and services on the other. The decision concerned an opposition brought by Danjaq against Mission Production's attempt to register the sign 'Dr. No' – the title of the first James Bond film and the name of James Bond's antagonist – as a trademark. Focusing on the essential origin function as a prerequisite for the acquisition of trademark rights, the Court stated that 'only signs which develop characteristic trade mark functions'[650] were eligible for trademark protection. Hence, protection of the signs 'Dr. No' and 'Dr. NO' as indicators of commercial source was only available if the signs developed such characteristic functions.[651] As Danjaq had failed to provide sufficient evidence in this regard, the Court concluded that 'Dr. No' and 'Dr. NO' did not indicate the commercial origin of films. Instead, they were identifiers of artistic origin distinguishing the 'Dr. No' film from other films in the James Bond series. The Court added that the capability of serving as a distinctive sign could not be inferred from the profits made with the film and its commercial success in the EU.[652] As the Picasso estate in *Picasso/Picaro*, Danjaq could not convince the Court that recognition as a literary and artistic work implied recognition as an identifier of commercial source.

The decision of the U.S. Supreme Court in *Dastar/Twentieth Century Fox* is a further example illustrating this point. The case concerned a TV series based on General Eisenhower's World War II book 'Crusade in Europe'. Although Fox had obtained the copyright to the series' first broadcast in 1949, it did not renew copyright in 1977 when the initial term of protection expired. In consequence, the original 1949 version entered the public domain. In 1988, Fox reacquired the television rights for the Crusade

648. Dusollier 2015, 161; Ohly 2008, 207-208.
649. See the examples given in section 8.2.1.
650. GCEU, 30 June 2009, case T-435/05, Danjaq/OHIM (Mission Productions), para. 26.
651. GCEU, *ibid.*, para. 26.
652. GCEU, *ibid.*, para. 25.

book.[653] When Dastar released a video set called 'World War II Campaigns in Europe' in 1995, Fox brought an action based on § 43(a)(1)(A) of the Lanham Act – the unfair competition provision in the U.S. trademark statute, which by its terms offers protection against false representations of origin likely to cause confusion.[654] Fox argued that Dastar's 1995 version caused actionable confusion because Dastar had failed to give proper credit to the original Crusade TV series even though its 1995 video set was a shortened and edited version of the original 1949 production. In fact, the screen credits of 'World War II Campaigns in Europe' only mentioned Dastar and Entertainment Distributing, a company owned by Dastar. Moreover, Dastar had listed its own employees as executive producers, producers, and associate producers.[655]

Therefore, the central question before the U.S. Supreme Court concerned the concept of 'origin of goods' underlying § 43(a)(1)(A). If the concept meant only the producer of the physical goods made available to the public, Dastar would have made no false representation because it was, in fact, the commercial origin of the 1995 videotapes. If, however, 'origin' could be understood to also include the creator of the underlying literary and artistic work – the original 1949 'Crusade in Europe' version – Fox might have been able to argue that Dastar was misleading the public into believing that it was the origin of the cultural expression embodied in the videotapes.[656]

Addressing this question, the Court took the dictionary meaning of origin – in the sense of the 'source of wares' – as a starting point.[657] It proceeded on the general assumption that consumers buying a branded product would not automatically assume that the company using the brand was the same entity that developed the idea for the product, or designed the product.[658] The Court recognized that in the case of communicative products (such as movies), consumers may in fact be concerned with knowing the creator of the content rather than the physical item at issue. But the Court considered that such a broadening of the origin concept underlying § 43(a)(1)(A) would cause a conflict between copyright and trademark law:

> The problem with this argument according special treatment to communicative products is that it causes the Lanham Act to conflict with the law of copyright, which addresses that subject specifically. The right to copy, and to copy without attribution, once a copyright has expired, like 'the right to make [an article whose patent has expired] – including the right

653. U.S. Supreme Court, 2 June 2003, Dastar/Twentieth Century Fox, 539 U.S. 23 (2003), 26.
654. For a discussion of the scope of the provision, see U.S. Supreme Court, *ibid.*, 29-31.
655. U.S. Supreme Court, *ibid.*, 27.
656. U.S. Supreme Court, *ibid.*, 31.
657. U.S. Supreme Court, *ibid.*, 31.
658. U.S. Supreme Court, *ibid.*, 32.

to make it in precisely the shape it carried when patented—passes to the public.'[659]

Focusing on the rule of a limited term of protection in copyright law, the Court warned of the erosion of the 'carefully crafted bargain' underlying copyright law: a bargain based on the enrichment of the public domain as a corollary of the enjoyment of protection.[660] Against this background, acceptance of a cause of action under § 43(a)(1)(A) would create a 'species of mutant copyright law that limits the public's "federal right to 'copy and to use'" expired copyrights'.[661] The result would be perpetual copyright protection causing imbalances in the system of intellectual property protection. The concept of 'origin of goods' in U.S. trademark legislation, therefore, had to be interpreted as a reference to the 'producer of the tangible goods that are offered for sale, and not to the author of any idea, concept or communication embodied in those goods'.[662]

The infringement test in the area of trademark protection against confusion, thus, allows a cautious approach to signs with cultural significance. First, recognition as an important cultural symbol need not be equated with recognition as a trademark. The fact that a given sign is a well-known literary and artistic work does not imply that it also constitutes a well-known identifier of commercial source. Second, a boundary line can be drawn between indications of artistic origin and indications of commercial origin. In cases about origin confusion, the infringement analysis need not cover indications concerning the author of the cultural expression underlying goods or services. It can be confined to indications of origin in the sense of a reference to the commercial provider of information products or services.[663]

Nonetheless, it would be inaccurate to conclude that trademark protection against confusion is unproblematic altogether. In the case of cultural material constituting not only a well-known literary and artistic work but also a strong identifier of commercial source, both arguments against protection against confusion lose their mitigating effect. Even if the infringement analysis focuses on recognition as a trademark and remains limited to 'origin' in the sense of indications of commercial origin of goods or services, the scope of protection against confusion will be considerable.[664] Again, fictional characters can serve as an example. The Mickey Mouse drawing is both a well-known work in the sense of copyright law and a well-known

659. U.S. Supreme Court, *ibid.*, 33.

660. U.S. Supreme Court, *ibid.*, 33-34.

661. U.S. Supreme Court, *ibid.*, 34.

662. U.S. Supreme Court, *ibid.*, 37. Cf. Ginsburg 2016, 57; Dusollier 2015, 164-165; Quanjel-Schreurs 2005, 133; Moffat 2004, 1473.

663. For a critique of this strict interpretation in the light of concerns about accuracy in market information and the author's attribution interest, see Ginsburg 2008, 485-491.

664. As to the impact of the strength of the mark on the confusion analysis, see Kur/Senftleben 2017, para. 5.106 and 5.151-5.155.

mark in the sense of trademark law.[665] In this situation, the cultural significance of the sign will not limit the scope of trademark protection against confusion because the trademark function of indicating the commercial origin of goods and services is strongly developed as well.

Moreover, the infringement test focusing on the existence of a likelihood of confusion does not necessarily offer room for declaring certain forms of use permissible for cultural reasons. Typical features of cultural expressions do not exclude confusion claims. In the famous French lawsuit *La vache qui rit*, for instance, a defence argument based on antithetical use of the protected sign was dismissed. The French Supreme Court held the view that a 'replica by contrast' ('La vache sérieuse') could not escape the verdict of infringement. Instead of constituting a valid defence argument, the contrast following from an antithetical use contributed to the creation of actionable consumer confusion.[666] The decision indicates that contrasting forms of use that often play a role in artistic contexts (parody and caricature can serve as examples) may fail to shield artists from allegations of infringement. Antithetical use may fall within the scope of trademark protection because the concept of actionable confusion includes the risk of consumers assuming an economic connection with the trademark owner.[667]

In *Adidas/Marca*, the CJEU further enhanced the risk of interferences with literary and artistic use by holding that the confusion analysis offered no room for overarching policy arguments, such as the need to reconcile trademark protection with competing cultural, social or economic interests. The Court left no doubt that a 'need for the sign to be available for other economic operators' did not constitute a factor relevant to the analysis.[668] Adidas had invoked trademark protection of its figurative three-stripes mark to inhibit competitors, such as Marca Mode, from marketing sports garments featuring two parallel stripes contrasting the basic colour of the sportswear at issue.[669] Seeking to defend the marketing of two-stripe products, Marca Mode had advanced the argument that widely used design elements, such as the stripe motif, had to be kept available for all traders. Because of this need to keep the stripe motif free, Adidas had to be prevented from asserting its broad exclusive rights against the use of two-stripe motifs. Assessing the

665. There seems to be little doubt that Mickey Mouse constitutes a well-known trademark in the sense of international trademark law and several national systems. For a discussion of the applicable criteria, see Senftleben 2009a, 50-55.

666. French Supreme Court, 5 January 1966, Chambre commerciale, JCP G, 1966, II, no. 14796, Fromageries Grosjean/Fromageries Bel ('La vache qui rit').

667. Cf. Jacques 2016, 480-481. For an example of a parody case where this risk played a decisive role, see England and Wales High Court, 10 October 2011, case HC11C03222, Ate My Heart/Mind Candy Limited, [2011] EWHC 2741 (Ch) (Justice Vos), paras 54-59. See also the comment by Jacques 2016, 475-476.

668. CJEU, 10 April 2008, case C-102/07, Adidas/Marca, para. 30.

669. CJEU, *ibid.*, paras 8-11.

impact of this 'requirement of availability' on Adidas' exclusive rights, the CJEU confirmed that there were:

> public interest considerations, connected in particular with the need for undistorted competition, which militate in favour of certain signs being used freely by all economic operators.[670]

These public policy considerations, the Court explained, were reflected in several grounds for refusal that are recognized in trademark law, such as the grounds relating to non-distinctive, descriptive and generic signs.[671] However, the Court refused to consider the requirement of availability also when determining the scope of protection. While the likelihood of confusion had to be appreciated globally, taking into account all factors relevant to the circumstances of the case, the fact that there was a need for the sign to be available for other traders could not be one of those relevant factors.[672] The Court also found that the public's perception of the sign as a decoration could not restrict anti-confusion protection when:

> despite its decorative nature, that sign is so similar to the registered trade mark that the relevant public is likely to perceive that the goods come from the same undertaking or, as the case may be, from economically-linked undertakings.[673]

Hence, the public's perception that a sign is a decoration does not always restrict protection against confusion. Decorative use does not fall outside the scope of applicable trademark rights from the outset. If an artist's decorative use of a cultural sign is likely to cause confusion because consumers have been taught to perceive the sign not only as an artwork but also as an indication of commercial source, the objective to prevent confusion prevails and the use may be declared infringing despite its decorative nature. An artistic work including Tintin and his dog Snowy may be found to infringe Hergé's trademark rights if, because of the strong development of the signs' function to indicate commercial origin, the public sees in the decorative use an indication that the work stems from Hergé or a commercially linked undertaking.[674] In the infringement analysis, the objective to prevent confusion, thus, has more weight than the freedom of decorative use even though, in the case of overlapping copyright and trademark protection, the alleged infringer may have chosen a trademarked

670. CJEU, *ibid.*, para. 22.
671. Article 7(1)(b), (c) and (d) EUTMR; Article 4(1)(b), (c) and (d) TMD.
672. CJEU, *ibid.*, para. 30.
673. CJEU, *ibid.*, para. 34.
674. See Court of Appeals of Paris, 3 September 2005, 13th Chamber, Section A, Paul B./Moulinsart, where the Court held that posters and postcards showing Tintin and Snowy amounted to infringement because these depictions were likely to cause confusion in the light of the registration of these characters as trademarks. See EUTMs no. 000145243, 001962646. Cf. Jacques 2016, 471 and 474-475.

sign with cultural significance for artistic reasons, and the assumption of a connection with the trademark owner may be the result of extensive advertising educating consumers to perceive the cultural sign as an indication of commercial origin. In fact, it is conceivable that consumers are only able to establish a link between the decorative sign and a particular commercial undertaking because the trademark proprietor taught them to associate the cultural sign with her enterprise. The ruling in *Adidas/Marca*, thus, entails the risk of a circular line of reasoning: decorative use in the cultural domain may be found to amount to infringement because consumers perceive the decorative sign as an indication of commercial origin. However, the reason for the link with a commercial undertaking in the minds of consumers is the trademark owner's marketing strategy aiming at the redefinition of the cultural sign as a badge of origin.

Hence, the *Adidas/Marca* decision paves the way for the use of trademark law as a self-service mechanism. For the acquisition of anti-confusion protection against decorative use of a cultural sign, it suffices to educate consumers to perceive the cultural sign as an indication of commercial source. On this basis, the trademark owner can argue that the decorative use is likely to mislead consumers into believing that there is a commercial connection. With regard to cultural signs that belonged to the public domain prior to the acquisition of trademark rights, the *Medusa* decision of the German Federal Court of Justice is of particular interest in this context. As already explained above (section 5.2.1), the case concerned Versace's picture trademark showing a stylized Medusa head. Having registered this trademark, among other goods and services, for building materials and furniture, Versace sought to prevent the defendant from marketing marble mosaics also showing different pictures of Medusa. Seeking to defend the use of Medusa heads as decorations for his products, the defendant referred to the 'Medusa Rondanini' – a Roman marble copy of the head of Medusa – which king Ludwig of Bavaria purchased from the heirs of marquis Rondanini and which, nowadays, is exhibited in the Glyptothek in Munich. The defendant argued that the Medusa heads on his marble mosaics were modelled on this museum item instead of constituting a copy of Versace's logo.[675]

In its trademark infringement analysis, the German Federal Court of Justice indicated that it was not prepared to deny trademark protection for the sole reason that Versace's logo was based on cultural material in the public domain.[676] The public domain status of an artistic work did not preclude a finding that the work had been used as a trademark by the defendant and thus in a way actionable under trademark law.[677] In line with CJEU jurisprudence, the Federal Court of Justice found that the decorative use at issue could

675. German Federal Court of Justice, 24 November 2011, case I ZR 175/09, 'Medusa', para. 5.
676. German Federal Court of Justice, *ibid.*, para. 15.
677. German Federal Court of Justice, *ibid.*, paras 19-20.

constitute relevant use as a trademark if the public was likely to perceive the decoration as an indication of commercial source. The answer to this question was dependent on the degree of distinctiveness: the stronger the distinctive character of Versace's trademark, the higher was the likelihood that the consuming public would no longer perceive the Medusa heads used by the defendant as mere decorations.[678] Applying these principles to the Versace logo, the Court denied use as a trademark because it had been established that only 5% of the relevant public knew the Versace logo.[679] Given this low degree of distinctiveness, the public was unlikely to recognize the Medusa heads on the products of the defendant as indications of commercial source. Instead, they would be perceived as mere design elements of the marble mosaics.[680] Versace's trademark action was thus dismissed.

Considering the importance of freedom of decorative use as a basis for cultural follow-on innovation, the *Medusa* decision yields mixed results. On the one hand, the German Federal Court of Justice explicitly confirmed that decorative use of a cultural symbol may constitute actionable use as a trademark. The inroads of trademark protection into the freedom of decorative use are thus considerable. While users of cultural material in the public domain can rely on freedom of use without any risk of exposure to an infringement action as long as the material is unencumbered with trademark rights, the situation becomes markedly different once trademark rights are granted. In principle, even a decorative inclusion of trademarked cultural material in a new creation may amount to relevant use in the sense of trademark law and give rise to an infringement action.

On the other hand, the Federal Court of Justice managed to contain this risk of losing an important area of freedom by pointing out that the plaintiff's trademark had to be sufficiently distinctive to justify the assumption that consumers would perceive the conflicting decorative sign as an indication of commercial source. This solution of the dilemma, however, has its price. Making the decision on actionable trademark use dependent on the degree of distinctiveness of the trademarked cultural sign, the Federal Court of Justice aligned the decision on permissible use with the marketing efforts of the trademark owner: the acquisition of a sufficient degree of distinctive character through advertising leads to the erosion of the use privilege. If Versace had managed to produce evidence of a high level of consumer recognition of its Medusa logo, the freedom of decorative use of the ancient 'Medusa Rondanini' would have been minimized. In principle, the trademark owner is thus free to broaden the scope of protection and conquer new territory in the field of decorative use through investment in advertising

678. German Federal Court of Justice, *ibid.*, para. 24.
679. German Federal Court of Justice, *ibid.*, paras 23-24.
680. German Federal Court of Justice, *ibid.*, para. 30.

campaigns that enhance consumers' recognition of public domain material as a trademark.

Therefore, the test of actionable trademark use developed in *Medusa* does not reliably preserve the freedom of decorative use. By contrast, users of trademarked cultural signs have to ascertain in each individual case whether the cultural sign concerned has become distinctive to such an extent that consumers are likely to perceive decorative use as an indication of commercial source. Imposing the burden of a refined distinctiveness test on users, the freedom of incorporating trademarked cultural expressions in new cultural productions can hardly be deemed robust enough to dispel concerns about an interference with remix activities in the cultural domain. To establish a sufficiently clear use privilege, the freedom of decorative use would have to be an 'easy case' involving less legal uncertainty and less dependence on marketing decisions taken by the trademark owner.[681]

Concerns about overbroad confusion claims have also been expressed in the U.S. Analysing the status quo reached in the field of trademark protection against confusion, Mark Lemley and Mark McKenna arrive at the conclusion that the extension of the confusion concept to confusion about affiliation or sponsorship poses a substantial threat to free speech interests:[682]

> [T]rademark law has taken the concept of confusion too far. Over the middle part of the twentieth century, courts expanded the range of actionable confusion beyond confusion over the actual source of a product – trademark law's traditional concern – to include claims against uses that might confuse consumers about whether the trademark owner sponsors or is affiliated with the defendant's goods. This expansion began for plausible reasons: consumers might be confused to their detriment in at least some cases in which the plaintiff and the defendant do not actually compete directly. But sponsorship and affiliation confusion has taken on a life of its own, leading courts to declare as infringing a variety of practices that might be confusing in some sense, but that do not affect consumers' decisionmaking process.[683]

Lemley and McKenna demonstrate that, once it is deemed sufficient that consumers would assume some relationship between the trademark owner and the alleged infringer based on the defendant's use of the trademark, the confusion action loses its boundaries.[684] It is no longer possible to draw a clear line between relationships about which confusion is relevant from a trademark perspective, such as confusion about the commercial origin of products or confusion about quality control, and other types of relationships

681. Cf. Benkler 1999, 363. For an economic analysis of the corrosive effect of uncertainty about the permissibility of a given form of use, see Depoorter 2004, 67-68.
682. Lemley/McKenna 2010, 416.
683. Lemley/McKenna 2010, 414.
684. Cf. Liu 2013, 1429-1438.

that do not justify a confusion claim.[685] The vague terms 'sponsorship' and 'affiliation' are elastic enough to encompass virtually any relationship between the parties. They transform trademark protection against confusion into a vehicle for infringement actions against any use of another's mark.[686]

Giving examples of confusion that led to lawsuits even though it should have been deemed irrelevant under trademark law, Lemley and McKenna refer to a Caterpillar tractor bulldozing the forest in a Tarzan movie and a confusion action based on the argument that this appearance of the trademarked product may cause consumers to think that Caterpillar did not care about the environment.[687] They also mention a humour magazine with parody advertising for a mythical product called 'Michelob Oily' that was attacked by the trademark owner not because consumers thought Michelob was actually selling this type of beer, but because a survey showed that a majority of consumers believed the magazine needed permission from Anheuser-Busch to run the fake advertising campaign.[688] Lemley and McKenna point out that these cases are not exceptional:

> these threats were not isolated incidents, and they shouldn't be quickly ignored. The recipients of all of these threats, like many others who receive similar objections, knew well that they had to take the asserted claims seriously because courts have sometimes been persuaded to shut down very similar uses.[689]

As the Tarzan and Michelob examples already indicate, the extension of confusion claims to sponsorship and affiliation pose particular threats to free expression.[690] In *Mutual of Omaha Insurance Company/Novak*, for instance, the U.S. Court of Appeals for the Eighth Circuit prohibited an antinuclear parody of Mutual of Omaha's Indian head logo on the ground that consumers were likely to believe that the insurance company 'went along' with the sale of T-shirts showing the parody 'in order to help make people aware of the nuclear war problem'.[691] The parody was thus found to cause confusion as to sponsorship.[692]

Developments in U.S. trademark law, thus, confirm that the hurdle to be surmounted for a successful anti-confusion claim against use in the cultural domain need not be particularly high. As in the EU, the underlying problem

685. Lemley/McKenna 2010, 422.
686. Lemley/McKenna 2010, 427. Cf. McGeveran 2015, 715.
687. Lemley/McKenna 2010, 417. Cf. U.S. District Court for the Central District of Illinois, 20 October 2003, Caterpillar/Walt Disney, 287 F. Supp. 2d 913, 917 (C.D. Ill. 2003). For further examples, see Assaf 2008, 71-72.
688. Lemley/McKenna 2010, 418. Cf. U.S. Court of Appeals for the Eight Circuit, 30 June 1994, Anheuser-Busch/Balducci Publications, 28 F.3d 769, 772-773 (8th Cir. 1994).
689. Lemley/McKenna 2010, 418.
690. Lemley/McKenna 2010, 441-442.
691. U.S. Court of Appeals for the Eighth Circuit, 30 December 1987, Mutual of Omaha Insurance Company/Novak, 836 F.2d 397, paras 12-13.
692. U.S. Court of Appeals for the Eighth Circuit, *ibid.*, paras 12-13.

lies in the alignment of the infringement analysis with the degree of distinctive character. The trademark owner can influence the scope of protection to a considerable degree. The more she invests in advertising, the higher the chances of making consumers believe that there must be some relationship between the trademark proprietor and the alleged infringer.[693] This mechanism is particularly problematic when it comes to branding of cultural signs. The more a trademark owner invests in the transformation of a cultural sign into a trademark, the more the cultural sign loses its original cultural meaning and, instead, functions as an identifier of commercial source (and sponsorship or other economic connections with this source). As a reward for the blurring of a sign's cultural meaning, trademark law thus offers a broader scope of protection against confusion. From the perspective of the cultural imperative, this incentive scheme is undesirable.

Hence, trademark protection of cultural signs is problematic even if it remains limited to the basic function of trademarks to indicate the commercial origin of goods and services. A sign's cultural significance may weaken its potential to serve as an indication of origin. Moreover, the concept of 'origin' underlying the infringement analysis need not be extended to indications of authorship. Nonetheless, the fact remains that, once a cultural sign has developed an independent origin function with regard to goods or services, the need to keep the sign free for cultural follow-on innovation is unlikely to prevail over the trademark rationale to ensure market transparency and protect consumers against confusion. Similarly, the intention to use the sign as a mere decorative element does not prevent a finding of infringement when the similarity with the registered trademark may cause confusion about a commercial link with the trademark owner – even if this link in the minds of consumers is only the result of advertising campaigns in which the trademark owner taught consumers to make a connection between the cultural sign and her enterprise. Trademark protection may thus reduce the breathing space for cultural follow-on innovation even if the scope of protection is confined to the trademark function of indicating commercial origin.

6.2.3 *Protection Against Dilution*

In contrast to trademark protection against confusion, protection against dilution does not concern the risk of misleading consumers into believing that goods or services of an unauthorized third party stem from the trademark proprietor. By contrast, protection against dilution concerns the economic and communication value of the trademark which has already been discussed above (section 6.1.1). Once the trademark proprietor has managed to create a favourable brand image, the trademark itself becomes an independent

693. Assaf 2008, 72-73.

communication product.[694] Against this background, the extension of trademark protection to a mark's economic and communication value affords the trademark owner the opportunity to control the communication surrounding the trademark and prevent interferences with her own marketing and communication strategy. Quite clearly, protection against dilution is particularly problematic from the perspective of cultural follow-on innovation. Anti-dilution protection enhances the trademark owner's control over the communication surrounding a protected sign and further restricts the possibility to use that sign in the context of cultural remix processes. If a sign with cultural significance obtains the status of a trademark eligible for protection against dilution, broad inroads are made into the freedom to use the sign in a cultural context.[695]

However, exclusive rights against trademark dilution are only available on the basis of specific eligibility and infringement criteria that regulate the access and scope of trademark protection in this area. In the absence of a trademark that functions as a powerful channel of communication with consumers, the trademark owner cannot rely on enhanced protection against dilution. To identify trademarks enjoying protection against dilution, most trademark systems ask whether the trademark is widely known among the consuming public.[696] International trademark law refers to 'well-known' trademarks in this context.[697] Article 16(2) TRIPS specifies that for determining whether a trademark is well known, 'the knowledge of the trademark in the relevant sector of the public, including knowledge that has been obtained as a result of the promotion of the trademark', must be taken into account. Article 2(2) JR WKM[698] clarifies that the concept of 'relevant sector of the public' should be understood to include consumers of the type of goods and services to which the mark applies, persons involved in the distribution of these goods and services, and business circles dealing with these goods and services. In a nutshell, this is a recommendation to focus on knowledge among the specific target audience and within the specific distribution chain of products to which the trademark is applied (niche knowledge). However, Article 4(1)(c) JR WKM creates room to 'require that the well-known mark be well known by the public at large' (general knowledge) with regard to the specific dilution actions of blurring, tarnishment and unfair freeriding. Article 4(1)(b)(ii) and (iii) JR WKM explicitly address these specific dilution

694. Kur/Senftleben 2017, para. 1.29-1.39; Ginsburg 2016, 75-77; Senftleben 2009a, 48-49; Bently 2008b, 15-41; Schroeder 2008, 161; Bone 2006, 549; Moskin 2004, 843-844; Dinwoodie 2002, 503-504; Fezer 2001, 827; Casparie-Kerdel 2001, 185-186; Lunney 1999, 437-439; Lemley 1999, 1694-1698; Brown 1999, 1619-1620; Dreyfuss 1990, 397-398; Lehmann 1986, 14-17.

695. Cf. Jacques 2016, 473.

696. Cf. Senftleben 2009a, 50-55; Beebe 2006, 1157.

697. Article 6bis PC and Article 16(2) and (3) TRIPS.

698. Cf. Kur 2000, 824.

actions, whereas Article 16(3) TRIPS does not clearly refer to blurring, tarnishment and unfair freeriding.[699]

As international law recommends a niche knowledge approach but also leaves room for a stricter general knowledge requirement, national policy-makers are free to set a high threshold and require that a trademark be known among the general consuming public to enjoy enhanced protection against dilution. U.S. trademark law is a prominent example of national legislation availing itself of this option and providing for a strict eligibility test to contain access to anti-dilution protection from the outset. According to Article 2 of the 2006 U.S. Trademark Dilution Revision Act, only 'famous marks' are eligible for protection against dilution by blurring or tarnishment. A mark is famous 'if it is widely recognized by the general consuming public of the United States as a designation of source of the goods or services of the mark's owner' (general knowledge). In consequence, niche fame among a specialized public, such as a specific target group of the product sold under the mark, is not sufficient.[700]

EU trademark law, by contrast, follows the opposite approach. A trademark owner seeking protection against dilution under Article 9(2)(c) EUTMR or Article 10(2)(c) TMD must show that her trademark has a 'reputation'. In principle, the CJEU could embrace this reputation requirement as a tool to limit access to enhanced protection against dilution from the outset. With a nuanced concept of reputation, the Court could ensure that anti-dilution protection is awarded only if a trademark has a brand image that is likely to be harmed or unfairly exploited because of its particularly high value and attractiveness.[701] Instead of establishing a strict reputation test, however, the threshold for assuming that a trademark has the necessary reputation is remarkably low in the EU. In *Chevy*, the CJEU explained that 'the market share held by the trade mark' and 'the size of the investment made by the undertaking in promoting it' had to be taken into account in this context.[702] With regard to the relevant public, the Court explained that:

> [t]he public amongst which the earlier trade mark must have acquired a reputation is that concerned by that trade mark, that is to say, depending on the product or service marketed, either the public at large or a more specialized public, for example traders in a specific sector.[703]

---

699. See Article 4(1)(b)(ii) and (iii) JR WKM concerning protection against use 'likely to impair or dilute in an unfair manner the distinctive character of the well-known mark' and use that 'would take unfair advantage of the distinctive character of the well-known mark'. Cf. Senftleben 2009a, 51-53. For a national implementation that does not provide for these specific anti-dilution actions, see Handler 2007, 307.
700. Beebe 2006, 1157.
701. Senftleben 2013b, 150-151; Senftleben 2009a, 54-55.
702. CJEU, 14 September 1999, case C-375/97, General Motors/Yplon ('Chevy'), para. 27.
703. CJEU, *ibid.*, para. 24.

Moreover, the Court clarified that:

> [t]he degree of knowledge required must be considered to be reached when the earlier mark is known by a significant part of the public concerned by the products or services covered by that trade mark.[704]

This clarification shows that the Court considers knowledge among the individual target group of the product concerned sufficient, even though this target group may be a specialized public in the case of specific goods or services. In line with Article 2(2) JR WKM, the Court favours a niche reputation approach. Further findings in *Chevy* confirm this conclusion. In respect of the necessary territorial expansion of the mark's reputation, the Court held the view that:

> [i]n the absence of any definition [in Article 10(2)(c) TMD] in this respect, a trade mark cannot be required to have a reputation 'throughout' the territory of the Member State. It is sufficient for it to exist in a substantial part of it.[705]

Hence, the CJEU developed a niche reputation approach focusing on knowledge among a specialized public in a substantial part of an EU Member State. If the case concerns an EUTM, the whole internal market is the reference point for determining whether the trademark has a reputation. However, the Court clarified in *Pago/Tirolmilch* that knowledge 'in a substantial part' can already be assumed when the EUTM is known throughout the territory of a Member State, such as Austria.[706] As a result, the trademark owner need not produce evidence of a reputation across all Member States or in a major part of the internal market. The anti-dilution action is readily available in all EU Member States where a commercially significant part of the relevant public knows the mark.[707] Introducing this low standard, the Court is far from exercising rigid access control. Instead of actively regulating access to enhanced protection against dilution, the Court makes the door to anti-dilution rights wide open.[708] The specific eligibility criterion of 'having a reputation' is applied flexibly instead of being employed to limit access to anti-dilution protection from the outset. Following this approach, the CJEU also fails to reduce the risk of anti-dilution claims against use in a cultural context. If trademark rights to a sign with cultural significance are granted, the trademark proprietor need not surmount a difficult hurdle to obtain enhanced protection against dilution. By contrast, it suffices to use the cultural sign in a way that makes it known as a trademark among a specialized public. In terms of territorial reach, this use

704. CJEU, *ibid.*, para. 26.
705. CJEU, *ibid.*, para. 28.
706. CJEU, 6 October 2009, case C-301/07, Pago/Tirolmilch, paras 29-30.
707. CJEU, 3 September 2015, case C-125/14, Iron & Smith/Unilever, paras 28-30. Cf. Kur/Senftleben 2017, para. 5.201-5.204.
708. Cf. the critique by Pollaud-Dulian 2001, 43.

need not cover the entire territory of the EU or a Member State. If a specialized public in a substantial part of the relevant territory knows the trademark, it becomes possible to bring an anti-dilution action against remix and reuse of the cultural sign concerned.

The erosion of a further prerequisite for an infringement action seems inevitable in the context of anti-dilution protection. As pointed out above, traditional protection against confusion requires a likelihood of confusion. Protection against dilution, however, is not primarily concerned with the prevention of confusing use. It aims at preserving the particular distinctive character and the repute of marks with a reputation. A trademark's particular distinctive character or repute, however, may be harmed or unfairly exploited without causing a risk of confusion. The mere allusion to the mark with a reputation can be sufficient. Accordingly, the CJEU adopted an elastic association test in *Adidas/Fitnessworld.*[709] As a result, enhanced protection against dilution becomes available when a competing sign calls to mind a mark with a reputation:

> [t]he fact that a sign is viewed as an embellishment by the relevant section of the public is not, in itself, an obstacle to the protection [of marks with a reputation against dilution] where the degree of similarity is none the less such that the relevant section of the public establishes a link between the sign and the mark.[710]

This ruling shows that a mere reference to a mark with a reputation may already be sufficient to trigger an anti-dilution claim. As the reference to use as an embellishment shows, decorative use falls within the scope of this broad association test. Moreover, an allusion to a trademark in the context of parody becomes actionable under the flexible test of 'establish[ing] a link between the sign and the mark'[711] (section 6.2.1). The above-described decision *Lila Postkarte* of the German Federal Court of Justice can serve as an example.[712]

As a result, protection against dilution is widely available in the EU. Under the low threshold requirement of niche reputation, a broad range of trademarks is eligible for anti-dilution protection. As discussed, knowledge among a specific target audience or within relevant circles of distribution already satisfies this criterion. The elastic association test of 'establishing a link between the sign and the mark' does not pose a substantial hurdle either. A mere reference to the trademark, an allusion in a parody, or use of decorative elements evoking the trademark can offer a sufficient basis for an anti-dilution claim. Moreover, a dilution claim does not require identity or

709. CJEU, 23 October 2003, case C-408/01, Adidas/Fitnessworld, para. 29.
710. CJEU, *ibid.*, para. 39.
711. CJEU, *ibid.*, para. 39.
712. See German Federal Court of Justice, 3 February 2005, case I ZR 159/02, 'Lila Postkarte', *GRUR* 2005, 583 (584) where the Court bases its assessment on the association test following from CJEU, *ibid.*, para. 39.

similarity of the goods or services involved. In the EU, protection is granted irrespective of whether the allegedly infringing sign is used 'in relation to goods or services which are identical with, similar to, or not similar to, those for which the trade mark is registered'.[713] Once a cultural sign attains the status of a mark with a reputation, the trademark proprietor can thus invoke protection across the entire spectrum of goods and services, including goods and services that concern activities in the cultural domain.

To finally obtain protection against dilution, however, the trademark proprietor must produce evidence that the allegedly infringing use takes unfair advantage of, or is detrimental to, the distinctive character or the repute of the mark with a reputation.[714] This remaining condition constitutes the last bastion against readily available protection against dilution, including allegedly infringing use in a cultural context. With regard to proof of detriment to the distinctive character of a mark with a reputation, the CJEU required in *Intel/CPM*:

> evidence of a change in the economic behaviour of the average consumer of the goods or services for which the earlier mark was registered consequent on the use of the later mark, or a serious likelihood that such a change will occur in the future.[715]

From a practical perspective, one may wonder how the required 'evidence of a change in the economic behaviour of the average consumer' can ever be produced.[716] Nonetheless, the CJEU upheld this approach by clarifying in later decisions that this concept had to be understood as an objective condition that could not be satisfied by deducing a change in economic behaviour from subjective elements, such as consumers' perceptions. In particular, the mere fact that consumers note the presence of a new sign similar to an earlier sign was not sufficient to fulfil this requirement.[717] The finding of an economic change had to be founded on 'an analysis of the probabilities' taking account of the normal practice in the relevant commercial sector. Mere suppositions were not enough.[718] Considering the described need to preserve breathing space for cultural forms of use, this strict criterion seems appropriate. As the CJEU relaxed the specific eligibility criterion of 'having a reputation' and adopted a flexible association test of 'establishing a link with the trademark', it is justified to set a high threshold when it comes to the final question of taking unfair advantage or causing detriment.

---

713. Article 9(2)(c) EUTMR and Article 10(2)(c) TMD.
714. Article 9(2)(c) EUTMR and Article 10(2)(c) TMD.
715. CJEU, 27 November 2008, case C-252/07, Intel/CPM, para. 77.
716. Cf. Bouvel 2008, 123; Quaedvlieg 2009a, 253; Quaedvlieg 2009b, 799; Middlemiss/Warner 2009, 326 (331-332).
717. CJEU, 14 November 2013, case C-383/12 P, Environmental Manufacturing/Elmar Wolf, para. 37.
718. CJEU, *ibid.*, para. 43.

The *Intel/CPM* decision, however, was followed by the *L'Oréal/Bellure* judgment in which the CJEU lowered this final threshold substantially. Dealing with comparison lists concerning cheap imitations of well-known L'Oréal perfumes, the Court stated that a mere attempt to 'ride on the coat-tails' of a mark with a reputation could be sufficient to assume that unfair advantage had been taken. The Court explained that:

> where a third party attempts, through the use of a sign similar to a mark with a reputation, to ride on the coat-tails of that mark in order to benefit from its power of attraction, its reputation and its prestige, and to exploit, without paying any financial compensation and without being required to make efforts of his own in that regard, the marketing effort expended by the proprietor of that mark in order to create and maintain the image of that mark, the advantage resulting from such use must be considered to be an advantage that has been unfairly taken of the distinctive character or the repute of that mark.[719]

The fundamental change with regard to the availability of anti-dilution protection becomes apparent the moment the relationship between the different final infringement criteria is considered. The three modes of infringement – detriment to distinctive character (blurring), detriment to repute (tarnishment), unfair advantage from distinctive character or repute (freeriding) – constitute alternative conditions in the context of Article 9(2)(c) EUTMR and Article 10(2)(c) TMD. For an infringement claim to be successful, it is sufficient to establish only one of these three distinct forms of actionable dilution.[720] By setting a low standard for the taking of unfair advantage, the Court thus creates a loophole which trademark proprietors can use when a showing of detriment is impossible under the described *Intel/CPM* standard. A trademark owner who does not succeed in providing 'evidence of a change in the economic behaviour of the average consumer' can insist on the taking of unfair advantage instead. For this alternative basis, it suffices to argue that the defendant attempts to ride on the coat-tails of the mark with a reputation.

With the creation of the flexible coat-tail formula in *L'Oréal/Bellure*, the CJEU, thus, abandoned the remaining bastion of final infringement criteria that could have limited the impact of anti-dilution claims based on Article 9(2)(c) EUTMR and Article 10(2)(c) TMD. As a result, brand owners invoking anti-dilution protection against use in a cultural context can benefit from a remarkably low eligibility criterion of having a reputation, an elastic association test covering referential and decorative use and, finally, a flexible unfair advantage criterion that is already fulfilled when a third party attempts

---

719. CJEU, 18 June 2009, case C-487/07, L'Oréal/Bellure, para. 49.
720. CJEU, 18 June 2009, case C-487/07, L'Oréal/Bellure, para. 38 and 42; CJEU, 22 September 2011, case C-323/09, Interflora/Marks & Spencer, para. 72. Cf. Kur/Senftleben 2017, para. 5.185.

to ride on the coat-tails of the mark with a reputation. Surveying these elastic conditions for protection against dilution, one can hardly deny that anti-dilution protection in the EU requires little more than use of a conflicting sign in some area of the market that triggers an association with a mark having a reputation in that market niche.[721] The CJEU thus offers brand owners broad control over the communication surrounding their trademarks. In consequence, the inroads into the freedom of remix and reuse in a cultural context are also broad when a sign with cultural significance acquires a reputation in the sense of EU trademark law.

Anti-dilution claims against use in a cultural context are not a mere theoretical option. In the U.S., for example, Mattel brought a lawsuit against the Danish band Aqua which had produced the song 'Barbie Girl' in 1997. In the song, one band member impersonated Barbie, singing in a high-pitched, doll-like voice. Another band member ('Ken') enticed Barbie to 'go party'. As the following text excerpt shows, the lyrics of the song played ironically with the Barbie world (and corresponding gender stereotypes) cultivated by Mattel:

> I'm a blonde bimbo girl, in a fantasy world
> Dress me up, make it tight, I'm your dolly
> You're my doll, rock and roll, feel the glamour in pink
> Kiss me here, touch me there, hanky-panky
> You can touch, you can play
> If you say 'I'm always yours', ooh ooh ...[722]

As 'Barbie Girl' had made it onto the Top 40 music charts, Mattel sought to stop the song's further dissemination and prevent an erosion of the carefully created Barbie image. Discussing the corresponding anti-dilution claim in *Mattel/MCA Records*, the U.S. Court of Appeals for the Ninth Circuit emphasized the need to safeguard freedom of expression. It stated that in the case of a trademark which also constituted a cultural icon, trademark rights should not entitle the trademark proprietor to prohibit the communication of ideas and points of view based on the expressive value of the trademark. The trademark owner should not have the right 'to control public discourse whenever the public imbues his mark with a meaning beyond its source-identifying function'.[723]

721. However, see also the practical considerations by Morcom 2009, 634-635, who emphasizes difficulties in establishing damage to the trademark after the CJEU decision about blurring in *Intel/CPM*. Nonetheless, the crucial point here is that the CJEU lowered the conditions for a showing of infringement substantially by providing the coat-tail formula – not requiring any evidence of damage – as a vehicle to bypass the higher infringement standard developed in *Intel/CPM*. The practical difficulties with regard to sufficient evidence of damage, therefore, have been reduced significantly.
722. See U.S. Court of Appeals for the Ninth Circuit, 24 July 2002, Mattel/MCA Records, 296 F.3d 894, 899 and Appendix reproducing the lyrics of the song.
723. U.S. Court of Appeals for the Ninth Circuit, *ibid.*, 901.

Nonetheless, the Court saw no possibility of denying harm under the blurring test in U.S. trademark law. While a reference to Barbie brought to mind only Mattel's doll prior to Aqua's song, it was clear that after the song's popular success, some consumers hearing Barbie's name would think of both the doll and the song, or perhaps of the song only. This, in turn, amounted to a 'classic blurring injury': as the mark no longer called to mind Mattel alone, it could not be denied that the mark's distinctiveness had been diminished.[724] To create breathing space for freedom of expression in these circumstances, the Court finally resorted to the defences in U.S. anti-dilution legislation, as in force at the time.[725] Discussing the defence of 'noncommercial use', the Court arrived at the conclusion that, in the light of the legislative history, this defence could be interpreted to encompass artistic and expressive speech that went beyond the mere proposal of a commercial transaction.[726] Ultimately, Aqua's Barbie parody, thus, was found not to amount to infringement.

Even though Aqua could escape the verdict of infringement by invoking the non-commercial use defence, the Barbie case demonstrates the broad scope of protection against dilution and its potential impact on use of protected signs in a cultural context. Once a cultural sign acquires the status of a mark enjoying protection against dilution, a trademark claim against remix and reuse in the cultural domain can no longer be ruled out.[727] As a result of a broad concept of dilution, the trademark owner obtains robust exclusive rights that require the invocation of defences to avoid a finding of infringement.

Besides the blurring argument that played a central role in *Mattel/MCA Records* (and could also be developed in the EU),[728] a tarnishment claim is also conceivable. In the Dutch case *Mercis and Bruna/Punt*, the publisher Mercis and Dick Bruna – author of the famous Dutch fictional character 'Miffy' used for toys, children's books and clothing – asserted copyright and trademark rights against the imitation of Miffy drawings in parodies placing Miffy in completely different contexts, including the depiction of Miffy as a 9/11 terrorist. The parodies had been posted on websites and weblogs hosted

---

724. U.S. Court of Appeals for the Ninth Circuit, *ibid.*, 903.
725. As to the evolution of a broader set of defences in U.S. trademark law, see Beebe 2006, 1157.
726. U.S. Court of Appeals for the Ninth Circuit, *ibid.*, 903-904. Cf. Ginsburg 2018b, 249-250.
727. For further U.S. case law showing the need to invoke fair use defences against allegations of trademark infringement in a cultural context, see Ginsburg 2018b, 248-252; Farley 2015, 23-24. Cf. the fair use analysis in U.S. Court of Appeals for the Ninth Circuit, 29 December 2003, Mattel/Walking Mountain Productions, 353 F.3d 792, 802-806 (9th Cir. 2003); U.S District Court for the Southern District of New York, 4 November 2002, Mattel/Pitt, 229 F. Supp. 2d 315, 322 (S.D.N.Y. 2002).
728. See the blurring test following from CJEU, 27 November 2008, case C-252/07, Intel/CPM, para. 29.

by Punt.nl.[729] Referring to the strong contrast following from the contexts chosen for the parodies and the underlying evidently humorous and ironical intention, the Court of Appeals of Amsterdam concluded that the Miffy imitations had to be qualified as permissible parodies in the sense of the exemption of use of copyrighted material 'in the context of a caricature, parody or pastiche' in Article 18b of the Dutch Copyright Act.[730] From a copyright perspective, the taking of individual features of the Miffy drawing was not decisive. Due to the distance created through the contrast with the original Miffy universe, the parodies could not be regarded as a simple copy. According to the Court, it was irrelevant in this regard that the parodies would not be perceived as funny by everybody.[731] The application of the parody exemption in the Dutch Copyright Act, moreover, implied that Dick Bruna could not invoke his moral rights, including the right to object to the distortion of his fictional character,[732] against the Miffy imitations.[733]

However, the action against the Miffy parodies was based not only on copyright protection but also on trademark rights. Besides a Benelux word mark concerning Miffy's original Dutch name 'Nijntje',[734] the publisher Mercis also relied on two figurative Benelux trademarks consisting of Miffy drawings.[735] This trademark claim was not doomed to fail from the outset even though consumers were unlikely to perceive the use of Miffy drawings for the purpose of parody as an indication of commercial source. The reason for this broad scope of protection lies in policy choices made in Benelux trademark law. The Benelux countries availed themselves of the possibility offered in Article 10(6) TMD to go beyond trademark rights against use that takes place in the course of trade and in relation to goods or services.[736] In addition, they extended the scope of protection to forms of use 'other than for the purposes of distinguishing goods or services'.[737] As a result, Mercis was

729. Court of Appeals of Amsterdam, 13 September 2011, case ECLI:NL:GHAMS:2011:BS7825, Mercis and Bruna/Punt, *AMI* 2012, p. 28, para. 4.1.

730. Court of Appeals of Amsterdam, *ibid.*, para. 4.13. For commentary on the development of the exemption of parody in Dutch copyright law and the role of the Miffy decision in this process, see De Cock Buning/Van Lingen 2014, 191; De Zwaan 2014, 195-196; Senftleben 2012a, 374-381.

731. Court of Appeals of Amsterdam, *ibid.*, para. 4.13.

732. See the national implementation of this moral right in Article 25(1)(d) of the Dutch Copyright Act (Auteurswet) on the one hand and the international provision in Article 6bis(1) BC on the other. As to the right of integrity in copyright's legal traditions in general and the Dutch tradition in particular, see Dietz 1995, 199; Dworkin 1995, 229; Kabel/Quaedvlieg 2012, 319-333.

733. Court of Appeals of Amsterdam, *ibid.*, para. 4.16.

734. Benelux trade mark no. 0578407, see www.tmdn.org/tmview/.

735. Benelux trade marks no. 0573738 and 0738985, see www.tmdn.org/tmview/.

736. These general conditions are prerequisites for a trademark claim under Article 10(2) TMD.

737. Article 2.20(2)(d) of the Benelux Convention on Intellectual Property which grants the right to prevent use 'for purposes other than those of distinguishing the goods or services, where use of the sign without due cause would take unfair advantage of or be

in a position to bring a trademark claim against a form of use that does not concern the traditional trademark function of indicating the origin of goods or services.[738] Given the potential negative repercussions of the terrorist version of Miffy on the brand image following from the friendly children's universe created by Dick Bruna, the case offered room for infringement arguments based on tarnishment. In *L'Oréal/Bellure*, the CJEU explained that this type of dilution harm could be found:

> when the goods or services for which the identical or similar sign is used by the third party may be perceived by the public in such a way that the trade mark's power of attraction is reduced. The likelihood of such detriment may arise in particular from the fact that the goods or services offered by the third party possess a characteristic or a quality which is liable to have a negative impact on the image of the mark.[739]

Dealing with this trademark claim, the Court of Appeals of Amsterdam faced the problem that the Benelux Convention on Intellectual Property[740] – containing the trademark legislation for the three Benelux countries – does not provide for an exemption of use 'in the context of a caricature, parody or pastiche' that corresponds with the aforementioned specific provision in the Dutch Copyright Act. Therefore, the Court had to resort to the open-ended defence of 'due cause' which is available in the Benelux system of protection against use 'other than for the purposes of distinguishing goods or services'.[741] In the case of a trademark parody, this defence may apply if the use can be justified in the light of the fundamental guarantee of freedom of expression.[742] Recalling its favourable assessment of the Miffy parodies in the light of applicable copyright standards, the Court of Appeals of Amsterdam used this 'due cause' defence as a vehicle to also reject the trademark claim. Considering the humorous intention, the absence of direct

---

detrimental to the distinctive character or the repute of the trademark'. As pointed out above, not only the requirement of 'use in the course of trade' but also the requirement of 'use in relation to goods or services' does not apply in this area of extended protection. Cf. Cohen Jehoram/Van Nispen/Huydecoper 2008, 366-367.

738. Court of Appeals of Amsterdam, *ibid.*, para. 4.19.
739. CJEU, 18 June 2009, case C-487/07, L'Oréal/Bellure, para. 40.
740. For the text of the Convention (also in English), see www.boip.int/en/document/benelux-convention-on-intellectual-property-bcip.
741. Article 2.20(1)(d) Benelux Convention on Intellectual Property. Cf. Vanovermeire 2009, 187-188.
742. For instance, see German Federal Court of Justice, 3 February 2005, case I ZR 159/02, 'Lila Postkarte', *GRUR* 2005, 583; German Federal Court of Justice, 11 March 2008, case VI ZR 7/07, 'Gen-Milch', *NJW* 2008, 2110; French Supreme Court, 8 April 2008, case 06-10961, Greenpeace/Esso; French Supreme Court, 8 April 2008, case 07-11251, Greenpeace/Areva. See also the commentary by Jacques 2016, 479 (who expresses concerns that the defence argument may be less robust when the use does not focus on a trademark which also serves as a company name); Ramsey/Schovsbo 2013, 671; Simon Fhima 2013, 293; Sakulin 2010, 247-282; Burrell/Gangjee 2010, 544; Geiger 2007, 317; Weckström 2007, 671.

competition, the sharp contrast with the original Miffy books and the absence of a risk of confusion, the Court was satisfied that the parodies constituted a legitimate form of free expression. The use of the Miffy trademarks was held to have been made with 'due cause' in the sense of Article 2.20(2)(d) of the Benelux Convention.[743]

Although the Miffy case, as the earlier Barbie case in the U.S., finally did not culminate in a finding of infringement, it illustrates the broad scope of anti-dilution claims and their potential impact on cultural follow-on innovation.[744] In *Mercis and Bruna/Punt*, the Court of Appeals of Amsterdam found neither direct competition nor a risk of confusion. Nonetheless, this was not sufficient to dismiss the trademark claim at the outset. Instead, the Court had to create room for the ironical play with the Miffy drawing on the basis of the defence of 'due cause'. Blurring and tarnishment are not the only causes of action that may be asserted against the remix and reuse of trademarked cultural icons, such as Barbie and Miffy. As explained, the EU system of protection against dilution affords owners of marks with a reputation the opportunity to invoke exclusive rights against unfair freeriding as an alternative basis for an anti-dilution lawsuit. This alternative avenue is particularly attractive because it does not require a showing of harm in the sense of evidence for a change in the economic behaviour of consumers.

To illustrate the practical impact of this alternative basis for an anti-dilution claim, one can consider a Japanese manga artist who seeks to show the artistic contrast between the Japanese manga tradition and the American superhero genre. For this purpose, she commences a new series of comic strips presenting a manga hero who fights against Superman.[745] As the inclusion of Superman is intended to trigger associations with DC Comics' original character, the manga comics fall within the broad EU concept of actionable use as a trademark (cf. section 6.2.1). The moment the comics are commercially exploited, use of the Superman drawing 'in the course of trade' can hardly be denied. Moreover, it is not sufficient to rebut trademark infringement arguments by pointing out that the public is unlikely to perceive the inclusion of Superman in the manga stories as an indication of commercial source. Protection against dilution is available even if no confusion about the commercial origin of the manga comics is caused. It is sufficient that the trademarked fictional character is called to mind.

The crucial question, then, is whether DC Comics can successfully develop an infringement argument based on blurring, tarnishment or unfair freeriding. If convincing evidence for a change in the economic behaviour of

743. Court of Appeals of Amsterdam, *ibid.*, para. 4.19.

744. Cf. Jacques 2016, 480, who points out that in French jurisprudence, the offensive nature of a parody may weigh against a finding of permissibility.

745. The Superman drawing is registered as a figurative trademark. For example, see the German trademark registration DD643100 covering various goods, including printed matter, magazines and books (available at https://register.dpma.de/DPMAregister/marke/einsteiger?lang=en).

consumers is unavailable to support a blurring or tarnishment claim,[746] the grant of protection against unfair freeriding in EU trademark law offers DC Comics an alternative basis for a trademark action. With regard to this infringement alternative, it suffices to assert that the manga publisher seeks to take unfair advantage of the brand image created by DC Comics. As explained above, protection against the taking of unfair advantage is available in situations where a third party attempts 'to ride on the coat-tails' of a mark with a reputation in order to benefit from the mark's 'power of attraction, its reputation and its prestige'.[747]

The power of persuasion of this line of argument must not be underestimated. In the decision *Styriagra*, the Austrian Supreme Court prohibited the marketing of pumpkin seeds with blue frosting under the trademark STYRIAGRA. As the blue frosting and the trademark called to mind Pfizer's well-known VIAGRA trademark and the blue Viagra pills, the Court was convinced that the defendant sought to profit unfairly from the strong reputation of Pfizer's trademark as a vehicle to draw the attention of consumers to his pumpkin product.[748] In this context, the Court rejected the argument that the use had taken place with 'due cause'. As the defendant's business was established and carried out in the Austrian state Styria, the trademark STYRIAGRA could be understood as an ironic blend of the name of the Austrian state where the pumpkin seeds came from, and the VIAGRA trademark of the plaintiff. To further support his parody argument, the defendant had also pointed out that his ironic play with Pfizer's trademark and the characteristic blue colour of Viagra pills created a sharp contrast between chemical and natural means of treating erectile dysfunction. The Austrian Supreme Court, however, remained unimpressed. While conceding that the due cause defence may be invoked to justify a trademark parody, it held that in these specific circumstances, the intention to take unfair advantage of the magnetism of Pfizer's highly distinctive trademark was predominant. In consequence, Pfizer's interest in trademark protection prevailed over the defendant's free speech interests.[749]

Similarly, the Court of Appeals of Amsterdam assumed unfair freeriding in *Rowling/Byblos* – the aforementioned case that concerned artistic remix (section 5.2.4). In the Netherlands, Byblos was about to launch the children's book 'Tanja Grotter and the Magical Contrabass' written by the Russian author Dimitri Yemets. In Byblos' book catalogue, Tanja Grotter was

746. As discussed above, the CJEU places quite a heavy burden of proof on trademark owners in the context of blurring and tarnishment claims. See CJEU, 27 November 2008, case C-252/07, Intel/CPM, para. 77; CJEU, 14 November 2013, case C-383/12 P, Environmental Manufacturing/Elmar Wolf, para. 37 and 43.

747. See CJEU, 18 June 2009, case C-487/07, L'Oréal/Bellure, para. 49.

748. Austrian Supreme Court, 22 September 2009, case 17Ob15/09v, 'Styriagra', para. 2.

749. Austrian Supreme Court, *ibid.*, para. 3.4.

presented as the Russian sister of the famous Harry Potter.[750] There was little doubt that the Tanja Grotter book leaned heavily on 'Harry Potter and the Sorcerer's Stone'. Comparing the story line, the setting of the respective wizard schools, the characters involved, the plot and the different events in the book, the Court of Appeals of Amsterdam arrived at the conclusion that the overall impression given by 'Tanja Grotter and the Magical Contrabass' conformed with the underlying 'Harry Potter and the Sorcerer's Stone' in too many respects to assume permissible use under applicable copyright standards.[751] To prevent the marketing of the Tanja Grotter book, however, J.K. Rowling and Time Warner relied not only on copyright protection but also on the trademark HARRY POTTER which Time Warner had registered, among other things, for printed matter and books.[752] Comparing the signs 'Tanja Grotter' and 'Harry Potter', the Court found that the signs were similar from an aural, visual and conceptual perspective.[753] The Court also confirmed a considerable degree of distinctiveness of the mark HARRY POTTER in respect of the book and film series.[754] Based on these findings, the Court readily assumed unfair freeriding. It was convinced that Byblos sought to derive unfair profit from the reputation of the HARRY POTTER mark.[755] As the Court had already rejected the invocation of the right of quotation in its copyright assessment,[756] Byblos' defence referring to a polemic discussion of societal conditions was doomed to fail.[757]

In the case of a manga including Superman, the manga producer thus faces a discouraging arsenal of dilution arguments provided by EU trademark law.[758] As the manga series seeks to create an artistic contrast with the traditional presentation of superheroes in American graphic novels, it is transformative in the sense that it places the fictional character in a new environment.[759] From a cultural perspective, use of this kind can be deemed

---

750. Court of Appeals of Amsterdam, 6 November 2003, case ECLI:NL:GHAMS:2003:AN7646, Rowling/Byblos, para. 4.1.
751. Court of Appeals of Amsterdam, *ibid.*, para. 4.7.3 and 4.7.7. Cf. Senftleben 2012a, 364.
752. Court of Appeals of Amsterdam, *ibid.*, para. 4.1. See EUTM no. 000935593. See also the various other title registrations relating to Harry Potter books: EUTMs 003276862, 001729557, 003121911, 003141231, 003426533, 003426558, 003426831, 005587951, 005956561 and 010110195.
753. Court of Appeals of Amsterdam, *ibid.*, para. 4.9.
754. Court of Appeals of Amsterdam, *ibid.*, para. 4.8.3.1.
755. Court of Appeals of Amsterdam, *ibid.*, para. 4.10.
756. For a more detailed discussion of this aspect of the decision, see Senftleben 2012a, 364; Frosio 2014, 381-382, who also gives examples of countries where the Harry Potter parody was deemed permissible.
757. Court of Appeals of Amsterdam, *ibid.*, para. 4.7.7 and 4.10.
758. Cf. the discussion of infringement criteria by Kur 2002, 605-607.
759. As to the notion of transformative use in U.S. copyright law which can serve as a reference point here, see Sag 2012, 47; Samuelson 2009, 2537; Beebe 2008, 156; Leval 1990, 1105; Litman 1997, 588; Nimmer 2003, 263.

desirable. It adds new connotations to pre-existing cultural material.[760] However, it is unclear whether a manga that includes the Superman drawing for the purpose of creating an artistic contrast between Japanese comics and the American superhero genre would survive a scrutiny in the light of the 'ride on the coat-tails' formula which constitutes the cornerstone of the unfair freeriding test developed by the CJEU. As in the Austrian *Styriagra* case and the Dutch *Tanja Grotter* decision, defence arguments based on freedom of expression may be rejected because of commercial exploitation.[761]

Against this background, the protection of marks with a reputation against the taking of unfair advantage is a feature of anti-dilution legislation that is particularly worrisome from the perspective of cultural follow-on innovation. When the remix of a trademarked cultural icon leads to a new work that is commercially exploited, it is easy to use the argument of unfair freeriding as a starting point to shed a negative light on the alleged infringer. The acceptance of unfair freeriding as an independent cause of action offers the claimant the opportunity to draw the picture of a parasitic user who advances the argument of artistic expression as a false pretence to reap where she has not sown.

The current system of EU trademark protection, however, even goes a step further. Apart from the outlined dilution actions which Article 9(2)(c) EUTMR and Article 10(2)(c) TMD make available for owners of marks with a reputation, CJEU jurisprudence paved the way for additional infringement arguments in the area of double identity. This infringement action is generally available with regard to all trademarks and, accordingly, whenever trademark rights in cultural signs are acquired. The double identity rule offers an infringement action against use of an identical sign for identical goods or services. With the broad function theory developed in *L'Oréal/Bellure*, the Court transformed the double identity rule of Article 9(2)(a) EUTMR and Article 10(2)(a) TMD into a further tool for the protection of communication, investment and advertising functions which the owner of trademark rights in a cultural sign may develop through marketing efforts.[762] This development

760. Cf. the analysis carried out by the U.S. Supreme Court, 7 March 1994, Campbell/Acuff-Rose, 510 U.S. 569, 579 (1994). See also Sag 2012, 47; Samuelson 2009, 2537; Beebe 2008, 156; Leval 1990, 1105; Litman 1997, 588; Nimmer 2003, 263.

761. See England and Wales High Court, 10 October 2011, case HC11C03222, Ate My Heart/Mind Candy Limited, [2011] EWHC 2741 (Ch), paras 77-78, where Justice Vos concludes that the commercial profit motive (concerning the exploitation of a children's song reminiscent of the Lady Gaga song 'Bad Romance') discredits defence arguments emphasizing the intention to parody the original song (para. 14). Cf. Jacques 2016, 476.

762. CJEU, 18 June 2009, case C-487/07, L'Oréal/Bellure, para. 58. For a discussion of the role of the broadened function theory in EU trademark law, see Basire 2014, 268-271; Kur 2014, 434; Senftleben 2014a, 518; Cohen Jehoram 2012, 1243; Hacker 2009, 333. As to the traditional focus of CJEU jurisprudence on the origin function, see CJEU, case C-206/01, *Arsenal Football Club* [2002] ECR I-10273, para. 51; case C-245/02, *Anheuser-Busch* [2004] ECR I-10989, para. 59; case C-48/05, *Adam Opel* [2007] ECR

gives rise to additional concerns about a corrosive effect on remix and reuse in the cultural domain.

As explained in section 6.1.1 above, the CJEU held in *L'Oréal/Bellure* that, besides the traditional function of indicating commercial origin, the communication, investment and advertising functions of a trademark also enjoyed protection in cases where the alleged infringer uses an identical sign for identical goods or services.[763] Hence, the Court expressly recognized the economic and communication value of a trademark as an independent subject matter of protection in double identity situations. As also stated above, the protection of communication, investment, and advertising functions is protection of the investment in the creation of a favourable brand image and the brand communication based on this image.

This development is relevant to the assessment of potential interferences of trademark protection with cultural follow-on innovation. Once the economic and communication value of a trademark is recognized as an independent subject matter of protection, the user of a protected sign can no longer escape an infringement claim in double identity situations by simply arguing that use in a cultural context is unlikely to mislead consumers into believing that there is a connection with the trademark owner. Even if no origin confusion is caused, the trademark proprietor can still argue that the use amounts to infringement because it damages the economic and communication value of the trademark. In consequence, a publication showing a biting parody of Mickey Mouse, Superman or Miffy – fictional characters registered in respect of printed matter, including books, newspapers and magazines[764] – may be held to be infringing even if the consuming public does not assume a commercial connection with the respective trademark proprietors.[765] In the absence of confusion, the infringement claim can be based on the argument that the parody damages the brand image resulting from investment in advertising and marketing activities. Under Article 9(2)(a) EUTMR and Article 10(2)(a) TMD, it is sufficient to show an 'adverse effect' on the communication, investment and advertising functions

I-1017, para. 21. As to this previous stage of development of the function theory, see Yap 2009, 86-87; Simon Fhima 2005, 401.

763. CJEU, 18 June 2009, case C-487/07, L'Oréal/Bellure, para. 58.

764. With regard to the Mickey Mouse drawing, see IR no. 296478. As to the Superman drawing, see https://register.dpma.de/DPMAregister/marke/einsteiger?lang=en for the German trademark registration DD643100. The Miffy drawing is registered in the Benelux for various goods, including printed matter, magazines and books. See https://register.boip.int/bmbonline/intro/show.do for the Benelux registration no. 0653451.

765. A trademark action against a biting parody is not a mere theoretical example. The aforementioned case *Mercis and Bruna/Punt*, for example, concerned a combined copyright and trademark claim against a parody showing Miffy as a 9/11 terrorist. See Court of Appeals of Amsterdam, 13 September 2011, case ECLI:NL:GHAMS:2011:BS7825, Mercis and Bruna/Punt, *AMI* 2012, p. 28.

of the affected trademark.[766] Hence, an interference with trademark-based communication, investment or advertising is enough to build a prima facie case of infringement.

In *Google France and Google*, the CJEU explained in respect of the advertising function that the trademark owner may have not only the objective of indicating the origin of its goods or services, 'but also that of using its mark for advertising purposes designed to inform and persuade consumers'.[767] In *Interflora/Marks & Spencer*, the Court elaborated with regard to the investment function that in addition to its origin and (potential) advertising function, a trademark may also be used 'to acquire or preserve a reputation capable of attracting consumers and retaining their loyalty'.[768] This investment function may overlap with the advertising function. Nonetheless, it had to be separated according to the Court because not only advertising was employed but also 'various commercial techniques' when the trademark was used to acquire or preserve a reputation.[769] As the Court did not comment on the communication function in any subsequent decision, this function still constitutes *terra incognita*. There can be little doubt, however, that the inclusion of the ancillary functions relating to trademark communication, investment and advertising strategies offer additional starting points for the development of infringement arguments.[770]

While it is not entirely clear whether, in the absence of any interference with the essential origin function, the CJEU would accept double identity infringement claims based exclusively on the erosion of communication, investment and advertising functions,[771] the decision in *Mitsubishi/Duma* already demonstrated quite clearly the Court's willingness to assume infringement when this is necessary to safeguard the possibility for trademark owners to use the mark to attract and retain consumers (advertising function) and exploit the trademark magnetism (investment function).[772] The case concerned debranding. All Mitsubishi trademark insignia had been removed from the goods before importation and sale on the EU market. Therefore, the origin function of the Mitsubishi trademarks could only play a subordinate role.[773] In this situation, the Court heavily relied on advertising and investment functions as avenues to arrive at an infringement action. The Court held that the marketing of the debranded goods were likely to substantially impede Mitsubishi's use of the registered marks to acquire a

766. CJEU, 18 June 2009, case C-487/07, L'Oréal/Bellure, para. 58.
767. CJEU, 23 March 2010, cases C-236/08-238/08, Google France and Google/Louis Vuitton et al., para. 91.
768. CJEU, 22 September 2011, case C-323/09, Interflora/Marks & Spencer, para. 60.
769. CJEU, *ibid.*, para. 61.
770. Cf. the above-cited description of the changing role of trademarks by Dreyfuss 1990, 397-398.
771. Ohly 2019, 336.
772. CJEU, 25 July 2018, case C-129/17, Mitsubishi/Duma, para. 46.
773. CJEU, *ibid.*, para. 45.

reputation and attract and retain consumers. After debranding, the marks could no longer serve as a factor in sales promotion or as an instrument of commercial strategy.[774] Moreover, the debranding would 'deprive the proprietor of the possibility of obtaining, by putting the goods on the EEA market first, the economic value of the product bearing that mark and, therefore, of its investment'.[775] In the light of this decision, it does not seem correct to downplay the impact of communication, investment and advertising functions on the infringement decision.[776] By contrast, arguments based on an impediment of communication, investment or advertising functions can tip the scales in favour of a finding of infringement.

For the condition of adverse effect to be an effective threshold against a protection automatism in double identity situations, it would have to constitute a strict requirement of detriment. Instead of the emergence of such a strict test, however, developments at the national level show that the formula of 'adverse effect' leaves room for different, more elastic interpretations. In *Grosse Inspektion für alle*, the German Federal Court of Justice deemed it sufficient for assuming detriment that the alleged infringer had tried to benefit from the power of attraction, the reputation and the prestige of the VW logo in an advertising campaign concerning car maintenance services. The Court held that:

> in general, the image transfer resulting from the exploitation of the reputation and distinctive character also weakens the distinctiveness of the senior mark with a reputation and, thereby, impairs its advertising function.[777]

On its merits, the German Federal Court of Justice thus equated the test of adverse effect in double identity situations with the test of unfair freeriding that is applied in anti-dilution cases falling under Article 9(2)(c) EUTMR and Article 10(2)(c) TMD. As explained, the CJEU stated in *L'Oréal/Bellure* that a mere attempt to 'ride on the coat-tails' of a mark with a reputation could be sufficient to assume that unfair advantage – in the sense of Article 10(2)(c) TMD – had been taken.[778]

To prevent trademark protection in double identity cases from impeding cultural follow-on innovation, it is important against this background to apply the threshold requirements of identical signs and identical goods or services strictly. In many cases, a parody concerning a trademark with cultural significance, such as Mickey Mouse, will not include an identical

774. CJEU, *ibid.*, para. 46.
775. CJEU, *ibid.*, para. 46.
776. See Ohly 2019, 336, who doubts that these accessory functions have much independent weight in the absence of a negative effect on the origin function.
777. German Federal Court of Justice, 14 April 2011, case I ZR 33/10, 'Grosse Inspektion für alle', para. 15.
778. CJEU, 18 June 2009, case C-487/07, L'Oréal/Bellure, para. 49.

copy of the Mickey Mouse drawing entered in the trademark register.[779] For a parody to be successful, it must make the target of its mockery clearly identifiable. In practice, however, this does not always require slavish copying of the trademarked symbol. In *Springender Pudel*, for example, the German Federal Court of Justice had to decide on the trademark registration of a Puma parody showing a jumping poodle instead of a jumping puma. In the characteristic typeset of the well-known Puma logo, the parody showed the word 'Pudel'[780] in place of the original word mark PUMA. The German Patent and Trademark Office had accepted the registration for various goods, including T-shirts, sportswear, handbags and printed matter. The registration thus covered goods, in respect of which the Puma logo was registered as well.[781] The question before the Court was whether Puma had to tolerate the registration of the poodle parody in the light of artistic freedom of expression.

Denying the entitlement to register the parody as a trademark, the German Federal Court of Justice emphasized that the registration primarily served commercial purposes. The Puma parody had been registered as a basis for selling T-shirts that had commercial success because of the funny play with the well-known Puma logo. While the aim to derive profit from Puma's reputation was evident, the humorous play with the Puma logo did not include elements of criticism, such as comments on Puma's products or production methods.[782] Weighing the fundamental protection of intellectual property against the freedom of artistic expression, the Court thus arrived at the conclusion that Puma was not obliged to accept the registration of the poodle logo as a trademark.[783]

With regard to the question of sign identity, the case provides an example of a logo parody which is funny because of several modifications of the original trademark. Quite clearly, this type of parody is not based on an identical copy of the registered logo. It falls outside the scope of the double identity rule. Considering the various deviations from the original Puma logo, the German Federal Court of Justice even denied a risk of direct or indirect confusion.[784] Similar parody cases arising from logo modifications

---

779. In principle, the infringement analysis in EU trademark law is based on a comparison of the allegedly infringing sign as used in the marketplace and the trademark as registered. Cf. Kur/Senftleben 2017, para. 5.108-5.124. For this reason, the Mickey Mouse drawing entered in the register constitutes the reference point for the analysis. See IR no. 296478.

780. Pudel is the German word for poodle.

781. German Federal Court of Justice, 2 April 2015, case I ZR 59/13, 'Springender Pudel', paras 1-3.

782. German Federal Court of Justice, *ibid.*, paras 46-51.

783. German Federal Court of Justice, *ibid.*, para. 51.

784. German Federal Court of Justice, *ibid.*, paras 27-31. As the Puma logo was well known, Puma could rely on enhanced protection against dilution instead. To advance the argument of dilution in the form of unfair freeriding, it was sufficient that the Puma parody called to mind the trademark. See German Federal Court of Justice, *ibid.*, paras 32-35.

can be found across the Atlantic. As mentioned in the preceding section, the U.S. Court of Appeals for the Eighth Circuit prohibited an antinuclear parody of Mutual of Omaha's Indian head logo in *Mutual of Omaha Insurance Company/Novak*. The parody was found to cause confusion as to sponsorship.[785] To create his antinuclear mockery, Novak had replaced the company name 'Mutual of Omaha' with the words 'Mutant of Omaha'. He had also added the indication 'Nuclear Holocaust Insurance'. In lieu of the Indian head which features prominently in the original logo, the parody depicted a side view of a feather-bonneted, emaciated human head. As in the German case *Springender Pudel*, the Mutual of Omaha parody had a commercial background. Novak had advertised and sold a considerable number of T-shirts, sweatshirts, caps, buttons, and coffee mugs with his parody before Mutual of Omaha obtained a preliminary injunction. As to the relationship between the signs, the U.S. Court of Appeals agreed with the District Court that Novak's design was 'very similar' to the original Mutual of Omaha logo. The Court deemed it decisive that the letters and styles of the phrases were virtually identical. Novak's 'Indian head' parody moreover depicted a side view of a head similar to the Indian head logo of the insurance company. Use of the word 'Mutant' in place of 'Mutual' was, in the context of Novak's parody, suggestive of Mutual of Omaha.[786] The degree of similarity between the signs was thus deemed higher than in the German case. Nonetheless, the antinuclear parody modified the original logo to such an extent that no sign identity was established.

In the context of assessing a potential corrosive effect of double identity protection on cultural remix and reuse, the comparison between the trademark and the allegedly infringing sign in parody cases, such as *Springender Pudel* and *Mutual of Omaha Insurance Company/Novak*, indicates that because of deviations from the trademarked signs at issue, protection in double identity cases will not always impact negatively on cultural follow-on innovation. As long as the test of identical signs is applied strictly, the described extension of EU double identity protection to communication, investment and advertising functions seems unlikely to impact use in the cultural domain. For instance, the use of a cultural sign in a parody will often involve the modification of the sign to create a contrast with the original work. If a cultural sign is registered as a trademark, the alteration of the sign for parodistic purposes will thus exclude the application of the double identity rule.

However, it must not be overlooked that the CJEU added some elasticity to the test of sign identity. In *LTJ Diffusion*, the Court took as a starting point that the requirement of identity implied that the two elements to be compared in double identity cases – the sign and the mark – should be

785. U.S. Court of Appeals for the Eighth Circuit, 30 December 1987, Mutual of Omaha Insurance Company/Novak, 836 F.2d 397, paras 12-13.

786. U.S. Court of Appeals for the Eighth Circuit, *ibid.*, para. 8.

the same in all respects. In principle, identity of signs could only be assumed where 'the sign reproduces, without any modification or addition, all the elements constituting the mark'.[787] Factoring the perception of the average consumer into the equation, however, the Court nonetheless arrived at a more lenient approach. In respect of the assessment of consumer perception, the Court had recourse to standards developed in the context of protection against confusion under Article 9(2)(b) EUTMR and Article 10(2)(b) TMD. Recalling previous findings in *Lloyd Schuhfabrik Meyer*, the Court pointed out that the sign produced an overall impression on the consumer, and that the consumer only rarely had the chance of making a direct comparison between the sign and the trademark. As the consumer, thus, had to rely on the imperfect picture which she had kept in mind, and her level of attention was likely to vary according to the category of goods or services in question, the perception of identity between the sign and the trademark could not be deemed to be the result of a direct comparison of all the characteristics of the sign and the mark.[788] Against this background, a more global assessment was appropriate which pays tribute to the fact that 'insignificant differences between the sign and the trade mark may go unnoticed by an average consumer'.[789]

Besides cases where a sign reproduces, without any modification or addition, all the elements constituting the trademark, the double identity rule of Article 9(2)(a) EUTMR and Article 10(2)(a) TMD, therefore, also covers situations where, viewed as a whole, the sign 'contains differences so insignificant that they may go unnoticed by an average consumer'.[790] In *Portakabin*, the CJEU had the opportunity to give a concrete example for the application of this standard. For keyword advertising purposes, Primakabin had selected not only the original trademark PORTAKABIN as a search term but also variations, namely 'portacabin', 'portokabin' and 'portocabin'.[791] While leaving the final word on the identity question to the referring national court, the CJEU observed that the versions with minor spelling mistakes could be regarded as containing differences which are so insignificant that they may go unnoticed by the average consumer.[792]

With the more elastic test of 'going unnoticed', the CJEU created a loophole for double identity claims targeting unauthorized use in the cultural domain. For this reason, it would be premature to jump to the conclusion that EU trademark protection in double identity situations is generally unproblematic. The above-described decision in *Mercis and Bruna/Punt*, for

787. CJEU, 20 March 2003, case C-291/00, LTJ Diffusion, paras 50-51.
788. CJEU, 22 June 1999, case C-342/97, Lloyd Schuhfabrik Meyer ('Lloyd/Loint's'), para. 26, on the one hand, and CJEU, 20 March 2003, case C-291/00, LTJ Diffusion, para. 52, on the other.
789. CJEU, 20 March 2003, case C-291/00, LTJ Diffusion, para. 53.
790. CJEU, *ibid.*, para. 54.
791. CJEU, 8 July 2010, C-558/08, Portakabin, para. 46.
792. CJEU, *ibid.*, para. 48.

instance, concerned seven parodies that placed Miffy in drug and terror contexts that were alien to the children's universe surrounding the original fictional character. As to the degree of copying, the District Court had concluded that in two parodies, the Miffy drawing had been copied literally except for certain additions.[793] In fact, it seemed to be an essential element of the humoristic effect of these parodies that the public may think at first sight that the parodies were genuine Miffy drawings. Only the sharp contextual contrast – drugs and terror – finally revealed the parodistic nature of the drawings. The test of sign identity can also play a role when it comes to the use of trademarked cultural symbols in appropriation art. At the core of this form of art lies the creation of new cultural material based on 'the taking over, into a work of art, of a real object or even an existing work of art'.[794] As this artistic practice involves substantial copying, it is not surprising that appropriation art has given rise to several lawsuits. The U.S. Court of Appeals for the Second Circuit, for instance, found copyright infringement in *Rogers/Koons* – a case concerning the three-dimensional sculptural piece 'String of Puppies' which Jeff Koons had based on Art Rogers' two-dimensional black-and-white photograph 'Puppies'. The photograph showed a couple on a bench holding eight new German Shepherd puppies. Giving instructions for the creation of the sculpture, Koons had insisted on detailed copying that captures the individual features of the photographic work.[795] However, Koons added colour in accordance with the shades of grey in the photograph. The little dogs, for example, appeared in shades of blue in the final sculpture. Moreover, Koons added flowers in the hair of the couple. To assess copyright infringement, the Court relied on the so-called ordinary observer test and asked whether 'the ordinary observer, unless he set out to detect the disparities, would be disposed to overlook them, and regard their aesthetic appeal as the same'.[796] On this basis, the Court arrived at the conclusion that small additions, such as the flowers in the hair of the couple, were insufficient to neutralize the impression that Koons' sculpture was overwhelmingly similar to the protected expression of Rogers' photograph.[797] Discussing the defence argument of fair use,[798] the Court added that 'the essence of Rogers' photograph was copied nearly *in toto*,

793. Court of Appeals of Amsterdam, 13 September 2011, case ECLI:NL:GHAMS:2011: BS7825, Mercis and Bruna/Punt, *AMI* 2012, 28, para. 4.11.

794. Wilson/Lack 2016, 20-21. For an analysis of intellectual property issues arising from almost literal copying in appropriation art cases, see Geiger 2018a, 6-7; Geiger 2018b, 428-431 and 434-437; Adler 2016, 559; Lucas/Ginsburg 2016, 5; Morley 2015, 385; Hudson Hick 2013, 1155; Jaszi 2009, 105; Bresler 2003, 15; Landes 2000, 1; Greenberg 1992, 1.

795. U.S. Court of Appeals for the Second Circuit, 2 April 1992, Rogers/Koons, 960 F.2d 301, section D and II. Cf. Hughes 1999, 938-939; Greenberg 1992, 23-33.

796. U.S. Court of Appeals for the Second Circuit, *ibid.*, section II.

797. U.S. Court of Appeals for the Second Circuit, *ibid.*, section II.

798. Section 107 of the U.S. Copyright Act.

much more than would have been necessary even if the sculpture had been a parody of plaintiff's work. In short, it is not really the parody flag that appellants are sailing under, but rather the flag of piracy'.[799]

On similar grounds, the District Court of Antwerp established copyright infringement in *Van Giel/Tuymans*. The case concerned the painting 'A Belgian Politician' which Luc Tuymans had based on Katrijn van Giel's photograph of the Belgian politician Jean-Marie Dedecker. Tuymans' painting reproduced the design, lighting and framing of the photograph.[800] To defend the copying, Tuymans pointed out that he had used a different format and a different colour gradation. He also expressed the view that through his individual way of painting, he had given the photograph a 'new status' and created a distance from the original work.[801] The Court, however, rejected the defence argument that 'A Belgian Politician' constituted a permissible parody.[802] Despite the distance which Tuymans sought to create, the Court held that the painting could not be deemed a parody 'from any perspective whatsoever'.[803] Tuymans' work was thus found to infringe Van Giel's copyright.

The finding of copyright infringement in *Rogers/Koons* and *Van Giel/Tuymans* does not imply that copying in appropriation art cases would automatically amount to trademark infringement under the EU double identity test of 'going unnoticed by an average consumer'.[804] Even though the infringement tests applied in U.S. copyright cases, such as the 'ordinary observer' test in *Rogers/Koons*,[805] resemble the EU trademark test of 'going unnoticed', the infringement analysis under the double identity rule of EU trademark law seems more fine-grained. In *BMW-Emblem*, for instance, the German Federal Court of Justice pointed out that the registration of a trademark in black and white only covered this black-and-white version. In line with EUIPO registration guidelines,[806] the Court saw no reason to assume that a trademark registration in black and white encompassed colour versions of the trademark. This starting point led to the conclusion that colour versions of the trademark were not identical with the registered black-and-white version and fell outside the scope of the double identity

799. U.S. Court of Appeals for the Second Circuit, *ibid.*, section III, 3 (emphasis in the original text). Cf. Farley 2015, 24-25.
800. District Court of Antwerp, 15 January 2015, case 14/4305/A, Van Giel/Tuymans, para. 4.
801. District Court of Antwerp, *ibid.*, paras 2-3.
802. In EU copyright law, the parody exception is laid down in Article 5(3)(k) ISD.
803. District Court of Antwerp, *ibid.*, para. 5.
804. CJEU, 20 March 2003, case C-291/00, LTJ Diffusion, para. 54.
805. U.S. Court of Appeals for the Second Circuit, 2 April 1992, Rogers/Koons, 960 F.2d 301, section II.
806. See https://euipo.europa.eu/ohimportal/en/guidelines.

rule.[807] If a cultural symbol is registered as a trademark, an appropriation artist may thus escape a finding of infringement under the double identity rule by adding colour or using colours different from the registered version of the cultural sign. Under the infringement standard developed in *BMW-Emblem*, for instance, no sign identity could be established in *Rogers/Koons* because Jeff Koons used colour for his sculptural piece whereas the photograph by Art Rogers was in black and white.

Appropriation art may also modify underlying source material to such an extent that a finding of infringement is beyond reach even under applicable copyright standards. In *Blanch/Koons*, for instance, the U.S. Court of Appeals for the Second Circuit held that Jeff Koons' inclusion of Andrea Blanch's fashion photograph 'Silk Sandals by Gucci' in his collage painting 'Niagara' was transformative to such a degree that the use had to be deemed fair and non-infringing under the U.S. fair use doctrine.[808] Koons had included the legs and feet from the photograph, inverted the orientation of the legs and added a heel to one of the feet. His intention was not the repackaging of a fashion photograph. Instead, the Court found that he had used the legs and feet 'as fodder for his commentary on the social and aesthetic consequences of mass media'.[809] Discussing the incorporation of photographs in paintings and collages, the U.S. Court of Appeals for the Second Circuit also reached nuanced results in *Cariou/Prince*. While the Court found that in the majority of cases, Richard Prince's use of photographs of Rastafarians made by Patrick Cariou could be deemed fair when considering the extent of the portions used and the changes made, the Court was unable to readily establish fair use in respect of five artworks with more substantial takings and a less transformative character.[810] In 'Graduation', for instance, Prince had confined his modifications to the addition of blue lozenges over the Rastafarian's eyes and mouth, and a picture of a guitar. Against this background, the Court had doubts whether these minimal alterations were sufficiently transformative and remanded the case to the lower court for a final determination.[811] When hypothetically applying the EU trademark test of identical signs to these cases, there can be little doubt that a finding of sign identity is unlikely. The various changes to 'Silk Sandals by Gucci' and the elements added in 'Graduation' would hardly 'go unnoticed by an average consumer'.[812] Most probably, Jeff Koons and Richard Prince could thus escape a finding of trademark infringement under

807. German Federal Court of Justice, 12 March 2015, case I ZR 153/14, 'BMW-Emblem', paras 15-17.
808. U.S. Court of Appeals for the Second Circuit, 25 October 2006, Blanch/Koons, 467 F.3d 244, 258-259.
809. U.S. Court of Appeals for the Second Circuit, *ibid.*, 248-249 and 252-253.
810. U.S. Court of Appeals for the Second Circuit, 25 April 2013, Cariou/Prince, 714 F.3d 694, section II. Cf. Morley 2015, 385; Farley 2015, 28-34.
811. U.S. Court of Appeals for the Second Circuit, *ibid.*, section II.
812. CJEU, 20 March 2003, case C-291/00, LTJ Diffusion, para. 54.

the EU double identity rule if they would modify trademarked source material to a comparable extent.

Nonetheless, EU trademark protection in double identity cases is not generally unproblematic from the perspective of cultural follow-on innovation. The spectrum of appropriation art offers examples of works that could give rise to a trademark claim based on the double identity rule. Andy Warhol's famous 1962 piece 'Campbell's Soup Cans', for instance, slavishly reproduces Campbell's soup containers, including all details of the Campbell logo. In this work, Warhol intentionally 'mimicked the repetition and uniformity of advertising by carefully reproducing the same image across each individual canvas'.[813] In 1981, Sherrie Levine began re-photographing works of several modernist photographers, such as Edward Weston, Walker Evans and Alexander Rodchenko. Levine's re-photographs only depart from the underlying source in size, surface and resolution. Hence, commentators point out that her re-photographs are 'almost indistinguishable from the originals'.[814] If this appropriation technique is applied to a photograph enjoying trademark protection,[815] the artistic use could thus fulfil the requirement of 'go[ing] unnoticed by an average consumer'[816] and fall within the province of the double identity rule. More recent examples show that the inclusion of trademarked source material in artworks can trigger an infringement claim. In the Netherlands, Louis Vuitton sued artist Nadia Plesner for the inclusion of an 'Audra' handbag – a handbag showing the famous LV logo in 'multicolor canvas' design – in a drawing of an undernourished African child holding not only the designer handbag but also a chihuahua dog. Mixing cruel reality with show business insignia known from Paris Hilton, Nadia Plesner sought to criticize insufficient media attention for problems and disasters that truly matter. With her work, she wanted to point to 'people who actually deserve and need attention'.[817]

For this purpose, Plesner started a campaign including the sale of 'Simple Living' T-shirts and posters showing the undernourished child with the handbag. With the proceeds of sales, she supported victims of the war in Darfur. Louis Vuitton, however, feared that the association with an armed conflict could have a corrosive effect on its prestigious brand image.[818] As

813. See the description of the work provided by the Museum of Modern Art, New York, available at https://www.moma.org/learn/moma_learning/andy-warhol-campbells-soup-cans-1962.

814. See the discussion of her work by van Leeuwen 2013. Cf. Hick 2013, 1178; Buccafusco/Bechtold/Sprigman 2017, 44-45.

815. For example, see German Federal Court of Justice, 24 April 2008, case I ZB 21/06, Marlene-Dietrich-Bildnis, which concerned an attempt to register a portrait photograph of the actress Marlene Dietrich as a trademark.

816. CJEU, 20 March 2003, case C-291/00, LTJ Diffusion, para. 53.

817. District Court of The Hague, 4 May 2011, case ECLI:NL:RBSGR:2011:BQ3525, Nadia Plesner/Louis Vuitton, para. 2.6.

818. See the facts reported in District Court of The Hague, *ibid.*, para. 2.1-2.8.

Louis Vuitton based its claims against Nadia Plesner on industrial design rights, the decision of the District Court of The Hague does not address the issue of trademark protection in double identity situations. Invoking the fundamental guarantee of (artistic) freedom of expression laid down in Article 10 ECHR, the Court arrived at the conclusion that Plesner's use of Louis Vuitton's handbag design did not amount to infringement.[819] Plesner thus escaped the verdict of infringement. However, she had to rely on a defence strategy based on freedom of expression as an external[820] limitation of Louis Vuitton's design rights. The infringement claim could not be rejected from the outset because use for artistic purposes does not fall outside the scope of industrial design rights altogether.

A similar scenario may have arisen if Louis Vuitton had brought the case on the basis of EU trademark law. The use of the LV logo on T-shirts and posters in the framework of the 'Simple Living' campaign may have been found to constitute prima facie infringement in the light of interferences with Louis Vuitton's trademark communication, investment and advertising strategy. If differences between a registered version of the LV logo and the depiction of the logo in 'Simple Living' may have gone unnoticed by an average consumer,[821] Louis Vuitton could even have invoked the double identity rule to support its claim. Nadia Plesner would thus have had to develop a defence strategy based on freedom of expression to justify her unauthorized use. Other works of Nadia Plesner could also give rise to a trademark dispute. In her painting 'Darfurnica',[822] she included not only the undernourished child with the Louis Vuitton handbag but also other references to trademarks and brands, such as Facebook's logo showing a white 'f' on dark blue background. As this logo is registered as an EUTM for various goods and services, including posters, printed matter, textiles and clothing,[823] a trademark claim based on the double identity rule does not seem a mere theoretical option.

Further examples of works that may trigger trademark infringement actions based on the double identity rule come to the fore when exploring the field of pop art. Roy Lichtenstein's paintings 'Look Mickey' and 'Popeye', for example, meticulously reproduce images of Mickey Mouse, Donald Duck and Popeye. Considering this reuse of cartoon characters, it cannot be ruled out that works of pop art may give rise to a trademark infringement action. If a work of pop art reproduces a cartoon character in the form that

819. District Court of The Hague, *ibid.*, para. 4.4-4.8.
820. As to the invocation of fundamental rights as external limitations of intellectual property rights outside the canon of exceptions and limitations in specific intellectual property legislation, see Geiger/Izyumenko 2019, 131; Schovsbo 2018, 571-573; Voorhoof 2002, 639-645; Dreier 2001a, 295.
821. Cf. CJEU, 20 March 2003, case C-291/00, LTJ Diffusion, para. 54.
822. For a reproduction and discussion of this painting, see District Court of The Hague, *ibid.*, para. 2.10.
823. EUTMs no. 009151226, 009724774 and 009776601.

has been registered as a trademark, the use for artistic purposes could lead to a claim based on the double identity rule. As it is the very purpose of pop art to erode the traditional distinction between 'high' and 'low' culture by creating works based on objects of mass culture,[824] the use of a trademarked depiction of a fictional character would not come as a surprise. The practice of obtaining trademark registrations with regard to different drawings of the same cartoon character enhances the risk of a trademark lawsuit.[825]

Finally, it is to be considered that the freedom of artistic remix concerns not only literary and artistic works as such but also their titles. Second authors embarking on remix and reuse activities may have to play not only with the contents and substance of a pre-existing work but also with the title of the work, the name of the author, and the names of main personages or fictional characters to make their point and convey their message to the public (section 5.2.4). The words forming a protected work title or name, however, will typically be included literally in a derivative work.[826] Works built on pre-existing cultural material often include names and titles stemming from the source material. Roy Lichtenstein's painting 'Look Mickey', for example, reproduces the trademarked name 'Mickey' and has a title including this name.[827] In the area of title use, trademark protection under the double identity rule can thus have a deep impact on cultural follow-on innovation.[828]

In sum, the far-reaching protection of the economic and communication value of trademarks in EU trademark law – under either the anti-dilution provisions of Article 9(2)(c) EUTMR and Article 10(2)(c) TMD or the double identity rule of Article 9(2)(a) EUTMR and Article 10(2)(a) TMD – offers a broad arsenal of tools which trademark proprietors who succeed in registering a cultural sign as a trademark can assert against remix and reuse in a cultural context. As explained, brand owners invoking anti-dilution protection against use in a cultural context can benefit from a remarkably low eligibility criterion of having a reputation, an elastic association test covering referential and decorative use and a flexible unfair advantage criterion that is already fulfilled when a third party attempts to ride on the coat-tails of the mark with a reputation. In double identity situations, it is no longer necessary to base infringement arguments on the traditional origin function. Instead,

824. See the description of this art movement on Wikipedia, available at https://en.wikipedia.org/wiki/Pop_art.

825. For example, see the different versions of Snoopy registered as EUTMs 000423178, 005468988, 008947715 and 010189025. For further examples of appropriation art that could give rise to trademark infringement actions, see Hick 2013, 1178.

826. Ohly 2019, 335.

827. For examples of Disney's registrations of the word mark MICKEY, see the registrations in France, no. 1567169 and 1128324, and Germany, no. 39716409. For the particulars of these registrations, see www.tmdn.org/tmview/.

828. Cf. Court of Appeals of Amsterdam, 26 juli 2001, ERB/Beukenoord, *AMI* 2002, 12, para. 2.14 and 2.22. Cf. Visser 2002, 15-16.

EU trademark law offers the protection of communication, investment and advertising functions as alternative avenues to arrive at prima facie infringement.

Surveying these elastic conditions for the protection of the economic and communication value of trademarks, it becomes apparent that the conceptual differences between copyright and trademark protection increasingly lose their practical importance in the EU. Copyright protection of Mickey Mouse is protection of the artistic content of the drawing. Trademark protection of the name MICKEY[829] and the Mickey Mouse drawing,[830] however, is not only protection as an indicator of commercial source but also protection of Disney's brand-based communication, investment and advertising efforts. Through the backdoor of brand image protection, trademark rights come closer and closer to the exclusive position awarded in copyright law. As a corollary, the extent of control over the communication surrounding a trademark is also increasingly approximated to the level of control which a copyright owner can exercise. With every extension of the scope of protection against dilution and every relaxation of the prerequisites for protection in double identity situations, the protection of signs with cultural significance as trademarks becomes more problematic from the perspective of cultural follow-on innovation. As the above analysis illustrates, it is disquieting how many steps EU trademark law has already taken in this direction.

6.2.4 ***Defences***

Although the developments described in the preceding sections show that EU trademark law offers various starting points for the development of infringement arguments against use in a cultural context, this does not mean that owners of trademarks with cultural significance will always have success with their claims. Instead, limitations of trademark protection may finally prevent a finding of infringement and serve as defences for artists using trademarked source material. Even if prima facie infringement is found, use of trademarked cultural material may be found permissible in the end. In the above-described case *Lila Postkarte* of the German Federal Court of Justice (section 6.2.1), the ironic play with Milka trademarks on postcards was ultimately found to have taken place with 'due cause' in the light of artistic freedom of expression.[831] In EU trademark law, the defence of 'due cause' is an open-ended limitation of protection against dilution that is available

829. See IR no. 983421, MICKEY; EUTMs no. 002827426 and 005240668, MICKEY MOUSE.
830. See IR no. 135377 and 296478; EUTMs no. 003335981 and 003332913.
831. German Federal Court of Justice, 3 February 2005, case I ZR 159/02, Lila Postkarte, *GRUR* 2005, 583 (585).

under Article 9(2)(c) EUTMR and Article 10(2)(c) TMD.[832] In Benelux trademark law, the 'due cause' defence is also available under Article 2.20(2)(d) of the Benelux Convention on Intellectual Property which, as explained in section 6.2.3, offers trademark owners the possibility of bringing infringement claims even if use does not serve the purpose of distinguishing goods or services in the course of trade.[833] In the above-described case *Mercis and Bruna/Punt* of the Court of Appeals of Amsterdam (section 6.2.3), the due cause defence prevented the condemnation of biting Miffy parodies, including the depiction of Miffy as a 9/11 terrorist.[834] In *Moët Hennessy/Cedric Art*, the Benelux Court of Justice went beyond parody cases and developed an *exceptio artis* on the basis of the due cause defence. This species of the due cause defence is capable of covering unauthorized use in pop art and appropriation art. The case concerned the use of the trademarked Dom Pérignon bottle[835] in stylized form and neon colours in paintings which, according to the artist Cédric Peers, played with pointillism and pop art.[836] Assessing this unauthorized use of Hennessy's trademark, the Benelux Court of Justice stated that artistic freedom – as an aspect of the artist's right to freedom of expression – could constitute a due cause when 'there is an artistic expression that is the original result of a creative shaping process'.[837] The Court added, however, that the artistic expression must not aim at harming the trademark or the proprietor of the trademark.[838]

Artists using trademarked source material may also invoke the defence of 'referential use' which was broadened in the framework of the 2015 EU trademark law reform and is now laid down in Article 14(1)(c) EUTMR and Article 14(1)(c) TMD.[839] In these provisions, the concept of referential use is described as use 'for the purpose of identifying or referring to goods or services as those of the proprietor of that trade mark'. If a reference to a trademarked cultural symbol is qualified as actionable use 'in the course of trade' and 'in relation to goods or services' (section 6.2.1), the broadened defence of referential use thus offers artists the opportunity to argue that the reference to the trademark is the result of an honest practice of using the sign. In the case of use in the cultural domain, such as use in a parody, this line of

832. Cf. Senftleben 2017c, 256-265; Kur/Senftleben 2017, para. 5.265-5.268 and 6.59-6.63; Di Cataldo 2011, 833.
833. Cf. Vanovermeire 2009, 187-188.
834. Court of Appeals of Amsterdam, 13 September 2011, case ECLI:NL:GHAMS:2011: BS7825, Mercis and Bruna/Punt, *AMI* 2012, 28, para. 4.19. See the due cause defence enshrined in Article 2.20(1)(d) of the Benelux Convention.
835. IR no. 323543.
836. See https://www.cedricgallery.com/ for examples.
837. Benelux Court of Justice, 14 October 2019, case A2018/1/8, Moët Hennessy/Cedric Art, para. 9.
838. Benelux Court of Justice, *ibid.*, para. 9.
839. As to the considerations underlying this legislative change, see Kur/Senftleben 2017, para. 6.39-6.41.

reasoning finds support in Recital 21 EUTMR and Recital 27 TMD which explicitly state that:

> [u]se of a trade mark by third parties for the purpose of artistic expression should be considered as being fair as long as it is at the same time in accordance with honest practices in industrial and commercial matters.

The referential use defence can thus serve as a final resort in cases where a conflict between trademark rights and artistic freedom of expression arises.[840] Infringement claims following the registration of cultural heritage material as a trademark will fail if use of the trademarked material for the purpose of remix in the cultural domain is deemed permissible under Article 14(1)(c) EUTMR or Article 14(1)(c) TMD. In respect of the spectrum of affected infringement actions, the field of application of the referential use defence is broader than the ambit of operation of the open-ended defence of due cause. While the scope of the due cause defence is limited to protection against dilution in the sense of Article 9(2)(c) EUTMR and Article 10(2)(c) TMD, the defence of referential use applies across all exclusive rights in EU trademark law. Hence, an artist can also assert the freedom of referential use in situations where an infringement claim is based on the double identity rule of Article 9(2)(a) EUTMR or Article 10(2)(a) EUTMR, and where the trademark proprietor invokes protection against confusion in the sense of Article 9(2)(b) EUTMR or Article 10(2)(b) TMD.

Despite this broad ambit of operation, however, it is an open question whether the referential use defence is capable of providing shelter for artists using a trademarked cultural sign in a derivative literary and artistic production. This use scenario may fall outside the scope of Article 14(1)(c) EUTMR and Article 14(1)(c) TMD because the artistic remix addresses the cultural dimension of the trademarked sign and not its additional, commercial connotations. Strictly speaking, references to the cultural sign as an artwork do not concern use 'for the purpose of identifying or referring to goods or services as those of the proprietor of that trade mark'. The artist does not aim at referring to the sign as an identifier of commercial source.[841] Instead, she bases her own contribution to the discourse in the artistic domain on the sign as a cultural artefact. Against this background, it becomes apparent that the configuration of the referential use defence is unsatisfactory.[842] While it may cover artistic comments on the role which a cultural sign plays as an indication of the commercial origin of goods or services and focal point of commercial communication, it fails to cover the artistic play

840. For a more detailed discussion of this point, see Schovsbo 2018, 555.
841. For U.S. case law where a similar point was made with regard to the nominative fair use defence in U.S. trademark law and the defence was deemed inapplicable for this reason, see U.S. Court of Appeals for the Ninth Circuit, 5 November 2008, E.S.S. Entertainment 2000/Rock Star Videos, 547 F.3d 1095 (9th Cir. 2008), Part II.A.
842. See also the critical comments made by Bohaczewski 2020, 869-872.

with the sign's pre-existing, cultural meaning that does not concern the trademark function of identifying goods or services of the trademark owner.

A further example of a general defence that is applicable to all exclusive rights granted in EU trademark law – but incapable of covering the artistic remix and reuse of trademarked cultural signs – is the defence of descriptive use. In line with Article 17 TRIPS which explicitly refers to 'fair use of descriptive terms', the proprietor of a trademark is not entitled under EU trademark law to prohibit a third party from using descriptive indications in the course of trade, provided that the use takes place in accordance with 'honest practices in industrial or commercial matters'.[843] The descriptive use defence laid down in Article 14(1)(b) EUTMR and Article 14(1)(b) TMD covers the use of 'signs or indications which […] concern the kind, quality, quantity, intended purpose, value, geographical origin, the time of production of goods or of rendering of the service, or other characteristics of the goods or services'.

If cultural signs, in respect of which trademark rights have been acquired, are used in a descriptive sense as indications of product characteristics, the use falls within the scope of this defence. The German indications 'Mozarttorte' (Mozart cake) and 'Mozartkugel' (Mozart ball), for example, are likely to be perceived as an indication of a particular type of cake or chocolate product by the consuming public in several EU Member States. Against this background, descriptive use of these indications – in the sense of use that seeks to provide information about product characteristics – is unlikely to give rise to a conflict with the trademark MOZART.[844] A similar conclusion can be drawn with regard to goods and services in the cultural domain. In the decision *Marlene Dietrich* – concerning an attempt to register a portrait photograph of the famous actress as a trademark – the German Federal Court of Justice held that a photograph of Marlene Dietrich constituted a descriptive indication of product characteristics in respect of books, magazines, photographs, posters, CDs, DVDs, musical performances and film productions.[845] Use of the portrait photograph as an indication of film, book or poster characteristics thus remains permissible even if

843. Article 14(1)(b) and (2) EUTMR and Article 14(1)(b) and (2) TMD.

844. Higher Court of Appeals of Munich, 26 July 2001, case 29 U 6000/00, 'Mozart', *GRUR-Rechtsprechungsreport* 2002, 12 (13). In the meantime, the EUTM MOZART which formed the basis of the dispute has been invalidated because of its descriptive character with regard to 'pastry and confectionary, chocolate products and sugar confectionary'. See GCEU, 9 July 2008, case T-304/06, Paul Reber/OHIM, para. 99. As to the distinction between use as a trademark and use as a product description, see Di Cataldo 2011, 833 (838-840).

845. German Federal Court of Justice, 24 April 2008, case I ZB 21/06, Marlene-Dietrich-Bildnis, paras 12-15.

trademark rights are acquired.[846] The descriptive use defence may also justify the unauthorized use of three-dimensional creations, such as sculptures.[847] As the CJEU elaborated in the decision *Henkel*, 'the possibility that the packaging might describe the characteristics of the product, including its quality, cannot be ruled out'.[848] In case a trademarked shape with cultural significance is used in a descriptive sense, Article 14(1)(b) EUTMR and Article 14(1)(b) TMD thus exempts the use from the control of the trademark proprietor.

As the concept of referential use, however, the concept of descriptive use has its limits. In many cases, artistic use of a trademarked sign with cultural significance will not concern the indication of product characteristics. Use of a trademarked Marlene Dietrich portrait in a parody or in appropriation art, for instance, does not constitute use for the purpose of describing product characteristics. It incorporates the trademark itself – in this case a portrait of the actress – in the product. In contrast to a label that is merely attached to the product (and may indicate certain product features), the portrait becomes a central element of the very contents of the product. This form of use is more aptly qualified as decorative use. It raises the question whether the descriptive use defence encompasses use of a trademarked sign as a product feature. Although the aforementioned jurisprudence addressing the descriptive use of shapes (which often form part of the product) may offer starting points for a more lenient approach,[849] decorative use of this nature is unlikely to fall within the scope of the descriptive use defence under the current approach taken by the CJEU.[850] As the Court tersely concluded in *Adidas/Marca*, the purely decorative use of a two-stripe motif on sports clothing 'is not intended to give an indication concerning one of the characteristics of those goods'.[851] Constituting design features, the stripes were not intended to indicate the characteristics of the sports and leisure garments.[852] Similarly, the Court excluded the application of the descriptive use defence in *Opel/Autec* on the ground that the faithful reproduction of the Opel logo on a scale model car could not be regarded as

846. In Marlene Dietrich, the German Federal Court of Justice denied trademark protection in respect of the mentioned goods and services because of a lack of distinctive character. See German Federal Court of Justice, *ibid.*, paras 12-15.
847. The registration of sculptures as trademarks is not a mere theoretical option. For a case concerning an attempt to register works of the famous Norwegian sculptor Gustav Vigeland, see EFTA Court, 6 April 2017, case E-5/16, Municipality of Oslo ('Vigeland'), paras 20-26.
848. CJEU, 12 February 2004, case C-218/01, Henkel/DPMA, para. 42.
849. CJEU, *ibid*, para. 42. See also Rosenblatt 2015, 625-626, who proposes an alternative approach based on genericity that could offer additional flexibility with regard to the use of cultural signs for expressive goods.
850. Kur/Senftleben 2017, para. 6.23-6.27; Bently/Sherman/Gangjee/Johnson 2018, 1068; Fezer 2009, 1602-1603.
851. CJEU, 10 April 2008, case C-102/07, Adidas/Marca, para. 48.
852. CJEU, *ibid.*, para. 48.

an indication of product characteristics. Instead, the logo became part of the product itself:

> However, the affixing of a sign which is identical to a trade mark registered, inter alia, in respect of motor vehicles to scale models of that make of vehicle in order to reproduce those vehicles faithfully is not intended to provide an indication as to a characteristic of those scale models, but is merely an element in the faithful reproduction of the original vehicles.[853]

Against this background, a reproduction of a trademarked cultural sign, such as a Marlene Dietrich portrait, in the context of a parody or in appropriation art is unlikely to be deemed an exempted descriptive indication of product characteristics in the sense of Article 14(1)(b) EUTMR and Article 14(1)(b) TMD.

Hence, an examination of the status quo reached in EU trademark law only brings to light one proven and tested backstop against infringement claims that target cultural follow-on innovation. The law provides for an open-ended defence of 'due cause' in Article 9(2)(c) EUTMR and Article 10(2)(c) TMD which artists already asserted successfully in several cases. This elastic defence is available in the area of protection against trademark dilution.[854] More general defences which are applicable in all infringement scenarios, including confusion cases and double identity situations, are laid down in Article 14(1)(b) and (c) EUTMR and Article 14(1)(b) and (c) TMD. They exempt descriptive and referential use from the control of the trademark owner. A closer look at the conceptual contours drawn in EU trademark law and practice, however, reveals that their effectiveness is doubtful in cases where an artist includes a trademarked cultural sign in a derivative work without the intention of referring to the sign as an indicator of the commercial origin of goods or services of the trademark proprietor. As the artist makes the cultural sign a part of the new work, this cultural remix scenario falls outside the scope of the descriptive use defence. When the artist invokes the sign's cultural meaning (and not its commercial trademark meaning), the use also goes beyond the concept of referential use that follows from a strict, literal reading of Article 14(1)(c) EUTMR and Article 14(1)(c) TMD. Outside the area of trademark protection against dilution, it is thus unclear which limitation of EU trademark rights could support remix and reuse of trademarked cultural signs in the artistic domain.

This sombre picture becomes even darker when it is considered that, even if the descriptive use defence or the referential use defence was applicable, artists would still have to surmount the additional hurdle of proving that their remix activity is 'in accordance with honest practices in industrial or commercial matters'. This general proviso is set forth in Article

853. CJEU, 25 January 2007, case C-48/05, Adam Opel/Autec, para. 44.
854. Cf. Żelechowski 2018, 128-131.

14(2) EUTMR and Article 14(2) TMD. As a result, both defences – the descriptive use argument and the referential use argument – only apply on condition that the use meet the additional requirement of honest commercial practices. Recital 21 EUTMR and Recital 27 TMD leave no doubt that this complicating factor impacts artistic remix and reuse:

> Use of a trade mark by third parties for the purpose of artistic expression should be considered as being fair as long as it is at the same time in accordance with honest practices in industrial and commercial matters.

Immediately, this legislative guideline raises the question whether the standard of honesty 'in industrial and commercial matters' can ever be an appropriate yardstick for the assessment of unauthorized use in an artistic context. From the perspective of the cultural imperative, the scrutiny is doomed to fail from the outset because industrial and commercial considerations, by definition, are inapt to clarify the legitimacy of use in the cultural domain. Considering Bourdieu's concept of different fields in society,[855] it is evident that the reference point is fundamentally wrong. The requirement of use in accordance with behavioural norms in the industrial and commercial sector cements the supremacy of the field of trade and commerce over the field of art and culture: even if use appears fair and legitimate in the light of cultural and artistic standards, it may still amount to trademark infringement because established industrial and commercial practices point in the opposite direction. The legislator allows the logic of commerce and trade to prevail over the logic of culture and art – an alarming decision that confirms and encourages the increasing erosion of the autonomy of the literary and artistic field (section 3.3.1.1).

Apart from these theoretical concerns, the honest commercial practices requirement poses substantial practical difficulties. An artist can hardly be expected to be aware of behavioural norms in industry and commerce. The proviso of honest commercial practices is thus not only undesirable because it obliges artists to align their cultural work with commercial standards of fairness and honesty but also impractical because artists do not have the knowledge necessary to ensure compliance with established industrial and commercial standards during the process of creation. Moreover, the information deficit weakens their strategic position in infringement proceedings. Even if the burden of establishing an incompatibility with honest commercial practices is placed on the trademark proprietor,[856] the artist must first ascertain which behavioural norms are applicable before she can develop pertinent counterarguments. While the trademark owner, by definition, is well acquainted with standards of honesty in industrial and commercial matters, the artist must first explore applicable behavioural norms. The use of

855. Bourdieu 1996, 134-135; Bourdieu 1992/1999, 253-255 and 368.

856. For arguments in favour of this distribution of the burden of proof, see Kur/Senftleben 2017, para. 6.78-6.79.

industrial and commercial standards as a yardstick for the assessment of cultural and artistic productions, thus, causes an information imbalance in favour of the trademark proprietor. In contrast to the artist, the trademark owner can remain in her own sector and play a home game.

Finally, the proviso of honest commercial practices is doubtful from a legal-doctrinal perspective. The CJEU tends to base the assessment of honesty on the same criteria which already informed the foregoing analysis of prima facie infringement. In *Gillette*, the Court held that use would fail to comply with honest practices in industrial and commercial matters if, for example:

- it is done in such a manner as to give the impression that there is a commercial connection between the third party and the trade mark owner;
- it affects the value of the trade mark by taking unfair advantage of its distinctive character or repute;
- it entails the discrediting or denigration of that mark;
- or where the third party presents its product as an imitation or replica of the product bearing the trade mark of which it is not the owner.[857]

While it is possible to draw a line between these elements and the EU catalogue of criteria for determining the legitimacy of comparative advertising,[858] the prohibition of use that gives the impression of a commercial connection with the trademark owner, and the ban on use that damages or takes unfair advantage of the mark's distinctive character or repute, correspond with infringement criteria in the field of trademark protection against confusion and dilution (cf. sections 6.2.2 and 6.2.3). The risk of circularity is obvious: by copying almost literally the criteria for establishing prima facie infringement, the CJEU subjects defences against allegations of infringement to additional scrutiny in the light of the same criteria that enabled the trademark owner to bring the infringement claim in the first place. This circular line of reasoning may render limitations of exclusive rights, such as the descriptive use defence and the referential use defence, moot in practice.[859] The CJEU, however, seems to accept this result. In the keyword advertising case *Portakabin*, the Court did not find it contradictory to conclude that:

> the circumstances under which a trade mark proprietor is, pursuant to Article 5(1) of Directive 89/104 [nowadays Article 10(2)(a) TMD],

857. CJEU, 17 March 2005, case C-228/03, Gillette/LA-Laboratories, para. 49.
858. Article 4(d), (f), (g) and (h) MCAD. Cf. Kur/Senftleben 2017, para. 6.72.
859. Cf. Kur/Senftleben 2017, para. 6.73; Senftleben/Bently/Dinwoodie et al. 2015, 339; Senftleben 2013b, 168-169; Simon Fhima/Jacob 2014, 274; Simon Fhima 2012, 501-502.

> entitled to prevent an advertiser from using a sign identical with, or similar to, that trade mark as a keyword may [...] easily correspond to a situation in which the advertiser cannot claim that it is acting in accordance with honest practices in industrial or commercial matters, and cannot therefore validly rely on the exception...[860] (comment within brackets added).

The corrosive effect of this jurisprudence on defences that could support use in the artistic domain is evident. The moment the same considerations that have led to a finding of prima facie infringement support a finding of incompliance with honest commercial practices, the requirement of use in accordance with honest practices in industrial and commercial matters degenerates into a torpedo which the trademark proprietor can employ to neutralize both the defence of descriptive use and the defence of referential use. To this day, this serious flaw in the EU approach to limitations of exclusive trademark rights has not been remedied satisfactorily. Annette Kur aptly summarizes the current state of the debate as follows:

> It is therefore important to emphasize that instead of applying those factors in the same way as when infringement is prima facie established, the interpretation must proceed in a more fine-grained fashion, taking account of the countervailing interests safeguarded by the limitations. This means that the concrete manner and dimensions of the use made must be appraised for their appropriateness and proportionality in view of all circumstances. Furthermore, the principle should be established that insofar as the limitations apply, use of the mark can only be qualified, but not entirely prohibited.[861]

In other words: the proviso of honest commercial practices remains a risk factor. In the light of freedom of expression,[862] a fine-grained, proportionality-based application of assessment factors that also inform the infringement analysis may add sufficient nuances to avoid a complete neutralization of defences, such as descriptive use and referential use. Nonetheless, it must not be overlooked that the symmetry of criteria for assessing prima facie infringement and honesty in industrial and commercial matters can easily lead to a situation where a finding of a likelihood of confusion or dilution already foreshadows the denial of compliance with honest commercial practices. In any case, the circularity in the approach taken by the CJEU weakens the effectiveness of defences and enhances the legal uncertainty for artists relying on a limitation of exclusive trademark rights to escape the verdict of infringement.

860. CJEU, 8 July 2010, C-558/08, Portakabin, para. 69.
861. Kur 2018, 105. Cf. also Kur/Senftleben 2017, para. 6.74; Senftleben/Bently/Dinwoodie et al. 2015, 339.
862. Recital 21 EUTMR and Recital 27 TMD.

In sum, the limitation infrastructure is wanting for several reasons. EU trademark law only provides for one defence that clearly has the potential to cover the creative remix and reuse of trademarked cultural signs in the artistic domain, namely the open-ended exemption of use with due cause that is available under Article 9(2)(c) EUTMR and Article 10(2)(c) TMD.[863] This defence, however, is confined to trademark protection against dilution. The descriptive use defence and the referential use defence in Article 14(1) EUTMR and Article 14(1) TMD have a broader scope. They are applicable across confusion, dilution and double identity contexts. However, they only cover use for the purpose of indicating product characteristics or referring to the cultural sign as an identifier of the commercial source of products stemming from the trademark owner. If the use concerns the inclusion of the cultural sign in a derivative work because of its cultural meaning and for the purpose of making it a part of the new work, the applicability of the descriptive use defence and the referential use defence is doubtful. Furthermore, both defences are subject to scrutiny in light of the general requirement of use in accordance with honest practices in industrial and commercial matters.[864] This additional condition causes considerable legal uncertainty. Artists can hardly be expected to be aware of behavioural norms in industry and commerce. Moreover, the same criteria that support a finding of prima facie infringement inform the assessment of honesty. As a result, the successful invocation of the descriptive use defence and the referential use defence is hanging by the thread of a fine-grained, proportionality-based application of assessment factors that already led to a finding of prima facie infringement.

Therefore, the current EU system of defences can hardly be deemed capable of giving artists reassurance that trademark rights do not pose a threat. A sufficiently robust set of limitations of protection is sought in vain. This shortcoming places a heavy burden on artists seeking to rebut infringement arguments. As defendants, they carry the burden of proving that all requirements for invoking a limitation of trademark rights are fulfilled. The legal uncertainty arising from the fragile character of currently available defences rests on their shoulders. They must demonstrate that the allegedly infringing use constitutes use with due cause[865] or falls within the scope of the EU concept of descriptive or referential use. Additional burdens can arise from the honest practices requirement. By stating that the defences for descriptive and referential use shall only apply where the use at issue is carried out in accordance with honest practices, Article 14(2) EUTMR and

863. However, see Bohaczewski 2020, 872-875, who even doubts the applicability of this defence argument.

864. Article 14(2) EUTMR; Article 14(2) TMD.

865. With regard to the distribution of the burden of proof in the context of the negative condition of 'due cause', see Kur/Senftleben 2017, para. 5.256.

Article 14(2) TMD seem to impose the burden of proof on the artist.[866] In practice, this would mean that an artist invoking the defence of descriptive or referential use must establish not only the prerequisites of the relevant limitation but also the absence of any possible element rendering her conduct incompatible with the standard of honest practices. This configuration of the interplay between limitations and honest practices test would amount to imposing a negative burden of proof which appears problematic in the light of considerations of equity and fairness.[867] Even if the obligation to plead and substantiate dishonesty in industrial and commercial matters is placed on the trademark owner, however, the artist must refute the evidence produced by the trademark owner and demonstrate compliance with the applicable standard of honesty. Hence, all above-described doubts about the scope of defences are detrimental to the artist and beneficial for the trademark owner.

6.3 DETERRENT EFFECT OF TRADEMARK PROTECTION

The survey of developments in EU trademark law in the preceding section 6.2 confirms the evolution of a scope of protection that raises serious concerns about an impediment of cultural follow-on innovation when it comes to overlapping copyright and trademark protection.[868] The described developments clearly reflect the continuous broadening of EU trademark protection and the increasing fluidity of infringement criteria that result from the recognition of a trademark's economic and communication value as an independent subject matter of protection. Once trademark law seeks to protect not only the basic origin function but also accessory functions related to communication, investment and advertising, it is hardly possible to maintain a strict gatekeeper requirement of 'use as a trademark' in the sense of use of an identical or confusingly similar sign for the purpose of indicating the commercial source of the alleged infringer's own goods or services. By contrast, the requirement of use as a trademark – use in the course of trade and use in relation to goods or services in EU terminology[869] – becomes more elastic and may already be satisfied when an unauthorized user evokes the trademark in the minds of consumers or refers to the trademark as being the source identifier of the trademark proprietor herself.[870] As a result of this relaxation of the requirement of use as a trademark, infringement claims against use in the cultural domain can hardly be stopped at an early stage of the infringement analysis. For example, it is no longer possible to readily

866. Kur/Senftleben 2017, para. 6.78.
867. Kur/Senftleben 2017, para. 6.79.
868. Cf. Schovsbo 2018, 576-577, who arrives at the same conclusion.
869. Article 9(2) EUTMR; Article 10(2) TMD.
870. Kur/Senftleben 2017, para. 5.50-5.56; Derclaye/Leistner 2011, 328.

assume that a parody – intentionally referring to a protected trademark to identify the target of the mockery – does not constitute actionable use as a trademark in the sense of EU trademark law (section 6.2.1).

In addition, the CJEU refuses to consider a potential 'need to keep free' in the framework of the infringement analysis. As a result, the test of a likelihood of confusion seems to leave no room for considering the need to keep signs free for cultural purposes.[871] Instead, even decorative use may amount to infringement, if consumers perceive the decorative sign as an indication of a connection with the trademark proprietor.[872] The objective to prevent confusion thus prevails over the freedom of decorative use even though an alleged infringer in the cultural domain may have chosen a sign with cultural significance (which also constitutes a trademark) for artistic reasons, and the assumption of a connection with the trademark owner may be the result of extensive advertising educating consumers to perceive the sign as an indication of commercial origin (section 6.2.2).

In the field of dilution, the objective to offer broad protection of a trademark's economic and communication value led to the relaxation of specific infringement criteria that regulate the availability and scope of exclusive rights. The threshold requirement for protection against dilution – the requirement of a mark 'having a reputation'[873] – is already fulfilled when a specialized public in a substantial part of the territory of registration knows the trademark at issue.[874] If the trademark owner does not succeed in producing evidence for a change in the economic behaviour of consumers, she can invoke the argument of unfair freeriding as an alternative basis for protection against dilution.[875] In the area of double identity, an adverse effect on the communication, investment or advertising function of the trademark can serve as an alternative basis for an infringement claim if use for cultural purposes is unlikely to cause confusion and does not encroach upon the origin function of the trademark (section 6.2.3).

The CJEU thus configurated EU trademark law in a way that allows broad protection of the economic and communication value of trademarks. As explained in section 6.1.2, the impact of this development must not be underestimated. The recognition of a trademark's economic and communication value in trademark law means that trademarks enjoy protection not only as identifiers of commercial source but also as communication tools. As communication also lies at the core of cultural remix processes, it is inaccurate to assume that, because of some safeguards, the EU trademark system is unlikely to make inroads into cyclic innovation in the cultural

871. CJEU, 10 April 2008, case C-102/07, Adidas/Marca, para. 30.
872. CJEU, *ibid.*, para. 34.
873. Article 9(2)(c) EUTMR and Article 10(2)(c) TMD.
874. CJEU, 14 September 1999, case C-375/97, General Motors/Yplon ('Chevy'), paras 24-28.
875. CJEU, 18 June 2009, case C-487/07, L'Oréal/Bellure, para. 49.

domain. The crucial point is that, as a result of CJEU jurisprudence, EU trademark law offers a whole panoply of arguments that can serve as starting points for an infringement claim. After the described relaxation of infringement criteria, a trademark action against use in the cultural domain no longer seems futile from the outset. Given the broad spectrum of arguments that could lead to a finding of prima facie infringement, artists must lean more heavily on limitations of trademark protection that can serve as defences. Considering the fragile limitation infrastructure in EU trademark law (section 6.2.4), however, the conclusion is inescapable that the grant of trademark rights to cultural signs causes a considerable risk of artists being exposed to infringement arguments that cannot easily be rebutted with the counterargument that they are obviously unfounded.[876] This exposure to a trademark action is a serious threat in and of itself.[877] It is likely to have a deterrent effect on cultural follow-on innovation even if judges do not rule in favour of trademark proprietors in the end. In various areas of creative activity, concerns have been articulated about a growing fear of artists to be sued for intellectual property infringement because of the reuse of pre-existing cultural material that still enjoys protection.[878] These fears can have a chilling effect on creativity and cultural diversity. An artist seeking to avoid potential lawsuits will refrain from the creation of works based on pre-existing material or limit takings from pre-existing material to an absolute minimum.[879] Therefore, the legal uncertainty arising from the elastic application of trademark infringement criteria in the jurisprudence of the CJEU leads to a climate that is not conducive to new cultural productions. Instead, it is likely to impoverish new cultural productions in terms of creative inputs.

In the above-described case *Lila Postkarte*, the defence of due cause finally saved the artistic play with Milka insignia. However, the fact remains that even though the use was found to constitute use in an artistic context, the

876. Cf. Peukert 2016, 425-426, who stresses the high degree of legal uncertainty arising from the current scope of trademark protection and insufficient reliability of limitations.
877. Cf. Lemley/McKenna 2010, 418-422 and 443; Calboli 2014a, 31.
878. Ramsey 2018, 427; Schovsbo 2018, 562; Adler 2016, 566; Cramer 2015; McGeveran 2015, 739-742; Aufderheide/Jaszi/Bello et al. 2014, 5; Frosio 2014, 378-380; Calboli 2014a, 31-32; Lemley/McKenna 2010, 418-422 and 443; Banerjee 2012, 564; Sakulin 2010, 292-293; McGeveran 2008, 1206-1207 and 1224-1225; Morrison 2008, 131-136; Hofrichter 2007, 1926; Gibson 2007, 913; Cohen 2006, 154-156; Aufderheide/Jaszi 2004, 29-30; Lessig 2004, 185-188; Coombe 2003, 1174; Amabile 1996, 115-120 and 231-232.
879. Cf. Adler 2016, 566, who stresses the chilling effect of legal uncertainty in the field of copyright: 'the disparate results in these cases, not to mention the high costs of litigating against a backdrop of uncertainty, help explain why a climate of "self-censorship" has taken hold in the art world'. The same conclusion is drawn by Aufderheide/Jaszi/Bello et al. 2014, 5, pointing out that artists 'pay a high price for copyright confusion and misunderstanding. Their work is constrained and censored, most powerfully by themselves, because of that confusion and the resulting fear and anxiety'.

elastic concept of use as a trademark developed by the CJEU prevented a judgment that put an end to the infringement action at an early stage.[880] The Court did not hold that the use did not constitute actionable trademark use from the outset. Instead, the parodist had to invoke the defence of due cause and argue the case in several instances until the German Federal Court of Justice took a final decision. The artistic use at issue thus led to a complex lawsuit even though the Milka trademarks had not been used as identifiers of commercial source. Similar problem scenarios – in the sense of lawsuits requiring several instances and placing substantial burden on artists before they finally prevail – can easily be found in the Benelux.[881] In many cases, however, artists and art centres will not have sufficient confidence and financial resources to take the risk of a lengthy lawsuit.[882] Florian Cramer gives the following example:

> Recently the Rotterdam art platform Roodkapje [Little Red Riding Hood] received mail from a lawyer. The content: a steep bill. For their annual programme 'Roodkapje Radicals' the curators advertised with an armed jihad fighter on a fake H&M poster. It was intended as a literal representation of the concept of radical chic, as a playful relativization of their own programme. But for H&M this was a violation of trademark law. When Roodkapje received the invoice from the H&M lawyer, they withdrew the poster. This is not a special event. Artists are regularly confronted with lawsuits[883] (explanation within brackets added).

These practical considerations must be taken into account when assessing the potential corrosive effect of trademark rights in cultural signs. In Germany, the necessity to consider infringement fears has explicitly been recognized in court decisions. Discussing the constitutional guarantee of

---

880. As to the importance to provide mechanisms that, in cases involving artistic freedom of expression, prevent lengthy lawsuits from the outset, see McGeveran 2008, 1224-1225; Lessig 2004, 185-188.

881. Benelux Court of Justice, 14 October 2019, case A2018/1/8, Moët Hennessy/Cedric Art, para. 9; Court of Appeals of Amsterdam, 13 September 2011, case ECLI:NL:GHAMS:2011:BS7825, Mercis and Bruna/Punt, *AMI* 2012, 28, para. 4.1, and District Court of The Hague, 4 May 2011, case ECLI:NL:RBSGR:2011:BQ3525, Nadia Plesner/Louis Vuitton, para. 2.1-2.8.

882. For a more detailed discussion of the chilling effect of cease-and-desist strategies, see Ramsey 2018, 427; Schovsbo 2018, 562; Dogan 2016, 1293; Greener 2015, 598; Calboli 2014a, 31-32; Lemley/McKenna 2010, 418-422 and 443; McGeveran 2008, 1206-1207; Lessig 2004, 185-188.

883. Cramer 2015: 'Onlangs kreeg het Rotterdamse kunstpodium Roodkapje post van een advocaat. De inhoud: een gepeperde rekening. Voor hun jaarprogramma "Roodkapje Radicals" adverteerden de curatoren met een bewapende jihadstrijder op een nepaffiche van H&M. Het was bedoeld als een letterlijke verbeelding van het begrip radical chic, als speelse relativering van hun eigen programma. Maar voor H&M was dit schending van het merkrecht. Toen Roodkapje de factuur van de H&M-advocaat kreeg, trokken zij het affiche in. Dit is geen bijzondere gebeurtenis. Geregeld krijgen kunstenaars rechtszaken aan hun broek' (translation from Dutch into English by Martin Senftleben).

artistic freedom of expression, the deterrent effect that arises from legal uncertainty surrounding a permitted use of protected material has explicitly been addressed by the German Federal Constitutional Court (Supreme Court in matters of constitutional law) in *Metall auf Metall*.[884] The decision was triggered by the jurisprudence which the German Federal Court of Justice (Supreme Court in matters of civil law) had developed with regard to sound sampling. The underlying lawsuit had been brought by the iconic German electronic music pioneers Kraftwerk. They asserted copyright and phonogram producer rights against the unauthorized use of a rhythmic sound fragment of two seconds which served as the basis of a continuous rhythmic sequence in Sabrina Setlur's song 'Nur mir'. The sound fragment stemmed from the piece 'Metall auf Metall' in Kraftwerk's 1977 album 'Trans Europa Express'.

In its earlier decisions in the *Metall auf Metall* saga,[885] the German Federal Court of Justice had held that sound sampling fell outside the scope of permitted free use and amounted to infringement of the neighbouring right of the phonogram producer if the unauthorized user was capable of producing the desired sound fragment himself.[886] In a further decision, the Court had specified that this criterion required an assessment of whether a sound producer with average equipment and talent, at the time of unauthorized use, would have been capable of producing an own recording which, from the perspective of the target audience, could be qualified as equal to the original sound fragment.[887] The German Federal Constitutional Court found that this assessment criterion encroached upon the guarantee of free artistic expression because it created too much legal uncertainty. The Court expressed the fear that:

> even in those cases where a reproduction equivalent to the original is not possible, artists will refrain from incorporating passages – which in such a case would be permissible even in the opinion of the [German] Federal Court of Justice – because of concerns about the overly great effort and expense, as well as the legal risk, involved in proving that reproducibility was impossible. The criterion of equivalent reproducibility therefore

884. German Federal Constitutional Court, 31 May 2016, case 1 BvR 1585/13, 'Sampling', para. 100.
885. For a more detailed discussion of the *Metall auf Metall* decisions in Germany, see Podszun 2016, 606-612; Leistner 2016, 772-777; Schippers 2014, 105; Conley/Braegelmann 2009, 1017; Dougherty 2007, 481.
886. German Federal Court of Justice, 20 November 2008, case I ZR 112/06, "Metall auf Metall I", 15, published in: *GRUR* 2009, 403.
887. German Federal Court of Justice, 13 December 2012, case I ZR 182/11, 'Metall auf Metall II', 16, *GRUR* 2013, 614.

has a deterrent effect that necessitates an especially effective constitutional review[888] (clarification within brackets added).

Hence, the deterrent effect that arises from legal uncertainty surrounding a permitted use must be factored into the equation. It is not sufficient that the statutory law provides for defences and that judges are willing to hear arguments based on these defences. It must also be considered whether artistic creators may nevertheless refrain from permissible use because the grant of intellectual property rights as such involves the risk of an infringement action. With regard to copyright/trademark overlaps, this means that even if courts may finally manage to arrive at reasonable solutions in cases involving use of trademarked cultural material, the fundamental difference remains that legal uncertainty about a potential trademark claim is surrounding the use of cultural material once trademark rights have been awarded.[889] The risk of potential trademark infringement is hanging above use made of affected cultural creations like the sword of Damocles. From a cultural perspective, the scenario in which an artwork belongs to the public domain and is entirely free is clearly preferable over a situation where trademark rights are granted and artists are exposed to the risk of an infringement claim.

6.4 CONCLUSION

In sum, advanced trademark systems, such as the EU trademark system, offer trademark owners various starting points for infringement claims against remix and reuse of trademarked signs with cultural significance. Use in the artistic domain may be deemed to cause confusion as to affiliation or sponsorship. Even if it does not cause confusion, a trademark action need not fail. If a trademark has acquired the status of a mark with a reputation, the trademark proprietor can still argue that use in the cultural domain damages, or takes unfair advantage of, the economic and communication value of the trademark. In cases where the allegedly infringing use concerns a sign that is identical to a cultural sign that has been registered as a trademark and identical goods or services, EU trademark law even offers protection of communication, advertising and investment functions without making it a prerequisite that the registered cultural sign has a reputation.[890]

Given this broadened spectrum of infringement arguments, the status quo reached in EU trademark law shows that protection of cultural signs as

888. German Federal Constitutional Court, 31 May 2016, case 1 BvR 1585/13, 'Sampling', para. 100. English translation available at: https://www.bundesverfassungsgericht.de/e/rs20160531_1bvr158513en.html.
889. McGeveran 2015, 738-742 and 754.
890. CJEU, 18 June 2009, case C-487/07, L'Oréal/Bellure, para. 58.

trademarks entails a serious risk of inroads into artistic freedom of expression. It is no longer accurate to describe trademark rights as defensive instruments that merely preserve a sign's function of indicating the commercial origin of goods or services. Instead, trademark rights have become exploitation instruments that come close to the exclusive rights in copyright law. As copyright, trademark rights offer the opportunity to exert considerable control over the communication surrounding a protected sign. Against this background, the deterrent effect of exposure to a trademark infringement action must not be underestimated when it comes to coexisting (section 5.2.3) or resurrected (section 5.2.1) trademark protection. If the trademark proprietor sends a cease-and-desist letter stating that use of a trademarked cultural sign amounts to infringement, this will often suffice to put an end to use in a cultural context. Growing fears of artists to be sued for intellectual property infringement reflect the dimension of this problem.[891]

As the scope of trademark rights in cultural signs is thus far from being unproblematic in advanced trademark systems that no longer confine protection to the traditional origin function, it is necessary to explore potential encroachments upon cyclic cultural innovation in more detail and discuss strategies to reduce the risk of a chilling effect on cultural creativity. In line with the distinction between intergenerational equity and public domain recognition as central elements of the cultural imperative (Chapter 3), the exploration of potential interferences with cultural follow-on innovation will take place in two steps. While Chapter 7 focuses on the risk of eroding the guarantee of intergenerational equity, Chapter 8 addresses the need to preserve and cultivate the public domain of literary and artistic expressions. The discussion of risk reduction strategies follows in Chapter 9.

891. For a more detailed discussion of the chilling effect of cease-and-desist strategies, see Ramsey 2018, 427; Schovsbo 2018, 562; Cramer 2015; McGeveran 2015, 739-742; Calboli 2014a, 31-32; Lemley/McKenna 2010, 418-422 and 443; McGeveran 2008, 1206-1207; Lessig 2004, 185-188.

Chapter 7
Perpetuation of the Protection of Cultural Expressions

The description of the cultural imperative in Chapter 3, the clarification of its relationship with the technical and trade imperatives of patent and trademark law in Chapter 4, and the assessment of the scope of trademark protection in Chapter 6 provide groundwork for the closer inspection of interferences of trademark rights with the cultural innovation cycle. As explained in Chapter 3, the current configuration of copyright law reflects two central principles which allow the protection system to function as an engine of cultural follow-on innovation: the guarantee of intergenerational equity and the recognition of the public domain. Indefinitely renewable trademark rights, however, may impede both preconditions for the proper functioning of the copyright system. They afford trademark owners the opportunity to perpetuate the protection of cultural expressions after copyright expiry (Mickey Mouse scenario, section 5.2.3). The principle of intergenerational equity, however, obliges authors to leave 'enough and as good'[892] *in common for following generations of authors (section 3.2.2). It implies that copyright holders do not withhold their works from the public domain once copyright protection expires. From the perspective of public domain recognition, it can be added that the obligation to leave 'enough and as good' also ensures the continuous enrichment of the public domain.*

892. Locke 1698, book II chapter 5 § 27. Cf. Gordon 1993, 1562-1564.

Trademark law, as already pointed out, does not set forth a limited term of protection. Instead, there is a possibility of renewing a trademark registration indefinitely.[893] *If, in case of subject matter enjoying cumulative protection under copyright and trademark law, trademark protection is renewed after the expiry of copyright protection, the intellectual creation concerned does not enter the public domain in its entirety. To the extent to which trademark rights persist, it may still not be used freely. The subject matter, therefore, only becomes part of the public domain insofar as acts of use are concerned that fall outside the scope of remaining trademark rights. Overlaps with trademark protection may thus encroach upon the rule of a limited term of protection in copyright law and impede the cultural innovation cycle. As trademark protection has a broad scope in advanced trademark systems (Chapter 6), the breadth of inroads into the public domain must not be downplayed. It is thus necessary to ascertain to what extent overlaps with trademark protection undermine the rule of a limited term of protection in copyright law.*

With regard to the technical innovation cycle, the same dilemma would arise in the case of overlapping trademark and patent protection. As copyright law, patent law provides only for a limited term of protection (section 4.1.1). In case of subject matter enjoying cumulative patent and trademark protection, trademark rights could still be renewed after the expiry of the patent monopoly. With a remaining risk of trademark infringement, use of technical know-how would not become entirely free. Theoretically, the rule of indefinite renewal in trademark law could thus interfere with both the cultural innovation cycle and the technical innovation cycle. This parallel makes it possible to discuss the potential conflict arising from a renewable term of trademark protection from a comparative perspective. Accordingly, section 7.1 will show that the trademark doctrine of utilitarian functionality which allows the categorical exclusion of technical product characteristics from trademark protection (section 4.2.2) provides an effective instrument to draw a boundary line between patent and trademark rights and prevent impediments of the technical innovation cycle. Section 7.2 will add that the doctrine of aesthetic functionality – the outright exclusion of aesthetic product features from trademark protection – can have a similar effect in respect of industrial designs and works of applied art.

Outside the realm of industrial designs and works of applied art, however, current trademark law does not contain specific safeguards against a far-reaching cumulation of copyright and trademark rights.

893. Article 18 TRIPS.

Moreover, an uncritical attitude vis-à-vis cumulative copyright and trademark protection often prevails in court decisions and literature (section 7.3). This status quo raises serious concerns about the inner consistency of the intellectual property system. Considering the efforts made to separate trademark protection from patent and industrial design protection, the question arises whether there are sufficient reasons for accepting the prolongation of protection in the case of literary and artistic works (section 7.4). Is the artificial perpetuation of exclusive rights relating to cultural expressions less problematic than an artificial perpetuation of exclusive rights relating to technical know-how and industrial designs? Is the cultural innovation cycle less vulnerable than innovation cycles in other domains of intellectual property, such as the domains of patents and industrial designs?

The discussion of these questions will show that the artificial perpetuation of exclusive rights in cultural expressions on the basis of trademark law is undesirable and causes an imbalance within the intellectual property system: whereas innovation cycles in the area of technical solutions and industrial designs are shielded from the corrosive effect of trademark rights, no comparable effort is made to safeguard the innovation cycle in the area of literary and artistic creativity. Instead of jumping to the conclusion that this imbalance must be remedied, however, section 7.5 will clarify whether the separation of copyright and trademark protection would involve costs that appear excessive and justify the maintenance of the status quo. Would an outright exclusion of literary and artistic works from trademark protection enhance the risk of consumer confusion to such an extent that it appears disproportionate? Would it frustrate ongoing investment in cultural creations after the expiry of copyright protection and, consequently, impoverish rather than enrich the cultural landscape? Weighing all arguments, a final assessment of the vulnerability of the cultural innovation cycle leads to the conclusion that there is a serious risk of trademark protection frustrating cultural follow-on innovation – a risk that requires appropriate countermeasures (section 7.6).

7.1. EXCLUSION OF INVENTIONS FROM TRADEMARK PROTECTION

Intellectual property law contains several provisions that shield the patent system from undesirable influences of other protection regimes. At the international level, such a provision can be found in the field of industrial designs. Article 25(1) TRIPS allows national legislators to exclude protection for industrial designs that are 'dictated essentially by technical or functional considerations'.[894] As already indicated, the trademark doctrine of utilitarian functionality points in the same direction. The EU manifestations of the doctrine – Article 7(1)(e) EUTMR and Article 4(1)(e) TMD – stipulate that signs consisting exclusively of 'the shape, or another characteristic, of goods which is necessary to obtain a technical result' shall not be registered or, if registered, shall be liable to be declared invalid. It can be deduced from Article 7(3) EUTMR and Article 4(4) TMD that technical product characteristics are also barred from acquiring distinctive character through continuous use in trade.[895] This categorical exclusion of trademark protection rests on several considerations: the objective to safeguard freedom of competition (7.1.1), the undesirability of an artificial perpetuation of exclusive rights in technical solutions after patent expiry (7.1.2) and the basic distinction between the mark and the product in trademark law (7.1.3).

7.1.1 *Freedom of Competition*

Attempts to acquire trademark rights to technical solutions after the expiry of patent protection have led to court decisions in various jurisdictions worldwide. In some cases, these attempts have even generated a whole series of decisions in different countries and regions. The law suit between Philips and Remington – about trademark protection for the head of a three-headed rotary electric shaver – is an example of such a legal saga.[896] In the EU, the *Philips/Remington* battle gave the CJEU the opportunity to clarify the rationale underlying the exclusion of technical product features. The Court

894. For commentary, see Kur 1996a, 151-152. For examples of national implementation, see Article 8(1) of the Community Designs Regulation No. 6/2002 of 12 December 2001: 'A Community design shall not subsist in features of appearance of a product which are solely dictated by its technical function.' A corresponding provision is set forth in Article 7(1) of Directive 98/71/EC of 13 October 1998 on the legal protection of designs. As to the scope of the exclusion of technical design features following from these provisions, see CJEU, 8 March 2018, case C-395/16, Doceram, paras 29-32. Cf. Koschtial 2005, 306-309.

895. CJEU, 18 June 2002, case C-299/99, Philips/Remington, para. 57 and 75; CJEU, 16 September 2015, case C-215/14, Nestlé/Cadbury ('Kit Kat'), paras 38-39; CJEU, 11 May 2017, case C-421/15 P, Yoshida Metal Industry/EUIPO, para. 35. Cf. also U.S. Supreme Court, 20 March 2001, TrafFix Devices/Marketing Displays, 532 U.S. 23, 33 (2001).

896. For instance, see Federal Court of Australia, 30 June 2000, Koninklijke Philips Electronics NV/Remington Products Australia Pty Limited [2000] FCA 876; 100 FCR 90, 101; CJEU, 18 June 2002, case C-299/99, Philips/Remington; Supreme Court of Canada, 17 November 2005, Kirkbi AG/Ritvik Holdings Inc., [2005] 3 S.C.R. 302, 2005 SCC 65; German Federal Court of Justice, 17 November 2005, case I ZB 12/04, 'Rasierer mit drei Scherköpfen', *GRUR Int.* 2006, 765.

explained that the utilitarian functionality doctrine in EU trademark law[897] served the purpose of preventing trademark protection 'from granting its proprietor a monopoly on technical solutions or functional characteristics of a product which a user is likely to seek in the products of competitors'.[898] The exclusion of shapes necessary to obtain a technical result was intended:

> to preclude the registration of shapes whose essential characteristics perform a technical function, with the result that the exclusivity inherent in the trade mark right would limit the possibility of competitors supplying a product incorporating such a function or at least limit their freedom of choice in regard to the technical solution they wish to adopt in order to incorporate such a function in their product.[899]

More generally, the CJEU underlined that the exclusion served the public interest by ensuring that 'a shape whose essential characteristics perform a technical function and were chosen to fulfil that function may be freely used by all'.[900] This additional statement can be placed in the context of the quid pro quo underlying patent law. After the expiry of protection, patented know-how enters the public domain. This is the price to be paid for the grant of protection and a precondition for the constant enrichment of the public domain of technical know-how as a result of the expiry of patents. Exclusive patent rights are granted on the condition that the patent owner accept the free availability of the invention once the limited period of patent protection ends. In this vein, the U.S. Supreme Court emphasized in *Dastar/Twentieth Century Fox* that it was necessary to shield the quid pro quo underlying patent law from the corrosive effect of trademark protection. The rights of a patentee were part of a 'carefully crafted bargain', under which, once the patent monopoly had expired, the public was free to use the invention at will. The Court explicitly warned of 'misuse or over-extension' of trademark protection into areas which, traditionally, formed the realm of patent law.[901]

---

897. The Court dealt with the shape exclusions in Article 3(1)(e) of the First Council Directive 89/104/EEC of 21 December 1988 to approximate the laws of the Member States relating to trademarks, *OJ* 1989 L 40, 1, which remained unchanged in Article 3(1)(e) TMD 1988. The current version of the EU functionality doctrine – laid down in Article 7(1)(e) EUTMR and Article 4(1)(e) TMD – encompasses not only the shape of products but also other characteristics.
898. CJEU, 18 June 2002, case C-299/99, Philips/Remington, para. 78. The Court confirmed this line of argument in CJEU, 14 September 2010, case C-48/09 P, Lego/Mega Brands, para. 43.
899. CJEU, *ibid.*, para. 79.
900. CJEU, *ibid.*, para. 80.
901. U.S. Supreme Court, 2 June 2003, Dastar/Twentieth Century Fox, 539 U.S. 23, 33-34 (2003), referring to U.S. Supreme Court, 20 March 2001, TrafFix Devices/Marketing Displays, 532 U.S. 23, 29 (2001).

7.1.2 *No Artificial Perpetuation of Exclusivity*

Addressing the relationship between patent and trademark protection, the CJEU clarified in *Philips/Remington* that the doctrine of utilitarian functionality 'reflects the legitimate aim of not allowing individuals to use registration of a mark in order to acquire or perpetuate exclusive rights relating to technical solutions'.[902] Hence it follows that the exclusion of 'the shape, or another characteristic, of goods which is necessary to obtain a technical result'[903] can be understood to draw a boundary line between patent and trademark protection. Patent law reigns supreme in the realm of technology. An inventor seeking protection of a technical solution is dependent on the patent system and may not, as an alternative, rely on trademark protection. Trademark law should not serve as a vehicle to perpetuate exclusive rights in technical solutions. Accordingly, the exclusion of technical product characteristics prevents trademark applicants from bypassing the patent rule of a limited term of protection. It safeguards the delicate balance between rights and freedoms in patent law and, ultimately, the technical innovation cycle.[904]

The CJEU confirmed this line of argument in *Lego/Mega Brands*. As patent protection for Lego brick functionality was no longer available after patent expiry, Lego sought trademark protection to maintain the exclusivity it had enjoyed under the patent regime. Discussing this attempt to obtain trademark rights, the CJEU pointed out that:

> the prohibition on registration as a trade mark of any sign consisting of the shape of goods which is necessary to obtain a technical result ensures that undertakings may not use trade mark law in order to perpetuate, indefinitely, exclusive rights relating to technical solutions.[905]

The CJEU even extended the exclusion of technical shapes from trademark protection by holding that the ground for refusal relating to shapes necessary to obtain a technical result could not be overcome by establishing that competitors could use alternative shapes to achieve the same technical result. The absolute ground for refusal applied irrespective of whether the shape at issue was the only one capable of obtaining the required technical result, or whether there were several shapes which were equivalent from a functional point of view.[906]

The U.S. Supreme Court took the same approach in *TrafFix Devices/ Marketing Displays*. The case concerned the question of whether trade dress protection (under the Lanham Act) was available for a technical mechanism built upon two springs ('dual-spring design') to keep temporary road and

902. CJEU, *ibid.*, para. 82.
903. Article 7(1)(e) EUTMR; Article 4(1)(e) TMD.
904. Cf. McKenna 2011, 828-830.
905. CJEU, 14 September 2010, case C-48/09 P, Lego/Mega Brands, para. 45.
906. CJEU, *ibid.*, paras 53-58.

other outdoor signs upright despite adverse wind conditions.[907] As Marketing Displays had managed to obtain two utility patents relating to the dual-spring design, the central question was whether, despite the technical character, there was room for trademark rights which the company could assert against TrafFix Devices: a competitor who had started copying the dual-spring solution after the expiry of the utility patents. Discussing this question, the U.S. Supreme Court relied on its earlier ruling in *Inwood Laboratories/Ives Laboratories* that a product feature was functional and could not serve as a trademark, 'if it is essential to the use or purpose of the article or if it affects the cost or quality of the article'.[908] The Court clarified that, where a design had to be deemed functional in the light of this *Inwood* formulation, there was 'no need to proceed further to consider if there is a competitive necessity for the feature'.[909]

With this statement, the Court referred to *Qualitex Co./Jacobson Products Co.*, where it had supplemented the *Inwood* test by observing that a design feature had to be declared functional 'if exclusive use of the feature would put competitors at a significant non-reputation-related disadvantage'.[910] While this *Qualitex* addition indicates that the objective to safeguard freedom of competition is an undercurrent of the exclusion of functional product features from trademark protection, the issue of a competitive necessity did not play a decisive role in *TrafFix* because the expired utility patents testified to the technical character of the dual-spring design at issue. The U.S. Supreme Court qualified the two utility patents as 'strong evidence' that the dual-spring design was functional from a technical perspective.[911] As the patent specification revealed that the dual-spring design achieved important operational advantages and affected the cost of the device,[912] utilitarian functionality could readily be inferred from the *Inwood* test. Hence, there was no need to consider, in addition, competitive disadvantages to support the categorical exclusion of the dual-spring design from trademark protection.[913]

The U.S. Supreme Court also clarified in *TrafFix* that competition-based considerations could not neutralize a finding of utilitarian functionality if utility patent rights had been granted for the product design at issue. After the expiry of patent protection, the prior patent owner could not escape the

907. U.S. Supreme Court, *ibid.*, 25-26 (2001).
908. U.S. Supreme Court, *ibid.*, 32-33, referring to U.S. Supreme Court, 1 June 1982, Inwood Laboratories/Ives Laboratories, 456 U.S. 844, 850, footnote 10 (1982).
909. U.S. Supreme Court, 20 March 2001, TrafFix Devices/Marketing Displays, 532 U.S. 23, 33 (2001).
910. U.S. Supreme Court, 28 March 1995, Qualitex Co./Jacobson Products Co., 514 U.S. 159, 165 (1995).
911. U.S. Supreme Court, 20 March 2001, TrafFix Devices/Marketing Displays, 532 U.S. 23, 29-30 (2001).
912. U.S. Supreme Court, *ibid.*, 31-32.
913. U.S. Supreme Court, *ibid.*, 33.

verdict of utilitarian functionality by arguing that there was no need for competitors to copy the technical features that enjoyed patent protection. Evidence of prior utility patents was sufficient to establish utilitarian functionality. It implied a competitive necessity to keep the technical solution free.[914] If a patent grant gives evidence of the technical character of the product feature at issue, a finding of utilitarian functionality is thus inescapable. It does not matter whether competitors can resort to alternative technical solutions that may achieve the same result:

> There is no need, furthermore, to engage, as did the Court of Appeals, in speculation about other design possibilities, such as using three or four springs which might serve the same purpose … Here, the functionality of the spring design means that competitors need not explore whether other spring juxtapositions might be used. The dual-spring design is not an arbitrary flourish in the configuration of [Marketing Display]'s product; it is the reason the device works. Other designs need not be attempted.[915]

Hence, the focus is on the technical character of the product feature for which trademark protection is sought. An intrinsic necessity to use this technical feature to give the trademark applicant's product the functionality it has is sufficient.[916] Like the CJEU, the U.S. Supreme Court seeks to generally foreclose the invocation of trademark protection to prolong exclusive rights relating to technical solutions – even if technical alternatives are available. As Mark McKenna notes in the light of the *TrafFix* decision:

> [f]unctionality, according to the Supreme Court, is not simply about competitive need for product features; it is also, even primarily, intended to police the boundary between trademark and patent law by channeling protection of useful product features exclusively to the patent system.[917]

In the EU and the U.S., the exclusion of product features necessary to obtain a technical result, thus, demarcates trademark law from patent law. Trademark law is not intended to serve as a vehicle for the 'evergreening' of intellectual property rights to technical solutions. By contrast, patent law has the final word on the term of protection in this area. Once patent protection expires, technical know-how enters the public domain. The courts on both sides of the Atlantic inhibit a former patent owner from invoking trademark law as an alternative means of protection. They seek to draw a boundary line

914. U.S. Supreme Court, *ibid.*, 33-34. Cf. Bone 2015, 212-213.
915. U.S. Supreme Court, 20 March 2001, TrafFix Devices/Marketing Displays, 532 U.S. 23, 33-34 (2001).
916. Cf. Bone 2015, 199, for a discussion between this 'intrinsic necessity' and a more general understanding of competitive necessity concerning the general class of the relevant product. As to the parallel discussion of this question in the EU, see Quaedvlieg 2013, 232-238.
917. McKenna 2011, 827-828.

between the domain of technology (patent law) and the domain of trade (trademark law) by categorically excluding trademark protection as a vehicle to artificially perpetuate the protection status after patent expiry.

7.1.3 *Distinction Between Mark and Product*

A further reason for the exclusion of technical shapes from trademark protection can be seen in the fact that trademark law is not intended to protect products as such. A trademark is a distinctive sign which is attached to goods or services to fulfil certain functions. Trademarks serve the purpose of identifying the commercial source of goods and services. They also offer an exclusive communication channel which the trademark owner can use to convey product-related information and advertising messages to consumers. The trademark is an element attached to the product. It relates to the product, but it should not cover the product itself.[918] This fundamental distinction between the mark and the product played a decisive role in the Canadian *Lego/Mega Brands* lawsuit that paralleled the court procedures in the EU until the Supreme Court of Canada rendered a final decision in 2005.[919]

With regard to the relationship between patent and trademark law, the Supreme Court of Canada pointed out that Lego's search for continuing protection of brick functionality after the expiry of patent rights carried with it the risk of discarding basic and necessary distinctions between different forms of intellectual property and their legal and economic functions. While patents protected new products and processes, the focus shifted from the product itself to the distinctiveness of its marketing in the case of trademarks.[920] The Court concluded that, on its merits, the *Lego/Mega Brands* case raised the question of whether a trademark could be the product itself.[921] Placing this question in the context of the doctrine of functionality, the Court invoked established case law, according to which 'no mark could consist of utilitarian features. Otherwise, it would make the wares a part of the mark and grant a monopoly on their functional features'.[922]

Acting on this maxim, the Supreme Court of Canada embraced the considerations concerning the invalidity of a mark consisting of the functional aspects of a Philips shaver in a decision taken by the Federal Court of

918. Kur/Senftleben 2017, para. 4.09; Kur 2001, 27. German Federal Court of Justice, 12 March 2015, case I ZR 153/14, BMW-Emblem, para. 28; German Federal Court of Justice, 13 June 2002, case I ZR 312/99, SYLT-Kuh, 8-9.
919. Supreme Court of Canada, 17 November 2005, Kirkbi AG/Ritvik Holdings Inc., [2005] 3 S.C.R. 302, 2005 SCC 65.
920. Supreme Court of Canada, *ibid.*, paras 37-39.
921. Supreme Court of Canada, *ibid.*, para. 39.
922. Supreme Court of Canada, *ibid.*, para. 46. As to the different lines of argument developed in this case, see Stratton/Lue 2006, 587; Levy 2006, 596; Macfarlane/Pallotta 2006, 575. Cf. Peukert 2012, 23-25, recognizing the distinction between the mark and the product as a basis for exclusions from trademark protection.

Canada in an earlier *Philips/Remington* lawsuit. In that earlier decision, the Federal Court of Canada had held that a trademark which went beyond distinguishing the products of its owner to the functional structure of the products themselves was 'transgressing the legitimate bounds of a trademark'.[923] In the light of this case precedent, the Supreme Court rejected not only trademark rights to Lego brick functionality but also Lego's additional claim invoking the common law tort of passing off:

> Granting such a claim in these circumstances would amount to recreating a monopoly contrary to basic policies of the laws and legal principles which inform the various forms of intellectual property in our legal system. The appellant is no longer entitled to protection against competition in respect of its product. It must now face the rigours of a free market and its process of creative destruction.[924]

This Canadian decision demonstrates that the exclusion of technical product characteristics from trademark protection can also be inferred from the fundamental distinction between the mark and the product in trademark law. From this perspective, technical functionality, being an essential utilitarian feature of the product itself, necessarily falls outside the scope of trademark protection. The exclusion is a corollary of the very nature of trademark rights which concern distinctive marketing instruments attached to the product, but not the product itself.

Similar considerations play a decisive role in Australia. In the absence of a functionality doctrine that could prevent the registration of utilitarian product features from the outset, Australian courts rely on the mark/product dichotomy to preclude a finding of actionable use as a trademark at the stage of the infringement analysis.[925] In *Koninklijke Philips Electronics/Remington Products Australia* – again a lawsuit about trademark protection for the Philips shaver system with a triple-headed shaving surface – the Full Court of the Federal Court of Australia recalled that the concept of 'trademark' implied that a mark was added 'as something distinct from the goods'.[926] The Court conceded that a mark may be closely bound up with the goods. For example, it may be written upon, stamped into or moulded onto the goods. Nonetheless, the mark always had to keep a separate identity. The various ways of using a trademark in relation to goods did not include the option of simply using the goods themselves as the trademark.[927] The Federal Court of Australia also gave reasons for drawing a boundary line between the mark and the product. On the one hand, trademark rights amounting to protection

923. Supreme Court of Canada, *ibid.*, para. 46, quoting Federal Court of Canada, Remington Rand Corp./Philips Electronics N.V. (1995), 64 C.P.R. (3d) 467 (F.C.A.), p. 478.

924. Supreme Court of Canada, *ibid.*, para. 69.

925. Handler 2018, 173-176.

926. Federal Court of Australia, 30 June 2000, Koninklijke Philips Electronics NV/ Remington Products Australia Pty Limited [2000] FCA 876; 100 FCR 90, 101.

927. Federal Court of Australia, *ibid.*, 101-102.

of the goods themselves may prevent other traders from legitimately producing similar goods. On the other hand, a mark consisting of nothing more than the goods was incapable of fulfilling the core function of a trademark, namely the task of distinguishing the commercial origin of the goods concerned.[928] In light of the missing categorical exclusion of functional product characteristics from trademark registration in Australia, the Court added that even if a functional product feature achieved registration, this did not imply that the manufacture and sale of similar artefacts by competitors constituted a form of using the protected sign in a trademark sense. Hence, Remington's unauthorized use of a three-headed shaver system could not be deemed actionable use of the mark as a trademark.[929]

As Michael Handler explains, the requirement of a separate identity of the trademark from the marked goods – traditionally known in Australia as the 'severability doctrine'[930] – has become a recurring theme in case law. In its 2009 judgment in *Sebel Furniture/Acoustic & Felts*, the Federal Court of Australia delineated the conceptual contours of the current[931] mark/product distinction in Australian trademark law as follows:

> A shape which is dictated by the nature of the goods or by the need to achieve some particular technical result or functional outcome cannot operate as a trade mark. In order to function as a trade mark, the shape must be something which is extra or which is added to the inherent form of the particular goods as something distinct which can denote origin. A shape cannot function as a trade mark if it is something that other traders may legitimately wish to use either because it is inherent to the particular goods (ie it is of their nature) or because it provides some technical or functional benefit to the goods.[932]

Therefore, developments in Canadian and Australian case law confirm that, besides the aim to safeguard freedom of competition and prevent an artificial prolongation of the limited term of patent protection, the conceptual requirement that a mark should be distinct and separable from the marked product supports the categorical exclusion of utilitarian product features from trademark protection.

7.1.4 Risk of Consumer Confusion

From the perspective of trademark law's central aim to ensure market transparency, however, the refusal of trademark protection for technical

928. Federal Court of Australia, *ibid.*, 101-102.
929. Federal Court of Australia, *ibid.*, 105. Cf. Handler 2018, 173.
930. Handler 2018, 175-176.
931. Handler 2018, 174.
932. Federal Court of Australia, 12 January 2009, Sebel Furniture Limited/Acoustic & Felts Pty Limited [2009] FCA 6; 80 IPR 244, 272.

product characteristics has certain drawbacks. As the Australian registration practice demonstrates, a shape necessary to obtain a technical result may be distinctive.[933] EU case law yields the same insight. The famous Lego toy brick, for instance, has been found to contain distinctive functional features which allow consumers to establish a link with the Lego company, and distinguish Lego bricks from those of other toy brick producers. In *Lego/Mega Brands*, the CJEU pointed out that it had not been disputed in the case that the Lego brick – despite its utilitarian functionality – had become distinctive in consequence of use in trade and that the shape of the brick constituted a sign capable of distinguishing Lego's goods from others with another origin.[934]

Given the distinctiveness which the brick had acquired through use, Lego's invocation of trademark protection did not appear pointless from the outset. The grant of trademark protection may even have been deemed necessary to protect consumers against confusion that may be caused by competitors using identical or similar shapes.[935] To safeguard freedom of competition and avoid an artificial perpetuation of patent rights, the CJEU, nonetheless, refrained from granting trademark rights. As the toy brick was functional from a technical perspective, it was categorically excluded from trademark protection (section 7.1.2). Hence, the Court took far-reaching measures to safeguard the technical innovation cycle while being well aware that this was not unlikely to reduce transparency on the toy brick market because the Lego brick, in fact, functioned as a source identifier. Although it had been established that the Lego brick had distinctive character, the trademark rationale of preventing consumer confusion could not prevail. Instead, the Court gave preference to the competing interest in unhindered access to technical know-how after the expiry of the patent monopoly.

As a result of the *Lego/Mega Brands* decision, the consuming public in the EU had to learn that the shape of the Lego brick was no longer exclusively reserved for the Lego company. Given the shape's distinctive character, it seems safe to assume that there have been incidents during this learning process where consumers were actually confused about the commercial origin of toy bricks offered in the marketplace. Nonetheless, the CJEU confirmed its position in later decisions. In *Yoshida Metal Industry/ EUIPO*, the Court stated explicitly that the doctrine of utilitarian functionality constituted an obstacle to trademark protection that:

> may prevent a sign consisting exclusively of the shape of goods which is necessary to obtain a technical result from being registered as a trade mark, even though that sign is capable of performing the essential function of a trade mark, that of guaranteeing the identity of the origin

933. Cf. Handler 2018, 174-176.
934. CJEU, 14 September 2010, case C-48/09 P, Lego/Mega Brands, para. 40.
935. Cf. Bone 2015, 228: '[c]ompetition is important, of course, but so too is avoiding harmful consumer confusion'.

> of the goods or services in question to the consumer by enabling him, without any possibility of confusion, to distinguish those goods or services from others which have another origin.[936]

In assessing the corrosive effect of this CJEU jurisprudence on market transparency, however, it must not be overlooked that the 'reasonably well-informed and reasonably observant and circumspect'[937] average consumer used as a yardstick by the Court can be expected to learn rather quickly of the expiry of patent protection and the free availability of the distinctive technical shape. Reasonably well-informed consumers are not unlikely to focus on other means of distinguishing the offers on the toy brick market, such as the individual trademarks used by the Lego company and its competitors. The potential corrosive effect on market transparency must therefore not be overestimated. It will be temporary.

7.1.5 Prevalence of the Technical Innovation Cycle

In sum, decisions in Australia, Canada, the EU and the U.S. show that trademark courts are alert to the risk of eroding the temporal limits of patent rights by offering trademark protection as an alternative. As judges in other regions, the CJEU embraces the doctrine of utilitarian functionality to inhibit trademark law from perpetuating exclusive rights to technical solutions. Considering the comparison of different configurations and preconditions for the proper functioning of intellectual property systems in Chapter 4, it can be said that these decisions reflect the supremacy of the technical imperative in intellectual property law: *the technical imperative supporting technological follow-on innovation prevails over the trade imperative of market transparency.*

Weighing the need to safeguard the technical innovation cycle (the core objective of patent law) against the guarantee of market transparency (the core objective of trademark law), the CJEU and courts in other regions give preference to the free availability of technology after patent expiry and accept the (temporary) diminution of market transparency with regard to technical signs that have acquired distinctive character as a result of use in trade. Even if technical subject matter has obtained distinctive character, trademark protection is denied to prevent trademark law from becoming an alternative avenue for acquiring or perpetuating intellectual property rights to technical solutions.[938]

---

936. CJEU, 11 May 2017, case C-421/15 P, Yoshida Metal Industry/EUIPO, para. 35. Cf. CJEU, 16 September 2015, case C-215/14, Nestlé/Cadbury ('Kit Kat'), paras 38-39.
937. CJEU, 22 June 1999, case C-342/97, Lloyd Schuhfabrik Meyer ('Lloyd/Loint's'), para. 26. Cf. Kur/Senftleben 2017, para. 5.166; Dinwoodie/Gangjee 2016, 339; Davis 2015, 16 and 21.
938. CJEU, 18 June 2002, case C-299/99, Philips/Remington, para. 57 and 75; CJEU, 16 September 2015, case C-215/14, Nestlé/Cadbury ('Kit Kat'), paras 38-39; CJEU, 11

Inevitably, this supremacy of the technical imperative impedes the functioning of intellectual property protection in the domain of trade. A risk of consumer confusion cannot be ruled out if technical subject matter which consumers perceive as an indication of commercial origin is nonetheless excluded from trademark protection. In such a case, the exclusion of technical product characteristics from trademark protection diminishes market transparency until the consuming public has learned that, due to the expiry of patent protection, the technical product feature is no longer exclusively assigned to one specific producer. However, the reasonably well-informed consumer used as a yardstick by the CJEU[939] can be expected to learn quickly of the expiry of patent protection and the free availability of the utilitarian product element for competitors of the original producer. Consumers will devote more attention to remaining means of distinguishing the offers in the marketplace, such as the individual trademarks used by the original producer and its competitors. Hence, the corrosive effect on market transparency is likely to remain limited. The diminution of market transparency will only be temporary.

7.2 EXCLUSION OF INDUSTRIAL DESIGNS AND WORKS OF APPLIED ART

The preceding section has shown that the doctrine of utilitarian functionality is an effective tool to keep technical subject matter outside the realm of trademark law. A finding of utilitarian functionality leads to a categorical ban on trademark protection that cannot be overcome by demonstrating the acquisition of distinctive character through use in trade. However, utilitarian functionality is not the only concept in trademark law that polices the border between trademark protection and other fields of intellectual property. Besides the exclusion of product features necessary to obtain a technical result, EU trademark law, for example, also excludes signs from protection which consist exclusively of 'the shape, or another characteristic, which gives substantial value to the goods'.[940] As the doctrine of utilitarian functionality in the field of technical solutions, this additional provision concerning substantial value features constitutes an outright, unconditional exclusion in the sense that it cannot be overcome through use in trade. Trademark protection remains excluded even if distinctive character is

May 2017, case C-421/15 P, Yoshida Metal Industry/EUIPO, para. 35; U.S. Supreme Court, 20 March 2001, TrafFix Devices/Marketing Displays, 532 U.S. 23, 33 (2001).

939. Kur/Senftleben 2017, para. 5.166; Dinwoodie/Gangjee 2016, 339; Davis 2015, 16 and 21.

940. Article 7(1)(e) EUTMR and Article 4(1)(e) TMD.

acquired as a result of use as a source identifier.[941] As a counterpart of the doctrine of utilitarian functionality, the exclusion of substantial value characteristics in EU trademark law can be regarded as a concept that offers room for considering aspects of aesthetic functionality in the context of a decision on the grant of trademark protection.[942]

A further parallel with the doctrine of utilitarian functionality concerns the rationales underlying the exclusion from trademark protection. The need to safeguard freedom of competition (section 7.2.1) and the objective to prevent the use of trademark rights as a vehicle to artificially prolong intellectual property protection that has expired (section 7.2.2) play a central role in the context of the exclusion of substantial value product characteristics as well. Moreover, the basic distinction between the mark and the product can serve as an additional explanation (section 7.2.3). The outright exclusion of substantial value characteristics also involves comparable costs in terms of market transparency. As in the case of technical product characteristics, a corrosive effect on market transparency can hardly be denied when product features of this kind are excluded from trademark protection even though they are inherently distinctive or have acquired distinctiveness through use in trade. At least temporarily, consumers may be confused when competitors of the original producer are free to use the same or a similar design (section 7.2.4).

In the context of the present enquiry, the exclusion of substantial value product characteristics constitutes an important further example of a norm in intellectual property law that forces the trade imperative of market transparency onto the sidelines. This further example is of particular importance because it concerns industrial designs and works of applied art. Insofar as an affected product design enjoys copyright protection,[943] the exclusion of

941. CJEU, 18 June 2002, case C-299/99, Philips/Remington, para. 75; CJEU, 20 September 2007, Benetton/G-Star, para. 26.

942. With regard to the connection between the exclusion of substantial value product characteristics in EU trademark law and the U.S. doctrine of aesthetic functionality, see Kur 2011, 3-6; Kur 2001, 36; Dinwoodie 1999, 691.

943. At the international level, works of applied art are expressly recognized as a work category eligible for copyright protection in Article 2(1) BC. The interplay between copyright protection and more specific protection regimes for industrial designs, however, is a matter which Articles 2(7) and 7(4) BC largely leave to national legislation, as long as copyright protection (with a minimum term of 25 years) remains available as a fallback option in the absence of a more specific protection regime for industrial designs. In many countries, the accumulation of copyright protection and more specific industrial design protection is possible. In countries following *la théorie de l'unité d'art*, this is even a corollary of the application of that theory. Cf. Gaubiac 1982, 3, with regard to the theory of unity; Quaedvlieg 1998, 49-52, with regard to differences between works and industrial designs. For an overview of the different approaches to the regulation of cumulative copyright and industrial design protection, see the various contributions to Derclaye 2018. As to the position in the EU, see CJEU, 12 September 2019, case C-683/17, Cofemel, para. 31 and 35-48 and 52-55. For the present enquiry, it is not decisive whether an industrial design affected by a shape exclusion in trademark

trademark protection on the basis of aesthetic functionality leads to the result that trademark rights are not available to perpetuate copyright exclusivity after the expiry of copyright protection. Hence, the cultural imperative supporting cultural follow-on innovation – with its rule of a limited term of protection – prevails over the trade imperative of market transparency that implies indefinitely renewable protection. The exclusion of substantial value product characteristics demonstrates that not only the need to safeguard the technical innovation cycle but also the interest in a well-functioning design innovation cycle can justify a temporary diminution of market transparency and the exposure of consumers to a temporary risk of confusion (7.2.5).

7.2.1 ***Freedom of Competition***

In *Hauck/Stokke* – the leading case on the conceptual contours of the exclusion of substantial value product characteristics in EU trademark law – the CJEU recalled the above-described decisions in *Philips/Remington* and *Lego/Mega Brands* (section 7.1.2) to explain the rationale underlying the categorical exclusion of aesthetically functional product features from trademark protection. As in the case of product features necessary to obtain a technical result, the exclusion of shapes giving substantial value to the goods serves the purpose of ensuring undistorted, free competition in EU law. Article 7(1)(e) EUTMR and Article 4(1)(e) TMD aim to prevent trademark protection not only from granting its proprietor a monopoly on technical solutions but also from serving as a means to monopolize other functional characteristics of a product 'which a user is likely to seek in the products of competitors'.[944]

In the U.S., similar considerations play a central role when assessing design features in the light of the doctrine of aesthetic functionality. In *Qualitex Co./Jacobson Products Co.*, the U.S. Supreme Court discussed trademark protection for a special shade of green gold which Qualitex had used for years to colour its dry cleaning press pads. Addressing the question of whether the specific colour of the laundry pads had to be deemed functional from an aesthetic perspective, the Court recalled its earlier statement in *Inwood Laboratories/Ives Laboratories* that a product feature was functional and could not serve as a trademark, 'if it is essential to the use

law enjoys copyright protection or more specific industrial design protection. In both cases, the protection will be granted only for a limited period of time whereas the acquisition of trademark rights would lead to potentially indefinite protection.

944. CJEU, 18 September 2014, case C-205/13, Hauck/Stokke, para. 18. Cf. CJEU, 18 June 2002, case C-299/99, Philips/Remington, para. 78; CJEU, 14 September 2010, case C-48/09 P, Lego/Mega Brands, para. 43.

or purpose of the article or if it affects the cost or quality of the article'.[945] Expanding on the meaning of this formula, the Court observed that a design feature had to be declared functional 'if exclusive use of the feature would put competitors at a significant non-reputation-related disadvantage' (cf. section 7.1.2).[946] As the CJEU in *Hauck/Stokke*, the U.S. Supreme Court thus underlined the objective to safeguard freedom of competition. In its later decision in *TrafFix Devices/Marketing Displays*, the Court confirmed the importance of an enquiry into competitive necessity by pointing out that it was 'proper to inquire into a "significant non-reputation-related disadvantage" in cases of esthetic functionality … '.[947] With regard to the dry cleaning pads at issue in *Qualitex Co./Jacobson Products Co.*, the U.S. Supreme Court arrived at the conclusion that, although colour could play an important role in making a product more desirable, aesthetic functionality could not always be found. Sometimes colour was not essential to a product's use or purpose and did not affect cost or quality. Hence, the aesthetic functionality doctrine following from *Qualitex* did not create an absolute bar to the use of colour alone as a mark.[948]

7.2.2 No Artificial Perpetuation of Exclusivity

Apart from considerations relating to freedom of competition, the aim to prevent an artificial perpetuation of intellectual property rights with a limited term is central to the enquiry into aesthetic functionality. In *Textilis*, the CJEU made it clear that aesthetic functionality could not readily be inferred from the fact that a sign – the case concerned a decorative pattern that was applied to fabric and paper[949] – was protected by copyright.[950] Instead, the copyright status had 'no bearing' on whether the sign consisted exclusively of a shape giving substantial value to the goods.[951] Therefore, the Court rejected the direct alignment of the enquiry into aesthetic functionality with copyrightability. This outcome, however, only indicates that the specific trademark criteria of aesthetic functionality cannot simply be set aside in the light of copyright protection. Instead, the trademark criterion of 'giv[ing]

945. U.S. Supreme Court, 28 March 1995, Qualitex Co./Jacobson Products Co., 514 U.S. 159, 165 (1995), quoting U.S. Supreme Court, 1 June 1982, Inwood Laboratories/Ives Laboratories, 456 U.S. 844, 850, footnote 10 (1982).
946. U.S. Supreme Court, 28 March 1995, Qualitex Co./Jacobson Products Co., 514 U.S. 159, 165 (1995).
947. U.S. Supreme Court, 20 March 2001, TrafFix Devices/Marketing Displays, 532 U.S. 23, 33 (2001).
948. U.S. Supreme Court, *ibid.*, 165.
949. CJEU, 14 March 2019, case C-21/18, Textilis, paras 12-14.
950. This defence argument had been advanced by the alleged infringer. See CJEU, *ibid.*, para. 19.
951. CJEU, *ibid.*, para. 45.

substantial value to the goods'[952] must be employed as a yardstick to determine whether it is necessary to prevent the erosion of the temporal limits of copyright. Expressing this objective in general terms, the Court stated in *Hauck/Stokke* that the exclusion of functional product characteristics in EU trademark law sought to:

> prevent the exclusive and permanent right which a trade mark confers from serving to extend indefinitely the life of other rights which the EU legislature has sought to make subject to limited periods.[953]

This general statement – addressing the temporal limits of rights in patent and copyright law alike – points in the direction of an important parallel between the rationales underlying the exclusion of technical product features (utilitarian functionality) and substantial value product features (aesthetic functionality). In both cases, the CJEU is prepared to apply the functionality doctrine broadly to preclude the acquisition of indefinitely renewable trademark rights. As explained in section 7.1.2, the Court held in *Lego/Mega Brands* that the exclusion of shapes necessary to obtain a technical result applied regardless of whether competitors could use alternative shapes to achieve the same technical result. The Court thus rejected the argument that the field of application of the absolute ground for refusal had to be confined to situations where the technical shape at issue was the only one capable of obtaining the required technical result. By contrast, the exclusion also applied when several shapes were available which were equivalent from a functional point of view.[954] Similarly, the CJEU opted for a broad scope of the exclusion of substantial value features in *Hauck/Stokke*. The case concerned trademark protection for the so-called Tripp Trapp children's chair consisting of sloping uprights and an L-shaped frame of uprights and sliding plates – a minimalist design which is not only aesthetically appealing but also offers other advantages, such as flexibility, safety and comfort. Given this mix of values inherent in the chair design, the lawsuit about the validity of a trademark registration which Stokke had obtained in the Benelux gave rise to the question whether, for invoking the exclusion of a shape giving substantial value to the goods, it was necessary that the shape's artistic or ornamental value constituted the main or predominant value.[955]

Answering this question, the CJEU made it clear that the scope of the exclusion of substantial value product characteristics could not be limited 'purely to the shape of products having only artistic or ornamental value'.[956] Otherwise, there was a risk that products having essential functional

952. Article 7(1)(e) EUTMR; Article 4(1)(e) TMD.
953. CJEU, 18 September 2014, case C-205/13, Hauck/Stokke, paras 19-20.
954. CJEU, 14 September 2010, case C-48/09 P, Lego/Mega Brands, paras 53-58.
955. CJEU, 18 September 2014, case C-205/13, Hauck/Stokke, para. 14.
956. CJEU, *ibid.*, para. 32.

characteristics as well as a significant aesthetic element would not be covered which, in turn, could compromise the objective to prevent the use of trademark law as a means of artificially extending the term of intellectual property rights which the legislator had limited in time.[957] This rejection of the argument that the exclusion of substantial value features only covered designs with predominant artistic or ornamental value gave rise to the further question which assessment criteria had to be taken into account when applying the doctrine of aesthetic functionality. In this regard, the Court clarified that the presumed perception of the design by the average consumer was not decisive but constituted a relevant assessment criterion.[958] Other criteria to be factored into the equation included:

- the nature of the category of goods concerned;
- the artistic value of the shape in question;
- the dissimilarity of the shape from other shapes in common use on the market concerned;
- a substantial price difference in relation to similar products; and
- the development of a promotion strategy which focuses on accentuating the aesthetic characteristics of the product in question.[959]

Hence, there can be little doubt that the CJEU aims at an open, flexible application of the exclusion of substantial value product characteristics.[960] Attempts to confine the analysis to specific criteria, such as a shape's artistic or ornamental value, are doomed to fail. With the formulation of a whole list of assessment criteria in *Hauck/Stokke*, the CJEU clearly expressed the need for a comprehensive analysis based on varied factors. In *Gömböc*, the Court confirmed its elastic multifactor approach by holding that – despite a technical background – even a shape forming 'the tangible symbol of a mathematic discovery' could be deemed functional from an aesthetic perspective, if the relevant public perceived the shape as 'special and striking'.[961] The fact that the product characteristic at issue did not concern the aesthetic merits of the shape was not decisive.[962]

The flexible *Hauck/Stokke* approach can be understood as a response to several aspects of previous decisions on the exclusion of substantial value shapes that had remained controversial. In *Bang & Olufsen*, the GCEU had confirmed the application of the value shape exclusion to a minimalist loudspeaker design for which Bang & Olufsen had sought protection before OHIM. The GCEU based its decision on the consideration that the shape at

957. CJEU, *ibid.*, paras 31-32.
958. CJEU, *ibid.*, para. 34.
959. CJEU, *ibid.*, para. 35.
960. Dinwoodie 2020, 31. See Ohly 2019, 327, for a critical comment on the broad scope of the open-ended exclusion criteria.
961. CJEU, 23 April 2020, case C-237/19, Gömböc, para. 45.
962. CJEU, *ibid.*, para. 46.

issue had very specific aesthetic characteristics and that Bang & Olufsen itself had presented the design as an essential element of the appeal of its product and its branding strategy. The Court was convinced that the shape was perceived as 'a kind of pure, slender, timeless sculpture for music reproduction', and that these characteristics made it 'an important selling point' falling under the exclusion of shapes giving substantial value to the goods in the sense of EU trademark law.[963] Hence, the *Bang & Olufsen* case testifies to the application of the exclusion of substantial value product characteristics in the area of aesthetic merit: the Bang & Olufsen loudspeaker design is excluded from trademark protection because of its outstanding aesthetic value which enhances the need to prevent trademark law from becoming an obstacle to free competition and an instrument for evergreening protection once industrial design rights and copyright expires.[964]

However, the case also sheds light on the dilemma which traditionally comes along with the concept of aesthetic functionality. If it is right to exclude shapes with a particular aesthetic value from trademark protection, then the exclusion, inevitably, becomes a punishment and disincentive for outstanding product design. The more aesthetically appealing an industrial design, the higher will be the risk of ineligibility for trademark protection. Less ambitious, average product design, by contrast, will attract trademark protection more easily because it is not exposed to the exclusion of substantial value product characteristics to the same extent. The final result – easier access to trademark protection for average design than for outstanding, pioneering design – appears unsatisfactory.[965]

One way of solving this dilemma is the abolition of the concept of aesthetic functionality. If the exclusion of substantial value product characteristics was abandoned altogether, the bias against high-quality product design would automatically disappear as well. In *Hauck/Stokke*, however, the CJEU developed an alternative solution. Rejecting the argument that the exclusion of substantial value product characteristics had to be confined to aesthetic functionality in the strict sense of a predominant artistic or ornamental value, the Court reduced the bias against aesthetically appealing product design by broadening the scope of the exclusion: not only shapes with artistic value are excluded from trademark protection but also shapes which have substantial value for other reasons, such as a departure from customary design solutions, a substantial price advantage, and a particular promotion effort.[966] After *Hauck/Stokke*, the doctrine of aesthetic functionality in the EU can hardly be accused of targeting aesthetically appealing product design in particular. Industrial design may be exposed to the exclusion of substantial value product characteristics for various other

963. GCEU, 6 October 2011, case T-508/08, Bang & Olufsen/OHIM, paras 74-75.
964. Cf. Kur 2011, 3-6; Kur 2001, 36; Dinwoodie 1999, 691.
965. Cf. Kur 2011, 17-18; Kur 2001, 36; Kur 1994, 191-193.
966. CJEU, 18 September 2014, case C-205/13, Hauck/Stokke, para. 35.

reasons. The list of assessment criteria established by the CJEU paves the way for a broader and less biased application of the exclusion in practice.

The *Benetton/G-Star* decision of the CJEU – another case predating the *Hauck/Stokke* judgment – already heralded the rejection of a concept of aesthetic functionality that confines the analysis to artistic or ornamental value. The case concerned the design of the G-Star 'Elwood' jeans which had been copied by Benetton. As a counterclaim to the infringement action brought by G-Star on the basis of two shape marks derived from the jeans design, Benetton sought the annulment of G-Star's trademarks on the ground that the shapes at issue determined the market value of the goods to a great extent as a result of 'their beauty or original character'. Hence, Benetton argued that the shapes gave substantial value to the jeans and had to be excluded from trademark protection for that reason.[967]

Hearing the case, the Dutch Supreme Court decided to stay the proceedings and refer prejudicial questions about the application of the exclusion of substantial value shapes to the CJEU. Previous decisions of the Benelux Court of Justice form the background to these prejudicial questions.[968] In the decision *Burberrys I*, the Benelux Court of Justice had drawn a distinction between the factors to be taken into account when excluding a shape from trademark protection because of its influence on the substantial value of the goods. According to the Benelux Court of Justice, a product's distinctive shape only fell within the scope of the exclusion:

> where the nature of the product is such that its appearance and shaping determine its market value entirely or substantially as a result of their beauty or original character. In this determination, the influence on the market value which does not result from the aesthetic attractiveness of the shape, but from the power of attraction that is connected with its recognition as a distinctive sign, must not be taken into consideration.[969]

Against this background, the *Benetton/G-Star* lawsuit gave rise to the question whether this traditional Benelux distinction had survived the harmonization of trademark law in the EU and remained relevant to the exclusion of substantial value product characteristics under harmonized EU trademark law. The Dutch Supreme Court asked whether the exclusion of substantial value product characteristics applied where the nature of the product was such that its appearance and shaping determined its market value entirely or substantially as a result of their beauty or original character, and whether the exclusion was inapplicable where, prior to the application for registration, the attractiveness of the relevant shape to the public had been

---

967. CJEU, 20 September 2007, case C-371/06, Benetton/G-Star, paras 10-11.
968. For an overview, see Vanovermeire 2009, 190-194.
969. Benelux Court of Justice, 14 April 1989, case A 87/8, Superconfex/Burberrys ('Burberrys I'), *NJ* 1989, no. 834, para. 16.

determined predominantly by the recognition of it as a distinctive sign.[970] Posing its prejudicial questions, the Dutch Supreme Court explicitly pointed out that the problem did not relate to the distinctive character of the contested marks.[971] From a Benelux perspective, the prejudicial question posed in *Benetton/G-Star*, therefore, concerned the repute understood as the power of attraction[972] which the design of the G-Star 'Elwood' jeans had acquired as a result of marketing activities making it known as a brand insignia. The CJEU answered this question by clarifying that the doctrine of aesthetic functionality had to be interpreted:

> as meaning that the shape of a product which gives substantial value to that product cannot constitute a trade mark under Article 3(3) of that directive [nowadays Article 4(4) TMD] where, prior to the application for registration, it acquired attractiveness as a result of its recognition as a distinctive sign following advertising campaigns presenting the specific characteristics of the product in question[973] (explanation within brackets added).

From a Benelux perspective, this answer misses the point. While the question submitted by the Dutch Supreme Court concerned acquired *attractiveness* (in the sense of brand magnetism), the CJEU's answer remained limited to acquired *distinctiveness* – even though the dictum still referred to 'acquired attractiveness'.[974] Due to a lack of conceptual refinement, the CJEU failed to discuss the traditional Benelux distinction between substantial value stemming from the shape's inherent beauty and substantial value arising from the recognition of a shape as a mark with a favourable brand image.[975] The CJEU avoided a more detailed discussion of the question in

---

970. CJEU, 20 September 2007, case C-371/06, Benetton/G-Star, para. 20.
971. CJEU, *ibid.*, para. 19.
972. As to the traditional understanding of 'repute' in the Benelux and its impact on the concept at EU level, see Kur/Senftleben 2017, para. 5.242-5.244, and Advocate General Jacobs, CJEU, 23 October 2003, case C-408/01, Adidas/Fitnessworld, Opinion of 10 July 2003, para. 38, stating that 'the concept of detriment to the repute of a trade mark […] describes the situation where – as it was put in the well-known Claeryn/Klarein decision of the Benelux Court of Justice – the goods for which the infringing sign is used appeal to the public's senses in such a way that the trade mark's power of attraction is affected'. The decision of the Benelux Court of Justice, 1 March 1975, case A 74/1, Claeryn/Klarein, *NJ* 1975, no. 472, dealt with a situation where ' … a sign similar to the [well-known] trademark [is] used under such circumstances that prejudice to the trademark owner may be caused by encroaching upon the trademark's potential for raising a desire to buy … '.
973. CJEU, 20 September 2007, case C-371/06, Benetton/G-Star, para. 28.
974. CJEU, *ibid.*, para. 28 and dictum.
975. Cf. Advocate General D.W. Feer Verkade, Dutch Supreme Court, 3 April 2009, case LJN BH1225, Benetton/G-Star II, Opinion of 23 January 2009, para. 2.5, wondering whether the former Benelux jurisprudence on this point (14 April 1989, case A 87/8, Superconfex/Burberrys ('Burberrys I'), *NJ* 1989, no. 834, para. 16) must be deemed overruled by the approach taken by the CJEU.

which way the acquisition of shape mark repute – in the sense of the acquisition of an attractive brand image – had to be taken into account when assessing the shape's impact on the value of the goods.[976] *Benetton/G-Star* only clarified that a product designer could not whitewash a product feature that is functional from an aesthetic perspective by focusing attention on this design element in advertising and educating consumers to recognize it as a distinctive sign.[977] Even if the advertising campaign has success and the design element acquires distinctiveness through use, the product feature remains aesthetically functional and ineligible for trademark protection.

In *Hauck/Stokke*, the CJEU came closer to a clarification of the impact of brand recognition. Condensing aspects of previous decisions, including *Benetton/G-Star*, the CJEU developed the described broad concept of aesthetic functionality that includes advertising drawing the attention of consumers to specific design elements. The assessment factors following from *Hauck/Stokke* comprise not only a shape's inherent beauty ('the artistic value of the shape in question') but also power of attraction that follows from advertising ('the development of a promotion strategy which focuses on accentuating the aesthetic characteristics of the product in question').[978] Because of the focus on aesthetic characteristics 'of the product in question',[979] however, it need not follow from *Hauck* that substantial value arising from recognition of a design element as a brand insignia leads to a finding of aesthetic functionality. In *Louboutin*, Advocate General Maciej Szpunar stated explicitly that the application of the absolute ground for refusal was not justified:

> where the advantage does not result from the intrinsic characteristics of the shape, but from the reputation of the mark or its proprietor. Indeed, the possibility of acquiring such a reputation is an important aspect of the system of competition which trade mark law helps to maintain.[980]

While *Hauck/Stokke* led to a broad and elastic concept of aesthetic functionality, the EU doctrine, thus, has certain limits. The accentuation of aesthetic product features in advertising may support a finding of aesthetic functionality when it draws the attention of the public to intrinsic aesthetic characteristics of the product and strengthens consumer recognition and appreciation of these aesthetic features. In line with the traditional Benelux approach,[981] however, the market value which does not result from the aesthetic attractiveness of the shape, but from the power of attraction that is

---

976. Cf. Kur 2011, 15-16.
977. Cf. Kur 2011, 15.
978. CJEU, 18 September 2014, case C-205/13, Hauck/Stokke, para. 35.
979. CJEU, *ibid.*, para. 35.
980. Opinion of Advocate General Maciej Szpunar, 22 June 2017, case C-163/16, Louboutin and Christian Louboutin, para. 72.
981. Cf. Benelux Court of Justice, 14 April 1989, case A 87/8, Superconfex/Burberrys ('Burberrys I'), *NJ* 1989, no. 834, para. 16.

connected with the recognition of design features as a mark with a favourable brand image, need not be taken into consideration. The EU concept of aesthetic functionality can be understood not to cover aspects of product design which consumers do not value because of their inherent beauty but because of the brand messages which these product features convey. Despite this room for a distinction between intrinsic aesthetic value and extrinsic brand value, it remains an open question how cases can be solved where the two aspects – inherent beauty and brand recognition – are intertwined to such an extent that they have become inseparable.[982]

7.2.3 *Distinction Between Mark and Product*

As explained above in the context of the exclusion of technical design elements (section 7.1.3), the mark/product dichotomy in trademark law can serve as an additional explanation for applying the functionality doctrine. Focusing on the artistic or ornamental value of product features, a parallel with the mark/product argument in the field of technical product characteristics can easily be drawn. In the case of a product that is intended to have a technical effect, the functioning of a shape achieving this technical effect constitutes an essential product feature.[983] Similarly, a shape's inherent beauty constitutes the very substance of a product that is intended to be aesthetically appealing. Therefore, the mark/product argument is also valid with regard to design elements that give substantial value to the goods because of their intrinsic artistic or ornamental value. In line with the CJEU jurisprudence discussed in the preceding section, the argument can be made even if consumer recognition and appreciation result from advertising 'accentuating the aesthetic characteristics of the product in question'.[984] The promotion strategy may draw the attention of the public to the value of design features. Over time, it may enhance the appreciation of the product design. Nonetheless, the mark/product distinction remains intact and the exclusion argument remains valid as long as the marketing effort concerns aesthetic product features that are intrinsic aspects of the outward appearance of the product – and not mere carriers of extrinsic brand value.

7.2.4 *Risk of Consumer Confusion*

Surveying the development of the functionality doctrine in EU trademark law, a remarkable pattern comes to the fore:

982. As to this dilemma, see Kur 2011, 15-16, who proposes to let brand recognition prevail and refrain from applying the doctrine of aesthetic functionality in this case.
983. Supreme Court of Canada, 17 November 2005, Kirkbi AG/Ritvik Holdings Inc., [2005] 3 S.C.R. 302, 2005 SCC 65, para. 39 and 46.
984. CJEU, 18 September 2014, case C-205/13, Hauck/Stokke, para. 35.

- the doctrine of utilitarian functionality is not confined to situations where a technical product feature is the only one capable of obtaining the required technical result. By contrast, the categorical exclusion of trademark protection also applies when competitors can use alternative shapes;[985]
- the doctrine of aesthetic functionality is not strictly confined to situations where product features have evident intrinsic artistic or ornamental value. By contrast, the exclusion also applies in other situations to be determined on the basis of a flexible list of assessment criteria, including situations where the value of the product feature is the result of a promotion strategy accentuating its aesthetic appeal.[986]

The CJEU thus prefers a broad, flexible interpretation of both branches of functionality: technical solutions falling under the exclusion of product characteristics necessary to obtain a technical result, and industrial designs and works of applied art falling under the exclusion of product characteristics giving substantial value to the goods.

With this preference for a broad, flexible interpretation, the CJEU also enhances the risk of consumer confusion arising from the application of the functionality doctrine. As explained above, the provisions in EU trademark law set forth unconditional, outright exclusions which apply even if the product feature at issue has distinctive character and is perceived as a source identifier by the consuming public.[987] As the Lego toy brick in *Lego/Mega Brands* (section 7.1.4),[988] the 'Tripp Trapp' children's chair that gave rise to the *Hauck/Stokke* lawsuit (section 7.2.2)[989] is an iconic and well-known industrial design. It seems plausible that consumers perceive the shape as an indication of commercial source in countries where the chair has success on the market. From the perspective of the trade imperative of market transparency, it would thus be consistent to register the chair design as a shape mark for the Stokke company, as the Benelux Office for Intellectual Property did with effect in the Benelux territory years ago.[990] In spite of its distinctive character, however, the chair design is subject to thorough

985. CJEU, 14 September 2010, case C-48/09 P, Lego/Mega Brands, paras 53-58.
986. CJEU, 18 September 2014, case C-205/13, Hauck/Stokke, paras 32-35; CJEU, 20 September 2007, case C-371/06, Benetton/G-Star, para. 28.
987. CJEU, 18 June 2002, case C-299/99, Philips/Remington, para. 57 and 75; CJEU, 16 September 2015, case C-215/14, Nestlé/Cadbury ('Kit Kat'), paras 38-39; CJEU, 11 May 2017, case C-421/15 P, Yoshida Metal Industry/EUIPO, para. 35. Cf. also U.S. Supreme Court, 20 March 2001, TrafFix Devices/Marketing Displays, 532 U.S. 23, 33 (2001).
988. CJEU, 14 September 2010, case C-48/09 P, Lego/Mega Brands, para. 40.
989. CJEU, 18 September 2014, case C-205/13, Hauck/Stokke, para. 7.
990. CJEU, *ibid.*, para. 7. To this day, the Tripp Trapp chair design is registered at the international level with effect in the Benelux (among other designated countries). See IR no. 767786.

scrutiny in light of the functionality factors developed by the CJEU.[991] With every expansion of the scope of the functionality doctrine, the CJEU enhances the risk of denying protection for a product feature which is distinctive and should be assigned to one individual undertaking from a market transparency perspective.

It is remarkable that the CJEU is prepared to run the risk of inroads into market transparency not only with regard to technical solutions but also with regard to industrial designs and works of applied art. Apparently, the spectre of consumer confusion does not appear so terrifying that the Court would not dare raising it when important countervailing objectives are at stake, such as the guarantee of undistorted, free competition and the need to avoid the use of trademark law as a vehicle to artificially perpetuate intellectual property rights with a limited term of protection.[992] If the flexible interpretation of the doctrine of aesthetic functionality is understood to indicate that the CJEU is prepared to put the consumer confusion mantra in trademark law into perspective altogether, this would be a radical paradigm shift in trademark law. The objective to protect consumers against confusion constitutes a sacrosanct core rationale of the trademark system and a powerful justification for the acceptance of new kinds of marks and the grant of protection against various forms of confusion.[993] A departure from this traditional position would be an upheaval. Once anti-confusion protection no longer forms an ultimate goal but becomes an objective of the protection system to be weighed against other important values, the discourse on trademark protection could be rationalized. Instead of blindly relying on the rhetoric of trademark protection being indispensable whenever a sign is perceived as a badge of origin, and sustaining a corresponding protection automatism,[994] a true balancing of interests could take place. The advantages to be derived from trademark protection in terms of enhanced market transparency could be weighed against disadvantages, such as restrictions of free competition and free speech following from potentially indefinite trademark rights.[995] Against this background, the flexible interpretation of the functionality

---

991. CJEU, *ibid.*, paras 23-25 and 32-35.
992. See the emphasis of these values in CJEU, *ibid.*, paras 18-19.
993. Cf. Kur/Senftleben 2017, para. 1.06-1.09; A. Griffiths 2008, 241; McKenna 2007, 1844; Economides 1988, 526.
994. As to the risk of a circular reasoning inferring a need for trademark protection from consumer perceptions shaped by the marketing strategies of brand owners, see Denicola 1982, 170; Ramsey 2003, 1150; McKenna 2007, 1899; Assaf 2008, 82-83; Lemley/McKenna 2010, 440; Senftleben 2013a, 812-813; Anemaet 2020, 188-189 and 211-212.
995. The need to balance trademark protection against competing free competition and speech interests has been described in more detail, for instance, by Ramsey/Schovsbo 2013, 671; Weckström 2007, 671. In *Gerolsteiner/Putsch*, the need for putting the consumer confusion rationale into perspective in the light of overriding interests has even been expressed openly by the CJEU itself. See CJEU, 7 January 2004, case C-100/02, Gerolsteiner/Putsch, para. 25: 'The mere fact that there exists a likelihood of aural confusion between a word mark registered in one Member State and an indication

doctrine – in spite of a risk of consumer confusion – comes as a welcome surprise and an important impulse for a thorough scrutiny of the role and appropriateness of the consumer confusion mantra in trademark law.

As pointed out above in the context of the exclusion of technical shapes (section 7.1.4), the corrosive effect on market transparency must not be overestimated when it comes to the denial of trademark protection for substantial value product characteristics which consumers perceive as source identifiers. The risk of consumer confusion will be temporary. The reasonably well-informed and reasonably observant and circumspect consumer taken as a yardstick by the CJEU[996] can be expected to learn quickly that affected product design no longer belongs exclusively to the original producer. Accordingly, the consuming public will look for other source identifiers which still provide reliable information on the commercial origin of the goods, such as the LEGO or STOKKE word mark attached to toy bricks and children's chairs.

Balancing a potential erosion of market transparency against a potential restriction of free and undistorted competition, this temporariness of potential consumer confusion appears as an important factor capable of tipping the scales in favour of free competition and a boundary line between trademark protection and industrial design protection for aesthetic product features. If the inroads made into market transparency can be expected to be only temporary, it seems difficult to justify the grant of trademark rights that would lead to a potentially indefinite monopolization of essential product features. Hence, the CJEU had sufficient reason to interpret not only the exclusion of technical product features but also the exclusion of substantial value product characteristics in a flexible manner. As the potential encroachment upon market transparency can be expected to remain temporary, this extension of a flexible interpretation to the domain of design and applied art does not give rise to concerns about a collapse of market transparency or an erosion of consumer reliance on trademarks. Consumers will simply focus on other trademarks attached to products with essential features that are ineligible for trademark protection because they represent substantial value. The Court is thus free to extend the impact of a broad, flexible functionality doctrine from the domain of technical solutions to the domain of industrial designs and works of applied art.

---

of geographical origin from another Member State is therefore insufficient to conclude that the use of that indication in the course of trade is not in accordance with honest practices.'

996. CJEU, 22 June 1999, case C-342/97, Lloyd Schuhfabrik Meyer ('Lloyd/Loint's'), para. 26. Cf. Kur/Senftleben 2017, para. 5.166; Dinwoodie/Gangjee 2016, 339; Davis 2015, 16 and 21.

7.2.5 Prevalence of the Design Innovation Cycle

In sum, the decision in *Hauck/Stokke* shows that the CJEU is prepared to prevent not only the erosion of the temporal limits of patent exclusivity but also the erosion of the temporal limits of exclusive rights relating to industrial designs and works of applied art.[997] The CJEU relies on the exclusion of substantial value characteristics to prevent trademark law from supporting attempts to artificially perpetuate exclusivity in this area. In *Gömböc*, the CJEU pointed out that the objective to prevent the evergreening of intellectual property rights with a limited term of protection did not automatically preclude the evolution of overlapping protection. The Court stated that 'such an objective does not mean that EU intellectual property law prevents the coexistence of several forms of legal protection'.[998] The Court also pointed out that the shape of a product could benefit from protection under trademark law if it fulfilled the conditions for registration as a trademark.[999] Applying the exclusion of substantial value characteristics broadly, however, the Court systematically thwarts attempts to acquire trademark rights to aesthetic product design. Therefore, the CJEU ostensibly gives trademark applicants the chance of cumulating industrial design and trademark protection with one hand (by upholding the principle that protection overlaps are possible) and takes it away with the other (by invoking aesthetic functionality to ban trademark rights to product design).

Placing this finding in the context of the analysis of core functions of intellectual property systems in Chapter 4, it can be concluded that – not only with regard to technical solutions but also in respect of industrial design – the functionality doctrine in trademark law allows the cyclic innovation paradigm of a limited term of protection to prevail over the trade imperative of market transparency. If the exclusion of substantial value product characteristics is invoked to ban trademark protection for industrial design and works of applied art,[1000] it may also be said that *the design imperative supporting cultural follow-on innovation in the area of aesthetic product appearance prevails over the trade imperative of market transparency.* The CJEU developed an elastic concept of aesthetic functionality that can be employed to keep industrial designs and works of applied art outside the trademark system. In this context, the CJEU accepts the (temporary) reduction of market transparency that can arise when the denial of trademark protection concerns a design that has acquired distinctive character through use in trade. Even if an industrial design or a work of applied art is distinctive, the

997. Ohly 2008, 216-217; Geier 2015, 188-193.
998. CJEU, 23 April 2020, case C-237/19, Gömböc, para. 51.
999. CJEU, *ibid.*, paras 52-53.
1000. As to overlapping industrial design and copyright protection, see the various contributions to Derclaye 2018. As to the position in the EU, see CJEU, 12 September 2019, case C-683/17, Cofemel, para. 31 and 35-48 and 52-55, and Koschtial 2005, 306-309. Cf. Gaubiac 1982, 3; Quaedvlieg 1998, 49-52.

functionality doctrine still imposes a ban on trademark rights to prevent trademark law from artificially perpetuating the exclusivity enjoyed under copyright law or specific industrial design legislation.

As in the above-discussed case of prevalence of the technical imperative (section 7.1.5), the supremacy of the design imperative in the area of industrial designs and works of applied art, inevitably, impedes the functioning of intellectual property protection in the domain of trade. A risk of consumer confusion cannot be ruled out, if trademark protection is denied with regard to a work of applied art which consumers perceive as an indication of commercial origin. The denial of trademark rights reduces market transparency until consumers have learned that, due to the expiry of copyright protection, the product appearance is no longer exclusively reserved for one specific producer. Facing competing offers of the same design in the marketplace, however, the reasonably well-informed consumer used as a yardstick by the CJEU can be expected to learn quickly to focus on other means of distinguishing the goods, such as the individual word marks used by the original producer and its competitors. Hence, the corrosive effect on market transparency is temporary and remains limited.

7.3 NO EXCLUSION OF LITERARY AND ARTISTIC WORKS IN GENERAL

As explained in section 4.1, both copyright and patent law are cyclic intellectual property systems. Their proper functioning depends on the expiry of protection. In cyclic intellectual property systems, a limited term of protection constitutes the price to be paid in exchange for the acquisition of protection.[1001] Otherwise, there would not be left 'enough and as good' in common for later creators and inventors.[1002] In the terminology developed in Chapter 3, this principle of intergenerational equity must be observed not only with regard to technical solutions but also in respect of literary and artistic works. Neither authors nor inventors should be offered the opportunity to use constant trademark renewal as a vehicle to escape the obligation of freeing their creations to the public domain. A limited term of protection is not only central to providing a constantly updated stock of freely available know-how for the continuous development of new inventions. It is also a prerequisite for a public domain of cultural expressions that is sufficiently rich to support the incessant creation of new literary and artistic works.

1001. Cf. U.S. Supreme Court, 2 June 2003, Dastar/Twentieth Century Fox, 539 U.S. 23, 33-34 (2003); German Federal Constitutional Court, 31 May 2016, case 1 BvR 1585/13, 'Sampling', *GRUR* 2016, 690, para. 87; EFTA Court, 6 April 2017, case E-5/16, Municipality of Oslo ('Vigeland'), para. 66. Cf. Vanovermeire 2009, 180.

1002. Locke 1698, book II chapter 5 § 27. Cf. Cohen 2006, 151-152; Lemley 1997, 997-998; Gordon 1993, 1562-1564.

Given this functional parallel, one might expect that the relationship between copyright and trademark protection is regulated in the same way as the relationship between patent and trademark protection: trademark law should prolong neither copyright nor patent exclusivity. Drawing a less rigid boundary line between copyright and trademark law leads to an imbalance within the intellectual property system. The cultural innovation cycle would be exposed to the freezing effect of potentially indefinite trademark protection (section 6.3) to a larger extent than its technical counterpart.[1003]

The broad application of the functionality doctrine that has been discussed in the preceding sections indicates that judges are aware of the need to avoid corrosive effects of potentially indefinite trademark protection on cyclic innovation processes in certain fields, such as technical know-how and industrial designs (sections 7.1.2 and 7.2.2). If the general objective to prevent encroachments upon intellectual property systems with a limited period of protection plays a crucial role in the context of technical solutions and industrial designs,[1004] one might assume that it is also central to other creations of the mind that enjoy protection only for a limited period, such as literary and artistic works in a more general sense. One might expect courts to take the steps necessary to prevent the corrosive effect of indefinite trademark protection not only in respect of technical solutions, industrial designs and works of applied art, but also with regard to books, paintings, drawings, musical compositions, films and other literary and artistic productions.[1005]

Nonetheless, the current intellectual property system treats these cases differently. While the functionality doctrine can be employed to prevent overlaps between patent and trademark protection and achieve a far-reaching separation of industrial designs and trademark protection, a comparably strong mechanism for policing the border between copyright and trademark protection has not evolved yet.[1006] In respect of literary and artistic works falling outside the category of works of applied art, the concept of aesthetic functionality has much less potential to achieve an outright exclusion of trademark rights (following section 7.3.1). In consequence, overlapping copyright and trademark protection is available in many cases even though the present scope of trademark protection raises serious concerns about a deterrent effect on cultural follow-on innovation (section 6.3). One reason for the acceptance of copyright/trademark protection overlaps in trademark law and practice may be the uncritical attitude which often prevails in literature (section 7.3.2). Moreover, trademark offices and courts seem confident that they can avoid overprotection on the basis of the general requirement of distinctiveness in trademark law (section 7.3.3). A closer analysis of

1003. Senftleben 2013a, 816-817 and 824-825.

1004. Cf. CJEU, 18 September 2014, case C-205/13, Hauck/Stokke, paras 19-20.

1005. See the illustrative list in Article 2(1) BC.

1006. Senftleben 2013a, 814-817.

distinctiveness as a bulwark against inappropriate copyright/trademark protection overlaps, however, raises serious doubts about this solution. As the example of fictional characters shows, the requirement of distinctiveness is an unreliable safeguard. It may even allow complete overlaps in the sense of trademark rights covering not only merchandising articles but also primary information products and services relating to cultural expressions (section 7.3.4).

7.3.1 Concept of Aesthetic Functionality Insufficient

It can be inferred from the foregoing discussion of the functionality doctrine that the concept of aesthetic functionality allows the prevention of copyright/trademark protection overlaps in certain cases. Works of applied art are subject to the exclusion of shapes and other product characteristics that give substantial value to the goods (section 7.2.2).[1007] The *Bang & Olufsen* case can serve as an example.[1008] If a product has substantial value because of the aesthetic appeal of its design elements, the doctrine of aesthetic functionality can prevent the acquisition of trademark rights. The risk of an artificial perpetuation of exclusive rights after the expiry of copyright protection is thus averted. However, the separation of copyright and trademark protection that can be achieved with the concept of aesthetic functionality has its limits.

Prior to the extension of the EU functionality doctrine to 'the shape, or another characteristic' in Article 7(1)(e) EUTMR and Article 4(1)(e) TMD, this was self-evident. Under the former EU trademark legislation, Article 7(1)(e) CTMR 2009 and Article 3(1)(e) TMD 2008 confined the scope of the doctrine to 'the shape which gives substantial value to the goods'. Traditionally, the word 'shape' was understood to require three-dimensionality. From the outset, the concept of aesthetic functionality was thus confined to three-dimensional creations. For a long time, this view prevailed. Under the Benelux exclusion of substantial value shapes which served as a model for

---

1007. With regard to the Benelux provision preceding the EU functionality doctrine, it was stated in a joint commentary of the Benelux governments that the exclusion of shapes which give substantial value to the goods 'was intended to set certain limits to the possibility of cumulating trademark protection with the protection following from copyright law or industrial designs law'. See Gemeenschappelijk Commentaar der Regeringen concerning Article 1(2) of the former Benelux Trademark Act, as quoted in Benelux Court of Justice, 14 April 1989, case A 87/8, Superconfex/Burberrys ('Burberrys I'), *NJ* 1989, no. 834, para. 12: 'beoogt een zekere mate van beperking op te leggen aan de mogelijkheid van samenloop van de merkenbescherming en de bescherming, die voortvloeit uit het auteursrecht of uit het tekeningen- en modellenrecht.' The Benelux Court of Justice, *ibid.*, para. 15, placed the provision in the context of freedom of competition.

1008. GCEU, 6 October 2011, case T-508/08, Bang & Olufsen/OHIM, paras 74-75.

the shape exclusions in EU trademark law,[1009] the question of three-dimensionality had arisen in a case concerning the exclusion of Burberrys' two-dimensional tartan pattern.[1010] At the time, the Benelux Court of Justice rejected an extension to two-dimensional creations and confined the functionality doctrine to three-dimensional shapes.[1011] In Germany, an attempt to extend the scope of the shape exclusions to two-dimensional subject matter was made in the aforementioned case concerning a portrait photograph of the actress Marlene Dietrich (section 6.2.4). Discussing a request to register the portrait in respect of photographs, posters, postcards and goods of a similar nature, the German Federal Patent Court argued that the Marlene Dietrich photograph constituted a mere reproduction of these goods, and invoked the exclusion of 'the shape which results from the nature of the goods themselves', as in force at that time, to deny registration.[1012] The Court expressed the view that the mark consisted of the product itself and sought to use the shape exclusion to foreclose the acquisition of trademark rights. In line with this approach, the shape exclusion would have been extended to a two-dimensional photograph. However, the decision was overruled by the German Federal Court of Justice which tersely concluded that the sign consisted of the reproduction of the head of Marlene Dietrich and did not consist of a shape resulting from the nature of a photograph, poster or postcard as such.[1013] Again, the scope of the shape exclusion – in this case the exclusion of nature shapes[1014] – was not broadened.

Prior to the amendment of EU trademark legislation, however, there was already a tendency to depart from the focus on three-dimensional subject

1009. In fact, the exclusion of substantial value product characteristics in EU trademark law was modelled on Article 1(2) of the former Benelux Trademark Act (Benelux Merkenwet). Cf. Cohen Jehoram/Van Nispen/Huydecoper 2008, 129-130.

1010. Benelux Court of Justice, 14 April 1989, case A 87/8, Superconfex/Burberrys ('Burberrys I'), *NJ* 1989, no. 9.

1011. Benelux Court of Justice, 16 December 1991, case A 90/4, Burberrys/Bossi ('Burberrys II'), *NJ* 1992, no. 596, paras 34-44. Cf. Cohen Jehoram/Van Nispen/Huydecoper 2008, 127-128, who considered an extension to two-dimensional shapes unlikely in the light of this case precedent.

1012. German Federal Patent Court, 9 November 2005, Porträtfoto Marlene Dietrich, para. 4.2.

1013. German Federal Court of Justice, 24 April 2008, Marlene-Dietrich-Bildnis, para. 11. For a similar development in U.S. law concerning use of Betty Boop's name on posters, dolls and clothing, see U.S. Court of Appeals for the Ninth Circuit, 23 February 2011, Fleischer Studios/A.V.E.L.A., 636 F.3d 1115, 1124 (9th Cir. 2011), invoking the doctrine of aesthetic functionality. This decision, however, was withdrawn and superseded in U.S. Court of Appeals for the Ninth Circuit, 19 August 2011, Fleischer Studios/A.V.E.L.A., 654 F.3d 958, 968 (9th Cir. 2011), 'Betty Boop'. Finally, aesthetic functionality was found with regard to the use of the name 'Betty Boop' on T-shirts and film posters. See U.S. District Court for the Central District of California, 14 November 2012, Fleischer Studios/A.V.E.L.A., 925 F. Supp. 2d 1067, 1074-1075 (C.D. Cal. 2012). Cf. Curtin 2018, 1017-1018 and 1022-1023.

1014. Article 3(1)(e)(i) TMD 2008.

matter. In *Pi-Design and Bodum/Yoshida*, the GCEU had to decide on the invalidity of the registration of a two-dimensional figurative sign – a graphic representation of handles of knives with black dots – as a Community trademark. The application for a declaration of invalidity was based on the argument that the black dots had to be understood to constitute dents necessary to obtain a technical result. Accordingly, the question arose whether the industrial design, being represented as a two-dimensional figurative sign, was subject to the exclusion of technical shapes in EU trademark law.[1015] The GCEU took the view that the wording of the shape exclusion in force at that time ('the shape of goods which is necessary to obtain a technical result') did not define the range of relevant signs. The provision made no distinction between three-dimensional shapes, two-dimensional shapes, or two-dimensional representations of three-dimensional shapes. For this reason, the Court held that the shape exclusion may apply to two-dimensional shapes.[1016] In light of the public policy objective underlying the exclusion of technical shapes, in particular the objective to safeguard freedom of competition, the exclusion applied to 'any sign, whether two- or three-dimensional, where all the essential characteristics of the sign perform a technical function'.[1017] On appeal, the CJEU overruled the GCEU decision because the Court had failed to devote attention to the actual use made of the trademark following its registration.[1018] The CJEU also referred to the conclusion that 'any sign, whether two- or three-dimensional' could fall under the exclusion of technical shapes.[1019] As no appeal claim had been brought against this element of the judgment, however, the CJEU did not comment on that outcome and left the more flexible interpretation developed by the GCEU intact.

Although the CJEU had not explicitly confirmed the extension of the shape exclusions to two-dimensional figurative signs in *Pi-Design and Bodum/Yoshida*, it seemed that EU courts did not exclude the possibility of applying the shape exclusions in EU trademark law more broadly. The case, however, concerned the specific problem of 'two-dimensional representations of three-dimensional shapes'.[1020] When this specific category is used in a trademark application, it would be arbitrary to determine the two- or three-dimensional nature of the design at issue on the basis of the representation mode. If the CJEU had confined the application of the shape exclusion to three-dimensional representations, a two-dimensional representation would have allowed trademark applicants to bypass the shape exclusion and thwart the underlying policy objectives. Due to these specific circumstances

1015. In this case, the relevant provision was Article 7(1)(e)(ii) CTMR 2009.
1016. GCEU, 8 May 2012, case T-416/10, Pi-Design and Bodum/Yoshida, para. 24.
1017. GCEU, *ibid.*, para. 27.
1018. CJEU, 6 March 2014, joined cases C-337/12P to C-340/12P, Pi-Design and Bodum/ Yoshida, para. 61.
1019. CJEU, *ibid.*, para. 51.
1020. GCEU, 8 May 2012, case T-416/10, Pi-Design and Bodum/Yoshida, para. 24.

surrounding the *Pi-Design and Bodum/Yoshida* decision, it remained unclear how elastic the exclusion of 'shapes' under former EU trademark legislation may become with regard to cultural signs. Could a Mickey Mouse or Donald Duck drawing – both registered as trademarks internationally[1021] – be qualified as an aesthetically functional two-dimensional shape or two-dimensional representation of a three-dimensional shape? Could perhaps even a melody be regarded as a musical shape falling under the shape exclusions?

In case of an affirmative answer, the EU doctrine of aesthetic functionality could have contributed more effectively to the separation of copyright and trademark protection. In *Louboutin*, however, the CJEU already indicated that it was reluctant to adopt a broad concept of 'shape' when assessing aesthetic functionality. Instead of extending the shape exclusion to colour features of a three-dimensional design – the red sole of Louboutin shoes – it held that the application of a particular colour to a specific location of a product did not mean that the sign at issue consisted of a 'shape' within the meaning of Article 3(1)(e) TMD 2008.[1022] In *Textilis*, the CJEU denied the application of the shape exclusion to the so-called Manhattan pattern: a series of two-dimensional decorative motifs affixed to fabric or paper. The Court saw no room for holding that the two-dimensional decorative motifs were indissociable from the shape of goods to which they were affixed. As fabric or paper did not have the same form as the decorative motifs, the shape exclusion was inapplicable.[1023] The EU doctrine of aesthetic functionality, thus, remained limited to two- or three-dimensional representations of three-dimensional shapes.

With the amendment of EU trademark legislation in December 2015, however, the prospect of a broader application of the doctrine of aesthetic functionality has become a reality.[1024] As explained, current EU trademark legislation provides for the exclusion of 'the shape, *or another characteristic*, which gives substantial value to the goods' (emphasis added).[1025] Hence, the doctrine of aesthetic functionality is no longer confined to shapes. Any essential product characteristic falls within its scope. Moreover, the approach to aesthetic functionality taken by the CJEU offers several starting points for a broad application of the exclusion of aesthetic product characteristics.[1026] As discussed in section 7.2.2, the Court already went beyond designs with predominant artistic or ornamental value and included other criteria, such as

1021. IR no. 135376, 135377 and 296478. For the particulars of the registrations, see www.wipo.int/madrid/en/search/.
1022. CJEU, 12 June 2018, case C-163/16, Louboutin and Christian Louboutin, para. 24.
1023. CJEU, 14 March 2019, case C-21/18, Textilis, paras 42-44.
1024. Cf. Kur/Senftleben 2017, para. 4.48. For a discussion of the extension of shape exclusions in the preparatory work for the new trademark legislation, see Knaak/Kur/von Mühlendahl 2011, para. 2.31 and 2.37.
1025. Article 7(1)(e) EUTMR; Article 4(1)(e) TMD.
1026. CJEU, 18 September 2014, case C-205/13, Hauck/Stokke, paras 31-32.

the nature of the category of goods concerned, dissimilarity from other common product features, the achievement of a substantial price difference and a promotion strategy accentuating aesthetic characteristics.[1027] In the light of this flexible approach, not only industrial designs but also texts, drawings, melodies and other literary and artistic works may fall under the broadened functionality doctrine.

Nonetheless, it is doubtful whether the extension of the traditional value shape exclusion to all kinds of product characteristics in current EU trademark legislation will lead to a separation of copyright and trademark protection that is comparable with the separation achieved in the field of patent/trademark and industrial design/trademark overlaps. As explained in section 7.2.2, copyright protection does not automatically imply that a cultural sign must be deemed functional from an aesthetic perspective. In *Textilis*, the CJEU made it clear that aesthetic functionality could not readily be inferred from the fact that a sign was protected by copyright. Instead, the copyright status had 'no bearing' on whether the sign consisted exclusively of a shape giving substantial value to the goods.[1028] The Court seems unlikely to depart from this position with regard to other product characteristics that are covered by the broadened functionality doctrine after the trademark law reform. In the absence of an alignment of the aesthetic functionality analysis with copyrightability, however, the configuration of the functionality doctrine itself limits its exclusionary effect. Despite the elasticity of the *Hauck/Stokke* criteria, the fact remains that the focus is on products and their particular characteristics. It is the very purpose of the factors developed by the CJEU to identify those characteristics that are essential to the goods. Not surprisingly, the functionality doctrine can be regarded as an exponent of the fundamental distinction between the mark and the product in trademark law (sections 7.1.3 and 7.2.3). It is capable of justifying an exclusion from trademark protection only if a cultural sign constitutes the very substance of goods, in respect of which trademark protection is sought. Only a mark which goes beyond distinguishing the products of its owner to the cultural expression which defines the very substance of the product is 'transgressing the legitimate bounds of a trademark'.[1029]

The requirement of defining the product itself – its substance – has a different impact on technical and cultural subject matter. A technical solution applied to a product will typically constitute an essential product feature. Due to the inseparable link between a technical solution applied to a product and

1027. CJEU, *ibid.*, para. 35.

1028. CJEU, 14 March 2019, case C-21/18, Textilis, para. 45.

1029. Cf. the language used with regard to 'the functional structure of the wares' by the Supreme Court of Canada, 17 November 2005, Kirkbi AG/Ritvik Holdings Inc., [2005] 3 S.C.R. 302, 2005 SCC 65, para. 46, quoting Federal Court of Canada, Remington Rand Corp./Philips Electronics N.V. (1995), 64 C.P.R. (3d) 467 (F.C.A.), 478.

the product itself, the doctrine of utilitarian functionality is capable of covering technical solutions to a large extent. It has an impressive potential to prevent overlapping patent and trademark protection because the conceptual contours of the doctrine match the parameters of overlap situations very well. Even though the scope remains limited to technical features that define the product, the doctrine of utilitarian functionality can achieve a far-reaching separation of patent and trademark protection (section 7.1.5). Cultural signs, by contrast, need not constitute an essential product feature in the sense of the functionality doctrine. The outward appearance of goods often constitutes an essential product feature. It may define the product itself. This is why the doctrine of aesthetic functionality is an effective tool for the exclusion of trademark protection when it comes to works of applied art that make a product appealing to the eye (section 7.2.5).[1030] However, the doctrine of aesthetic functionality is inapplicable when a literary and artistic work does not form a central part of the product. Inevitably, the radius of an exclusion based on aesthetic functionality ends where a literary and artistic work is attached to a good as a mere label.[1031]

In contrast to technical solutions and a product's outward appearance, texts, drawings, paintings or music may be applied to goods as non-essential, external elements – without influencing product properties. A melody used as a sound mark to sell chocolate, for instance, is detached from the characteristics of the goods. The link forged in the minds of consumers merely stems from advertising. The characteristics of the marketed product do not depend on the musical work in any way.[1032] In the aforementioned *Marlene Dietrich* decision, the German Federal Court of Justice recognized explicitly that a portrait photograph of the actress did not have to be placed prominently on the articles at issue. It could also be used as a label attached to the goods.[1033] If merely used as a label, however, a cultural sign can hardly ever be found to add substantial value in the sense of the functionality doctrine.[1034] Otherwise, the value which the sign represents in the form of the label would be sufficient to assume aesthetic functionality and invoke the exclusion based

1030. Vanovermeire 2009, 195-203.

1031. Cf. Ohly 2019, 328; Curtin 2018, 1021; Stieper 2012, 1091.

1032. Examples of this kind are not of a theoretical nature. In Germany, for instance, the beer producer Licher has consistently used 'Solveig's Song' from Edvard Grieg's 'Peer Gynt Suite' in advertising since the 90s. See https://www.youtube.com/watch?v=dfGGjk1QEeM. Ohly 2008, 206, gives the additional example of Kenneth J. Alford's 'Colonel Bogey March' which German consumers are likely to associate with the herbal digestive 'Underberg' as a result of continuous use in trade. See https://www.underberg.com/en/.

1033. German Federal Court of Justice, 24 April 2008, case I ZB 21/06, Marlene-Dietrich-Bildnis, paras 19-22. See also the confirmation of this point in German Federal Court of Justice, 31 March 2010, case I ZB 62/09, Marlene-Dietrich-Bildnis II, paras 20-28; German Federal Court of Justice, 8 March 2012, case I ZB 13/11, 'Neuschwanstein', *GRUR* 2012, 1044, para. 20.

1034. Ohly 2019, 328; Curtin 2018, 1021; Stieper 2012, 1091.

on substantial value considerations. This, in turn, would lead to a circular line of reasoning and the exclusion of any sign with brand value from trademark protection. For example, the attachment of the Coca Cola logo to soft drinks would also lead to an exclusion of trademark rights because the brand goodwill of the logo adds substantial value to the product.[1035] To avoid this absurd result, use as a label necessarily falls outside the scope of the aesthetic functionality doctrine.

CJEU jurisprudence points in the direction of an even broader neutralization of the doctrine of aesthetic functionality. If substantial value cannot be deduced objectively from the sign's impact on product characteristics, but only follows from the subjective appreciation of the sign's appearance on the product, aesthetic functionality may be unavailable as a ground for refusal as well. In *Neuschwanstein*, the CJEU discussed whether the name of the famous Bavarian castle constituted a descriptive characteristic of souvenir articles displaying the indication 'Neuschwanstein'. In this respect, the Court drew a distinction between general, objective characteristics of everyday goods sold as souvenir items,[1036] and the subjective appreciation following from the fact that the attachment of the name 'Neuschwanstein' may call to mind fond memories of a castle visit:

> In so far as the name 'Neuschwanstein' designates the castle which bears that name, it must be considered that merely affixing that name on, inter alia, the goods concerned enables the relevant public to regard those everyday consumer goods also as souvenir items. The fact that they constitute souvenirs through the mere affixing of that name is not, in itself, an essential descriptive characteristic of those goods. Accordingly, it is not reasonable to conclude that, in the mind of the relevant public, the memory to which the name 'Neuschwanstein' relates is an indication of a quality or an essential characteristic of the goods and services covered by the contested trade mark.[1037]

Admittedly, the Court did not directly address aesthetic functionality. If these considerations are applied mutatis mutandis to aesthetic product features, however, the decision indicates that a fictional character affixed to a merchandising article, such as a scarve, hat, shirt or cup, need not automatically be deemed functional from an aesthetic perspective. As long as the sign's added value only stems from subjective appreciation in the minds of consumers, such as the ability to evoke positive feelings or pleasant memories of a cultural event, its impact on product characteristics may be

---

1035. Cf. England and Wales Court of Appeal, 1 November 2017, London Taxi Corporation, [2017] EWCA Civ 1729, *GRUR Int.* 2018, 150, para. 75 (Justice Floyd); U.S. Court of Appeals for the Ninth Circuit, 11 August 2006, Au-tomotive Gold/Volkswagen of America, 457 F.3d 1062, 1073-1074 (9th Cir. 2006).

1036. CJEU, 6 September 2018, case C-488/16P, Bundesverband Souvenir – Geschenke – Ehrenpreise ('Neuschwanstein'), paras 42-43.

1037. CJEU, *ibid.*, paras 45-46.

insufficient to invoke the doctrine of aesthetic functionality. Following the *Neuschwanstein* distinction between general, objective characteristics of scarves, hats, shirts and cups,[1038] and the subjective appreciation of scarves, hats, shirts and cups bearing souvenir insignia, a product feature that only leads to subjective appreciation is not a characteristic that could be relevant to the assessment of aesthetic functionality. As it is not inherent to the nature of the product, it must remain outside the equation. As long as substantial value is 'determined by the free will of the buyer and is focused solely on that buyer's intentions',[1039] the *Neuschwanstein* decision – if understood to have relevance beyond the question of descriptiveness – precludes a finding of aesthetic functionality.

With its focus on characteristics that define the objective properties of the product, the doctrine of aesthetic functionality thus fails to encompass scenarios in which cultural signs are merely attached to goods as labels or influence a product's value only subjectively by evoking positive feelings or fond memories. In this respect, the conceptual contours of the doctrine do not match the parameters of overlap situations. The possibility of adding cultural signs to products as separate elements or features – separate in the sense that they do not have a direct impact on objective product characteristics – constitutes a major difference with technical solutions and industrial designs which, because of their very nature, define product properties and form part of the product itself.

Hence, the diversity of literary and artistic works poses particular problems. In contrast to aesthetic product design, other cultural expressions – texts, drawings, paintings, melodies, etc. – need not define the product as such.[1040] Due to its focus on essential product characteristics, the functionality doctrine is incapable of separating trademark protection from copyright protection in this case. Therefore, a remarkable imbalance comes to the fore: while the doctrine of utilitarian functionality shields the technical innovation cycle from the corrosive effect of renewable trademark protection (section 7.1.5), and the doctrine of aesthetic functionality achieves a similar result with regard to cyclic innovation in the field of industrial design (section 7.2.5), the functionality doctrine fails to draw a comparable boundary line between copyright and trademark protection outside the realm of works of applied art.[1041] From this perspective, a new initiative is needed to safeguard cultural innovation when literary and artistic creativity does not concern aesthetic product design. It is important to supplement the functionality doctrine with other grounds for refusal that are capable of keeping cultural expressions outside the scope of trademark law if they do not define

1038. CJEU, *ibid.*, para. 42.
1039. CJEU, *ibid.*, para. 44.
1040. Cf. Ohly 2019, 328; Curtin 2018, 1021; Stieper 2012, 1091.
1041. Senftleben 2013a, 816-817 and 824-825.

objective product characteristics. Otherwise, a registration strategy presenting cultural expressions as mere labels remains a loophole for the acquisition of trademark rights and an impediment of cultural follow-on innovation.

7.3.2 Uncritical Attitude in Literature

Literature statements, however, often overlook the discrepancy between effective tools to safeguard cyclic innovation in the areas of technology and industrial design, and missing instruments to avoid inroads into cultural follow-on innovation outside the field of product aesthetics. Instead, a rather uncritical view on cumulative copyright and trademark protection often prevails. The possibility of combining copyright and trademark protection is frequently mentioned without much commentary on potential risks for cyclic cultural innovation processes and accepted on the ground that trademark rights do not offer protection for a cultural creation as such, but only for certain functions which the cultural creation fulfils as a distinctive sign in respect of goods and services to which it is attached.[1042] The acceptance of cumulative protection can thus be justified by pointing out that copyright and trademark rights serve different functions and, accordingly, provide for exclusive rights that differ in scope.[1043] Focusing on formal eligibility for protection under copyright and trademark law, Tobias Cohen Jehoram, Constant van Nispen and Tony Huydecoper arrive at an even broader, more general entitlement of intellectual property holders to cumulate copyright and trademark protection:

> In principle, there is no objection against cumulation or concurrence of trademark rights and copyrights and the benefits of the two protection regimes exist independently for the two rights. The proprietor of these rights satisfied all requirements stipulated by the different laws, so that there is no reason to limit the protection under one of the legal regimes for the sole reason that another legal protection exists.[1044]

Based on an economic analysis, Gideon Parchomovsky and Peter Siegelman even recommend the encouragement of rights cumulation strategies that allow intellectual property owners to employ trademark protection and brand loyalty as tools to leverage patents, trade secrets and copyrights. Parchomovsky and Siegelman argue that, by enabling companies to create brand loyalty, trademark protection puts pressure on patent and copyright

1042. Ginsburg 2018b, 261-264; Ginsburg 2016, 60-63; Stieper 2012, 1090-1091; Mende/Isaac 2012, 144; Peukert 2012, 111-113; Reeskamp 2010, 33; Bercovitz 2001, 612.

1043. Ohly 2019, 332; McGuire 2011, 774; Derclaye/Leistner 2011, 314-315 and 320; Bercovitz 2001, 612. For a statement pointing in the same direction, see Kur 2017, 1086. However, see also the focus on appropriate checks and balances in Kur 2001, 45 and 50.

1044. Cohen Jehoram/Van Nispen/Huydecoper 2010, 556.

owners to increase the number of sales during the limited term of protection. As patent and copyright owners must prepare for the post-protection period, they assume that right holders will lower the price of their products during the protection period (and reduce the social deadweight loss generated by the intellectual property monopoly) in an attempt to broaden their loyal customer base.[1045] After patent or copyright expiry, the broadened group of loyal customers offers compensation for lost monopoly profits in the form of willingness to pay more for the branded product even though the monopoly position no longer exists. The broadening of the customer base, thus, allows patent and copyright owners to secure supra-competitive profits once the limited protection period comes to an end. As a result, it finally pays off to refrain from maximum monopoly pricing during the term of patent and copyright protection.[1046] As Mark McKenna has shown, however, Parchomovsky and Siegelman's economic model rests on oversimplified and doubtful assumptions.[1047] They concede themselves that the expected welfare-enhancing effect of additional trademark protection (lower prices and less deadweight loss) is likely to be small in the case of copyright/trademark overlaps because, in comparison with patented products, brand loyalty has less impact.[1048] The possibility of repeat sales is missing in the case of literary and artistic works. Moreover, the long duration of copyright renders term extensions following from renewable trademark protection 'virtually meaningless'.[1049] Nonetheless, they advocate the combination of patent and copyright protection with trademark rights.[1050]

The widespread practice of cumulating copyright and trademark protection can also lead to intuitive support for the protection overlap as a given fact. Considering the traditional acceptance of trademark rights to cultural creations, Caspar van Woensel refrained from a critical analysis in his dissertation. He simply pointed out that it had become a well-established practice in recent decennia to allow the trademark registration of cultural heritage signs that belong to the public domain and are attractive because of their reputation and beauty.[1051] In later publications, Van Woensel departed from this initial position which readily accepted trademark rights to cultural signs in the light of existing rights acquisition strategies. Instead, he argued for the introduction of a 'white list' of names and pictures that should be kept free from 'trademark pretensions' because of cultural and societal relevance. He gave the example of the name and portrait of Anne Frank in this context.[1052]

1045. Parchomovsky/Siegelman 2002, 1474.
1046. Parchomovsky/Siegelman 2002, 1474-1475.
1047. McKenna 2009a, 884-890.
1048. Parchomovsky/Siegelman 2002, 1499.
1049. Parchomovsky/Siegelman 2002, 1499.
1050. Parchomovsky/Siegelman 2002, 1500 and 1503-1505.
1051. Van Woensel 2007, 294.
1052. Van Woensel 2013, 376.

Besides statements which readily accept the cumulation of rights as a corollary of formal eligibility for protection under copyright and trademark law or seek to justify the protection conglomerate in the light of functional differences between copyright and trademark rights or purported economic benefits, the debate also led to the development of more nuanced approaches. Annette Kur stated that the cumulation of different intellectual property rights was only unproblematic as long as the individual protection regimes involved were balanced in the sense that the prerequisites for obtaining protection were appropriately aligned with the contents and limits of exclusive rights.[1053] The decision on overlapping protection required a thorough scrutiny of the checks and balances offered by the protection regimes involved. If these checks and balances were sufficient to prevent excessive protection that obstructs competition, the cumulation of rights was acceptable.[1054] Otherwise, overlapping protection raised the problem of 'asymmetric convergence' and required appropriate countermeasures.[1055] This assessment standard paves the way for tailor-made solutions. Instead of bright-line rules, the acceptance of overlaps depends on a thorough scrutiny of the protection systems involved. As long as a sufficient arsenal of legal safeguards against excessive protection are available, it is possible to afford intellectual property owners the opportunity to combine copyright and trademark protection.[1056]

Turning to more critical statements, Feer Verkade expressed concerns about the corrosive effect of overlapping protection on the individual balance and structure of copyright and trademark law. Instead of affording rights owners the opportunity to always enjoy the 'best of both worlds', they should be bound to accept the 'one world' offered by each individual law.[1057] Hence, potentially indefinite trademark protection should not be available as a vehicle to undermine the limited term of copyright protection and the absence of formalities in copyright law should not allow the circumvention of the registration requirement in Benelux trademark law.[1058] Seeking to prevent one protection regime from blurring the conceptual contours of the other, Verkade proposes to determine on a case-by-case basis whether the

1053. Kur 2002, 596-599; Kur 2001, 45 and 50. See also Ohly 2019, 332, who emphasizes the need to limit the scope of protection in accordance with the specific functions of trademark law. In the U.S., McKenna 2009a, 884, expresses a similar view.

1054. Kur 2001, 44.

1055. Kur 2001, 42-44.

1056. For a similar approach, see Ohly 2008, 205-208, who is confident that the absolute grounds for refusal and the requirements for establishing infringement in trademark law provide an adequate arsenal of legal tools to arrive at appropriate solutions case by case. Dinwoodie 2002, 518-521, also argues for a policy-based development of tailor-made solutions and 'doctrinal mediation'. See also Derclaye/Leistner 2011, 306-308, 313-314 and 328, who follow in the footsteps of Kur's approach.

1057. Verkade 1998, 72.

1058. Verkade 1998, 72.

trademark or copyright aspect should take precedence.[1059] Following this approach, a rights owner is thus prevented from asserting copyright and trademark protection cumulatively even if the creation at issue is eligible for protection under both regimes. After the expiry of copyright, for instance, the copyright rule of a limited term of protection is a factor weighing against 'precedence' of trademark protection.[1060] In this way, Verkade seeks to ensure that the work enters the public domain – at least in the case of genuine cultural expressions, such as fictional characters. He gives the example of 'Dik Trom': the main character and title of a famous Dutch children's book series.[1061] Similarly, Antoon Quaedvlieg proposed a solution based on the degree to which a work 'falls under the core competence of copyright and the less it has to do with the commercial world of the trademark'.[1062] The application of this yardstick may lead to the denial of trademark protection for works of art (made in one single copy), literary characters, work titles and cartoon characters.[1063]

Laura Heymann proposed to curb benefits accruing from cumulative intellectual property protection 'by calibrating remedies to the nature of the harm incurred'.[1064] Following this approach, judges should attempt to divine the nature of the harm that the plaintiff seeks to remedy, for instance by considering the course of conduct or litigation history. They should also look at the relationship between the intellectual property right asserted and the remedy sought. Considering the underlying nature of the harm at issue, they should identify the remedy 'best designed to ameliorate that harm'[1065] and only provide this specific remedy. In this way, Heymann seeks to prevent an overbroad grant of protection based on the various labels which owners of overlapping rights may apply to their infringement claims.[1066]

The spectrum of comments on trademark/copyright protection overlaps, finally, comprises proposals seeking to eliminate cumulative copyright and trademark protection for literary and artistic works altogether. As Benjamin Raue has shown, a categorical ban on the cumulation of rights can follow from a strong preference for freedom of competition based on the public interest in the optimal use of intellectual resources and the encouragement of follow-on innovation after the expiry of the limited term of copyright protection.[1067] Alternatively, the quid pro quo in copyright law – the grant of

1059. Verkade 1998, 73.
1060. For a similar approach focusing on an international standard, see Köklü/Nérisson 2016, 573-577.
1061. Verkade 1998, 73.
1062. Quaedvlieg 2004, 54. Cf. Geier 2015, 150-151.
1063. Quaedvlieg 2004, 53-54.
1064. Heymann 2013, 273. Dinwoodie 2020, 34, also recommends the further exploration of this option.
1065. Heymann 2013, 275.
1066. Heymann 2013, 275.
1067. Raue 2010, 82-83, 121-123 and 199-201.

exclusive rights on condition that the work be released into the public domain when copyright expires – can underpin an outright exclusion of trademark rights. Irene Calboli proposed the development of a 'comprehensive doctrine, which could deny *ex ante* the possibility of applying trademark protection on copyrighted, or formerly copyrighted, works as a violation of the copyright bargain in the [U.S.] Constitution … '.[1068] She also recommended a ban on the registration of signs as trademarks that 'are or were copyrighted'.[1069] If the constant enrichment and cultivation of the public domain is qualified as an element of *ordre public*, continued trademark protection after copyright expiry can also be deemed impermissible because it withholds literary and artistic works from the public domain and causes a conflict with public order and morality for this reason.[1070] Interestingly, this latter approach offers an alternative to a strategy based on a broad application of the doctrine of aesthetic functionality. As the functionality doctrine, a conflict with *ordre public* leads to a categorical exclusion of literary and artistic works from trademark protection – categorical in the sense that the registration obstacle cannot be overcome by acquiring distinctiveness through use in trade.

7.3.3 *Court Reliance on Distinctiveness*

In practice, courts seem reluctant to adopt positions leading to the full separation of copyright and trademark protection when it comes to literary and artistic works in the more general sense of books, writings, paintings, drawings, sculptures, musical compositions and other 'classical' work categories.[1071] Even nuanced approaches, such as Verkade's proposal to determine the predominant protection aspect case by case, have difficulty to make their way into court decisions.[1072] Instead, judges seem to favour the rather uncritical attitude in respect of cumulative copyright and trademark protection which comes to the fore in many literature statements.

As pointed out above, this approach creates a sharp contrast between the treatment of technical solutions and industrial designs/works of applied art on the one hand and literary and artistic works (other than works of applied art) on the other. In *Philips/Remington*, the CJEU referred to the 'legitimate aim of not allowing individuals to use registration of a mark in order to acquire or perpetuate exclusive rights relating to technical solutions'.[1073] In

1068. Calboli 2014a, 32.
1069. Calboli 2014a, 33. Cf. Calboli 2014b, 77-80.
1070. Van Woensel 2007, 412-413; Klinkert/Schwab 1999, 1073; Nordemann 1997, 391; Osenberg 1996, 102-104.
1071. See the illustrative list in Article 2(1) BC.
1072. However, see Mende/Isaac 2012, 146-147, who report instances where courts in the UK sought to confine claims to one protection regime only.
1073. CJEU, 18 June 2002, case C-299/99, Philips/Remington, para. 82.

Hauck/Stokke, the Court, more broadly, invoked the objective 'to prevent the exclusive and permanent right which a trade mark confers from serving to extend indefinitely the life of other rights which the EU legislature has sought to make subject to limited periods'.[1074] Even though copyright is such a right with a limited period of protection, a comparably clear statement with regard to the relationship between copyright and trademark protection for literary and artistic works is sought in vain. In *Dior/Evora*, the CJEU saw 'no need to consider the question whether copyright and trade mark rights may be relied on simultaneously in respect of the same product...'.[1075] The case concerned the advertising of parallel imports. Dior asserted cumulative copyright and trademark protection of perfume packaging and bottles to shield its exclusive distribution network. It asserted both rights against Evora advertising showing the protected packaging and perfume flacons. Admittedly, the case did not concern one of the aforementioned 'classical' work categories but works of applied art. Nonetheless, it gave the CJEU the chance to comment on overlapping copyright and trademark protection.[1076] The Court, however, contented itself with a reference to earlier case law, according to which copyright was exhausted and could not be relied upon to prevent or restrict the importation of protected works which had been lawfully marketed in another EU Member State. In light of the exhaustion principle, the Court deemed it sufficient to clarify that:

> the protection conferred by copyright as regards the reproduction of protected works in a reseller's advertising may not, in any event, be broader than that which is conferred on a trade mark owner in the same circumstances.[1077]

The CJEU, thus, bypassed the problem of protection overlaps[1078] and solved the case at the level of limitations of protection.[1079] As the exhaustion

1074. CJEU, 18 September 2014, case C-205/13, Hauck/Stokke, paras 19-20.
1075. CJEU, 4 November 1997, case C-337/95, Dior/Evora, para. 58.
1076. The sixth prejudicial question posed by the Dutch Supreme Court in this case (see CJEU, *ibid.*, para. 14) clearly referred to both aspects of protection: 'Do the provisions of Article 30 and 36 of the EC Treaty preclude the proprietor of a (picture) trade mark or a holder of copyright relating to the bottles and packaging used for his goods from making it impossible, *by invoking the trade mark right or copyright*, for a reseller who is free further to commercialize those goods to advertise the goods in a manner customary to retail traders in the relevant sector? Is this the case also where the reseller, as a result of the manner in which he uses the trade mark in his advertising material, *damages the luxurious and prestigious image of the trade mark* or the publication or reproduction take place in circumstances such that *damage may be done to the person entitled to the copyright*?' (emphases added).
1077. CJEU, *ibid.*, para. 58.
1078. In his comment on the decision, Verkade 1998, 74 (footnote 28), points out that the Court 'passes over the *general problem of cumulation* but nevertheless rules on the significant escalation of the principle where branded articles which are also copyright-protected are depicted in advertising' (emphasis in the original text).
1079. As to this solution of the case and the resulting need for horizontal fair use limitations, see Kur 2001, 48-49.

of trademark rights entails the freedom of resellers to make use of the trademark to inform the public about the further commercialization of the goods involved,[1080] the same freedom must be available under copyright law. The overarching EU principle of free movement of goods and services in the internal market supports this finding.[1081]

While the *Dior/Evora* decision of the CJEU can hardly be regarded as the final word on the preconditions for invoking cumulative copyright and trademark protection,[1082] the GCEU provided guidelines in this regard in *Danjaq/OHIM (Mission Productions)*. The case concerned an opposition brought by Danjaq against Mission Production's attempt to register the sign 'Dr. No' – the title of the first James Bond film and the name of Bond's antagonist – as a trademark. Commenting on the possibility of copyright/trademark protection overlaps in this context, the Court pointed out that:

> [t]he same sign may be protected as an original creative work by copyright and as an indicator of commercial origin by trade mark law. It is therefore a matter of different exclusive rights based on distinct qualities, that is to say the original nature of a creation, on the one hand, and the ability of a sign to distinguish the commercial origin of the goods and services, on the other.[1083]

Hence, the GCEU adhered to the aforementioned literature approach accepting the protection overlap on the ground that trademark rights do not offer protection for a cultural creation as such, but only for certain functions which the cultural creation fulfils as a distinctive sign in respect of goods and services to which it is attached.[1084] In this vein, the Court stated that 'only signs which develop characteristic trade mark functions'[1085] were eligible for trademark protection and rejected trademark rights to 'Dr. No' because the sign would be perceived as a mere descriptive reference to the film and not as an identifier of commercial source.[1086] While an explicit confirmation of this position is still missing, CJEU decisions point in a similar direction. In *Gömböc*, the CJEU recalled that it was necessary to prevent indefinitely renewable trademark rights from evergreening other intellectual property

1080. CJEU, 4 November 1997, case C-337/95, Dior/Evora, para. 38.
1081. CJEU, *ibid.*, paras 57-58. As to the free movement of goods and services as an overarching harmonizing principle, see the comments by Dinwoodie 2020, 32; Derclaye/Leistner 2011, 291.
1082. As pointed out by Kur 2001, 48 (footnote 108), the CJEU was not bound by the prejudicial questions to positively confirm the cumulative availability of copyright and trademark protection.
1083. GCEU, 30 June 2009, case T-435/05, Danjaq/OHIM (Mission Productions), para. 26.
1084. Stieper 2012, 1090-1091; Peukert 2012, 111-113.
1085. GCEU, *ibid.*, para. 26.
1086. GCEU, *ibid.*, paras 25-28. For a discussion of similar developments in the U.S., see Heymann 2013, 251-256.

rights with a limited term of protection.[1087] This statement, however, did not inhibit the Court from concluding that 'such an objective does not mean that EU intellectual property law prevents the coexistence of several forms of legal protection'.[1088] Hence, there is room for holding that cumulative copyright and trademark protection is possible when a literary and artistic work has the distinctive character necessary to serve as a trademark. This, in turn, would confirm the GCEU approach regarding the overlap question as a matter of 'different exclusive rights based on distinct qualities'.[1089]

Similar considerations play a role in national court decisions. The Dutch Supreme Court, for instance, traditionally permits the cumulative assertion of copyright and trademark claims unless one of the two legal regimes explicitly excludes an amalgam of rights.[1090] The Court added that a holder of rights under trademark and copyright law could invoke both rights simultaneously only if he had a distinct interest in the protection following from each individual right.[1091] Considering the conceptual differences between copyright and trademark protection which the GCEU highlighted in *Danjaq*, this condition need not constitute a substantial hurdle. As explained, the cumulation of rights is often considered acceptable because copyright protects a cultural creation as such, whereas trademark law only protects trademark functions.[1092] The Dutch Supreme Court relied on similar considerations to justify the acceptance of combined copyright and trademark claims. While copyright was capable of covering the cultural creation as such, trademark rights only related to certain distinctive elements. For this reason, the Dutch Supreme Court was satisfied that both trademark and copyright protection were important to a plaintiff invoking both rights.[1093] The result is a rather low, if not negligible, threshold for accumulating copyright and trademark protection.[1094] If – despite the problematic extension of protected trademark functions to communication, investment and

1087. CJEU, 23 April 2020, case C-237/19, Gömböc, para. 50. As explained above, the Court had already made this general point in CJEU, 18 September 2014, case C-205/13, Hauck/Stokke, paras 19-20.
1088. CJEU, 23 April 2020, case C-237/19, Gömböc, para. 51.
1089. GCEU, 30 June 2009, case T-435/05, Danjaq/OHIM (Mission Productions), para. 26. Cf. CJEU, 23 April 2020, case C-237/19, Gömböc, para. 53, which emphasizes the need to satisfy the distinctiveness requirement.
1090. Dutch Supreme Court, 16 April 1999, case LJN ZC2889, Bigott-Batco/Doucal, para. 3.9. Cf. Cohen Jehoram/Van Nispen/Huydecoper 2010, 556.
1091. Dutch Supreme Court, 8 September 2006, case LJN AV3384, Benetton/G-Star, para. 3.11: 'Uitgangspunt is dat een rechthebbende op zowel een merkrecht als een auteursrecht beide naast elkaar kan handhaven, mits de rechthebbende belang heeft bij de aan elk van die rechten verbonden bescherming (Article 3:303 BW).' Cf. Quanjel-Schreurs 2007, 80-83.
1092. Stieper 2012, 1090-1091; Peukert 2012, 111-113.
1093. Dutch Supreme Court, 8 September 2006, case LJN AV3384, Benetton/G-Star, para. 3.11.
1094. Cf. Visser 2002, 17.

advertising (section 6.1) – the formal difference between the purpose and scope of protection is already sufficient to justify the cumulation of rights, there seems to be no substantial obstacle to the assertion of cumulative protection in case of subject matter capable of constituting both an original work and a trademark.

Hence, courts in the EU do not seem hesitant to hear claims based on cumulative copyright and trademark protection. As the CJEU saw no need to clarify the matter in *Dior/Evora*, the lower GCEU and the national courts in the EU are free to develop elastic tests of eligibility for combined claims, such as the legal interest requirement introduced by the Dutch Supreme Court. Judges seem sympathetic to combined copyright and trademark claims because intellectual property law does not unequivocally reject overlaps between the two protection regimes. In addition, judges seem confident that they can find nuanced solutions even if they permit the cumulative assertion of copyright and trademark protection. The *Marlene Dietrich* decision of the German Federal Court of Justice can serve as an example. As explained above (section 7.3.1), the German Federal Court of Justice – in contrast to the Federal Patent Court in its lower instance decision – saw no need to apply the functionality doctrine to exclude trademark rights to a portrait photograph of the actress Marlene Dietrich in respect of photographs, posters, postcards and goods of a similar nature. Overruling the Patent Court's decision, the Federal Court of Justice clarified first that the exclusion of shapes resulting from the nature of the goods was inapplicable.[1095] In a second step, the Court developed its alternative solution. Having rejected the nature shape exclusion, the Court relied on the general requirement of distinctiveness to refuse trademark protection in respect of goods and services concerning the work and life of the actress. This approach is consistent with earlier decisions where the Court had denied distinctiveness of cultural signs in respect of cultural productions because the public – well acquainted with the predominant cultural meaning of the sign – would perceive it as a mere description of product characteristics and not as an indication of commercial source (section 6.2.4).[1096] Following this approach in *Marlene Dietrich*, the Federal Court of Justice denied distinctiveness with regard to books, magazines, photographs, posters, CDs, DVDs, musical performances and film productions on the ground that the photograph was incapable of indicating a commercial source. In respect of these goods and services, the public would perceive it as a mere indication of product

1095. German Federal Court of Justice, 24 April 2008, case I ZB 21/06, Marlene-Dietrich-Bildnis, para. 11. Cf. Article 7(1)(e)(i) EUTMR; Article 4(1)(e)(i) TMD.

1096. For relevant case precedents, see German Federal Court of Justice, 5 December 2002, case I ZB 19/00, Winnetou, 6; German Federal Court of Justice, 23 January 2003, case I ZR 171/00, 'Winnetous Rückkehr', 10.

characteristics.[1097] In other words, the Court argued that the cultural meaning of the photograph – showing the head of Marlene Dietrich – rendered the sign descriptive and incapable of serving as a trademark in respect of goods and services closely related to the work and life of the actress.

This solution, however, has its price. In contrast to a categorical exclusion following from the application of the functionality doctrine, the hurdle of a lack of distinctiveness can be surmounted once the sign becomes distinctive as a result of use in trade.[1098] The Marlene Dietrich photograph may acquire the capacity to distinguish goods and services related to the life and work of the actress through continuous use.[1099] The German Federal Court of Justice added that the portrait photograph was inherently distinctive with regard to merchandising articles, such as scarves, hats, shirts and shoes. In this respect, it rejected the view expressed by the Federal Patent Court that consumers would perceive the portrait as a mere marketing tool and fail to understand that it served as an indication of commercial source.[1100] The Federal Court of Justice emphasized instead that the photograph did not necessarily need to be placed prominently on the articles. It could also be used as a label attached to the goods. Given this option of use as a badge of origin, distinctive character could not be denied.[1101]

Hence, the German Federal Court of Justice walked a fine line in *Marlene Dietrich*. To avoid overbroad access to trademark rights in the absence of a categorical ban (that could have followed from the functionality doctrine), the Court drew a distinction between goods and services closely related to the life and work of Marlene Dietrich on the one hand and merchandising articles which are only loosely connected with the actress on the other. While trademark rights can readily be awarded in respect of merchandising articles, the sign is descriptive and ineligible for trademark protection in respect of music, books, films and photos – unless distinctive character is obtained as a result of the sign's use in trade. The Court, thus, seems to hope that by declaring the portrait photograph descriptive in respect of goods and services that are closely related to the life and work of Marlene Dietrich, the corrosive effect of trademark rights on the cultural innovation

1097. German Federal Court of Justice, 24 April 2008, case I ZB 21/06, Marlene-Dietrich-Bildnis, paras 12-15.
1098. Article 4(4) TMD; Article 7(3) EUTMR.
1099. German Federal Court of Justice, *ibid.*, para. 17.
1100. German Federal Patent Court, 9 November 2005, case 29 W (pat) 147/03, Porträtfoto Marlene Dietrich, *GRUR* 2006, 333, para. 8.1 and 8.2.
1101. German Federal Court of Justice, 24 April 2008, case I ZB 21/06, Marlene-Dietrich-Bildnis, paras 19-22. See also the confirmation of this point in German Federal Court of Justice, 31 March 2010, case I ZB 62/09, Marlene-Dietrich-Bildnis II, paras 20-28; German Federal Court of Justice, 8 March 2012, case I ZB 13/11, 'Neuschwanstein', *GRUR* 2012, 1044, para. 20.

cycle can be minimized.[1102] This equation, however, contains several risk factors. Will use as a trademark for merchandising articles really be confined to use on labels attached to scarves, hats, shirts and shoes? Will the trademark owner refrain from sending cease-and-desist letters to competitors also selling merchandising articles with a portrait of the actress as long as these competitors attach different labels to the goods to indicate a different commercial origin? Will the trademark owner send cease-and-desist letters also to authors and producers in the core field of music, books, films and photos even though trademark rights have been denied in this regard? Will affected authors and producers simply ignore the threat of legal action after consulting the trademark register? Will the trademark owner assert even broader protection going beyond the list of registered goods and services by alleging that the trademark has become a mark with a reputation enjoying protection with regard to all kinds of goods and services (section 6.2.3)?[1103] How will affected authors and producers react to such a further substantiation of the trademark claim?

Moreover, the initial denial of trademark rights in respect of music, books, films and photos need not discourage further investment in the sign with regard to culturally important market sectors. A trademark proprietor who already acquired rights in respect of merchandising articles may see the option of strengthening the sign's distinctive character with regard to cultural productions through use in trade as an invitation to make further investments presenting the portrait photograph as a source identifier also in this core area of cultural activity.[1104] In case of successful marketing and advertising efforts, trademark rights may finally be granted with regard to music, books, films and photos on the basis of distinctive character acquired as a result of use.[1105] The trademark owner may thus obtain trademark rights which can have a direct impact on the core area of cultural creativity related to the life and work of Marlene Dietrich after the expiry of copyright protection. Opting for an approach based on the requirement of distinctive character, the

---

1102. For a similar approach based on genericity instead of descriptiveness, see Rosenblatt 2015, 625-626.

1103. Article 9(2)(c) EUTMR; Article 10(2)(c) TMD. For an example of such an expansive trademark exploitation strategy, see Curtin 2018, 991-995.

1104. As to this rights acquisition strategy, see Curtin 2018, 965 and 988-992; Senftleben 2017b, 707; Ramsey 2003, 1150. Cf. also Denicola 1982, 170; McKenna 2007, 1899; Lemley/McKenna 2010, 440; Senftleben 2013a, 812-813; Anemaet 2020, 188-189 and 211-212.

1105. This risk could only be avoided by applying – in respect of expressive goods – a ground for refusal that cannot be overcome through use in trade. See Rosenblatt 2015, 625-626, who develops such an approach on the basis of the exclusion of generic signs in U.S. trademark law which is more robust than in an EU context because it cannot be overcome by establishing secondary meaning. Cf. Beebe 2012, 82-83; Ramsey 2003, 1121-1122. The situation is different in the EU because genericity no longer places an obstacle to a trademark registration once distinctiveness is acquired through use in trade. See Article 4(4) TMD; Article 7(3) EUTMR.

German Federal Court of Justice, thus, solved the dilemma arising from a protection overlap only provisionally. The Court did not manage to find a solution that is sustainable in the sense that it also minimizes the risk of a corrosive effect on the cultural innovation cycle for the future.[1106] When copyright to the portrait photograph finally expires, the trademark portfolio may have grown to such an extent that it also covers music, books and films. In comparison with an outright exclusion of trademark rights following from the invocation of the functionality doctrine (section 7.3.1), the distinctiveness-based solution of the German Federal Court of Justice is weaker because it offers the possibility of developing an aggressive enforcement strategy on the basis of trademark rights granted with regard to merchandising articles (section 6.3). It also keeps open the backdoor of extending trademark protection to goods and services of cultural importance through continuous use in trade.

Irrespective of these deficiencies, it has become a widespread practice in the EU to avoid a categorical exclusion of cultural signs from trademark protection and refuse the grant of rights – based on a lack of distinctiveness – only in respect of goods and services that are directly connected with the cultural expression in question. A further example of this approach can be found in the Benelux. In the *Anne Frank* cases between the Swiss Anne Frank Foundation and the Benelux Office for Intellectual Property, the Court of Appeals of Brussels had to decide on the registration of the signs 'Het dagboek van Anne Frank' ('The Diary of Anne Frank') and 'Het achterhuis' ('The Secret Annex') in respect of books, films and guided tours. As the goods and services were directly linked with Anne Frank's writings and her account of the life of a Jewish family hiding in concealed office rooms from the Nazi terror in Amsterdam, the Benelux Office for Intellectual Property had refused the registration on the grounds that the signs were descriptive and devoid of distinctive character.[1107] Confirming this office decision, the Court of Appeals of Brussels pointed out that the titles of literary works constituted an integral part of the works themselves and created a link with their contents.[1108] Against this background, the public would not perceive the signs as identifiers of commercial source but as mere references to Anne Frank's books. For this reason, the titles 'The Diary of Anne Frank' and 'The Secret Annex' were incapable of serving as distinctive signs with regard to books, films and guided tours.[1109] Agreeing also with the Benelux Office that the signs were descriptive, the Court referred to the *Philips/Remington* decision of the CJEU and recalled the public interest in keeping certain signs

1106. See also Curtin 2018, 993-994, who demonstrates against the background of office practice in the U.S. that the application of descriptiveness as a ground for refusal is not consistent in cases involving cultural signs.

1107. Court of Appeals of Brussels, 3 October 2013, cases 2013/7132 and 2013/7133, Anne Frank Foundation/Benelux Office for Intellectual Property, para. 1.

1108. Court of Appeals of Brussels, *ibid.*, para. 5.

1109. Court of Appeals of Brussels, *ibid.*, para. 6 and 10.

free for competitors and the public at large.[1110] The Court warned of the risk of artificially perpetuating copyright exclusivity after the expiry of copyright protection, and granting the Anne Frank Foundation an indefinitely renewable exclusive right with regard to a work belonging to the universal cultural heritage – a monopoly position which not even Anne Frank's heirs enjoy.[1111] Finally, the Court rejected the argument advanced by the Swiss Anne Frank Foundation that the signs had acquired distinctive character in respect of books, films and guided tours as a result of the use made of them in trade.[1112]

The Court's line of reasoning clearly reflects the intention to prevent an artificial perpetuation of copyright exclusivity and keep the titles 'The Diary of Anne Frank' and 'The Secret Annex' free. Nonetheless, the decision cannot conceal that the requirement of distinctive character is a weak safeguard in comparison with the categorical exclusion of trademark rights that would follow from the application of the functionality doctrine. While emphasizing the inaptness of the signs to distinguish books, films and guided tours related to Anne Frank's hiding place and writings, the Court acknowledged that a trademark registration of book titles was possible in respect of goods and services that are independent of the works they identify.[1113] As the German Federal Court of Justice in the *Marlene Dietrich* decision,[1114] the Court of Appeals of Brussels thus conceded that a trademark registration in respect of merchandising articles was conceivable.[1115] Moreover, the decision contains a separate section discussing whether 'The Diary of Anne Frank' and 'The Secret Annex' had acquired distinctive character vis-à-vis books, films and guided tours through use in the course of trade.[1116] While the Court finally denied this question, the attention devoted to this point shows that signs with cultural significance may become distinctive as a result of continuous use in trade – even in respect of goods and services that are directly connected with their cultural meaning.

At EU level, the Swiss Anne Frank Foundation already had success in registering the original Dutch book titles – 'Het achterhuis' and 'Het dagboek van Anne Frank' – in respect of books, films, theatre productions and guided tours.[1117] In contrast to the Court of Appeals of Brussels,[1118] the EUIPO did

1110. Court of Appeals of Brussels, *ibid.*, para. 7, and CJEU, 18 June 2002, case C-299/99, Philips/Remington, para. 78.
1111. Court of Appeals of Brussels, *ibid.*, para. 7 and 10.
1112. Court of Appeals of Brussels, *ibid.*, para. 8.
1113. Court of Appeals of Brussels, *ibid.*, para. 5.
1114. German Federal Court of Justice, 24 April 2008, case I ZB 21/06, Marlene-Dietrich-Bildnis, paras 19-22.
1115. Court of Appeals of Brussels, 3 October 2013, cases 2013/7132 and 2013/7133, Anne Frank Foundation/Benelux Office for Intellectual Property, para. 5.
1116. Court of Appeals of Brussels, *ibid.*, para. 8.
1117. See EUTM no. 012451787 (HET ACHTERHUIS) and EUTM no. 012452281 (HET DAGBOEK VAN ANNE FRANK) which cover various goods and services in classes 9, 16 and 41.
1118. As the CJEU, 6 September 2018, case C-488/16P, Bundesverband Souvenir – Geschenke – Ehrenpreise ('Neuschwanstein'), para. 72, pointed out, the EU trademark

not deny distinctive character and granted trademark rights in areas of literary and artistic creativity where the book titles play a crucial role. This office decision demonstrates how fragile the basic requirement of distinctive character is. Even with respect to central literary and artistic activities, such as film and book productions, the requirement of distinctiveness is incapable of keeping cultural signs free. Even in these core areas of artistic creativity, it remains an unreliable safeguard: an obstacle which trademark applicants can overcome through continuous use in trade. From the perspective of cultural follow-on innovation, this result is highly problematic. It confirms that the cultural innovation cycle is exposed to the risk of trademark rights with a deterrent effect (section 6.3) to a larger extent than innovation cycles in the fields of technology and industrial design where the functionality doctrine precludes the acquisition of trademark rights much more reliably (sections 7.1.5 and 7.2.5).

In the *Anne Frank* cases, the Court of Appeals of Brussels explicitly sought to achieve the same objectives which the CJEU had formulated when invoking the functionality doctrine in *Philips/Remington*: sufficient room for free competition and an embargo on the perpetuation of intellectual property rights which expire after a limited term of protection.[1119] In contrast to the *Philips/Remington* case involving a patent/trademark overlap, however, the Court of Appeals of Brussels had no functionality argument at its disposal that could have ruled out trademark rights regardless of whether the sign in question was distinctive.[1120] The Court thus had to resort to the general requirement of distinctive character which can be satisfied once distinctive character is obtained in consequence of the use made of a sign in trade. Moreover, distinctive character can hardly be denied in respect of goods and services which are not directly related to the cultural expression concerned. The bulwark against copyright/trademark overlaps is thus less fortified than the bastion against patent/trademark overlaps.[1121]

---

system is 'an autonomous system with its own set of objectives and rules peculiar to it; it applies independently of any national system'. Hence, the EUIPO was not bound to follow the decision on distinctiveness taken by the Court of Appeals of Brussels on the basis of the harmonized Benelux trademark system.

1119. See Court of Appeals of Brussels, 3 October 2013, cases 2013/7132 and 2013/7133, Anne Frank Foundation/Benelux Office for Intellectual Property, para. 7, on the one hand, and CJEU, 18 June 2002, case C-299/99, Philips/Remington, para. 78 and 82, on the other.

1120. As to this feature of the functionality doctrine, see CJEU, *ibid.*, para. 57 and 75; CJEU, 16 September 2015, case C-215/14, Nestlé/Cadbury ('Kit Kat'), paras 38-39; CJEU, 11 May 2017, case C-421/15 P, Yoshida Metal Industry/EUIPO, para. 35. Cf. also U.S. Supreme Court, 20 March 2001, TrafFix Devices/Marketing Displays, 532 U.S. 23, 33 (2001).

1121. In this sense also Van Woensel 2013, 374-375, who points out that an outright exclusion, such as the exclusion because of a conflict with morality or public order, is missing in respect of the Anne Frank signs.

The aforementioned decision of the GCEU in *Danjaq/OHIM (Mission Productions)* can serve as a third example illustrating the unsatisfactory reliance of the courts on the requirement of distinctive character in cases involving cultural material. As indicated above, the GCEU was called upon to decide on an opposition brought against Mission Production's application for registration of the words 'Dr. No' at EU level. Mission Productions sought to register 'Dr. No' in respect of film apparatus, recording discs, vehicles, leather goods, clothing and beverages. Danjaq's opposition was based on the argument that it was the proprietor of the earlier well-known marks 'Dr. No' and 'Dr. NO' and that it had acquired non-registered trademark and film title rights relating to the use of these signs to designate films, DVDs, videos, comic books, music recordings, books, posters and action figures.[1122]

As explained above, the GCEU took as a starting point that, in principle, the cumulation of copyright and trademark rights was possible.[1123] Turning to an assessment of the signs 'Dr. No' and 'Dr. NO' against this background, the Court pointed out, however, that the accumulation of protection under different intellectual property regimes did not occur automatically. The protection as an indicator of commercial source was only available for signs developing characteristic trademark functions.[1124] As Danjaq had failed to provide evidence in this regard, the Court concluded that 'Dr. No' and 'Dr. NO' did not indicate the commercial origin of films, but rather their artistic origin. For the average consumer, the signs only distinguished the 'Dr. No' film from other films in the James Bond series. In contrast to the signs '007' and 'James Bond', consumers would not perceive the indications 'Dr. No' and 'Dr. NO' as source identifiers. In particular, the capability of serving as a distinctive sign could not be inferred from profits made with the film and its commercial success in the EU.[1125] Also with regard to comic books, music recordings, books, posters, model cars and watches, the signs 'Dr. No' and 'Dr. NO' did not constitute trademarks, but mere references to the film indicating that the goods concerned the film music, the film character, the car used in the film, the watch relating to the film in the fortieth anniversary edition of the James Bond series, etc. The signs 'Dr. No' and 'Dr. NO' had thus to be deemed descriptive, whereas other signs, namely 'James Bond', '007' and the James Bond gun symbol, could be regarded as source identifiers which Danjaq had used for the marketing of those goods.[1126]

Given the absence of use as a source identifier, the GCEU rejected Danjaq's argument that the signs 'Dr. No' and 'Dr. NO' constituted well-known trademarks or non-registered trademarks on which an opposition

1122. GCEU, 30 June 2009, case T-435/05, Danjaq/OHIM (Mission Productions), paras 2-3.
1123. GCEU, *ibid.*, para. 24 and 26.
1124. GCEU, *ibid.*, para. 26.
1125. GCEU, *ibid.*, para. 25.
1126. GCEU, *ibid.*, paras 27-28.

could be based.[1127] The Court also rejected Danjaq's additional claim invoking title protection under the national laws of several EU Member States as a ground for opposition. Relying on general statements about regular broadcasts and substantial profits in the EU, Danjaq had not provided sufficient evidence with regard to the extent of use in the markets concerned, in particular in Germany and Sweden. For a successful invocation of national title rights, details of relevant cinema and TV programming would have been necessary to give proof of the extent of use.[1128] Hence, Danjaq's opposition failed altogether.

With regard to the question of protection overlaps and the role of distinctiveness, the decision yields mixed results. On the one hand, it is remarkable that the Court rejected Danjaq's trademark claims not only with regard to goods and services concerning the core area of cultural expression involved, namely film and book productions,[1129] but also in respect of several merchandising articles, in particular model cars and watches.[1130] Given this outcome, one might be tempted to conclude that the GCEU managed to apply the basic requirement of distinctiveness more effectively than the German Federal Court of Justice in *Marlene Dietrich* and the Court of Appeals of Brussels in the *Anne Frank* cases. In the decisions of the latter courts, the acquisition of trademark rights in respect of merchandising articles had been deemed possible.[1131] On the other hand, the GCEU qualified other signs with a comparable cultural meaning, namely 'James Bond' and '007', as distinctive in respect of all the goods and services at issue: merchandising articles and core information products, such as films and books.[1132] In the case of 'James Bond' and '007', the requirement of distinctive character thus proved completely ineffective as a safeguard against protection overlaps. The reason for this opposite result lies in the Court's general assumption that signs having both qualities – constituting an artistic creation and fulfilling trademark functions – are automatically eligible for cumulative copyright and trademark protection.[1133] Considering this starting point, the denial of trademark rights to 'Dr. No' is merely the result of a schematic application of this basic principle and the trademark test of distinctiveness. It does not reflect a general intention to prevent copyright/trademark overlaps. By contrast, the confirmation that 'James Bond' and '007' are valid trademarks

1127. GCEU, *ibid.*, para. 31 and 36.
1128. GCEU, *ibid.*, paras 43-45.
1129. GCEU, *ibid.*, para. 25 and 27.
1130. GCEU, *ibid.*, para. 28.
1131. German Federal Court of Justice, 24 April 2008, case I ZB 21/06, Marlene-Dietrich-Bildnis, paras 19-22; Court of Appeals of Brussels, 3 October 2013, cases 2013/7132 and 2013/7133, Anne Frank Foundation/Benelux Office for Intellectual Property, para. 5.
1132. GCEU, 30 June 2009, case T-435/05, Danjaq/OHIM (Mission Productions), para. 25 and 27.
1133. GCEU, *ibid.*, para. 26.

shows the Court's willingness to accept double protection whenever a cultural sign is consistently used as an identifier of commercial use in trade.

On balance, the requirement of distinctive character, thus, again appears as a weak safeguard against cumulative copyright and trademark protection.[1134] It only offers a makeshift solution that leaves the final word on the acquisition of trademark rights to a company's marketers and their decision to use a cultural sign as an indication of commercial source in the sense of trademark law. The decision in *Danjaq/OHIM (Mission Productions)* is striking in this regard because the rejection of trademark rights to the sign 'Dr. No' concerned an opposition against Mission Productions' attempt to register the same sign as a trademark. Rejecting Danjaq's trademark rights to 'Dr. No', the Court eliminated not only the basis for the opposition but also one of the obstacles to the trademark registration sought by Mission Productions. Ironically, the decision thus refused trademark rights and enhanced the chances of obtaining them at the same time.[1135]

As to the registration of cultural signs in respect of merchandising articles, it is important to add a final nuance in the light of developments in CJEU jurisprudence. As explained, the *Marlene Dietrich* case before the German Federal Court of Justice and the *Anne Frank* cases before the Court of Appeals of Brussels led to the insight that cultural signs may be deemed inherently distinctive in respect of merchandising articles.[1136] An initial trademark registration covering merchandising articles, thus, offers a gateway for acquiring trademark rights and familiarizing the public with use of the sign as an identifier of commercial source. Through continuous use in trade, the trademark proprietor may later be able to extend the scope of protection to cultural goods and services. In *Neuschwanstein*, the CJEU further encouraged this strategy of cultural heritage branding. As discussed in section 7.3.1, the Court held that the souvenir function which buyers ascribe subjectively to a product bearing the name of the famous 'Neuschwanstein' castle in Bavaria was not an objective characteristic inherent to

---

1134. With regard to the concept of distinctiveness in U.S. trademark law, see Curtin 2018, 996-1003, who arrives at the same conclusion and recommends the development of more robust grounds for refusal.

1135. Nowadays, the sign DR. NO is registered as EUTM no. 004810438 for Danjaq LLC. The registration took place in February 2011 – after the decision of the GCEU – and covers, among other things, cleaning preparations, perfumery, cosmetics, hair styling products, jewellery, watches, stationery, artist's materials, party bags and decorations, live performances and exhibitions, and the provision of cinema and theatre facilities. A showing of distinctiveness acquired through use was not necessary for obtaining this registration.

1136. German Federal Court of Justice, 24 April 2008, case I ZB 21/06, Marlene-Dietrich-Bildnis, paras 19-22; Court of Appeals of Brussels, 3 October 2013, cases 2013/7132 and 2013/7133, Anne Frank Foundation/Benelux Office for Intellectual Property, para. 5.

the nature of that product.[1137] The memory evoked in the minds of consumers was not sufficient to qualify the name 'Neuschwanstein' as a descriptive indication of a product quality or an essential product characteristic.[1138]

If this line of reasoning is applied mutatis mutandis to souvenir and merchandising articles bearing famous artworks, it confirms and broadens the registrability of cultural signs in respect of goods in this category. In the German *Neuschwanstein* decision that preceded the CJEU judgment, the German Federal Court of Justice had been more careful. The German Federal Court of Justice held the view that even though 'Neuschwanstein' constituted the distinctive name of a famous building, the consuming public would fail to understand the indication 'Neuschwanstein' as an indication of commercial source on souvenir articles. It would merely perceive the name as a reference to the famous castle.[1139] As explained, the CJEU overruled this national decision. The registration of cultural signs for souvenir and merchandising articles is thus possible even if the goods are directly connected with a cultural event, such as the performance of a musical. The counterargument of the German Federal Court of Justice that may prevent the acquisition of trademark rights – namely the argument that the consuming public may perceive the sign on event souvenirs as a mere descriptive reference to the musical – has been rejected by the CJEU.[1140] The doors to trademark rights in respect of merchandising and souvenir articles are thus wide open.

7.3.4 *No Prevalence of the Cultural Innovation Cycle*

In sum, it can be concluded that in the case of cultural signs stemming from general work categories, such as books, paintings, drawings, musical compositions and films, the cumulation of copyright and trademark protection is often possible. As these signs need not define product characteristics (but may be attached to goods as mere labels), the functionality doctrine is incapable of categorically banning trademark rights.[1141] The remaining obstacle – the trademark requirement of distinctiveness – is a hurdle which trademark applicants can surmount in many cases. Cultural signs may be deemed inherently distinctive in respect of merchandising articles and goods

1137. CJEU, 6 September 2018, case C-488/16P, Bundesverband Souvenir – Geschenke – Ehrenpreise ('Neuschwanstein'), para. 44.
1138. CJEU, *ibid.*, paras 45-46.
1139. German Federal Court of Justice, 8 March 2012, case I ZB 13/11, 'Neuschwanstein', *GRUR* 2012, 1044, para. 15. Cf. Ruess 2018, 1150.
1140. CJEU, 6 September 2018, case C-488/16P, Bundesverband Souvenir – Geschenke – Ehrenpreise ('Neuschwanstein'), paras 45-46.
1141. Cf. Ohly 2019, 328; Curtin 2018, 1021; Stieper 2012, 1091.

and services that are not connected with cultural productions.[1142] While the test of distinctiveness may restrict trademark rights to cultural goods and services that are directly related to the primary information products embodying the cultural sign concerned, even this remaining safeguard against overly broad protection overlaps is lost in the case of cultural signs that are consistently used as indicators of commercial origin, such as fictional characters (Mickey Mouse scenario, section 5.2.3) and work titles (Winnetou scenario, section 5.2.4). In this case, the goods and services covered by the trademark registration may encompass the exploitation of the books, films and music containing the cultural expression at stake.[1143] As a result, trademark law substantially enhances the risk of an artificial perpetuation of intellectual property protection after the expiry of the limited term of copyright.

As cyclic innovation in technology and aesthetic product appearance, however, cultural follow-on innovation in the area of general work categories depends on a limited term of protection to ensure the constant enrichment of the public domain and the free availability of fresh sources and building blocks for new creations (Chapter 3). Nonetheless, the trade imperative of market transparency prevails. Once a trademark applicant manages to establish distinctive character, trademark rights to a cultural sign stemming from a book, music or film production may be granted. Unlike the technical imperative supporting follow-on innovation in the field of technology (section 7.1.5) and unlike the design imperative supporting cyclic innovation in the field of product appearance (section 7.2.5), *the cultural imperative supporting follow-on innovation in the area of general work categories, such as books, paintings, drawings, musical compositions and films, does not prevail over the trade imperative of market transparency.*[1144] There is no elastic ground for refusal that categorically excludes literary and artistic works in a more general sense – not only works of applied art – from trademark protection. When it comes to cultural signs stemming from books, paintings, drawings, musical compositions, films, etc., judges are reluctant to accept the reduction of market transparency that would follow from a denial of trademark protection for creations that have acquired distinctive character through use in trade. While a temporary destabilization of market transparency is tolerated in the area of inventions and industrial designs (sections 7.1.5 and 7.2.5), the opposite result comes to the fore in the field of literary and artistic works other than works of applied art. Once a cultural sign in this broader category has become distinctive as a result of the use made of it in

1142. German Federal Court of Justice, 24 April 2008, case I ZB 21/06, Marlene-Dietrich-Bildnis, paras 19-22; Court of Appeals of Brussels, 3 October 2013, cases 2013/7132 and 2013/7133, Anne Frank Foundation/Benelux Office for Intellectual Property, para. 5.

1143. GCEU, 30 June 2009, case T-435/05, Danjaq/OHIM (Mission Productions), para. 25 and 27.

1144. Assaf 2008, 3.

trade, the absence of an outright ban on trademark rights allows companies to employ trademark law as a tool to artificially perpetuate the exclusivity enjoyed under copyright law and pose obstacles to cyclic cultural innovation processes. Affected cultural signs do not enter the public domain. They do not become freely available for remix and reuse in the artistic domain.

From the perspective of the cultural imperative, this is disquieting. The possibility of creating copyright/trademark protection overlaps exposes the cultural innovation cycle to the chilling effect of indefinitely renewable trademark rights (section 6.3) to a significantly greater extent than comparable innovation processes in the areas of technology and product design. As a result, an imbalance is caused within the intellectual property system. From a functional perspective, the protection regimes for inventions, industrial designs, and literary and artistic works are comparable in the sense that they all seek to support cyclic innovation (section 4.1.1). Nonetheless, the current intellectual property system does not make a comparable effort to shield all these cyclic systems from the corrosive effect of static trademark protection.[1145] Trademark law aims at a stable distribution of intellectual resources instead of fostering reuse and remix (section 4.2.3). As long as copyright/trademark protection overlaps are accepted, the copyright system thus has to cope with an impediment of cultural follow-on innovation whereas this burden is alleviated in the domains of patents and industrial designs.

7.3.5 *No Justification for Overlap Acceptance*

Considering the foregoing analysis, the question arises whether there is a sound justification for the discrepancy between the approach taken with regard to inventions and industrial designs on the one hand and the carelessness that prevails with regard to literary and artistic works on the other. As explained above (section 7.3.2), the acceptance of overlapping copyright and trademark protection for literary and artistic works often rests on the assumption that trademark rights do not offer protection for a cultural creation as such, but only for certain functions which the cultural creation fulfils as a distinctive sign in respect of goods and services to which it is attached (following section 7.3.5.1). An alternative attempt to justify the acceptance of copyright/trademark overlaps concerns the substitutability of literary and artistic works in the context of cultural follow-on innovation. If it is assumed that artists seeking to base new creations on pre-existing literary and artistic works can easily find alternatives for unavailable source material, the need to prevent the acquisition of trademark rights may appear less pressing than in the case of technical solutions and industrial designs (section 7.3.5.2). Moreover, the mark/product dichotomy which offers an additional reason for the categorical exclusion of trademark rights to

1145. Senftleben 2013a, 825.

inventions and industrial designs (sections 7.1.3 and 7.2.3) is unavailable in the field of literary and artistic works. While technical solutions and aesthetic design features typically define product characteristics, a literary and artistic work may be attached to goods as a mere label (section 7.3.5.3). Attempts to justify cumulative copyright and trademark protection may also emphasize the risk of consumer confusion that may arise if trademark rights are refused with regard to literary and artistic works that have acquired distinctive character through use (section 7.3.5.4). Finally, it may even be asserted that indefinitely renewable trademark rights have beneficial effects because they offer ongoing economic incentives for continued investment in literary and artistic works (section 7.3.5.5).

As the following analysis will show, none of these arguments is convincing. In addition, the artificial perpetuation of copyright exclusivity on the basis of trademark rights can be deemed unfair. A copyright owner can use the long period of copyright protection strategically to impregnate a literary and artistic work with the source-identifying function necessary to obtain trademark rights. Against this background, the acquisition of trademark rights appears as a dysfunctional advantage that is derived unfairly from the monopoly position awarded in copyright law (section 7.3.5.6).

7.3.5.1 Rejection of Different Rights Arguments

As explained above (section 7.3.3), the GCEU pointed out in *Danjaq/OHIM (Mission Productions)* that the same sign may be protected as an original creative work by copyright and as an indicator of commercial origin by trademark law. According to the Court, this was a matter of:

> different exclusive rights based on distinct qualities, that is to say the original nature of a creation, on the one hand, and the ability of a sign to distinguish the commercial origin of the goods and services, on the other.[1146]

On its merits, the application of an amalgam of copyright/trademark protection in respect of literary and artistic works is thus based on the conviction that differences in the configuration of the protection regimes – a focus on originality in the case of copyright law and a focus on trademark functions in the case of trademark law – justify the award of double protection. The argument of 'different exclusive rights based on distinct qualities' also implies that there is no true protection overlap. With the expiry of copyright, the protection of the cultural creation as such comes to an end. Remaining trademark protection covers a different aspect, namely its trademark functions. However, this argument is only valid as long as differences in the configuration of copyright and trademark protection really lead to different outcomes in practice. Once trademark protection becomes so

1146. GCEU, 30 June 2009, case T-435/05, Danjaq/OHIM (Mission Productions), para. 26.

robust that, despite the focus on trademark functions, it de facto amounts to protection of a cultural creation as such, the argument of 'different exclusive rights based on distinct qualities' can be unmasked as mere rhetoric. With every function that is added to the portfolio of protected trademark functions, the argument loses its power of persuasion. As discussed in section 6.1.1, EU trademark law offers protection of a trademark's communication, investment, and advertising functions. This protection concerns the investment in the creation of a valuable brand image and the brand communication based on this image. With the recognition of these accessory functions, the CJEU broadened the control of the trademark owner over the communication surrounding a protected sign and brought the scope of trademark rights closer to the scope of copyright.[1147] The recognition of communication, investment and advertising functions shows that trademarks are more than a mere badge of origin. The focus is no longer on the prevention of use that is likely to cause confusion. By contrast, trademark rights are of particular interest because they offer the chance of capitalizing on the brand image and recouping the substantial investment made in its creation. In other words, trademark rights are exploitation rights.[1148] They have become comparable to the exploitation rights granted in copyright law. Considering the various starting points for trademark claims against use in the cultural domain (section 6.2), it can hardly be denied that the position of the trademark proprietor comes closer and closer to the position bestowed upon an owner of copyright.[1149]

With regard to the justification of copyright/trademark overlaps by reference to the theory of 'different exclusive rights based on distinct qualities',[1150] this shift from the aim to prevent use of confusingly similar signs to profit maximization after the creation of a valuable brand image is of particular interest. It contradicts the assumption that copyright offers protection of a cultural expression as such, whereas trademark protection only amounts to protection of certain functions which the cultural expression fulfils as a badge of origin. Once the communication, investment and advertising functions are taken into account, the trademark itself is recognized as a product in its own right.[1151] The protection of the economic and communication value of a trademark constitutes protection of the communication surrounding a trademark. In case of a sign with cultural significance, this means protection of the communication surrounding a cultural sign 'as

1147. CJEU, 18 June 2009, case C-487/07, L'Oréal/Bellure, para. 58.

1148. Kur/Senftleben 2017, para. 1.29-1.39; Ginsburg 2016, 75-77; Senftleben 2009a, 48-49; Bently 2008b, 15-41; Schroeder 2008, 161; Bone 2006, 549; Moskin 2004, 843-844; Dinwoodie 2002, 503-504; Fezer 2001, 827; Casparie-Kerdel 2001, 185-186; Lunney 1999, 437-439; Lemley 1999, 1694-1698; Brown 1999, 1619-1620; Dreyfuss 1990, 397-398; Lehmann 1986, 14-17.

1149. Cf. Liu 2013, 1433-1440.

1150. GCEU, 30 June 2009, case T-435/05, Danjaq/OHIM (Mission Productions), para. 26.

1151. Dreyfuss 1990, 397-398.

such'. Hence, the alleged conceptual difference between exclusive rights in copyright and trademark law vanishes. A mere reproduction of a cultural creation is sufficient to bring a copyright claim.[1152] Similarly, a mere reference to a cultural creation that is registered as a trademark may be sufficient to file an infringement lawsuit in a trademark system that protects not only a trademark's traditional origin function but also its various communication functions (section 6.2).

Trademark rights that survive copyright expiry can thus serve as a means to perpetuate former copyright exclusivity to a considerable extent. The situation differs markedly from the regular copyright scenario in which a literary and artistic work enters the public domain in its entirety. As use of a literary and artistic work enjoying cumulative copyright and trademark protection does not become entirely free after copyright expiry, the modalities for reusing an affected cultural expression are altered fundamentally. Concerns about a chilling effect of protection overlaps on creativity and cultural diversity are not unfounded. An artist seeking to avoid potential lawsuits will refrain from the use of trademarked source material or limit takings to an absolute minimum. The considerable risk of trademark infringement that remains after copyright expiry is likely to thwart new cultural productions or at least impoverish them in terms of creative inputs (section 6.3). The argument based on the different nature and scope of exclusive rights in trademark law is thus misleading. The theory of 'different exclusive rights based on distinct qualities'[1153] neglects the transformation of trademark rights into brand exploitation instruments. It justifies copyright/trademark protection overlaps on the basis of an outdated understanding of trademarks as mere indicators of commercial source. Hence, the argument must be rejected.

7.3.5.2 Substitutability Revisited

Substitutability arguments must fail as well. As discussed in section 4.1.3, the cultural innovation cycle can hardly be deemed less vulnerable than innovation processes in other domains of intellectual property. It would be wrong to assume that literary and artistic works can be substituted more easily than technical solutions or industrial designs. Trademark rights are likely to harm the cyclic evolution of new cultural productions to the same extent as they would harm the cyclic evolution of new technical knowledge. General perceptions of the domain of technology and the domain of culture must not lead to inaccurate assumptions in this context. While it may be right to characterize technical knowledge as the result of exact, objective science and cultural productions as the result of subjective, intuitive imagination,[1154]

1152. Article 9(1) BC.
1153. GCEU, 30 June 2009, case T-435/05, Danjaq/OHIM (Mission Productions), para. 26.
1154. Quaedvlieg 1987, 21-22.

this fundamental difference does not justify the assumption that there is also a fundamental difference with regard to the substitutability of intellectual creations stemming from these distinct domains. The opposite is true. Cultural signs are non-substitutable from the perspective of second authors who depend on the sign to create a derivative work and develop a new artistic position. If a given literary and artistic work is not available for this purpose, the cultural innovation step will simply not take place (section 4.1.3). The objectivity of the technological domain, on the one hand, and the subjectivity of the cultural domain, on the other, only means that the assessment of non-substitutability is objective in the case of technical solutions (because it depends on objective, technical necessities), whereas it is subjective in the case of literary and artistic works (because it depends on an artist's individual appreciation of pre-existing cultural material). Because of the subjectivity of the assessment in the cultural domain, however, there is reason to undertake even broader efforts to shield the cultural innovation cycle from the corrosive effect of trademark rights (section 4.1.4). Hence, the discrepancy between the rejection of patent/trademark overlaps (section 7.1.5) on the one hand and the acceptance of copyright/trademark overlaps on the other cannot be justified by declaring literary and artistic works substitutable. The assumption of substitutability is wrong when considering the vulnerability of remix processes in the cultural domain.

Moreover, it is to be considered that the functionality doctrine is applicable in patent cases even if a technical solution is substitutable (section 7.1.2). The CJEU addressed the substitutability issue in *Lego/Mega Brands*. The Court held that a trademark applicant could not avoid the verdict of utilitarian functionality by establishing that competitors could use alternative shapes to achieve the same technical result.[1155] The U.S. Supreme Court adopted the same approach in *TrafFix Devices/Marketing Displays*.[1156] Therefore, the substitutability question has been decided in a way that allows a broad exclusion of technical solutions from trademark protection. The functionality doctrine is applicable even if technical alternatives with equal functionality are available. As in the field of technology, however, there is substantial reason to keep cultural signs outside the realm of indefinitely renewable trademark protection even if alternatives are available: the more remix activities become possible after the expiry of copyright, the richer the cultural discourse about the meaning and interpretation of the literary and artistic creation at issue.[1157] Therefore, it would be inconsistent (and a confirmation of the bias against cyclic cultural innovation within the intellectual property system) to consider substitutability decisive when a trademark application concerns a literary and artistic work: first, cultural

1155. CJEU, 14 September 2010, case C-48/09 P, Lego/Mega Brands, paras 53-58.

1156. U.S. Supreme Court, 20 March 2001, TrafFix Devices/Marketing Displays, 532 U.S. 23, 33-34 (2001).

1157. Cf. Cohen 2006, 154.

source material is non-substitutable from the perspective of an artist embarking on the creation of a derivative work; second, alternatives do not preclude the application of the functionality doctrine in patent cases. Given the need to make at least the same effort to ensure freedom of remix in the cultural domain (section 4.1.4), the existence of alternatives cannot justify the grant of trademark protection in copyright cases.

7.3.5.3 Mark/Product Dichotomy Not Decisive

The preceding sections clarified that, as trademark rights to technical solutions and aesthetic product design, trademark rights to cultural signs must be rejected because the grant of broad rights in advanced trademark systems, such as EU trademark law, would artificially perpetuate exclusive rights after the expiry of copyright protection and restrict the availability of non-substitutable source material for cultural follow-on innovation. In addition, however, the outright exclusion of trademark rights to inventions and industrial designs rests on the mark/product dichtotomy in trademark law (sections 7.1.3 and 7.2.3). This third factor is not readily applicable to literary and artistic works. While technical solutions and aesthetic design features typically constitute product characteristics, a cultural sign stemming from a literary or artistic production, such as a work title, painting, drawing or a melody, may be attached to goods as a mere label or promotion jingle. Cultural signs need not define the substance of the product (section 7.3.1).[1158]

This difference, however, does not justify the acceptance of indefinitely renewable trademark rights after copyright expiry. Even if a label depicting an artwork does not constitute an essential product characteristic from the perspective of the functionality doctrine in trademark law, the grant of trademark rights may still impede cultural follow-on innovation. Once trademark rights are awarded because a label does not define product characteristics, the trademark proprietor may bring infringement claims with a deterrent effect on cultural remix activities (section 6.3). From the perspective of cyclic cultural innovation, the difference in the assessment matrix that follows from the mark/product distinction in trademark law is thus immaterial. Considering the substantial risk of an encroachment upon artistic freedom of remix, it is not sufficient to emphasize that technical solutions and industrial designs define product characteristics, whereas literary and artistic works may be used as labels. The acceptance of cumulative copyright and trademark protection does not become plausible simply because literary and artistic works need not constitute decisive product features from a trademark perspective.

1158. Cf. Ohly 2019, 328; Curtin 2018, 1021; Stieper 2012, 1091.

7.3.5.4 Risk of Consumer Confusion Not Decisive

However, a categorical exclusion of trademark rights to literary and artistic works would lead to the denial of trademark protection even if a cultural sign has acquired distinctive character. The refusal of trademark rights may enhance the risk of consumer confusion. There are literary and artistic works, such as Mickey Mouse, that do constitute not only important cultural creations but also signs with a strong distinctive character. The drawback of potential consumer confusion, however, is willingly accepted to safeguard follow-on innovation in the area of technology and aesthetic product design. Even if an invention or industrial design is distinctive, trademark rights will still be denied to prevent trademark law from becoming a means of artificially perpetuating the limited term of patent or industrial design protection (sections 7.1.4 and 7.2.4). In consequence, society as a whole must bear the costs of reduced market transparency and an enhanced risk of consumer confusion if technical solutions and industrial designs are perceived as indicators of commercial source.

This policy decision raises the question of whether the costs for society resulting from an enhanced risk of consumer confusion is so much higher in the case of literary and artistic works that the objective of consumer protection should prevail. For several reasons, the answer can hardly be in the affirmative. If consumers are expected to understand that Lego brick functionality[1159] and the design of the 'Tripp Trapp' children's chair[1160] cannot be exclusively reserved for Lego and Stokke on the basis of trademark law (sections 7.1.4 and 7.2.4), and competitors enjoy the freedom to copy the renowned brick and the renowned chair despite the distinctive character of the respective intellectual creations, the same commitment of society can be expected with regard to literary and artistic works such as Mickey Mouse and the Mona Lisa. Not only in the case of technical solutions and industrial designs but also in the case of literary and artistic works, overlapping trademark protection should be denied and resulting incidents of consumer confusion should be accepted as costs that are unavoidable and justified in the light of the objective to safeguard cultural follow-on innovation.[1161]

As pointed out in the context of the exclusion of technical solutions and industrial designs (sections 7.1.4 and 7.2.4), the destabilization of market transparency should not be exaggerated anyhow. The denial of trademark protection can be expected to have only a temporary disturbing effect. Consumers will learn quickly that a cultural sign no longer enjoys protection after copyright expiry and focus on other means of distinction, such as a separate word mark attached to information products embodying the cultural

1159. CJEU, 14 September 2010, case C-48/09 P, Lego/Mega Brands, para. 40.
1160. CJEU, 18 September 2014, case C-205/13, Hauck/Stokke, para. 7.
1161. Liu 2013, 1432-1436.

creation concerned.[1162] A parallel with the Lego brick illustrates this point. After the denial of trademark protection for Lego brick functionality,[1163] consumers are likely to check more carefully whether a toy brick bears the LEGO word mark. They will base their purchasing decision on this trademark instead of simply relying on the brick design. Similarly, consumers will check more carefully whether a comic book featuring Mickey Mouse bears the DISNEY word mark or logo once the famous mouse drawing enters the public domain. The inroads made into market transparency, thus, will remain limited. An artificial perpetuation of Lego's patent monopoly or Disney's copyright monopoly via trademark law, by contrast, would continue as long as the respective trademark proprietors renew their trademark rights. Hence, it appears disproportionate to allow the grant and maintenance of trademark rights: the risk of a temporary diminution of market transparency does not outweigh the risk of a potentially indefinite impairment of cultural follow-on innovation.

Finally, enterprises are likely to change their branding strategy. Once trademark protection for cultural creations is unequivocally excluded to safeguard cyclic cultural innovation, enterprises can be expected to invest less in marketing based on literary and artistic works. They will desist from presenting a literary and artistic work not only as an information product but also as an indicator of commercial source. Instead, they are likely to cultivate separate badges of origin that are immune to the expiry of copyright protection. Moreover, the creative industry will educate consumers to focus on these specific source identifiers instead of teaching them to recognize a literary or artistic work as an identifier of commercial source. In other words, the denial of trademark rights to cultural creations will reduce incentives for transforming literary and artistic works into trademarks.[1164] Accordingly, the risk of consumer confusion that may arise from a refusal of trademark rights also vanishes because consumers will never have been taught to perceive cultural creations as indicators of commercial origin.

7.3.5.5 No Incentive to Continue Investment

In the discussion about trademark rights in cultural signs, it has also been argued that the possibility of perpetuating copyright exclusivity after the expiry of the limited term of copyright protection provides an incentive for continued investment in the quality, reputation and appeal of literary and artistic creations, such as fictional characters. Discussing economic benefits of copyright evergreening, Richard Posner pointed out that:

1162. Liu 2013, 1436; Raue 2010, 200.
1163. CJEU, 14 September 2010, case C-48/09 P, Lego/Mega Brands, paras 53-58.
1164. Cf. Curtin 2018, 965 and 988-992; Anemaet 2020, 188-189 and 211-212; Senftleben 2017b, 707; Senftleben 2013a, 812-817; Lemley/McKenna 2010, 440; Assaf 2008, 82-83; McKenna 2007, 1899; Ramsey 2003, 1150; Denicola 1982, 170.

> the dichotomy between the cost of creating an expressive work, which is incurred up front, and the cost of disseminating it, incurred after it is created, can be overstated. Maintaining a market for 'Mickey Mouse' requires continued expenditures on advertising and promotion and continual minor modifications in the character itself designed to maintain the character's appeal in the face of changing tastes. These expenditures may not be forthcoming if the character is freely copiable.[1165]

Following this line of reasoning, it could be said that economic benefits accruing from continued investment in cultural creations justify the use of trademark law to artificially perpetuate copyright exclusivity after the expiry of copyright protection.[1166] It is doubtful, however, whether these purported benefits are substantial enough to outweigh the societal costs arising from an impairment of cultural follow-on innovation.

If a literary or artistic work is still commercially exploited at the end of the long term of copyright protection, the copyright holder is likely to have obtained a robust position on the relevant market. It would be surprising if the copyright holder did not manage to establish a particularly strong product development, marketing and distribution machinery during the life of the author and (at least) 50 years after her death.[1167] Against this background, the question arises whether Posner's assumption of an end of investment is realistic. Why should the copyright holder give up investing in a cultural creation for the sole reason that copyright protection is no longer available? With her strong position on the market and a refined exploitation machinery, the copyright holder is in an ideal position to compete with newcomers on the market who enjoy the freedom of using the cultural creation after copyright expiry but have no comparable market share and no comparable distribution network. Who could have less difficulty to face the rigours of free competition than the copyright holder who can rely on benefits and goodwill accumulated during the long period of copyright protection?

It can hardly be asserted against these considerations that the copyright holder need not have secured a strong market position and a successful exploitation machinery when copyright protection finally expires. This is not decisive. If the copyright holder is rather unsuccessful in her marketing efforts and has a weak position on the market at the moment of copyright expiry, the time seems ripe to put an end to the copyright monopoly anyway. If the copyright holder is incapable of successful marketing even though she enjoys all advantages of a copyright monopoly, it seems preferable to open

1165. Posner 2005, 61. Cf. Landes/Posner 2003a, 228; Landes/Posner 2003b, 471.
1166. The argument can be supplemented with the additional consideration that the interest of passive consumers in stability – instead of recoding – of the meaning of literary and artistic productions must be factored into the equation as well. Cf. Hughes 1999, 926-928, 940-947 and 952-958.
1167. Article 7(1) BC.

the market and enable free competition to see whether competitors can develop better products and services that are more in line with consumer tastes and make better use of the cultural creation concerned. It would be illogical to allow the copyright holder to artificially perpetuate copyright, continue an unsuccessful exploitation strategy and inhibit competitors from developing more innovative products and services in the cultural domain.

Given the long duration of copyright protection, it must also be pointed out that Posner's basic assumption of particularly strong efforts in respect of 'advertising and promotion and continual minor modifications'[1168] is questionable. As the copyright holder enjoys the advantages of a monopoly, she may be tempted to confine investment in the cultural creation to a minimum. The economic benefits of an artificially prolonged term of protection would thus remain minimal as well. Exposing the copyright holder to the challenges of free competition after copyright expiry, by contrast, will change the situation for the better. Being confronted with offers of newcomers who are now free to develop competing products, the copyright holder will be obliged to adopt a more ambitious approach and enhance her investment in advertising, promotion and product development. Hence, it is not self-evident that an artificial perpetuation of copyright on the basis of trademark law leads to more expenditure. By contrast, the economic benefits may be much higher when the former copyright holder is exposed to competition.[1169]

In sum, the economic benefits for society are most probably higher when no artificial perpetuation of copyright takes places after copyright expiry. If the copyright holder has a strong market position at the end of copyright protection, she is in an ideal position to face free competition. Being confronted with competing offers by newcomers, the copyright holder will strengthen her efforts to defend her market share and become more innovative. The economic benefits for society will thus be higher. If the copyright holder has a weak market position at the end of the term of copyright, she has proven to be incapable of developing successful products even though enjoying the advantages of a copyright monopoly. Hence, it seems right to allow free competition and give competitors the opportunity of showing that they can exploit the cultural creation in a more innovative way. Also in this alternative scenario, free competition will enhance economic benefits because copyright can no longer be used to block new products and services. Posner's economic argument of perpetual protection

1168. Posner 2005, 61.

1169. See the analysis of positive public domain effects by Heald/Erickson/Kretschmer 2015, 29-31; Buccafusco/Heald 2013, 37, who conclude that '[a]lthough there may be costs associated with movement into the public domain, allowing open access to public domain works will yield considerable benefits. These benefits should dramatically outweigh the costs'. Cf. Lunney 2018, 191-193; Netanel 2008, 200-205. As to the potential damage which trademark protection causes because it requires consistent use of the same signs, see Calboli 2018, 305-307. She refers to the risk of 'trapping' brand owners in their own brand insignia and blocking necessary innovation steps.

securing continued investment is thus unconvincing. It does not have sufficient weight to cast doubt upon the conclusion that trademark protection should be denied to avoid an artificial perpetuation of copyright protection and safeguard the process of cultural follow-on innovation.

7.3.5.6 Improper Acquisition of Trademark Rights

In addition, it must not be overlooked that the perpetuation of copyright exclusivity on the basis of indefinitely renewable trademark rights is unfair from several perspectives. First of all, the acquisition of trademark rights to cultural signs can be unmasked as an attempt to derive unfair benefits when copyright protection finally comes to an end. As explained in section 3.2, the acceptance of a limited term of protection is inherent in the functional design of the copyright system. Acceptance of this quid pro quo is a prerequisite for acquiring copyright protection in the first place. From the perspective of intergenerational equity among authors, a limited term of protection constitutes the price to be paid for the acquisition of copyright (section 3.2.2).[1170] A copyright owner who seeks to artificially prolong the term of copyright exclusivity on the basis of trademark law withholds her cultural creation from the public domain and deprives subsequent generations of authors of the freedom to remix this creation without exposure to a potential trademark infringement claim. From this perspective, it is unfair to use trademark law to escape the obligation to release literary and artistic works in their entirety into the public domain when copyright expires. A copyright owner pursuing this evergreening strategy seeks to deprive second author of the freedom of remix which she enjoyed herself when making the literary and artistic work at issue. Moreover, the copyright owner refuses to pay the price (in the form of public domain enrichment) for the enjoyment of copyright protection.

It may even be said that a copyright owner who strives for the acquisition of trademark rights during the term of copyright protection seeks to obtain trademark rights surreptitiously. Considering the long term of copyright protection,[1171] the copyright owner has plenty of time to use the copyright monopoly strategically to establish a strong link between the protected sign and her enterprise in the minds of consumers. As the audience witnesses the use of the sign in connection with the products of the copyright owner for this long period, it does not come as a surprise if, at the end of the term of copyright protection, the consuming public is well aware that products bearing the cultural sign stem from the copyright owner.[1172] In fact, the opposite – no sufficient connection with the copyright owner's enterprise

1170. U.S. Supreme Court, 2 June 2003, Dastar/Twentieth Century Fox, 539 U.S. 23, 33-34 (2003); German Federal Constitutional Court, 31 May 2016, case 1 BvR 1585/13, 'Sampling', *GRUR* 2016, 690, para. 87; EFTA Court, 6 April 2017, case E-5/16, Municipality of Oslo ('Vigeland'), para. 66. Cf. Vanovermeire 2009, 180.

1171. Article 7(1) BC.

1172. As to the debate of this point in the U.S., see McKenna 2009a, 885-890.

– would be surprising. For the copyright owner, it is thus easy to imprint the sign on the memory of consumers not only as a cultural icon but also as an identifier of commercial source. Because of the exclusive position granted in copyright law, the copyright holder need not fear any major interruption during the process of establishing secondary meaning. In contrast to other cases where distinctiveness is acquired through use in trade, the copyright owner can easily control the communication surrounding the sign. She need not compete with other market participants who also wish to use the sign in trade.

Hence, the acquisition of trademark rights appears as a dysfunctional, unfair advantage that is derived from the monopoly position awarded in copyright law. To prevent this protection excess, the law should render evergreening strategies based on trademark rights unattractive from the outset. Therefore, it makes sense to categorically deny trademark rights to literary and artistic works in order to frustrate efforts to transform cultural expressions into indications of commercial origin during the term of copyright protection. If the law no longer offers the prospect of trademark rights, copyright owners will abandon the strategy of turning a cultural sign into an identifier of commercial source. In consequence, the sign becomes entirely free at the end of the term of copyright protection and fully available for cultural follow-on innovation.

7.4 CONCLUSION

Trademark law fails to offer adequate safeguards against an artificial perpetuation of copyright exclusivity after the expiry of copyright protection. While the functionality doctrine prevents overlaps between patent and trademark protection[1173] and leads to a far-reaching separation of industrial design and trademark protection,[1174] a comparably strong mechanism for policing the border between copyright and trademark protection has not evolved yet.[1175] In the case of cultural signs stemming from books, paintings, drawings, musical compositions and films, the cumulation of copyright and trademark protection is often possible. As these signs need not define product characteristics (but may be attached to goods as mere labels), the functionality doctrine is incapable of banning trademark rights. The remaining obstacle – the requirement of distinctive character – is a hurdle which trademark applicants can surmount in many cases. Cultural signs may be deemed inherently distinctive in respect of merchandising articles and goods

1173. CJEU, 18 June 2002, case C-299/99, Philips/Remington, para. 82; CJEU, 14 September 2010, case C-48/09 P, Lego/Mega Brands, para. 45 and 53-58; U.S. Supreme Court, 20 March 2001, TrafFix Devices/Marketing Displays, 532 U.S. 23, 33-34 (2001).

1174. CJEU, 18 September 2014, case C-205/13, Hauck/Stokke, paras 19-20.

1175. Senftleben 2013a, 814-817.

and services that are not connected with cultural productions.[1176] While the test of distinctiveness may restrict trademark rights to cultural goods and services that are directly related to the primary information products embodying the cultural sign concerned, even this remaining safeguard against overly broad protection overlaps is lost in the case of cultural signs that are consistently used as indicators of commercial origin, such as fictional characters and work titles. In this case, the goods and services covered by a trademark registration may encompass the exploitation of the books, films and music containing the cultural expression at stake. The corrosive effect on cultural follow-on innovation is self-evident.

In *Gömböc*, the CJEU stated that the rules of EU law concerning the registration of industrial designs and trademarks were independent, 'without any hierarchy existing as between those rules'.[1177] From a formalistic point of view, the Court could easily make the same statement with regard to the originality test in EU copyright law[1178] and the enquiry into distinctiveness in trademark law. The foregoing analysis of legal instruments used to separate intellectual property regimes, however, unmasks this insistence on equal status as mere rhetoric. Through the backdoor of the functionality doctrine, the CJEU introduces a hierarchy between cyclic innovation in the area of industrial designs and follow-on creativity in the area of literary and artistic works (other than works of applied art). The Court applies aesthetic functionality flexibly to prevent trademark rights to design solutions that give substantial value to the goods. Until now, however, the Court has failed to develop comparable legal tools to separate trademark and copyright protection in the case of general work categories, such as books, paintings, drawings, musical compositions, films, etc. Cyclic innovation in the field of these general categories of literary and artistic works, thus, has a lower rank in CJEU jurisprudence and is exposed to the corrosive effect of trademark protection (section 6.3) to a larger extent.

In practice, the acceptance of overlapping copyright and trademark protection for literary and artistic works often rests on the assumption that trademark rights do not offer protection for a cultural creation as such, but only for certain functions which the cultural creation fulfils as a distinctive sign in respect of goods and services to which it is attached. However, this argument is only valid as long as differences in the configuration of copyright and trademark protection really lead to different outcomes in practice. Trademark rights in advanced protection systems, such as the EU trademark system, have become so robust that, despite the focus on trademark

---

1176. German Federal Court of Justice, 24 April 2008, case I ZB 21/06, Marlene-Dietrich-Bildnis, paras 19-22; Court of Appeals of Brussels, 3 October 2013, cases 2013/7132 and 2013/7133, Anne Frank Foundation/Benelux Office for Intellectual Property, para. 5.

1177. CJEU, 23 April 2020, case C-237/19, Gömböc, para. 54.

1178. Cf. CJEU, 16 July 2009, case C-5/08, Infopaq/DDF, para. 45; CJEU, 1 December 2011, case C-145/10, Painer, para. 89.

functions, they de facto offer exploitation rights that are comparable with the copyright monopoly. As the non-hierarchy argument, the different rights argument, thus, is a charade. Considering the metamorphosis of trademark rights into exploitation rights that allow far-reaching control over the communication surrounding protected signs, it is not convincing to justify copyright/trademark overlaps by emphasizing differences in the configuration of the respective protection regimes.

Moreover, cultural follow-on innovation is as vulnerable as innovation processes in the area of technology and product design. It would be wrong to assume that, in contrast to technical solutions, literary and artistic works are substitutable when it comes to processes of cultural follow-on innovation. In the context of inventions and industrial designs, an outright exclusion of trademark protection does not even depend on the existence of alternatives for competitors. Against this background, the grant of trademark rights to cultural signs cannot be justified by assuming that artists seeking to base new creations on pre-existing cultural expressions can easily find alternatives for unavailable source material. Admittedly, however, the mark/product dichotomy which offers an additional reason for the categorical exclusion of inventions and industrial designs from trademark protection is unavailable in the field of literary and artistic works. While technical solutions and industrial designs typically define product characteristics, a literary and artistic work may be attached to goods as a mere label. This formal difference, however, does not change the equation with regard to an impediment of cultural follow-on innovation and the risk of encroaching upon freedom of expression. Once trademark rights are awarded, the trademark proprietor can threaten artists with trademark infringement claims, interfere with open, dialogic communication in the artistic domain and curtail freedom of expression. Considering these fundamental concerns, arguments based on the formal distinction between the mark and the product in trademark law do not offer a sufficient basis for declaring copyright/trademark overlaps acceptable and granting trademark rights to cultural signs.

It is to be conceded, however, that an exclusion of literary and artistic works from trademark protection may temporarily give rise to incidents of consumer confusion when, in fact, a cultural creation has acquired distinctive character as a result of use in trade. However, this risk of potential consumer confusion is willingly accepted to safeguard cyclic innovation processes in the domains of inventions and industrial designs. There is no compelling reason to decide otherwise when it comes to literary and artistic works. The destabilization of market transparency can be expected to have only a temporary disturbing effect. Consumers will learn quickly that a cultural sign no longer enjoys protection after copyright expiry and focus on other means of distinction, such as a separate word mark attached to information products embodying the cultural creation concerned.

Moreover, it is not convincing to assert that indefinitely renewable trademark rights offer ongoing economic incentives for continued investment in literary and artistic works. As the copyright owner enjoys a long period of copyright protection, she can be expected to be well prepared for the rigours of free competition after copyright expiry. Instead of killing investment, the end of copyright will strengthen efforts to preserve the traditional market dominance by investing in new and improved versions of the cultural expression at stake. Seeking trademark protection, the copyright owner only tries to escape the obligation to leave 'enough and as good'[1179] in common for second authors. The enrichment of the public domain, however, is the price to be paid for the enjoyment of copyright protection.[1180] As the long monopoly period following from copyright protection allows the copyright owner to use market exclusivity strategically to impregnate a literary and artistic work with the source-identifying function necessary to obtain trademark rights, the acquisition of trademark rights appears as a dysfunctional, unfair advantage that is derived from the monopoly position awarded in copyright law.

In sum, the analysis shows that the different treatment of cyclic cultural innovation in intellectual property law cannot be justified. As the innovation imperatives in patent and design law, the cultural imperative in copyright law should prevail over the commercial imperative of market transparency and the grant of indefinitely renewable trademark rights. To remedy the current imbalance in the intellectual property system, it is necessary to introduce a mechanism for the categorical exclusion of literary and artistic works from trademark protection that is as effective as the functionality doctrine in the area of inventions and industrial designs. In this way, it becomes possible to ensure an equal treatment of cyclic innovation systems and shield processes of cultural follow-on innovation adequately from the corrosive effect of static trademark protection.

1179. Locke 1698, book II chapter 5 § 27. Cf. Gordon 1993, 1562-1564.

1180. U.S. Supreme Court, 2 June 2003, Dastar/Twentieth Century Fox, 539 U.S. 23, 33-34 (2003).

Chapter 8

Reappropriation of Cultural Expressions in the Public Domain

As elaborated in Chapter 3, the cultural imperative in copyright law rests on two fundamental principles: the guarantee of intergenerational equity and the recognition of the public domain. In the preceding Chapter 7, the corrosive effect of cumulative copyright and trademark protection on the guarantee of intergenerational equity has been analysed in more detail. The examination dealt with the risk of artificially perpetuating protection after copyright expiry. After this analysis, the time is ripe to change the perspective and address the second element of the cultural imperative: the recognition of the public domain. While the guarantee of intergenerational equity seeks to prevent copyright owners from using coexisting trademark protection to escape their obligation to observe the temporal limits of copyright, the principle of public domain recognition seeks to ensure that trademark law is not used as a vehicle to reappropriate cultural material that has already become part of the public domain. The focus is on the preservation of the public domain of cultural expressions – in the sense of measures to prevent trademark rights from drying out freely available sources of inspiration and diminishing the potential of cultural public domain material to serve as a basis for dialogue and discussion in the literary and artistic field. While the guarantee of intergenerational equity ensures that cultural material enters *the public domain, the principle of public domain recognition ensures that public domain material* stays *in the public domain.*

After the introduction of different concepts of 'public domain' that can serve as reference points for the analysis (following section 8.1), problems arising from trademark rights to literary and artistic works in the public domain will be analysed in more detail (section 8.2). In addition, the objective to provide a robust and diverse public domain can be understood to encompass the positive obligation to cultivate and further enrich the public domain. As trademarks may become iconic symbols with cultural significance (section 5.2.5), it must be asked whether trademark protection should be phased out when this happens (section 8.3). The analysis will lead to proposals for the further improvement of the intellectual property system in the light of the need to preserve a robust and diverse public domain of cultural expressions (section 8.4).

8.1 CONCEPTUAL CONTOURS OF THE PUBLIC DOMAIN

The discussion on public domain recognition addresses the situation where new intellectual property rights are established with regard to cultural expressions in the public domain. The cultural material concerned may be unprotected because it stems from a time where copyright protection did not exist. It may also be unprotected because copyright protection lapsed and the work entered the public domain. In both cases, the acquisition of new intellectual property rights, such as trademark rights, inevitably curtails a formerly unlimited freedom of use. It may imperil cultural follow-on innovation. Considering these contours of the problem, it is advisable to clarify first the concept of 'public domain'. In particular, the question arises whether cultural material only belongs to the public domain as long as it is completely unencumbered by trademark rights, or whether it is sufficient to preserve areas of free use for cultural purposes in trademark law. In scholarly literature, reflections on the meaning and function of the public domain have led to different definitions of the area of freedom called the 'public domain'.[1181] Providing an overview, Pamela Samuelson identified various conceptions,[1182] including strict definitions focusing on the legal status of being free from any intellectual property right (following section 8.1.1), and more elastic definitions asking whether and to what extent material can be used freely, notwithstanding the existence of intellectual property rights

1181. For a discussion of different conceptions of the public domain, see the contributions to Guibault/Hugenholtz 2006; Boyle 2003; Lange 1981, 147; Litman 1990, 965. As to the debate on the freedom of speech underpinning, see Zimmerman 2004, 297; Benkler 2003, 173. For an overview of different aspects of the public domain in relation to trademark law, see Peukert 2012, 18-37.

1182. Samuelson 2006a, 101 (145-154). As to problems in tracing the conceptual contours of the public domain, see Samuelson 2006b, 13-17.

(section 8.1.2). Obviously, these conceptual differences influence the assessment of risks caused by the grant of trademark rights to cultural material in the public domain. Following a legal status approach, trademark protection would have to be excluded altogether in order to preserve the public domain. Under a freedom of use approach, trademark rights may be acceptable as long as they do not encroach upon the freedom of using cultural material for the purpose of creating new cultural productions. To arrive at appropriate guidelines for the preservation of the public domain of cultural expressions, the different public domain conceptions thus offer important reference points.

8.1.1 *Legal Status Perspective*

Under typical legal status definitions, in order for any literary or artistic work to be considered 'public domain', it must be completely unencumbered by intellectual property rights.[1183] From this perspective, it is highly problematic when trademark rights are acquired in respect of cultural material that has never enjoyed, or no longer enjoys, copyright protection. As explained in section 4.2.2, traces of public domain recognition in trademark law, such as the requirement of genuine use, are incapable of dispelling concerns about an encroachment upon the public domain.[1184] In the absence of a limited term of protection, trademark law appears as the 'ultimate threat' to a public domain understood as a reservoir of cultural expressions free from any intellectual property rights. Awarding intellectual property rights that may potentially last in eternity, trademark law has the potential of putting an end to this public domain status once and for all.

The crucial question, then, is whether trademark law offers sufficient safeguards against the acquisition of trademark rights to signs with cultural significance. Do the criteria for determining eligibility for trademark protection offer sufficient room for excluding cultural signs from protection that should remain in the public domain? This question brings basic protection requirements into focus, such as distinctiveness and a sufficiently clear and precise representation on the trademark register. It also refers to the possibility of excluding signs categorically from registration and protection as trademarks on the basis of absolute grounds for refusal, such as public order and morality,[1185] and the functionality doctrine (sections 7.1 and 7.2). If the legal status perspective is adopted as a basis for the assessment of trademark rights in cultural heritage signs, the central question, thus, is how the acquisition of trademark rights can be avoided from the outset.

1183. Cf. Dusollier 2015, 136-137.
1184. Cf. the problem analysis by Wilf 1999, 1-5.
1185. Cf. EFTA Court, 6 April 2017, case E-5/16, Municipality of Oslo ('Vigeland'), paras 92-96.

8.1.2 Freedom of Use Perspective

In contrast to the legal status perspective, public domain concepts focusing on freedom of use offer a more expansive view. They do not require that cultural public domain material remain entirely free from trademark rights. Besides material that is unencumbered by intellectual property rights, the freedom of use approach allows the consideration of areas of freedom that result from measures to keep certain forms of use outside the scope of the exclusive rights of the trademark proprietor. This approach allows the inclusion of freedoms that remain intact even if trademark rights are acquired with regard to cultural public domain material.[1186] The perspective shifts from the threshold requirements for obtaining trademark protection to inherent limits of exclusive rights and defences that explicitly permit certain forms of unauthorized use and are capable of preserving freedom of use once trademark protection has been granted.

More specifically, the freedom of use perspective requires an analysis of the interplay between inherent limits of exclusive rights as implicit safeguards of user freedoms and the development of defences as explicit safeguards of user freedoms. The more flexible the requirements for a showing of prima facie infringement, the weaker are the inherent limits of exclusive trademark rights, and the stronger is the need for the adoption of defences that explicitly exempt certain forms of use from the control of the trademark owner.[1187] As Graeme Dinwoodie posited against the background of U.S. trademark law:

> However, as the scope of trademark protection expands and the metes and bounds of protection become more uncertain, we cannot rely exclusively on creative interpretation of the prima facie cause of action to establish limits. Trademark law must more consciously develop defenses that reflect the competing values at stake in trademark disputes.[1188]

The analysis of trademark law from the broader perspective of freedom of use, thus, sheds light on a broader range of public domain preservation tools. With regard to both instruments – inherent limits of exclusive rights and explicit defences – it is to be noted, however, that despite the preservation of freedom of use, the cultural signs concerned enjoy protection as trademarks. Inherent limits and defences may safeguard the freedom to

1186. For a public domain conception of this type, see Benkler 1999, 361-162, where he argues for including 'use generally considered permissible, absent peculiar facts to the contrary'. Cf. also the similar approach developed by Merges 2004, 183-184.

1187. Senftleben 2013a, 819.

1188. Dinwoodie 2009, 152. Cf. Knaak/Kur/von Mühlendahl 2011, para. 2.260-2.262, proposing the inclusion of an explicit limitation regarding honest referential use that, besides comparative advertising, would cover use for purposes of indicating replacement or service, use for purposes of commentary and criticism, and parody.

use protected signs for specific forms of cultural follow-on innovation. However, these preservation tools are incapable of preserving signs as part of an information commons that can freely be shaped and defined in the course of an open communication process in the artistic domain (cf. section 3.3.2.4).[1189] Due to the grant of exclusive rights, the trademark owner is likely to influence or even dictate the communication process surrounding the protected sign. As a holder of exclusive rights, the trademark proprietor obtains a position in the communication arena that is stronger than the position of other speakers.[1190]

8.2 ASSESSMENT OF PRESERVATION TOOLS

The overview of public domain conceptions in the preceding section has shed light on several legal instruments that can be employed in trademark law to avoid an impoverishment of the public domain of cultural expressions. The freedom of use perspective offers room for a nuanced analysis. Following this approach, trademark rights remain unproblematic as long as legal instruments seeking to ensure freedom of use in the artistic domain are robust enough to qualify this freedom as a public domain space in its own right. The freedom of use perspective may lead to the conclusion that the grant of trademark protection does not diminish the reservoir of cultural signs available for artistic remix and reuse. To escape the verdict of an encroachment upon the public domain, trademark law can delimit exclusive rights in such a way that artists need not fear a reduction of their freedom of use (section 8.2.1). Alternatively, trademark law may provide for robust and reliable defences that effectively preserve freedom of use in the artistic domain (section 8.2.2).

However, the more detailed discussion of these legal instruments in the following sections will yield the insight that, at least in advanced trademark systems, such as the EU system, both legal mechanisms do not offer artists sufficient legal certainty to dispel concerns about inroads into the public domain. Under current EU trademark law, the only remaining option, therefore, is recourse to the stricter legal status perspective. For a cultural sign to form part of the public domain from this perspective, it must be unencumbered by intellectual property rights. The acquisition of trademark rights, automatically, puts an end to the public domain status. This remaining

1189. Cf. Dusollier 2018, 180, emphasizing the need for a public sphere paradigm that safeguards 'a public space for discussion and creation'.

1190. Cf. Curtin 2018, 1008-1009. With regard to the question of the extent to which the trademark owner is capable of shaping the perception of the consuming public, see Gangjee 2013, 51-56; Tan 2013, 225; Ramsey 2010b, 851; Gerhardt 2010, 101; Heymann 2009, 651; Litman 1999, 15-16; Wilf 1999, 4-5; Kozinski 1993, 960; Dreyfuss 1990, 415 and 424.

option, thus, requires the use of absolute grounds for refusal to categorically exclude public domain material from trademark protection (section 8.2.3).

8.2.1 INHERENT LIMITS OF TRADEMARK RIGHTS

With regard to inherent limits of the exclusive rights of trademark owners, the risk assessment undertaken in Chapter 6 has already shown that every expansion of trademark rights, inevitably, reduces the ambit of operation and the degree of legal certainty which inherent limits can offer. The enhancement of protection is the reverse of the cultivation of inherent limits of exclusive rights. The more extensive and flexible the exclusive rights of trademark owners, the less efficient will be the safe harbour function which inherent limits can fulfil with regard to use in the cultural domain. In a trademark system that only provides for traditional protection against confusion, the inherent limits of exclusive rights – the confinement to use in the course of trade, use as a mark and use likely to cause confusion – might function as effective safeguards that exempt references to the protected mark in non-confusing artistic contexts from the control of the trademark owner.

In a system offering protection of more extravagant proportions, however, the inherent limits of exclusive rights may be reduced to such an extent that they lose that safeguarding function. Current EU trademark law is an example of an advanced trademark system in which inherent limits of exclusive rights, such as the gatekeeper requirements of 'use in the course of trade' and 'use in relation to goods or services' have lost much of their potential to contain access to trademark protection from the outset. As explained in section 6.2.1, the requirements of use in the course of trade and use in relation to goods or services are applied flexibly by the CJEU. They do not prevent trademark owners from attacking use in the artistic domain that is not – and is not intended to be – perceived as indications of commercial source. On the contrary, mere references to a protected sign can be sufficient to allow the trademark owner to bring an infringement action.

As to the breadth of exclusive rights, it would be wrong to assume that trademark rights relating to public domain material are unproblematic because the scope of protection against confusion and dilution will always remain limited. As discussed in section 6.2.2, the CJEU held in *Picasso/ Picaro* that the renown of a cultural creation may constitute such a rich conceptual reference that it greatly reduces the recognition of the sign as a trademark.[1191] One may thus be tempted to concede that in the case of cultural public domain material, the distinctive character will normally be so weak that specific prerequisites for the invocation of protection against confusion and dilution – in particular the need to demonstrate a likelihood of confusion and the need to demonstrate a reputation justifying protection

1191. CJEU, 12 January 2006, case C-361/04P, 'Picasso/Picaro', para. 27.

against dilution – constitute obstacles that will inhibit a trademark owner from bringing a lawsuit against use in the artistic domain.[1192]

This line of reasoning, however, neglects the elasticity of distinctive character as a parameter for determining the scope of protection. The fact that a sign is not inherently distinctive because of strong cultural connotations does not preclude the possibility of transforming the sign into a strong source identifier through continuous use in trade. In the *Vigeland* case before the EFTA Court, for instance, the Municipality of Oslo attempted to register numerous works of the famous Norwegian sculptor Gustav Vigeland after copyright had expired.[1193] The statements submitted by Oslo showed clearly that the city was confident to have made sufficient investments in the framework of continuous city branding to turn Vigeland's works into strong source identifiers.[1194] In France, Vermeer's famous 'Milkmaid' has been used for the marketing of dairy products to such an extent that it seems safe to assume that the cultural icon has become a well-known mark.[1195] The example shows that even a famous artwork can be impregnated with marketing messages and transformed into a powerful trademark.[1196]

Turning to experiences in the U.S., Justin Hughes mentions Cinderella and Snow White as examples of cultural icons that have been redefined in the social consciousness by Disney's versions of the fairy tales.[1197] Jane Ginsburg refers to the decision of the District Court for the Southern District of New York in *Frederick Warne/Book Sales* where the Court dealt with Warne's assertion that, as the publisher of Beatrix Potter's well-known series of Peter Rabbit children's books, it had acquired trademark rights in a 'sitting rabbit' illustration appearing within 'The Tale of Peter Rabbit'. Based on the registration of three book covers under the Lanham Act, Warne also claimed book trademark rights in the 'running rabbit', the 'dancing squirrel', and the 'reading mouse'.[1198] Considering its marketing efforts, Warne was confident

1192. Dusollier 2015, 161; Ohly 2008, 207-208. For case law making this point, see U.S. District Court for the Southern District of New York, 19 December 1979, Frederick Warne/Book Sales, 481 F. Supp. 1191, 1198 (S.D.N.Y. 1979).

1193. EFTA Court, 6 April 2017, case E-5/16, Municipality of Oslo ('Vigeland'), paras 28-30.

1194. Report for the Hearing, Judge-Rapporteur Baudenbacher, 5 October 2016, case E-5/16, Municipality of Oslo ('Vigeland'), para. 32.

1195. EUTM no. 002998334 concerning, among other goods, dietetic foodstuffs and baby food; vegetables, fruits, meat, poultry, game, fish and seafood; milk products; coffee, tea, cocoa and chocolate products; bakery products, snack foods, breakfast cereals and ice cream. Cf. Bianchi 2017.

1196. As to the trademark registration of La Latière, see also IR no. 414494 and the French semi-figurative mark 99796048. The breadth of trademark protection against dilution – going beyond the core market of dairy products – is not mentioned in the analysis conducted by Dusollier 2015, 162.

1197. Hughes 1999, 963, also gives examples where, according to his analysis, no such redefinition has occurred.

1198. U.S. District Court for the Southern District of New York, 19 December 1979, Frederick Warne/Book Sales, 481 F. Supp. 1191, 1193 (S.D.N.Y. 1979).

that the characters portrayed in eight illustrations, particularly the 'running rabbit', had attained 'a place in the public esteem comparable to Mickey Mouse, Peter Pan, and Raggedy Ann and Andy'.[1199] After copyright expiry, Warne sought to prevent Book Sales from using the 'running rabbit' and the 'sitting rabbit' as corner ornaments and cover illustrations for the publication of a large and colourful Peter Rabbit volume. While the Court doubted that 'a British cony, however endearing, could gain as important a place in American hearts as Mickey Mouse',[1200] it conceded that the Peter Rabbit illustrations may have acquired secondary meaning and come to represent the goodwill and reputation of Warne as the publisher of the children's books.[1201] The Court thus recognized that cultural signs may be transformed into powerful trademarks – despite strong cultural connotations – and left the door open for evidence of secondary meaning and consumer confusion.[1202] As Warne had not furnished this evidence, however, the issue of secondary meaning remained unresolved.[1203] Rebecca Curtin recalls a further decision of the same Court which goes a step further. In *Wyatt Earp Enterprises/ Sackman*, the District Court for the Southern District of New York allowed the producer of an ABC television show (starring Hugh O'Brian as the famous historical lawman) to assert trademark rights to the name 'Wyatt Earp' against the sale of Wyatt Earp costumes. In this context, the Court held that 'the name of Wyatt Earp has been battered into the public consciousness by the television program to an extent far beyond any fame or notoriety ever previously attached to the marshal's name'.[1204] The Court was thus willing to assume the existence of trademark rights and recognition, and accept the transformation of the cultural sign into a brand.[1205]

A trademark taken from the public domain may thus be developed into a strong badge of origin over time. This is inherent in the configuration of the distinctiveness test in trademark law. In addition, the acquisition of a considerable degree of distinctive character and a broad scope of trademark protection does not seem particularly difficult when a trademark consists of a sign that has cultural significance but is not widely known among the consuming public.[1206] A symbol, shape or melody stemming from a culturally important but relatively unknown work in the public domain is unlikely to have a strong cultural connotation capable of weakening the

1199. U.S. District Court for the Southern District of New York, *ibid.*, 1194.

1200. U.S. District Court for the Southern District of New York, *ibid.*, 1194.

1201. U.S. District Court for the Southern District of New York, *ibid.*, 1195.

1202. Cf. Calboli 2014a, 28.

1203. U.S. District Court for the Southern District of New York, *ibid.*, 1196. Cf. Ginsburg 2016, 58-59; Dusollier 2015, 160-161.

1204. U.S. District Court for the Southern District of New York, 10 January 1958, Wyatt Earp Enterprises/Sackman, 157 F. Supp. 621, 624 (S.D.N.Y. 1958). Cf. Curtin 2018, 1009.

1205. For further examples of U.S. case law pointing in the same direction, see Calboli 2014a, 28-29.

1206. Ohly 2008, 207.

recognition of the sign as an indication of commercial source. Who thinks of Nike, the Greek goddess of victory, when seeing the trademark NIKE?[1207] Who is aware of culturally important signs of indigenous communities?

Given the relatively low threshold for acquiring anti-dilution protection in the EU (see the discussion of niche reputation in section 6.2.3), there is also a substantial risk of unknown signs with cultural significance becoming eligible for enhanced protection against dilution. Once reputation is established, EU trademark law offers anti-dilution protection covering blurring, tarnishment and unfair freeriding across all goods and services and, thus, in competitive and non-competitive situations (section 6.2.3). For a claim based on the taking of unfair advantage, it suffices to argue that 'a third party attempts, through the use of a sign similar to a mark with a reputation, to ride on the coat-tails of that mark'.[1208] Moreover, the CJEU refuses to consider the need to keep protected signs free in the context of the infringement analysis. In *Adidas/Marca*, the Court explained that it was clear that:

> the requirement of availability is extraneous both to the assessment of the degree of similarity between the mark with a reputation and the sign used by the third party and to the link which may be made by the relevant public between that mark and the sign. It cannot therefore constitute a relevant factor for determining whether the use of the sign takes unfair advantage of, or is detrimental to, the distinctive character or the repute of the trade mark.[1209]

Surveying these developments in EU trademark law, it becomes apparent that the inherent limits of exclusive rights – use in the course of trade, use as a trademark, use likely to cause confusion and use likely to cause dilution – have become elastic and unreliable safeguards of freedom of use for cultural purposes. In many cases of use in a cultural context, it will be difficult to rule out the threat of a trademark infringement claim on the basis of inherent limits of trademark rights. In comparison with a situation where cultural material stays in the public domain altogether, the inroads made into the freedom of use for cultural follow-on innovation are considerable. As pointed out in section 6.3, considerable legal uncertainty about a potential trademark claim is surrounding the use of cultural material once it has been appropriated by virtue of trademark law. The risk of potential trademark infringement is hanging above use made of affected cultural expressions like the sword of Damocles.

1207. With regard to these and further examples, see Assaf 2009, 2-3; Assaf 2008, 11-12; Senftleben 2010a, 101-102.

1208. CJEU, 18 June 2009, case C-487/07, L'Oréal/Bellure, para. 49. For a critical comment on intuitive protection against freeriding as a species of unjust enrichment law, see Lemley/McKenna 2010, 137.

1209. CJEU, 10 April 2008, case C-102/07, Adidas/Marca, para. 43.

Given this legal uncertainty, the inherent limits of exclusive trademark rights in EU trademark law are no longer robust enough to preserve an area of freedom that could legitimately be regarded as part of the public domain. Public domain definitions accounting for freedom of use draw a boundary line between clear cases of freedom of use that can be seen as part of the public domain, and unclear cases that cannot be included. As Yochai Benkler explains, the freedom of use perspective of the public domain only includes 'the range of uses of information that any person is privileged to make absent individualized facts that make a particular use by a particular person unprivileged'.[1210] More concretely, the freedom of use approach only regards as public domain space:

> the range of privileged uses that are 'easy cases.' Uses of information commonly perceived as permissible absent special circumstances, such as a brief quotation in a critical review or lending a book to a friend, fall within the functional definition of the public domain. Uses that are privileged because of highly particularized facts would not fall within that definition.[1211]

Considering the explained elasticity and unreliability of inherent limits of exclusive rights in EU trademark law, user freedoms that may result from the requirements of use in the course of trade, use in relation to goods or services, use likely to cause confusion and use likely to cause dilution are no longer 'easy cases' in the sense of this public domain definition. Rather than constituting uses 'commonly perceived as permissible absent special circumstances', the remix and reuse of cultural expressions qualify as 'uses that are privileged because of highly particularized facts'[1212] once the cultural signs concerned have attracted trademark protection in the EU. Inherent limits of exclusive rights in the EU trademark system are thus not reliable enough to declare the acquisition of trademark rights to public domain material unproblematic. If cultural heritage signs are registered, the broad scope of trademark protection creates considerable legal uncertainty. This legal uncertainty is likely to erode the freedom of use which artists could enjoy in the absence of trademark rights. The inherent limits of trademark protection in advanced trademark systems, such as the EU trademark system, are thus insufficient to prevent an encroachment upon the public domain.

8.2.2 *Defences*

The critical assessment of inherent limits of trademark rights raises the question of whether the explicit recognition of defences in EU trademark law could be sufficient to eliminate the risk of a corrosive effect on artistic

1210. Benkler 1999, 362.
1211. Benkler 1999, 362-363.
1212. Benkler 1999, 362-363.

productions. Considering the previous discussion of this point (section 6.2.4), however, there can be little doubt that, despite the recognition of defences for 'due cause',[1213] 'descriptive use'[1214] and 'referential use',[1215] and despite the emphasis on freedom of expression as a guiding principle for the application of trademark rights,[1216] an unambiguous, sufficiently mature *exceptio artis* is sought in vain. Instead, the risk of infringement that arises from the grant of trademark rights to cultural signs is likely to have a deterrent effect on cultural follow-on innovation even if an artist can rely on a defence (section 6.3). As a finding of due cause or permissible descriptive or referential use depends on highly particularized facts, such as honesty in industrial and commercial matters[1217] and a loyal position in respect of the trademark owner (section 6.2.4),[1218] there is sufficient room to destabilize the reassurance of non-infringement that could follow from the adoption of exceptions to exclusive rights. In other words: the defences in EU trademark law are far from constituting 'easy cases' in the sense of public domain concepts including freedom of use.[1219] As the inherent limits of trademark rights discussed in the preceding section, they are incapable of dispelling concerns about infringement threats once trademark rights are obtained with regard to cultural signs in the public domain. Given the volatility of freedom of use guarantees in EU trademark law, it would be wrong to follow the freedom of use approach and qualify trademark rights to cultural public domain material as unproblematic simply because artists can invoke defences.

8.2.3 *Arguments for a Categorical Exclusion of Public Domain Material*

From the perspective of cultural follow-on innovation, an outright exclusion of cultural signs from trademark protection is clearly preferable over the fragile freedom of use guarantees that have been discussed in the preceding sections. Inherent limits of exclusive rights and defences are not reliable and robust enough in EU trademark law to regard them as public domain spaces in the sense of the freedom of use approach (section 8.1.2). Accordingly, the only remaining tool for effective public domain preservation is the denial of trademark rights in cultural public domain material from the outset. If a cultural sign remains unencumbered by trademark rights, it is entirely free

1213. Article 10(2)(c) EUTMR; Article 9(2)(c) TMD.
1214. Article 14(1)(b) EUTMR; Article 14(1)(b) TMD.
1215. Article 14(1)(c) EUTMR; Article 14(1)(c) TMD.
1216. Recital 21 EUTMR and Recital 27 TMD. Cf. Schovsbo 2018, 568 and 578-579.
1217. Article 14(2) EUTMR; Article 14(2) TMD.
1218. CJEU, 8 July 2010, C-558/08, Portakabin, para. 69; CJEU, 17 March 2005, case C-228/03, Gillette/LA-Laboratories, para. 49.
1219. Benkler 1999, 362-363.

for artistic remix and can support a truly open communication process that is not subject to the trademark owner's control (section 3.3.2.4).[1220] With the registration of cultural signs as trademarks, by contrast, the freedom of remix is sacrificed in favour of a scenario in which trademark rights can serve as a basis for an infringement action. Given the extravagant proportions of trademark rights in the EU (section 6.2), the climate change in respect of cultural remix will be considerable.[1221]

The elimination of infringement threats, however, is not the only argument in favour of a categorical exclusion of cultural heritage signs from trademark protection. In addition, this approach prevents unfair freeriding on positive, valuable connotations which cultural signs may have acquired in the artistic domain (section 8.2.3.1). It also prevents intentional or unintentional censorship of derivative cultural productions (section 8.2.3.2) and reduces the exposure of cultural signs to commercial marketing messages that may render them unattractive for use in the artistic domain (8.2.3.3). The prospect of a 'sign renaissance' – use in product marketing leading to a revived and intensified interest in a cultural sign – does not outweigh the detriment that results from the reduction of the artistic discourse potential of affected cultural signs (8.2.3.4).

8.2.3.1 Prevention of Unfair Freeriding

Cultural symbols are already predefined: they have cultural meanings that may make them desirable from the perspective of a trademark owner's brand development strategy. Literary and artistic works often have rich and positive connotations: an aura that helps selling goods. Investing in the acquisition of trademark rights to such a work, an enterprise can benefit from the favourable image which the cultural material already has.[1222] Given the popularity of the sign, the process of brand image creation need not be started from scratch.[1223] The establishment of a link with the cultural work offers the chance of an image transfer that may outweigh the costs of advertising necessary to acquire distinctiveness through use in trade.[1224] Vermeer's friendly and caring 'Milkmaid' helps Nestlé to sell dairy products.[1225] A

1220. Cf. Dusollier 2018, 180-183; Dusollier 2015, 167-168.
1221. Senftleben 2017b, 688.
1222. Senftleben 2017b, 697; Assaf 2008, 12 and 17; Klinkert/Schwab 1999, 1071. For an example of an art-based advertising campaign, see Bugdahl 2010, 374-375, who describes the campaign launched by the Swedish vodka brand ABSOLUT.
1223. Cf. Norwegian Board of Appeal for Industrial Property Rights, 13 November 2017, cases 16/00148, 16/00149, 16/00150, 16/00151, 16/00153 and 16/00154, 'Vigeland', para. 23.
1224. Cf. EFTA Court, 6 April 2017, case E-5/16, Municipality of Oslo ('Vigeland'), para. 75.
1225. EUTM no. 002998334 concerning, among other goods, dietetic foodstuffs and baby food; vegetables, fruits, meat, poultry, game, fish and seafood; milk products; coffee, tea, cocoa and chocolate products; bakery products, snack foods, breakfast cereals and ice cream. Cf. Bianchi 2017.

Rembrandt portrait and the name 'van Gogh' enhance the attractiveness of brushes, pencils and other artists' materials offered under these trademarks.[1226] Even if an artwork has no direct connection with the goods or services to which it is attached as a mark, it still serves as a reliable 'eye-catcher' drawing consumers' attention to the products ennobled by the presence of artistic expression.[1227] Arguably, the enhanced value to be gained in the case of cultural signs with positive pre-existing connotations allows bigger investments than in regular cases of brand development – investments capable of setting aside the cultural renown and 'particularly rich conceptual reference' which the CJEU qualified as an obstacle to a high degree of distinctiveness in *Picasso/Picaro* (sections 6.2.2 and 8.2.1).[1228]

Therefore, the risk of freeriding on positive cultural connotations which a sign has as a result of its evolution in the cultural domain must not be underestimated.[1229] To minimize this risk, it is advisable to exclude trademark rights to cultural signs from the outset. Once it is clear that trademark rights are unavailable, the trademark system no longer provides dysfunctional incentives.[1230] If cultural signs in the public domain are categorically excluded from trademark protection, a brand developer investing in cultural symbols can no longer expect to receive trademark rights as a reward. As a result, the investment becomes less secure and less attractive. The prospect of trademark protection no longer spurs investment in signs with rich cultural connotations.[1231]

8.2.3.2 Prevention of Censorship

A further argument in favour of the strict legal status concept of the public domain – requiring public domain material to be unencumbered by trademark rights – follows from an analysis of the censorship risk that arises from the grant of trademark rights. Inevitably, the grant of trademark rights gives the trademark proprietor an elevated position in the discourse about the affected cultural creation (section 3.3.2.4). The broader the scope of trademark protection as a result of investment in advertising and marketing,

1226. EUTM no. 000119180 and German registration no. 94061 concerning, among other goods, colours, lacquers, inks, sheet and powder metals for painters and artists, paper, printed matter, bookbinding materials, photographs, materials for artists and painters, brushes, pastels and pencils. Cf. Bugdahl 2010, 373.
1227. See the examples given by Bugdahl 2010, 372-374, attesting to the use of famous artworks as trademarks for unrelated goods and services.
1228. CJEU, 12 January 2006, case C-361/04P, 'Picasso/Picaro', para. 27. Cf. Wandtke/Bullinger 1997, 578.
1229. Cf. Curtin 2018, 962-963; Litman 1999, 1718.
1230. Ramsey 2018, 465-466.
1231. Cf. Denicola 1982, 170; Ramsey 2003, 1150; McKenna 2007, 1899; Assaf 2008, 82-83; Lemley/McKenna 2010, 440; Senftleben 2013a, 812-813; Anemaet 2020, 188-189 and 211-212.

the stronger the trademark owner's influence on the communication surrounding affected cultural signs.[1232] A trademark enjoys broader protection against confusion when it has a strong distinctive character (section 6.2.2).[1233] It enjoys protection against dilution that goes beyond identical and similar goods and services when it acquires the status of a well-known, famous or reputed mark (section 6.2.3).[1234] This gradual expansion of communication power entails the risk of censorship. Intentionally or unintentionally, the trademark proprietor will bring trademark claims against those forms of unauthorized use which, from her point of view, denigrate the trademarked cultural sign (and, therefore, damage the reputation of the trademark), whereas the trademark owner is likely to refrain from taking action against artists whose derivative works do not interfere with her own strategy for the development of the message and meaning of the sign (and, thus, are no threat to the value and renown of the trademark).[1235]

This enforcement behaviour inevitably results from the registration of a cultural sign as a trademark and subsequent use of the cultural sign as a tool to convey marketing messages to consumers. It does not seem decisive whether the trademark proprietor is a commercial enterprise or a public body.[1236] Even if the owner of the trademark right is a state, municipality or museum, and even if the objective underlying the acquisition of trademark rights is art custodianship rather than cultural heritage grabbing,[1237] the risk of censorship – in the sense of enforcement measures seeking to prevent interferences with the trademark proprietor's own vision of the sign – cannot be ruled out. A public body, such as a state-owned cultural heritage institution, is likely to refrain from infringement claims in cases where unauthorized remix and reuse complies with its own understanding of the message and meaning of the cultural sign. Conversely, it is likely to bring an

1232. For a discussion of the growing impact of trademark rights on communication based on the protected sign, see Senftleben 2011b, 383; Ramsey 2003, 1095; Dreyfuss 1990, 397.

1233. Kur/Senftleben 2017, para 4.346-4.347; McCarthy 2004, 1170-1172.

1234. As to these different threshold requirements for the acquisition of protection in the area of dissimilar goods and services in international, U.S. and EU law, see Senftleben 2009a, 50-55.

1235. Cf. Senftleben 2017b, 688-689.

1236. See Ohly 2019, 333 and 338-339, who rejects a categorical exclusion of trademark rights but confirms that trademark protection is not the right vehicle to allow public bodies to preserve cultural heritage. For a concrete example, see Regional Court of Magdeburg, 19 April 2005, case 7 O 703/05, 'Himmelsscheibe von Nebra 2' where the German State Saxony-Anhalt (owner of trademark rights in the ancient Nebra Sky Disk) brought a lawsuit against book covers showing the trademarked Sky Disk. While the State of Saxony-Anhalt asserted its trademark rights, the Court deemed copyright protection decisive which Saxony-Anhalt had acquired as a result of the first publication of the Nebra Sky Disk after its discovery. Cf. Ohly 2008, 209-210.

1237. For a more detailed discussion of this situation, see Senftleben 2017b, 685-689.

infringement action if it finds unauthorized use in a derivative work irreconcilable with its own understanding of the cultural sign.[1238]

8.2.3.3 Prevention of Sign Devaluation

In addition to the described risk of censorship, the grant of trademark rights is likely to devalue cultural public domain material as a basis of cultural follow-on innovation because it leads to the attachment of commercial marketing messages.[1239] Due to the configuration of the trademark system, use of the cultural sign as a marketing instrument is inevitable once trademark rights are awarded. To maintain the trademark right, the owner must make genuine use of the sign in the sense of trademark law. Otherwise, the trademark registration is exposed to the risk of cancellation after an uninterrupted period of non-use (a period of five years in the EU).[1240] The requirement of genuine use has two facets in the EU. On the one hand, the trademark proprietor is obliged to use the trademark to create or preserve an outlet for the goods or services, in respect of which the mark is registered.[1241] On the other hand, the use must be in accordance with the essential trademark function of indicating the commercial origin of these goods or services.[1242] Once a cultural sign is registered as a trademark, the owner of the registration is therefore bound to develop the sign as a badge of origin and marketing tool for the goods and services involved. A recent EUIPO decision concerning the registration of Banksy's 'Flower Thrower' as a trademark confirms that even if an artist registers an artwork with the intention to safeguard freedom of remix and prevent traders from commercial use, he cannot escape the obligation to use the artwork for product marketing himself. If the intention of genuine use in the sense of trademark law is missing, the trademark registration is liable to be declared invalid because of bad faith.[1243]

The legal obligation to embark on genuine use and add commercial marketing messages, however, is only the tip of the iceberg. When a commercial undertaking registers a cultural sign with the intention to make genuine use and transform the sign into a badge of origin, the legal certainty resulting from trademark protection is likely to encourage even broader investment in brand-based advertising seeking to attach lifestyle messages to

---

1238. Senftleben 2017b, 689.
1239. Cf. Assaf 2008, 21-23.
1240. Cf. Kur/Senftleben 2017, para. 6.176-6.182. Article 19(1) TRIPS sets forth an international minimum standard of 'at least' three years of non-use.
1241. CJEU, 11 March 2003, case C-40/01, Ajax/Ansul, para. 36 and 43. Cf. Kur/Senftleben 2017, para. 6.154.
1242. CJEU, 8 June 2017, case C-689/15, Gözze Frottierweberei, para. 42. Cf. Kur/Senftleben 2017, para. 6.156.
1243. EUIPO Cancellation Division, 14 September 2020, cancellation no. 33 843 C (invalidity), Full Colour Black/Pest Control Office ('Banksy'), 10-12 and 15.

affected signs (section 6.1.1). When a cultural sign in the public domain is adopted as a trademark, these marketing efforts will blur cultural connotations (section 3.3.2.4) which the sign had prior to the acquisition of trademark rights. Commercial messages conveyed by the trademark owner may even gradually supersede the sign's cultural meaning.[1244]

In the light of an economic analysis of the interplay between intellectual property protection and the public domain, this development may seem unproblematic at first glance: the more complex and diverse a sign's denotations, the higher might be its value. Eli Salzberger describes this potential positive effect as follows:

> Let us assume that the government changes the designation of particular common land into private property, this piece of land is subsequently purchased by an individual on which she builds an architectural masterpiece. This new building is privately owned in the sense that no one can enter the building, use it, sell it, or eliminate it save its private owner or under her permission. But the pleasure of viewing the building for the rest of the community, the inspiration it creates, its contribution to future architectural plans can be regarded as an enlargement of the public domain.[1245]

In this vein, it might be argued that the grant of trademark protection enriches a sign in the public domain because it offers incentives to add complex commercial meanings to a formerly undeveloped sign.[1246] In the case of an undefined sign which the trademark owner charges with source-identifying and lifestyle messages, the branding process may lead to an enhancement of language tools and rhetoric devices.[1247] As recognized above, iconic trade symbols may trigger complex associations that make them attractive source material for literary and artistic productions seeking to reflect current societal conditions (section 5.2.5).

However, a different scenario arises when branding initiatives concern signs which already have complex meanings because of their evolution in the cultural domain.[1248] The question, then, is whether potential benefits accruing from the grant of trademark protection outweigh the detriment flowing from the risk of losing cultural connotations that may be relevant to the

1244. Assaf 2008, 11-12 and 21-23.
1245. Salzberger 2006, 55.
1246. Cf. M. Richardson, 193, who argues for the adoption of an incentive rationale in trademark law that seeks to stimulate popular brand culture and the creation of new brand language.
1247. Cf. Dreyfuss 2020, 328-329.
1248. Cf. Landes/Posner 1988, 272-273, who recognize benefits accruing from incentives to invest resources in the invention of 'new words'. Arguably, the same argument cannot be made with regard to the recoding of signs which already have a rich spectrum of meanings. However, see Richardson 2004, 213, for a positive assessment of recoding because of additional connotations.

discourse in the artistic domain.[1249] With regard to cultural material in the public domain, it is doubtful that branding will enrich language and offer additional rhetoric devices. A sign with cultural significance already has complex meanings and connotations attached to it.[1250] It can hardly be compared with the undeveloped common land which Salzberger takes as a starting point in his explanation of potential positive effects. If the complex meanings and rich connotations evoked by a cultural sign are blurred or even suppressed as a result of the acquisition of trademark protection and the attachment of marketing messages,[1251] the sign's expressive value will be reduced rather than being enhanced. The attachment of marketing messages will thus devaluate the sign and reduce its potential to play an independent role in the process of cultural follow-on innovation.

As explained in section 3.3.2.4, this devaluation has far-reaching societal repercussions. An artwork can unmask defects of existing societal conditions and prepare society for the transition to a better community. Given this fundamental importance of literary and artistic productions, particular importance must be attached to the preservation of the cultural meaning of artworks as a basis for dialogue and discussion in the artistic domain. Once a work of art is created, society should seek not to interfere with the artistic discourse. Otherwise, an important impulse for required social and political changes will be lost. The sociological analysis of processes of creation in section 3.3.1.3 confirms this assumption. It underlines the need for a new generation of artists to define its position vis-à-vis the reservoir of pre-existing cultural expressions.[1252] The commercial messages added by the trademark owner after the acquisition of trademark rights to cultural public domain material overshadow the discourse in the artistic domain. Inevitably, the attachment of commercial marketing messages influences the perception of the public: the sign is no longer exclusively seen as an artwork but also as an identifier of commercial source, symbol of a particular lifestyle, etc. This risk must not be underestimated. Second authors who want to build their creations on the trademarked sign cannot escape the commercial connotations which the sign has as a result of use in trade. In consequence, the discussion and reinterpretation of the sign in the literary and artistic domain and its use as a reference point for future artistic creativity become more difficult.

Artists who feel that the commercial connotations added by the trademark owner thwart their intended artistic expression will avoid the sign and use other cultural creations instead. While their artistic creativity is unlikely to stop altogether, it will go in different directions: second authors will no longer make an effort to reflect on the cultural message and

1249. Cf. Assaf 2008, 77.
1250. CJEU, 12 January 2006, case C-361/04 P, Picasso/Picaro, para. 27.
1251. Cf. Assaf 2009, 2-3; Senftleben 2010a, 75; Wandtke/Bullinger 1997, 578.
1252. Bourdieu 1992/1999, 370-372.

importance of the trademarked sign. They will focus on other sources of inspiration. Once impregnated with commercial connotations, cultural signs are rendered less attractive for use in the artistic domain because the remix of the sign's artistic expression is no longer possible without evoking its commercial facets. In consequence, the sign's potential to serve as a basis for artistic dialogue – and societal change – will never be explored in its entirety. Society loses potentially important reflections on a cultural sign which – in the absence of use as a trade symbol – could have come to light in the artistic discourse: one of the seeds for cultural follow-on innovation will never grow into the tree that could have come into existence without commercial interference. Inevitably, the branches depending on the cultural dimension of the sign will remain underdeveloped. Because of the communication power of the trademark owner (section 6.3) and the commercial redefinition of the sign's meaning, artists are likely to refrain from using the sign as a source of inspiration and a building block of new works. This problem may be particularly severe with regard to a country's own cultural heritage. When attempts to register cultural signs as trademarks concern domestic cultural symbols,[1253] the grant of trademark rights renders these domestic reference points for cultural follow-on innovation unattractive in the eyes of artists looking for source material for new creations. Trademark rights in domestic cultural symbols bring in its wake a disincentive to use these symbols in derivative literary and artistic works. In consequence, the grant of trademark rights may hamper the renewal of the domestic cultural landscape.

Admittedly, research in the field of cognitive science has shown that dilutive use of a sign can reinforce, rather than chip away, the strength of its original meaning. With regard to dilutive use of well-known marks, Rebecca Tushnet has pointed out that:

> exposure to near variants or uses in other contexts makes the trademark more familiar and thus more easily retrieved from memory. This process can add value in the same way that marketers think preexisting associations carried by descriptive or suggestive terms add value to a trademark. Words with multiple associations may be more easily activated, or reference to one word may 'prime' us to recall a similar word. Tiffany's-the-restaurant may make us think of Tiffany's-the-jeweler when we are at lunch thinking of gifts for Mother's Day.[1254]

Relying on brand-extension research, Tushnet also stresses that use of variants of a protected sign in a dubious context is unlikely to tarnish a strong brand as long as there is no source confusion and the brand messages are robustly embedded in the minds of consumers:

1253. For example, see EFTA Court, 6 April 2017, case E-5/16, Municipality of Oslo ('Vigeland'), paras 20-26.

1254. Tushnet 2008, 537. Cf. Lemley/McKenna 2010, 429-432.

> If consumers are given a reason to distinguish an authorized extension or cobranded product from the core brand – for example, a name like Courtyard by Marriott instead of Marriott or Coke BlaK instead of Coke – they will do so, and negative opinions about the extension will not return to harm opinions of the core brand. If consumers seize on such fine distinctions for authorized line extensions, it seems implausible that, absent confusion, they will transfer negative opinions between unrelated products or services.[1255]

Applying these insights to cultural signs mutatis mutandis, it may be said that use of a cultural sign in a commercial marketing context may enhance the familiarity of consumers with the cultural symbol. It may render the sign more easily accessible in the memory of the public. Consumers are likely to think not only of marketing messages but also of the sign's cultural meaning when it appears in commercial communication. Even use of a cultural sign in an objectionable, negative context need not erode the favourable, positive image which the sign may have as a result of its evolution in the cultural domain.

While these considerations unmask trademark dilution and brand erosion arguments as mere rhetoric,[1256] they fail to address the central concern underlying the present enquiry. The risk of devaluating cultural symbols through use in commercial communication arises even if the use makes consumers more familiar with the sign and its cultural meaning, and even if the use does not automatically kill cultural connotations. Inevitably, the sign becomes a hybrid. The time of its unchallenged existence as a cultural artefact is over. With the communication power following from the grant of exclusive trademark rights (section 6.2), commercial connotations enter the picture. If the activities of the trademark owner comply with the outlined genuine use requirements, the audience detecting the trademarked sign in a derivative artwork will inevitably think of the enterprise of the trademark owner and the pictures and marketing messages which the trademark owner evokes in advertising. An artist including the sign in a derivative work can hardly elude these commercial connotations. As Katya Assaf points out:

> the essence of the first task [the task of trademark developers to educate consumers to perceive the sign as a trademark] is to create a strong associative link between the trademark and the respective products or services in the consumer's mind. If the trademark consists of an existing cultural sign, this process will inevitably interfere with its meaning. This interference happens due to the reciprocal forces existing in the semantic field; while some of the cultural sign's initial meaning comes to be

1255. Tushnet 2008, 543-544.
1256. Tushnet 2008, 562-565.

embedded in the trademark, the trademark also casts a shadow on the cultural sign[1257] (explanation within brackets added).

Hence, the mere existence of commercial connotations is problematic – regardless of their interplay with the sign's cultural meaning. The moment commercial marketing messages are added, the damage consisting of a 'shadow on the cultural sign' is done: the cultural sign is devalued as a basis for artistic remix and reuse that seeks to play with the sign's original, cultural meaning.[1258] As the trademark owner creates an amalgam of commercial and cultural connotations, it is no longer possible to refer to the sign's cultural meaning in isolation. An artist wishing to do so must realize that her intended artistic comment may be doomed to fail because of the additional commercial connotations that blur the perception of the sign and the perception of the derivative work. This corrosive effect of commercial marketing messages is particularly strong when trademark rights are granted. In contrast to incidental and variable use in advertising, indefinitely renewable trademark rights enhance the risk of continuous and consistent use as an identifier of commercial source and carrier of commercial marketing messages. Hence, the corrosive effect is unlikely to vanish. In the case of trademark rights, the damage to the communication process in the cultural domain will be much more enduring than in the case of incidental use in advertising. Trademark rights impose a lasting burden on use of the sign in the artistic discourse. They impregnate the sign with commercial messages.

It is doubtful whether the commercial meanings added by the trademark owner can outweigh the loss of dialogic communication potential for artistic purposes and derivative works that could have evolved from reflections on the sign's cultural dimension. Admittedly, the connotations stemming from genuine trademark use may serve as an alternative reference point for artistic creativity. An artist may find the hybrid nature of a trademarked cultural sign inspiring. The resulting derivative work, however, must not be confused with a comment on the sign's cultural meaning. It is a play with the sign's hybrid nature: the fact that the sign triggers an amalgam of cultural and commercial associations. This, however, is unlikely to compensate for the loss of artistic expression based on the cultural meaning of the devalued sign. For a critical comment on the omnipresence of commercial messages in modern society, a wide variety of genuine commercial symbols is available: signs that have been devised as trademarks and carriers of commercial messages from the outset (section 5.2.5). Moreover, it seems cynical to first allow commercial messages to permeate artworks and justify this process afterwards by pointing to critical artistic comments on the devaluation of affected signs. Without the acceptance of trademark rights and the commercial redefinition

1257. Assaf 2008, 11.
1258. Cf. Curtin 2018, 998.

of artworks, the critical artistic comment would not have been necessary. The problem would not have arisen in the first place.

On balance, the adoption of cultural heritage signs as trademarks – and the termination of the public domain status – thus reduces the value of affected signs for dialogic communication in the cultural domain. Marketing messages which the trademark proprietor attaches to a sign with cultural significance will inevitably blur and suppress its cultural dimension and erode the sign's artistic discourse potential over time (section 3.3.2.4).[1259] Again, there is a remarkable difference between inherent limits of exclusive rights and defences on the one hand (freedom of use concept of the public domain, section 8.1.2) and an outright exclusion from protection on the other (legal status concept of the public domain, section 8.1.1). A categorical denial of trademark rights keeps cultural signs in the public domain entirely free from trademark rights and avoids incentives for the attachment of commercial marketing messages. The grant of trademark protection, by contrast, provides a strong incentive for the attachment of marketing messages and triggers the described problematic process of devaluing the sign and reducing its artistic discourse potential. From the outset, inherent limits of trademark rights and defences that exempt certain forms of use from the control of the trademark owner are thus incapable of contributing to the preservation of cultural public domain material as effectively as the outright denial of protection. An approach based on inherent protection limits and defences does not bar the acquisition of trademark rights. Hence, it encourages the trademark owner to impregnate the cultural sign with commercial marketing messages.

8.2.3.4 Counterargument of Sign Renaissance

To add a nuance to the assessment of sign devaluation in consequence of use as a trademark, it is important to note, in line with Rebecca Tushnet's analysis of the impact on consumers' minds,[1260] that the use of a cultural symbol in a commercial context may also have positive effects. In particular, it may lead to a 'renaissance' of the sign: a cultural sign that has sunk into oblivion may be rediscovered and become known to a broad audience as a result of use in advertising.[1261] The consuming public, including artists, may take use in advertising as a starting point to learn more about the sign and its creator. Nonetheless, this welcome renaissance must not culminate in the

1259. Assaf 2009, 2-3; Senftleben 2010a, 101-102; Wandtke/Bullinger 1997, 578.

1260. Tushnet 2008, 537.

1261. Cf. Dutch Supreme Court, 28 October 1948, Bureau I.E./Churchill's Cigars ('Winston Churchill'), *Bijblad bij de industriële eigendom* 1949, 24. This may also be derived, mutatis mutandis, from the conclusions drawn by Tushnet 2008, 537-542. Cf. also Dreyfuss 2020, 328-329, who emphasizes the potential of branding initiatives to create new language and rhetorical devices. This argument, however, overlooks that cultural signs already have a rich spectrum of meanings because of their evolution in the

grant of trademark rights. By contrast, it only seems beneficial as long as the communication process surrounding the sign remains open. Inevitably, the revitalization of the sign in the public mind gives the advertiser a head start and significant advantage in the definition of the sign's meaning. It forges a strong link between the sign and the advertiser's commercial messages. As the advertiser becomes a centre of gravity in the communication process, it is of crucial importance to open up the discourse concerning the rediscovered sign as soon as possible.[1262] Speakers in the cultural domain – in particular artists looking for sources of inspiration and building blocks for new creations – must have the chance of rising to supreme definition powers in the debate. Pushing the advertiser's commercial messages aside with their artistic comments and references to the sign's cultural dimension, they can recultivate the sign as a cultural symbol and reference point of literary and artistic creativity.

The regulation of advertising leaves room for this reintegration of the rediscovered sign in the cultural domain. Use in advertising does not bestow upon the advertiser an exclusive right that could serve as a basis for lawsuits against speakers in the cultural domain. While the owner of trademark rights obtains an exclusive right to prohibit unauthorized use of the sign and an incentive to invest in the development of the sign as a commercial symbol (sections 6.1.1 and 6.2), the use in advertising only means that the advertiser has availed himself of the freedom – enjoyed not only by him but also by any other speaker – to use public domain material freely. The freedom of using public domain material in advertising does not prevent artists from freely using the same sign for artistic purposes. Moreover, the freedom of use in advertising does not provide incentives to invest in the sign as a commercial symbol. It does not lead to an exclusive right that offers sufficient legal certainty for substantial investment in the attachment of lasting commercial connotations to the sign. Even more importantly, it does not lead to a legal position which the advertiser can invoke to substantiate threats of infringement when sending cease-and-desist letters to artists using the sign for their work. A user in the cultural domain can re-establish the sign's cultural meaning without exposure to allegations of trademark infringement. Therefore, the mere invocation of freedom to use public domain material in advertising does not change the rules of the communication process as fundamentally as the grant of exclusive trademark rights. It does not give one individual speaker outstanding communication control.

---

cultural domain. Branding blurs and erodes this pre-existing set of connotations (see preceding section 8.2.3.3). For a discussion wondering about positive long-term effects, see Hughes 1999, 959-960.

1262. Cf. Curtin 2018, 1012-1013, who emphasizes the need to ensure freedom of competition among producers of literary and artistic productions wishing to build upon public domain characters.

The award of trademark rights, by contrast, gives the advertiser the described exclusive position and broad definition power to shape the meaning of cultural public domain material. Instead of opening up the communication process, the grant of trademark rights cements the advertiser's hegemony in the communication process for an indefinite time. Trademark protection means that one player in the communication process has far-reaching control and strong incentives to invest in the development of her own messages and the suppression of the messages of others. The grant of trademark rights, thus, thwarts the objective to reintegrate the sign in the cultural domain. It nullifies the benefits that could have accrued from the sign's rediscovery. The risk of trademark infringement is likely to stifle initiatives to reuse and remix the sign (section 6.3). Therefore, the potential benefits of a sign renaissance in a commercial context do not constitute a valid argument against concerns about the devaluation of cultural signs in a commercial context. In particular, it would be wrong to assume that a sign renaissance justifies the grant of trademark rights. The opposite is true. The recognition of exclusive rights would frustrate the reintegration of the rediscovered sign in the artistic discourse. The far-reaching definition power of the advertiser who renews the interest of the general public in a forgotten cultural sign must not be stable. If the advertiser remains the centre of gravity in the communication process, the perception of the sign will be shaped by the advertiser's commercial messages. The opportunity to recultivate not only the sign but also its artistic discourse potential (section 3.3.2.4) will be lost. As trademark protection affords the advertiser the opportunity to reign supreme in the communication process, it eliminates the stimulus for cultural follow-on innovation that could have followed from the rediscovery of the sign.

8.3 CULTIVATION OF THE PUBLIC DOMAIN

So far, the scrutiny of trademark protection in the light of the objective to preserve a rich and robust public domain for cultural follow-on innovation has led to the insight that appropriate countermeasures are necessary to prevent trademark rights from removing cultural heritage signs from the public domain and diminishing the reservoir of signs that are available for remix in the artistic domain. However, apart from this defensive task – the prevention of trademark protection from encroaching upon the public domain – the copyright rationale to offer a rich and robust public domain as a basis for cyclic cultural innovation may also include a more ambitious, assertive aspect. Public domain recognition in the sense of the cultural imperative in copyright law may be understood to require that trademarks fall into the public domain once they have acquired a strong cultural meaning (following section 8.3.1). For example, this positive enrichment obligation could concern the trademark COCA COLA which has acquired an iconic status not only as a trademark but also as a cultural symbol. It may thus be argued that COCA COLA should become freely available to broaden the range of signs that can serve as source material for cultural follow-on innovation (section 8.3.2).

8.3.1 TERMINATION OF TRADEMARK RIGHTS TO ICONIC TRADE SYMBOLS

Quite clearly, the discussion of a need to phase out trademark protection because of cultural significance is a thought experiment. A new ground for revoking trademark protection because of cultural significance could hardly be reconciled with existing international norms in the field of trademark law. As it would not fall within the scope of Article 6*quinquies*(B) No. 2 PC, it could hardly be invoked in cases of *telle quelle* protection.[1263] As it does not presuppose the absence or loss of distinctiveness, it may also be deemed incompatible with the guarantee of indefinite renewal in Article 18 TRIPS and the description of protectable subject matter in Article 15 TRIPS. Therefore, the current intellectual property system does not seem to offer room for terminating trademark rights to enrich the reservoir of freely available source material for cultural follow-on innovation.

Despite the theoretical nature of a phase-out discussion, however, an enquiry into the termination of trademark rights is important in the context of the analysis of the copyright/trademark interface because it reveals a peculiar hierarchy of values in intellectual property law. In the light of the rationales underlying trademark protection, it seems radical to consider the termination of trademark protection at all. Trademark rights are indefinitely renewable in order to ensure market transparency. As explained in section 4.2.1, a static, potentially endless grant of protection in trademark law is indispensable to achieve the overarching goals of fair competition, consumer protection and a well-functioning marketplace. Given these core rationales, there can be little doubt that policymakers would hardly ever accept and implement a phase-out mechanism that puts an end to trademark rights because of cultural significance. In addition, it has already been pointed out in section 5.2.5 that the termination of trademark protection may be undesirable even from the perspective of cultural follow-on innovation. If trademark protection is phased out because of cultural significance and trademark proprietors stop using affected trademarks as commercial badges of origin, this will deprive iconic trade symbols of their very function in commerce and trade. This loss of the commercial *raison d'être*, however, may also deprive genuine trade symbols of their value for the artistic discourse. Arguably, the particular contrast which the use of a trade symbol

1263. For a more detailed discussion of this international protection mechanism, see Ng-Loy 2018, 147-164; Kunz-Hallstein 2006, 487; Beier 1992, 243; Ladas 1975, 1211-1240; Bodenhausen 1969, 113-119.

in an artwork evokes – the contrast arising from the use of an everyday industrial object in the context of art – is only possible as long as the trade symbol is clearly defined and perceived as an industrial object – and not as an artwork.[1264] Against this background, iconic trade symbols that have evolved in the commercial domain were qualified as a separate category of signs above: a category that is distinct from cultural signs (section 5.2.5).

Nonetheless, it is tempting to embark on the described thought experiment and discuss the termination of trademark protection for iconic trade symbols as a means to broaden the pool of public domain material which artists can use freely without any exposure to a trademark infringement risk. This enquiry is of particular interest because it reflects the prevalence of the commercial imperative of market transparency over the cultural imperative of public domain enrichment in intellectual property law. The current intellectual property system does not categorically deny trademark rights to cultural public domain material. In principle, it allows the termination of the public domain status once distinctive character is acquired through use in trade (section 4.2.2.2). The public domain status of cultural expressions is thus sacrificed to support the commercial imperative of market transparency. By contrast, the inverse scenario – an obligation on trademark owners to relinquish their rights to support the cultural imperative of public domain enrichment – is regarded as odd and inconsistent. While the intellectual property system deprives the public domain of cultural expressions that have been developed into source identifiers in trade, it fails to bring trade symbols into the public domain that have become powerful cultural icons.

Seeking to justify this different treatment of cultural and commercial concerns, it may be said, as already explained, that the trademark owner will stop investing in a trademark and the maintenance of a specific brand image once the trade symbol enters the public domain and no longer functions as an exclusive, reliable badge of origin (section 6.1.1).[1265] It may also be argued that the whole symbol will be devalued and finally lost – not only for marketing purposes but also for cultural purposes – when the end of investment by the trademark proprietor is equated with the end of the specific meaning that has elevated the trademark to a cultural icon. In this vein, the erosion of trademark protection for iconic trade symbols entails the risk of eroding commercial connotations and lifestyle messages that may constitute important reference points for statements in works of art. On its merits, the argument rests on the assumption that Campbell's soup can would be less useful as a reference point for artistic expression, such as Andy Warhol's work (section 5.2.5), once the Campbell Soup Company can no longer exert control over the iconic Campbell's logo on the basis of trademark rights.

1264. As to this contrast between the realm of art and the world of consumer goods, see Bürger 1974, 82-85.
1265. Cf. Posner 2005, 61.

Nuancing this line of argument, however, it is important to consider the broad spectrum of additional connotations which a trademark may receive when it enters the public domain. Once the commercial meaning – the sign's initial *raison d'être* – is no longer cultivated, this need not lead to a situation where the sign is immediately rendered unattractive for use in artworks. The richness of associations and meanings attached to a trademark does not exclusively depend on the trademark proprietor. By contrast, it is the result of a joint effort of trademark owners and consumers. As already pointed out in section 4.2.2, it is the consuming public that frequently imbues trademarks with connotations distinct from and sometimes unrelated to the advertising messages conveyed by the trademark owner.[1266] From this perspective, a general entitlement to the use of iconic trademarks – as public domain material – in social and cultural discourse appears as a corollary of the public's contribution to the creation of trade symbols with complex meanings and connotations that have transformed affected trademarks into symbols with particular cultural significance.[1267]

The end of the trademark protection status, therefore, implies that the communication process surrounding the sign becomes more democratic. The predominance of the trademark owner comes to an end and the sign becomes a generally available carrier of meanings which every member of the public – not only the former trademark owner but also consumers and artists – can shape and influence. As a result of this open, dialogic communication process, the initial trademark meaning of the sign will fade away. Commercial marketing messages are likely to give way to reflections on the lifestyle and attitude that have been associated with the initial mark. In other words: the sign's role as a cultural icon will continuously supersede the sign's source-identifying function. Gradually, the open communication process following from the incorporation of the sign into the public domain will destruct its trademark meaning. Nonetheless, the termination of trademark protection does not automatically erode the full spectrum of connotations evoked by the sign. At least during a transitory phase – when the commercial lifestyle messages of the former trademark owner are still intact – the public domain status of the formerly protected trade symbol may instigate a more open and diverse discussion that adds new connotations and strengthens existing nuances of the sign's meaning.

Therefore, the reason for considering iconic trade symbols a separate category of signs that is distinct from cultural signs (section 5.2.5) and the reason for shying away from the termination of trademark rights because of cultural significance do not lie in a sudden and complete loss of meaning. By

1266. Litman 1999, 15-16. Cf. Peukert 2019, 1181-1182; Gangjee 2013, 51-56; Tan 2013, 225; Gerhardt 2010, 101; Ramsey 2010b, 851; Heymann 2009, 651; Wilf 1999, 4-5; Kozinski 1993, 960; Dreyfuss 1990, 415 and 424. However, see also the critical comments on the limitation of trademark rights made by Richardson 2004, 193.

1267. Wilf 1999, 40-46.

contrast, it is the result of a weighing process. The benefits which society may derive from a richer spectrum of fully developed cultural connotations do not seem to outweigh the detriment of losing a strong identifier of commercial source. The broadening of the reservoir of reference points for artistic creativity seems to have less weight in intellectual property law and less importance to society. Under current societal conditions, it is conceivable to see the Mona Lisa being registered as a trademark (as a result of the acquisition of distinctive character through use in trade) and her cultural connotations being washed away over time (as a result of intensive use in product marketing), whereas it seems inconceivable to see the COCA COLA trademark falling into the public domain (as a result of a finding of particular cultural significance) and its source-identifying function being washed away over time (in an entirely open communication process that is no longer dominated by the trademark owner).

8.3.2 *Limitation of Trademark Rights Because of Expressive Genericity*

Admittedly, there is an alternative explanation why trademark rights to iconic trade symbols are not systematically phased out once these symbols acquire cultural significance. For trademark law to satisfy the cultural interest in freedom to use iconic trade symbols in an artistic context, it may be sufficient to exempt use in the cultural domain from the control of the trademark proprietor. A new set of rules that brings trademark protection to an end altogether may appear excessive. This becomes apparent when potential grounds for revoking trademark protection are considered. In principle, a new rule for phasing out trademark protection because of cultural significance could be modelled on existing rules that address generic signs. In the framework of the international regulation of *telle quelle* protection, Article 6*quinquies*(B) No. 2 PC allows the denial or invalidation of trademark protection when a trademark consists exclusively of signs or indications which 'have become customary in the current language or in the bona fide and established practices of the trade of the country where protection is claimed'. This international standard governing protection of trademarks duly registered in the country of origin 'as is' in other Paris Union countries,[1268] made its way into domestic trademark legislation and has become widespread in trademark systems around the globe.[1269]

For this traditional concept of genericity to serve as a vehicle to bring trademarks with cultural significance into the public domain, it would have to be broadened substantially. A starting point for this step can be found in

1268. For a more detailed discussion of this international protection mechanism, see Ng-Loy 2018, 147-164; Kunz-Hallstein 2006, 487; Beier 1992, 243; Ladas 1975, 1211-1240; Bodenhausen 1969, 113-119.

1269. For an overview, see the contributions to Senftleben 2012b.

literature. As Rochelle Dreyfuss already pointed out thirty years ago, trademarks serve as status symbols representing particular attitudes, preferences and aspirations. They may be capable of evoking 'vibrant, evocative metaphors.'[1270] However, the fact that trademarks may become information shortcuts that condense a highly complex amalgam of connotations does not automatically mean that they are generic in the sense of the traditional concept underlying Article 6*quinquies*(B) No. 2 PC. Traditional genericity relating to use as a generic term in a current language or trade practice differs markedly from the expressive genericity which Dreyfuss describes. She distinguishes between use of the 'signalling function' of trademarks which corresponds with the traditional function of indicating the commercial origin of goods or services, and use of the 'expressive function' of trademarks which concerns use of the trademark as a shortcut for a certain image, lifestyle or attitude:

> In referring to 'Barbie' in order to indicate that she was treated like a beautiful but empty-headed accessory, [Joan] Kennedy exploited a set of meanings that are quite different from the ones invoked by Mattel, and I label this use of the trademark 'expressive'.[1271]

Hence, 'expressive genericity' does not mean that the trademark as such has become a generic element of the current language. By contrast, it refers to a specific form of using trademarks in a metaphorical sense: not as identifiers of commercial source but as symbols of personal or societal conditions.[1272] The concept of 'expressive genericity' is incongruent with the concept underlying Article 6*quinquies*(B) No. 2 PC because it does not presuppose a loss of the capacity to distinguish goods or services. Expressive genericity refers to a metaphorical play with associations which a trademark evokes. Despite the cultural connotations allowing this play, the trademark can still serve as a reliable and distinctive indicator of commercial source. The distinction between a trademark's 'signalling function' and its 'expressive function' in Dreyfuss' concept of expressive genericity is of particular importance against this background. It paves the way for a less draconic strategy to accommodate the cultural interest in iconic trade symbols. Instead of revoking trademark rights altogether, it seems possible to maintain protection of the signalling function of iconic trade symbols, while still offering artists freedom to use the expressive, metaphorical aspect of trade symbols on the basis of a robust exemption of artistic use in trademark law. Arguably, a limitation of trademark rights that enables artistic use of the expressive aspect of iconic trade symbols can serve as an alternative avenue

1270. Dreyfuss 1990, 397-398.
1271. Dreyfuss 1990, 400. Cf. Lemley/McKenna 2010, 442.
1272. Cf. Assaf 2008, 58-61.

to support cultural follow-on innovation.[1273] As Rochelle Dreyfuss concludes:

> it should be possible to build upon the defences that trademark law has constructed for the competitive vocabulary a parallel set of principles to protect expressive speech. In a regime that recognized the facility to compartmentalize, signaling functions would be analysed according to the conventional Polaroid principles, and the newly developed doctrines would operate to allocate rights when trademarks are used expressively. Proprietary rights to marks would then be protected across the entire signaling spectrum, except in instances in which expressive communication was suppressed by the loss of vocabulary.[1274]

This defence-based solution – drawing a distinction between infringing signalling use and free expressive use of iconic trade symbols – has the additional advantage of leaving the source-identifying function of affected trade symbols intact. The sign can survive as a trademark and the trademark owner can continue investing in the maintenance of the brand image which the trademark evokes. In consequence, the trade symbol remains available as a vehicle to symbolize the world of consumerism and materialism in artworks – not only temporarily until the open communication process in the public domain submerges the trademark meaning (see preceding section) but also permanently as long as the trademark owner uses the sign as a brand in trade. Therefore, the defence-based approach preserves the opportunity for artists to create a particular contrast in their literary and artistic work by incorporating iconic trade symbols which represent the world of commerce (section 5.2.5).

8.4 CONCLUSION

Trademark law poses a particular threat to the objective to recognize and preserve a rich and robust public domain as a central element of the cultural imperative in copyright law. Inevitably, the removal of cultural heritage signs from the public domain erodes the absolute freedom of use following from the public domain status. The prospect of acquiring trademark rights may encourage freeriding on the rich spectrum of connotations which cultural signs offer as a result of their evolution in the artistic domain. Moreover, the use of cultural material for marketing purposes is likely to erode the artistic discourse potential of affected signs and devalue them as sources of inspiration and building blocks of new artistic works. Against this background, it is essential to take appropriate measures to avoid an encroachment upon the public domain of cultural expressions. Otherwise, cultural heritage

1273. Cf. Assaf 2008, 79-80.
1274. Dreyfuss 1990, 418.

signs may be removed from the public domain and redefined in commercial contexts during a potentially indefinite period of trademark protection. Cyclic cultural innovation, by contrast, would become more difficult.

As to the arsenal of countermeasures that may be taken into consideration, the discussion about the concept of 'public domain' in literature has shed light on a broad spectrum of preservation mechanisms that differ in degree of effectiveness. An outright, categorical exclusion of cultural heritage signs from trademark protection is the most effective public domain preservation tool. It ensures that cultural heritage signs cannot be removed from the public domain through the acquisition of trademark rights. The adoption of this measure is in line with the legal status definition of the public domain which makes absence of any intellectual property right a precondition for awarding public domain status.

Less far-reaching preservation tools enter the picture when the public domain is understood to encompass robust user freedoms that remain after the acquisition of trademark protection. Because of several inherent limits – the confinement to use in the course of trade, use as a trademark, use likely to cause confusion and use likely to cause dilution – exclusive trademark rights need not have a broad scope. User freedoms that are implicitly derived from these inherent limits of trademark rights may play an important role in the preservation of artistic freedom of use. Forms of using protected signs may also be exempted from the control of the trademark owner explicitly by adopting exceptions to exclusive rights that provide a defence in infringement cases. However, the foregoing analysis has shown that recourse to inherent limits of exclusive rights and defences against infringement claims are only sufficient in trademark systems that focus on protection against confusion and refrain from transforming trademark rights into exploitation instruments that come close to the absolute rights against use and copying granted in copyright and patent law.[1275] Inherent limits of exclusive rights will become less reliable safeguards with every expansion of trademark protection. In the EU trademark system, for instance, the protection of investment in the creation of a valuable brand image has broadened the scope of protection to such an extent that remaining inherent limits of exclusive rights are rendered incapable of guaranteeing freedom of artistic use. The weaker the inherent limits of exclusive trademark rights become in advanced trademark systems, the stronger the need for the adoption of exceptions that explicitly exempt culturally relevant forms of use from the control of the

1275. With regard to this tendency in advanced trademark systems, see Peukert 2016, 415-418; Gangjee 2013, 43-47; Senftleben 2013b, 146-156; Vanovermeire 2009, 187-188; Senftleben 2009a, 45; Moskin 2004, 842; Fezer 2003, 457; Pollaud-Dulian 2001, 43; Strasser 2000, 375; Hughes 1999, 1006; Brown 1999, 1619; Dreyfuss 1990, 397.

trademark owner.[1276] Specific defences against infringement claims, however, only constitute appropriate preservation tools in the sense of public domain concepts that take account of freedom of use if they are reliable and robust to such an extent that artistic use becomes an 'easy case'[1277] in which non-infringement is found regularly. The various conditions surrounding the due cause defence and the descriptive and referential use defences in EU trademark law, however, complicate the invocation of these defences substantially and preclude the assumption that they effectively preserve a public domain space of artistic use.

Moreover, it is to be considered that both – inherent limits of exclusive rights and explicit exceptions that serve as defences – do not bar the acquisition of trademark rights. As a result of the grant of protection, the trademark owner will be able to influence or even dictate the communication process surrounding the protected sign. Commercial connotations may be added to the sign that reduce its value for cultural forms of use or even suppress its potential to serve as a reference point for open, dialogic communication in the literary and artistic domain. Given the predominance of the trademark proprietor, the communication concerning affected cultural expressions is no longer as open and free as it would have been in the absence of the grant of trademark rights. Hence, there is a qualitative difference between inherent limits of exclusive rights and specific defences on the one hand and the categorical exclusion of cultural signs from trademark protection on the other. An effective exclusion keeps signs free from trademark protection and does not provide an incentive for the attachment of marketing messages. This incentive is offered, however, when trademark protection is granted. Inherent limits of, and limited exceptions to, the exclusive rights of trademark owners are thus incapable of preserving cultural signs as part of an information commons that can freely be shaped and defined in the course of an open, dialogic communication process.[1278] The contribution of these legal mechanisms to the preservation of the public domain is limited in comparison with an effective exclusion from trademark protection.

In the light of these results of a scrutiny of trademark law on the basis of different public domain definitions, a clear hierarchy of preservation tools comes to the fore. From the perspective of the cultural imperative in copyright law, it is preferable to exclude cultural heritage signs categorically from trademark protection. This is the most effective strategy to preserve the public domain of cultural expressions and ensure the openness of the communication process surrounding these expressions in the artistic domain. A solution based on implicit or explicit limitations of exclusive rights only constitutes the second-best option. Even if a trademark system succeeds in

1276. Senftleben 2013a, 819.
1277. Benkler 1999, 362.
1278. Cf. Dusollier 2018, 180-183; Dusollier 2015, 167-168.

setting robust and reliable limits to exclusive rights, the fact remains that the trademark proprietor obtains the opportunity to remove cultural signs from the public domain and embark on the attachment of commercial marketing messages. The trademark proprietor is a privileged speaker in the communication arena. He has more impact on the communication process than other speakers because he can avail himself of exclusive rights to influence the perception of the affected sign. The adoption of limitations is thus less effective than the categorical denial of trademark rights.

The assessment is different, however, in the field of iconic trade symbols. Once a trade symbol has acquired cultural significance, it may be argued from the perspective of public domain enrichment that trademark protection should be revoked to broaden the reservoir of freely available source material for cultural follow-on innovation and allow unrestricted remix activities in the literary and artistic domain. Practically speaking, however, the termination of trademark rights because of cultural significance is beyond reach in the light of international protection standards. Moreover, the end of trademark protection would deprive the trade symbol of its *raison d'être*. After the sign has fallen into the public domain, its commercial meaning is likely to vanish because the trademark proprietor loses his dominant position in the communication process and the opportunity to maintain a specific brand image with complex lifestyle messages. As trade symbols are commercial creations, the ultimate loss of trademark meaning entails the risk of also losing important reference points for cultural follow-on innovation. Once the sign is no longer perceived as a commercial symbol, artists can no longer employ the sign to create a contrast between the world of art and the world of commerce. Hence, a peculiar situation arises where the loss of commercial meaning reduces the possibilities for artists to comment on societal conditions. Given this result, it is preferable not to revoke trademark protection when trademarks become iconic trade symbols with cultural significance. Instead, the cultural significance of the sign should be made available for artistic remix activities by developing reliable and robust inherent limits of, or exceptions to, trademark rights that support unauthorized metaphorical use of the expressive meaning of iconic trade symbols in literary and artistic productions. In this regard, the freedom of use approach to public domain preservation is thus preferable.

Chapter 9
Risk Reduction

The analysis of the corrosive effect of trademark protection for cultural signs in the preceding chapters has led to the insight that appropriate countermeasures are necessary to avoid an undesirable impediment of the cultural innovation cycle. Hence, the time has come to discuss the practical implementation of risk reduction instruments in trademark law. The following section 9.1 will discuss the categorical exclusion of trademark rights to cultural signs. The outright exclusion of trademark protection would prevent interferences with cultural follow-on innovation from the outset. Section 9.2 will address the less severe measure of limiting the scope of trademark rights with regard to use in the cultural domain. The spectrum of legislative solutions available for this latter approach ranges from the cultivation of inherent limits of exclusive rights (preventing the trademark owner from establishing prima facie infringement) to the development of robust defences that allow artists to rebut infringement arguments.

9.1 IMPLEMENTATION OF CATEGORICAL EXCLUSION OF CULTURAL SIGNS

A categorical exclusion of trademark rights to cultural signs would eliminate the problem of copyright/trademark protection overlaps altogether. However, it would also have a deep impact on current trademark registration practices, in particular in the field of fictional characters (cf. Chapter 1). Therefore, it is important to evaluate the implementation parameters of this far-reaching legislative measure. A first question arising from the foregoing analysis concerns the right point in time for the exclusion of trademark protection. In the case of cultural signs that have already entered the public domain, the answer to this question is straightforward. As the legislative measure serves the purpose of preserving the public domain status of a sign that is unencumbered by intellectual property rights (section 8.1.1), the exclusion of trademark rights must necessarily have effect *ex ante*. In the case of cultural signs that still enjoy copyright protection, the determination of the point in time for excluding trademark protection is less clear. The mere fact that trademark rights should not be available as a vehicle to prolong the copyright monopoly does not automatically determine the point in time for taking appropriate countermeasures. Trademark protection may be excluded categorically from the outset. Alternatively, trademark protection may be phased out after copyright expiry. Accordingly, the following section 9.1.1 discusses the choice between an *ex ante/ex post* solution in the case of contemporary creations, such as fictional characters.

The next point is the identification of a ground for refusal in trademark law that would ensure that the envisaged *ex ante/ex post* exclusion of cultural signs becomes operative in practice. In this context, the current reliance of trademark offices and courts on the basic requirement of distinctiveness to regulate access to trademark protection for cultural signs is problematic. In many cases, this practice allows the acquisition of trademark rights because cultural signs are found to be inherently distinctive with regard to goods or services that are unrelated to cultural productions, or because a cultural sign has acquired distinctiveness as a result of use (section 7.3.3). To achieve a robust, categorical exclusion of cultural signs from trademark protection, it is necessary to develop a ground for refusal that allows trademark offices and courts to deny the registration of cultural signs once and for all – regardless of whether the sign concerned is inherently distinctive or acquires distinctive character in consequence of use in trade (sections 7.4 and 8.4).[1279] Accordingly, sections 9.1.2 and 9.1.3 explore the potential of different registration requirements and grounds for refusal to serve as a basis for this categorical exclusion of cultural signs from trademark protection.

After the development of appropriate exclusion instruments, section 9.1.4 addresses the option of employing the international communication mechanism following from Article 6*ter* PC to universalize the ban on the acquisition of trademark rights to cultural signs. On the basis of Article 6*ter* PC, it might become possible to establish an international 'white list'[1280] of cultural expressions that have to be kept outside the trademark system. A summary of results concludes the discussion (section 9.1.5).

1279. Anemaet 2016, 331-332; Senftleben 2013a, 824-825.
1280. Cf. Van Woensel 2013, 376.

9.1.1 *Need for an Exclusion* Ex Ante

In the case of cultural heritage signs that belong to the public domain and are encumbered by intellectual property rights, the implementation of an effective, categorical ban on trademark rights, evidently, requires *ex ante* countermeasures: to preserve the sign's public domain status – in the strict sense of an absence of any intellectual property right (section 8.1.1) – an outright exclusion is necessary that prevents the acquisition of trademark rights from the outset. As concluded in section 8.4, there should be a possibility for trademark examiners and judges to foreclose the grant of trademark rights upfront by rejecting trademark applications that concern public domain material.

In respect of fictional characters and other contemporary creations in the field of literature and art, however, the situation is more complex. As these works still enjoy copyright protection and have not become part of the public domain yet, it is conceivable to permit cumulative copyright and trademark protection during the term of copyright protection and introduce an *ex post* solution that requires measures against trademark protection only at the very end of the term of copyright. Hence, the question arises whether it would be sufficient to put an end to trademark protection when copyright expires, or whether it is preferable to adopt an *ex ante* approach that excludes the acquisition of trademark rights from the outset, as in the case of cultural heritage signs. As a result, protection overlaps would never come into existence and no further action would be necessary when copyright protection finally expires.

Obviously, the horizontal application of a rule of *ex ante* prevention of trademark protection would lead to a consistent exclusion practice across the whole spectrum of cultural signs: the categorical exclusion of trademark rights from the outset would cover cultural signs that already entered the public domain (Mona Lisa scenario, section 5.2.1) and cultural signs that still enjoy copyright protection (Mickey Mouse scenario, section 5.2.3). Despite this advantage of horizontal application, one might be tempted to assume that in cases of contemporary creations, it is sufficient and preferable to put an end to trademark protection once copyright expires. This *ex post* solution minimizes the impact of the exclusion on trademark protection in practice. As long as copyright is available, the copyright owner remains free to transform a literary and artistic work into a trademark, obtain trademark rights and develop lucrative merchandising strategies.

Nonetheless, there are good reasons to strike at the root of the problem and opt for an *ex ante* solution that excludes the acquisition of trademark rights to contemporary cultural creations from the outset. As long as trademark law offers the prospect of trademark rights to cultural signs, the creative industry will embark on the use of contemporary cultural creations as identifiers of commercial source. If, following an *ex post* approach, trademark protection expires together with the copyright monopoly at the end of the term of copyright, this transformation of cultural signs into brands enhances the risk of consumer confusion (section 9.1.1.1). Moreover, the attachment of commercial marketing messages during the term of copyright is likely to reduce the potential of affected cultural creations to serve as reference points for open, dialogic communication in the artistic domain (section 9.1.1.2). The option of acquiring trademark rights during the term of copyright also reinforces the predominance of mainstream media productions and reduces the appetite of potential audiences for a broader spectrum of literary and artistic productions playing with the cultural creation at issue (section 9.1.1.3). From a practical perspective, it can be added that cumulative expiry rules, such as a rule that mandates the cumulative expiry of copyright and trademark protection at the end of the copyright term, have not survived in the past. They seem to constitute fragile safeguards against an artificial perpetuation of copyright exclusivity (section 9.1.1.4). An *ex post* rule of combined copyright and trademark expiry may also require the introduction of registration formalities that are prohibited in copyright law (section 9.1.1.5) or be qualified as an impermissible truncation of trademark registration or renewal terms (section 9.1.1.6). In sum, the alternative of an *ex ante* rule that precludes the acquisition of trademark rights from the outset is preferable (section 9.1.1.7).

9.1.1.1 Prevention of Consumer Confusion

As already indicated, the application of an *ex post* solution in the case of contemporary cultural creations – permitting protection overlaps during the period of copyright protection – will inevitably increase exit costs when the term of copyright finally expires. As trademark rights would only be excluded *ex post*, the regulation of copyright/trademark overlaps still provides a strong incentive for copyright owners to seek additional trademark protection during the term of copyright. In consequence, cultural creations would still be developed into powerful brands. Considering the long period of copyright protection, the risk of losing trademark protection at the end of the term is unlikely to have a deterrent effect on investment in cultural creations seeking to present cultural material as an identifier of commercial source.[1281] Hence, consumers would still be exposed to marketing campaigns aiming to educate them to perceive a cultural sign as a trademark. This, in turn, has its price when trademark protection – in line with the *ex post* approach – finally expires together with copyright. Once consumers have been taught to perceive a cultural sign as an identifier of commercial source in trade, this commercial meaning of the sign enhances the risk of consumer confusion. After the joint expiry of copyright and trademark protection, consumers will first have to learn that the cultural sign

1281. Cf. the discussion of the investment horizon in the field of literary and artistic productions by Poort/Theeuwes 2010, 142-143.

no longer refers to one individual commercial source. At least for a transition period, market transparency will be reduced (section 7.3.5.4).

An *ex ante* solution preventing the grant of trademark rights to cultural creations from the outset avoids these higher costs for society. Once it is made impossible to obtain trademark rights to contemporary cultural creations, the marketing of related products must necessarily be based on other indicators of commercial source. These other badges of origin – constituting no cultural creations but genuine trademarks (traditional word marks, e.g.) – will survive the expiry of copyright. When copyright protection comes to an end, consumers can then still base their purchasing decisions on these alternative source identifiers irrespective of the fact that the contemporary cultural creation as such has become free and third parties enjoy the freedom of offering remixes. Hence, the *ex ante* exclusion of trademark protection for cultural creations – the upfront denial of trademark rights – is an important precautionary measure against consumer confusion. From the outset, it discourages businesses from using cultural creations as trademarks. Instead, it requires the development of alternative identifiers of commercial source for the sale and promotion of cultural productions. As these alternative badges of origin constitute genuine trademarks, they survive the expiry of copyright protection and remain capable of ensuring market transparency.

9.1.1.2 Preservation of Artistic Discourse Potential

A further advantage of an *ex ante* solution – the denial of trademark rights to cultural material from the outset – lies in the reduction of the corrosive effect of commercial messages on the genuine cultural meaning of literary and artistic works. An *ex post* solution – permitting copyright/trademark overlaps during the term of copyright protection – inevitably causes harm: it imperils the process of defining and redefining literary and artistic works through use, reuse and remix in the cultural domain. As the acquisition of trademark rights to cultural creations remains possible under an *ex post* approach, it seems safe to assume that enterprises would still seek to develop cultural signs into brands by attaching commercial connotations, in particular messages relating to the origin and quality of goods or services, and advertising messages. These commercial messages reduce the artistic discourse potential of affected cultural creations (section 3.3.2.4). They interfere with the evolution of meanings and connotations in an open, dialogic cultural communication process (section 8.2.3.3).

9.1.1.3 Reduced Reinforcement of Mainstream Media Productions

With regard to the cultural communication process, it must also be considered that the focus on the prevention of an artificial extension of the copyright monopoly via trademark law can easily hide the fact that damage can also arise from the merchandising of cultural works as such. As Guy Pessach has argued, merchandising strengthens our attachment to mainstream media productions, narrows our horizon and, ultimately, reduces our appetite for alternative, independent productions:

> My only purpose is to show how broad intellectual property protection establishes a circular dynamic effect under which the cultural solidarity value of media products is leveraged and maintained by its related nonmedia commodified products. Such processes, especially when occurring in large-scale measures, tend to steer audience attention to a limited track of media products, thereby preventing consumers from being open and attentive to the contents of other types of media products that are not part of, and do not fit into, this corporate media dynamic. Consequently, alternative media products will have difficulties in reaching the attention of people who highly value commodified elements, regardless of the fact that these elements themselves are not related to the pure creative and communicative content of the media product.[1282]

Cumulative copyright and trademark protection is thus not only problematic when copyright protection expires and trademark rights become a vehicle to artificially prolong exclusive rights. Damage may already be done before. The grant of trademark rights during the term of copyright protection may spur merchandising tactics based on literary and artistic works.[1283] If cultural creations also become powerful brands, this marketing success is not unlikely to lead to continuous product diversification until consumers find themselves in a whole universe of 'nonmedia commodified products' in the sense of Pessach's critique which may shape their tastes in the area of media productions and reduce their appetite for alternatives and a broader spectrum of cultural creations:

> Just as Mickey Mouse, the cartoon character, promotes the t-shirt, the t-shirt of Mickey Mouse promotes and supports the solidarity value of Mickey Mouse, the cartoon character, within feature media products.[1284]

From this perspective, the exclusion of trademark rights at the end of the term of copyright comes too late: mainstream consumer tastes have already been reinforced during the period of copyright protection to such an extent that the final cumulative expiry of copyright and trademark protection is an insufficient compensation. Independent media productions with less merchandising potential simply have no chance to compete with the

1282. Pessach 2003, 1102-1103. See also Coombe/Herman 2001, 922.
1283. Cf. Coombe 2003, 1175-1176.
1284. Pessach 2003, 1101.

solidarity network of merchandising articles surrounding mainstream media productions.[1285]

Considering Bourdieu's sociological analysis of the field of literary and artistic production (section 3.3.1.1), it can be added that this bias in favour of mainstream media productions causes an imbalance in the ongoing fight between independent, autonomous and dependent, profit-oriented authors for predominance in the literary and artistic field. As explained above, the intellectual property system ought to be neutral in this power struggle (section 3.3.1.3). Hence, it is not advisable to encourage merchandising activities based on literary and artistic works by granting not only copyright but also trademark rights during the long period of copyright protection. Instead, it is preferable to exclude trademark protection *ex ante* – by denying trademark rights to cultural signs from the outset. In this way, additional incentives for intensified merchandising efforts going beyond the support offered by copyright protection itself are also excluded from the outset.

9.1.1.4 Fragility of Cumulative Expiry Rules

It is to be added that national experiences with rules of combined expiry for different types of intellectual property shed light on practical problems that also cast doubt upon the sustainability of an *ex post* correction of overlapping copyright and trademark protection at the moment of copyright expiry.[1286] Until December 2003, the Uniform Benelux Law on Designs and Models contained a rule of cumulative expiry of overlapping copyright and industrial design protection. Upon expiry of the term of sui generis industrial design rights in the Benelux, coexisting copyright protection lapsed as well unless a declaration of continued copyright entitlement was filed with the Benelux Office within a time period starting one year prior to expiry and ending three months thereafter.[1287] The declaration served the purpose of ensuring register transparency. It was registered and published to clarify that the extinction of an industrial design in the register, in this particular case, did not imply that copyright had expired as well.[1288]

The problem with this Benelux rule lay in the fact that, at the time, the term of sui generis industrial design protection under harmonized Benelux legislation amounted to a maximum of 15 years.[1289] Article 7(4) BC,

1285. Cf. Benkler 2003, 183-184; Coombe/Cohen 1999, 1052.

1286. Cf. the critical comments by Heymann 2013, 250-256, who bases her analysis on an analysis of U.S. case law.

1287. Articles 21(3) and 24 of the Benelux Drawings and Designs Law, as in force until 1 December 2003. Cf. CJEU, 20 October 2016, case C-169/15, Montis Design, paras 13-15; Van Gompel 2017, 69; Spoor/Verkade/Visser 2019, 115; Van Oerle/Hagemans 2000, 124-125.

1288. Van Oerle/Hagemans 2000, 125.

1289. In line with Article 10 of Directive 98/71/EC of the European Parliament and of the Council of 13 October 1998 on the legal protection of designs, the maximum term of

however, provides for an international minimum term of copyright protection for works of applied arts of 25 years. Thus, the Benelux rule of expiry of both copyright and industrial design protection after 15 years fell short of the international minimum standard in the area of copyright law.[1290] The possibility of depositing a declaration of continued copyright entitlement could not remedy this shortcoming because it raised another issue of compliance with international copyright law: the obligation to file a declaration with the office as a prerequisite for upholding copyright could be seen as a prohibited formality in the sense of Article 5(2) BC.[1291] Against this background, the Dutch Supreme Court had already declared the cumulative expiry rule inapplicable with regard to nationals of other Berne Union countries prior to its final abandonment.[1292] On 1 December 2003, the rule of combined expiry of copyright and industrial design protection in the Benelux was abolished altogether.[1293]

Similar developments can be observed in the UK. Prior to 31 July 2016, Section 52 of the UK Copyright, Designs and Patents Act 1988 contained a provision that confined the term of copyright protection to 25 years with regard to artistic works that had been used as the basis for industrially manufactured designs. The threshold for assuming industrial mass production was the manufacture of 50 articles.[1294] The legal mechanism applied to achieve the term reduction was a defence to infringement actions. After the end of a period of 25 years calculated from the end of the calendar year in which the industrially manufactured designs were first marketed, Section 52(2) ensured that the underlying artistic work 'may be copied by making articles of any description, or doing anything for the purpose of making articles of any description, and anything may be done in relation to articles so made, without infringing copyright in the work'. Competitors were thus free to use the artistic work as a design template for manufacturing articles at an industrial scale as well.[1295]

Introducing a 25-year term, Section 52(2) implemented the shorter term of protection for works of applied art that is permissible under Article 7(4) BC. At the same time, it approximated the period of copyright protection to the maximum term of protection that is available in the EU in respect of

sui generis industrial designs protection nowadays amounts to 25 years in the Benelux. See Article 3.14(2) of the Benelux Convention on Intellectual Property.

1290. Van Gompel 2017, 72-73.

1291. CJEU, 20 October 2016, case C-169/15, Montis Design, paras 38-41. Article 5(2) BC prohibits formalities with regard to 'the enjoyment and the exercise' of copyright. Cf. Van Gompel 2017, 73-75; Van Gompel 2011, 19-20 and 175-176, with regard to the category of renewal formalities.

1292. Dutch Supreme Court, 26 May 2000, case LJN AA5967, Cassina/Sedeti, *NJ* 2000, no. 671. Cf. Spoor/Verkade/Visser 2019, 115.

1293. Spoor/Verkade/Visser 2019, 115.

1294. Bently/Sherman/Gangjee/Johnson 2018, 815; Dinwoodie 2002, 510.

1295. Dinwoodie 2020, 29; Bently 2018, 218-219.

registered industrial designs. Article 10 DD provides for 'one or more periods [of protection] of five years each, up to a total term of 25 years from the date of filing'. As already indicated, Section 52 was abandoned in 2016.[1296] The reason for the abolition was the CJEU decision in *Flos* where the Court declared the harmonized 70-year term of copyright protection applicable to industrial designs.[1297] The CJEU also held that it was incompatible with EU law to render copyright protection unenforceable for a transitional period of 10 years or longer with regard to products manufactured on the basis of designs that had fallen into the public domain under domestic industrial design legislation prior to the implementation of the harmonized 70-year term.[1298] In the UK, *Flos* was understood to preclude the maintenance of Section 52.[1299]

Across the Atlantic, the discussion on cumulative expiry rules can be placed in the context of the 'doctrine of election' that evolved in the U.S. in the first half of the twentieth century. As Jeanne Fromer and Mark McKenna explain, the doctrine of election obliged creators of works of applied art to 'elect just one form of intellectual property protection, even if they would seem to qualify for multiple forms'.[1300] The obligation to choose one specific protection regime related to both the copyright/design patent overlap and the design patent/trademark overlap.[1301] The focus on just one intellectual property right was deemed necessary to avoid discrepancies with regard to the scope and term of protection. In particular, U.S. courts sought to preclude an extension of the monopoly following from the grant of design patent rights.[1302]

By the mid-twentieth century, however, the climate surrounding the election question changed because of the U.S. Supreme Court decision in *Mazer/Stein*. The case concerned statuettes which the plaintiff used as a basis for the mass production of lamps. Seeking to escape the verdict of copyright infringement, the defendants argued that the invocation of copyright – instead of a design patent – constituted misuse of copyright.[1303] The U.S. Supreme Court, however, disagreed. It held that:

> the patentability of the statuettes, fitted as lamps or unfitted, does not bar copyright as works of art. Neither the Copyright Statute nor any other says that because a thing is patentable it may not be copyrighted. We should not so hold.[1304]

1296. Bently/Sherman/Gangjee/Johnson 2018, 815-816.
1297. CJEU, 27 January 2011, case C-168/09, Flos, paras 40-41. See Article 1(1) TD.
1298. CJEU, *ibid.*, paras 62-65.
1299. Bently 2018, 223-225.
1300. Fromer/McKenna 2018, 203; Heymann 2013, 251-252.
1301. Fromer/McKenna 2018, 204.
1302. Fromer/McKenna 2018, 203-204; Du Mont/Janis 2018, 376-377.
1303. U.S. Supreme Court, 8 March 1954, Mazer/Stein, 347 U.S. 201, 206 (1954). Cf. Ginsburg 2018a, 303-306; Heymann 2013, 252.
1304. U.S. Supreme Court, 8 March 1954, Mazer/Stein, 347 U.S. 201, 217 (1954).

With the *Mazer/Stein* ruling as a compass, lower courts subsequently departed from the doctrine of election.[1305] The U.S. Court of Customs and Patent Appeals held in *Mogen David Wine* that:

> trademark rights, or rights under the law of unfair competition, which happen to continue beyond the expiration of a design patent, do not 'extend' the patent monopoly. They exist independently of it, under different law and for different reasons. The termination of either has no legal effect on the continuance of the other.[1306]

The abandonment of the doctrine of election, thus, brought in its wake the confirmation that trademark rights could survive the expiry of other intellectual property rights with a limited term of protection. The further decision in *In re Yardley* made it clear that existing copyright registrations did not bar the acquisition of design patent protection.[1307] Again, the rejection of the doctrine of election culminated in the confirmation that the protection periods of the two intellectual property regimes remained independent. According to the Court, the mere fact that 'the copyright will persist beyond the term of any design patent which may be granted does not provide a sound basis for rejecting appellant's design patent application'.[1308]

These national experiences indicate that once an intellectual property right is awarded, legislators and courts find it particularly difficult to synchronize the end of protection with the expiry of rights in another, overlapping protection regime. In the light of this result, it appears preferable from the perspective of the cultural imperative to avoid the grant of concurrent trademark rights and the evolution of protection overlaps from the outset. A rule of joint expiry of copyright and trademark protection seems too fragile to give sufficient reassurance that trademark offices and courts will put an end to the corrosive effect of overlapping trademark protection when copyright lapses.

9.1.1.5 Calculation of Copyright Term and Prohibition of Formalities

In addition, the discussion of experiences with rules of combined expiry in the preceding section sheds light on two problems arising from international copyright and trademark protection standards: first, a rule of cumulative expiry of trademark rights (together with copyright) raises issues of register

1305. Du Mont/Janis 2018, 378; Heymann 2013, 252-254; Mues 1974, 568-573.

1306. U.S. Court of Customs and Patent Appeals, 12 March 1964, In re Mogen David Wine Corporation, 328 F.2d 925, 930 (C.C.P.A. 1964). Cf. Heymann 2013, 253.

1307. U.S. Court of Customs and Patent Appeals, 28 March 1974, In re Yardley, 493 F.2d 1389, 1394 (C.C.P.A. 1974). Cf. Du Mont/Janis 2018, 378-380; Heymann 2013, 253-254; Mues 1974, 543-544.

1308. U.S. Court of Customs and Patent Appeals, *ibid.*, 1395. Cf. Fromer/McKenna 2018, 204.

transparency that may require the introduction of formalities that are prohibited under international copyright law. Second, the early expiry of trademark rights may be incompatible with the international guarantee of specific trademark protection intervals and renewal options (following section 9.1.1.6).

The first issue – prohibited formalities in international copyright law – arises from the need for trademark offices to ensure clarity about the termination of trademark rights as a result of copyright expiry. As Article 5(2) BC prohibits formalities in the field of copyright, it exempts copyright owners from the obligation to register their creations and other information that could allow the determination of the date of copyright expiry. As a result, a rule of cumulative copyright and trademark expiry would confront trademark offices with legal uncertainties resulting from the prohibition of formalities in copyright law.[1309] Copyright comes into being by virtue of the mere act of creation. The acquisition and maintenance of copyright does not depend on the fulfilment of registration and renewal requirements.[1310] In line with the international rules laid down in the Berne Convention, the term of copyright protection is the life of the author and fifty years after her death.[1311] The making available to the public or the work's creation may serve as alternative reference points for the calculation of the term in the case of film works and anonymous/pseudonymous works.[1312] Shorter periods of protection may apply to photographic works and works of applied art.[1313] National law may provide for longer terms, such as 70 years *post mortem auctoris*.[1314] In the case of works of joint authorship, the death of the last surviving author is decisive for the calculation of the term.[1315]

An office seeking to determine at which point in time the trademark registration of a cultural sign lapses in consequence of copyright expiry would thus have to consider a whole bundle of potentially complex rules.[1316] Additional difficulties arise from transition rules accompanying copyright term extensions and the interplay of national and international norms.[1317] In any case, trademark offices would have to ascertain the identity of the natural person who created the cultural sign in cases where the standard rule of a term based on the author's life applies. If information about the work's

1309. Article 5(2) BC.
1310. Van Gompel 2011, 18-20, 175-176 and 194-195.
1311. Article 7(1) BC.
1312. Article 7(2) and (3) BC.
1313. Article 7(4) BC. However, see the departure from a shorter term of protection for photographic works in Article 9 WCT.
1314. For instance, see Article 1(1) TD. Cf. CJEU, 27 January 2011, case C-168/09, Flos, paras 39-40. As to the term extension in the U.S., see U.S. Supreme Court, 15 January 2003, Eldred/Ashcroft, 537 U.S. 186, 202 (2003). Cf. Austin 2003, 163.
1315. Article 7bis BC.
1316. Cf. Liu 2013, 1450-1453.
1317. For instance, see CJEU, 20 October 2016, case C-169/15, Montis Design, paras 34-45. Cf. Van Gompel 2017, 72-75; Dusollier 2015, 144-149.

creator is provided in connection with a trademark registration,[1318] offices would still have to find reliable information on the author's death. As the expiry of trademark rights together with copyright is not in favour of the trademark proprietor, the office can hardly rely on (potentially incorrect) declarations made by the trademark proprietor in this regard, for instance in the context of registration renewals. In the absence of other mechanisms ensuring accurate information, the office would thus have to base the cancellation of cultural signs on its own research.[1319] A rule of *ex ante* denial of trademark protection for cultural signs, by contrast, would not give rise to comparable problems. It would not impose the burden of calculating the term of copyright protection on trademark offices. As it would prevent the acquisition of trademark rights upfront, the copyright issue of prohibited formalities would not arise in the first place.

9.1.1.6 Truncation of Trademark Registration or Renewal Term

The second issue – a truncated term of trademark protection – arises from international standards in the field of trademark law. Article 18 TRIPS states that the initial registration of a trademark, and each renewal of registration, shall be for a term of no less than seven years. It also states that the registration of a trademark shall be renewable indefinitely. Article 13(5) STLT adds that the duration of the initial period of a trademark registration, and the duration of each renewal period, shall be ten years. A rule of combined expiry of copyright and trademark protection may be incompatible with these standards. The expiry of trademark rights at the end of the term of copyright may put an end to trademark protection prior to a registration or renewal interval of seven or ten years. It would also deprive the trademark proprietor of the possibility of indefinite renewal.

The above example of a former Benelux rule of cumulative expiry of copyright and industrial design protection (section 9.1.1.4) sheds light on the

1318. The introduction of a requirement to provide information on the natural person who created a trademark seems possible in the light of registration practices in the area of patent law where information on the inventor of a technical solution can be a standard element of the patent registration. For instance, see Arts. 60(1), 62 and, in particular, Article 81 of the European Patent Convention 2000. It is to be noted, however, that current international standards in the area of trademark registrations do not offer room for indications concerning the creator of a trademark. Article 3(4) of the Singapore Treaty on the Law of Trademarks may even be understood to prohibit the adoption of this additional element as a prerequisite for trademark applications.

1319. The debate on the problem of orphan works in copyright law has shown how burdensome and costly search obligations with regard to the author of a literary and artistic work can be. Cf. Van Gompel 2007, 669; Sherman 2007, 13. For an example of minimum search standards in the area of orphan works, see Article 3(2) and the Annex of Directive 2012/28/EU of the European Parliament and of the Council of 25 October 2012 on Certain Permitted Uses of Orphan Works.

conflict with international minimum standards that may result from an early termination of the term of protection. In the case of the Benelux system, the problem was an early termination of copyright protection relating to works of applied art – falling short of the international minimum term of 25 years that is laid down in Article 7(4) BC. If trademark rights are first granted in an *ex post* expiry system and later cancelled because of the expiry of copyright, a similar conflict arises with regard to the international guarantee of protection terms following from the registration or renewal of trademarks. As *ex post* exclusion systems do not bar trademark registrations of cultural signs from the outset, it is possible to obtain an initial trademark registration of a sign with cultural significance. Moreover, several renewals may take place before the end of copyright finally puts an end to trademark protection. *Ex post* expiry systems may thus be deemed incompatible with Article 18 TRIPS and Article 13(5) STLT because they terminate trademark registrations regardless of whether the initial registration term, or a subsequent renewal term, is still running. A further conflict arises from the fact that *ex post* exclusion systems deprive the trademark proprietor of the possibility to renew the trademark registration indefinitely.

These potential conflicts with international trademark law need not be insurmountable hurdles. In spite of the international minimum standards set forth in Article 18 TRIPS and Article 13(5) STLT, it is generally accepted that trademark rights may be cancelled in certain circumstances. For instance, Article 19 TRIPS provides for the cancellation of an existing trademark registration in case of non-use. In the context of the international rules on *telle quelle* protection, Article 6*quinquies*(B) No. 2 and 3 PC reflects the possibility of cancelling a trademark registration when the sign concerned has become generic, or when it is contrary to morality or public order.[1320]

Arguably, a cultural sign that is registered as a trademark may be regarded as having become generic from a cultural perspective once copyright protection expires.[1321] In trademark law, however, this assumption may appear as an inconsistent legal fiction with regard to the basic origin function of affected trademarks (cf. section 8.3.2). The expiry of copyright does not deprive a cultural sign of distinctive character that has been acquired in years of use as a trademark. In particular, copyright expiry does not automatically change the perception of consumers who have learned to understand a cultural sign as an indication of commercial origin. In line with the rules of copyright law, however, the fact that the cultural sign has entered the public domain and ought to become freely available for all may be seen

1320. Ng-Loy 2018, 147-164; Kunz-Hallstein 2006, 487; Beier 1992, 243; Ladas 1975, 1211-1240; Bodenhausen 1969, 113-119.

1321. For a more detailed discussion of the need for a concept of cultural genericity in trademark law, see Dreyfuss 1990, 397.

as a sufficiently strong reason for a normative correction.[1322] Assuming genericity after copyright expiry, it becomes possible to bring trademark law in line with the rule of a limited term of protection in copyright law. The cancellation option reflected in Article 6*quinquies*(B) No. 2 PC could then serve as a vehicle to implement this legal fiction in trademark law.

Alternatively, it could be assumed that the continuation of trademark protection after copyright expiry would lead to a conflict with principles of morality and public order. If the rule of a limited term of copyright protection is qualified as a crucial element of public order (section 9.1.2.4),[1323] an attempt to bypass this rule by insisting on coexisting trademark protection could be sufficient to justify the cancellation of trademark protection. The option to invalidate trademark rights to safeguard public order is reflected in Article 6*quinquies*(B) No. 3 PC.

Doubts about compliance with Article 18 TRIPS and Article 13(5) STLT may thus be dispelled. Nonetheless, it becomes apparent that an *ex post* exclusion of trademark protection at the moment of copyright expiry may be exposed to allegations of incompliance with international standards regulating intervals and renewals of trademark protection.[1324] An *ex ante* system denying the grant of trademark rights from the outset is more consistent and preferable from this perspective. In an *ex ante* system, trademark rights to cultural signs would never be granted. By definition, compliance questions triggered by the early termination of an initial term of trademark registration, or subsequent renewal terms, would not arise. The question of depriving trademark owners of the possibility of indefinite renewal would never become relevant. As no trademark right is granted in the first place, the end of protection as a result of copyright expiry would not give rise to speculations about a violation of Article 18 TRIPS or Article 13(5) STLT.

9.1.1.7 *Ex Ante* Exclusion Preferable

On balance, the adoption of an *ex ante* system that excludes the acquisition of trademark rights to cultural material from the outset has several advantages. In comparison with an *ex post* system granting trademark rights first and putting an end to these rights when coexisting copyright protection expires, an *ex ante* system:

– does not offer the prospect of trademark protection for cultural signs. Therefore, it does not provide incentives for investment in cultural signs seeking to educate consumers to perceive a cultural sign as an

1322. EFTA Court, 6 April 2017, case E-5/16, Municipality of Oslo ('Vigeland'), para. 66.
1323. For case law pointing in this direction, see EFTA Court, *ibid.*, para. 96.
1324. Cf. Ohly 2019, 332, who sees no room for justifying an *ex post* termination of trademark rights if the rights owner enjoyed cumulative protection during the term of copyright.

indication of commercial source. An *ex post* system, by contrast, would offer the prospect of trademark protection for the relatively long period of copyright protection. Accordingly, it provides incentives for adding a source-identifying function to cultural material. This, in turn, would enhance the costs for society when trademark protection finally comes to an end together with copyright protection. It enhances the risk of consumer confusion;

- avoids incentives for the attachment of commercial meanings to cultural signs. If trademark rights are not available for signs with cultural significance, investment in the development of the sign as a commercial symbol becomes less secure. Under an *ex post* approach, enterprises enjoying cumulative copyright and trademark protection are likely to develop cultural signs into brands by attaching commercial connotations, in particular messages relating to the origin and quality of goods or services, and advertising messages. If trademark protection is denied from the outset, this blurring of the sign's cultural dimension (and reduction of the sign's potential for dialogic communication in the artistic domain) is less likely to occur in the first place;
- reduces the incentive for rights owners to transform cultural signs into powerful brands for merchandising purposes. If trademark rights are unavailable from the outset, cultural creations are less likely to become tools for the marketing of merchandising articles that strengthen consumers' attachment to mainstream media productions and reduce their appetite for alternatives and a broader spectrum of cultural creations;
- avoids the adoption of an *ex post* system that is unlikely to offer a sustainable long-term solution in the light of experiences with past national rules of cumulative expiry of intellectual property rights;
- does not impose the burden on trademark offices to ascertain the end of the term of copyright protection in the case of cultural signs. Under an *ex post* system, trademark offices would have to monitor the term of copyright protection in order to determine the expiry of trademark protection. For this purpose, they would have to apply the complex rules of copyright law on the calculation of the term of protection. They would also have to carry out searches with regard to the death of all authors of cultural signs in the register;
- avoids the risk of violating the international prohibition of copyright formalities in Article 5(2) BC and the risk of incompliance with international trademark law arising from the fact that a rule of joint copyright/trademark expiry may truncate trademark registration or renewal terms, and thwart the trademark rule of indefinite renewal.

Hence, *ex ante* systems are preferable. There are substantial reasons to avoid the acquisition of trademark rights to cultural material upfront.[1325] Signs with cultural significance should be kept outside the trademark protection regime from the outset. This means that it is possible to follow a harmonized approach: in the case of cultural heritage signs that belong to the public domain and are encumbered by intellectual property rights, it is self-evident that an exclusion *ex ante* is necessary to preserve the sign's public domain status (section 8.1.1). For the reasons given in the preceding sections, an *ex ante* exclusion is also preferable when it comes to contemporary cultural creations, such as fictional characters, which still enjoy copyright protection and have not become part of the public domain yet. The present analysis, thus, paves the way for a harmonized exclusion practice across the whole spectrum of cultural signs: the exclusion of trademark rights from the outset should cover cultural signs that already entered the public domain (Mona Lisa scenario, section 5.2.1). However, it should also cover signs that still enjoy copyright protection (Mickey Mouse scenario, section 5.2.3).

9.1.2 ***Exclusion Instruments***

After clarifying that an *ex ante* exclusion system is preferable with regard to both cultural heritage signs and contemporary cultural creations, the question arises which legal instruments are available to achieve the desired outright exclusion of trademark protection across the whole spectrum of cultural signs. Does current trademark law provide for grounds for refusal that could be employed for this purpose?

Considering the critical remarks about the basic requirement of distinctiveness that have already been made above (section 7.3.3), it does not come as a surprise that a refusal based on a lack of distinctive character can hardly be deemed sufficient in this context. An exclusion of cultural material from trademark protection because of missing distinctiveness is not reliable and robust enough to achieve a lasting exclusionary effect (section 9.1.2.1). An exclusion based on a conflict with public order or morality, by contrast, would effectively bar trademark protection even if distinctive character has been acquired in consequence of continuous use in trade (section 9.1.2.2). Furthermore, both – subjective morality criteria (section 9.1.2.3) and objective public order criteria (section 9.1.2.4) – would allow judges to openly express cultural concerns that support the denial of trademark protection. They would no longer be obliged to hide behind conventional trademark criteria for assessing a sign's distinctiveness.

The practical implementation of the required morality and public order concept, however, raises additional questions. As trademark offices and

1325. Cf. Calboli 2014a, 32-34; Raue 2010, 82.

courts can hardly be expected to embark on an in-depth analysis of the artistic merits of a sign for which trademark protection is sought, it becomes necessary to explore the potential of the originality test in copyright law to serve as a compass for identifying cultural signs that have to be kept free in the light of applicable public order and morality criteria. Given the low threshold for obtaining copyright following from the elasticity of the originality test, this examination brings situations into focus where a distinctive sign attracts copyright protection accidentally even though it has specifically been devised to serve as a trademark (section 9.1.2.5). In addition, specific problems arise in trademark systems which do not provide for public order and morality as absolute grounds for refusal. The U.S. trademark system can serve as an example (section 9.1.2.6). A discussion of compliance of the proposed strategy for implementing an outright exclusion of trademark rights with international law concludes the analysis (section 9.1.2.7).

9.1.2.1 Refusal Based on Lack of Distinctiveness Insufficient

For a sign to constitute a trademark, it must be capable of distinguishing the goods or services of one undertaking from those of other undertakings.[1326] Signs that do not fulfil this basic eligibility criterion, such as non-distinctive, descriptive and generic signs,[1327] remain outside the protection system. In principle, the basic requirement of distinctive character can thus have an exclusionary effect. A cultural sign that lacks distinctive character is not eligible for trademark protection and will remain unencumbered by trademark rights. However, a cultural sign that is not inherently distinctive may acquire the capacity to distinguish goods or services as a result of use in trade.[1328] This additional rule destabilizes the exclusionary effect of the distinctiveness requirement: trademark protection relating to cultural signs may result from marketing efforts that educate consumers to perceive a formerly non-distinctive, descriptive or generic sign as a reference to one particular commercial source.[1329] Once the required link is established in the

1326. Article 15(1) TRIPS.

1327. These categories of signs ineligible for trademark protection are reflected in the absolute grounds for refusal of many countries. See the various contributions to Senftleben 2012b. See also the international regulation of *telle quelle* protection in Article 6quinquies(B) No. 2 and 6quinquies(A)(1) Paris Convention. Pflüger 2011, 235-241; Kunz-Hallstein 2006, 487; Beier 1992, 243; Ladas 1975, 1211-1240; Bodenhausen 1969, 113-119.

1328. Article 15(1) TRIPS; Article 4(4) TMD; Article 7(3) EUTMR. Nonetheless, national law may exclude the acquisition of trademark rights through use in trade with regard to certain types of signs lacking distinctive character. U.S. trademark law, for instance, does not offer the possibility of acquiring distinctive character through use in the case of generic signs. Cf. Beebe 2012, 82-83; Ramsey 2003, 1121-1122.

1329. Cf. Ohly 2008, 217, who describes this risk with regard to industrial designs and works of applied art.

minds of consumers, the sign may be protected as a trademark. The exclusion from trademark protection is thus *conditional* on the absence of acquired distinctiveness.

Considering the market transparency rationale underlying trademark law (section 4.2.1), it may be said that trademark law seeks to recognize the marketing efforts made by an individual trader and protect consumers against confusion by providing for the possibility of acquiring distinctiveness through use in trade. The moment a cultural sign is perceived as a reference to one particular commercial source, it seems to become necessary, from this perspective, to inhibit other traders from using that particular sign.[1330] In consequence, the exclusion of cultural signs from trademark protection that results from the basic protection requirement of distinctiveness is not absolute. It depends on how trademark offices and courts determine whether distinctive character has been acquired as a result of continuous use of a cultural sign in trade.

Recognizing the public policy dimension of the basic requirement of distinctiveness, the CJEU explicitly placed the rejection of signs lacking distinctive character in the context of a need to keep these signs free for all. In *Windsurfing Chiemsee*, the Court explained that absolute grounds for refusal concerning descriptive signs served the public interest, insofar as:

> descriptive signs or indications relating to the categories of goods or services in respect of which registration is applied for may be freely used by all, including as collective marks or as part of complex or graphic marks.[1331]

Given this need to keep descriptive signs available, the Court delineated the scope of the respective absolute grounds for refusal rather broadly (section 5.1). It held that, for the registration of a geographical name to be prohibited, it was not necessary to give evidence of a real, current or serious need to leave the indication free. By contrast, it was sufficient that the geographical name was liable to be used as an indication of geographical origin with regard to a certain category of goods or services in the future.[1332] The particular importance which the CJEU attaches to the requirement of distinctive character as a means of preventing the acquisition of trademark rights to certain categories of signs also comes to the fore in the Court's jurisprudence on non-traditional trademarks. In *Henkel*, the Court pointed out that average consumers were not:

1330. For a critique of the circularity in this line of argument, see Ramsey 2003, 1150; Denicola 1982, 170.

1331. CJEU, 4 May 1999, cases C-108/97 and C-109/97, Windsurfing Chiemsee, para. 25.

1332. CJEU, *ibid.*, paras 35-37.

in the habit of making assumptions about the origin of goods based on the shape of their packaging, in the absence of any graphic or word element.[1333]

Therefore, it could prove more difficult to establish distinctive character in the case of product packaging for which trademark protection is sought. Only a trademark which significantly departed from the norm or customs of the sector and thereby fulfilled the function of an indication of commercial origin was not devoid of distinctive character.[1334] In the above-described *Libertel* decision (section 4.2.2.2), the Court used the same line of argument with regard to colour per se.[1335] Distinctiveness without any prior use was inconceivable save in exceptional circumstances, and particularly where the number of goods or services for which the mark was claimed was very restricted and the relevant market very specific.[1336]

In these decisions on non-traditional marks, the CJEU seems to require proof for the acquisition of distinctive character as a result of use in trade to keep these signs outside the trademark system and safeguard the public domain.[1337] As explained in section 4.2.2.2, the Court acknowledged in *Libertel* that there was a public interest in not unduly restricting the availability of colours for competitors.[1338] However, it is doubtful whether this effort to keep signs available on the basis of the requirement of distinctiveness is sufficient. While this is not intended, the jurisprudence of the CJEU may encourage marketing campaigns based on product packaging or colour per se – marketing efforts that aim to change the perception of consumers.[1339] The more often the public is confronted with a shape mark or abstract colour mark, the more alert it will be to the fact that, besides standard word and figurative marks, shapes and colour per se may also

1333. CJEU, 12 February 2004, case C-218/01, Henkel/DPMA, para. 52; CJEU, 8 April 2003, cases C-53/01 to C-55/01, Linde and others, para. 48.
1334. CJEU, 12 February 2004, case C-218/01, Henkel/DPMA, para. 49.
1335. CJEU, 6 May 2003, case C-104/01, Libertel, para. 65.
1336. CJEU, *ibid.*, para. 66.
1337. The hurdle to be surmounted, however, need not necessarily be high. For instance, see German Federal Court of Justice, 9 July 2009, case I ZB 88/07, 'ROCHER-Kugel', *GRUR* 2010, 138, para. 43: 'In the case of a shape mark having characteristics that depart from the basic shape of the type of goods concerned, there is, as a general rule, no reason to assume that the threshold for acquiring distinctive character is particularly high.' Accordingly, the fact that 62% of the relevant public recognized the shape mark was deemed sufficient. With regard to colour per se, the German Federal Patent Court held that, in a small market segment, a recognition of the color mark by 50% of the relevant public is sufficient in light of a considerable market share of the applicant on that particular market. See German Federal Patent Court, 9 December 2008, case 33 W (pat) 57/07, 'Farbe Lila', *GRUR* 2010, 71.
1338. CJEU, 6 May 2003, case C-104/01, Libertel, para. 55.
1339. Ramsey 2003, 1150. Cf. also Denicola 1982, 170; McKenna 2007, 1899; Lemley/McKenna 2010, 440; Senftleben 2013a, 812-813; Anemaet 2020, 188-189 and 211-212.

indicate the commercial source of goods and services. The CJEU may thus have to revise its own assumptions about the distinctiveness of shapes and colour per se in the near future. Arguably, the assumption of consumers not being 'in the habit' of perceiving signs of this type as a badge of origin loses power of persuasion with every trader who succeeds in linking a specific shape or colour with her enterprise as the origin of goods or services in the minds of consumers.[1340]

Similar problems arise when the basic requirement of distinctiveness is employed as a vehicle to ensure that signs with cultural significance remain free from trademark protection. In the field of signs belonging to the public domain, the *Mona Lisa* decision of the German Federal Patent Court can serve as an example. The case concerned an attempt to register the famous Leonardo da Vinci's painting as a trademark. Rejecting this trademark application, the German Federal Patent Court held that the applicant had failed to establish the requisite distinctiveness. Because the painting was frequently used by third parties in advertising, the public would regard the Mona Lisa as a mere advertising instrument rather than as an indication of source.[1341] The Court also held that, because of frequent use in advertising, the painting had become customary in established trade practices.[1342] However, the Court was unwilling to accept that the registration of the Mona Lisa was contrary to public policy or accepted principles of morality. In the Court's view, the appropriation of the Mona Lisa on the basis of trademark law would not violate the principle that cultural expressions should remain freely available for the public after the expiry of copyright protection. The additional argument of a conflict with public policy or accepted principles of morality was thus rejected.[1343]

A similar pattern arose in the *Nachtwacht* (Night Watch) decision of the Court of Appeals of The Hague. The case concerned an application to register the famous painting of Rembrandt van Rijn as a trademark for the marketing of the chemical element strontium. Despite the fact that use of the Night Watch in respect of this chemical product seems quite exotic, the Court arrived at the conclusion that the painting could not be deemed inherently distinctive. It lent weight to the fact that the Benelux Office for Intellectual

---

1340. Given the widespread recognition of Milka lilac (EUTM no. 000031336) and Deutsche Telekom magenta (EUTM no. 000212787) as abstract colour marks in the EU, it may already be asked whether it is still correct to deny inherent distinctiveness in the case of eccentric colours, even though there is increased consumer awareness that colour may serve as an indication of commercial source. UPS brown (EUTM no. 000962076) constitutes an additional example indicating that an abstract colour may serve as a source identifier, even if it is much less exceptional.

1341. German Federal Patent Court, 25 November 1997, case 24 W (pat) 188/96, Mona Lisa, *GRUR* 1998, 1021.

1342. German Federal Patent Court, *ibid.*, 1023. For case comments, see Senftleben 2010a, 102-104; Assaf 2009, 5; Ohly 2008, 206; Klinkert/Schwab 1999, 1067; Nordemann 1997, 389.

1343. German Federal Patent Court, *ibid.*, 1023.

Property had demonstrated frequent use of the Night Watch as a decorative element on various goods.[1344] On this basis, the Court concluded that the average consumer of strontium would immediately recognize a reproduction of the Night Watch on the packaging of strontium as one of the most famous paintings of the world and fail to understand that the sign was intended to indicate the commercial origin of the goods. Instead, the consumer would perceive the sign as a mere decoration.[1345] As the German Federal Patent Court in *Mona Lisa*, the Court of Appeals of The Hague saw no need to base its rejection of trademark rights not only on a lack of distinctiveness but also on a conflict with *ordre public*. The Benelux Office for Intellectual Property had explicitly invoked this additional ground for refusal.[1346] Nonetheless, the Court refrained from a discussion of a conflict with public policy or accepted principles of morality even though it was fully aware that a denial of rights because of a lack of distinctive character would leave open the backdoor of acquiring distinctiveness – and trademark protection – in consequence of use in the course of trade.[1347]

The rejection of public policy and principles of morality as further grounds for refusal in *Mona Lisa* and *Nachtwacht* has far-reaching consequences. The exclusion of cultural heritage signs because of a lack of distinctive character following from the painting's widespread use in advertising is weak because cultural signs can acquire distinctive character as a result of use in trade (section 7.3.3).[1348] The decisions of the German Federal Patent Court and the Court of Appeals of The Hague, thus, offer the chance of overcoming the registration obstacle through intensive use in product marketing and advertising. Once consumers have been taught to perceive the Mona Lisa and the Night Watch as source identifiers referring to the applicant's enterprise, a registration of the famous paintings becomes possible. Furthermore, the assessment of distinctive character may differ from trademark examiner to trademark examiner. The verdict of a lack of distinctive character in the Benelux, for instance, did not prevent the EUIPO from assuming inherent distinctive character and granting EU-wide trademark rights to the Night Watch for the sale of strontium.[1349] An exclusion

---

1344. Court of Appeals of The Hague, 29 August 2017, case 200.205.771/01, ECLI:NL:GHDHA:2017:2446, Chiever/Benelux-Organisatie voor de Intellectuele Eigendom ('Nachtwacht'), para. 12.
1345. Court of Appeals of The Hague, *ibid.*, para. 12.
1346. Court of Appeals of The Hague, *ibid.*, para. 1.4.
1347. Court of Appeals of The Hague, *ibid.*, paras 8-9.
1348. Nonetheless, Basire 2018, 435, prefers a solution based on the requirement of distinctiveness and the assumption that consumers will perceive cultural signs as descriptive or decorative product elements. This solution, however, does not address the destabilizing effect of the possibility to acquire distinctiveness through continuous use in trade.
1349. EUTM no. 016613903. As the CJEU, 6 September 2018, case C-488/16P, Bundesverband Souvenir - Geschenke – Ehrenpreise ('Neuschwanstein'), para. 72, pointed out, the EU trademark system is 'an autonomous system with its own set of objectives and

based on a conflict with public policy and principles of morality would be more robust. Proof of the acquisition of distinctive character through use is not sufficient to surmount this registration hurdle. In contrast to a refusal based on a lack of distinctiveness, the rejection of trademark rights on the ground that the application is contrary to public policy or accepted principles of morality leads to an outright exclusion – irrespective of whether the painting is distinctive or not. Instead of following this secure route, the German Federal Patent Court and the Court of Appeals of The Hague deemed it sufficient to rely on the basic requirement of distinctive character. Hence, they failed to permanently eliminate the risk of a removal of the Mona Lisa and the Night Watch from the public domain.

With regard to contemporary cultural creations, similar conclusions have already been drawn above (section 7.3.3). In *Marlene Dietrich*, the German Federal Court of Justice denied distinctiveness with regard to books, magazines, photographs, posters, CDs, DVDs, musical performances and film productions on the ground that the photograph of the actress lacked the capability of indicating commercial source. In respect of these goods and services, the public would perceive it as a mere indication of product characteristics.[1350] This solution of the case has its price. Relying on descriptiveness as a ground for refusal, the Court did not rule out the possibility of the Marlene Dietrich photograph becoming distinctive with regard to goods and services related to the life and work of the actress at a later stage.[1351] Moreover, the Court held that the portrait photograph was inherently distinctive with regard to merchandising articles, such as scarves, hats, shirts and shoes.[1352]

In the *Anne Frank* cases, the Court of Appeals of Brussels followed a similar line of argument. As the goods and services in question – books, films and guided tours – were directly connected with Anne Frank's writings, the Court held that the public would not perceive the signs 'The Diary of Anne Frank' and 'The Secret Annex' as identifiers of commercial source.[1353] While emphasizing the inaptness of the signs to distinguish books, films and guided tours related to Anne Frank's hiding place and writings, however, the Court acknowledged that a trademark registration of book titles was possible in

---

rules peculiar to it; it applies independently of any national system.' Hence, the EUIPO was not bound to follow the decision on distinctiveness taken by the Court of Appeals of Brussels on the basis of the harmonized Benelux trademark system.

1350. German Federal Court of Justice, 24 April 2008, case I ZB 21/06, Marlene-Dietrich-Bildnis, paras 12-15.

1351. German Federal Court of Justice, 24 April 2008, case I ZB 21/06, Marlene-Dietrich-Bildnis, para. 17.

1352. German Federal Patent Court, *ibid.*, para. 8.1-8.2 and 19-22. See also the confirmation of this point in German Federal Court of Justice, 31 March 2010, case I ZB 62/09, Marlene-Dietrich-Bildnis II, paras 20-28.

1353. Court of Appeals of Brussels, 3 October 2013, cases 2013/7132 and 2013/7133, Anne Frank Foundation/Benelux Office for Intellectual Property, para. 6 and 10.

respect of goods and services that are independent of the works they identify.[1354] The Court also conceded that a trademark registration in respect of merchandising articles was conceivable.[1355] Moreover, the decision contains a separate section discussing whether 'The Diary of Anne Frank' and 'The Secret Annex' had acquired distinctive character vis-à-vis books, films and guided tours through use in the course of trade.[1356]

Hence, the same problem arises that has already been identified in the area of non-traditional types of marks where the CJEU assumes that consumers are not 'in the habit' of perceiving shapes or colour per se as indications of commercial origin unless the applicant succeeds in providing sufficient evidence of distinctiveness acquired through use. While this jurisprudence seems intended to keep certain categories of signs – non-traditional marks in the decisions of the CJEU, signs with high cultural significance in the described *Mona Lisa*, *Night Watch*, *Marlene Dietrich* and *Anne Frank* decisions – free from trademark protection, the use of the requirement of distinctive character for this purpose may have the opposite effect. Enterprises may regard the prospect of acquiring trademark rights as a result of use in trade as an invitation to invest in marketing and advertising activities based on the very signs which the courts want to keep free. They may strive to make a cultural symbol part of the trademark experience they are offering to consumers. The mere possibility of acquiring trademark rights in consequence of use may be sufficient to support business activities that lead to the registration of cultural signs as trademarks instead of putting an end to attempts to obtain trademark rights to cultural expressions.[1357] The fact that artworks often have particularly rich and positive connotations may further encourage branding strategies targeting cultural signs. The enhanced value to be gained once trademark protection is acquired allows bigger investments than in regular cases of brand development (section 8.2.3.1). The prospect of acquiring trademark rights through use in trade may thus lead to marketing campaigns seeking to exploit positive cultural connotations.[1358] Developments in the Netherlands confirm that enterprises may have a strong interest in the exploitation of signs belonging to the cultural heritage. In the *Nachtwacht* case before the Court of Appeals of The Hague, it was explicitly pointed out that the registration initiative had been started as a test case for several clients with an interest in clarifying whether they were free to adopt iconic artworks as trademarks.[1359] Hence, concerns about industry initiatives

1354. Court of Appeals of Brussels, *ibid.*, para. 5.
1355. Court of Appeals of Brussels, *ibid.*, para. 5.
1356. Court of Appeals of Brussels, *ibid.*, para. 8.
1357. EFTA Court, 6 April 2017, case E-5/16, Municipality of Oslo ('Vigeland'), para. 75.
1358. The EFTA Court, *ibid.*, para. 65, explicitly recognized this risk of freeriding following from 'commercial greed'.
1359. Court of Appeals of The Hague, 29 August 2017, case 200.205.771/01, ECLI:NL:GH-DHA:2017:2446, Chiever/Benelux-Organisatie voor de Intellectuele Eigendom ('Nachtwacht'), para. 4.

aiming at the exploitation of positive cultural connotations are not unfounded.[1360]

The requirement of a lack of distinctive character can hardly prevent this particular form of freeriding (section 8.2.3.1). It does not avoid the acquisition of trademark rights in situations where an enterprise employs a cultural symbol as a figurehead for its product marketing to take advantage of the positive connotations which the cultural symbol already has. On the contrary, it rewards this trademark acquisition strategy by granting trademark rights once distinctive character follows from continuous use in trade. With their reliance on the basic requirement of distinctive character in cases involving cultural material, courts turn a blind eye to this form of freeriding on positive cultural connotations that may spur investment in the use of cultural signs as brand elements.

In addition, it is to be considered that the requirement of distinctiveness as a basic threshold for the acquisition of trademark rights fails to cover the entire spectrum of cultural public domain material. The *Mona Lisa* case of the German Federal Patent Court concerned a famous cultural symbol belonging to mankind's universal cultural heritage. In the light of the popularity of the painting and its widespread use in advertising, the Court could reject the registration attempt on the grounds that the sign had become a customary marketing tool and constituted a non-distinctive, generic sign. In *Nachtwacht*, the recognition of the sign as a famous part of mankind's universal cultural heritage allowed the Court of Appeals of The Hague to develop a similar argument. In the case of cultural material that is not well known, however, this line of argument is not available.[1361] For example, the registration of a culturally important but not widely known melody taken from a classical piece of music could hardly be rejected based on the argument that the sign has been used so frequently in a commercial context that consumers are unlikely to perceive it as a reference to an individual commercial source.[1362] By contrast, the assumption of inherent distinctiveness seems inescapable when use of the melody for marketing purposes is new for the consuming public. When an exclusive link between the sign and an individual commercial source can be established in the minds of consumers, it makes no difference from a trademark perspective whether an

1360. Cf. Curtin 2018, 962-963; Litman 1999, 1718.

1361. Vgl. zu ähnlichen Zweifeln an den durch das BPatG aufgestellten Klinkert/Schwab 1999, 1067 (1068).

1362. Examples of this kind are not of a theoretical nature. In Germany, for instance, the beer producer Licher has consistently used 'Solveig's Song' from Edvard Grieg's 'Peer Gynt Suite' in advertising since the 90s. See https://www.youtube.com/watch?v=dfGGjk1QEeM. Ohly 2008, 206, gives the additional example of Kenneth J. Alford's 'Colonel Bogey March' which German consumers are likely to associate with the herbal digestive 'Underberg' as a result of continuous use in trade. See https://www.underberg.com/en/.

enterprise develops its own melody for advertising purposes or uses a pre-existing melody taken from the classical public domain repertoire.

Moreover, the requirement of distinctive character may fail to cover the entire spectrum of goods and services. As the above-described outcome of the *Marlene Dietrich* decision of the German Federal Court of Justice and the *Anne Frank* cases of the Court of Appeals of Brussels shows, courts may assume a lack of inherent distinctiveness in respect of goods and services that are directly related to the cultural symbol, such as books, posters, CDs and DVDs, films, musical performances, film productions and guided tours. However, they are not reluctant to grant trademark rights with regard to merchandising articles. Hence, the process of brand development can begin. On the basis of trademark rights covering merchandising articles, the trademark owner can start to invest in the sign, attach commercial meanings, and transform the cultural symbol into a brand that may acquire distinctive character in respect of directly related goods and services, such as books and films, over time (section 7.3.3).

Considering these weaknesses of the requirement of distinctive character as a safeguard against the adoption of cultural signs as trademarks, court and office decisions denying trademark rights on the ground that the requisite distinctive character is missing must not hide the fact that a lack of distinctive character is not a cultural ground for refusal that allows courts and offices to name the true reason for not awarding trademark rights. In the case of cultural signs, it would be desirable to have room to articulate prevailing cultural concerns candidly, in particular the risk of artificially extending protection beyond the temporal limits of copyright, encouraging the privatization of parts of the cultural heritage, supporting the undesirable redefinition of important cultural expressions in commercial contexts, and providing incentives for unfair freeriding on the status, reputation and favourable image of cultural expressions.[1363]

Considering these clear articulations of cultural reasons for denying trademark protection, the argument of a lack of distinctive character can be unmasked as mere pretence. In *Mona Lisa* and *Nachtwacht*, the German Federal Court of Justice and the Court of Appeals of The Hague rightly pointed out that the famous paintings were used frequently in marketing and advertising contexts. Therefore, they had reason to assume widespread use by various enterprises and could cast doubt upon the capacity of the signs to identify one particular commercial source. From the perspective of the cultural imperative, however, it is cynical to solve the case on this basis. On its merits, the Courts argued that the Mona Lisa and the Night Watch could escape registration as trademarks because commercial use of these cultural

1363. Senftleben 2017b, 698; Wandtke/Bullinger 1997, 578. For arguments pointing in a similar direction, see van Woensel 2007, 412-413; Nordemann 1997, 391; Osenberg 1996, 102-103. According to Ohly 2008, 207, and Seifert 2000, 1018, by contrast, the existing regulatory instruments in trademark law are sufficient.

symbols had already become commonplace.[1364] The basic requirement of distinctiveness was effective because many commercial actors had already usurped the cultural sign at stake. The trademark registration was rejected because other traders may want to use the cultural symbols in their advertising as well. However, the enquiry into distinctiveness did not offer room for denying trademark protection because freeriding on the reputation and positive image of the cultural signs at issue, the attachment of commercial connotations and the corresponding reduction of their potential for dialogic communication in the artistic domain were inacceptable (section 3.3.2.4).[1365]

In sum, the application of the basic requirement of distinctive character is thus unsatisfactory. The exclusionary effect is incomplete because it does not cover the whole spectrum of goods and services. Moreover, it is unreliable because a lack of distinctiveness can be overcome through use in trade. In the case of relatively unknown cultural signs, the test of distinctiveness may fail to serve as a safeguard against the acquisition of trademark rights altogether. Finally, the exclusion of cultural material from trademark protection on the basis of the requirement of distinctiveness also prevents courts and trademark offices from clearly articulating prevailing cultural interests and concerns. Instead, they must keep within inadequate assessment standards resulting from the test of distinctiveness, such as widespread use in a commercial context implying a non-distinctive, descriptive or generic character, or a need to keep the sign free for other traders who may want to use the cultural symbol in advertising and product marketing as well. These shortcomings make the requirement of distinctive character unsuitable for the task of effectively preventing the acquisition of trademark rights to contemporary cultural creations and cultural signs in the public domain. It would be desirable to have more effective tools to avoid the acquisition of trademark rights.

9.1.2.2 Refusal Based on Public Order or Morality Preferable

The discussion of the exclusionary effect of distinctive character has brought to light two central parameters for the assessment of the effectiveness of grounds for refusal in trademark law. First, a ground for refusal may be weak because it can be overcome through continuous use in trade. Second, it may be weak because it does not apply across all goods and services. In both cases, the ground for refusal leaves loopholes for the acquisition of trademark rights and the undesirable redefinition of cultural signs in a commercial context. Considering these two parameters, the basic requirement of distinctiveness proves to be particularly weak because it has both

1364. For a similar critique of argumentation patterns in trademark cases addressing cultural signs, see Curtin 2018, 963.

1365. Assaf 2009, 5.

shortcomings: it can be overcome through use in trade and often remains confined to goods and services that have a connection with the cultural sign in question.

A strong ground for refusal – in the sense of reliably precluding the acquisition of trademark rights to cultural signs altogether – would have to score high with regard to both dimensions. Public order and morality could be such a strong antipode to the weak gatekeeper requirement of distinctiveness. This ground for refusal is immune against the acquisition of distinctive character through use in trade. If a trademark registration is contrary to public order or morality, it does not matter whether the sign is distinctive. Second, a refusal based on public order or morality can cover the whole spectrum of goods and services. If the *registration* of a cultural sign as a trademark is deemed offensive (rather than the sign as such), this finding bars the acquisition of trademark rights regardless of the goods and services involved.[1366] In contrast to the basic requirement of distinctiveness, public order and morality are thus grounds for refusal with a particularly strong exclusionary effect.[1367]

At the international level, Article 6*quinquies*(B) No. 3 PC reflects these grounds for refusal in the context of *telle quelle* protection by pointing out that Paris Union countries are not obliged to accept for registration and protection signs duly registered in other countries of the Union 'when they are contrary to morality or public order...'. Given this international recognition of public order and morality as legitimate reasons for denying trademark protection, it is not surprising that these grounds for refusal have made their way into national trademark laws around the globe.[1368] The prevention of copyright/trademark overlaps on the basis of public order and morality, thus, has the additional advantage of universal applicability. If public order and morality can serve as grounds for denying trademark rights to cultural signs, countries seeking to safeguard the cultural innovation cycle need not create new legal instruments. Trademark offices and courts can invoke public order and morality as well-established grounds for refusal to exclude trademark rights. In the EU, for instance, Article 7(1)(f) EUTMR and Article 4(1)(f) TMD bar from registration trademarks 'which are contrary to public policy or to accepted principles of morality'.

Experiences with this ground for refusal, however, show that judges and examiners may be hesitant to argue that considerations of public order or morality militate against the grant of trademark rights to cultural signs. In the

1366. Cf. GCEU, 15 March 2018, case T-1/17, La Mafia Franchises/EUIPO, para. 40, for the same result based on the particularly offensive nature of a sign.

1367. Cf. Peukert 2019, 1191-1192, who confirms the importance of considerations based on public order and morality from the theoretical perspective of resistance against the increasing commodification of intellectual creations that are not primarily made for sale, such as works of art.

1368. For an overview of the use of these grounds for refusal in different regions of the world, see Senftleben 2012b.

decision *Winston Churchill*, for example, the Dutch Supreme Court rejected the argument that registration of the name and portrait of Winston Churchill as a trademark for cigars was contrary to morality or public order.[1369] The Court found that even though some may perceive the use of Churchill's name and portrait for tobacco marketing as a crudity, others may find it acceptable. Moreover, use for this purpose may keep the memory of this popular statesman alive.[1370] As explained in section 9.1.2.1, the German Federal Patent Court also rejected the public order and morality argument in respect of an attempt to register the Mona Lisa as a trademark. Instead, the Court assumed a lack of distinctive character and denied trademark protection for this reason.[1371] The Court of Appeals of The Hague adopted the same approach in the *Nachtwacht* case.[1372]

These decisions seem grounded in traditional assumptions about the field of application of public order and morality as grounds for refusal.[1373] The guidelines developed by the Grand Board of Appeal of OHIM, for instance, indicate that the focus has traditionally been on the offensive character of the sign as such, or the offensive character of use of a particular sign in respect of objectionable goods or services.[1374] The test for refusing trademark rights to a cultural sign would thus culminate in the question of whether a sufficiently broad part of the relevant public considers the sign in and of itself offensive, or finds use of the sign in relation to certain goods or services inacceptable. With regard to signs of symbolic value, the GCEU decision in *Couture Tech/OHIM ('Soviet coat of arms')* illustrates this field of application. In this case, trademark protection was sought for a figurative sign showing the coat of arms of the former Soviet Union.[1375] The application had been rejected by OHIM on the ground that in Latvia and Hungary, the registration of official symbols of the former USSR would cause a conflict with public policy. Confirming this decision, the GCEU pointed out that in the assessment of a sign's offensive character, national circumstances had to be factored into the equation that were likely to

1369. Dutch Supreme Court, 28 October 1948, Bureau I.E./Churchill's Cigars ('Winston Churchill'), *Bijblad bij de industriële eigendom* 1949, 24.

1370. Dutch Supreme Court, *ibid.*, 24.

1371. German Federal Patent Court, 25 November 1997, case 24 W (pat) 188/96, Mona Lisa, *GRUR* 1998, 1022-1023.

1372. Court of Appeals of The Hague, 29 August 2017, case 200.205.771/01, ECLI:NL:GH-DHA:2017:2446, Chiever/Benelux-Organisatie voor de Intellectuele Eigendom ('Nachtwacht'), para. 1.4 and 8-9.

1373. For an overview of this traditional approach, see Geiger/Machado Pontes 2017, 8-11; Kur/Senftleben 2017, para. 4.205-4.218; ECS 2017, 459-460.

1374. BoA, 6 July 2006, case R 495/2005-G, *Jebaraj Kenneth trading as Screw You/OHIM* (SCREW YOU), para. 30. See also BoA, 25 March 2003, case R 111/2002-4, *Dick Lexic Ltd. v. OHIM* (DICK & FANNY).

1375. GCEU, 20 September 2011, case T-232/10, *Couture Tech Ltd/OHIM* ('Soviet coat of arms'), paras 2-3.

influence the perception of a mark by the relevant public.[1376] As it seemed obvious that a substantial part of the public in Hungary and Latvia would consider the mark offensive, the application for registration had to be refused.[1377]

This traditional focus on the offensive nature of the sign for which protection is sought narrows the field of application with regard to cultural signs. Obviously, a sign consisting of the Mona Lisa, the Night Watch, Mickey Mouse or Harry Potter is not scandalous in and of itself. Under the traditional approach, cultural signs can thus only be refused in extreme cases where the sign is placed in an objectionable context, for instance, because of the goods or services involved. An attempt to register a sign derived from Pablo Picasso's famous painting 'Guernica' for the sale of weapons might be such an example where the goods concerned contradict the meaning of the affected cultural sign.[1378] As long as the traditional focus on the scandalous nature of the sign as such, or an objectionable context arising from the goods or services, is not abandoned in favour of a more flexible approach, public order and morality can hardly play the highly effective role with regard to cultural signs which these grounds for refusal could have because they are immune against the acquisition of distinctiveness through use in trade.

A national precursor of a more elastic application of public order and morality can be found in the area of religious signs. In *Messias*, for example, the German Federal Patent Court denied the registration of the word mark MESSIAS for clothing, shoes and hats. In this case, the sign as such was not offensive. The Court focused on the fact that the trademark registration would lead to commercial use of the religious sign in trade.[1379] In *Budha*, the German Federal Patent Court assumed that significant parts of the German public would perceive the word BUDHA (which the trademark applicant sought to register for perfumery, cosmetics, jewellery, watches, clothing, shoes and hats) as a reference to the Buddha as the founder of buddhism. As the grant of trademark rights would lead to the commercial exploitation of the word 'Budha', the Court held that the trademark application was contrary to the religious or ethical values of significant parts of the German public. The relevant public would perceive the registration as offensive.[1380] The focus, therefore, switched from the offensive nature of the sign to the offensive nature of the registration as a trademark and the subsequent commercialization of the religious sign.

Similar impulses for a broader application of public order and morality as grounds for refusal in cases involving cultural signs can follow from the

1376. GCEU, *ibid.*, para. 36 and 53.

1377. GCEU, *ibid.*, paras 57-62.

1378. See the discussion of this example by ECS 2017, 459-460.

1379. German Federal Patent Court, 2 November 1993, case 27 W (pat) 85/92, 'Messias', *GRUR* 1994, 377.

1380. German Federal Patent Court, 17 January 2007, case 28 W (pat) 66/06, 'Budha', 5.

milestone ruling of the EFTA Court in *Vigeland*. The EFTA Court was called upon to assess an attempt to register several artworks made by Gustav Vigeland – one of the most eminent Norwegian sculptors – as trademarks. The reason for the initiative to acquire trademark rights was the expiry of the term of copyright protection.[1381] The prejudicial questions came from the Norwegian Board of Appeal for Industrial Property Rights. The Board of Appeal was wondering about the application of several grounds for refusal.[1382] Among other works, the underlying trademark application concerned Vigeland's 'Monolith' (*Monolitten*) and 'Angry Boy' (*Sinnataggen*) – popular works which feature prominently in the Vigeland Installation in the centre of Oslo's Frogner Park. Interestingly, the registration initiative had not been taken by a trademark 'troll' seeking to obtain rights to popular artistic works for the sole purpose of threatening users with infringement claims and pressing for excessive licence fees without any intention to make genuine use of the works itself.[1383] By contrast, the trademark application had been filed by the Municipality of Oslo. In respect of this remarkable step, Oslo submitted arguments to the EFTA Court which were derived from a distinction between Vigeland's artistic work on the one hand and the city's commercial marketing efforts on the other. In particular, Oslo argued that:

> [a]ll of the shapes have been exclusively connected to, and used by or through, the Municipality since the death of Gustav Vigeland in 1943. Many of these shapes are well known and valuable, in particular, due to the efforts and investments made by the Municipality.[1384]

Hence it seems that from the perspective of the Municipality of Oslo, the rights to Vigeland's works ought to be due to the city – even after copyright expiry – because of the efforts made to ensure that the works became well known. Oslo stated that no other entity could have justifiable interests to the commercial exploitation of Vigeland's works against this background.[1385] The Municipality also pointed out that it had specifically been chosen by Gustav Vigeland to administer and safeguard his artistic reputation and memory.[1386] Nonetheless, considerations of art custodianship, such as the

---

1381. EFTA Court, 6 April 2017, case E-5/16, Municipality of Oslo ('Vigeland'), para. 20. Gustav Vigeland died on 12 March 1943.

1382. EFTA Court, *ibid.*, paras 28-30.

1383. For a case that has arisen from this practice, see Higher Court of Appeals of Dresden, 4 April 2000, case 14 U 3611/99, 'Johann Sebastian Bach', *NJW* 2001, 615. The case concerned the registration of the name and portrait of Johann Sebastian Bach as a trademark for various goods and services, including glassware, porcelain and crockery. While the trademark proprietor had not commenced using the sign himself, he systematically asserted his trademark rights against users referring to Johann Sebastian Bach. Cf. the background information given by Götting 2001, 615.

1384. Report for the Hearing, Judge-Rapporteur Baudenbacher, 5 October 2016, case E-5/16, Municipality of Oslo ('Vigeland'), para. 32.

1385. Report for the Hearing, *ibid.*, para. 36.

1386. Report for the Hearing, *ibid.*, para. 36.

need to preserve the cultural dimension of Vigeland's works by preventing third parties from attaching undesirable commercial connotations, did not play a central role in the submission to the EFTA Court.[1387] Instead, Oslo insisted that:

> it should be assessed whether the value and fame of the work are related to characteristics and qualities of the artwork alone, or if the value and renown may be attributed to investments and efforts made by the Municipality.[1388]

With this strategy, the city of Oslo had little success in its own country. The Norwegian Industrial Property Office remained unimpressed and refused the trademark application on the grounds that Vigeland's works were non-distinctive, descriptive and functional. The shape of the works added substantial value to at least some of the goods, in respect of which registration was sought.[1389] Instead of dispelling these concerns, the Board of Appeal decided to supplement the list of grounds for refusal with a further argument. It expressed the view that a trademark registration of works belonging to the cultural heritage may be contrary to public policy or accepted principles of morality, and wondered which factors should inform the decision on these grounds for refusal.[1390]

Answering this prejudicial question, the EFTA Court took several important steps towards a more flexible application of public order and morality as grounds for denying trademark rights to cultural signs. First, the EFTA Court adhered to a legal status definition of the public domain (section 8.1.1). For a cultural creation to be part of the public domain, it had to be unencumbered by intellectual property rights.[1391] According to the EFTA Court, the legal status of 'absence of individual protection for, or exclusive rights to, a work'[1392] is the normal status of literary and artistic works and the period of copyright protection is an anomaly during which the work is withheld from a free and entirely open communication process.[1393] Precursors of this approach can be found in the domestic law of EU Member States. As explained in section 3.3.2.4, the German Federal Constitutional Court, for instance, also held that a work, once published, becomes an independent factor influencing the cultural and intellectual perception of its age which increasingly evaporates in the process of its communication until the time of protection finally expires.[1394]

1387. Report for the Hearing, *ibid.*, paras 31-42.
1388. Report for the Hearing, *ibid.*, para. 37.
1389. EFTA Court, 6 April 2017, case E-5/16, Municipality of Oslo ('Vigeland'), para. 27.
1390. EFTA Court, *ibid.*, paras 28-30.
1391. EFTA Court, *ibid.*, para. 66.
1392. EFTA Court, *ibid.*, para. 66.
1393. EFTA Court, *ibid.*, para. 66.
1394. German Federal Constitutional Court, 31 May 2016, case 1 BvR 1585/13, 'Sampling', *GRUR* 2016, 690, para. 87. Cf. Peukert 2019, 1180-1181; Cohen 2006, 154-155; Kreile 1993, 257-258; Kirchhof 1988, 34-35.

Second, the EFTA Court clarified the policy objectives which formed the basis of its approach. In the Court's view, the determination of a fixed time frame of copyright protection after which anyone can draw from ideas and creative content of others without limitation served the principles of legal certainty and protection of legitimate expectations.[1395] It also served the general interest in 'protecting creations of the mind from commercial greed' and 'ensuring the freedom of the arts'.[1396] These policy considerations are broader than the reasons given by the CJEU for policing the border between trademark rights and patent or industrial design protection. As explained in sections 7.1 and 7.2, the CJEU held that the functionality doctrine in EU trademark law served the purpose of ensuring undistorted, free competition and preventing the artificial perpetuation of intellectual property rights with a limited term of protection.[1397] In comparison with this competition-based explanation of a dividing line between trademark rights and other forms of intellectual property protection, the EFTA Court's reference to 'commercial greed' and 'freedom of the arts' adds important aspects. It takes into account the need to prevent the pursuit of profit maximization from suppressing the evolution of free, autonomous art.[1398] As a result, concerns about follow-on innovation in the artistic domain can be factored into the equation. The analysis need no longer be confined to competition-based considerations.

Third, the EFTA Court recalled the remarkable development of EU trademark protection in recent years: from a protection system that focuses on the protection of consumers against origin confusion to a protection regime that recognizes investment in brand development as an independent objective of protection (section 6.1.1).[1399] While explicitly referring to remaining differences in the configuration of copyright and trademark protection,[1400] this modern understanding of the trademark system led to a clear articulation of the risk of wrong incentives for investment in cultural heritage grabbing:

> The possibility of acquiring distinctiveness through use provided for in Article 3(3) of the Trade Mark Directive may lead undertakings, which seek to transfer the appeal of formerly copyright protected works to their goods or services, to try to appropriate the work through targeted marketing campaigns.[1401]

1395. EFTA Court, *ibid.*, para. 65.
1396. EFTA Court, *ibid.*, para. 65.
1397. CJEU, 18 September 2014, case C-205/13, Hauck/Stokke, paras 18-20; CJEU, 18 June 2002, case C-299/99, Philips/Remington, para. 78; CJEU, 14 September 2010, case C-48/09 P, Lego/Mega Brands, para. 43. Cf. Kur 2011, 6-10.
1398. Cf. Senftleben 2017, 25-28; Bourdieu 1992/1999, 103-105, 342-345 and 530-533.
1399. EFTA Court, 6 April 2017, case E-5/16, Municipality of Oslo ('Vigeland'), para. 72. Cf. Kur/Senftleben 2017, para. 1.12-1.39.
1400. EFTA Court, *ibid.*, para. 62.
1401. EFTA Court, *ibid.*, para. 75. As to the risk of dysfunctional cumulation, see also ECS 2017, 458.

Therefore, the Court did not jump to the conclusion that trademark protection could hardly ever have a corrosive effect on cultural follow-on innovation because trademarks were merely identifiers of commercial source (section 7.3.5.1). By contrast, the understanding of trademark law as an incentive and investment scheme – and trademark rights as brand exploitation instruments[1402] – yielded the insight that the mere possibility of acquiring distinctiveness through use in trade could lead to rights acquisition strategies that aim at the exploitation of positive cultural connotations attached to cultural signs. In line with its earlier reference to the need to protect cultural creations from 'commercial greed', the Court thus warned against 'targeted marketing campaigns' seeking to derive profit from valuable cultural meanings.[1403]

On the basis of these considerations, the EFTA Court finally embarked on a closer inspection of public order and morality as grounds for refusing trademark rights to Vigeland's artworks. In this context, the Court made a first contribution to the further development of public order and morality as grounds for refusal by clearly distinguishing two aspects: a refusal based on grounds of public policy requires an assessment of objective criteria, whereas a refusal based on accepted principles of morality implies the examination of subjective values.[1404]

As to the subjective criterion of a conflict with accepted principles of morality, the Court underlined the necessity to examine on a case-by-case basis how the relevant public would perceive the sign at issue. In line with the traditional approach outlined above,[1405] the Court posed the question of whether Vigeland's works – in and of themselves – would be considered offensive by reasonable consumers with average sensitivity and tolerance thresholds.[1406] Quite clearly, this question could be answered in the negative.[1407] The EFTA Court, however, went beyond this standard analysis and added an important nuance by holding that:

> certain pieces of art may enjoy a particular status as prominent parts of a nation's cultural heritage, an emblem of sovereignty or of the nation's

1402. Kur/Senftleben 2017, para. 1.29-1.39; Ginsburg 2016, 75-77; Senftleben 2009a, 48-49; Bently 2008b, 15-41; Schroeder 2008, 161; Bone 2006, 549; Moskin 2004, 843-844; Dinwoodie 2002, 503-504; Fezer 2001, 827; Casparie-Kerdel 2001, 185-186; Lunney 1999, 437-439; Lemley 1999, 1694-1698; Brown 1999, 1619-1620; Dreyfuss 1990, 397-398; Lehmann 1986, 14-17.

1403. EFTA Court, *ibid.*, para. 65 and 75.

1404. EFTA Court, *ibid.*, paras 84-86. As to the innovative character of the decision, see Geiger/Machado Pontes, 11-12, who place the judgment in the context of previous EU office practice.

1405. For an overview, see Geiger/Machado Pontes 2017, 8-11; Kur/Senftleben 2017, para. 4.205-4.218; ECS 2017, 459-460.

1406. EFTA Court, *ibid.*, paras 89-90 and 93.

1407. EFTA Court, *ibid.*, para. 91.

> foundations and values. A trade mark registration may even be considered a misappropriation or a desecration of the artist's work, in particular if it is granted for goods or services that contradict the values of the artist or the message communicated through the artwork in question. Therefore, the possibility cannot be ruled out that trade mark registration of an artwork may be perceived by the average consumer in the EEA State in question as offensive and therefore as contrary to accepted principles of morality.[1408]

This addition is remarkable. With this statement, the EFTA Court departed from the traditional focus on the scandalous nature of the sign itself. A refusal based on accepted principles of morality may also follow from a finding that the relevant public perceives the trademark registration of an artwork as offensive.[1409] In this way, the EFTA Court substantially broadened the field of application of the ground of refusal. It extended the above-described broader perspective – including the possibility of the public perceiving the registration for use in commerce as offensive – from religious signs[1410] to signs with cultural significance. While in the past the offensive nature of the cultural sign or its attachment to scandalous goods or services was decisive,[1411] the offensive nature of the attempt to register a cultural sign as a trademark offers an alternative avenue for a refusal based on a conflict with morality in line with the approach taken by the EFTA Court.[1412]

As to the second aspect – the objective criterion of a conflict with public policy – the EFTA Court noted that 'public policy' referred to principles and standards regarded to be of a fundamental concern to the state and the whole of society. Therefore, a refusal based on public policy required exceptional circumstances, namely 'a genuine and sufficiently serious threat to a fundamental interest of society'.[1413] Nonetheless, the Court saw room for applying this ground for refusal in the context of artwork registrations:

> An artwork may be refused registration, for example, under the circumstances that its registration is regarded as a genuine and serious threat to certain fundamental values or where the need to safeguard the public domain, itself, is considered a fundamental interest of society.[1414]

1408. EFTA Court, *ibid.*, para. 92.
1409. EFTA Court, *ibid.*, para. 92. For the discussion of a similar concept of "cultural offensiveness" that has evolved in New Zealand in respect of signs of indigenous peoples, see Frankel 2005, 87-91.
1410. German Federal Patent Court, 17 January 2007, case 28 W (pat) 66/06, 'Budha', 5.
1411. BoA, 6 July 2006, case R 495/2005-G, *Jebaraj Kenneth trading as Screw You/OHIM* (SCREW YOU), para. 30. See also BoA, 25 March 2003, case R 111/2002-4, *Dick Lexic Ltd. v. OHIM* (DICK & FANNY).
1412. EFTA Court, 6 April 2017, case E-5/16, Municipality of Oslo ('Vigeland'), para. 93. Cf. Basire 2018, 435.
1413. EFTA Court, *ibid.*, paras 94-96.
1414. EFTA Court, *ibid.*, para. 96.

As in the context of accepted principles of morality, the EFTA Court stated that a genuine and serious threat to public policy could follow from the trademark registration of an artwork.[1415] The Court thus confirmed the substantial broadening of the scope of the ground for refusal: not only the nature of the sign at issue but also the registration attempt as such can be sufficient to justify a refusal based on public order.

However, the EFTA Court could hardly carry out a more concrete assessment of the situation surrounding the application filed by the Municipality of Oslo. Given the discretion enjoyed by the national authorities in this respect, it was for the Norwegian office and courts to determine whether these requirements were met in the *Vigeland* case. Interestingly, the Czech Republic had submitted a statement to the Court referring to 'a fundamental interest of society in leaving certain famous pieces of art available to everyone, such as well-known and outstanding creations of mind that are part of the universal cultural heritage'.[1416] This statement shows that national authorities may be willing to adopt the approach developed by the EFTA Court. In fact, the Norwegian Board of Appeal for Industrial Property Rights finally denied the trademark registration of Vigeland's artworks on the basis of public order considerations. The Board of Appeal saw a conflict with public order arising from the registration of Vigeland's works as trademarks:

> due to the signs depicting works of art which hold considerable cultural value to Norwegian society, and partly because the temporal limitation of the copyright protection period pursuant to the Copyrights Act is meant to safeguard fundamental societal considerations...[1417]

The Board of Appeal thus combined two lines of reasoning which the EFTA Court had declared valid in the context of the public order assessment. First, the Board of Appeal held that, because of significant cultural value, the registration of Vigeland's artworks threatens fundamental values of Norwegian society. Second, the Board stated that the temporal limitation of copyright constituted a fundamental interest of Norwegian society.[1418] Offering further support for its refusal of trademark protection, the Board also pointed to unfair competitive advantages that could follow from freeriding on the positive reputation which the artworks had already acquired during the term of copyright protection:

> [n]ot only are there no costs in connection with development of a trademark, but the sign is in itself already known as a work of art and

1415. EFTA Court, *ibid.*, para. 96.

1416. Report for the Hearing, Judge-Rapporteur Baudenbacher, 5 October 2016, case E-5/16, Municipality of Oslo ('Vigeland'), para. 118.

1417. Norwegian Board of Appeal for Industrial Property Rights, 13 November 2017, cases 16/00148, 16/00149, 16/00150, 16/00151, 16/00153 and 16/00154, 'Vigeland', para. 14.

1418. Cf. the arguments recognized by the EFTA Court, 6 April 2017, case E-5/16, Municipality of Oslo ('Vigeland'), para. 96.

connected to something positive. As a result, there is no need to build consumer recognition of the mark or to generate the positive associations required for reoccurring purchases...[1419]

Finally, the Board made it clear that the intention of art investment and art custodianship did not constitute a legitimate interest in trademark law that could supersede the considerations and fundamental societal interests underlying the limitation of the term of copyright protection.[1420]

This final outcome[1421] shows that the EFTA Court has provided important, exemplary lines of argument in *Vigeland* for a more systematic exclusion of artworks from trademark protection on the basis of public policy or morality. The Court added public order and morality to the canon of grounds for refusal that can inform the assessment of registration attempts relating to signs with cultural significance. As already pointed out, this solution is more robust and complete than a refusal based on a lack of distinctiveness. The acquisition of distinctive character through use in trade does not affect a refusal based on public order or morality. As the Norwegian Board of Appeal finally qualified the *registration* of Vigeland's artworks – not the artworks themselves and not the context arising from use in respect of specific goods or services – as contrary to public order, the refusal of trademark rights also applies across the whole spectrum of goods and services. As the focus is on the mere fact of registration for use in commerce, any trademark registration is impermissible regardless of the goods or services involved. In addition, considerations of public policy and morality, as developed by the EFTA Court, offer trademark offices and courts room to clearly articulate cultural concerns in the context of a rejection of trademark protection. With the *Vigeland* decision, it becomes possible to state candidly that trademark law is not intended to serve as a basis for freeriding on the reputation and positive image of cultural symbols, the erosion of an artworks' artistic discourse potential as a result of exposure to commercial marketing strategies, and the impairment of the unhindered, open communication process surrounding the sign in the cultural domain. From the perspective of the cultural imperative, the *Vigeland* decision is thus an important step in the right direction.[1422]

The EFTA Court also outlined the limits of its approach. The application of public order and morality as grounds for refusal should not lead to a rejection automatism. According to the Court, the fact that an artwork had previously enjoyed copyright protection 'may not in itself form the basis for

1419. Norwegian Board of Appeal for Industrial Property Rights, *ibid.*, para. 23.
1420. Norwegian Board of Appeal for Industrial Property Rights, ibid., para. 24. Cf. Basire 2018, 435.
1421. The Municipality of Oslo did not appeal the decision of the Norwegian Board of Appeal for Industrial Property Rights. The decision of the Board thus remained the final word in the matter.
1422. Senftleben 2017b, 716-717.

refusing trade mark registration'.[1423] Moreover, no threat to the need to safeguard the public domain could be found in the case of works that were primarily created to serve as signs to be registered as trademarks (where cumulative copyright and trademark protection is merely incidental, cf. section 9.1.2.5), or in the case of signs which, albeit based on a work pertaining to the public domain, contained additional elements that transformed or diffused the original work to such an extent that consumers were unlikely to confuse the sign with the original creative work (cf. section 9.1.2.4).[1424]

9.1.2.3 Subjective Morality Criteria

A closer inspection of the central lines of reasoning developed by the EFTA Court reveals the remarkable potential of public order and morality considerations for achieving a categorical exclusion of cultural signs from trademark protection across the whole spectrum of goods and services. With regard to morality as a ground for refusal, the EFTA Court provided two core arguments for an outright exclusion:

- the relevant public may perceive the registration as a trademark as offensive because certain pieces of art enjoy a 'particular status as prominent parts of a nation's cultural heritage, an emblem of sovereignty or of the nation's foundations and values'[1425] (morality ground 1);
- the relevant public may perceive the registration as a trademark as offensive because it would lead to a 'misappropriation or a desecration of the artist's work, in particular if it is granted for goods or services that contradict values of the artist or the message communicated through the artwork in question'[1426] (morality ground 2).

At first sight, the latter argument focusing on misappropriation or desecration (morality ground 2) may appear narrow. Quite clearly, the scenario mentioned above – an attempt to register a distinctive element of Pablo Picasso's 'Guernica' for the marketing of weapons – would fall within this category. However, this example also illustrates potential limits of the approach. While consumers may regard the registration in respect of weapons as a desecration of the artwork in the light of the painting's message, the outcome may be different when the trademark application concerns goods and services that do not contradict the values conveyed by the painting. If interpreted strictly, the desecration argument will thus fail in many cases.

1423. EFTA Court, 6 April 2017, case E-5/16, Municipality of Oslo ('Vigeland'), para. 88.
1424. EFTA Court, *ibid.*, paras 97-98.
1425. EFTA Court, *ibid.*, para. 92.
1426. EFTA Court, *ibid.*, para. 92.

However, the EFTA Court used the words 'in particular'[1427] to introduce the scenario in which goods or services contradict values communicated through the artwork. This specific example does not prevent the invocation of the desecration argument in other cases. As explained in section 8.2.3.3, the registration of a cultural sign as a trademark triggers a redefinition process in the commercial domain that is undesirable from the perspective of the cultural imperative. The attachment of marketing messages blurs a sign's cultural meaning and reduces its potential to serve as a reference point for the discourse in the artistic domain. The original message of the artwork may even be suppressed and lost in the end.[1428] In other words, it may be argued that, regardless of the goods and services involved, the grant of trademark rights to cultural signs *always* leads to a desecration of the artist's work, namely the desecration following from the attachment of commercial marketing messages that interfere with the sign's cultural meaning – the values and messages conveyed by the artist through the artwork.[1429]

When the desecration aspect of morality ground 2 is understood in this broader sense, the ground for refusal applies irrespective of the goods and services. As explained in section 8.2.3.3, a trademark registration entails the obligation to make genuine use of the registered sign as a trademark. This, in turn, requires the attachment of commercial marketing messages to the affected sign. The desecration of an artwork is thus inherent in the grant of trademark protection. Viewed from this perspective, the argument applies across all goods and services and has the potential to categorically exclude cultural signs from trademark protection. Consumers may perceive the attachment of marketing messages to a sign with cultural significance as offensive because it suppresses the sign's cultural meaning and desecrates the artwork in this way.

The second aspect of morality ground 2 – the EFTA Court referred not only to 'desecration' but also to 'misappropriation' of the artist's work[1430] – can have a broad exclusionary effect as well. In *Shield Mark/Kist* – a case before the CJEU that concerned an attempt to register, among other signs, the first nine notes of Ludwig van Beethoven's piano piece 'Für Elise' as a trademark – Advocate General Dámaso Ruiz-Jarabo Colomer addressed the misappropriation risk. He expressed the view that it was difficult to accept:

> that a creation of the mind, which forms part of the universal cultural heritage, should be appropriated indefinitely by a person to be used on

1427. EFTA Court, *ibid.*, para. 92.

1428. Assaf 2009, 2-3; Senftleben 2010a, 75; Wandtke/Bullinger 1997, 578.

1429. Cf. Frankel 2005, 88 and 94, who describes the formal recognition of cultural offensiveness – in the sense of the use of cultural symbols in inappropriate commercial contexts – with regard to symbols of Māori culture in the trademark legislation of New Zealand.

1430. EFTA Court, *ibid.*, para. 92.

the market in order to distinguish the goods he produces or the services he provides with an exclusivity which not even its author's estate enjoys.[1431]

In the light of this statement, it is conceivable that consumers with a similar feeling of unease regard the registration of a cultural sign as an offensive misappropriation of the artist's work by third parties who – unlike the author's heirs – do not have a family connection. In this line of reasoning, the ground for refusal, again, applies across the whole spectrum of goods and services and leads to an outright exclusion of trademark protection. At the same time, Colomer's statement may set limits to the misappropriation approach. What if an author's estate itself files the trademark application? Would the close connection with the author legitimize the registration attempt in the eyes of the relevant public? If so, the misappropriation argument would be rendered inapplicable. This, however, need not lead to a trademark registration. The desecration argument offers an alternative basis for an outright exclusion. As other trademark proprietors, the author's estate is bound to make genuine use of the cultural sign once it is registered as a trademark. The registration exposes the affected sign to the risk of desecration as a result of use for commercial marketing purposes. The refusal of trademark rights, thus, follows from the need to avoid the desecration of the artist's work. The fact that, in this case, the author's estate registers the sign and controls the use in commerce does not eliminate the desecration risk.

On balance, the amalgam of desecration and misappropriation considerations which the EFTA Court applied to establish morality ground 2 can thus have a far-reaching exclusionary effect. It can be a powerful legal instrument to keep cultural signs outside the trademark system. The exclusionary effect will be particularly strong when the commercial redefinition of the sign's meaning in the context of use in trade (section 8.2.3.3) is qualified as a desecration of the artist's work.

Morality ground 1 refers to a scenario where the relevant public finds the trademark registration offensive because the affected sign constitutes a prominent part of a nation's cultural heritage, an emblem of sovereignty or an emblem of a nation's foundations and values.[1432] From the outset, this ground for a refusal is confined to signs with a particular status. It is incapable of covering all kinds of signs with cultural significance. Nonetheless, practical experiences with cases involving signs that are important national cultural heritage, emblems of sovereignty or emblems of a nation's foundations and values, show that there is room for a broader application of this line of argument. In the above-described *Nachwacht* case, for instance, the Court of Appeals of The Hague explicitly pointed out that the Night

1431. Opinion of Advocate General Colomer, 3 April 2003, case C-283/01, Shield Mark/Kist, para. 52.

1432. EFTA Court, *ibid.*, para. 92.

Watch was 'carved in the collective memory of the inhabitants of the Benelux'.[1433] Nonetheless, the Court refrained from a refusal based on a conflict with morality and relied on a lack of distinctiveness instead.[1434] As explained in section 9.1.2.1, this is a missed opportunity to arrive at a robust exclusion of trademark protection that applies across all goods and services and regardless of the acquisition of distinctive character through use. As the painting plays such a prominent role in the collective memory of the Benelux population, it would only have been a small step to assume that Benelux consumers would perceive the registration of the Night Watch – one of the most prominent parts of their cultural heritage – as offensive.

By the same token, the Court of Appeals of Brussels could have excluded 'The Diary of Anne Frank' and 'The Secret Annex' categorically from the trademark register in the aforementioned *Anne Frank* cases (section 9.1.2.1). Focusing on the outstanding cultural heritage status and the connection of the works with central values in a democratic, open society, it would have been consistent to invoke principles of morality, as developed in the *Vigeland* decision of the EFTA Court, and put an end to trademark registration initiatives once and for all – irrespective of the acquisition of distinctive character through use and regardless of the goods and services involved. Instead, the Court of Appeals of Brussels opted for a temporary, fragile solution and refused the registration in respect of directly related goods and services on the grounds that the signs were descriptive and devoid of distinctive character.[1435]

Hence it becomes apparent that trademark judges and examiners are not exhausting the full potential of morality considerations relating to a sign's particular status in the pantheon of a nation's cultural heritage, emblems of sovereignty or symbols of state foundations and societal values. This is striking because the importance of cultural signs falling within this category goes beyond the cultural domain. The status requirements following from this ground for refusal have a social and political dimension. In the light of these additional facets, it should not be too difficult to identify relevant signs in practice. Given their prominent role in the realm of cultural heritage, state sovereignty or national foundations and values, offices and courts enquiring into a potential conflict with morality need not be art experts to take a decision on the need to impose a categorical ban on the registration of relevant signs as trademarks (section 5.2.1).

The objective to avoid the acquisition of trademark rights to important cultural heritage signs, emblems of sovereignty and symbols of state

1433. Court of Appeals of The Hague, 29 August 2017, case 200.205.771/01, ECLI:NL:GH-DHA:2017:2446, Chiever/ Benelux-Organisatie voor de Intellectuele Eigendom ('Nachtwacht'), para. 12.

1434. Court of Appeals of The Hague, *ibid.*, paras 8-9.

1435. Court of Appeals of Brussels, 3 October 2013, cases 2013/7132 and 2013/7133, Anne Frank Foundation/Benelux Office for Intellectual Property, para. 6 and 10.

foundations and societal values (morality ground 1) is an important addition to the invocation of morality to prevent the misappropriation or desecration of the artist's work (morality ground 2). As already indicated, it supplements cultural concerns with social and political considerations. While misappropriation and desecration arguments focus on a sign's meaning in the cultural domain, the consideration of a sign's status as national cultural heritage, an emblem of sovereignty, or a symbol of state foundations and values allows the social and political dimension of cultural signs to enter the picture. Taken together, the two categories of morality considerations identified by the EFTA Court offer a broad spectrum of reference points for the enquiry into a conflict with morality.

As to the limits of the approach, it seems that the example given by the EFTA Court itself does not pose particular difficulties. As explained, the Court referred to literary and artistic works that were primarily created to serve as signs to be registered as trademarks – a situation where cumulative copyright and trademark protection arises incidentally.[1436] Signs of this nature, however, seem to fall outside the described morality approach from the outset. If it has been the very intention of the artist to design a logo for the distinction of goods or services of an enterprise, the registration as a trademark does not contradict the artist's values and genuine cultural expression. Moreover, a sign of this nature is unlikely to acquire the status of national cultural heritage, an emblem of sovereignty, or a symbol of state foundations and values. Accordingly, neither morality ground 2 (misappropriation or desecration) nor morality ground 1 (cultural heritage, sovereignty, foundations and values) applies. The sign remains unaffected by the morality considerations following from the EFTA Court's *Vigeland* decision.

While the trademark design scenario is thus unlikely to play a major role, the broadest limit of the described morality approach results from the basic configuration of the refusal concept itself. As the EFTA Court pointed out, a conflict with morality is a subjective criterion – subjective in the sense that the perception of reasonable consumers with average sensitivity and tolerance thresholds is decisive.[1437] Accordingly, an examiner or judge following in the footsteps of the EFTA Court cannot posit readily that the registration of a given work of art would lead to the misappropriation or desecration of the artist's work. The central question is whether the relevant public would find the registration attempt inacceptable for this reason. In the case of artworks, the necessity to assess the situation through the lens of consumer perception raises further questions about the level of knowledge and sensitivity of the relevant public. Can consumers be expected to recognize the risk of a redefinition and devaluation of cultural signs as a

1436. EFTA Court, *ibid.*, paras 97-98.
1437. EFTA Court, *ibid.*, paras 89-90 and 93. Cf. CJEU, 27 February 2020, case C-240/18P, Constantin Film/EUIPO ('Fack Ju Göhte'), para. 42; GCEU, 15 March 2018, case T-1/17, La Mafia Franchises/EUIPO, para. 26.

result of use as trademarks? Do consumers have sufficient knowledge of the values and messages underlying affected artworks? Even if these works are not widely known?

In other words, it is important to clarify the reference point for the assessment. Quite clearly, an assessment based on the perception of consumers with sufficient awareness of matters of art and culture may enhance the potential of morality considerations to achieve a categorical exclusion of cultural signs from trademark protection, whereas an assessment based on the perception of consumers not caring too much about matters of art may reduce this potential and limit the exclusionary effect of the ground for refusal. In practice, the consumer standard that is currently applied in the EU to assess conflicts with accepted principles of morality is the 'reasonable person with average thresholds of sensitivity and tolerance'.[1438] According to the CJEU, the assessment from the perspective of this consumer must shed light on the 'fundamental moral values and standards' to which society adheres at the time of assessment: the prevailing 'social consensus'.[1439] In *Constantin Film*, the CJEU emphasized that this determination should not be confined to an abstract assessment of the allegedly scandalous sign. The case concerned an attempt to register the title of the German film 'Fack Ju Göhte' (a phonetic transcription of 'Fuck you, Goethe' in German).[1440] Considering the enormous success of the comedy among the German-speaking public and its worldwide educational use by the Goethe Institute,[1441] the Court insisted on an assessment that includes the 'concrete and current social context' to ascertain whether the relevant public finds the sign acceptable despite its vulgar nature.[1442] As there were no indications that the film title had caused a controversy in Germany or Austria, the CJEU saw no reason to assume a conflict with morality.[1443]

Quite clearly, the consideration of the 'concrete and current social context' surrounding a sign allows empirical findings to enter the picture, such as the popularity of a film with a vulgar title and its use by a renowned cultural institution. The consumer standard on which the assessment is to be based, however, is far from empirical reality. The qualification of relevant consumers as 'reasonable' with 'average thresholds of sensitivity and tolerance'[1444] indicates that this consumer is a normative fiction. As Graeme Dinwoodie and Dev Gangjee rightly observed with regard to normative connotations of the average consumer in the infringement analysis:

1438. EFTA Court, *ibid.*, para. 90; CJEU, 27 February 2020, case C-240/18P, Constantin Film/EUIPO ('Fack Ju Göhte'), para. 42; GCEU, 15 March 2018, case T-1/17, La Mafia Franchises/EUIPO, para. 26.
1439. CJEU, *ibid.*, para. 39.
1440. CJEU, *ibid.*, para. 46.
1441. CJEU, *ibid.*, para. 52.
1442. CJEU, *ibid.*, para. 43.
1443. CJEU, *ibid.*, paras 52-53.
1444. CJEU, *ibid.*, para. 42.

> [t]he more that the reasonably well-informed and reasonably observant and circumspect consumer is a normative fiction, the greater the scope for the CJEU to create legal rules that establish EU-wide standards. The more empirical that question becomes, then the greater the role of national courts and the more likely that divergent market realities in Europe will result in different outcomes with adverse effects on the creation of an integrated market.[1445]

Applying this insight to the prototype of a reasonable consumer with average sensitivity and tolerance thresholds in morality cases, it can thus be said that the assessment of consumer perception need not depend exclusively on empirical findings. Normative assumptions can influence the determination of the degree of sensitivity and tolerance that is ascribed to the relevant consumer. In the case of cultural signs, these normative assumptions can include a higher degree of sensitivity vis-à-vis the corrosive effect of trademark protection on cultural follow-on innovation (section 6.3).

The inclusion of normative considerations in the assessment is not unusual.[1446] In *La Mafia Franchises*, the GCEU had to decide on the offensive nature of a figurative trademark showing a red rose and the slogan 'La Mafia se sienta a la mesa' for restaurant services offered in themed restaurants, clothing and footwear, and business management and organization consultancy services.[1447] As the words 'La Mafia' constituted the dominant element of the mark,[1448] the analysis focused on the question how the relevant public – reasonable consumers with average sensitivity and tolerance thresholds – would perceive that sign. The GCEU emphasized that the word element 'La Mafia' was understood worldwide as a reference to a criminal organization involved in illegal activities, such as drug and arms trafficking, money laundering and corruption, and not shying away from intimidation, physical violence and murder.[1449] The Court went on to explain that such criminal activities breached the very values on which the EU was founded, in particular the values of respect for human dignity and freedom (Article 2 of the Treaty on European Union) and the right to life, integrity of the person, liberty and security (Articles 2, 3 and 6 CFR). Those values were indivisible and made up the spiritual and moral heritage of the EU.[1450] In sharp contrast to the illicit practices of the criminal organization, the connection with the sentence 'se sienta a la mesa' ('takes a seat at the table'

1445. Dinwoodie/Gangjee 2016, 367.
1446. For instance, see the assessment in GCEU, 20 September 2011, case T-232/10, *Couture Tech Ltd/OHIM* ('Soviet coat of arms'), paras 57-62, where the Court derived a conflict with accepted principles of morality from legislation prohibiting the use of the type of signs for which registration was sought.
1447. GCEU, 15 March 2018, case T-1/17, La Mafia Franchises/EUIPO, paras 1-3.
1448. GCEU, *ibid.*, para. 32.
1449. GCEU, *ibid.*, para. 35.
1450. GCEU, *ibid.*, para. 36.

in Spanish) trivialized the violence of Mafia activities by referring to the idea of sharing a meal and, thus, conviviality and relaxation.[1451] Based on these findings and normative considerations, the Court arrived at the conclusion that:

> the contested mark, considered as a whole, refers to a criminal organisation, conveys a globally positive image of that organisation and, therefore, trivialises the serious harm done by that organisation to the fundamental values of the European Union […]. The contested mark is therefore likely to shock or offend not only the victims of that criminal organisation and their families, but also any person who, on EU territory, encounters that mark and has average sensitivity and tolerance thresholds.[1452]

On its merits, the Court thus inferred from normative values reflected in primary EU legislation that the relevant public had to find the mark scandalous. In the light of the values at stake, it was inconceivable for the Court that any EU citizen could accept the trademark registration. The way in which the Court dealt with counterarguments pointing to acceptance of references to the Mafia in the creative sector confirms this impression. The GCEU remained unimpressed by the defence argument that the Mafia was often the subject of fictional accounts in literature and in cinema, and that the registration was not intended to shock or offend, but to allude to the 'Godfather' film series on which the concept of the themed restaurants using the figurative mark was based.[1453] The Court dismissed these arguments by stating that the existence of Mafia books and films in no way altered the perception of the harm done by that organization.[1454] It thus disregarded starting points for an enquiry into the empirical reality of consumer perception and, instead, relied on normative considerations focusing on the seriousness of the crimes committed by the criminal organization. Arguably, an empirical analysis could have led to a different outcome. Use of Mafia insignia in films and books impacts consumer perception and raises the question of whether a reasonable consumer with average sensitivity and tolerance thresholds would place the contested Mafia trademark in the context of the Mafia genre in the creative sector (and find the trademark acceptable), or see a connection with the organization's crimes (and find the trademark inacceptable).

With regard to the question whether the registration of cultural signs as trademarks gives rise to a conflict with morality, the decision in *La Mafia Franchises* offers important insights. It shows that normative considerations can play a crucial role. The assessment need not follow the dictates of

1451. GCEU, *ibid.*, para. 45.
1452. GCEU, *ibid.*, para. 47.
1453. GCEU, *ibid.*, paras 39-42.
1454. GCEU, *ibid.*, para. 43.

empirical findings reflecting consumer perception. By contrast, the normative construct of a reasonable consumer with average sensitivity and tolerance thresholds allows judges and examiners to make assumptions about the perception of a contested sign in the light of societal values. Hence, the analysis need not remain limited to the question how consumers of flesh and blood actually perceive the sign. Instead, it is decisive which perception one would expect from the prototype of a reasonable consumer with average sensitivity and tolerance thresholds who knows and cares about overarching societal values. This normative colouring paves the way for a value-based evaluation of cultural signs with the status of important cultural heritage, an emblem of state sovereignty or a symbol of societal foundations and values (morality ground 1). It also offers the opportunity of a value-based assessment when the risk of artwork misappropriation or desecration (morality ground 2) is central to the analysis and the enquiry into consumer perception must address concerns about an undesirable redefinition and devaluation of cultural signs in the commercial domain of trade (section 8.2.3.3). The focus on the 'concrete and current social context' in *Constantin Film*[1455] does not preclude the inclusion of normative considerations. As the CJEU also pointed out in *Constantin Film*, the yardstick for assessing the concrete and current social context remains the 'reasonable person with average thresholds of sensitivity and tolerance'.[1456] This reasonable person, however, is the 'normative fiction'[1457] that offers room for the inclusion of normative considerations, such as sufficient sensitivity regarding the risk of blurring and suppressing the cultural meaning of affected signs and devaluing them for the discourse in the artistic domain (section 8.2.3.3).

Based on this normative understanding of the consumer prototype and applicable sensitivity and tolerance thresholds, morality considerations can thus have a remarkable potential to support an outright exclusion of cultural signs from trademark protection. However, *La Mafia Franchises* also indicates that morality arguments are the stronger the more fundamental the values associated with the sign at issue. Morality considerations can certainly acquire particular importance in the case of cultural heritage signs and renowned artworks that play a central role in a country's cultural landscape and the discourse in the artistic domain. Morality ground 1 – referring to national cultural heritage and symbols of sovereignty, state foundations and values – explicitly requires an elevated societal status of the affected sign. Morality ground 2 – the misappropriation and desecration argument – also seems the stronger the higher the societal impact and recognition of a work of art.

1455. CJEU, 27 February 2020, case C-240/18P, Constantin Film/EUIPO ('Fack Ju Göhte'), para. 43.
1456. CJEU, *ibid.*, para. 42.
1457. Dinwoodie/Gangjee 2016, 367.

Against this background, a refusal based on a conflict with morality seems less convincing when the registration attempt concerns symbols of contemporary mainstream culture. The denial of a conflict with accepted principles of morality in *Constantin Film* reflects the limited power of persuasion of the morality argument in this context.[1458] Even if normative considerations are factored into the equation, it appears artificial to conclude that a reasonable consumer with average sensitivity and tolerance thresholds would qualify an animation film producer's registration of a fictional character as a misappropriation or desecration of the artist's work. While this argument may still have success when a fictional character is based on a traditional story or fairy tale which the public regards as national cultural heritage, it appears weak when the fictional character has newly been created to feature prominently in the film and the artist has specifically designed the character for this purpose.

The analysis, thus, yields mixed results. On the one hand, it seems plausible that the relevant public would regard the attachment of commercial marketing messages to signs belonging to mankind's universal cultural heritage or a country's individual treasury of cultural symbols as an offensive act of misappropriation or desecration (Mona Lisa scenario, section 5.2.1). On the other hand, the same line of reasoning will often be unconvincing when a trademark registration is sought for new literary and artistic creations of contemporary mainstream culture (Mickey Mouse scenario, section 5.2.3). Therefore, trademark judges and examiners can put the morality criteria following from the *Vigeland* decision to good use in the field of cultural heritage signs and other works of art with an elevated societal status. The morality criteria are less strong, however, when contemporary mainstream creations are at issue, such as fictional characters. A conflict with principles of morality, thus, does not have the same exclusionary effect across the whole spectrum of cultural signs. This does not mean that creations falling into the Mickey Mouse category can hardly ever be excluded from trademark protection on the basis of the *Vigeland* criteria. However, it is necessary to employ other lines of reasoning for this purpose, such as arguments supporting the finding of a conflict with public order.

9.1.2.4 Objective Public Order Criteria

In *Vigeland*, the EFTA Court characterized public order considerations as objective criteria in the sense of not requiring an assessment through the prism of consumer perception.[1459] The assessment can thus focus directly on the objective to cultivate the public domain and safeguard the cultural

1458. CJEU, 27 February 2020, case C-240/18P, Constantin Film/EUIPO ('Fack Ju Göhte'), paras 52-53.

1459. EFTA Court, 6 April 2017, case E-5/16, Municipality of Oslo ('Vigeland'), paras 84-86.

innovation cycle – regardless of whether consumers would find the registration of a cultural sign objectionable for these reasons. As to relevant public order criteria, the Court provided the following central arguments for an outright exclusion of cultural signs from trademark protection:

- the registration as a trademark would pose a genuine and sufficiently serious threat to 'certain fundamental values',[1460] 'a fundamental interest of society'[1461] or 'a fundamental concern to the State and the whole of society'[1462] (public order ground 1);
- the registration as a trademark would run counter to the need to safeguard the public domain which amounts to a genuine and serious threat if this need 'itself, is considered a fundamental interest of society'[1463] (public order ground 2).

As the morality argument, these lines of reasoning have the potential to effectively achieve a categorical exclusion of cultural signs from trademark protection across the whole spectrum of goods and services (section 9.1.2.2). Public order ground 2 – referring to public domain preservation as a fundamental interest of society – directly addresses the cultural concerns at stake. It can be seen as a special case of the broader reference to fundamental interests, values and concerns of society in public order ground 1. On its merits, public order ground 2 deals with a specific scenario where a legal system recognizes public domain preservation and cultivation as a fundamental societal interest in its own right – with the consequence that attempts to reappropriate cultural public domain material on the basis of trademark law, and attempts to prevent literary and artistic works from entering the public domain at the end of copyright protection, automatically give rise to a conflict with this element of *ordre public*.

As to theoretical groundwork capable of elevating public domain preservation and cultivation to an independent element of public order, David Lange's plea for public domain recognition offers an important starting point. As discussed in section 3.2.1, Lange argued that 'no exclusive interest should ever have affirmative recognition unless its conceptual opposite is also recognized. Each right ought to be marked off clearly against the public domain'.[1464] It is easy to draw a line between this statement and the quid pro quo in copyright law: the grant of copyright has the corollary that the protected creation enters the public domain at the end of the term of protection. The grant of copyright and the enrichment of the public domain

1460. EFTA Court, *ibid.*, para. 96.
1461. EFTA Court, *ibid.*, para. 95.
1462. EFTA Court, *ibid.*, para. 94.
1463. EFTA Court, *ibid.*, para. 96.
1464. Lange 1981, 150.

are two sides of the same coin.[1465] One way of recognizing this interdependence between copyright protection and public domain enrichment is the inclusion of public domain preservation and cultivation in the canon of principles that underpin the proper functioning of the legal system and form part of the public order. In this vein, Séverine Dusollier explicitly recognized that, in order to immunize the public domain of cultural expressions from renewed commodification on the basis of trademark rights:

> the registration of a trademark should be denied when it would lead to the reconstitution of a monopoly akin to that provided formerly by copyright and preventing use of the work in creative expression. The public interest or general interest could be taken into account as a ground for such a refusal.[1466]

To strengthen the arsenal of legal tools contributing to public domain preservation, Dusollier proposes the qualification of the public domain as a *res communis*: a legal status that implies the prohibition of 'a recapture of the work as a whole' and guarantees 'collective use of the work' in the sense of an entitlement of each member of the public to use, modify, exploit, reproduce and create new works from public domain material.[1467] In the light of the *Vigeland* decision, a refusal of trademark protection because of a conflict with *ordre public* appears as a first step in the right direction from this perspective. Commenting on the above-described *Mona Lisa* decision of the German Federal Patent Court,[1468] Wilhelm Nordemann argued for a broad concept of public order, including the entirety of all legally binding laws that are currently in force. As copyright legislation belongs to this circle of binding laws, Nordemann argued that a trademark proprietor's exclusive right to a work in the public domain had to end where the assertion of the trademark right would run counter to the free use of the public domain material concerned – irrespective of whether the use took place in the private sphere or in commerce.[1469] Based on this recognition of copyright's public domain principle as an element of *ordre public*, Nordemann saw room for limiting the exclusive right of trademark owners in cases where the exercise of this right would impede use in the cultural domain.[1470]

1465. See the invocation of this 'carefully crafted bargain' in U.S. Supreme Court, 2 June 2003, Dastar/Twentieth Century Fox, 539 U.S. 23 (2003), 33-34.
1466. Dusollier 2015, 163.
1467. Dusollier 2015, 167.
1468. German Federal Patent Court, 25 November 1997, case 24 W (pat) 188/96, Mona Lisa, *GRUR* 1998, 1021-1023.
1469. Nordemann 1997, 391. Cf. also Klinkert/Schwab 1999, 1073; Osenberg 1996, 102-104. For an overview of the debate in Germany, see Geier 2015, 158-162.
1470. According to Nordemann 1997, 391, this limitation would only have effect when the trademark owner seeks to prohibit use in relation to cultural productions, such as use on a book cover. For an approach seeking to establish the public domain principle in international intellectual property law, see Köklü/Nérisson 2016, 573-577.

Nordemann's broad concept of public order is in line with the concept of 'constitutional order' in the German Constitution (Grundgesetz). Article 2(1) of the German Constitution guarantees a person's general freedom of action.[1471] With regard to this fundamental freedom, the German Federal Constitutional Court held that the concept of 'constitutional order' was not confined to the norms of the Grundgesetz or fundamental constitutional principles. It encompassed every legal norm which formally and substantially complied with the Grundgesetz.[1472] A person's freedom to act, in other words, falls within the constitutional guarantee of freedom as long as it keeps within the legal framework set by the entirety of legal norms satisfying the requirements of the Constitution. Applying this line of reasoning to the problem of copyright/trademark overlaps, it may be said that the registration of public domain material as a trademark and the invocation of trademark rights to a cultural sign after the expiry of copyright protection are illegitimate actions and in conflict with public order because they thwart the public domain principle (limited term of protection) in copyright law – a copyright rule that is formally and substantially in conformity with constitutional norms. This line of argument goes beyond Nordemann's proposal of a mere limitation of trademark rights. It employs public order – understood broadly as a reference to all legally binding laws that comply with a country's constitution – to arrive at an outright exclusion of cultural signs from trademark protection.

With regard to the evident counterargument that not only copyright but also trademark law has the status of legally binding and constitutional legislation, Friedrich Klinkert and Florian Schwab argued convincingly in the German debate about the *Mona Lisa* decision that, as an absolute ground for refusal in trademark law, a conflict with public order provided room within the trademark system to take account of the public domain principle stemming from copyright law. Given this openness of the trademark system, the recognition of copyright's public domain principle did not presuppose a higher rank of copyright legislation. Deference to copyright's public domain principle in trademark law simply ensured the most harmonious interplay of two sets of laws with the same rank in the norm hierarchy.[1473] As use of a broad concept of public order leads to the most consistent calibration of the relationship between copyright and trademark legislation, this solution is better than an interpretation that would neglect the public domain principle when taking registration decisions in trademark law.

1471. Article 2(1) Grundgesetz, available in English at https://www.gesetze-im-internet.de/englisch_gg/, reads as follows: 'Every person shall have the right to free development of his personality insofar as he does not violate the rights of others or offend against the constitutional order or the moral law.'

1472. German Federal Constitutional Court, 16 January 1957, case 1 BvR 253/56, 'Elfes', BVerfGE 6, 32 (37-38), *NJW* 1957, 297.

1473. Klinkert/Schwab 1999, 1070-1071.

Risk Reduction

Besides these legal-doctrinal arguments for the inclusion of copyright's public domain principle in the concept of *ordre public*, the discussion of the cultural imperative in Chapter 3 offers strong policy-based arguments for the recognition of public domain preservation and cultivation as fundamental interests of society and parts of the public order. As pointed out in aesthetic theory (section 3.3.2), literary and artistic creations have the potential to mirror shortcomings of present society and raise a desire for changes for the better. An artwork can unmask defects of existing societal conditions and prepare society for the transition to a better community.[1474] Therefore, the recognition of the need to preserve a rich and robust public domain of cultural expressions is of particular importance to society. It ensures that alternative visions of society that are evoked in literary and artistic works remain intact – visions that may provide impulses for societal changes. A robust public domain of cultural expressions is central to the artistic discourse. It serves as a source of inspiration and basis of new acts of creation. These new creative efforts will lead to fresh cultural productions which, as the pre-existing works on which they are built, mirror shortcomings of reality and offer the prospect of a better society.

Hence, the societal importance of public domain preservation and cultivation must not be underestimated. As cultural expressions in the public domain serve as a reservoir for new literary and artistic productions and the copyright rule of a limited term of protection ensures a constant enrichment and renewal of this reservoir, there can be little doubt that public domain preservation (preventing trademark proprietors from adopting public domain material as trademarks) and public domain cultivation (preventing copyright holders from withholding their creations from the public domain after copyright expiry) can constitute fundamental interests of society in the sense of the *Vigeland* decision.[1475] As the registration of literary and artistic works as trademarks would run counter to the need to safeguard the public domain and support the described societal interests, it can be deemed a genuine and serious threat to a fundamental societal value that raises a conflict with public order.

A survey of reference points for the inclusion of public domain preservation and cultivation in the circle of fundamental interests of society that form part of *ordre public*, thus, yields two central lines of argument. On the one hand, it may be posited that, as a legally binding and constitutional rule, copyright's public domain principle – the obligation to leave the public

---

1474. Schiller 1794-1795, 35 (Letter 9); Adorno 1970, 32-34.

1475. Norwegian Board of Appeal for Industrial Property Rights, 13 November 2017, cases 16/00148, 16/00149, 16/00150, 16/00151, 16/00153 and 16/00154, 'Vigeland', para. 14. Cf. EFTA Court, 6 April 2017, case E-5/16, Municipality of Oslo ('Vigeland'), para. 96.

domain of cultural expressions intact as a basis for the artistic discourse,[1476] and the obligation to release a literary and artistic work into the public domain in exchange for the enjoyment of exclusive rights during the term of copyright protection – falls within the scope of the concept of public order. On the other hand, it may be said that artists can only fulfil their fundamental societal role – the role of identifying shortcomings in social and political conditions and giving impulses for the improvement of these conditions – on the basis of a rich and diverse public domain of cultural expressions. Trademark protection, however, allows the privatization and redefinition of literary and artistic works in the commercial domain (section 8.2.3.3). This erosion of the cultural dimension of affected works leads to a conflict with public order because it compromises society's fundamental interest in alternative visions of society that can serve as a basis for the artistic discourse, new artworks and critical reflections of societal conditions (section 3.3.2.4). This second argument is not confined to genuine works of art. It also covers works arising from contemporary mainstream productions. Even if a cultural symbol has a commercial background and does not offer an alternative vision of society itself, it may still constitute an important reference point for critical reflection in a work of art (section 5.1).

To this day, these arguments remain underdeveloped in case law. In *Medusa* – the decision of the German Federal Court of Justice where the defendant referred to the ancient 'Medusa Rondanini' to demonstrate that he had not copied Versace's Medusa logo (section 6.2.2) – the Court tersely concluded that the public domain status of a sign did not prevent its use as a trademark. In infringement proceedings, the judge was bound by the office decision to grant trademark rights and could not rely on a sign's public domain status to deny actionable trademark use.[1477] In *Mona Lisa*, the German Federal Patent Court expressed doubts about a conflict with public order because a denial of trademark rights based on this ground for refusal would prevent not only third parties from registering literary and artistic works as trademarks but also the works' authors themselves.[1478] This line of reasoning neglects the quid pro quo underlying the grant of copyright protection. In exchange for the enjoyment of copyright, an author and his heirs[1479] are bound to relinquish exclusive rights to her creation at the end of

1476. As to underlying copyright theory, see Locke 1698, book II chapter 5 § 27; Gordon 1993, 1562-1564.

1477. German Federal Court of Justice, 24 November 2011, case I ZR 175/09, 'Medusa', paras 19-20.

1478. German Federal Patent Court, 25 November 1997, case 24 W (pat) 188/96, Mona Lisa, *GRUR* 1998, 1021 (1023).

1479. Viewed from this perspective, the counterargument advanced by Ohly 2008, 207, who wants to give an author's heirs the opportunity to acquire trademark rights is invalid. As the author himself, the heirs would neglect copyright's quid pro quo and refuse to pay the price for the enjoyment of copyright during the limited term for which copyright legislation provides.

the term of protection, and let her work enter the public domain (section 3.2). Unless a literary and artistic work is specifically created to serve as a trademark and enjoys copyright protection only incidentally (the limitation of public order arguments pointed out by the EFTA Court, cf. section 9.1.2.5),[1480] authors can hardly assert a legitimate interest in coexisting trademark protection that could continue after copyright expiry and push aside society's interest in the enrichment of the public domain of cultural expressions. The argument developed by the German Federal Patent Court is thus invalid. An author's interest in trademark protection does not pose an obstacle to the invocation of public order as a ground for refusing trademark rights. On the contrary, there is substantial reason to rely on public order considerations and safeguard a rich and diverse public domain by inhibiting both – third parties and authors (including their heirs) – from acquiring trademark rights.[1481] Even if an author states that he has no intention to curtail freedom of remix, the registration of an artwork as a trademark remains illegitimate. In the light of the deterrent effect of trademark protection (section 6.3), the artist cannot dispel concerns about the use of trademark rights to censor derivative works and erode copyright's public domain principle. For instance, Banksy's attempt to register the 'Flower Thrower' as a trademark is in conflict with public order even though the artist explicitly encourages the 'copying, borrowing and uncredited use […] for amusement, activism and education purposes'.[1482] Banksy cannot whitewash the erosion of the temporal limits of copyright protection by consenting to certain forms of remix.

Departing from its cautious approach in *Mona Lisa*, the German Federal Patent Court recognized in *Neuschwanstein* that indications of buildings or objects with outstanding cultural significance – belonging to the national or world cultural heritage – were elements of the public domain that should not be exposed to monopolization and commercialization following from the grant of trademark rights.[1483] Considering the cultural, architectural, political and historical importance of Neuschwanstein castle in Bavaria, the Court had no doubt that there was a strong public interest in the free availability of the name 'Neuschwanstein'. To prevent the grant of an unjustified legal monopoly, the German Federal Patent Court assumed a general need to keep this name free. It declared the indication 'Neuschwanstein' devoid of

1480. EFTA Court, 6 April 2017, case E-5/16, Municipality of Oslo ('Vigeland'), paras 97-98.

1481. See also the critique expressed by Klinkert/Schwab 1999, 1070, who maintain that, even if it was legitimate to give the author a privileged position, this specific author privilege could not justify the Court's reluctance to invoke public order as a ground for refusal against trademark applications filed by third parties.

1482. EUIPO Cancellation Division, 14 September 2020, cancellation no. 33 843 C (invalidity), Full Colour Black/Pest Control Office ('Banksy'), 11.

1483. German Federal Patent Court, 4 February 2011, case 25 W (pat) 182/09, 'Neuschwanstein', *GRUR* 2011, 922 (925).

distinctive character.[1484] The German Federal Court of Justice, however, rejected this argument. It saw no room for recognizing a general need to keep free – going beyond established grounds for refusing non-distinctive and descriptive signs – to prevent the acquisition of trademark rights to indications of subject matter with outstanding cultural significance. In the opinion of the German Federal Court of Justice, such a general need to keep free could not be derived from the cultural heritage status of relevant buildings and objects, such as Neuschwanstein castle. Moreover, it could not be based on the public domain principle in copyright law.[1485] Therefore, the German Federal Court of Justice overruled the decision of the German Federal Patent Court and rejected the concept of a general need to keep public domain material free.[1486]

In the aforementioned decision *Winston Churchill* (section 9.1.2.2) – concerning the registration of Churchill's name and portrait as trademarks for cigars – the Dutch Supreme Court held that, in principle, the unauthorized communication of a portrait to the public may amount to an offence under Article 35 of the Dutch Copyright Act (Auteurswet, as in force at the time of the decision) and conflict with public order for this reason.[1487] Hence, the Court acknowledged that the infringement of a norm of copyright law (Articles 19 to 21 of the Dutch Copyright Act set forth provisions regulating the protection of portraits) can give rise to a conflict with public order. In the concrete case, however, the requirements for the assumption of an offence were not fulfilled.[1488] Moreover, the facts of the case did not offer starting points for the Court to discuss whether an encroachment upon copyright's public domain principle could come into conflict with public order even though the Dutch Copyright Act did not (and still does not) contain criminal provisions seeking to safeguard the quid pro quo underlying the grant of protection. The *Winston Churchill* decision, thus, did not address the public order considerations developed above.[1489] The aforementioned *Nachtwacht* decision of the Court of Appeals of The Hague also remained silent on the issue even though the Benelux Office for Intellectual Property had explicitly invoked public order as one of the relevant grounds for refusal in that case.[1490] As indicated above (section 9.1.2.1), the Court was reluctant to

1484. German Federal Patent Court, *ibid.*, 925.

1485. German Federal Court of Justice, 8 March 2012, case I ZB 13/11, 'Neuschwanstein', *GRUR* 2012, 1044, paras 28-30.

1486. Cf. Lerach 2018, 461.

1487. Dutch Supreme Court, 28 October 1948, Bureau I.E./Churchill's Cigars ('Winston Churchill'), *Bijblad bij de industriële eigendom* 1949, 24.

1488. Dutch Supreme Court, *ibid.*, 24-25.

1489. For a rejection of the public order argument in the Benelux context, see Vanovermeire 2009, 180-183.

1490. Court of Appeals of The Hague, 29 August 2017, case 200.205.771/01, ECLI:NL:GH-DHA:2017:2446, Chiever/Benelux-Organisatie voor de Intellectuele Eigendom ('Nachtwacht'), para. 1.4.

discuss the public order dimension of the need to safeguard the public domain. Instead, it relied on a lack of distinctive character to deny trademark rights.[1491]

In U.S. case law, copyright's quid pro quo – the interdependence of protection and public domain enrichment – features more prominently. As pointed out in section 4.1.2, the U.S. Supreme Court emphasized in *Dastar/Twentieth Century Fox* that it was necessary to shield the quid pro quo underlying copyright (and patent) law from the corrosive effect of protection regimes with potentially indefinite rights. In this context, the Court explicitly referred to the 'carefully crafted bargain' that regulated the interplay between the grant of copyright and freedom of use after copyright expiry.[1492] In its earlier decision in *Graham/John Deere* (see section 4.1.1), the U.S. Supreme Court had already recognized the need to preserve the public domain of technical know-how in the context of patent law. According to the Court, Congress may not authorize the issuance of patents whose effects were to remove existent knowledge from the public domain, or restrict free access to materials already available.[1493] However, the Court clarified in *Eldred/Ashcroft* and *Golan/Holder* that this passage of its earlier decision was not intended to put a categorical ban on legislation that, as a result of an extension of the term of copyright protection, delayed the entry of existing works into the public domain,[1494] or restored copyright to works that had already entered the public domain for the purpose of achieving compliance with international minimum standards of copyright protection.[1495] The statement made in *Graham/John Deere* only addressed 'an invention's very eligibility for patent protection'.[1496] In *Golan/Holder*, the U.S. Supreme Court finally concluded that, for the purpose of allowing the U.S. to adhere to the Berne Convention, expand markets for U.S. authors and invigorate protection against copyright piracy abroad,[1497] it was legitimate to remove foreign literary and artistic works from the U.S. public domain by reviving copyright protection.[1498]

With regard to the question of whether use of trademark law to reappropriate public domain material or extend exclusive rights to cultural signs after copyright expiry may be qualified as incompatible with public order, this U.S. jurisprudence yields mixed results. On the one hand, *Eldred/Ashcroft* and *Golan/Holder* seem to indicate that the Supreme Court

1491. Court of Appeals of The Hague, ibid., paras 8-9.

1492. U.S. Supreme Court, 2 June 2003, Dastar/Twentieth Century Fox, 539 U.S. 23 (2003), 33-34.

1493. U.S. Supreme Court, 21 February 1966, Graham/John Deere Co., 383 U.S. 1, 5-6 (1966).

1494. U.S. Supreme Court, 15 January 2003, Eldred/Ashcroft, 537 U.S. 186, 202 (2003).

1495. U.S. Supreme Court, 18 January 2012, Golan/Holder, 565 U.S. 302, 321 (2012).

1496. U.S. Supreme Court, *ibid.*, 321.

1497. U.S. Supreme Court, *ibid.*, 324.

1498. U.S. Supreme Court, *ibid.*, 315-321 and 328-329.

may accept a delay in public domain enrichment and the removal of cultural signs from the public domain.[1499] On the other hand, it must not be overlooked that these decisions concerned the grant of an extended or revived term of copyright protection. Hence, the basic principle of a limited term of protection was not at issue. Neither *Eldred* nor *Golan* addressed potential threats to public order that may arise from the grant of indefinitely renewable trademark rights. In respect of a trademark scenario with potentially perpetual protection, the concerns about an erosion of copyright's 'carefully crafted bargain'[1500] which the Court expressed in *Dastar/Twentieth Century Fox* may finally prevail.[1501] Moreover, it is noteworthy that the enquiry into a conflict with public order is one of the questions that informs the decision on a sign's eligibility for trademark protection. Even if the passage taken from *Graham/John Deere* was only meant to address 'an invention's very eligibility for patent protection',[1502] this specific focus does not render it inapplicable in a trademark scenario. By contrast, it is the very purpose of the public order enquiry to clarify whether cultural signs can be deemed eligible for trademark protection. In combination with *Dastar*, the decision in *Graham/John Deere* may thus serve as a basis for holding that the grant of trademark rights whose effects are to remove cultural signs from the public domain conflicts with public order because they undermine copyright's carefully crafted bargain.[1503] Therefore, U.S. case law offers starting points for the recognition of public domain preservation and cultivation as elements of *ordre public*.

In the EU, similar reference points can be found in CJEU jurisprudence. To preserve the public domain of technical knowledge, the Court held in *Philips/Remington* that it was a legitimate aim to prevent individuals from using 'registration of a mark in order to acquire or perpetuate exclusive rights relating to technical solutions'[1504] (section 7.1.2). In *Hauck/Stokke*, the Court recognized the more general objective to prevent the exclusive and permanent right which a trademark confers 'from serving to extend indefinitely the life of other rights which the EU legislature has sought to make subject to limited periods'[1505] (section 7.2.2). As copyright constitutes such a right with a limited term of protection, *Hauck/Stokke* lays groundwork for a CJEU

1499. Cf. Dusollier 2015, 154-157.

1500. U.S. Supreme Court, 2 June 2003, Dastar/Twentieth Century Fox, 539 U.S. 23 (2003), 33-34.

1501. Cf. Calboli 2014a, 32-33.

1502. U.S. Supreme Court, 18 January 2012, Golan/Holder, 565 U.S. 302, 321 (2012).

1503. Cf. the corresponding lines of reasoning in U.S. Supreme Court, 21 February 1966, Graham/John Deere Co., 383 U.S. 1, 5-6 (1966), and U.S. Supreme Court, 2 June 2003, Dastar/Twentieth Century Fox, 539 U.S. 23 (2003), 33-34.

1504. CJEU, 18 June 2002, case C-299/99, Philips/Remington, para. 82.

1505. CJEU, 18 September 2014, case C-205/13, Hauck/Stokke, paras 19-20.

decision in which the Court invokes public order considerations to exclude cultural signs from trademark protection.[1506]

The fact that *Philips/Remington* and *Hauck/Stokke* concerned technical and aesthetic functionality need not be an obstacle. As Annette Kur has shown, there is a link between the exclusion of signs because of functionality, and the exclusion of signs because of a conflict with public order.[1507] The connecting piece of legislation is Article 6*quinquies*(B) PC. Under the international rule of *telle quelle* protection laid down in Article 6*quinquies*(A)(1) PC, a country of the Paris Union is bound to accept every trademark duly registered in the country of origin for filing and subsequent protection in the same form (*telle quelle*).[1508] However, the country where protection is sought is free to deny registration or invalidate a trademark stemming from another Paris Union country on the basis of one of the grounds for refusal listed in Article 6*quinquies*(B) PC: the mark infringes earlier rights of third parties (No. 1); the mark is non-distinctive, descriptive or generic (No. 2); the mark is deceptive or contrary to morality or public order (No. 3). In addition to these internationally recognized grounds for refusal, Article 7(1)(e) EUTMR and Article 4(1)(e) TMD explicitly allow the denial of trademark protection – and thus also the denial of *telle quelle* protection in the sense of Article 6*quinquies*(A)(1) PC – if a sign is functional. Hence, the question arises whether a denial based on the functionality doctrine is in line with the international guarantee of *telle quelle* protection even though functionality is not listed as a ground for refusal in Article 6*quinquies*(B) PC.

Obviously, one way of solving this dilemma is to argue that a refusal based on functionality constitutes a specific case – a subcategory – of one of the grounds for refusal enumerated in Article 6*quinquies*(B) PC. In *Rasierer mit drei Scherköpfen* – a case about *telle quelle* protection of the head of Philips' three-headed rotary electric shaver (see section 7.1.1 for a discussion of other lawsuits dealing with this technical design feature) – the German Federal Court of Justice opted for Article 6*quinquies*(B) No. 2 PC and placed the functionality doctrine in the context of distinctiveness-based grounds for refusal that safeguard the need to keep non-distinctive, descriptive and generic signs free.[1509] As Annette Kur rightly observed, this decision is inconsistent because a lack of distinctive character can be overcome through

1506. Cf. Quaedvlieg 2006, 511-512, discussing the 'public interest in *ending* protection' (emphasis in the original text) and whether the CJEU could recognize 'a reflex on trademark law'.

1507. Kur 2011, 18-20.

1508. For a discussion of the scope of this obligation and, more specifically, the reduction of the obligation to acceptance of the form of the mark, see Ng-Loy 2018, 161-162. Cf. Kunz-Hallstein 2006, 487; Beier 1992, 243; Ladas 1975, 1211-1240; Bodenhausen 1969, 113-119.

1509. German Federal Court of Justice, 17 November 2005, case I ZB 12/04, 'Rasierer mit drei Scherköpfen', *GRUR Int.* 2006, 765, para. 15.

use in trade.[1510] A refusal based on utilitarian functionality, by contrast, leads to an outright exclusion of the sign concerned – irrespective of whether the sign is distinctive.[1511] Therefore, the correct international basis for explaining the application of the functionality doctrine in decisions about *telle quelle* protection is Article 6*quinquies*(B) No. 3 PC: public order and morality.[1512] A conflict with public order or morality results in a categorical exclusion of trademark protection that remains unaffected by the acquisition of distinctive character through use. The integration of functionality in Article 6*quinquies*(B) No. 3 PC is also more consistent than the assumption that freedom to exclude functional signs from trademark registration can be created by positing that besides the category of signs inherently capable of distinguishing goods or services and eligible for registration under Article 15(1) TRIPS, there is a category of signs inherently *in*capable of distinguishing goods or services and *in*eligible for registration, namely signs that are functional.[1513]

Adopting the approach based on Article 6*quinquies*(b) No. 3 PC, *Philips/Remington* and *Hauck/Stokke* can be qualified as CJEU decisions that deal with utilitarian and aesthetic functionality as specific subcategories of public order and morality. From this perspective, the objective featuring prominently in these decisions, namely the objective to prevent trademark rights 'from serving to extend indefinitely the life of other rights which the EU legislature has sought to make subject to limited periods',[1514] is a species of public order considerations. Given this link between public order and the functionality discussion in *Philips/Remington* and *Hauck/Stokke*, it is only a small step for the CJEU to reject trademark rights to literary and artistic works on the ground that the grant of trademark protection would artificially extend the limited period of protection prescribed in EU copyright law[1515] and conflict with public order for that reason. As functionality proves to be a subcategory of public order criteria in the light of Article 6*quinquies*(B) PC, it is consistent to extend the public domain rationale known from *Philips/Remington* and *Hauck/Stokke* to literary and artistic works under the general heading of public order.

Admittedly, the CJEU explicitly recognized in *Butterfly Music* and *Flos* that the introduction of a harmonized 70-year term of copyright protection[1516] in the EU may have the effect of 'protecting afresh works or subject

1510. Kur 2011, 20; Kur 2017, 1086. Cf. Article 7(3) EUTMR; Article 4(4) TMD.

1511. CJEU, 18 June 2002, case C-299/99, Philips/Remington, para. 57; CJEU, 20 September 2007, case C-371/06, Benetton/G-Star, paras 25-27; CJEU, 14 September 2010, case C-48/09 P, Lego/Mega Brands, para. 47.

1512. Kur 2011, 20; Kur 2017, 1086.

1513. De Carvalho 2014, 316-317.

1514. CJEU, 18 September 2014, case C-205/13, Hauck/Stokke, paras 19-20. Cf. CJEU, 18 June 2002, case C-299/99, Philips/Remington, para. 82.

1515. Article 1(1) TD.

1516. Article 1(1) TD.

matter which had entered the public domain'.[1517] As the U.S. Supreme Court in *Eldred/Ashcroft* and *Golan/Holder*,[1518] the CJEU thus accepted inroads into the public domain to achieve overarching policy goals, in particular EU harmonization and internal market objectives.[1519] This jurisprudence, however, need not prevent the Court from generalizing the public domain rationale known from *Philips/Remington* and *Hauck/Stokke*. As the U.S. decisions, *Butterfly Music* and *Flos* only concerned the extension and restoration of a limited term of copyright protection – without questioning the basic principle of a limited term as such.[1520] Trademark law, however, offers potentially perpetual protection. The grant of trademark rights would undermine copyright's public domain principle altogether. With regard to this more fundamental assault on the public domain, the CJEU remains free to take measures on the basis of *Philips/Remington* and *Hauck/Stokke* and qualify the acquisition of indefinitely renewable trademark rights as incompatible with public order.

As U.S. case law, the jurisprudence of the CJEU, thus, offers starting points for the inclusion of public domain preservation and cultivation in the circle of public order considerations that can lead to a categorical exclusion of cultural signs from trademark protection. Against this background, the *Vigeland* decision of the EFTA Court can pave the way for a new approach. Highlighting the possibility of recognizing the need to safeguard the public domain as a fundamental interest of society,[1521] it may inspire decisions that invoke public order as a ground for refusing trademark rights to cultural signs.[1522] As explained in section 9.1.2.2, the Norwegian Board of Appeal for Industrial Property Rights already gave an example of this new approach. The Board of Appeal qualified the attempt to register Vigeland's sculptures as being contrary to public order because of the considerable cultural value of the artworks and the fundamental societal considerations underlying the temporal limitation of copyright protection.[1523] This final word in the *Vigeland* case demonstrates the effectiveness of public order ground 2 as a means to keep cultural signs outside the trademark system: the scenario

1517. CJEU, 29 June 1999, case C-60/98, Butterfly Music, paras 18-20; CJEU, 27 January 2011, case C-168/09, Flos, para. 42.
1518. U.S. Supreme Court, 15 January 2003, Eldred/Ashcroft, 537 U.S. 186, 202 (2003); U.S. Supreme Court, 18 January 2012, Golan/Holder, 565 U.S. 302, 321 (2012).
1519. CJEU, 29 June 1999, case C-60/98, Butterfly Music, paras 9-10 and 24; CJEU, 27 January 2011, case C-168/09, Flos, para. 42.
1520. CJEU, 29 June 1999, case C-60/98, Butterfly Music, paras 18-20; CJEU, 27 January 2011, case C-168/09, Flos, para. 43 and 46.
1521. EFTA Court, 6 April 2017, case E-5/16, Municipality of Oslo ('Vigeland'), para. 96.
1522. Senftleben 2017b, 716-717. As to experiences in New Zealand with a concept of 'cultural offensiveness' that covers traditional cultural expressions, cf. Handler 2012, 242; Frankel 2008, 455-456; Frankel 2005, 90-93.
1523. Norwegian Board of Appeal for Industrial Property Rights, 13 November 2017, cases 16/00148, 16/00149, 16/00150, 16/00151, 16/00153 and 16/00154, 'Vigeland', para. 14.

where a legal system recognizes public domain preservation and cultivation, in and of itself, as a fundamental interest of society.

Interestingly, developments in EU copyright law may give further impulses for elevating the need to preserve and cultivate the public domain to an element of *ordre public*. With the amendment of EU copyright law in the 2017 Directive on Copyright in the Digital Single Market, a new provision entered the picture that explicitly recognizes the necessity to ensure that cultural expressions in the public domain are not encumbered with new layers of copyright protection for the same expression. Article 14 DSMD provides that:

> when the term of protection of a work of visual art has expired, any material resulting from an act of reproduction of that work is not subject to copyright or related rights, unless the material resulting from that act of reproduction is original in the sense that it is the author's own intellectual creation.

Evidently, the provision seeks to prevent copyright evergreening. Recital 53 DSMD directly refers to the underlying public domain principle in copyright law:

> The expiry of the term of protection of a work entails the entry of that work into the public domain and the expiry of the rights that Union copyright law provides in relation to that work. In the field of visual arts, the circulation of faithful reproductions of works in the public domain contributes to the access to and promotion of culture, and the access to cultural heritage. In the digital environment, the protection of such reproductions through copyright or related rights is inconsistent with the expiry of the copyright protection of works...

Hence, Article 14 DSMD is intended to preserve the public domain by barring copyright claims based on 'faithful reproductions' of cultural expressions in the public domain.[1524] It clarifies that the mere reproduction of public domain material does not revive copyright. The photographer is not entitled to assert copyright to the reproduction.[1525] This new copyright rule – no new term of protection for verbatim reproductions – makes an aspect of copyright's public domain principle visible in statutory law and, arguably, requires corresponding measures in trademark law.[1526] If EU legislation explicitly excludes the revival of copyright protection, trademark offices and

1524. Cf. Holthuis/Van den Eijnde 2019, 133-134; Keller 2019, 172-173, who also address protection regimes for non-original photographs that are available in some EU Member States. For an example of this protection at the national level, see German Federal Court of Justice, 20 December 2018, case I ZR 104/17, 'Museumsfotos', *GRUR* 2019, 284. For a broader case law overview and in-depth analysis, see Wallace/Euler 2020, 825-834.
1525. Cf. ECS 2020, 3.
1526. Cf. Keller 2019, 172.

courts must not bypass and thwart this recognition of the need to preserve the public domain by awarding trademark rights to cultural expressions that have entered the public domain. With Article 14 DSMD, the objective to preserve the public domain obtains a formal, statutory position. The provision can be understood to express a public domain principle which, as an overarching principle of EU intellectual property law, forms part of *ordre public*.[1527] Moreover, it can be assumed that the CJEU already confirmed the impact of this overarching principle on trademark law in *Philips/Remington* and *Hauck/Stokke*.[1528] As Article 14 DSMD itself, these decisions of the CJEU can be seen as manifestations of the public domain principle in EU intellectual property law. Considering that the functionality doctrine discussed in *Philips/Remington* and *Hauck/Stokke* is a subcategory of public order,[1529] it is consistent to also align the assessment of a conflict with public order with the public domain principle. If trademark protection is sought with regard to reproductions of artworks that are in the public domain, these trademark applications should be refused on the ground that the grant of trademark rights would thwart the public domain principle underlying copyright law (and other intellectual property regimes with a limited term of protection). The grant of trademark rights would conflict with the need to preserve and cultivate the public domain as an element of public order, as expressed in Article 14 DSMD, *Philips/Remington* and *Hauck/Stokke*.

In the context of trademark law, however, it would be inappropriate to follow the confinement of Article 14 DSMD to non-original reproductions. The exclusion of copyright revival in Article 14 DSMD no longer applies when the reproduction is 'original in the sense that it is the author's own intellectual creation'. In line with Recital 53, this proviso confines the scope of Article 14 DSMD to 'faithful reproductions' that do not reflect a sufficient degree of free, creative choices to satisfy the originality test in EU copyright law.[1530] If this confinement to non-original verbatim reproductions was applied in trademark law, it would lead to a situation where copies of public domain artworks that contain creative additions or modifications, such as stylized versions, would escape the verdict of a conflict with *ordre public*. This limitation of the scope of the rule is problematic in light of the breadth of trademark rights. The trademark proprietor can bring an infringement claim not only against the use of an identical copy of the protected mark but

1527. Cf. Nordemann 1997, 391; Klinkert/Schwab 1999, 1073; Osenberg 1996, 102-104. See also Wallace/Euler 2020, 836-838, for a discussion of the broader context and public interests surrounding Article 14 DSMD.

1528. CJEU, 18 September 2014, case C-205/13, Hauck/Stokke, paras 19-20. Cf. CJEU, 18 June 2002, case C-299/99, Philips/Remington, para. 82.

1529. Kur 2011, 20; Kur 2017, 1086.

1530. ECS 2020, 3; Holthuis/Van den Eijnde 2019, 134. As to the copyright originality test in the EU, see CJEU, 16 July 2009, case C-5/08, Infopaq/DDF, para. 45; CJEU, 1 December 2011, case C-145/10, Painer, para. 89. With regard to the eligibility of artwork photographs for copyright protection, see Margoni 2014, 51-53.

also against the use of conflicting signs that are merely similar from an aural, visual or conceptual perspective.[1531] To effectively prevent the reappropriation of public domain artworks and interferences with cultural follow-on innovation, it is thus necessary to go beyond 'faithful reproductions' and also inhibit the registration of signs that are merely similar to a public domain artwork. In other words, compliance with public order should only be found if the reproduction of a public domain artwork is so loosely connected with the original work that the trademark proprietor could not base an infringement claim on sign similarity when seeking to prevent artists from using the original work in new literary and artistic productions. In this vein, the EFTA Court required the use of signs which, if based on a work pertaining to the public domain, contained additional elements that transformed or diffused the original work to such an extent that consumers were unlikely to confuse the sign with the original creative work.[1532] The registration attempt should only survive scrutiny in the light of public domain preservation as an element of public order if it concerns a sign that differs from the public domain artwork at issue to such an extent that, according to trademark infringement standards (sections 6.2.2 and 6.2.3), reproductions of the original work in artistic remix activities would no longer fall within the scope of the trademark right. If these guidelines are taken into account, Article 14 DSMD can contribute in a meaningful way to the recognition of public domain preservation and cultivation as elements of public order in the EU.

As explained at the beginning of this section, the recognition of the public domain principle, in and of itself, as an element of *ordre public* (public order ground 2) is only one aspect of the approach which the EFTA Court developed in *Vigeland*.[1533] Public order ground 2 is a special case of the broader, more general public order ground 1: the scenario where a trademark registration poses a genuine and sufficiently serious threat to 'certain fundamental values',[1534] 'a fundamental interest of society'[1535] or 'a fundamental concern to the State and the whole of society'.[1536] If a legal system does not recognize the need to safeguard the public domain, in and of itself, as a fundamental interest of society, other values, interests or concerns can thus still support a refusal based on a conflict with public order. The above analysis of reasons for a categorical exclusion of literary and artistic works from trademark protection reflects several of these values, interests and concerns. The objective to prevent unfair freeriding on positive connotations which signs may have as a result of their evolution in the cultural domain (section 8.2.3.1), for instance, can be placed in the broader context of

1531. Cf. Kur/Senftleben 2017, para. 4.337-4.345 and 5.106.
1532. EFTA Court, *ibid.*, paras 97-98.
1533. EFTA Court, 6 April 2017, case E-5/16, Municipality of Oslo ('Vigeland'), para. 96.
1534. EFTA Court, *ibid.*, para. 96.
1535. EFTA Court, *ibid.*, para. 95.
1536. EFTA Court, *ibid.*, para. 94.

society's fundamental interest in undistorted competition.[1537] The same may be said about the necessity to take measures against the improper acquisition of trademark rights on the basis of sign recognition that has been obtained during the long term of copyright protection (section 7.3.5.6). In addition to these considerations relating to the prevention of unfair competitive advantages, the fundamental interest in freedom of expression enters the picture.[1538] Exclusive trademark rights that are employed as censorship instruments (section 8.2.3.2), commercial meanings that devalue cultural signs as reference points for open, dialogic communication in the artistic domain and building blocks of new literary and artistic creations (section 8.2.3.3) and infringement risks that pose an obstacle to the reuse and remix of domestic cultural symbols (section 6.3) are examples of encroachments upon freedom of expression that may follow from the grant of trademark rights to cultural signs. Given the human rights dimension and the fundamental importance of freedom of expression to society, it seems justified to apply public order as a ground for refusal to eliminate these risks.[1539]

As the morality considerations discussed in the preceding section, the concept of public order following from the EFTA Court's *Vigeland* decision, thus, has a remarkable potential to achieve a categorical exclusion of cultural signs from trademark protection. Unlike a scrutiny in the light of morality standards, public order criteria are not inherently limited by the need to conduct the analysis through the prism of consumer perception. By contrast, trademark tribunals can directly invoke fundamental values, interests and concerns that militate against the grant of trademark protection. The described lines of argument – based on the public domain principle in EU intellectual property law, copyright's quid pro quo, the risk of losing alternative visions of society, the need to ensure undistorted competition and the guarantee of freedom of expression – broaden the ambit of operation of public order as a ground for refusal. The EFTA Court expressed the view that

---

1537. Modern concepts of undistorted, fair competition recognize, besides the traditional protection of competitors and consumers, the public interest in the efficient functioning of competition – in the sense of a protection of market participants' freedom of action and decision. Cf. Höpperger/Senftleben 2007, 74-76; Henning-Bodewig 2005, 425-426; Ohly 2004, 894-896; Ullmann 2003, 821.

1538. Articles 11 and 13 CFR; Article 10 ECHR. Cf. section 3.1. See the discussion of freedom of expression as guiding principles for the development of EU trademark law by Senftleben/Bently/Dinwoodie et al. 2015, 337. As to the general potential of fundamental rights to ensure an appropriate calibration of intellectual property protection, see the groundwork laid by Geiger 2004b, 268; Geiger 2006, 371.

1539. Cf. the debate on how to reconcile trademark protection with freedom of expression. See Bohaczewski 2020, 856; Żelechowski 2018, 115-135; Senftleben 2015, 354; Ramsey/Schovsbo 2013, 671; Simon Fhima 2013, 293; Sakulin 2010; Geiger 2010a, 163; Burrell/Gangjee 2010, 544; Nasser 2009, 188; Bently 2008, 1205; Dreyfuss 2008, 261; Geiger 2007, 317; Ramsey 2010a, 405; Weckström 2007, 671; Gulasekaram 2005, 887; Leval 2004, 187; Timbers/Huston 2003, 1278; Aoki 1997, 523; Dreyfuss 1990, 415-418.

'registration of a sign as a trade mark may only be refused as contrary to public policy in accordance with [EU trademark legislation] in exceptional circumstances'.[1540] Considering the societal values, interests and concerns discussed above, however, the threshold of exceptionality need not be high. From the perspective of the cultural imperative, an exceptional situation that calls for caution arises whenever trademark protection is requested in respect of a cultural sign. The public order criteria have the potential to pave the way for this cautious approach.

As discussed in the preceding section, the morality criteria following from the *Vigeland* decision are strong in respect of cultural heritage signs and other important works of art (Mona Lisa scenario, section 5.2.1). However, they are weak in respect of contemporary mainstream creations (Mickey Mouse scenario, section 5.2.3). The public order criteria, by contrast, offer a solid basis for the exclusion of trademark protection in respect of both categories of cultural signs. The registration of works of art (Mona Lisa scenario) raises concerns about the loss of alternative visions of society. The registration of icons of contemporary mainstream culture (Mickey Mouse scenario) gives rise to concerns about the erosion of copyright's quid pro quo. In both cases, the need to prevent unfair competitive advantages and the risk of an encroachment upon freedom of expression offer additional arguments for particular caution and a denial of trademark rights. Hence, the public order considerations following from *Vigeland* have a universal field of application.

9.1.2.5 Declaration of Non-Use in a Cultural Context

As to the issue of practical implementation, guidelines for detecting conflicts with morality have already come to light in section 9.1.2.3. A refusal based on a conflict with morality requires the identification of artworks that constitute prominent parts of a nation's cultural heritage, emblems of sovereignty or symbols of a nation's foundations and values. It also requires an assessment of sign misappropriation or desecration through the prism of consumer perception. The morality argument is the stronger the more elevated the status of the cultural sign concerned. In particular, a conflict is likely to arise when an attempt is made to register signs belonging to mankind's universal cultural heritage or a country's individual treasury of cultural symbols. This group of signs seems congruent with the circle of signs that have been characterized as self-evident conflict cases in the discussion of the Mona Lisa scenario in section 5.2.1. Arguably, a trademark examiner or judge will have little difficulty to recognize signs in this category in a trademark application. If, in line with the recommendation in section 9.1.2.3, the attachment of commercial marketing messages is generally deemed offensive, the identification of a sign with the elevated status of

1540. EFTA Court, *ibid.*, para. 96.

universal cultural heritage or a sign with particular cultural importance at the national level will almost inevitably lead to the verdict of a conflict with principles of morality.

The practical implementation of the described public order criteria is more delicate: trademark offices may find it hard to identify problem scenarios where a trademark registration would undermine the public domain principle in intellectual property law or copyright's quid pro quo, blur alternative visions of society, grant an unfair competitive advantage or impede freedom of expression and cultural follow-on innovation. In practice, it seems advisable to translate these abstract criteria into more concrete guidelines for examiners and judges. The accomplishment of this task is more complex than in the case of morality criteria because an exclusion based on public order considerations, as explained in the preceding section, has a broader field of application. While the morality criteria concern predominantly the exclusion of cultural heritage signs and other works of art (Mona Lisa scenario), the multifaceted public order criteria cover not only this category of signs but also contemporary symbols of mainstream culture (Mickey Mouse scenario). Surveying the factors for identifying signs in the Mona Lisa and the Mickey Mouse category, as discussed in sections 5.2.1 and 5.2.3, several shared criteria come to the fore that may be put to good use in the public order analysis, such as the question of whether the sign at issue:

- is exhibited in an art museum or features in a contemporary mainstream production;
- has already served as a basis for parodies, remixes or other forms of mash-up;
- displays typical style features of artworks or cultural mainstream creations;
- clearly meets copyright's originality test because it reflects a high degree of free, creative choices;
- could theoretically serve as an embellishment to improve the outward appearance of a product;
- would describe the contents of a product when applied to goods or services in the cultural domain.

If the application of these criteria brings to light a sign's cultural significance, arguments for the assumption of a conflict with public order can be derived from the need to prevent the aforementioned negative consequences (erosion of the public domain principle and copyright's quid pro quo, blurring and suppression of alternative visions of society, unfair competitive advantages, curtailment of freedom of expression, impediment of cultural follow-on innovation). If these arguments carry weight in light of the cultural significance of the sign at issue, it becomes possible to exclude the sign from trademark protection. However, the decision process is not intended to lead to an inescapable exclusion automatism (section 5.2.1). The degree to which the aforementioned factors support a finding of cultural significance is decisive for the decision on the exclusion of the sign from trademark protection. If the sign at issue does not appear particularly relevant to cultural follow-on innovation in the light of the described factors, an exclusion is less plausible than in the case of a sign that clearly has relevance to the discourse in the artistic domain when it is viewed through the prism of the assessment factors. Therefore, the factors are tools to assess the degree of cultural significance and support the decision to exclude a sign from trademark protection. They are not inerrant indicators of cultural significance that dictate a categorical exclusion from trademark protection whenever a sign scores in one of the assessment categories.

To clarify the interplay of the different assessment factors, it seems important to revisit an issue that has already been mentioned above. As explained in sections 2.2 and 5.2.1, copyright's originality test is not congruent with the limits of the domain of literature and art. The fact that a given creation satisfies the test of originality can hardly inform the final decision on the cultural nature of a sign for which trademark protection is sought. The originality test has been overstretched and now encompasses even industrial creations outside the realm of literature and art: 'non-literature' and 'non-art' falling outside the spectrum of cultural signs discussed in Chapter 5. Trade symbols can serve as examples. The logo and design of Campbell's soup can, for instance, may attract copyright protection in countries applying a low originality threshold.[1541] As explained in section 5.2.5, however, this trade symbol should not be qualified as a cultural sign. While Andy Warhol's work gives evidence of artistic remix, the Campbell logo and the soup can design do not constitute museum items or pieces of art (in contrast to Andy Warhol's paintings). They are industrial creations made for use in commerce. It would be wrong against this background to deny trademark protection for distinctive features, such as the Campbell logo (section 5.2.5). Instead, it is necessary to offer sufficient room for artistic remix activities within the trademark system (sections 8.3.2. and 9.2.1.6).

On the one hand, it is thus important to warn of the risk of attaching too much importance to copyright's originality test. Originality must not become an overpowering factor in the assessment of conflicts with public order that overshadows all other factors. On the other hand, concerns about the breadth of the originality concept in copyright law must not discredit originality as a factor in the public order enquiry altogether. If an enquiry based on the multifactor test does not yield evidence of a sign's museum status, link with a literary or artistic production, previous use in cultural remix activities, etc., the originality test will inevitably play an important role in determining cultural significance and assessing the risk of a conflict with public order.

1541. For example, see the discussion of potential copyright protection for Diesel's coin pocket label in District Court of The Hague, 22 May 2019, case ECLI:NL:RB-DHA:2019:5189, Diesel/Calvin Klein Europe, para. 4.15.

Moreover, the application of the originality test may provide important impulses for the recalibration of the currently inflated intellectual property system. Copyright protection for non-literature and non-art is the result of the continuous relaxation of the originality test and the corresponding expansion of the notion of 'literary and artistic work' (section 2.2). One of the problems arising from this continuous expansion of the realm of copyright is the growth of protection overlaps. The denial of trademark rights to literary and artistic works on the basis of public order criteria is a countermeasure seeking to alleviate the problems arising from overlapping copyright and trademark protection. The originality test is an important vehicle to implement this countermeasure in practice because, despite all shortcomings, its application seems still easier and less problematic than the alternative of an open assessment of artistic merit. Against this background, it would be contradictory if copyright protection for non-literature and non-art could thwart this initiative. This would mean that the very category of works that is an exponent of the problematic expansion of intellectual property domains could frustrate the implementation of a promising measure against a problem arising from this expansion, namely dysfunctional copyright/trademark overlaps. As a result, the intellectual property system would be trapped in a vicious circle: the problem (of overlapping protection) could not be solved because of one of the origins of the problem (the continuous relaxation of the originality test in copyright law).

Therefore, it is important to include the originality factor in the assessment of conflicts with public order. The inclusion of originality allows the development of a strategy to activate the internal self-healing forces of the intellectual property system (section 2.3). Confronted with the task of conducting the originality test in the framework of trademark examinations, trademark offices are exposed to the flaws of an overly elastic criterion for determining eligibility for copyright protection. As it appears paradoxical to deny trademark registrations of trade symbols, such as the Campbell logo, on the ground that they must be kept free for cultural follow-on innovation, trademark offices are likely to sharpen the conceptual contours of originality and devise an originality test for the identification of conflicts with public order that is stricter than the copyright test.[1542] In sections 5.2.1 and 5.2.3, it has already been proposed to focus on 'easy' cases: creations that clearly

1542. Admittedly, the CJEU, 12 September 2019, case C-683/17, Cofemel, para. 31 and 35-48 and 52-55, rejected assessment criteria based on a specific aesthetic effect in the field of industrial design protection. Accordingly, national systems which traditionally applied a threshold criterion of a higher degree of artistic merit in cases of industrial design have abandoned these specific criteria. Cf. German Federal Court of Justice, 16 June 2016, case I ZR 222/14, 'Geburtstagskarawane', *GRUR* 2016, 1291, para. 44. This development concerning the regulation of copyright/design protection overlaps, however, need not preclude an assessment based on a high degree of free, creative choices (a reflection of enhanced artistic merit) for the purpose of identifying cultural signs in a trademark context. Moreover, the previous German practice of requiring a higher

meet the originality test because they display a high degree of free, creative choices.[1543] Following this approach, the tension within the intellectual property system – caused by the relaxation of the originality test in copyright law – becomes a burden for the operations of a central institutional player: intellectual property offices. Burdening trademark offices with the application of an overbroad originality concept in copyright law, the self-healing of the system can begin. Trademark offices will have to question the originality test as a reliable indicator of cultural significance. Their stricter application of the test in the public order context – requiring a high degree of free, creative choices or even a redesign of the test – may inspire judges in regular copyright cases to adopt stricter standards as well. From this bird's-eye perspective, it thus makes sense to impose the task on trademark offices to conduct an originality analysis. It is desirable to activate the self-healing forces of the intellectual property system in this way.

However, it is also important to address a practical difficulty that comes along with the inclusion of originality as an assessment factor in the public order analysis. This final challenge evolves from the fact that the acquisition of copyright does not depend on the fulfilment of formal requirements. As formalities are prohibited,[1544] copyright emerges automatically from the mere act of creation. Given the described low standard of originality, copyright may come into being with regard to creations that have never been intended to serve cultural purposes. It may even be forced on owners of intellectual creations who have no intention of availing themselves of the protection title. In the case of an industrial object constituting neither literature nor art, the copyright owner may have no particular interest in copyright protection and prefer trademark protection instead. If, for example, a logo is designed specifically for use as a source identifier in trade, the owner of the logo will primarily seek trademark protection because this form of intellectual property protection corresponds with the intended use.[1545] In such a situation, it seems odd to deny trademark protection. Otherwise, a genuine commercial creation – intended to serve as a trademark from the outset – would artificially be kept outside the trademark system even though its owner wants to focus on use as a trademark.

To solve this dilemma, it is necessary to discuss the responsibility for distinguishing between genuine literary and artistic works on the one hand

---

degree of artistic merit (cf. German Federal Court of Justice, *ibid.*) demonstrates that this type of assessment criteria is manageable in practice.

1543. As to the application of this test in the EU, see in particular CJEU, 16 July 2009, case C-5/08, Infopaq/DDF, para. 45; CJEU, 1 December 2011, case C-145/10, Painer, para. 89.

1544. Article 5(2) BC. As to the scope of the prohibition of formalities concerning the acquisition of copyright, see Van Gompel 2011, 194-199.

1545. Cf. Bercovitz 2001, 615-616. As explained, the EFTA Court, 6 April 2017, case E-5/16, Municipality of Oslo ('Vigeland'), paras 97-98, saw no basis for excluding trademark protection in this specific situation.

and genuine identifiers of commercial source on the other. So far, the analysis has been based on the assumption that it would be a natural task of trademark offices to detect encroachments upon cultural follow-on innovation (in the framework of assessing conflicts with public order) in the course of the trademark examination process. As a result, the burden of proof is placed on the office. The trademark examiner must develop convincing arguments that support the denial of trademark protection for public order reasons. This requires the discussion of factors that make the existence of a conflict plausible, such as an interference with copyright's quid pro quo. However, little attention has been devoted to the option to oblige the trademark applicant to demonstrate the absence of cultural significance. Trademark offices are expected to make an encroachment upon cultural follow-on innovation plausible, whereas the applicant need not show that such an encroachment is unlikely. When assessed critically, this approach replicates the general bias against cultural concerns within the intellectual property system by placing the burden of proof on trademark offices. It presupposes a need to justify the exclusion of a sign from trademark protection for cultural reasons instead of expecting trademark applicants to justify their request for a trademark registration when their creations qualify as literary and artistic works.

Apart from these theoretical considerations, there are practical reasons: it will often be impossible for trademark examiners to fathom the applicant's subjective intentions. A logo designed for the purpose of use as a mark may constitute a literary and artistic work in a traditional sense and even satisfy the stricter originality test (high degree of free, creative choices) applied by the trademark office. It is thus a hybrid: depending on the context in which the sign is further developed after its creation, it may become a genuine trademark or remain a cultural object (see the example of Tony the Tiger in section 5.2.5 above). It is thus insufficient to assess the properties of the sign for which trademark protection is sought. If the trademark examiner has no additional sources of information, such as information about a connection with a literary and artistic production or earlier use in the context of cultural remix activities, he can only venture his best guess regarding the motive underlying the application for registration. In such a case, it is necessary to shift the burden of proof and place the obligation on the trademark applicant to formally declare that a sign which qualifies as a literary and artistic work is a genuine commercial creation that has specifically been made to serve as a trademark.

Hence, the examination of trademark applications in the light of the described multifactor test must be carried out in two steps. The first step is the ex officio examination of the sign for which trademark protection is sought. This analysis can yield sufficient information for the trademark office to reject the application. If cultural relevance is evident – for instance, due to an obvious connection with a cultural production, such as a film, book or opera – the trademark office can directly deny the registration on the ground that the sign clearly constitutes a cultural object and that its trademark registration would run counter to the public domain principle in copyright law and cause a conflict with public order. Because the sign's cultural dimension is evident in this situation, the examiner need not rely on the ambiguous originality test. Signs stemming from cultural productions, such as artworks featuring prominently in a museum and characters of comic books and cartoon films, can readily be excluded from trademark protection. As they have already been used and exploited as literary and artistic works, or already served as a basis for cultural remix activities, the request for trademark protection can be unmasked as an attempt to bypass the limits of copyright protection, in particular the limited term of protection.

If, however, the application of the multifactor test does not lead to clear results and the sign at issue must be deemed eligible for copyright protection because it satisfies the stricter version of the originality test developed by the trademark office, it becomes the task of the trademark applicant to dispel concerns about a conflict with public order by furnishing proof that the grant of trademark protection will not interfere with copyright's public domain principle. In this second step of the procedure, the office should oblige the trademark application to sign a *declaration of non-use in a cultural context.* The registration should depend on a formal declaration that the applicant will not use the hybrid sign at issue, meeting both the (stricter) originality test and the test of distinctiveness, in a cultural context.[1546]

To ensure that such a declaration of non-use in a cultural context binds the applicant to focus on use of the hybrid sign as a mark, the declaration should be entered in the register. A departure from the declared intention should have severe consequences: if use of the sign for cultural purposes takes place at a later stage, the trademark should become subject to invalidation. If protection as a literary and artistic work is invoked with regard to the sign, this assertion of copyright should be equated with use in a cultural context and seen as a breach of the declaration to focus on use as a mark which the trademark owner gave at the application stage. Accordingly, a defendant facing the copyright claim should be entitled to a counterclaim putting an end to trademark protection with effect *ex tunc.*[1547] As the trademark owner herself invokes copyright and derives protection from the cultural aspect of the sign, she is obliged to also accept the limits of protection in the cultural domain, namely the limits of copyright protection. Under these circumstances, the loss of trademark rights is a

1546. As to the option of introducing such formal declarations as 'mere procedural requirement[s]' in EU trademark law, see CJEU, 29 January 2020, case C-371/18, Sky and Others, para. 86.

1547. Cf. Article 62(2) EUTMR.

corollary of the obligation to acquiesce in the conceptual limits of copyright.[1548] Claiming copyright, the owner of a hybrid sign gives clear evidence of her intention to avail herself of the protection following from the cultural aspect of the sign. The moment benefits are derived from the entitlement to copyright protection, there is sufficient reason to also ask the price for this protection title, consisting of a limited term of protection.[1549] The invocation of copyright protection, thus, should constitute a ground for invalidating trademark protection with regard to the hybrid sign concerned.

The introduction of this copyright-related ground for invalidation is likely to have a disciplining effect on the current practice of accumulating and enforcing whole bundles of intellectual property rights. As the declaration of non-use in a cultural context is recorded in the trademark register, a defendant confronted with a copyright claim can easily find out whether a counterclaim aiming at the invalidation of the trademark registration is possible. Once the invocation of copyright entails the risk of losing trademark rights with effect *ex tunc*, the rights owner will consider carefully whether it is advisable to enforce copyright. Hence, the practice of combining copyright and trademark claims is rendered less attractive because it comes at the price of losing trademark protection. It is thus possible to solve the problem of rather accidental, unintended copyright protection for works designed to serve as trademarks – arising from the absence of registration requirements in copyright law – by making the registration as a trademark subject to a declaration of non-use in a cultural context. As long as the trademark owner refrains from the invocation of copyright, the obtained trademark rights remain intact. Once copyright is enforced, however, the rights owner is exposed to the risk of losing trademark protection altogether.

To implement the declaration of non-use in a cultural context and establish the described legal consequences in practice, the decision of the CJEU in *Sky* can serve as a signpost. Discussing bad faith, the CJEU stated that EU Member States were free to introduce obligations to make declarations with regard to use intentions during the application procedure. The

1548. This solution comes close to the proposal of McKenna 2009a, 891-894, to oblige companies to elect between different forms of intellectual property protection at the product level – instead of allowing the cumulation of different rights with regard to different product features.

1549. Cf. Dinwoodie 2020, 28-29; Derclaye/Leistner 2011, 309-310; Moffat 2004, 1532. As to case law pointing in this direction, see U.S. Supreme Court, 2 June 2003, Dastar/Twentieth Century Fox, 539 U.S. 23, 33-34 (2003). It is also possible to draw a parallel with the line of argument in U.S. Supreme Court, 20 March 2001, TrafFix Devices/Marketing Displays, 532 U.S. 23, 30-31 (2001), where the Court denies trade dress protection (based on the Lanham Act) on the ground that, with regard to the product feature at issue, the claimant had already invoked patent protection in an earlier infringement case. In EU trademark law, the framework for introducing the proposed declaration system follows from CJEU, 29 January 2020, case C-371/18, Sky and Others, para. 83 and 86.

ruling in *Sky* concerned an obligation to declare a bona fide intention of putting the registered sign to genuine use.[1550] However, the judgment can be understood in a more general sense. It offers a basis for introducing obligations to make declarations on the intended use of trademarked signs as long as these declarations remain 'mere procedural requirement[s]'[1551] and do not function as independent grounds for refusal or invalidity besides the statutory grounds listed in Article 4 TMD and Articles 7 and 59 EUTMR.[1552] The decision in *Sky*, thus, offers room for the introduction of an obligation to declare non-use in a cultural context when trademark protection is sought for a hybrid sign that fulfils both the originality test and the requirement of distinctiveness. The qualification as a 'mere procedural requirement' need not make the declaration a toothless tiger. With regard to the obligation to declare a bona fide intention of genuine use, the CJEU explained in *Sky* that:

> the infringement of such an obligation to make such a statement may constitute evidence for the purposes of establishing possible bad faith on the part of the trade mark applicant when he or she filed the trade mark application.[1553]

Hence, it is not decisive that the infringement of an obligation to make a declaration with regard to use intentions cannot constitute an independent ground for refusal or invalidity under current EU trademark law. Nonetheless, it may provide the evidence necessary to invoke one of the existing statutory grounds. In particular, the refusal to declare non-use in a cultural context and the invocation of copyright contrary to such a declaration could be regarded as proof of a registration that is deficient because of a conflict with public order.[1554] If a trademark applicant refuses to declare non-use in a cultural context at the application stage, this reluctance may be regarded as an indication that the applicant is likely to exploit the cultural aspect of the sign. This, in turn, supports a refusal of the trademark application because the applicant seeks to neglect copyright's quid pro quo. Obviously, the applicant wants to reap the fruits of copyright protection without paying the price of a limited term of protection.[1555] The refusal to sign the declaration of non-use in a cultural context can thus be regarded as evidence of the trademark applicant's intention to erode copyright's quid pro quo and acquire trademark protection in conflict with *ordre public* (section 9.1.2.4). If the hybrid sign is first registered together with the declaration of non-use in a cultural context,

1550. CJEU, *ibid.*, para. 86.
1551. CJEU, *ibid.*, para. 86.
1552. CJEU, *ibid.*, para. 83 and 86.
1553. CJEU, *ibid.*, para. 86.
1554. Articles 59 and 7(1)(f) EUTMR and Article 4(1)(f) TMD.
1555. For an alternative approach pointing out the merits of trademark protection against confusion, see Heymann 2013, 259-260. This alternative view, however, overlooks the current proportions of trademark protection and its corrosive effect on cultural follow-on innovation. Cf. section 6.3.

the later invocation of copyright provides evidence that the trademark registration was contrary to public order and must be invalidated with effect *ex tunc* at that later stage.

In *Sky*, the CJEU explicitly recognized the freedom of Member States to introduce use declarations in the context of bad faith. Therefore, an alternative option is the implementation of the described declaration of non-use in a cultural context as a species of bad faith. In this scenario, the refusal to sign the declaration would provide evidence of the trademark applicant's intention to acquire trademark protection in bad faith: as a means of threatening users in the cultural domain and impeding cultural follow-on innovation. If the applicant signs the declaration and registers the sign together with the declaration of non-use in a cultural context, the subsequent invocation of copyright protection in respect of the hybrid sign concerned would have to be qualified as evidence of bad faith at the application stage justifying the invalidation of the trademark registration with effect *ex tunc*. The crux of this bad faith solution, however, lies in the current limitations of the bad faith concept. Instead of providing room for cultural concerns and considerations relating to copyright's quid pro quo, the CJEU aligns the bad faith analysis with trademark functions and the trademark concept of genuine use (cf. section 9.1.3.4). A bad faith implementation strategy would thus require a substantial recalibration of the bad faith test that is currently applied. Considering these difficulties and the foregoing exploration of the remarkable potential of public order to serve as a tool for defending copyright's quid pro quo and safeguarding cultural follow-on innovation (section 9.1.2.4), an implementation strategy based on public order is more consistent.

In sum, the implementation of public order as a ground for refusing trademark rights to cultural signs does not pose insurmountable hurdles. Trademark offices can identify relevant signs on the basis of the criteria developed in section 5.2.1 (Mona Lisa scenario) and section 5.2.3 (Mickey Mouse scenario). As explained in these sections, the criteria for identifying cultural signs must not be misunderstood as bright-line rules. They are intended to assist examiners and judges in the assessment of the cultural dimension of signs without dictating the final decision. In some cases, originality may be a decisive factor. As the criteria of the originality test are not fully aligned with the contours of the domain of literature and art, however, a recalibration of the test is inescapable. Instead of invoking the elastic notion of originality that has evolved in copyright law, it is advisable to apply the test strictly and require a high degree of free, creative choices in the context of the public order analysis. This recalibration provides an important impulse for the critical reassessment of the elastic originality concept that evolved in copyright law. It may have welcome repercussions on the further development of originality as a central tool to regulate access to copyright protection. In cases where the factor analysis does not yield a clear result because the sign at issue has specifically been designed to serve as a trademark and eligibility for copyright protection is an accidental, unintended side effect of the absence of registration requirements in copyright law, the office should make registration as a trademark dependent on a formal declaration of non-use in a cultural context. This declaration should be recorded in the trademark register. If copyright is invoked with regard to a trademark registered under these circumstances, the trademark should be liable to be declared invalid, for instance in consequence of a counterclaim brought by the defendant in the copyright infringement action.

9.1.2.6 No Implementation Obstacle in the U.S.

The foregoing discussion shows that it is possible to operationalize public order and morality criteria (sections 9.1.2.3 and 9.1.2.4) in a way that allows trademark examiners and judges to use these absolute grounds for refusal to prevent the acquisition of trademark rights to cultural signs. While several practical obstacles have proved surmountable in the preceding section, specific implementation problems arise in trademark systems that do not recognize public order and morality as grounds for refusal. In the U.S., for instance, the Supreme Court eroded the morality clause (placing a ban on the registration of trademarks consisting of, or comprising, 'immoral […] or scandalous matter')[1556] and the disparagement clause (prohibiting the registration of marks which 'may disparage […] persons, living or dead, institutions, beliefs, or national symbols, or bring them into contempt, or disrepute').[1557] Instead of recognizing the important role which these grounds for refusal may play in the field of cultural signs, developments in the U.S. thus point in the opposite direction. Not surprisingly, commentators wonder whether the invocation of public order and morality to deny trademark rights to cultural signs would be unconstitutional in the U.S.[1558]

A closer look at the decisions, however, reveals that these concerns are unfounded. In *Matal/Tam*, the U.S. Supreme Court dealt with the request of the rock band 'The Slants' to register their band name as a trademark. The word 'slants' is a derogatory term for persons of Asian descent. Seeking to reclaim the term and deprive it of its denigrating force, the Asian-American band members had adopted this word as the name of their group. Despite the intention to purify the term, the USPTO invoked the disparagement clause

1556. Lanham Act, 15 U.S. Code § 1052(a), as in force prior to U.S. Supreme Court, 24 June 2019, Iancu/Brunetti, 588 U.S. __ (2019), section II.

1557. Lanham Act, 15 U.S. Code § 1052(a), as in force prior to U.S. Supreme Court, 19 June 2017, Matal/Tam, 582 U.S. __ (2017), section IV.

1558. Dreyfuss 2020, 325; Ginsburg 2018b, 258. With regard to similar developments and concerns in the EU, see Żelechowski 2020, 318. Insofar as CJEU jurisprudence, such as CJEU, 27 February 2020, case C-240/18P, Constantin Film/EUIPO ('Fack Ju Göhte'), para. 56, can be understood to point in the same direction (cf. Żelechowski, *ibid.*, 318), the following arguments demonstrating that there is no implementation obstacle apply mutatis mutandis in the context of EU trademark law.

and rejected the trademark application on the ground that the word 'slants' slurs Asian-Americans.[1559] This fact pattern prompted a court decision focusing on the speech-suppressing use of the disparagement clause. The U.S. Supreme Court concluded that:

> [t]he Government has an interest in preventing speech expressing ideas that offend. And, as we have explained, that idea strikes at the heart of the First Amendment. Speech that demeans on the basis of race, ethnicity, gender, religion, age, disability, or any other similar ground is hateful; but the proudest boast of our free speech jurisprudence is that we protect the freedom to express 'the thought that we hate'.[1560]

Hence, the U.S. Supreme Court condemned the disparagement clause because it feared inroads into freedom of speech. More specifically, the Court saw a risk of viewpoint discrimination undermining the First Amendment principle that the government 'may not prohibit the expression of an idea simply because society finds the idea itself offensive or disagreeable'.[1561] Moreover, the Court held that, as an overly broad 'happy-talk' norm, the disparagement clause could affect any trademark that disparages any person, group or institution, including trademarks like 'Down with racists', 'Down with sexists' and 'Down with homophobes'.[1562]

Assessing the impact of *Matal/Tam* on the proposed use of public order and morality as grounds for refusal in cases concerning cultural signs, it is important to note at the outset that the interface between the U.S. disparagement clause and the criteria developed in the preceding sections is small. A connection may be established with morality ground 2 which, as explained in section 9.1.2.3, addresses the situation where a trademark registration is deemed offensive because it would lead to a 'misappropriation or a desecration of the artist's work, in particular if it is granted for goods or services that contradict values of the artist or the message communicated through the artwork in question'.[1563] *Matal/Tam*, however, does not impact the other criteria developed in sections 9.1.2.3 and 9.1.2.4. Even with regard to the desecration argument underlying morality ground 2, the decision need not remain the final word. Arguably, the free speech equation is markedly different from the assessment made by the U.S. Supreme Court when trademark rights in cultural signs are at issue. As pointed out above, the fact pattern in *Matal/Tam* favoured an approach focusing on speech constraints which the trademark applicant may experience. The rock band 'The Slants' wanted to reclaim the derogatory term 'slants'. Therefore, the denial of the trademark registration appeared as a discriminatory measure suppressing a

1559. U.S. Supreme Court, 19 June 2017, Matal/Tam, 582 U.S. __ (2017), section I.D. Cf. Beebe/Fromer 2019, 173-175.

1560. U.S. Supreme Court, *ibid.*, section IV.

1561. U.S. Supreme Court, *ibid.*, section III.C.

1562. U.S. Supreme Court, *ibid.*, section IV.

1563. EFTA Court, 6 April 2017, case E-5/16, Municipality of Oslo ('Vigeland'), para. 92.

specific form of trademark-based communication. Paving the way for the grant of the trademark right, the U.S. Supreme Court supported the efforts of Simon Tam to obtain a stronger position in the discourse surrounding the term 'slants' – a position that may allow him to add new, positive connotations to the derogatory term. Hence, the U.S. Supreme Court sought to prevent a speech-suppressing use of the disparagement clause. As a result, it enhanced the freedom of speech of the trademark applicant.

If, by contrast, the desecration argument (morality ground 2, see section 9.1.2.3) is invoked to deny the registration of a cultural sign as a trademark, the use of morality as a ground for refusal *furthers* freedom of speech. The denial of the trademark registration may reduce the trademark applicant's arsenal of communication tools. Admittedly, the trademark applicant is deprived of the opportunity to strengthen her position in the discourse surrounding the cultural sign on the basis of exclusive rights to prohibit use by others. On balance, however, this decision safeguards and enhances the freedom of speech of other participants in the debate, in particular artists. Denying trademark rights, the communication process concerning the cultural sign remains open.[1564] No individual trademark owner obtains a position that is stronger than the position of other speakers. As explained in section 3.3.2.4, the denial of trademark protection preserves the artistic discourse potential of the cultural sign: its potential to serve as a basis for open, dialogic communication in the cultural domain. The denial of trademark rights also reduces the risk of constant use for marketing purposes that impregnates the sign with commercial messages devaluing the sign as a reference point for artistic remix (section 8.2.3.3). Finally, the denial of trademark protection forecloses the acquisition of trademark rights that may have a deterrent effect on artistic expression (section 6.3).[1565] The free speech equation is thus different. The detriment to the trademark applicant is outweighed by considerable benefits for other speakers, in particular artists. It is also outweighed by benefits for society. Preserving the artistic discourse potential of cultural signs, society can reap the fruits of an open, dialogic process of discussing and remixing artworks – an open process that is not dominated by one individual speaker with an interest in specific commercial connotations.

While the disparagement argument in *Matal/Tam* concerned the risk of negative viewpoint discrimination against one individual voice and the decision reflected the intention to enhance the impact of one individual speaker, the use of desecration arguments in cases involving cultural signs serves the purpose of preventing positive discrimination in favour of commercial speakers which may use exclusive trademark rights to suppress artist speech. Instead of discriminating against the trademark applicant, it is a non-discriminatory measure that preserves equal access to the discourse

1564. Cf. Ramsey 2018, 468-469.
1565. Ramsey 2018, 426-427.

and equal impact of all speakers on the process of attaching meaning and connotations to a cultural sign. The U.S. Supreme Court may have been right in the *Matal/Tam* scenario. To guard Simon Tam from viewpoint discrimination, it seemed necessary to prevent the application of the disparagement clause. In cases concerning the registration of cultural signs as trademarks, however, the opposite is true.[1566] To protect artists and other speakers from discrimination in favour of trademark owners and commercial speech interests, it is necessary to embrace morality as a ground for refusal (for instance, in the form of the desecration argument) and put an end to the trademark registration attempt.

A closer look at the free speech matrix underlying *Matal/Tam*, thus, reveals that the outright verdict of unconstitutionality was short-sighted. The U.S. Supreme Court overlooked the dualism that is inherent in morality-based grounds for refusal. While the denial of trademark rights because of disparagement or desecration may culminate in undesirable viewpoint discrimination in some cases, it prevents an undesirable superiority of commercial speech over artistic speech in cases involving cultural signs. When the registration of artworks as trademarks is at issue, the denial of trademark rights on the basis of morality arguments has a speech-enhancing effect. The invocation of morality as a ground for refusal is desirable to prevent positive discrimination in favour of commercial speakers that leads to exclusive trademark rights at the expense of open dialogic communication in the cultural domain. Therefore, *Matal/Tam* must not be misunderstood as a decision that bars the use of morality arguments to deny trademark rights in cultural signs. To prevent *positive* viewpoint discrimination that allows commercial speech to suppress artistic speech, it is indispensable to draw on the full panoply of morality arguments, including the desecration argument developed in section 9.1.2.3.

Unfortunately, the U.S. Supreme Court has not yet seized the opportunity to change its course and add the described nuances with regard to cultural signs. In *Iancu/Brunetti*, the Court held that the Lanham Act's ban on the registration of trademarks consisting of, or comprising, 'immoral […] or scandalous matter' was unconstitutional as well.[1567] With this further decision, the Court came closer to the morality criteria discussed in section 9.1.2.3. As in *Matal/Tam*, however, the facts underlying the decision offered no room for considering speech-enhancing use of morality as a ground for refusal to prevent positive discrimination in favour of trademark owners that may impede artistic freedom of expression. *Iancu/Brunetti* concerned the attempt of the artist and entrepreneur Erik Brunetti to register the trademark FUCT as a brand name for his clothing line. Brunetti argued that the four letters had to be pronounced one after the other: F-U-C-T. The USPTO,

1566. Ramsey 2018, 465-469.
1567. Lanham Act, 15 U.S. Code § 1052(a). See U.S. Supreme Court, 24 June 2019, Iancu/Brunetti, 588 U.S. __ (2019), section II.

however, argued that the brand name constituted the 'equivalent of [the] past participle form of a well-known word of profanity' and had 'decidedly negative sexual connotations'.[1568] Again, the risk of an encroachment upon the trademark applicant's freedom of speech occupied centre stage. Potential inroads into the freedom of speech of other participants in the discourse surrounding a sign for which trademark protection is sought, such as artists in the case of cultural signs, did not enter the picture and remained beyond reach for the U.S. Supreme Court.

As the problem pattern was similar to *Matal/Tam*, the U.S. Supreme Court could follow the same line of reasoning. It invoked the free speech postulate that '[t]he government may not discriminate against speech based on the ideas or opinions it conveys'.[1569] Surveying office practice in the field of immoral and scandalous marks, the Court concluded that the morality clause in the Lanham Act led to viewpoint-based discrimination:

> So the Lanham Act allows registration of marks when their messages accord with, but not when their messages defy, society's sense of decency or propriety. Put the pair of overlapping terms together and the statute, on its face, distinguishes between two opposed sets of ideas: those aligned with conventional moral standards and those hostile to them; those inducing societal nods of approval and those provoking offense and condemnation. The statute favors the former, and disfavors the latter. 'Love rules'? 'Always be good'? Registration follows. 'Hate rules'? 'Always be cruel'? Not according to the Lanham Act's 'immoral or scandalous' bar.[1570]

Hence, the prohibition of trademark registrations concerning immoral or scandalous marks could not survive scrutiny in the light of the First Amendment in the U.S. As *Matal/Tam*, however, the decision did not discuss the specific speech dilemma arising from the registration of cultural signs as trademarks. The speech restrictions which a trademark registration may impose on other speakers – artists in the case of cultural signs (cf. sections 3.3.2.4, 8.2.3.3 and 6.3) – fell outside the equation. Therefore, neither *Matal/Tam* nor *Iancu/Brunetti* prevent the U.S. Supreme Court from embracing morality-based grounds for refusal, as developed in section 9.1.2.3, in a future decision that concerns the freedom of speech of third parties (in particular artists). For a change of course, a fact pattern is necessary that offers the Court the opportunity to consider the corrosive effect of positive discrimination in favour of commercial speech (following from the grant of exclusive rights) instead of simply addressing negative discrimination against the trademark applicant.

1568. U.S. Supreme Court, *ibid.*, section I.
1569. U.S. Supreme Court, *ibid.*, section II.
1570. U.S. Supreme Court, *ibid.*, section II. For an in-depth analysis of USPTO practice in the field of immoral and scandalous marks, see Beebe/Fromer 2019, 182-197.

With regard to substantive assessment criteria, it is important to add that the application of morality-based grounds for refusal does not entail viewpoint-based discrimination in the case of cultural signs. If applied broadly in line with the guidelines developed in section 9.1.2.3, the registration attempt as such is considered offensive. It does not matter which goods or services are involved. Accordingly, the trademark office need not determine whether the public finds the commercial use of Picasso's 'Guernica' scandalous in respect of weapon, while it accepts use of the painting as a marketing tool for other goods and services. The decision can be based on the consideration that the risk of commercial marketing messages suppressing dialogic cultural communication requires a registration ban across all goods and services (section 9.1.2.3). This position does not discriminate against commercial speakers.[1571] It only prevents the acquisition of exclusive trademark rights that would give commercial speakers a stronger position in the communication process than artists. Rightly understood, the categorical denial of the Guernica registration – regardless of the goods and services involved – is a measure preventing positive discrimination in favour of commercial speakers – positive discrimination that would impede open, dialogic communication in the cultural domain (section 3.3.2.4).

Hence, *Matal/Tam* and *Iancu/Brunetti* do not pose lasting obstacles to the cultivation of morality as a ground for refusal when trademark applicants seek to register cultural signs as trademarks. By contrast, they confirm that the broad application of morality criteria, as proposed in section 9.1.2.3, is appropriate to avoid viewpoint-based discrimination that depends on an interpretation of the message and meaning of artworks. From the outset, *Matal/Tam* and *Iancu/Brunetti* also leave the public order criteria unaffected that have been developed in section 9.1.2.4. The U.S. Supreme Court decisions concerned the disparagement clause and the morality clause in the Lanham Act. They have no bearing on the use of *ordre public* as a ground for refusal in cases concerning cultural signs. The public order and morality criteria following from the discussion in sections 9.1.2.3 and 9.1.2.4, thus, can be implemented in the U.S. It is wrong to assume that *Matal/Tam* and *Iancu/Brunetti* foreclose this development in U.S. trademark law and practice.

9.1.2.7 Compliance with International Law

After the clarification of implementation options in the preceding sections, a final point of concern that merits attention is compatibility with international trademark law. Admittedly, the control of access to trademark protection for cultural signs on the basis of fully developed public order and morality criteria (sections 9.1.2.3 and 9.1.2.4) impacts existing rights acquisition

1571. As to the concept of viewpoint discrimination in the U.S., see Ramsey 2018, 418-419; Calvert 2019, 48-49 and 81-82.

strategies. As already pointed out, the cumulation of copyright and trademark protection has become a standard strategy in the field of character merchandising. Fictional characters feature prominently in trademark registers. The denial of trademark rights *ex ante* (at the gate to the trademark universe, as discussed in section 9.1.1) – and not only *ex post* (after the expiry of copyright protection) – entails a considerable climate change that may raise questions about compliance with international trademark norms. Article 15(1) TRIPS states that:

> [a]ny sign, or any combination of signs, capable of distinguishing the goods or services of one undertaking from those of other undertakings, shall be capable of constituting a trademark. Such signs, in particular words including personal names, letters, numerals, figurative elements and combinations of colours as well as any combination of such signs, shall be eligible for registration as trademarks. Where signs are not inherently capable of distinguishing the relevant goods or services, Members may make registrability depend on distinctiveness acquired through use.

Considering the reference to 'being capable of distinguishing' as a central criterion for identifying signs that are eligible for trademark protection, this provision, at first glance, seems to contain a de facto obligation to register cultural signs when they are inherently distinctive in respect of certain goods or services or have acquired distinctiveness in consequence of use in trade.[1572] However, Article 15(2) TRIPS clarifies that WTO Members may deny registration of a trademark on 'other grounds' as long as these other grounds do not derogate from the provisions of the Paris Convention. The option reflected in Article 6*quinquies*(B) No. 3 PC – the possibility of denying a trademark registration because the mark is contrary to morality or

1572. Article 15(1) TRIPS itself makes it clear that WTO Members are free to make registrability depend on distinctiveness acquired through use in the case of signs that are not inherently capable of distinguishing the relevant goods or services. Cultural signs are often regarded as descriptive indications in respect of cultural productions. At least after the acquisition of distinctive character through use, however, Article 15(1) TRIPS seems to offer little room to escape the obligation to register the sign (see also the discussion of this weakness of distinctiveness as an exclusion instrument in section 9.1.2.1). De Carvalho 2014, 295, argues nonetheless that the international rule addressing the acquisition of distinctiveness through use means that signs which are not inherently distinctive may be excluded from trademark registration altogether. He sees the registration of signs which have acquired distinctiveness through use as an option for WTO Members but not as an obligation: 'The first case consists of marks whose distinctiveness is not inherent but which have acquired it through use. Those signs are still distinctive, but not inherently. WTO Members may make registrability of those signs available. It is a faculty, not an obligation.' If this view is adopted, international law would thus allow the outright exclusion of cultural signs from trademark protection to the extent that they can be deemed descriptive vis-à-vis certain goods and services, such as goods and services that are directly related to the cultural production at issue.

public order[1573] – is thus available in this context. In an *ex ante* exclusion system, it can be argued that the registration of a cultural sign as a trademark would conflict with morality or public order because use in a commercial context would violate and finally erase the cultural meaning of relevant signs, and the registration as a trademark would set in motion an indefinitely renewable protection automatism that encroaches upon the rule of a limited term of copyright protection (sections 9.1.2.3 and 9.1.2.4). Even if a cultural sign is distinctive, the exclusion *ex ante* can thus be justified.

Additional room for the exclusion of cultural signs *ex ante* follows from the fact that Article 6*quinquies*(B) PC – while reflecting standard grounds for refusal that have become widespread in national legislation[1574] – has a limited ambit of operation. As explained above, it only applies in situations of *telle quelle* protection where the registration of a trademark 'duly registered in the country of origin' is requested in another Paris Union country 'as is'.[1575] The general rule governing national registration systems follows from Article 6(1) PC: Paris Union Members are free to determine the conditions for the filing and registration of trademarks in domestic legislation.[1576] As to the interplay between this freedom of Paris Union Members and the obligations concerning protectable subject matter in the sense of Article 15(1) TRIPS, guidance can be found in the WTO dispute settlement case *United States – Section 211 Omnibus Appropriations Act of 1998*.[1577] Discussing the impact of Article 15(1) TRIPS on the discretion left to national legislation under Article 6(1) PC, the Appellate Body emphasized that Article 15(1) TRIPS should not be misunderstood as a protection automatism requiring the registration of any distinctive sign:

> Identifying certain signs that are capable of registration and imposing on WTO Members an obligation to make those signs eligible for registration in their domestic legislation is not the same as imposing on those Members an obligation to register automatically each and every sign or combination of signs that are capable of and eligible for registration under Article 15.1. This Article describes which trademarks are 'capable of' registration. It does not say that all trademarks that are capable of registration 'shall be registered'. This Article states that such signs or combinations of signs 'shall be eligible for registration' as trademarks.

1573. Kunz-Hallstein 2006, 487; Beier 1992, 243; Ladas 1975, 1211-1240; Bodenhausen 1969, 113-119.
1574. For an overview covering different regions of the world, see Senftleben 2012b, 294-295.
1575. Article 6*quinquies*(B) PC read in connection with Article 6*quinquies*(A)(1) PC. Cf. Bodenhausen 1969, 114.
1576. Bodenhausen 1969, 87-88. WTO Appellate Body, 2 January 2002, WTO Document WT/DS176/AB/R, United States – Section 211 Omnibus Appropriations Act of 1998, para. 132.
1577. Cf. Correa 2007, 179-180.

> It does not say that they 'shall be registered'. To us, these are distinctions with a difference. And, as we have said, supporting these distinctions is the fact that the title of this Article speaks of subject matter as 'protectable', and not of subject matter 'to be protected'. In this way, the title of Article 15 expresses the notion that the subject matter covered by the provision is subject matter that qualifies for, but is not necessarily entitled to, protection.[1578]

Taking this insight as a starting point, the Appellate Body defined the relation between Article 15(1) TRIPS and Article 6(1) PC as follows:

> If Article 15.1 required the registration of any and every sign or combination of signs that meets the distinctiveness criteria specified in that Article, then WTO Members would be deprived of the legislative discretion they enjoy under Article 6(1) of the Paris Convention (1967). In our view, Article 15.1 of the TRIPS Agreement limits the right of Members to determine the 'conditions' for filing and registration of trademarks under their domestic legislation pursuant to Article 6(1) only as it relates to the distinctiveness requirements enunciated in Article 15.1.[1579]

Therefore, WTO Members remain free to determine specific conditions for the registration of trademarks as long as the rule of eligibility for registration in case of distinctiveness, as a general principle, remains intact. *United States – Section 211 Omnibus Appropriations Act of 1998* concerned the denial of registration on the ground that the applicant was not the owner of the trademark.[1580] This specific condition was deemed permissible by the Appellate Body because it did not preclude the registration of distinctive signs 'so long as the application for registration as a trademark is not made by a person who is not the legitimate owner of the sign or combination of signs according to United States law'.[1581]

Admittedly, the denial of registration because of the need to keep cultural signs free from trademark protection goes beyond the ownership question. It would generally exclude relevant cultural signs from registration, whereas the ownership obstacle discussed in *United States – Section 211 Omnibus Appropriations Act of 1998* could be overcome by the owner of the trademark herself. Nonetheless, an extension of the argument to cultural signs seems defensible. As the Appellate Body explains itself, Article 15(1) TRIPS does not impose a registration automatism on WTO Members: not each and every sign that 'qualifies for' registration under Article 15(1) TRIPS

1578. WTO Appellate Body, *ibid.*, para. 155.
1579. WTO Appellate Body, *ibid.*, para. 165.
1580. WTO Appellate Body, *ibid.*, para. 166.
1581. WTO Appellate Body, *ibid.*, para. 166.

must be deemed 'entitled to' registration.[1582] Hence, it is sufficient that the principle of eligibility for registration is upheld outside the domain of cultural signs. Besides arguments based on a conflict with morality or public order derived from Article 6*quinquies*(B) No. 3 PC, the general freedom of WTO Members to determine conditions for registration on the basis of Article 6(1) PC thus provides additional room for an *ex ante* exclusion of cultural signs.

Finally, it must not be overlooked that despite international obligations that may follow from Article 15(1) TRIPS, lawmakers in WTO Member States seem to agree that functional signs can be excluded from trademark registration even if they have acquired distinctiveness as a result of use in trade.[1583] As explained in section 9.1.2.4, the refusal of trademark protection because of aesthetic functionality, from an international perspective, is a special case of a denial of trademark rights on the basis of considerations of public order and morality. In the context of *telle quelle* protection under Article 6*quinquies*(A)(1) PC, the international basis for applying the functionality doctrine is the reference to public order and morality in Article 6*quinquies*(B) No. 3 PC.[1584] In the case of functional signs, the functionality doctrine – as a specific aspect of public order and morality – thus already prevails over a registration automatism derived from Article 15(1) TRIPS. Against this background, it is consistent to let public order and morality prevail as well when the question of *telle quelle* protection arises with regard to cultural signs.

Under existing international protection standards, a categorical exclusion of cultural signs from trademark protection can thus be grounded in the robust freedom of national lawmakers to regulate access to the trademark protection system on the basis of morality and public order criteria. In situations concerning *telle quelle* protection, this follows from Article 6*quinquies*(B) No. 3 PC. In domestic contexts, it follows from the general freedom to determine conditions for the registration of trademarks offered by Article 6(1) PC. The existing practice of excluding functional signs from registration even if they are distinctive (in the sense of Article 15(1) TRIPS) confirms the use of this breathing space for the implementation of a categorical ban on trademark rights at the national level. As functionality is a special subset of public order and morality criteria, the same approach is permissible and consistent under international trademark law with regard to cultural signs.

1582. WTO Appellate Body, *ibid.*, para. 155.

1583. See the examples given in sections 7.1 and 7.2 and the contributions to Senftleben 2012b. With regard to EU Member States, see CJEU, 11 May 2017, case C-421/15 P, Yoshida Metal Industry/EUIPO, para. 35; CJEU, 16 September 2015, case C-215/14, Nestlé/Cadbury ('Kit Kat'), paras 38-39; CJEU, 14 September 2010, case C-48/09 P, Lego/Mega Brands, para. 40.

1584. Kur 2011, 20; Kur 2017, 1086.

9.1.3 *Interplay with Other Grounds for Refusal*

The foregoing analysis has identified considerable room for the application of public order and morality as grounds for refusing trademark rights to cultural signs. Invoking public order and morality, trademark offices and courts can overcome the weaknesses of decisions based on a lack of distinctive character. As explained in section 9.1.2.2, distinctiveness and public order/morality appear as two poles of the spectrum of grounds for refusal in trademark law. Distinctiveness is particularly weak because the refusal can be overcome through use in trade and normally remains limited to specific goods and services. Public order and morality are particularly strong because the refusal is immune to the acquisition of distinctive character through use in trade and can apply across all goods and services.[1585] However, public order and morality are not the only grounds for refusal capable of developing a stronger exclusionary effect than a refusal based on a lack of distinctiveness. Between the two poles of distinctiveness (weak) and public order/morality (strong), there are several other registration requirements and grounds for refusal that may contribute to the prevention of undesirable overlaps between copyright and trademark protection. General registration requirements, such as visual perceptibility (following section 9.1.3.1), can have the potential to keep certain categories of cultural signs outside the trademark system altogether. Moreover, it is worthwhile to explore concepts, such as aesthetic functionality (section 9.1.3.2), high symbolic value (section 9.1.3.3) and bad faith (section 9.1.3.4) to provide an overview of exclusion mechanisms which trademark offices and courts have at their disposal. Do these additional registration requirements and grounds for refusal have added value? Are they capable of complementing or reinforcing a refusal based on public order or morality?

9.1.3.1 Visual Perceptibility

In line with Article 15(1) TRIPS, trademark offices may require, as a condition of registration, that 'signs be visually perceptible'. Evidently, this practical requirement is particularly relevant to non-traditional types of marks. A sound is not visually perceptible. Therefore, the optional TRIPS requirement of visual perceptibility can serve as a vehicle to exclude musical works from trademark protection altogether.[1586] However, it must not be overlooked that this registration requirement does not allow fine-grained decisions. Inevitably, the strict application of visual perceptibility as a gatekeeper requirement bars all kinds of sounds from trademark protection – regardless of cultural significance. Moreover, trademark policymakers move away from a strict focus on visual perceptibility. Many trademark systems

1585. Anemaet 2016, 331-332; Senftleben 2013a, 824-825.
1586. Senftleben 2013a, 826.

opt for the more flexible requirement of graphical representation[1587] and accept standard musical notation as a valid mode of representing sound marks.[1588] As a result of the 2015 EU trademark law reform,[1589] Article 4(b) EUTMR and Article 3(b) TMD require that signs be represented on the trademark register 'in a manner which enables the competent authorities and the public to determine the clear and precise subject matter of the protection afforded to its proprietor'.[1590] While this open-ended standard may be deemed more restrictive than the previous requirement of graphical representation in the case of colour combinations,[1591] it can easily be satisfied in the case of sound marks when the registration system has been digitized and allows for the upload of sound files. A sound file can accurately represent even most advanced musical creations that may be difficult to capture in a sufficiently clear and precise manner with standard musical notation.

9.1.3.2 Aesthetic Functionality

As already pointed out in section 9.1.2.4, the functionality doctrine – including the concept of aesthetic functionality – is a subcategory of public order and morality from the perspective of international trademark law. In the context of *telle quelle* protection under Article 6*quinquies*(A)(1) PC, the correct international basis for explaining the application of the functionality doctrine is the reference to public order and morality in Article 6*quinquies*(B) No. 3 PC.[1592] Given this close connection between the functionality doctrine and a refusal based on public order or morality, the question arises which added value the concept of aesthetic functionality could have. As discussed in section 7.3.1, the functionality doctrine focuses on product characteristics that are essential in the sense that they define the product at issue.[1593] Cultural signs, however, may be used in a marketing context as labels or advertising jingles without defining the properties of the goods concerned.[1594] The functionality doctrine, thus, fails to offer a general

1587. See the various contributions to Senftleben 2012b.

1588. As to the use of standard musical notation, see CJEU, 27 November 2003, case C-283/01, Shield Mark/Kist, para. 64. The requirement of graphical representation may still pose an insuperable obstacle to the registration of smell marks. See CJEU, *ibid.*, para. 73.

1589. Cf. Kur/Senftleben 2017, para. 4.05; Senftleben 2020, 209.

1590. This standard has been derived from CJEU, 12 December 2002, case C-273/00, Sieckmann, para. 55. See the explicit reference to the 'Sieckmann' criteria in Recital 10 EUTMR and Recital 13 TMD. Cf. Kur/Senftleben 2017, para. 4.20-4.22.

1591. CJEU, 29 July 2019, case C-124/18 P, Red Bull/EUIPO, paras 43-47; GCEU, 30 November 2017, cases T-101/15 and T-102/15, Red Bull/EUIPO, para. 118. Cf. Senftleben 2020, 209-210.

1592. Kur 2011, 20; Kur 2017, 1086.

1593. This inherent limitation of the concept offers various starting points to reject a broad application to cultural signs. Cf. Hughes 2015, 1264-1267; Kurtz 1986, 505.

1594. Cf. Ohly 2019, 328; Curtin 2018, 1021; Stieper 2012, 1091.

safeguard against trademark rights to cultural signs. If relevant signs are used in product marketing without influencing the aesthetic properties of the goods, the concept of aesthetic functionality is incapable of fulfilling the role of an effective filter mechanism that prevents the acquisition of trademark rights.

Nonetheless, it may be desirable to further develop the doctrine of aesthetic functionality as a ground for refusal that complements public order and morality.[1595] While considerations of public order and morality offer various starting points for denying trademark rights to cultural heritage signs in the public domain, the spectrum of morality arguments is less broad when it comes to contemporary mainstream creations that still enjoy copyright protection (see the more detailed discussion in section 9.1.2.3). With regard to cultural creations in the latter category, including fictional characters, the doctrine of aesthetic functionality could play an important role, if rightly applied. As explained in section 7.3.1, the EU concept of aesthetic functionality was traditionally limited to the exclusion of 'the shape which gives substantial value to the goods'.[1596] The current, amended version covers all kinds of product characteristics. It provides for the outright exclusion from trademark protection of 'the shape, *or another characteristic*, which gives substantial value to the goods' (emphasis added).[1597] Besides artistic value, the nature of the category of goods concerned, dissimilarity from other common product features, the achievement of a substantial price difference, and the development of a promotion strategy accentuating aesthetic characteristics constitute relevant assessment factors.[1598]

This range of criteria offers room to argue that a cultural sign stemming from a contemporary mainstream production 'gives substantial value' in the sense of the amended EU concept. First of all, this line of reasoning may be valid with regard to primary information products in which a contemporary mainstream creation is embodied. Arguably, an attempt to register a Spider-Man drawing for film productions can be refused on the ground that the fictional character lies at the core of the information product for which protection is sought. Accordingly, the Spider-Man drawing can be qualified as a feature giving substantial value to the goods. The same can be said about the registration of a Harry Potter drawing for Harry Potter books and the registration of a famous melody from 'The Phantom of the Opera' for recordings of the musical. A flexible application of aesthetic functionality may also foreclose the possibility of obtaining trademark protection with

1595. See Wandtke/Bullinger 1997, 577, proposing the development of a far-reaching aesthetic functionality exclusion of cultural material from trademark protection based on the mark/product dichotomy in trademark law. For a similar proposal under U.S. trademark law, see Curtin 2018, 1004-1005.
1596. Article 7(1)(e)(iii) CTMR 2009 and Article 3(1)(e)(iii) TMD 2008.
1597. Article 7(1)(e)(iii) EUTMR and Article 4(1)(e)(iii) TMD.
1598. CJEU, 18 September 2014, case C-205/13, Hauck/Stokke, paras 34-35.

regard to merchandising articles. Arguably, the particular value of merchandising articles relating to cultural productions is typically due to cultural signs that stem from the original information products, such as films, books and musicals.[1599] Often they feature prominently on the merchandising articles themselves. For example, a Mickey Mouse drawing will immensely enhance the value of a T-shirt because of the popularity of the famous fictional character known from comic books and cartoon films. Therefore, it seems plausible to invoke the exclusion of 'the shape, or another characteristic, which gives substantial value to the goods'[1600] as a ground for refusal with regard to the registration of Mickey Mouse as a trademark in respect of merchandising articles showing that cultural sign.[1601]

As pointed out in section 7.3.1, however, this line of reasoning only remains intact as long as the CJEU desists from extending the *Neuschwanstein* approach to the enquiry into aesthetic functionality. In *Neuschwanstein*, the CJEU discussed whether the name of the famous Bavarian castle constituted a descriptive characteristic of souvenir articles displaying the indication 'Neuschwanstein'. In this respect, the Court drew a distinction between general, objective characteristics of everyday goods sold as souvenir items,[1602] and the subjective appreciation following from the fact that the attachment of the name 'Neuschwanstein' may call to mind fond memories of a castle visit.[1603] According to the Court, the souvenir function ascribed to a product bearing the name 'Neuschwanstein' was not an objective characteristic inherent to the nature of that product, since that function was determined 'by the free will of the buyer and was focused solely on that buyer's intentions'.[1604] The fact that the name 'Neuschwanstein' transformed regular goods into souvenir articles could not be deemed an essential descriptive characteristic of the goods concerned. The memory evoked in the minds of consumers was not sufficient to qualify the name 'Neuschwanstein' as an indication of a product quality or an essential product characteristic.[1605]

If these considerations are applied mutatis mutandis to the doctrine of aesthetic functionality, the *Neuschwanstein* decision may have the result that a fictional character affixed to a merchandising article, such as a scarve, hat, shirt or cup, can no longer be deemed functional from an aesthetic perspective. As long as the sign's added value only stems from subjective appreciation, such as the ability to evoke positive feelings or pleasant

1599. Curtin 2018, 1005. Cf. U.S. District Court for the Central District of California, 14 November 2012, Fleischer Studios/A.V.E.L.A., 925 F. Supp. 2d 1067, 1074-1075 (C.D. Cal. 2012), 'Betty Boop'.
1600. Article 7(1)(e)(iii) EUTMR; Article 4(1)(e)(iii) TMD.
1601. Cf. Curtin 2018, 970; Liu 2013, 1436.
1602. CJEU, 6 September 2018, case C-488/16P, Bundesverband Souvenir – Geschenke – Ehrenpreise ('Neuschwanstein'), paras 42-43.
1603. CJEU, *ibid.*, paras 45-46.
1604. CJEU, *ibid.*, para. 44.
1605. CJEU, *ibid.*, paras 45-46.

memories of a cultural event, its impact on product characteristics may be insufficient to invoke the doctrine of aesthetic functionality. In the light of *Neuschwanstein*, a product feature that only leads to subjective appreciation is not a characteristic that could be relevant to the assessment of aesthetic functionality. If, in the eye of the end consumer, the substantial value of a fictional character on a merchandising article only follows from the subjective appreciation of positive feelings evoked by the character,[1606] the *Neuschwanstein* approach neutralizes the doctrine of aesthetic functionality. To avoid this erosion of the effectiveness of aesthetic functionality as a ground for refusal, the CJEU would thus have to refrain from extending the *Neuschwanstein* approach (which the Court developed in the context of an enquiry into descriptiveness) to the analysis of aesthetic functionality.

The *Neuschwanstein* decision, however, is not the only hurdle that must be surmounted to arrive at an effective application of the doctrine of aesthetic functionality to merchandising articles bearing a popular cultural sign. For the doctrine of aesthetic functionality to apply, the cultural sign for which trademark protection is sought must constitute 'the shape, or another characteristic' of merchandising articles.[1607] This requirement poses difficulties when a cultural sign is attached to a product as a mere label. As explained in section 7.3.3, the German Federal Court of Justice acknowledged in *Marlene Dietrich* that the photograph of the actress for which trademark protection was sought did not have to be placed prominently on merchandising articles. It could also be used as a label attached to the goods. Given this option of use as a badge of origin, distinctive character could not be denied.[1608] Similar considerations can easily thwart the application of the doctrine of aesthetic functionality. If Mickey Mouse is attached to T-shirts only as an inside-neck label, it seems difficult to argue that the drawing constitutes a product characteristic. As discussed in section 7.3.1, the link with the product is too loose to justify the invocation of aesthetic functionality as a ground for refusal.

In practice, the crux of the matter lies in the fact that trademark applications usually do not contain a detailed description of the contents of the products, in respect of which the registration is sought. The applicable international standard laid down in Article 3(1)(a)(xv) STLT only requires, as a maximum obligation that applicants have to accept,[1609] an indication of:

> the names of the goods and/or services for which the registration is sought, grouped according to the classes of the Nice Classification, each group preceded by the number of the class of that Classification to which

1606. CJEU, *ibid.*, para. 44.

1607. Article 7(1)(e)(iii) EUTMR and Article 4(1)(e)(iii) TMD.

1608. German Federal Court of Justice, 24 April 2008, case I ZB 21/06, Marlene-Dietrich-Bildnis, paras 19-22. See also the confirmation of this point in German Federal Court of Justice, 31 March 2010, case I ZB 62/09, Marlene-Dietrich-Bildnis II, paras 20-28.

1609. Article 3(4) Singapore Treaty of the Law of Trademarks.

that group of goods or services belongs and presented in the order of the classes of the said Classification.

According to this international standard, trademark offices are supposed to handle registration issues on the basis of rather general indications of goods and services.[1610] A trademark examiner confronted with a request to register a Spider-Man drawing in respect of films would thus have to insinuate that the applicant will use the cultural sign for Spider-Man films to arrive at a refusal based on aesthetic functionality. In the case of merchandising articles, the examiner would have to assume that a depiction of Spider-Man would feature prominently on the articles instead of merely serving as an inconspicuous label.

EU law offers several reference points for such a critical approach. In *Postkantoor*, the CJEU had to decide whether a trademark application concerning a Dutch composite word consisting of descriptive components ('post' and 'office') had to be refused even though the word resulting from the combination of descriptive elements could not be regarded as the only and most usual Dutch indication of the characteristics of the goods and services concerned. The Court answered that for a refusal based on the need to keep descriptive signs free, it was sufficient that the sign at issue, if not already in use as a regular description of the goods or services concerned, could be used for such descriptive purposes in the future.[1611] Therefore, a word had to be refused registration 'if at least one of its possible meanings designates a characteristic of the goods or services concerned'.[1612]

Extending this approach to aesthetically functional signs, it could be argued that a cultural sign (e.g., a Spider-Man drawing) must be refused registration if it is functional with regard to at least one of its possible applications to primary information products (Spider-Man films) or merchandising articles (Spider-Man T-shirt). In *Postkantoor*, the CJEU also held that it was inacceptable if trademark offices registered a mark 'only in so far as the goods or services concerned do not possess a particular characteristic'.[1613] The development of such a registration practice would cause legal uncertainty about the extent of protection.[1614] Hence, the *Postkantoor* decision can also be understood to prevent trademark offices from registering a cultural sign only in respect of those goods of a certain category (films), in respect of which the mark is not functional (namely films not featuring Spider-Man). The final result could thus be an outright exclusion of

1610. As to the use of general indications in the EU, see Article 33(5) EUTMR; Article 39(5) TMD. Cf. CJEU, 19 June 2012, case C-307/10, Chartered Institute of Patent Attorneys ('IP Translator'), paras 53-56 and 61-62.

1611. CJEU, 12 February 2004, case C-363/99, Koninklijke KPN/Benelux-Merkenbureau ('Postkantoor'), para. 95.

1612. CJEU, *ibid.*, para. 97.

1613. CJEU, *ibid.*, para. 114.

1614. CJEU, *ibid.*, para. 115.

trademark protection for primary information products on the ground that the cultural sign is aesthetically functional at least in respect of those information products in which the cultural sign itself plays a central role.

In case law, this approach has not been established as a standard rule yet. In *Marlene Dietrich II* – a further case in the German line of decisions concerning the registration of a portrait of the famous actress as a trademark (see section 7.3.3) – the German Federal Court of Justice was reluctant to adopt the *Postkantoor* approach.[1615] The case was not about aesthetic functionality. It concerned the right test for deciding whether the portrait photograph was devoid of distinctive character in respect of merchandising articles. While the German Federal Patent Court had denied registration on the ground that current marketing practices did not support the assumption that the portrait photograph – once registered for merchandising articles – would only be used as a distinctive label,[1616] the German Federal Court of Justice rejected this argument by pointing out that the *Postkantoor* approach only concerned descriptive signs in the sense of Article 3(1)(c) TMD 2008.[1617] With regard to signs devoid of distinctive character in the sense of Article 3(1)(b) TMD 2008, a broader approach was necessary: the analysis could not be confined to usual ways of using the sign in trade.[1618] Instead, the trademark office had to assess the future prospects of the sign being perceived as a source identifier by the consuming public when it was attached to the goods in places where badges of origin typically were to be found. For a favourable prognosis, it was sufficient that there was a possibility of attaching the sign in a way which consumers would readily understand as use as a mark.[1619] In the framework of the registration procedure, the assumption of distinctive character in the context of an assessment concerning Article 3(1)(b) TMD 2008, thus, did not require a finding that each and every way of applying the sign to the goods would constitute use which the public perceives as trademark use.[1620]

On its merits, the German Federal Court of Justice, therefore, developed rules for assessing signs which are potentially devoid of distinctive character that are the reverse of the approach to descriptive signs following from the CJEU's *Postkantoor* decision. Instead of basing its analysis on the least favourable way of attaching the sign to the goods (namely, in a descriptive way), a trademark office following the German Federal Court of Justice would have to assess the future prospects of the sign being perceived as a

1615. German Federal Court of Justice, 31 March 2010, case I ZB 62/09, 'Marlene-Dietrich-Bildnis II', para. 15.
1616. German Federal Court of Justice, *ibid.*, paras 8-10.
1617. German Federal Court of Justice, *ibid.*, para. 15.
1618. German Federal Court of Justice, *ibid.*, para. 18, referring to CJEU, 16 September 2004, case C-329/02P, SAT.1/OHIM, para. 36; CJEU, 15 September 2005, case C-37/03P, BioID/OHIM, para. 62.
1619. German Federal Court of Justice, *ibid.*, para. 19 and 21.
1620. German Federal Court of Justice, *ibid.*, para. 21.

trademark on the basis of the most favourable way of attaching the sign to the goods (namely, in a potentially distinctive way). When this outcome of the *Marlene Dietrich II* decision is placed in the context of aesthetic functionality, the trademark examiner would thus have to assume, in favour of the applicant, use as a label that does not influence product characteristics (Mickey Mouse as a mere inside-neck label) instead of taking use as a feature of the goods themselves as a point of departure for the analysis (Mickey Mouse on the front of a T-shirt). In principle, the German Federal Court of Justice still upholds this approach. In its 2012 *Neuschwanstein* decision (the final outcome of a national procedure that preceded the *Neuschwanstein* lawsuit before the CJEU),[1621] the German Federal Court of Justice explicitly referred to *Marlene Dietrich II* as a valid reference point for the enquiry.[1622] The Court added, however, that the specific nature of the sign and the goods at issue had to be taken into account. Without factual evidence to the contrary, it could not be assumed that the famous name of Neuschwanstein castle would be presented on merchandising articles in a way that allows consumers to perceive the sign as a badge of origin.[1623]

In the area of aesthetic functionality, developments in CJEU jurisprudence support this more realistic appraisal of the way in which a cultural sign will appear on products in the marketplace. Instead of accepting purported modes of appearance that favour the trademark applicant, the CJEU insisted in *Simba Toys/EUIPO* on an analysis based on real-life features of the sign for which protection was sought. In *Simba Toys/EUIPO*, Seven Towns had filed an application for the registration of the famous Rubik's Cube as a trademark for three-dimensional puzzles.[1624] However, the graphical representation submitted for this purpose only showed the shape of the cube and its surfaces with the characteristic grid structure. It did not reveal the technical functionality of the Rubik's Cube, namely the rotating capability of its individual elements.[1625] Hence, the question was whether the assessment of utilitarian functionality had to be confined to the graphical representation not indicating any technical feature, or whether the trademark examiner was free to factor the real-life appearance of the cube into the equation and consider the technical effect following from the rotating capability of the cube's individual elements. Answering this question, the CJEU held that:

> since it is not disputed that the sign at issue consists of the shape of actual goods and not of an abstract shape, the General Court should have

1621. As to the CJEU decision, see CJEU, 6 September 2018, case C-488/16P, Bundesverband Souvenir – Geschenke – Ehrenpreise ('Neuschwanstein'). For critical comments on the silence of the CJEU decision on substantive arguments advanced by the German Federal Court of Justice, see Ruess 2018, 1151.

1622. German Federal Court of Justice, 8 March 2012, case I ZB 13/11, 'Neuschwanstein', *GRUR* 2012, 1044, para. 20.

1623. German Federal Court of Justice, *ibid.*, para. 21.

1624. CJEU, 10 November 2016, case C-30/15P, Simba Toys/EUIPO, para. 8.

1625. CJEU, *ibid.*, para. 7.

> defined the technical function of the actual goods at issue, namely a three-dimensional puzzle, and it should have taken this into account when assessing the functionality of the essential characteristics of that sign.[1626]

Therefore, the CJEU required an assessment including the real-life appearance of the product and the technical function of its individual elements. The examiner was not bound to refrain from considering the technical functionality of the actual goods simply because the applicant had chosen a graphical representation that did not indicate that functionality. It was immaterial in this context that the registration was sought for three-dimensional puzzles in general – without being restricted to those that have a rotating capability – and that Seven Towns did not append to its trademark application a description specifying that the shape at issue had a rotating capability. To avoid the grant of an overbroad exclusive right, these facts could not preclude:

> account from being taken of the technical function of the actual goods represented by the sign at issue for the purpose of examining the functionality of the essential characteristics of that sign, as the proprietor of that mark would otherwise be allowed to broaden the scope of the protection arising from the registration thereof to cover every type of puzzle with a similar shape, namely any three-dimensional puzzle with cube-shaped elements, regardless of the principles by which it functions.[1627]

The Rubik's Cube was thus exposed to an enquiry into utilitarian functionality based on the technical features known from the three-dimensional puzzle sold on the market. Seven Towns could not hide behind a mode of representation that concealed the rotating capability of the cube's individual elements. As to the correct way of identifying essential real-life characteristics of a sign for which trademark protection is sought, the CJEU clarified in *Gömböc* that the presumed consumer perception could not be decisive. It only constituted 'a relevant criterion of assessment'.[1628] As already explained in section 5.2.1, trademark examiners must base their decision on 'objective and reliable information'.[1629] With regard to technical features, the Court mentioned a product description submitted at the time of filing, data relating to patent rights that have been conferred earlier, survey evidence and expert opinions, as well as scientific publications, catalogues or websites describing the technical features of the product.[1630]

1626. CJEU, *ibid.*, para. 47.
1627. CJEU, *ibid.*, para. 52.
1628. CJEU, 23 April 2020, case C-237/19, Gömböc, paras 30-31.
1629. CJEU, *ibid.*, para. 34 and 41.
1630. CJEU, *ibid.*, para. 34.

With regard to cultural signs and an enquiry into aesthetic functionality, trademark offices and courts could theoretically adopt a similar approach to rebut an applicant's argument that a cultural sign would only be attached to goods as a label without any impact on product characteristics. Considering market reality, the decisions in *Simba Toys* and *Gömböc* seem to offer trademark examiners and judges the opportunity to respond that experiences with merchandising articles show that fictional characters often feature prominently on the goods themselves and that, for this reason, the enquiry into aesthetic functionality must be extended to this form of use. In consequence, trademark applicants could no longer escape scrutiny in the light of aesthetic functionality by arguing that a cultural sign would only serve as a source identifier on a label.[1631]

Even if the approach taken in *Simba Toys* and *Gömböc* could be generalized and applied broadly in the area of aesthetic functionality,[1632] however, the fact remains that cultural signs can be applied flexibly to goods. In contrast to technical elements, a literary and artistic work can be affixed to various places of a product. Hence, position marks may offer a final resort for applicants seeking to register a cultural sign in respect of primary information products and merchandising articles. To preclude a scrutiny in the light of aesthetic functionality based on the least favourable way of attaching the cultural sign to the goods, the applicant could specify that the cultural sign would be used as a label constituting a position mark and indicate precisely where that position mark would be placed on the goods.[1633]

In practice, CJEU jurisprudence poses additional obstacles to an assessment focusing on the least favourable way of attaching a cultural sign to goods (the mode of use that would support a finding of aesthetic functionality). In *AS/Deutsches Patent- und Markenamt ('#darferdas?')*, the CJEU discussed which mode of placing a sign on goods was relevant to the assessment. The case concerned the question of whether the enquiry had to be based on use of the hashtag #darferdas? on the front or the label of clothing.[1634] The Court explained that, at the time of filing, trademark applicants were not obliged to indicate or even know precisely which use they would make of the sign after registration.[1635] Therefore, the assessment

---

1631. Cf. Ohly 2019, 328.

1632. Given current national practices, it does not seem safe to assume that this will happen without further CJEU decisions addressing aesthetic functionality explicitly. With regard to the exclusion of nature shapes because of functionality, the German Federal Court of Justice, 25 October 2007, case I ZB 22/04, 'Milchschnitte', *GRUR* 2008, 510, paras 15-16, for instance, traditionally takes the opposite approach and bases the assessment on the general category of goods concerned.

1633. This option was also discussed in *Marlene Dietrich II*. See German Federal Court of Justice, *ibid.*, para. 11.

1634. CJEU, 12 September 2019, case C-541/18, AS/Deutsches Patent- und Markenamt ('#darferdas?'), para. 7, 8 and 31.

1635. CJEU, *ibid.*, para. 22.

had to take into account the customs in the economic sector concerned and include all forms of use with practical significance:

> When it is apparent from those customs that several uses are practically significant in that economic sector, those authorities must […] take into consideration those various uses in order to determine whether the average consumer of the goods or services covered will perceive that sign as an indication of the commercial origin of those goods or services.[1636]

The Court also pointed out that a cautious approach was necessary to prevent registrations based on very specific and unlikely forms of use.[1637] In the light of the facts which the German Federal Court of Justice had submitted together with its prejudicial questions, however, the CJEU explicitly confirmed with regard to clothing that use of the sign #darferdas? on the front and the label of T-shirts could both be regarded as practically significant types of placement on the product.[1638] The current approach taken by the CJEU, thus, precludes an assessment based exclusively on the appearance of cultural signs on the front of goods, such as T-shirts and other merchandising articles, unless use as a label can be deemed unlikely and irrelevant in the economic sector concerned. A broad application of the *Simba Toys* and *Gömböc* approach to arrive at a finding of aesthetic functionality seems difficult against this background.

It is also to be considered that a further category of goods has not entered the picture yet: goods that are unrelated to the cultural sign and do not constitute typical merchandising articles. When the registration of a Mickey Mouse, Spider-Man or Harry Potter drawing, or a Phantom of the Opera melody, is sought in respect of cars, the conclusion seems inescapable that the cultural sign does not define the characteristics of the product. Its popularity may enhance consumers' willingness to buy the car. In *Hauck/ Stokke*, however, the CJEU included promotion strategies in its concept of aesthetic functionality only insofar as they concern product characteristics. The Court mentioned 'the development of a promotion strategy which focuses on accentuating the aesthetic characteristics of the product in question'.[1639] The use of a cultural sign as a marketing tool without a direct impact on the aesthetic characteristics of the product falls outside this category. Inevitably, the doctrine of aesthetic functionality thus fails to prevent certain forms of using a cultural sign as a trademark. To avoid this result, it would be necessary to relax the focus on material product characteristics. A starting point for this step follows from *Copad/Dior* where the CJEU discussed the scope of the concept of 'the quality of the goods

1636. CJEU, *ibid.*, paras 24-25.
1637. CJEU, *ibid.*, paras 26-28.
1638. CJEU, *ibid.*, paras 29-31.
1639. CJEU, 18 September 2014, case C-205/13, Hauck/Stokke, para. 35.

manufactured' that is relevant to the assessment of a licensee's contravention of provisions of a trademark licensing contract.[1640] The Court stated that:

> the quality of luxury goods such as the ones at issue in the main proceedings is not just the result of their material characteristics, but also of the allure and prestigious image which bestows on them an aura of luxury.[1641]

In *Coty Germany*, the CJEU explicitly confirmed this broadening of the quality concept.[1642] Besides material characteristics, the 'allure and prestigious image' forms part of the quality of luxury goods in the view of the Court.[1643] Extending this broad concept to cultural signs, it may be argued that, even if a cultural sign is attached as a mere label to unrelated goods (goods outside the cultural sector that are not regularly used as merchandising articles), it still bestows a particular 'aura' on the goods, namely the aura evoked by the literary and artistic production from which the sign is taken. From this perspective, it seems possible to conclude that the cultural sign gives substantial value to the goods (and must be deemed aesthetically functional for this reason) if the aura associated with the underlying literary and artistic production makes the product attractive to consumers.

However, this relaxation of the requirement of a 'shape, or another characteristic, which gives substantial value to the goods' in Article 7(1)(e) EUTMR and Article 4(1)(e) TMD would also exclude any other sign with a favourable aura from trademark protection, including signs with genuine brand value. As explained in section 7.3.1, the attachment of the Coca Cola logo to soft drinks would also lead to an exclusion of trademark rights because the brand value of the logo adds substantial value to the product. Hence, use as a label on unrelated goods can hardly be brought within the scope of the aesthetic functionality doctrine, even if *Copad/Dior* is used as a source of inspiration.

On balance, it becomes apparent that the EFTA Court was right in the *Vigeland* case. The EFTA Court cast doubt upon aesthetic functionality as a tool to prevent the acquisition of trademark rights to cultural signs because this ground for refusal does not cover services from the outset and seems incapable of precluding a registration in respect of goods that are unrelated to the sign's initial cultural context.[1644] The EFTA Court concluded that the exclusion of trademark protection on the basis of substantial value considerations failed to 'ensure that works, in general, are kept within the public domain'.[1645] The current analysis confirms this result: the doctrine of

1640. Article 25(2)(e) EUTMR and Article 25(2)(e) TMD.
1641. CJEU, 23 April 2009, case C-59/08, Copad/Dior, para. 24.
1642. CJEU, 6 December 2017, case C-230/16, Coty Germany, para. 25.
1643. Cf. the description of the marketing and branding strategies applied by the luxury perfume industry given by Machnicka 2012, 141-143.
1644. EFTA Court, 6 April 2017, case E-5/16, Municipality of Oslo ('Vigeland'), para. 81.
1645. EFTA Court, *ibid.*, para. 81.

aesthetic functionality has little to add to the public order and morality criteria discussed in sections 9.1.2.3 and 9.1.2.4. Nonetheless, aesthetic functionality may be converted into a more effective ground for refusal when the trademark applicant seeks a registration in respect of primary information products to which a cultural sign relates.

9.1.3.3 High Symbolic Value

Aesthetic functionality is not the only ground for refusal which, from the perspective of international *telle quelle* protection (Article 6*quinquies*(A)(1) and (B) No. 2 and 3 PC), has a close connection with public order and morality. Under the umbrella of the overarching concept of public order and morality, EU Member States, for instance, enjoy the freedom of denying protection for trademarks including 'a sign of high symbolic value, in particular a religious symbol'.[1646] As in the case of functionality, Article 6*quinquies*(B) No. 3 PC offers an international basis for applying this ground for refusal in *telle quelle* protection scenarios. The exclusion of signs with high symbolic value may be understood to cover not only signs with a religious meaning, such as holy names, pictures and icons, but also cultural signs which, in the light of a country's history and traditions, are perceived as national symbols.[1647] Historical and cultural monuments may fall within the scope of this broader concept.[1648]

The close conceptual connection with public order and morality is self-evident. As discussed in sections 9.1.2.3 and 9.1.2.4, a conflict with morality arises when the relevant public perceives the registration as a trademark as offensive because certain pieces of art enjoy a 'particular status as prominent parts of a nation's cultural heritage, an emblem of sovereignty or of the nation's foundations and values'[1649] (morality ground 1). A sign conflicts with public order when its registration as a trademark would pose a genuine and sufficiently serious threat to 'certain fundamental values',[1650] 'a fundamental interest of society'[1651] or 'a fundamental concern to the State and the whole of society'[1652] (public order ground 1). An attempt to register a 'sign of high symbolic value' or a 'religious symbol' is likely to fall within

1646. Article 4(3)(b) TMD.
1647. For an in-depth analysis of this optional ground for refusal in EU law and a plea for its implementation at the national level, see Van Woensel 2007, 227-249 and 452-456.
1648. For instance, see Article 11(1), sub 11, of the Trademark Law of Bulgaria referring to 'marks which consist of or include the name or a representation of historical and cultural monuments of the Republic of Bulgaria, as specified by the Ministry of Culture'.
1649. EFTA Court, 6 April 2017, case E-5/16, Municipality of Oslo ('Vigeland'), para. 92.
1650. EFTA Court, *ibid.*, para. 96.
1651. EFTA Court, *ibid.*, para. 95.
1652. EFTA Court, *ibid.*, para. 94.

the province of these public order and morality considerations and trigger a refusal.

As a conflict with public order or morality, the optional ground for refusal for EU Member States poses an insurmountable hurdle to trademark protection. It constitutes an outright exclusion of signs of high symbolic value and religious symbols – irrespective of whether the sign has acquired distinctive character through use in trade.[1653] EU Member States that adopted this optional ground for refusal include Bulgaria, Czech Republic, Greece, Hungary, Italy, Latvia, Poland, Portugal and Slovakia.[1654] In the Benelux, it has not made its way into trademark legislation despite a strong plea for its inclusion in literature.[1655] It is also noteworthy that in the EUTMR, the specific ground for refusal relating to high symbolic value and religious symbols is sought in vain.[1656]

Quite clearly, the conceptual overlap with public order and morality criteria begs the question which added value the ground for refusal may have in respect of public order and morality. The option to exclude signs of high symbolic value and religious symbols from trademark protection does not in itself constitute a sufficiently broad cultural ground for refusal. A sign with cultural significance may qualify as an important national symbol and fall under the exclusion of signs with high symbolic value. Cultural signs without high symbolic value or religious meaning, however, remain unaffected. Nonetheless, the optional ground for refusal may have a role to play as a catalyst sensitizing examiners and judges to the importance of keeping important symbols, including cultural symbols, free from trademark protection. The adoption of this optional ground for refusal has a clarifying effect: it highlights the importance of a specific facet of public order and morality considerations. Making the symbolic value aspect of public order ground 1 and morality ground 1 visible in trademark legislation, it draws the attention of trademark offices and courts to cultural signs with outstanding importance and makes high symbolic value a regular assessment factor to be taken into account in the context of trademark registrations.

However, the limited scope of the optional ground for refusal is also worrisome. If national legislation adopts the exclusion of signs with high

---

1653. Article 4(4) TMD and Article 7(3) EUTMR only offer the possibility of obtaining trademark rights as a result of the acquisition of distinctive character as a result of use in trade with regard to non-distinctive, descriptive and generic signs.

1654. See Article 11(1), sub 11, of the Trademark Act of Bulgaria, Sec. 2(1)(i) Act on Trademarks of the Czech Republic, Article 3(2)(a) of the Trademark Act of Greece, Article 3(2)(c) of the Trademark Law of Hungary, Article 10 of the Trademark Law of Italy, Article 6(1), sub 9, of the Trademark Law of Latvia, Article 131(2)(v) of the Trademark Law of Poland, Article 238(4)(b) of the Industrial Property Code of Portugal, Sec. 5(1)(j) of the Trademarks Act of Slovakia. These laws are available online at www.wipo.int/clea.

1655. Van Woensel 2007, 452-456.

1656. Article 7(1) EUTMR is silent on high symbolic value and religious meaning as absolute grounds for refusal.

symbolic value and religious symbols, this may be misunderstood as an indication that the legislator has considered the question of signs with particular value, including cultural value, and decided to confine the exclusion of signs in this category to signs with high symbolic or religious meaning. As a result, signs with cultural value, but without high symbolic value or religious meaning, may be deemed registrable because they fall outside the specific ground for refusal addressing this category of signs. As a vehicle to arrive at a categorical exclusion of cultural signs from trademark protection, the adoption of high symbolic value as an optional ground for refusal is thus a double-edged sword. It can have a beneficial effect if understood correctly: as a facet of the broader concept of public order and morality and an invitation to develop not only this specific ground for refusal but also the full spectrum of public order and morality criteria developed in sections 9.1.2.3 and 9.1.2.4. If, by contrast, the adoption of a specific ground for refusal addressing high symbolic value is misunderstood as the lawmaker's final word on the exclusion of signs with particular value, including cultural value, it confines the analysis to a small fraction of signs that are relevant to cultural follow-on innovation, and thwarts the objective to develop a broader basis for the exclusion of cultural signs from trademark protection.

9.1.3.4 Bad Faith

In *Vigeland*, the UK submitted an observation highlighting the potential contribution of bad faith as a ground for refusal[1657] in cases concerning cultural signs:

> Moreover, the Government of the United Kingdom argues that registration may also be denied under the 'bad faith' provision pursuant to Article 3(2)(d) of the Directive [Article 3(2)(d) TMD 2008; Article 4(2) TMD] if registration of marks that are cultural works is sought merely to obtain a monopoly, and not with any intention of using the marks as trade marks[1658] (text within brackets added).

It is easy to draw a line between this ground for refusal and cases where a trademark 'troll' seeks to register signs with cultural significance for the sole purpose of threatening users with infringement claims and obtaining licence fees in this way. In such a case of 'cultural heritage grabbing', a refusal or invalidation of trademark rights because of bad faith comes into play.[1659] The CJEU applies bad faith as a ground for refusal when 'relevant and consistent

1657. Article 4(2) TMD.

1658. Report for the Hearing, Judge-Rapporteur Baudenbacher, 5 October 2016, case E-5/16, Municipality of Oslo ('Vigeland'), para. 139-140.

1659. Ohly 2008, 207; Vanovermeire 2009, 186. Cf. CJEU, 11 June 2009, case C-529/07, Lindt/Hauswirth, para. 53. For a more detailed analysis of bad faith trademark registrations, see Tsoutsanis 2005; Helm 1996, 593.

indicia' support the assumption that the trademark proprietor has filed the application:

> not with the aim of engaging fairly in competition but with the intention of undermining, in a manner inconsistent with honest practices, the interests of third parties, or with the intention of obtaining, without even targeting a specific third party, an exclusive right for purposes other than those falling within the functions of a trade mark, in particular the essential function of indicating origin recalled in the previous paragraph of the present judgment.[1660]

This formula offers a basis for applying bad faith as a ground for refusal when the trademark applicant seeks to register cultural signs for the sole purpose of bringing infringement claims against users, including users in the cultural domain. In *Lindt/Hauswirth*, the CJEU identified several factors that are relevant to the identification of bad faith applications. In particular, it may be relevant that the applicant knows or must know that a third party is using a sign identical or similar to the sign for which registration is sought and that the applicant intends to prevent that third party from continuing to use the sign.[1661]

However, the UK statement also sheds light on the weak point of the bad faith argument: it is difficult to rely on bad faith unless it becomes apparent that the trademark proprietor has no intention of making genuine use of affected cultural signs in trade.[1662] The decision of the Higher Court of Appeals of Dresden in *Johann Sebastian Bach* clearly reflects the destabilizing effect of this requirement. As discussed in section 6.2.1, the Court saw clear indications that the signs concerning Johann Sebastian Bach (and various other cultural signs) had been registered for the sole purpose of preventing others from use and forcing them to enter into licensing agreements – without any true intention of using the signs in trade.[1663] Nonetheless, the Court found no basis for assuming bad faith. As the registration had occurred in 1999 and the case was decided in 2000, an obligation to put the trademarks to genuine use had not arisen yet. Instead, the trademark proprietor could rely on the possibility of acquiring trademark rights in the EU on the basis of mere registration – with the requirement of genuine use becoming an issue only five years after completion of the registration procedure.[1664] The fact that the trademark owner had not developed plans for the use of the Bach signs to create or preserve an 'outlet

1660. CJEU, 29 January 2020, case C-371/18, Sky and Others, para. 75.
1661. CJEU, 11 June 2009, case C-529/07, Lindt/Hauswirth, para. 44. Cf. Ohly 2019, 333-334; Kur 2017, 1090.
1662. This prerequisite is also highlighted in CJEU, *ibid.*, para. 44, where the Court explicitly refers to the condition of 'without intending to use it'.
1663. Higher Court of Appeals of Dresden, 4 April 2000, case 14 U 3611/99, 'Johann Sebastian Bach', *NJW* 2001, 615 (617).
1664. Article 18(1) EUTMR and Article 16(1) TMD.

for the goods or services'[1665] at the time of filing the application was thus insufficient to assume bad faith. Instead, the Higher Court of Appeals of Dresden felt bound by the registration decision taken by the German Patent and Trademark Office.[1666]

In *Sky*, the CJEU confirmed that trademark applicants were not required 'to indicate or even to know precisely' which use they would make of the mark in the five-year period following registration.[1667] The Court added that EU Member States were free to impose an obligation on applicants to formally declare their bona fide intention to put registered signs to genuine use (section 9.1.2.5). According to the Court, the infringement of such an obligation may constitute evidence of possible bad faith. However, the mere infringement of the obligation to make the declaration could not constitute an independent ground for invalidity of the trademark.[1668] Therefore, the problem arising from the five-year grace period remains. Instead of effectively barring the acquisition of trademark rights *ex ante* – before damage is done to the process of cultural follow-on innovation (section 9.1.1.7) – bad faith can serve as a weapon against trademark trolls and cultural heritage grabbing only after the true intentions of the trademark owner have become manifest.[1669] At this later point in time, artists may already have shied away from use of affected cultural signs because of cease-and-desist letters and infringement lawsuits instigated by the trademark owner (section 6.3).

Against this background, the current concept of bad faith does not constitute an effective tool to exclude cultural signs from trademark protection and safeguard the cultural innovation cycle. As long as bad faith only covers the trademark owner's intention of putting registered signs to genuine use in trade, the contribution of bad faith arguments to the maintenance of cyclic cultural innovation will remain limited – at least during the five-year period following the trademark registration procedure. During this time, the trademark owner has the opportunity to develop genuine use activities under current EU trademark law. Hence, the trademark owner also has the chance of threatening users, including users in the cultural domain, with infringement claims.

The aforementioned bad faith formula which the Court used in *Sky* also renders the bad faith argument inapplicable when the trademark applicant has

1665. CJEU, 11 March 2003, case C-40/01, Ajax/Ansul, para. 37.
1666. Higher Court of Appeals of Dresden, *ibid.*, 617-618.
1667. CJEU, 29 January 2020, case C-371/18, Sky and Others, para. 76.
1668. CJEU, *ibid.*, para. 86. For case law reflecting circumstances that may justify the assumption of bad faith, see England and Wales High Court, 6 February 2018, case HC-2016-001587, Sky/Skykick, [2018] EWHC 155 (Ch), para. 209-225, where Justice Arnold concludes in light of the UK requirement of a declaration of bona fide intention of genuine use and the available body of UK case law that 'at least in certain circumstances, it may constitute bad faith to apply to register a trade mark without any intention to use it in relation to the specified goods or services' (at 225).
1669. Ohly 2008, 207.

the aim of engaging fairly in competition and embarking on use for purposes falling within the functions of trademarks.[1670] From the outset, the current bad faith test is aligned with trademark categories of legitimate use. If a company adopts a cultural sign as a trademark and submerges its cultural meaning in the course of massive marketing campaigns, the current, trademark-centric criteria do not offer starting points for invoking bad faith. As EUIPO's invalidation decision in *Banksy* has shown, the absence of an intention to impregnate a cultural sign with commercial marketing messages leads to the verdict of bad faith.[1671] The aim to suppress cultural connotations in the process of transforming a cultural sign into a brand, by contrast, is not regarded as use in bad faith in the sense of trademark law. The current bad faith assessment encourages the redefinition of cultural signs in trade (section 8.2.3.3). Marketing campaigns and the attachment of commercial connotations are preconditions for the maintenance of trademark rights. These activities are fully consistent with the expectation that the trademark proprietor will employ the sign as a marketing tool in commerce. This trademark logic inhibits the bad faith assessment, as currently applied by the CJEU, from lending weight to cultural concerns, such as the risk of an impediment of dialogic cultural communication (section 3.3.2.4), unfair freeriding on positive cultural connotations (section 8.2.3.1), censorship based on the trademark owner's vision of affected cultural signs (section 8.2.3.2) and the impregnation of cultural signs with commercial marketing messages that devalue the sign as a reference point for the artistic discourse (section 8.2.3.3).

At best, bad faith may complement public order and morality arguments under specific circumstances.[1672] As explained in section 9.1.2.5, it may serve as an implementation vehicle to combine the obligation to declare non-use in a cultural context, as proposed above, with the legal consequence of invalidity when the trademark owner asserts copyright contrary to the non-use declaration. This application of bad faith in connection with a declaration of non-use in a cultural context, however, would require a substantial broadening of the concept of bad faith. On balance, the bad faith argument, as currently applied, is thus wanting. It may offer some *ex post* support in cases of cultural heritage grabbing. However, it is incapable of fulfilling the role which public order and morality criteria can play *ex ante* when trademark applicants seek to register cultural signs as trademarks. To allow bad faith to play the role discussed in connection with a declaration of non-use in a cultural context (section 9.1.2.5), a substantial broadening of the bad faith concept would be necessary.

1670. CJEU, 29 January 2020, case C-371/18, Sky and Others, para. 75.

1671. EUIPO Cancellation Division, 14 September 2020, cancellation no. 33 843 C (invalidity), Full Colour Black/Pest Control Office ('Banksy'), 10-12 and 15.

1672. See Ohly 2019, 333-334 and Kur 2017, 1090, for proposals aiming at a broader, more flexible application of bad faith criteria.

9.1.4 *Communication under Article 6ter PC*

In addition to the registration requirements and grounds for refusal discussed in the preceding section, it is advisable to explore the option of qualifying cultural signs with outstanding national importance as state emblems in the sense of Article 6*ter* PC (section 9.1.4.1). This regulatory approach offers the prospect of an international communication system for cultural signs with outstanding importance that should be kept outside the trademark systems of Paris Union countries and WTO Members (following section 9.1.4.2). As the following discussion will show, however, the communication system following from Article 6*ter* PC is inappropriate because it entails the risk of undesirable state control over notified cultural signs (section 9.1.4.3). The 2003 UNESCO Convention for the Safeguarding of the Intangible Cultural Heritage[1673] provides a more convincing template for the establishment of an international 'white list'[1674] of cultural signs to be kept free from trademark protection (section 9.1.4.4).

9.1.4.1 Cultural Signs as State Emblems

Besides the entitlement to deny the registration of signs that would be contrary to morality or public order under the *telle quelle* protection rule of Article 6*quinquies*(B) No. 3 PC, international trademark law provides for the refusal of trademark protection in the case of official emblems. Article 6*ter*(1)(a) PC excludes from registration and use as trademarks, or elements of trademarks, 'armorial bearings, flags, and other State emblems, of the countries of the Union, official signs and hallmarks indicating control and warranty adopted by them, and any imitation from a heraldic point of view'. Article 6*ter*(1)(b) PC extends this rule to emblems of international intergovernmental organizations.[1675] Therefore, international trademark law recognizes the need to exclude certain official signs from trademark protection. As a refusal based on public order or morality, this mechanism for excluding trademark protection is unconditional in the sense that the obstacle to registration cannot be overcome through use in the course of trade.

As to the scope of the exclusion of official emblems, it is noteworthy that domestic legislation can broaden the range of signs that are kept outside of trademark law on the basis of a filter mechanism resembling Article 6*ter* PC. EU trademark law offers a good starting point for exploring these

1673. The text of the Convention is available at https://ich.unesco.org/en/convention.

1674. Cf. Van Woensel 2013, 376.

1675. For a description of this additional exclusion mechanism, see WIPO Document SCT/15/3, dated 14 October 2005, "Article 6ter of the Paris Convention: Legal and Administrative Aspects", available online at www.wipo.int/sct. For commentary, see Cf. Pflüger 2011, 229-233; Pacek 2009, 673; Ladas 1975, 1240-1247; Bodenhausen 1969, 94-99; Ronga 1966, 148.

ramifications.[1676] In the area of official signs and emblems, EU Member States are free to adopt an absolute ground for refusal referring to badges, emblems and escutcheons which are of public interest but not covered by Article 6*ter* PC.[1677] This optional ground for refusal may be invoked with regard to the official emblems of lower public entities, such as provinces and municipalities, and other public institutions, such as the police and the fire brigade.

The reason for the adoption of Article 6*ter* PC at the international level was not only the consideration that the registration or use of official emblems would encroach upon the right of a state to control the use of symbols of its sovereignty but also the fear that such use 'might mislead the public with respect to the origin of goods to which such marks would be applied'.[1678] The use of emblems of states and international intergovernmental organizations could give the false impression of a connection with the government bodies concerned. It may mislead consumers into believing that products or services[1679] marketed under such emblems have the approval or support of a state or international intergovernmental organization. This risk of a false impression of quality control or sponsorship may not only arise from the use of 'classical' symbols of state sovereignty, such as the flags and armorial bearings explicitly mentioned in Article 6*ter*(1) PC, but also in cases where other signifiers of state power are used, such as historical monuments, cultural artefacts, names and portraits of monarchs and political leaders. Therefore, the question arises whether it would make sense to bring a broader range of signs – including signs with cultural significance – within the scope of the unconditional exclusion from trademark protection following from Article 6*ter* PC.[1680]

1676. As to the basic exclusion mechanism based on Article 6*ter* PC, see Article 3(1)(h) TMD and Article 7(1)(h) CTMR. The scope of this absolute ground for refusal has been clarified in CJEU, 16 July 2009, cases C-202/08 P and 208/08 P, American Clothing Associates/OHIM, para. 47 and 80.
1677. Article 4(3)(c) TMD. For example, see § 8(2) No. 6 of the Trademark Law of Germany; Article 5 of the Trademark Law of Malta, Article 131(2)(ii) of the Trademark Law of Poland, Article 238(4)(a) of the Industrial Property Code of Portugal, Article 5(1)(i) and (k) of the Trademark Law of Spain. These laws are available at www.wipo.int/clea. The additional ground for refusal is also applied at EUTM level. See Article 7(1)(i) EUTMR.
1678. Bodenhausen 1969, 96.
1679. The application of Article 6*ter* PC not only to trademarks but also to service marks has been confirmed explicitly in Article 16 TLT and Article 16 STLT. Cf. WIPO 2005, para. 32. With regard to protection against both use as trade and service marks in the EU, see Kur/Senftleben 2017, para. 4.226.
1680. As to the meaning of the word 'emblem' in Article 6*ter* PC, see Bodenhausen 1969, 96.

9.1.4.2 Prospect of an International 'White List'

In comparison with the exclusion mechanisms offered by the concept of morality (section 9.1.2.3) and public order (section 9.1.2.4), Article 6*ter* PC has important added value. The provision itself reflects the close connection with considerations of public order and morality. Article 6*ter*(10) PC clarifies that the specific exclusion mechanism with regard to emblems of states and international intergovernmental organizations 'shall not prevent the countries from exercising the right given in paragraph (3) of Article 6*quinquies*, Section B ... '. Accordingly, marks incorporating emblems protected under Article 6*ter* PC may alternatively be denied registration or invalidated at the national level on the grounds that they are contrary to morality or public order, or of a deceptive nature.[1681] In the light of the deliberations at the 1925 The Hague Conference for the Revision of the Paris Convention,[1682] WIPO described the interplay between Article 6*ter* PC and Article 6*quinquies*(B) No. 3 PC as follows:

> The reference to Article 6quinquies(B)(3) of the Paris Convention seems to indicate that Article 6ter could be understood to deal with a special case of marks contrary to morality or public order, namely marks that unduly incorporate emblems or signs of States or international intergovernmental organizations. On the basis of the lex specialis principle, it could be argued that Article 6ter, to the extent that it contains specific provisions with regard to such emblems and signs, would preempt the application of the general principle reflected in Article 6quinquies(B)(3). To avoid that interpretation Article 6ter(10) makes it clear that Article 6quinquies(B)(3) remains applicable.[1683]

Hence, Article 6*ter* PC can be understood as a specific mechanism dealing with a category of signs that may also give rise to scrutiny from the perspective of morality or public order – without excluding the possibility of invoking the general public order and morality rule laid down in Article 6*quinquies*(B) No. 3 PC. The added value of the specific 6*ter* mechanism clearly comes to the fore in paragraph 3(a) of the provision which confirms agreement of the countries of the Paris Union:

> to communicate reciprocally, through the intermediary of the International Bureau, the list of State emblems, and official signs and hallmarks indicating control and warranty, which they desire, or may hereafter desire, to place wholly or within certain limits under the protection of this Article, and all subsequent modifications of such list. Each country of the Union shall in due course make available to the public the lists so

1681. WIPO 2005, para. 38.
1682. BIRPI 1925, 460.
1683. WIPO 2005, para. 39.

communicated. Nevertheless such communication is not obligatory in respect of flags of States.

Considering the aim of preventing trademark rights to cultural signs, a communication under Article 6*ter* PC appears attractive because it could universalize the exclusionary effect of public order/morality considerations. Once a cultural sign falling within the scope of Article 6*ter* PC has been circulated via the International Bureau of WIPO,[1684] countries belonging to the Paris Union and, by virtue of Article 2(1) TRIPS, Members of the WTO are bound to refuse and invalidate the sign's registration and prohibit its use as a trademark unless they have transmitted an objection in line with Article 6*ter*(4) PC. Article 6*ter*(9) PC even adds a more general prohibition of unauthorized use of armorial bearings in trade 'when the use is of such a nature as to be misleading as to the origin of the goods'. This broader prohibition is not limited to use as a trademark.[1685]

The application of the communication mechanism following from Article 6*ter* PC may thus lead to the establishment of an international 'white list' of cultural signs to be kept free from trademark protection. In 2013, Caspar van Woensel already proposed the introduction of a white list of names and images with particular symbolic importance, such as the name and portrait of Anne Frank, at Benelux level.[1686] In 2004, Jeremy Phillips and Ilanah Simon Fhima had argued for measures against signs with problematic, politically sensitive meanings: a 'black list' of signs to be banned from trademark registers, advertising campaigns and product packaging.[1687] Their focus was on names and symbols of Nazi and fascist regimes, such as signs relating to Adolf Hitler and Benito Mussolini.[1688] The idea of a list of signs to be kept free is thus not entirely new.[1689] While insignia of dictatorships and other totalitarian regimes – candidates for a blacklist – will hopefully no longer obtain the status of state emblems anywhere in the world, it seems worthwhile against this background to explore the potential of Article 6*ter* PC to serve as a vehicle for the establishment of an international white list of cultural signs to be kept outside the trademark system across Paris Union and WTO Members.

1684. For a more detailed description of the communication process, see WIPO 2005, paras 40-49.

1685. WIPO 2005, para. 37, gives the example of use 'as decorative elements on the packaging or design of goods, or in advertising material'.

1686. Van Woensel 2013, 376.

1687. According to Phillips/Simon Fhima 2004, 328-330, the 'black list' system would have to be introduced based on a 'no-mark' approach that would be policed by a pan-European agency across all classes of goods and services.

1688. Phillips/Simon Fhima 2004, 327-328.

1689. With regard to the option of using Article 6ter PC in the field of traditional cultural expressions, see Osei-Tutu 2017, 1062 and 1070-1071.

9.1.4.3 Undesirable State Control

A closer look at Article 6*ter* PC, however, reveals that besides the promising communication mechanism, the provision poses several problems that make the use of this path to a white list undesirable. First, the conceptual contours of Article 6*ter* PC hardly offer sufficient room to cover the wide variety of cultural expressions that may be relevant to the cultural innovation cycle. The inherent limits of Article 6*ter* PC clearly come to the fore when considering the objectives on which the provision is based. As Georg Bodenhausen explains in the light of the debate at the 1925 The Hague Revision Conference, the objective underlying the provision is:

> to exclude the registration and use of trademarks which are identical or present a certain similarity to State emblems, an expression which, in view of the word 'other,' includes armorial bearings and flags of the State concerned. The reasons for this are that such registration or use would violate the right of the State to control the use of symbols of its sovereignty and furthermore might mislead the public with respect to the origin of goods to which such marks would be applied.[1690]

The aim to realize the objectives pointed out by Bodenhausen justifies the communication of official state insignia which consumers perceive as signifiers of state power (and potentially misleading indications of state approval or support). Bodenhausen's statement even reflects a more general concern about the misappropriation of symbols of sovereignty.[1691] Admittedly, this calibration of the provision allows the international notification of certain cultural signs. As discussed in section 9.1.2.3, sovereignty is an aspect of morality considerations which the EFTA Court mentioned explicitly in the *Vigeland* decision. The Court referred to a scenario where the relevant public may perceive the registration as a trademark as offensive because certain pieces of art enjoy a 'particular status as prominent parts of a nation's cultural heritage, an emblem of sovereignty or of the nation's foundations and values'.[1692] If a cultural sign is regarded as an emblem of sovereignty, it is thus possible, from this perspective, to exclude the sign from trademark protection because of a conflict with morality. In addition, the sign can be communicated to Paris Union and WTO Members under Article 6*ter* PC. However, it is also evident that an exclusion based on the objective to offer a state control over its official emblems and avoid the false

1690. Bodenhausen 1969, 96.

1691. Cf. CJEU, 16 July 2009, cases C-202/08 P and C-208/08 P, American Clothing Associates/OHIM (Maple Leaf), para. 40, where the Court agrees with Advocate General Ruiz-Jarabo Colomer that the essential functions of state emblems include 'that of identifying a State and that of representing its sovereignty and unity'.

1692. EFTA Court, 6 April 2017, case E-5/16, Municipality of Oslo ('Vigeland'), para. 92.

impression of state approval or support would only cover cultural expressions which the consuming public perceives as references to state power. Only a small fraction of cultural signs seems to fulfil this criterion.

The EFTA Court referred not only to artworks as emblems of state sovereignty but also to artworks that are core elements of a nation's cultural heritage, and symbols of a nation's foundations and values. Cultural signs in these latter categories may have nationwide importance. Besides concerns arising from morality criteria, their use as trademarks may trigger an enquiry into a conflict with public order (section 9.1.2.3).[1693] But they hardly constitute official emblems in the sense of Article 6*ter* PC. The consuming public in the Benelux, for example, may strongly object to the employment of Rembrandt's 'Night Watch' as a commercial trade symbol.[1694] The same may perhaps be said about use of Vigeland's 'Monolith' as an identifier of commercial source in Norway.[1695] It is doubtful, however, that the public in the Benelux and Norway would perceive these cultural signs as official emblems indicating state power and control. Not surprisingly, lawmakers in the EU deemed it necessary to supplement the exclusion following from Article 6*ter* PC[1696] with the above-described (optional) ground for refusal relating to signs with high symbolic value and religious symbols (section 9.1.3.3).[1697] Apparently, cultural signs do not constitute state emblems simply because they have symbolic value in a given society. Article 6*ter* PC is thus incapable of contributing in a meaningful way to the cross-border prevention of trademark rights to cultural signs.

The inherent limits of the core concept of 'state emblem', however, is not the only argument against an Article 6*ter* PC communication avenue for cultural signs. Second – and even more importantly – the qualification of a cultural sign as an official emblem in the sense of Article 6*ter* PC implies acceptance of a state claim to affected cultural signs. As explained, Bodenhausen refers to negotiating history reflecting the 'right of the State to control the use of symbols of its sovereignty … '.[1698] Communicating a cultural sign under Article 6*ter* PC, a state calls upon other states to keep the communicated sign free from trademark protection. Making the communication, however, the notifying state declares its entitlement to exert control over the use of the cultural sign. Therefore, the freedom from trademark rights goes hand in hand with potential state control. Article 6*ter*(1) PC

1693. EFTA Court, *ibid.*, paras 94-96.

1694. Cf. Court of Appeals of The Hague, 29 August 2017, case 200.205.771/01, ECLI:NL:GHDHA:2017:2446, Chiever/ Benelux-Organisatie voor de Intellectuele Eigendom ('Nachtwacht'), para. 12.

1695. Norwegian Board of Appeal for Industrial Property Rights, 13 November 2017, cases 16/00148, 16/00149, 16/00150, 16/00151, 16/00153 and 16/00154, 'Vigeland', para. 14.

1696. Article 7(1)(h) EUTMR and Article 4(1)(h) TMD.

1697. Article 4(3)(b) TMD.

1698. Bodenhausen 1969, 96.

explicitly refers to international agreement on the refusal or invalidation of trademark registrations, and the prohibition of use as trademarks or elements of trademarks 'without authorization by the competent authorities'. As Bodenhausen notes with regard to this feature, the competent state authorities 'may allow the use of such emblems, signs or hallmarks in certain trademarks, probably of their own nationals'.[1699]

Hence, the communication under Article 6*ter* PC goes far beyond the passive prevention of trademark rights. It entails the risk that states may actively regulate the use of communicated cultural signs.[1700] This gives rise to concerns about censorship. Intentionally or unintentionally, a state is likely to prohibit use which, from its point of view, denigrates the communicated cultural sign, and allow use that corresponds with its own understanding of the message and meaning of the sign (section 8.2.3).[1701] In addition, state involvement may lead to the attachment of additional connotations that devalue affected signs in the eyes of artists looking for building blocks for new creations. Given the current trend towards nation branding,[1702] a state may wish to include cultural signs in a broader marketing strategy with a corrosive effect on the sign's potential to serve as a basis for the artistic discourse leading to new artworks (section 8.2.3.3). In the light of this risk of state control, a white list approach based on Article 6*ter* PC appears undesirable.

A third objection follows from the scope of protection offered in Article 6*ter*(1)(a) PC. The ban on trademark rights covers replicas of state emblems and 'any imitation from a heraldic point of view'. On the one hand, this configuration of the prohibition confirms that the drafters did not have cultural signs in mind. The assessment of art imitations 'from a heraldic point of view' makes little sense unless the artwork itself is a coat of arms. On the other hand, the confinement to heraldic imitations leaves loopholes for the registration of variants which – without amounting to infringement from a heraldic point of view – are sufficiently similar to enable the consuming public to clearly identify the underlying work of art.[1703] As the EFTA Court pointed out in *Vigeland*, however, trademark rights should only be accepted in the case of signs which, albeit based on a cultural sign, contain additional elements that transform or diffuse the original work to such an extent that consumers are unlikely to confuse the sign with the original creative work

1699. Bodenhausen 1969, 95.
1700. For example, see the Swissness legislation, available at https://www.ige.ch/en/law-and-policy/national-ip-law/indications-of-source/swiss-indications-of-source/swissness.html. Cf. Abegg 2018, 565-590.
1701. Senftleben 2017b, 688-689.
1702. Cf. Coombe 2005, 42-47.
1703. For example, the use of roundish shapes or different colours, or the omission of certain elements of a state emblem, may render Article 6*ter* PC inapplicable. Cf. Kur/Senftleben 2017, para. 4.232-4.233.

(cf. section 9.1.2.4).[1704] Apart from the attractive communication mechanism that may lead to an international white list of cultural signs to be kept outside the trademark system, Article 6*ter* PC is thus inappropriate for several reasons: it fails to cover a sufficiently broad range of cultural signs, involves the risk of state control, and sets forth imitation criteria that are inapt for the task of preventing trademark rights to cultural signs.

9.1.4.4 Template for an Alternative Notification System

As Article 6*ter* PC does not offer a proper basis for the establishment of an international white list of cultural signs to be kept free from trademark protection, the question arises which alternative system could potentially serve as a model. As discussed in section 9.1.4.2, a white list of cultural signs could play an important role. It would allow the exchange of information about cultural signs which, from the perspective of notifying institutions, should remain unencumbered by trademark rights. The white list could thus provide guidance for examiners and judges who must decide on the grant of trademark protection.

Surveying the spectrum of international notification and information systems, a promising prototype for the creation of an appropriate communication system for cultural signs comes to light in the 2003 UNESCO Convention for the Safeguarding of the Intangible Cultural Heritage.[1705] According to Article 2(2) of the Convention, relevant intangible cultural heritage is manifested *inter alia* in oral traditions and expressions, performing arts, social practices, rituals and festive events, knowledge and practices concerning nature and the universe, and traditional craftsmanship. Article 2(3) clarifies that safeguarding measures seek to ensure the viability of relevant intangible cultural heritage, 'including the identification, documentation, research, preservation, protection, promotion, enhancement, transmission, particularly through formal and non-formal education, as well as the revitalization of the various aspects of such heritage'. Article 11(b) reflects the task of Contracting States to 'identify and define the various elements of the intangible cultural heritage present in its territory, with the participation of communities, groups and relevant non-governmental organizations'. In line with Articles 12 and 29, these domestic elements of intangible cultural heritage are included in inventories that are updated on a regular basis and addressed in periodical reports to the Intergovernmental Committee for the Safeguarding of the Intangible Cultural Heritage.[1706] To achieve international visibility, Article 16(1) provides that:

1704. EFTA Court, 6 April 2017, case E-5/16, Municipality of Oslo ('Vigeland'), paras 97-98.
1705. The text of the Convention is available at https://ich.unesco.org/en/convention.
1706. As to the composition and tasks of the Committee, see Articles 5 to 8 of the Convention.

> [i]n order to ensure better visibility of the intangible cultural heritage and awareness of its significance, and to encourage dialogue which respects cultural diversity, the Committee [the Intergovernmental Committee for the Safeguarding of the Intangible Cultural Heritage], upon the proposal of the States Parties concerned, shall establish, keep up to date and publish a Representative List of the Intangible Cultural Heritage of Humanity.

As the Committee meets annually to evaluate nominations submitted by Contracting States, the Representative List is supplemented with further cultural practices and intangible heritage expressions each year.[1707]

In comparison with communications under Article 6*ter* PC, this system following from the Convention for the Safeguarding of the Intangible Cultural Heritage has clear advantages.[1708] It rests on an open-ended circumscription of cultural practices and expressions of intangible heritage that are eligible for inclusion in the list (Article 2(2)). Moreover, the communication mechanism focuses on international visibility and an international exchange of information on relevant intangible cultural heritage (Article 16(1)). If this template were used to establish an international white list of cultural signs, it would thus overcome the constraints resulting from the confinement of Article 6*ter* PC to state emblems (by using an open-ended circumscription of relevant cultural signs instead) and eliminate the risk of state control over communicated signs (by limiting itself to a mere exchange of cultural signs that ought to be kept outside the trademark system). Finally, Article 11(b) of the Convention indicates that, within a given national system, the identification of cultural signs for inclusion in the white list should constitute an inclusive process with the involvement of artistic communities, groups and relevant non-governmental organizations. By analogy with Article 16(1) of the Convention, an international committee composed of representatives of art communities stemming from different states could then take a final decision on the addition of a cultural sign to the white list.

Hence, a template for an international communication system that would overcome the weaknesses of Article 6*ter* PC is available. Its practical implementation, however, would require not only international consensus on the underlying concept of 'cultural sign' and the purely informatory purpose of the communication system[1709] but also willingness among the trademark

---

1707. See the database available at https://ich.unesco.org/en/lists.
1708. In the sense of providing a template for the development of an appropriate international communication system. As to the need to supplement preservation mechanisms under the Convention with protection tools in intellectual property law if protection against misappropriation is sought or exploitation of intangible cultural heritage is intended, see Ubertazzi 2017, 563-568; Hilty 2009b, 885.
1709. Cf. Osei-Tutu 2017, 1072, with regard to the problem that the communication system is a toothless tiger failing to offer any concrete protection against misappropriation.

institutions of Paris Union and WTO Members to accept the white list as guidance in cases that concern the denial of trademark rights in cultural signs.

9.1.5 *Conclusion*

The assessment of existing legal instruments in the preceding sections has yielded important guidelines for the practical implementation of a categorical exclusion of cultural signs from trademark protection. The current reliance of trademark examiners and judges on the basic requirement of distinctiveness is problematic. In the trademark pantheon of absolute grounds for refusal, a lack of distinctiveness is a particularly weak exclusion argument because it often remains limited to specific goods and services, such as goods and services that are directly related to the literary or artistic production at issue. Moreover, it can be overcome through continuous use of a cultural sign in trade. Constituting a genuine category of trademark law, the requirement of distinctiveness, by definition, is also incapable of providing an appropriate forum for discussing concerns about an impediment of follow-on innovation in the cultural domain. Instead of permitting the direct articulation of cultural concerns about the acquisition of trademark rights, the test of distinctiveness only gives trademark offices and courts the chance to let these concerns prevail in the guise of an argument based on market transparency. They must hide the central point – concerns about an impediment of cultural follow-on innovation – behind a rhetoric of lacking distinctiveness.

To force the trademark system to process this cultural concern more appropriately, it must be translated into a code that is readable in the light of trademark terminology. Therefore, a ground for refusal is needed that allows offices and courts to clearly express a cultural argument against the registration and protection of a cultural sign as a trademark without being obliged to repackage that argument as a concern about distinctive character. For example, offices and courts should be able to base a refusal on the argument that the grant of trademark rights to signs with cultural significance entails an inacceptable risk of blurring and finally erasing the sign's cultural meaning as a result of the attachment of marketing messages, interfering with open, dialogic communication in the artistic domain, freeriding on favourable cultural connotations which the sign already has, obtaining unfair competitive advantages because of this freeriding and, ultimately, artificially perpetuating copyright after the expiry of the limited term of copyright protection and impeding the cultural innovation cycle.

As the analysis has shown, a refusal based on morality or public order is an important step in this direction. If the refusal focuses on the offensive nature of the attempt to register a cultural sign as a trademark, it applies across the whole spectrum of goods and services. Moreover, it is robust in the sense that continuous use in trade does not enable the trademark applicant to surmount the registration obstacle. Following in the footsteps of the EFTA Court decision in *Vigeland*, morality and public order can also be conceptualized in a way that offers quite some room for a refusal in cases involving cultural signs. More specifically, the *Vigeland* decision provides four central exclusion arguments:

(1) the relevant public may perceive the registration as a trademark as offensive because certain pieces of art enjoy a 'particular status as prominent parts of a nation's cultural heritage, an emblem of sovereignty or of the nation's foundations and values'[1710] (morality ground 1);
(2) the relevant public may perceive the registration as a trademark as offensive because it would lead to a 'misappropriation or a desecration of the artist's work, in particular if it is granted for goods or services that contradict values of the artist or the message communicated through the artwork in question'[1711] (morality ground 2);
(3) the registration as a trademark would pose a genuine and sufficiently serious threat to 'certain fundamental values',[1712] 'a fundamental interest of society'[1713] or 'a fundamental concern to the State and the whole of society'[1714] (public order ground 1);
(4) the registration as a trademark would run counter to the need to safeguard the public domain which amounts to a genuine and serious threat if this need 'itself, is considered a fundamental interest of society'[1715] (public order ground 2).

In contrast to decisions based on an assessment of distinctive character, these considerations of morality and public order give trademark offices and courts the opportunity to clearly articulate cultural concerns – in particular the need to prevent an impediment of cultural follow-on innovation – in the context of a rejection of trademark protection. As discussed in the preceding sections, these exclusion arguments make it possible to state candidly that trademark law is not intended to serve as a basis for freeriding on the reputation and positive image of cultural symbols, the reduction of a sign's artistic discourse potential as a result of exposure to commercial marketing strategies, and the impairment of the unhindered, open communication process surrounding the sign in the cultural domain.

The attachment of commercial meanings in the course of marketing campaigns, for example, may be qualified as a desecration of the artist's work in the sense of morality ground 2. Unfair freeriding on positive

1710. EFTA Court, 6 April 2017, case E-5/16, Municipality of Oslo ('Vigeland'), para. 92.
1711. EFTA Court, *ibid.*, para. 92.
1712. EFTA Court, *ibid.*, para. 96.
1713. EFTA Court, *ibid.*, para. 95.
1714. EFTA Court, *ibid.*, para. 94.
1715. EFTA Court, *ibid.*, para. 96.

connotations of cultural signs may be seen as an interference with society's fundamental interest in undistorted competition that justifies the invocation of public order ground 1. The use of trademark rights to prevent the remix and reuse of cultural signs in the artistic domain may be deemed inacceptable from the perspective of freedom of expression – a fundamental interest of society that may be defended on the basis of public order ground 1. In the case of signs with a particular status in society – the status of important cultural heritage, an emblem of sovereignty or a symbol of a nation's foundations and values – morality ground 1 allows a refusal based on the social and political dimension of cultural signs. Finally, public order ground 2 applies in legal systems where the safeguarding of the public domain – in and of itself – is qualified as a fundamental interest of society, for instance, to preserve alternative visions of society that are evoked in literary and artistic works and should remain intact to provide impulses for societal change.

Public order and morality, thus, offer various starting points for trademark examiners and judges to arrive at a categorical exclusion of cultural signs from trademark protection. In comparison with the broad spectrum of exclusion arguments provided by public order and morality, other grounds for refusal have a rather limited potential to keep cultural signs free. Aesthetic functionality constitutes a special case of public order and morality considerations. However, the concept focuses on product characteristics. While literary and artistic works may form essential product elements, they may also be attached to products as mere labels or remain loosely connected to the product as a mere sound mark. Hence, the ambit of operation of aesthetic functionality is confined to situations where a cultural sign features prominently in or on the product itself, for instance as the main (fictional) character of a comic book or animation film, or as a central decorative element that gives value to merchandising articles.

Specific grounds for refusal that focus on a particular status of cultural signs, such as high symbolic value, have a rather limited scope from the outset: by definition, these grounds for refusal only cover cultural signs that meet the specific status requirement set forth in relevant provisions. Signs with high cultural significance but without high symbolic value fall outside the scope of the specific exclusion mechanism that made its way into EU trademark law. While a status-based ground for refusal, such as the denial of protection in the case of signs with high symbolic value, may be effective within its limited field of application, it must not be regarded as a *lex specialis* precluding the invocation of more general public order and morality considerations. Otherwise, the introduction of a specific, status-based ground for refusal would be a Trojan Horse thwarting the objective to arrive at a broader exclusion of various types of cultural signs.

Finally, bad faith may pose an obstacle to the acquisition of trademark rights in cases of cultural heritage grabbing. However, this exclusion mechanism is largely rendered ineffective in many trademark systems, including the trademark regimes in the EU, because of the grace period of permissible non-use that follows the trademark registration. Until the end of this grace period, the cultural heritage grabber can maintain the trademark registration without developing genuine use activities in the marketplace. For this reason, it can be particularly difficult for trademark offices and courts to establish bad faith at the moment where the trademark application is received. As trademark proprietors can wait several years before finally embarking on genuine use in the marketplace, it is not sufficient for the denial of trademark rights that, at the time of applying for a trademark registration, the applicant has not already made preparations for product marketing based on the cultural sign.

While a refusal of trademark rights based on aesthetic functionality, high symbolic value or bad faith adds little to public order and morality considerations, the communication of emblems of states and international intergovernmental organizations under Article 6*ter* PC sheds light on an important complementary feature of sign exclusion mechanisms in the field of trademark law: the prospect of using notifications of cultural signs to establish a 'white list' of cultural expressions to be kept free across Paris Union and WTO Members. The closer inspection of this communication avenue, however, yields the insight that the employment of the existing 6*ter* system for the purpose of preventing trademark rights to cultural signs is undesirable. The communication under Article 6*ter* PC leads not only to the exclusion of notified signs but also to the exertion of state control. It cannot be ruled out that a state uses 6*ter* communications strategically to claim the right of authorizing and regulating the use of notified cultural signs. Ultimately, the qualification of cultural signs as 'state emblems' may culminate in the inclusion of notified signs in nation branding campaigns with a corrosive effect on the sign's potential to serve as a basis for open, dialogic communication in the artistic domain.

In sum, considerations of public order and morality, by far, are the most promising vehicles to achieve an outright exclusion of cultural signs from trademark protection under existing trademark legislation. The public order and morality criteria that can be distilled from the *Vigeland* decision of the EFTA Court offer trademark offices and courts considerable room for the application and further development of this ground for refusal in cases involving cultural signs. It is thus advisable to explore the full potential of public order and morality as grounds for refusing trademark rights to cultural signs. As also pointed out in the foregoing analysis, public order and morality decisions should aim at preventing the acquisition of trademark rights and the evolution of overlapping copyright/trademark protection *ex ante*. Ideally, public order and morality criteria fulfil a gatekeeper function that is comparable with the role of utilitarian and aesthetic functionality in the field of technical solutions and industrial designs. From the outset, they should ensure the exclusion of trademark rights to works of art (Mona Lisa scenario described in section 5.2.1) and creations of contemporary mainstream culture

(Mickey Mouse scenario described in section 5.2.3) in cases where cultural significance is self-evident and relevant factors weigh clearly in favour of the exclusion of trademark protection.

Considering the above-described risk of copyright protection coming into being accidentally with regard to logos and other signs that are specifically made to serve as identifiers of commercial source, an additional rule is necessary to refine the application of public order and morality considerations. When it comes to these hybrid signs, trademark applicants should have the opportunity to formally declare that the sign will not be used in a cultural context. This declaration of non-use in a cultural context should be registered together with the sign itself. If copyright protection is later invoked in respect of a sign registered under these circumstances, this enforcement step should automatically qualify as use in a cultural context. As the trademark proprietor avails herself of protection stemming from the cultural aspect of the sign, the trademark should become liable to be declared invalid and the defendant facing the copyright claim should be able to bring a counterclaim demanding this invalidation. Hence, the implementation of cultural grounds for refusal on the basis of public order or morality should not only provide for the *ex ante* exclusion of trademark protection but also for a later invalidation in cases where a declaration of non-use in a cultural context has been made.

9.2 IMPLEMENTATION OF LIMITATIONS OF TRADEMARK RIGHTS

The analysis of potential interferences of trademark protection with intergenerational equity (Chapter 7) and public domain recognition (Chapter 8) has led to the insight that the categorical exclusion of cultural signs from trademark protection is the most effective – but also the most far-reaching – measure to prevent impediments of cultural follow-on innovation (Chapter 6). However, the discussion of exclusion mechanisms in the preceding chapter has also shown that the assessment of a sign's cultural significance need not automatically lead to the conclusion that the sign should be kept outside the trademark protection system altogether. The decision on the exclusion of trademark protection depends on a detailed assessment in the light of various factors (section 9.1.2.5). This multifactor test is intended to alert trademark examiners and judges to a sign's potential cultural significance. It must not be misunderstood as an inescapable bright-line rule that dictates the denial of trademark rights whenever a sign scores in one of the above-described assessment categories. If a sign's cultural importance is self-evident and the factors clearly tip the scales in favour of an outright exclusion of trademark protection, the denial of trademark rights is inescapable from the perspective of the cultural imperative. If, by contrast, the analysis yields mixed results, a more nuanced approach is necessary that may lead to the grant of trademark rights (section 9.1.2.5). In this latter case, the limitation of trademark rights is the only remaining option to support remix and reuse in the cultural domain.[1716]

Hence, it is conceivable that a trademark examiner conducting the multifactor analysis to assess the degree of a sign's cultural significance arrives at the conclusion that, despite some risk of hampering cultural remix activities, the concern about an impediment of cultural follow-on innovation does not have sufficient weight to justify a complete refusal of trademark rights (section 5.2.1). With regard to these cases – where trademark rights are finally granted even though negative repercussions on cultural remix activities cannot be ruled out – it is important to introduce safeguards in trademark law to reduce the potential corrosive effect on cyclic cultural innovation. More concretely, it is necessary to set limits to trademark rights that discourage the assertion of trademark rights against processes of cultural follow-on innovation or give artists the chance of defending unauthorized use against infringement claims. This regulatory response – the development of safety valves in trademark law – constitutes the only legal instrument that is currently available with regard to iconic trade symbols that have acquired cultural significance (sections 5.2.5 and 8.3.2).

As already indicated, legislators and judges seeking to limit trademark rights can pursue two different strategies: on the one hand, they can rely on inherent limits of the exclusive rights granted in trademark law as implicit obstacles to infringement claims. On the other hand, they can develop explicit, statutory exceptions to trademark rights that serve as defences for users in the cultural domain (sections 8.2.1 and 8.2.2). To implement the first approach, a strict test of use as a mark is necessary that fulfils the function of a general prerequisite for trademark infringement claims. This test would have to play the role of a gatekeeper criterion that must be satisfied before more specific infringement criteria, such as a likelihood of confusion or a likelihood of dilution, are even taken into consideration. The strict test of use as a mark would thus preclude a finding of prima facie infringement unless the trademark proprietor succeeds in demonstrating that the allegedly infringing use has relevance in the context of trademark law (following section 9.2.1). The second approach seeks to alleviate the problems arising from an amalgam of copyright and trademark protection by providing for robust defences that exempt artistic remix of protected signs from the control of trademark owners. This solution is less satisfactory because it places the burden of providing proof of legitimate artistic use on the individual creator who is confronted with a trademark infringement claim that does not appear unfounded from the outset (section 9.2.2).

1716. For approaches which generally prefer the adoption of limitations of protection over the outright exclusion of trademark rights, see Dreyfuss 2020, 330-331; Ohly 2019, 335-338.

9.2.1 Strict Requirement of Use as a Trademark

As discussed in section 6.2.1, advanced trademark systems, such as the EU trademark system, are likely to deprive the test of 'use as a mark' of its potential to function as a bulwark against infringement claims targeting use in the cultural domain. Instead of limiting trademark claims to cases where the alleged infringer employs the trademark to indicate the commercial origin of its own goods or services, mere references to the trademark may be sufficient to qualify use in a cultural context as actionable even though the consuming public understands that the reference to the trademark is not intended to indicate commercial source. The CJEU ruling in *Adidas/Fitnessworld* illustrates the status quo reached in EU trademark law. The CJEU held in this case that decorative use of a sign similar to a protected mark may already be sufficient to trigger protection against dilution.[1717] A mere link with the trademark – in the sense of use that calls to mind the protected sign – may be deemed actionable in accordance with this assessment standard (section 6.2.3).[1718] An elastic concept of actionable use also prevails in the context of protection against confusion. In *Adidas/Marca*, the CJEU held that the public's perception that a sign is a decoration could not constitute a restriction on anti-confusion claims when, despite its decorative nature, the sign used by the alleged infringer was so similar to the trademark that the relevant public may assume an economic link with the trademark owner (section 6.2.2).[1719] The decision on use as a trademark, thus, depends on the marketing efforts of the trademark proprietor and the resulting degree of trademark recognition.[1720] Investing heavily in advertising campaigns that educate consumers to establish a link with the trademark whenever they see a similar sign, the trademark owner can shape consumer perception in a way that enhances the chances of surmounting the hurdle of use as a mark and proving prima facie infringement. Use as a mark, thus, is a fragile gatekeeper criterion that fails to offer a robust area of freedom that could dispel concerns about an encroachment upon freedom of expression in the artistic domain. Instead, it leads to a bias in favour of the trademark owner who can increase the success rate of infringement claims by investing in the recognition of a cultural sign as a trademark.

To remedy this shortcoming, it would be necessary to shape the test of trademark use in a way that achieves the opposite result: a bias in favour of users who embark on the remix of trademarked cultural signs in the artistic

1717. CJEU, 23 October 2003, case C-408/01, Adidas/Fitnessworld, para. 39.

1718. German Federal Court of Justice, 3 February 2005, case I ZR 159/02, 'Lila Postkarte', *GRUR* 2005, 583 (584).

1719. CJEU, 10 April 2008, case C-102/07, Adidas/Marca, para. 34.

1720. German Federal Court of Justice, 24 November 2011, case I ZR 175/09, 'Medusa', para. 23. Cf. Court of Appeals of Amsterdam, 26 juli 2001, ERB/Beukenoord, *AMI* 2002, 12, para. 2.16-2.18; Visser 2002, 15-16.

domain.[1721] As the discussion of public domain concepts has shown (section 8.2.1), artistic use would have to constitute an 'easy case' – a case that is commonly deemed non-actionable unless there are 'individualized facts that make a particular use by a particular person unprivileged'.[1722] Hence, the test of use as a mark would have to render the trademark owner incapable of establishing prima facie infringement when artistic use calls to mind a sign which the public recognizes not only as a protected trademark but also as a sign with cultural significance, such as the Mona Lisa (section 5.2.1) or Mickey Mouse (section 5.2.3). In such a case, the sign's cultural aspect should be decisive. It should tip the scales in favour of the unauthorized user in the cultural domain unless the trademark proprietor produces evidence of 'individualized facts' that make the particular use at issue unprivileged even though it takes place in a cultural setting.

To attain this recalibration of the trademark use requirement, it is advisable to follow an approach that focuses on the cultural aspect of a trademarked cultural sign and attaches particular importance to the specific circumstances of use in the artistic domain. The so-called Rogers test that evolved in U.S. jurisprudence offers a useful starting point for this change of perspective (following section 9.2.1.1). The 'Rogers' test, however, concerns an immunity against confusion claims. To arrive at a horizontal trademark use requirement that also covers dilution claims, it is important to extend the concept. In this regard, it must be considered that use in a cultural setting will normally concern the cultural, expressive meaning of a cultural sign. It does not seek to damage or exploit the trademark magnetism of the sign but its rhetoric uniqueness – the specific set of meanings and connotations which a cultural sign evokes as a result of its evolution in the cultural domain (section 9.2.1.2). This insight offers a basis for the establishment of a robust legal presumption in favour of users in the cultural domain: where a trademarked cultural sign is used in connection with a literary or artistic production, it is appropriate to presume that the use does not amount to actionable use as a trademark (section 9.2.1.3). In practice, the establishment of this legal presumption imposes the burden on the trademark proprietor to demonstrate 'individualized facts' that justify a departure from the rule of non-actionable use in a cultural context – a test of trademark relevance that serves as a threshold requirement for access to protection against confusion (section 9.2.1.4) and protection against dilution (section 9.2.1.5) alike. The application of this gatekeeper requirement is also appropriate when iconic trade symbols are employed as metaphors in the context of cultural expression (section 9.2.1.6).

The practical implementation of this strict test of use as a mark, however, can pose particular difficulties. EU trademark law requires compliance with 'honest practices' in industrial and commercial matters in

1721. Cf. Kur 2002, 602-603.
1722. Benkler 1999, 362-363.

connection with artistic expression.[1723] The proviso of honest practices reflects a problematic superiority of behavioural norms of the sector of trade and industry over behavioural standards in the cultural domain. To prevent an erosion of the desirable bias in favour of artistic use, it is necessary to weave the gatekeeper criteria for establishing 'use as a mark' into the fabric of the test of honest practices (section 9.2.1.7). This strategy – the establishment of a robust bias in favour of users in the cultural domain and the alignment of the honest practices proviso with this bias – yields a gatekeeper requirement that is specific enough to escape the criticism which more ambitious plans to introduce a general test of use as a mark have triggered (section 9.2.1.8). A specific gatekeeper requirement for claims against artistic use has clear advantages over an approach relying on traditional defences, such as descriptive and referential use. Instead of preventing the trademark owner from building a valid infringement claim from the outset, defences only offer an immunity after the trademark owner confronted the artist with a valid claim of prima facie infringement. The deterrent effect of trademark rights (section 6.3) is thus reduced to a lesser extent (section 9.2.1.9).

9.2.1.1 U.S. *Rogers* Test as a Template

The debate on cultivating 'use as a mark' as a general threshold requirement for infringement claims in trademark law offers useful guidance for initiatives to reduce the corrosive effect of trademark rights on cultural follow-on innovation. Relying on the search costs rationale in trademark law,[1724] Stacey Dogan and Mark Lemley state that:

> [l]imiting trademark rights to a right to prevent confusing uses of the mark as a brand helps to ensure that trademark rights remain tied to their search costs rationale – only those individuals or companies who are using the mark to advertise their own products or services have the motive and opportunity to interfere with the clarity of the mark's meaning in conveying product information to consumers, and so only those uses ought to be of concern to trademark law.[1725]

Introducing a general gatekeeper criterion of use as a mark, Dogan and Lemley thus seek to limit trademark claims, from the outset, to situations where the alleged infringer deliberately uses another's mark to market her own goods or services. The benefits of this approach for users in the cultural domain are obvious. As Dogan and Lemley emphasize, a trademark use requirement with this configuration – focusing on 'misleading branding'[1726] – serves the purpose of preventing trademark rights:

1723. Recital 21 EUTMR; Recital 27 TMD. Cf. Schovsbo 2018, 568.
1724. Cf. Kur/Senftleben 2017, para. 1.08-1.11.
1725. Dogan/Lemley 2004, 798.
1726. Dogan/Lemley 2008a, 542.

> from being used as a weapon against parodists, newspapers, dictionaries, artists, and the wide variety of people who use trademarks as part of their mode of expression.[1727]

Nonetheless, it is doubtful whether the criterion of 'misleading branding' already constitutes the magical formula necessary to stop trademark claims against use in the cultural domain at an early stage of the infringement analysis. The problem with misleading branding as a yardstick is that the test remains in the orbit of the trademark universe. The assessment remains aligned with the infringement categories of trademark law. Therefore, it is difficult to cover the full range of use that is potentially actionable from a misleading branding perspective: not only direct confusion but also confusion about affiliation and sponsorship, etc. (section 6.2.2). Dogan and Lemley, for example, understand their misleading branding concept to encompass 'those who themselves use marks in a way that suggests some affiliation between themselves and the trademark holder'.[1728] Similarly, Margreth Barrett defines actionable trademark use as 'application of a mark in a manner that invites consumers to associate the mark with goods or services that the user is offering for sale or distribution and to rely on it for information about the source, sponsorship, or affiliation of those goods or services'.[1729]

These statements bring the test of misleading branding close to the problematic approach taken by the CJEU. As in *Adidas/Marca*, a finding of non-actionable decorative use seems to be hanging by a thread. The moment the degree of trademark recognition is strong enough to make consumers think about 'some affiliation' with the trademark owner, the decorative use may already lose the immunity from trademark infringement claims. In *Adidas/Marca*, the CJEU saw a risk that, despite a decorative context, the consuming public may assume an economic link with the trademark owner if the degree of similarity between the decorative sign and the registered trademark was high.[1730] This concern seems to have been the primary reason for the Court to align the analysis with the degree of trademark recognition. The CJEU concluded that the appreciation of a likelihood of confusion in the case of decorative use depended:

> not solely on the degree of similarity between the trade mark and the sign, but also on the ease with which the sign may be associated with the mark having regard, in particular, to the recognition of the latter on the market.[1731]

1727. Dogan/Lemley 2008a, 555.
1728. Dogan/Lemley 2004, 799.
1729. Barrett 2006, 375.
1730. CJEU, 10 April 2008, case C-102/07, Adidas/Marca, para. 34.
1731. CJEU, 10 April 2008, case C-102/07, Adidas/Marca, para. 36.

The test of misleading branding, thus, entails the risk of losing sight of the cultural dimension of the allegedly infringing use and focusing on the degree of trademark recognition instead. In the *Medusa* decision of the German Federal Court of Justice (section 6.2.2), the application of the assessment standard following from CJEU jurisprudence led to a focus on the degree to which consumers were able to recognize Versace's Medusa logo as a trademark. As it had been established that not more than 5% of the buyers of marble mosaics knew the Versace logo, the Court held that consumers were unlikely to perceive the decorative use of a Medusa head as an indication of commercial source.[1732] The owner of trademark rights to a cultural sign with a higher degree of trademark recognition, however, would have had less difficulty to demonstrate that the decorative use 'may be associated with the mark'[1733] in the sense of the CJEU decision in *Adidas/Marca*. Accordingly, the owner of a trademark with a stronger source-identifying function in the relevant sector may succeed in establishing prima facie infringement.

Obviously, the mechanical reliance on the degree of trademark recognition as a yardstick for identifying actionable trademark use neglects the individual context in which the use takes place. Instead of aligning the test of trademark use with the degree of trademark recognition, the decorative context should play a decisive role. The trademark use concept that is applied in Australia can serve as a source of inspiration in this regard. As Michael Handler explains on the basis of the decision of the High Court of Australia in *The Shell Co. of Australia Ltd./Esso Standard Oil (Australia) Ltd.*, an objective judgment is necessary:

> by reference to likely consumer reaction, taking into account the particular manner and context of the defendant's use. The converse of the trademark use requirement is that other types of use, such as nominative, descriptive, or decorative use, will not infringe.[1734]

Hence, the individual circumstances – 'the particular manner and context' – should play a decisive role. If an allegedly infringing use is made in connection with a literary and artistic production, this specific decorative context should allow the unauthorized user to escape the verdict of actionable use as a trademark even if the use concerns a cultural sign which consumers can easily recognize as a trademark. The decorative use may still call to mind the trademark. Consumers may fully understand that they see a sign with a source-identifying function. Nonetheless, the specific cultural

1732. German Federal Court of Justice, 24 November 2011, case I ZR 175/09, 'Medusa', para. 23.

1733. CJEU, 10 April 2008, case C-102/07, Adidas/Marca, para. 36.

1734. Handler 2018, 170, referring to High Court of Australia, 23 November 1961, The Shell Co. of Australia Ltd./Esso Standard Oil (Australia) Ltd., [1963] 109 CLR 407, 422 (Kitto J.).

context – a trademarked cultural sign used in a literary and artistic production – should prevent a finding of actionable use as a trademark.

Dogan and Lemley come closer to this result when they propose to focus attention on the 'non-branding way'[1735] of use. Following this guideline, the Court of Appeals of Amsterdam could have been short on the infringement question in the *Mercis and Bruna/Punt* case that concerned the use of the fictional character Miffy in biting parodies (section 6.2.3).[1736] Instead of lending weight to the evocation of the trademarked fictional character in the minds of consumers, the Court could have put an end to the infringement claim at an early stage by emphasizing that the alleged infringers used Miffy in a decorative way for the purpose of achieving a sharp contrast with the intact children's world in Miffy comic strips.[1737] The specific decorative context arising from a link with an artistic production would have inhibited the claimant Mercis from demonstrating use as a trademark and proving prima facie infringement. As a result, the parodist would not have been confronted with a valid infringement claim that required the invocation of the open-ended defence of 'due cause' (section 6.2.4). Instead of a rule saying that decorative use is only permissible if the artist succeeds in substantiating a due cause,[1738] the decision in *Mercis* would have led to the insight that trademark claims against decorative use of trademarked fictional characters in an artistic setting are futile because the specific decorative context precludes a finding of actionable use as a mark. As a result, the legal certainty surrounding the remix of fictional characters, such as Miffy, would have been enhanced.

Hence, the different nature of use in the cultural domain should occupy centre stage. An approach focusing on the cultural context surrounding the use seems capable of creating considerable breathing space for the remix of cultural signs in literary and artistic productions even if these signs have been transformed into strong trademarks. The trademark owner may emphasize that consumers are likely to see not only a cultural symbol but also an indicator of commercial source. However, this argument no longer tips the scales in favour of a finding of actionable use as a mark. Once the decorative nature of the use and the specific context arising from a connection with a literary and artistic production are the kingpin of the analysis, it becomes possible to arrive at a general presumption of non-infringement and an effective shield against trademark infringement claims: presumably, use of a trademarked cultural sign in the cultural domain does not amount to trademark infringement.

1735. Dogan/Lemley 2008a, 542.

1736. Court of Appeals of Amsterdam, 13 September 2011, case ECLI:NL:GHAMS:2011 :BS7825, Mercis and Bruna/Punt, *AMI* 2012, 28, para. 4.1.

1737. In fact, this consideration played an important role in the court decision anyway. See Court of Appeals of Amsterdam, *ibid.*, para. 4.19.

1738. Court of Appeals of Amsterdam, *ibid.*, para. 4.19.

To create a trademark use requirement that achieves this result, it is necessary to go beyond the criterion of misleading branding (which rests on a trademark category of infringement) and adopt an expressive use test (which brings the literary and artistic dimension of the use into focus). For this important step, the so-called Rogers test that evolved in U.S. law provides a useful starting point.[1739] In *Rogers/Grimaldi*, the U.S. Court of Appeals for the Second Circuit was called upon to decide on an infringement claim brought by the actress Ginger Rogers against the use of her name in the title of Federico Fellini's film 'Ginger and Fred'. The film told the story of two fictional Italian cabaret performers – Pippo and Amelia – who imitated Ginger Rogers and Fred Astaire and became known in Italy as 'Ginger and Fred'. Seeking to make a satiric comment on television variety shows, the film focused on a televised reunion of Pippo and Amelia many years after their retirement. Ginger Rogers based her infringement claim on the argument that the film's title created the false impression that she was associated with the film production.[1740]

Dealing with this claim, the Court of Appeals emphasized the expressive dimension of film titles. Judge Newman explained that filmmakers frequently relied on 'word-play, ambiguity, irony, and allusion in titling their works'.[1741] The Court also lent weight to the interest of the audience in sufficient breathing space for free expression. The subtleties of a title could enrich the understanding of the work. Consumers of artistic works had a dual interest against this background: on the one hand, the interest in not being misled and, on the other hand, the interest in enjoying the results of the filmmaker's freedom of expression. For all these reasons, the Court concluded that the expressive element of titles of literary and artistic works required more protection than the labelling of ordinary commercial products:

> We believe that in general the [Lanham] Act should be construed to apply to artistic works only where the public interest in avoiding consumer confusion outweighs the public interest in free expression[1742] (text within brackets added).

From the outset, the Court thus established a bias in favour of users in the cultural domain. Instead of allowing concerns about misleading branding to occupy centre stage, the Court was willing to let the interest in free expression prevail. This approach corresponds with the strategy recommended above: to offer sufficient room for artistic remix and reuse within the trademark system, it is necessary to depart from the traditional focus on trademark categories of infringement (such as misleading branding) and

1739. Cf. McGeveran 2015, 745-749.

1740. U.S. Court of Appeals for the Second Circuit, 5 May 1989, Rogers/Grimaldi, 875 F.2d 994 (2nd Cir. 1989), 997.

1741. U.S. Court of Appeals for the Second Circuit, *ibid.*, 998.

1742. U.S. Court of Appeals for the Second Circuit, *ibid.*, 999.

factor an element into the equation that permits the expressive nature of the use to tip the scales in favour of the artistic user and against a finding of infringement. In *Rogers/Grimaldi*, this approach culminated in the creation of an assessment framework which later became known as the 'Rogers' test:[1743]

> In the context of allegedly misleading titles using a celebrity's name, that balance will normally not support application of the [Lanham] Act unless the title has no artistic relevance to the underlying work whatsoever, or, if it has some artistic relevance, unless the title explicitly misleads as to the source or the content of the work[1744] (text within brackets added).

In other words: as long as the unauthorized use is relevant to the derivative literary and artistic production from an artistic point of view, it does not amount to infringement – except where the use clearly reflects the intention to mislead the audience as to the commercial origin of the work at issue. Hence, permitted use in an artistic context is the rule; infringing use is the exception. Only if the unauthorized use explicitly misleads the public, an infringement claim can have success.[1745]

When this 'Rogers' test is compared with the approach following from CJEU jurisprudence, the difference clearly comes to the fore. As explained above, the CJEU held in *Adidas/Marca* that, even if allegedly infringing use takes place in a decorative context, the consuming public may still assume an economic link with the trademark owner (and be exposed to an actionable risk of confusion) if the degree of similarity between the decorative sign and the registered trademark was high.[1746] The CJEU also held that the infringement analysis depended on the degree of recognition of the affected trademark in the relevant market sector.[1747] Under the *Adidas/Marca* approach, it would thus have been sufficient for Ginger Rogers to emphasize that her name was well known in the film business. On this basis, she could have argued that, given this strong recognition, use of her name in the film title 'Ginger and Fred' was likely to cause confusion as to affiliation or sponsorship. The high degree of recognition of her name would have played a crucial role in establishing infringement.

Devoting attention to artistic relevance and requiring evidence of 'explicitly misleading' use in *Rogers/Grimaldi*, the U.S. Court of Appeals for the Second Circuit, by contrast, focused on the question whether there were clear indications that the name 'Ginger' had been included in the film title for the very purpose of giving the false impression that Ginger Rogers endorsed

1743. Cf. Dinwoodie 2021, 1-2; Calboli 2014b, 72-76.
1744. U.S. Court of Appeals for the Second Circuit, *ibid.*, 999.
1745. Dinwoodie 2021, 2-3.
1746. CJEU, 10 April 2008, case C-102/07, Adidas/Marca, para. 34.
1747. CJEU, *ibid.*, para. 36.

and supported the film production. As there was no evidence that the film title was explicitly misleading in this sense, the Court found no infringement:

> The title 'Ginger and Fred' contains no explicit indication that Rogers endorsed the film or had a role in producing it. The survey evidence, even if its validity is assumed, indicates at most that some members of the public would draw the incorrect inference that Rogers had some involvement with the film. But that risk of misunderstanding, not engendered by any overt claim in the title, is so outweighed by the interests in artistic expression as to preclude application of the Lanham Act. We therefore hold that the sponsorship and endorsement aspects of Rogers' Lanham Act claim raise no 'genuine' issue that requires submission to a jury.[1748]

Hence, the specific test of artistic relevance and explicitly misleading use de facto neutralized the confusion claim which the actress had based on the risk of consumers assuming a connection between her and the Fellini film. While the CJEU created room for infringement arguments based on affiliation and sponsorship in *Adidas/Marca*, the U.S. Court of Appeals for the Second Circuit suppressed these arguments in *Rogers/Grimaldi* by setting the bar high and requiring a form of use that is explicitly misleading. The perspective of the two Courts is fundamentally different. The CJEU lends weight to the degree of recognition of the protected sign and allows this recognition to prevail over the expressive component of decorative use. The Second Circuit, by contrast, lends weight to the expressive nature of the allegedly infringing use and allows this expressive component to function as a legal presumption of non-infringement that can only be rebutted by demonstrating blatant infringement: a showing of explicitly misleading use under the guise of literary and artistic expression.

In a nutshell, the CJEU assesses decorative use in the light of trademark categories of infringement, such as the degree of distinctive character, whereas the 'Rogers' test changes the perspective and introduces artistic relevance as a factor capable of outperforming these traditional trademark infringement criteria. From the perspective of cultural follow-on innovation, this latter approach – allowing artistic relevance to pose a substantial obstacle to trademark infringement claims – is preferable. Therefore, the decision in *Rogers/Grimaldi* is of particular interest. As the 'Rogers' test focuses on artistic relevance, it could serve as a template for the calibration of the gatekeeper requirement of use as a mark in cases involving trademarked cultural signs.

Subsequent developments in U.S. case law confirm that the 'Rogers' test can provide a useful model for devising a threshold requirement of use as a mark that supports remix and reuse of trademarked cultural signs in the cultural domain. In *Rogers/Grimaldi*, the 'Rogers' test emerged as an

1748. U.S. Court of Appeals for the Second Circuit, *ibid.*, 1001.

assessment tool for an anti-confusion claim in a specific area. As explained, the case concerned the allegedly misleading use of a celebrity's name in a film title.[1749] The U.S. Court of Appeals for the Second Circuit, however, did not hesitate to broaden the test's ambit of operation several months later in *Cliffs Notes/Bantham Doubleday* – a case that concerned book parodies in study guide format which imitated distinctive elements of the covers of Cliffs Notes' study guides for short stories, plays and books.[1750] Dealing with the satiric play with the format and style of Cliffs Notes' books, the Second Circuit pointed out that the case did not raise the question of whether a title was false advertising but whether the appearance of a work's cover was confusingly similar to the elements of an earlier cover enjoying trademark protection. The Court also recognized that in *Cliffs Notes/Bantham Doubleday*, the element of parody entered the picture which had not been present in *Rogers/Grimaldi*. These differences, however, did not inhibit the Second Circuit from relying on the 'Rogers' test. To the contrary, the Court emphasized that it was appropriate to weigh the public interest in free expression against the public interest in avoiding consumer confusion in any case where an expressive work was alleged to infringe a trademark right under the U.S. Lanham Act:

> Thus, we hold that the Rogers balancing approach is generally applicable to Lanham Act claims against works of artistic expression, a category that includes parody.[1751]

Applying the 'Rogers' test, the Court then dismissed the infringement claim as a matter of law even though the district judge had found a strong likelihood of confusion. In this context, the Second Circuit recalled that trademark owners had to tolerate more and surmount a higher hurdle when artistic expression was involved:

> taking into account that somewhat more risk of confusion is to be tolerated when a trademark holder seeks to enjoin artistic expression such as a parody, the degree of risk of confusion between Spy Notes and Cliffs Notes does not outweigh the well-established public interest in parody … And although the district court found a strong likelihood of confusion between the cover of Spy Notes and that of Cliffs Notes, based on its review of the eight Polaroid factors, that determination is a legal conclusion which is reviewable by this court as a matter of law.[1752]

Further scope extensions followed from decisions in which other appeal courts in the U.S. took over the 'Rogers' test developed by the Second

1749. U.S. Court of Appeals for the Second Circuit, *ibid.*, 999.
1750. U.S. Court of Appeals for the Second Circuit, 5 September 1989, Cliffs Notes/Bantham Doubleday Dell Publishing Group, 886 F.2d 490 (2nd Cir. 1989), 492. Cf. Dinwoodie 2021, 2-3.
1751. U.S. Court of Appeals for the Second Circuit, *ibid.*, 495-496.
1752. U.S. Court of Appeals for the Second Circuit, *ibid.*, 498.

Circuit. In *E.S.S. Entertainment 2000/Rock Star Videos*, the U.S. Court of Appeals for the Ninth Circuit dealt with 'Grand Theft Auto: San Andreas' – a video game mimicking, in cartoon style, the look and feel of actual urban neighbourhoods, including East Los Angeles where one can find the strip club 'Play Pen Gentlemen's Club'. As the real-life environment served as a source of inspiration, the corresponding game environment – East 'Los Santos' – also contained a strip club which the game designers called 'Pig Pen'.[1753] Not amused by this virtual counterpart, the operator of the strip club in Los Angeles, E.S.S. Entertainment 2000, sued Rock Star Videos for trademark infringement arguing that the unauthorized use of a variation of the Play Pen logo and trade dress in the video game was likely to cause confusion among consumers as to whether E.S.S. Entertainment endorsed, or was associated with, the video depiction.[1754]

Again, this case scenario deviated from previous situations in which the 'Rogers' test had been applied. Most importantly, Rock Star Videos had not included the name 'Pig Pen' in the title or cover of the video game. This difference, however, was not decisive for the Ninth Circuit. The Court held that:

> [a]lthough [the 'Rogers'] test traditionally applies to uses of a trademark in the title of an artistic work, there is no principled reason why it ought not also apply to the use of a trademark in the body of the work[1755] (text within brackets added).

This extension to use in the body of a literary and artistic work is of particular importance to the current quest for an appropriate gatekeeper requirement of use as a mark. The remix and reuse of trademarked cultural signs in the cultural domain will often concern use in the body of literary and artistic works. The decision in *E.S.S. Entertainment 2000/Rock Star Videos* demonstrates that the 'Rogers' test is capable of covering this remix scenario.

Moreover, the decision clarified the conceptual contours of the artistic relevance test. In *Rogers/Grimaldi*, the Second Circuit had established the rule that trademark protection against expressive use was unavailable unless the protected sign had 'no artistic relevance to the underlying work whatsoever'.[1756] This element of the 'Rogers' test can become a risk factor. If judges insist on a high degree of artistic relevance, a trademark proprietor can easily refute the defencc argument by arguing that use of her trademarked cultural sign is not sufficiently relevant to the literary and artistic production containing the sign without authorization. In *E.S.S. Entertainment 2000/Rock Star Videos*, the operator of the real world strip club argued that

1753. U.S. Court of Appeals for the Ninth Circuit, 5 November 2008, E.S.S. Entertainment 2000/Rock Star Videos, 547 F.3d 1095 (9th Cir. 2008), 1096-1097.

1754. U.S. Court of Appeals for the Ninth Circuit, *ibid.*, 1097.

1755. U.S. Court of Appeals for the Ninth Circuit, *ibid.*, 1099.

1756. U.S. Court of Appeals for the Second Circuit, 5 May 1989, Rogers/Grimaldi, 875 F.2d 994 (2nd Cir. 1989), 999.

the inclusion of the virtual 'Pig Pen' strip club had not enough artistic relevance to the video game because the game did not address and deal with the 'Play Pen Gentlemen's Club' as such.[1757] The Ninth Circuit, however, remained unimpressed. Instead of requiring that the imitation of 'Play Pen' look and feel had to be highly relevant to the video game from the perspective of artistic content, the Court emphasized that the 'Rogers' test referred to 'no artistic relevance […] whatsoever'.[1758] Accordingly, the level of artistic relevance merely had to be 'above zero'.[1759] As Rock Star Video's artistic goal was the development of a cartoon-style parody of East Los Angeles, the digital recreation of a critical mass of East Los Angeles businesses and buildings, including a strip club similar to the 'Play Pen Gentlemen's Club' in the real world, had at least 'some artistic relevance'.[1760] Therefore, the unauthorized use met the 'Rogers' test and could escape the verdict of infringement.[1761]

The 'Rogers' test also offered a robust immunity from infringement claims in the more recent decision *Twentieth Century Fox Television/Empire Distribution*. In this case, Fox sought a declaratory judgment that its TV show 'Empire' and various related activities did not violate the trademark rights of Empire Distribution, a respected record label known for album releases in the urban music genre, including hip hop, rap, and R&B. The TV show portrayed a fictional hip hop music label – 'Empire Enterprises' – based in New York. It served as a basis for additional marketing and merchandising activities ranging from music releases and live performances to the sale of shirts and champagne glasses bearing the TV 'Empire' brand.[1762] Discussing Empire Distribution's counterclaims for trademark infringement, the U.S. Court of Appeals for the Ninth Circuit seized the opportunity to further expand the 'Rogers' test:

> Although it is true that these promotional efforts technically fall outside the title or body of an expressive work, it requires only a minor logical extension of the reasoning of Rogers to hold that works protected under its test may be advertised and marketed by name, and we so hold.[1763]

This step may seem remarkable in light of the wide variety of promotion activities which Fox had developed.[1764] Nonetheless, the inclusion of advertising and marketing efforts makes sense when looking at the

1757. U.S. Court of Appeals for the Ninth Circuit, 5 November 2008, E.S.S. Entertainment 2000/Rock Star Videos, 547 F.3d 1095 (9th Cir. 2008), 1100.
1758. U.S. Court of Appeals for the Ninth Circuit, *ibid.*, 1100.
1759. U.S. Court of Appeals for the Ninth Circuit, *ibid.*, 1100.
1760. U.S. Court of Appeals for the Ninth Circuit, *ibid.*, 1100.
1761. U.S. Court of Appeals for the Ninth Circuit, *ibid.*, 1101.
1762. U.S. Court of Appeals for the Ninth Circuit, 16 November 2017, Twentieth Century Fox Television/Empire Distribution, 875 F.3d 1192 (9th Cir. 2017), 1195.
1763. U.S. Court of Appeals for the Ninth Circuit, *ibid.*, 1197.
1764. Cf. Dinwoodie 2021, 4-5.

'Rogers' test as an instrument to shield use of trademarked cultural signs in a cultural context against trademark infringement claims. As pointed out in section 6.2.1, cultural activities require not only freedom to create new works on the basis of pre-existing material but also freedom to bring these new works to the attention of the public and create a market for them.[1765] It is not sufficient that an artist enjoys the freedom of using trademarked material in her atelier or studio. To avoid an impediment of cultural follow-on innovation, it is also necessary that the artist be free to sell and promote the resulting literary and artistic work.

The case scenario of *Twentieth Century Fox Television/Empire Distribution* seems extreme because Fox created a fictitious 'Empire' brand and used it as a marketing tool in the very sector where Empire Distribution had established its business. When a trademarked cultural sign is incorporated in a derivative literary and artistic work, however, use of the cultural sign in advertising and promotion activities will appear less extreme because the sign has a pre-existing, cultural meaning and the promotion activities are likely to evoke this cultural dimension of the sign (and not its later trademark function). Vermeer's 'Milkmaid' can serve as an example. As explained in section 8.2.1, the 'Milkmaid' painting is known as a trademark for dairy products in France. Nevertheless, French consumers are unlikely to perceive use of the 'Milkmaid' in advertising and merchandising activities as use of the trademark as long as the advertising and merchandising efforts concern a derivative literary and artistic production addressing Vermeer's masterpiece. Given the cultural context of the use, the public will make a connection with the sign's cultural meaning.

Besides the extension of the 'Rogers' test to promotion and merchandising activities, the decision in *Twentieth Century Fox Television* is of particular interest because the Ninth Circuit clarified that the test does not require a reference to the sign as a trademark. For its fictional TV music label, Fox had chosen the word 'Empire' because the show's setting was the Empire State New York and its subject matter was a figurative music and entertainment empire.[1766] Therefore, Fox did not refer to 'Empire' as a trademark of Empire Distribution. It used the word for different reasons. The absence of referential use in a trademark sense, however, did not offer Empire Distribution the opportunity to rebut the defence argument. The Ninth Circuit pointed out that no 'referential requirement' appeared in the text of the 'Rogers' test. Accordingly, the Court held that such a requirement

---

1765. German Federal Constitutional Court, 31 May 2016, case 1 BvR 1585/13, 'Sampling', para. 68; German Federal Constitutional Court, 13 June 2007, case 1 BvR 1783/05, 'Roman Esra', BVerfGE 119, 1 (21-22); German Federal Constitutional Court, 17 July 1984, case 1 BvR 816/82, 'Anachronistischer Zug', BVerfGE 67, 213 (224); German Federal Court of Justice, 21 February 2019, case I ZR 98/17, 'HHole (for Mannheim)', *GRUR* 2019, 609, para. 35.

1766. U.S. Court of Appeals for the Ninth Circuit, 16 November 2017, Twentieth Century Fox Television/Empire Distribution, 875 F.3d 1192 (9th Cir. 2017), 1198.

would be inconsistent.[1767] Fox could rely on the 'Rogers' test even though the word 'Empire' was only relevant to its TV show for thematic and geographic reasons. To win the case, it was not necessary that the word 'Empire' was used as a reference to Empire Distribution's trademark and that the trademark aspect of the sign had artistic relevance to the TV production.[1768]

With regard to use of the 'Rogers' test as a shield when trademarked cultural signs are used in a cultural setting, it is of particular importance to deny a requirement of use for the purpose of referring to the sign as a trademark. As discussed in section 6.2.4, an artist incorporating a trademarked cultural sign into a derivative work may choose the sign because of its cultural meaning. In consequence, the artist does not use the sign to identify or refer to goods or services (or policies) of the trademark proprietor.[1769] A requirement of referential use in a trademark sense would thus render the 'Rogers' test inapplicable in standard situations where trademarked cultural signs appear in an artistic context. Against this background, the rejection of a referential use requirement in *Twentieth Century Fox Television/Empire Distribution* confirms that the 'Rogers' test, as developed by U.S. courts, could provide a useful reference point for devising an appropriate threshold requirement of use as a mark in cases where trademarked cultural signs are remixed in the artistic domain.

Interestingly, U.S. case law also sheds light on the outer limits of the 'Rogers' test. In *Gordon/Drape Creative*, the Ninth Circuit dealt with the unauthorized use of Christopher Gordon's catchphrases 'Honey Badger Don't Care' and 'Honey Badger Don't Give a S---'. The two statements had become immensely popular as a result of Gordon's repeated use of the phrases in his YouTube video 'The Crazy Nastyass Honey Badger'. Gordon had started selling various goods bearing the phrases – ranging from T-shirts and mugs to costumes and plush toys. After obtaining a trademark registration for HONEY BADGER DON'T CARE, Gordon also granted licences, including licences for the production and marketing of greeting cards. Although its own negotiations with Gordon had not led to a licensing agreement, Drape Creative did not refrain from designing and producing greeting cards in which both phrases featured prominently with slight variations, such as 'Honey Badger don't give a $#*%!' or 'Honey Badger and me just don't care. Happy Birthday'. For this reason, Gordon brought a trademark action against Drape Creative.[1770] Discussing the unauthorized use of the catchphrases, the Ninth Circuit arrived at the conclusion that

1767. U.S. Court of Appeals for the Ninth Circuit, *ibid.*, 1198.

1768. U.S. Court of Appeals for the Ninth Circuit, *ibid.*, 1198.

1769. Cf. the referential use defence laid down in Article 14(1)(c) EUTMR and Article 14(1)(c) TMD.

1770. U.S. Court of Appeals for the Ninth Circuit, 20 November 2018, Gordon/Drape Creative, 909 F.3d 257 (9th Cir. 2018), 910-911.

incompliance with the 'Rogers' test could not be ruled out because of explicitly misleading use:

> In this case, we cannot decide as a matter of law that defendants' use of Gordon's mark was not explicitly misleading. There is at least a triable issue of fact as to whether defendants simply used Gordon's mark with minimal artistic expression of their own, and used it in the same way that Gordon was using it – to identify the source of humorous greeting cards in which the bottom line is 'Honey Badger don't care'.[1771]

On its merits, the Court thus saw a risk of whitewashing a mere imitation. The Ninth Circuit found that the phrases had artistic relevance to the greeting cards. The first criterion of the 'Rogers' test was fulfilled.[1772] Following the 'Rogers' approach, however, a finding of artistic relevance does not preclude the verdict of infringement if the use 'explicitly misleads as to the source or the content of the work'.[1773] Assessing this second criterion, the Ninth Circuit stated that greeting card consumers would perceive the phrases, as presented in Drape Creative's cards, as indications of commercial origin. Drape Creative had not employed the trademark in a context that differed from the context in which Gordon used the catchphrases himself.[1774] Moreover, Drape Creative had not added enough own expressive content to the work beyond the mark itself:

> But using a mark as the centerpiece of an expressive work itself, unadorned with any artistic contribution by the junior user, may reflect nothing more than an effort to 'induce the sale of goods or services' by confusion or 'lessen […] the distinctiveness and thus the commercial value of' a competitor's mark.[1775]

Gordon/Drape Creative, thus, adds an important nuance. In many cases, the cultural context in which an artist places a trademarked sign will create a contrast with the commercial trade environment in which the sign functions as a mark. This contrast will often suffice to avoid the impression of an indication of commercial source from the outset.[1776] If, however, the artistic use does not differ from the form in which the trademark owner uses the mark himself, it is decisive whether the artist has made a contribution of its own that dispels concerns about mere plagiarism and explicitly misleading use.

1771. U.S. Court of Appeals, *ibid.*, IV.C.
1772. U.S. Court of Appeals, *ibid.*, IV.B.
1773. U.S. Court of Appeals for the Second Circuit, 5 May 1989, Rogers/Grimaldi, 875 F.2d 994 (2nd Cir. 1989), 999.
1774. U.S. Court of Appeals for the Ninth Circuit, 20 November 2018, Gordon/Drape Creative, 909 F.3d 257 (9th Cir. 2018), IV.C.
1775. U.S. Court of Appeals for the Ninth Circuit, *ibid.*, IV.C.
1776. See the examples of earlier, valid 'Rogers' scenarios given by U.S. Court of Appeals for the Ninth Circuit, *ibid.*, IV.C.

This nuance does not render the 'Rogers' test unsuitable.[1777] As explained, the current enquiry serves the purpose of identifying appropriate criteria for a gatekeeper requirement of use as a mark that is capable of shielding cultural follow-on innovation from the potential corrosive effect of trademark rights to cultural signs. The concept of cultural follow-on innovation implies that pre-existing material, such as a trademarked cultural sign, is used as a basis to create new and fresh literary and artistic expression (section 3.3). The additional assessment factor evolving from the decision in *Gordon/Drape Creative* is compatible with this concept. A test that requires use as a mark as a precondition for trademark infringement claims need not permit mere imitations that are clearly misleading from a trademark perspective. Instead, it is consistent to ask whether an artist using a trademark provides an artistic perspective that places the sign in a different context – different from the setting in which the sign functions as a trademark. This assessment criterion need not prevent artists from using literal copies of trademarks in their works. In appropriation art, for instance, the artistic recontextualization – creating a difference from the regular trademark context – follows from the process of taking over a trademarked symbol into a work of art (cf. section 6.2.3).[1778] In 'Campbell's Soup Cans', Andy Warhol slavishly reproduced the Campbell logo. Nonetheless, the artistic context of this repetitive copying led to a distance from the commercial trade context in which the logo normally appears. This contrast prevents the impression of an indication of commercial source.

If the trademark incorporated into a work of art is a cultural symbol, the creation of an artistic setting that differs from the trademark context is even easier. It is sufficient that the artist, instead of addressing the trademark aspect of the sign, addresses its cultural dimension. In *Gordon/Drape Creative*, the Ninth Circuit stated:

> If an artist pastes Disney's trademark at the bottom corner of a painting that depicts Mickey Mouse, the use of Disney's mark, while arguably relevant to the subject of the painting, could explicitly mislead consumers that Disney created or authorized the painting, even if those words do not appear alongside the mark itself.[1779]

If the artist refrains from putting Disney's mark, however, a depiction of Mickey Mouse in a derivative artwork is unlikely to support a finding of explicitly misleading use. Mickey Mouse is not only a cultural symbol but also a Disney trademark (section 5.2.3). Nonetheless, the artistic remix context of the use will normally prevent the impression of employing Mickey Mouse as an identifier of commercial source – unless the artist, as pointed out

1777. Cf. Dinwoodie 2021, 6-8.
1778. Wilson/Lack 2016, 20-21.
1779. U.S. Court of Appeals for the Ninth Circuit, *ibid.*, IV.C.

in the 'Rogers' test,[1780] intentionally seeks to give the impression of a Disney product and explicitly misleads the public.

In sum, the 'Rogers' test that evolved in U.S. case law appears as an appropriate model for a test of use as a mark – as a gatekeeper requirement preventing trademark infringement claims against users in the cultural domain upfront – for several reasons. The 'Rogers' test:

- introduces artistic relevance as an assessment factor in the trademark infringement analysis instead of repeating traditional infringement criteria of trademark law, such as the degree of distinctiveness;
- creates a bias in favour of users in the artistic domain[1781] by requiring a showing of explicitly misleading use instead of deeming any risk of confusion sufficient, including the risk of some consumers assuming an economic link with the trademark owner;
- covers use in the title and body of derivative works, as well as use for marketing and merchandising purposes;
- does not require a reference to the trademark function of a trademarked cultural sign. It also applies when the sign is used to address its cultural meaning;
- allows artists to prevent a finding of explicitly misleading use (and trademark infringement) by placing the trademarked cultural sign in an artistic context that differs from the commercial context in which the sign functions as a trademark.

9.2.1.2 Extension to Dilution Scenarios

Despite all these merits, it must not be overlooked that the 'Rogers' test has been configurated in a way that does not cover the full spectrum of trademark infringement actions. As the criterion of explicitly misleading use indicates,[1782] the test is designed to offer an immunity from claims based on a risk of confusion (section 6.2.2). In *Rogers/Grimaldi*, the U.S. Court of Appeals for the Second Circuit left no doubt that, with this criterion, it sought to identify instances where 'the public interest in avoiding consumer confusion outweighs the public interest in free expression'.[1783] Hence, the 'Rogers' test leaves artists empty-handed when they are confronted with an infringement claim based on trademark dilution (section 6.2.3). The threshold criterion of use as a mark, however, should provide a general immunity and make it possible to stop all types of infringement claims at an early stage – before the trademark owner can establish prima facie infringement.

1780. U.S. Court of Appeals for the Second Circuit, 5 May 1989, Rogers/Grimaldi, 875 F.2d 994 (2nd Cir. 1989), 999.

1781. Dinwoodie 2021, 9.

1782. U.S. Court of Appeals for the Second Circuit, *ibid.*, 999.

1783. U.S. Court of Appeals for the Second Circuit, *ibid.*, 999.

In the U.S., the limited scope of the 'Rogers' test clearly came to the fore in *Mattel/MCA Records* where the Ninth Circuit dealt with an infringement action against the Danish band Aqua which had ridiculed Mattel's Barbie universe and corresponding gender stereotypes with its song 'Barbie Girl' (see the description of the case in section 6.2.3).[1784] While the Court could reject Mattel's confusion claim on the basis of the 'Rogers' test,[1785] it saw no possibility to do the same with regard to Mattel's dilution claim:

> the injury from dilution usually occurs when consumers aren't confused about the source of a product… Whereas trademark law targets 'interference with the source signaling function' of trademarks, dilution protects owners 'from an appropriation of or free riding on' the substantial investment that they have made in their marks[1786] (emphasis in the original).

Considering the 'Rogers' test inapplicable, the Ninth Circuit went on to discuss harm flowing from dilution in the form of blurring: as the word 'Barbie' no longer called to mind Mattel alone but also Aqua's ironic song, the mark's distinctiveness had been diminished.[1787] To create breathing space for freedom of expression, the Court finally resorted to the defence of 'noncommercial use' in U.S. anti-dilution legislation, as in force at the time, and declared the Barbie lampoon permissible on this basis (cf. section 6.2.3).[1788]

Due to its confinement to confusion cases, the 'Rogers' test only offers a partial solution in the quest for an appropriate gatekeeper requirement of use as a mark. Its inapplicability in dilution cases is worrisome. Damage-based dilution claims – blurring and tarnishment (section 6.2.3) – are not the only risk factors. In *Mattel/MCA Records*, the Ninth Circuit also referred to freeriding on the substantial investment which owners of marks with a reputation made to create powerful brands.[1789] In the EU, this latter branch of anti-dilution protection plays a crucial role. The elastic 'coat-tail formula' which the CJEU developed in *L'Oréal/Bellure* offers broad access to freeriding actions (section 6.2.3).[1790] In the keyword advertising case *Interflora/Marks & Spencer*, it became apparent that an act of taking unfair advantage may already be inferred from the mere selection of a mark with a reputation as a search term triggering a competitor's advertising:

1784. U.S. Court of Appeals for the Ninth Circuit, 24 July 2002, Mattel/MCA Records, 296 F.3d 894 (9th Cir. 2002), 899.
1785. U.S. Court of Appeals for the Ninth Circuit, *ibid.*, 902.
1786. U.S. Court of Appeals for the Ninth Circuit, *ibid.*, 903.
1787. U.S. Court of Appeals for the Ninth Circuit, *ibid.*, 903.
1788. U.S. Court of Appeals for the Ninth Circuit, *ibid.*, 903-904.
1789. U.S. Court of Appeals for the Ninth Circuit, *ibid.*, 903.
1790. CJEU, 18 June 2009, case C-487/07, L'Oréal/Bellure, para. 49. Cf. Kur/Senftleben 2017, para. 5.245.

> In those circumstances, [...] it cannot be denied that, where a competitor of the proprietor of a trade mark with a reputation selects that trade mark as a keyword in an internet referencing service, the purpose of that use is to take advantage of the distinctive character and repute of the trade mark.[1791]

The considerable infringement risk arising from this line of reasoning is evident: if this freeriding argument is extended to the inclusion of a mark with a reputation in an artwork, the mere selection of a cultural sign that also constitutes a trademark with a reputation may already be sufficient to establish prima facie infringement.[1792] In fact, a line can be drawn between this freeriding scenario and the sponsorship and affiliation scenario discussed in the preceding section: if the degree of a mark's distinctiveness is decisive for a finding of confusion about an economic link with the trademark owner,[1793] the analysis is fully aligned with trademark categories of infringement. The cultural nature of the use, however, is likely to be neglected. The same may be said about an enquiry into unfair freeriding that relies on the mechanical selection test which the CJEU adopted in *Interflora/ Marks & Spencer*.

To prevent a rash decision on prima facie infringement not only in the area of confusion but also in the field of dilution, it is indispensable to expand the 'Rogers' approach to dilution claims. The underlying recipe for minimizing the corrosive effect of trademark protection remains the same. In light of the expressive nature of the allegedly infringing use and the free expression values at stake, it is appropriate to establish a bias in favour of users in the cultural domain: a legal presumption of non-infringement which the trademark owner can only rebut by showing that the artist has deliberately chosen the mark with a reputation to damage, or derive unfair advantage from, its distinctiveness or repute. The damage or freeriding must not be a mere side effect of the artistic comment involving a mark with a reputation. By contrast, it must be the very purpose underlying the artist's selection of the trademark.

To lay a solid foundation for this expansion of the legal presumption of non-actionable use to dilution scenarios, it is important to analyse the circumstances surrounding the use of a trademarked cultural sign in an artistic context in more detail. As explained in the preceding section, a strict threshold requirement of use as a mark, such as the 'Rogers' requirement of explicitly misleading use, can support remix in the cultural domain even if a cultural sign has been transformed into a strong identifier of commercial source. In *Twentieth Century Fox/Empire Distribution*, the Ninth Circuit recalled in respect of trademark protection against confusion that 'consumers

1791. CJEU, 22 September 2011, case C-323/09, Interflora/Marks & Spencer, para. 86. Cf. Kur/Senftleben 2017, para. 5.248.

1792. Article 9(2)(c) EUTMR and Article 10(2)(c) TMD.

1793. CJEU, 10 April 2008, case C-102/07, Adidas/Marca, para. 36.

are less likely to mistake the use of someone else's mark in an expressive work for a sign of association, authorship, or endorsement'.[1794] A corresponding argument for assuming non-infringement in dilution cases is required for the extension of the 'Rogers' approach to cases concerning anti-dilution protection. Instead of allowing the sign's trademark aspect to dominate the analysis, the cultural context of the use must be decisive. To achieve this goal, it must be made plausible that the selection of a mark with a reputation for use in an artwork, as a rule, is made for the purpose of artistic expression and not for the purpose of causing damage or taking unfair advantage. Hence, it is necessary to explain in more detail why an artist's selection of a trademarked cultural sign with a reputation can be presumed not to be the result of a decision to deliberately damage the mark or unfairly exploit its reputation.

An answer to this question can be derived from Rochelle Dreyfuss' discussion of the rhetoric uniqueness of trademarks. As explained in section 8.3.2, Dreyfuss stresses the importance of breathing space for freedom of expression in trademark law and proposes the development of a specific arsenal of defences that shield expressive forms of trademark use from infringement claims. Establishing a specific set of defences, she seeks to arrive at a scenario where trademark protection is available 'across the entire signaling spectrum, except in instances in which expressive communication was suppressed by the loss of vocabulary'.[1795] Evidently, this approach rests on a distinction between 'signalling' and 'expressive' forms of use. According to Dreyfuss, a trademark fulfils a 'signalling' function when it distinguishes the goods and services of the trademark owner from those manufactured by others. 'Expressive use', by contrast, concerns the employment of the trademark as a metaphor or symbol representing a particular societal or personal condition.[1796] Again, the Joan Kennedy statement mentioned above (section 8.3.2) can serve as an example. Saying that she felt like a 'Barbie doll', Kennedy sought to express that she was treated like a 'beautiful but empty-headed accessory' when she was with Edward Kennedy.[1797] Obviously, the word 'Barbie' was not used to identify Mattel as the commercial source of products in this context. Kennedy employed the word 'Barbie' as a metaphor for a female stereotype. Even though this reference to Barbie found its way into a commercially exploited biography, Dreyfuss concludes in the light of the expressive nature of the use that:

1794. U.S. Court of Appeals for the Ninth Circuit, 16 November 2017, Twentieth Century Fox Television/Empire Distribution, 875 F.3d 1192 (9th Cir. 2017), 1197-1198.

1795. Dreyfuss 1990, 418.

1796. Dreyfuss 1990, 400. Cf. Assaf 2008, 58-61.

1797. Dreyfuss 1990, 397 and 400.

> the absence of a connection between the presence of the word 'Barbie' and a decision to purchase the book means that the word was not being used in what I have defined as its signaling sense.[1798]

With regard to the current enquiry into arguments for the expansion of the 'Rogers' approach to dilution claims, it is important to add that Kennedy did not choose the Barbie trademark to damage the brand image or derive unfair advantage from its magnetism. She selected the mark to express herself. The associations evoked by the word 'Barbie' provided an important shortcut to explain a personal feeling and condition.

Besides the distinction between 'signalling' use that is actionable and 'expressive' use that should remain unaffected by trademark infringement claims, Dreyfuss' analysis is of particular interest because she also develops criteria for the assessment of hybrid forms of use that do not belong to the 'signalling' or 'expressive' pole of the spectrum but are located somewhere between the extremes:

> courts entertaining hybrid use cases would first decide whether there is an expressive component to the challenged use and then consider how central the trademark is to the usage. If the mark is found to be rhetorically unique within its context, it would be considered expressively – but not necessarily competitively – generic, and the trademark owner would not be permitted to suppress its utilization in that context.[1799]

Interestingly, these criteria for hybrid cases follow a logic that seems similar to the 'Rogers' approach. First, the analysis focuses attention on the 'expressive component' of the use. Second, it asks which role the trademark plays in the expressive context and raises the issue of rhetoric uniqueness. The Ninth Circuit stated that in confusion cases, the 'Rogers' test only required minimal artistic relevance 'above zero'.[1800] Dreyfuss' test for hybrid cases appears as a refined version of this marginal threshold requirement. It offers a useful basis for explaining why artists using a cultural sign that has become a trademark with a reputation are unlikely to make this choice because they seek to damage or exploit the trademark's distinctiveness or repute. First, the connection with a literary or artistic work implies the existence of 'an expressive component' in the sense of Dreyfuss' concept. Second, cultural signs, such as Mickey Mouse (section 5.2.3) and the Mona Lisa (section 5.2.1), routinely fulfil the criterion of 'rhetoric uniqueness'.

This requirement refers to the mix of core denotations (dictionary definitions in the case of words) and additional connotations which a sign receives as a result of its 'history, derivation and identification with

1798. Dreyfuss 1990, 400.

1799. Dreyfuss 1990, 418.

1800. U.S. Court of Appeals for the Ninth Circuit, 5 November 2008, E.S.S. Entertainment 2000/Rock Star Videos, 547 F.3d 1095 (9th Cir. 2008), 1100.

users'.[1801] An enquiry into rhetoric uniqueness must 'establish the set of denotations and connotations associated with a mark and determine whether there exists another effective mechanism for invoking that set'.[1802] Hence, rhetoric uniqueness raises the question whether the specific amalgam of central and peripheral meanings which a sign evokes is unique in the sense that the sign plays a crucial role in the communication process because it allows the speaker to make a specific point. For a sign to be rhetorically unique, it must be the most effective means of triggering a specific spectrum of associations which a speaker needs to contribute to the discourse.[1803] As the discussion of non-substitutability of literary and artistic works in section 4.1.3 has already shown, cultural signs regularly meet this requirement: in principle, each aesthetic position reflected in a cultural sign is indispensable when considering the preconditions for the creation of derivative works. For contributing to the discourse in the cultural domain, authors of derivative works depend on the 'particularly rich conceptual reference'[1804] which a pre-existing cultural sign provides. The specific spectrum of cultural meanings attached to a cultural sign supports the conclusion that there is no alternative (and equally effective) mechanism for invoking that particular mix of denotations and connotations.

Hence, cultural signs can generally be deemed 'rhetorically unique'. They allow speakers in the cultural domain to make a particular point based on the specific mix of core denotations and additional connotations which the sign has as a result of its evolution in the cultural domain.[1805] In the light of Dreyfuss' criteria, it is thus possible to answer the question why use of trademarked cultural signs for the purpose of damaging or unfairly exploiting their distinctiveness or repute is exceptional in artistic contexts even if the sign has acquired the status of a mark with a reputation. As a rule, use in the artistic domain is not the result of an attempt to blur, tarnish or derive unfair advantage from the distinctiveness or repute of the sign's trademark dimension. Instead of analysing the use through the prism of these trademark categories of infringement, it is crucial to recognize the rhetoric uniqueness of trademarked cultural signs. Artists depend on this rhetoric uniqueness to express themselves. To contribute to the discourse in the cultural domain, they include the sign in their work to trigger the specific set of meanings which the sign offers as a rhetorically unique communication tool. Although the sign has both cultural and commercial connotations, it can thus be said that an artist is unlikely to choose a trademarked cultural sign with a reputation deliberately to damage or take unfair advantage of the sign's trademark distinctiveness and repute. Instead, potential damage or advantage

1801. Dreyfuss 1990, 413.
1802. Dreyfuss 1990, 421.
1803. Dreyfuss 1990, 421.
1804. CJEU, 12 January 2006, case C-361/04P, 'Picasso/Picaro', para. 27.
1805. Cf. Dreyfuss 1990, 413 and 418.

is a side effect of an artistic statement which – given the sign's rhetoric uniqueness – would not be possible without the possibility of evoking the specific denotations and connotations of the cultural sign. As a rule, the purpose of an artist's use of a trademarked cultural sign is not blurring, tarnishment or unfair freeriding. By contrast, the selection of the sign is an artistic necessity because the sign offers a rhetorically unique basis for cultural follow-on innovation (section 4.1.3).

9.2.1.3 Definition of Trademark Use Requirement

Against this background, it is possible to draw a parallel with the decision in *Rogers/Grimaldi* and establish a corresponding presumption of non-infringement that can only be rebutted in exceptional circumstances.[1806] Given the rich denotations and connotations of cultural signs – the rhetoric uniqueness which makes them indispensable communication tools for cultural follow-on innovation[1807] – it is appropriate to posit that, as a rule, the public interest in free expression must prevail over the trademark proprietor's interest in protection against dilution when a trademarked cultural sign is used in the cultural domain. This is only different in the exceptional situation where an artist – instead of relying on the sign's rhetorically unique denotations and connotations to make an artistic statement – deliberately uses the sign to damage or exploit the sign's trademark distinctiveness and repute.

As the 'Rogers' test, the adoption of this legal presumption introduces a bias in favour of artists in the trademark infringement analysis. As explained in section 9.2.1.1 with regard to trademark protection against confusion, the application of the 'Rogers' test would abolish the bias in favour of the trademark owner that follows from the focus on the degree of trademark recognition in current EU case law, such as the CJEU decision in *Adidas/Marca*.[1808] Similarly, a presumption of non-dilution based on the rhetoric uniqueness of cultural signs would abolish the bias in favour of proprietors of trademarked cultural signs with a reputation that follows from the mechanical assumption of actionable freeriding in CJEU decisions, such as *Interflora/Marks & Spencer*.[1809] In confusion as well as dilution contexts, the legal presumption of non-actionable use poses a hurdle which the trademark owner must first surmount before he can bring a claim against use in an artistic context: the trademark proprietor must convincingly rebut the presumption of permissible use. Only if the trademark owner succeeds in demonstrating that – despite the cultural setting – an artist aims at causing

1806. U.S. Court of Appeals for the Second Circuit, 5 May 1989, Rogers/Grimaldi, 875 F.2d 994 (2nd Cir. 1989), 999.
1807. Dreyfuss 1990, 413, 418 and 421.
1808. CJEU, 10 April 2008, case C-102/07, Adidas/Marca, para. 36.
1809. CJEU, 22 September 2011, case C-323/09, Interflora/Marks & Spencer, para. 86.

consumer confusion or damaging and unfairly exploiting the sign's trademark distinctiveness or repute, he can rebut the legal presumption of use in an expressive,[1810] non-branding[1811] way. Only then, the trademark owner can save the claim from being dismissed as unfounded from the outset.

Using the 'Rogers' test as a template, the gatekeeper requirement for trademark infringement claims that establishes this legal presumption can be defined as follows: use of a trademarked cultural sign in a cultural context will normally not constitute actionable use as a mark unless the cultural sign has no artistic relevance to the underlying work whatsoever, or, if it has some artistic relevance, unless the use of the cultural sign explicitly misleads as to the source of the derivative literary and artistic work, or deliberately blurs, tarnishes or takes unfair advantage of the distinctiveness or repute which the cultural sign has acquired as a trademark.[1812]

The requirement of rhetoric uniqueness[1813] does not form part of this trademark use test. As explained in the preceding section, cultural signs, such as Mickey Mouse (section 5.2.3) and the Mona Lisa (section 5.2.1), generally satisfy the test of rhetoric uniqueness. Because of their evolution in the cultural domain, they offer a mix of core denotations and additional connotations that makes them unique, non-substitutable communication tools in the artistic discourse. As the proposed test of use as a mark focuses on trademarked cultural signs, it is not necessary to ascertain this status of a rhetorically unique communication instrument in each individual case. Instead, it is sufficient – in line with the configuration of the 'Rogers' test – to ask whether the inclusion of the trademarked cultural sign has at least some artistic relevance to the derivative work of the unauthorized user: a minimal level of relevance 'above zero'.[1814]

In practice, the application of this upfront test of use as a mark means that the trademark owner must first overcome the hurdle of demonstrating that use in the cultural domain has trademark relevance *at all*. Even if a cultural sign acquires a strong distinctive character or even the status of a mark with a reputation, the legal presumption of non-actionable use in a decorative, expressive context remains an obstacle to the assertion of trademark rights. The sign's spectrum of cultural denotations and connotations – the fact that the sign conveys not only commercial but also cultural messages – places a lasting burden on the invocation of trademark rights when the use occurs in a cultural setting. It functions as a barrier to infringement claims.

1810. Dreyfuss 1990, 418.
1811. Dogan/Lemley 2008a, 542.
1812. Cf. the 'Rogers' formula developed by the U.S. Court of Appeals for the Second Circuit, 5 May 1989, Rogers/Grimaldi, 875 F.2d 994 (2nd Cir. 1989), 999.
1813. Dreyfuss 1990, 413 and 418.
1814. U.S. Court of Appeals for the Ninth Circuit, 5 November 2008, E.S.S. Entertainment 2000/Rock Star Videos, 547 F.3d 1095 (9th Cir. 2008), 1100.

As a result, use of a trademarked cultural sign in an artistic, decorative context becomes a robust user freedom (section 8.2.1) – a case that is commonly deemed non-actionable unless there are 'individualized facts that make a particular use by a particular person unprivileged'.[1815] When a trademarked cultural sign is used in connection with a literary and artistic production, the legal presumption of non-actionable use ensures that the use is routinely qualified as use other than as a mark. Hence, a confusion or dilution claim is doomed to fail. To rebut this legal presumption, the trademark proprietor must demonstrate 'individualized facts' that make the particular use at issue unprivileged. More concretely, the trademark owner must show that the cultural, expressive setting is a pretext for explicitly misleading or deliberately diluting use.

9.2.1.4 Impact on Confusion Analysis

With regard to the traditional analysis in anti-confusion cases, the presumption of use other than as a mark in favour of users in the cultural domain adds an important nuance. Neither the degree of similarity between the signs involved nor the degree of distinctive character is decisive. It is not enough to show that the cultural sign has become a (highly) distinctive mark. It is not enough that consumers see not only a cultural sign but also a reference to a trademark. By contrast, the immunity of artistic remix activities from trademark infringement claims follows from the specific cultural context in which the use takes place. As long as the sign is not explicitly employed as a misleading badge of origin in respect of the literary and artistic production itself (the artist's own goods or services), the trademark owner cannot rebut the legal presumption of non-actionable use other than as a mark.

In *Adidas/Marca*, the infringement question arose from the use of a two-stripe motif on sportswear that competed with Adidas' three-stripe garments.[1816] Given Adidas' extensive marketing efforts, the CJEU suspected that, despite the decorative nature of the use, the similarity of the signs could mislead consumers into believing that the two-stripe products came from Adidas or an economically linked undertaking.[1817] In *Opel/Autec*, by contrast, the CJEU attached importance to the fact that consumers of small-scale toy cars expected scale models to copy all details of the real car and even accorded:

> great importance to absolute fidelity to the original, so that that consumer will understand that the Opel logo appearing on Autec's products indicates that this is a reduced-scale reproduction of an Opel car.[1818]

1815. Benkler 1999, 362-363.
1816. CJEU, 10 April 2008, case C-102/07, Adidas/Marca, para. 11.
1817. CJEU, ibid., para. 34.
1818. CJEU, 25 January 2007, case C-48/05, Opel/Autec, para. 23.

Even though the unauthorized use included an identical copy of the highly distinctive Opel logo (which Opel had registered not only for motor vehicles but also for toys), the Court assumed that the specific decorative context eliminated a risk of direct or indirect confusion.[1819] This latter scenario corresponds with the scenario arising from the application of the proposed trademark use requirement and the corresponding legal presumption of non-actionable use in cases where a trademarked cultural sign is used in the context of a literary or artistic production. Generalizing the assumption that consumers will not perceive the sign as an indication of origin when it appears in a cultural context, the legal presumption of non-actionable use renders the trademark owner incapable of bringing an anti-confusion claim even if an exact copy of the trademarked cultural sign is used and the sign has become highly distinctive.

The only escape route for the trademark owner is evidence of exceptional circumstances. The trademark owner must demonstrate that consumers are explicitly misled into believing that the cultural sign is a badge of origin despite the cultural setting of the use.[1820] Departing from the CJEU decision in *Adidas/Marca*,[1821] it is not sufficient for the trademark owner to emphasize that, given large investments in educating consumers to perceive the cultural sign as a trademark, the consuming public is likely to assume a commercial connection with his enterprise. As a result of branding efforts, the sign's denotations and connotations may constitute an amalgam of cultural and commercial aspects – meanings stemming from the sign's evolution in the cultural domain and meanings following from later use for marketing purposes in the domain of trade. It is also conceivable that the derivative literary and artistic production deliberately plays with this blend of cultural and commercial dimensions of the sign. As long as this play remains at the expressive side of Dreyfuss' distinction between 'expressive' and 'signalling' use,[1822] however, the trademark owner cannot rebut the presumption of non-actionable use in the cultural domain.

In practice, it is only possible to establish prima facie infringement if the trademark proprietor manages to demonstrate that the artist has included explicit indications of commercial origin which falsely identify the trademark owner as the commercial source of the artwork. In *Gordon/Drape Creative*, the Ninth Circuit gave the example of an artist pasting Disney's trademark at the bottom corner of a painting depicting Mickey Mouse.[1823] Given the rhetoric uniqueness of Mickey Mouse as a cultural sign (section

1819. CJEU, *ibid.*, paras 23-24.
1820. This is in line with the distribution of the burden of proof under the 'Rogers' test. See U.S. Court of Appeals for the Ninth Circuit, 20 November 2018, Gordon/Drape Creative, 909 F.3d 257 (9th Cir. 2018), II.
1821. CJEU, 10 April 2008, case C-102/07, Adidas/Marca, para. 36.
1822. Cf. Dreyfuss 1990, 418.
1823. U.S. Court of Appeals for the Ninth Circuit, 20 November 2018, Gordon/Drape Creative, 909 F.3d 257 (9th Cir. 2018), IV.C.

9.2.1.2), the reproduction of the fictional character in a derivative work – even though constituting itself a well-known Disney trademark[1824] – is not sufficient to establish explicitly misleading use. As long as the trademarked cultural sign is used in an expressive way – for the purpose of making a point on the basis of its rhetorically unique mix of denotations and connotations – the trademark owner cannot succeed in demonstrating actionable use as a mark. The unnecessary addition of Disney's logo in the bottom corner, by contrast, reflects the intention to cause confusion and offers Disney a starting point to rebut the presumption of non-actionable use in an artistic context. Hence, the confusion claim can only have success if the artwork contains additional, explicitly misleading features.

Besides the 'Rogers' test that evolved in the U.S., Australian trademark law sets forth a trademark use requirement that comes close to the gatekeeper criterion that is proposed here. In *Christodoulou/Disney*, the Federal Court of Australia arrived at the conclusion that Disney's use of the book title 'The Hunchback of Notre Dame' which the plaintiff had registered for entertainment services did not constitute actionable use as a trademark even though Disney used this title commercially for the marketing of a film and related information products, such as soundtrack albums, story books, comic strips and sheet music.[1825] The Court summarized its findings as follows:

> The purpose and nature of each use is to describe the respondents' products accurately. The uses are not for the purposes of indicating a relevant connection in the course of trade or to distinguish the respondents' goods from those of other traders. The uses do not amount to 'use(s) as a trade mark' within the meaning of s 120 of the Act. Therefore, in each case the use complained about was not use as a trade mark.[1826]

In line with earlier case law, in particular the decision of the Full Court of the Federal Court of Australia in *Musidor/Tansing* (rejecting actionable use of the mark THE ROLLING STONES which had been registered for CDs),[1827] the Federal Court based this conclusion on the specific context and descriptive nature of the allegedly infringing use.[1828]

The proposed trademark use requirement with its legal presumption of non-actionable use would function in a similar way when it comes to decorative use of a trademarked cultural sign in a literary or artistic production. Instead of focusing on the recognition of the sign as a trademark,

1824. IR no. 296478.

1825. Federal Court of Australia, 4 October 2005, Christodoulou/Disney Enterprises Inc., [2005] 156 FCR 344, para. 20.

1826. Federal Court of Australia, *ibid.*, para. 71.

1827. Federal Court of Australia, 5 August 1994, Musidor BV/Robert William Tansing (trading as Apple Music House), [1994] 52 FCR 363.

1828. Federal Court of Australia, 4 October 2005, Christodoulou/Disney Enterprises Inc., [2005] 156 FCR 344, para. 42 and 71. Cf. Handler 2018, 171.

the specific cultural context occupies centre stage and tips the scales in favour of the defendant. In *Christodoulou/Disney*, Disney invoked the trademark use requirement as a defence argument. The presumption of use other than as a mark that is proposed here, by contrast, places the burden of proof on the plaintiff. In the absence of evidence which makes explicitly misleading branding for the purpose of distinguishing the artist's own goods or services plausible, the trademark owner cannot overcome the legal presumption of non-actionable use. Hence, the trademark owner must establish that, despite the cultural context, the use has trademark relevance. As Michael Handler states against the backdrop of trademark use case law in Australia, courts embarking on this analysis should demand 'cogent evidence, based on the specifics of the defendant's conduct'.[1829] As explained, the trademark owner must show that the allegedly infringing use explicitly seeks to cause confusion among consumers about the artwork's true commercial origin.[1830]

9.2.1.5 Impact on Dilution Analysis

In the area of protection against dilution, the trademark owner can rely on a broader range of arguments to substantiate that the cultural, expressive setting is only a pretext for damaging or unfairly exploiting the mark's distinctiveness or repute. From the perspective of EU trademark law, the actionable harm consists of damaging, or taking unfair advantage of, the highly distinctive character or the repute of the mark.[1831] For this type of harm, it is not necessary that consumers actually confuse the sign used in a cultural context with the protected trademark. According to established CJEU case law, it suffices that the use calls to mind the trademarked cultural sign. The mere risk of association is enough to assume that the use has trademark relevance (section 6.2.3).[1832]

The proposed trademark use requirement and the corresponding legal presumption of non-actionable use in favour of users in the cultural domain, however, provide an effective shield against these arguments. These factors substantially change the equation. Instead of accepting the traditional trademark logic of anti-dilution claims based on mere association – the fact that the sign used in a cultural setting calls to mind the protected mark – the trademark owner must develop a different line of argument that addresses the literary and artistic dimension of the trademarked sign. More concretely, the trademark proprietor must demonstrate that, even though the sign constitutes a rhetorically unique, non-substitutable communication tool in the cultural

1829. Handler 2018, 183.
1830. Cf. Handler 2018, 183, who proposes a similar standard with regard to non-traditional types of marks, such as shape features and colours.
1831. Cf. the spectrum of infringement arguments available under Article 9(2)(c) EUTMR and Article 10(2)(c) TMD.
1832. CJEU, 23 October 2003, case C-408/01, Adidas/Fitnessworld, para. 39.

domain (section 9.2.1.2),[1833] the artist deliberately selected the sign for a different reason, namely for the purpose of damaging or unfairly exploiting the distinctiveness or repute which the sign has acquired as a trademark.[1834] In the different context of defence arguments (justifying unauthorized use only after prima facie infringement has been established), the Benelux Court of Justice already came close to this solution in *Moët Hennessy/Cedric Art*. As explained in section 6.2.4, the Court held that 'artistic expression that is the original result of a creative shaping process'[1835] did not amount to trademark infringement unless the artistic expression aimed at harming the trademark or the proprietor of the trademark.[1836] The Court thus brought the question into focus whether the artist deliberately aimed at causing damage. As a result, it is no longer sufficient to argue that the unauthorized use, in a general and unspecific sense, calls to mind a well-known identifier of commercial source. The trademark owner must show that the use is accompanied by circumstances – 'individualized facts'[1837] – that make it plausible that the artist has chosen the sign in bad faith – with the intention to blur, tarnish or take unfair advantage of its strong recognition as a trademark. For this demonstration of actionable use despite the cultural setting, it is not sufficient that the selection of a cultural sign which also constitutes a well-known mark has the side effect of damaging the brand image or attracting extra attention for the artwork.

Again, Vermeer's famous 'Milkmaid' can serve as an example. As indicated above (8.2.1), the iconic artwork has been used for the marketing of dairy products to such an extent in France that it seems safe to assume that it has become a well-known mark.[1838] If the 'Milkmaid' painting features prominently in a literary and artistic work, however, the legal presumption of non-actionable use (other than as a mark) prevents the trademark owner from simply basing a dilution claim on the argument that French consumers, when seeing the artwork, will inevitably think of the Milkmaid trademark for dairy products. In particular, it is not enough to argue that, given the association in the minds of consumers, the use is likely to damage, or derive unfair advantage from, the brand image. By contrast, the trademark owner can only establish prima facie infringement if she manages to demonstrate that the 'Milkmaid' has been incorporated in the artwork for the very purpose of damaging the brand image or deriving unfair profit from the sign's trademark dimension. The efforts of the trademark owner are doomed to fail if the

1833. Dreyfuss 1990, 413 and 418.
1834. For a similar approach in existing case law in the EU, see Benelux Court of Justice, 14 October 2019, case A2018/1/8, Moët Hennessy/Cedric Art, para. 9.
1835. Benelux Court of Justice, 14 October 2019, case A2018/1/8, Moët Hennessy/Cedric Art, para. 9.
1836. Benelux Court of Justice, ibid., para. 9.
1837. Benkler 1999, 362-363.
1838. Cf. Bianchi 2017. As to the trademark registration of La Latière, see the international word mark IR 414494 and the French semi-figurative mark 99796048.

Vermeer painting has been chosen for expressive reasons: to make a point on the basis of its rhetorically unique mix of denotations and connotations in the cultural domain. Even if these expressive reasons lead to a derivative work which, from the trademark owner's perspective, damage the brand image (the commercial aspect of the sign), the infringement claim cannot have success as long as the trademark owner cannot substantiate that the artist has chosen the sign for this very purpose, and not for an artistic, critical comment. As a result of branding efforts of the trademark owner, the sign's denotations and connotations may constitute an amalgam of cultural and commercial aspects – meanings stemming from the sign's evolution in the cultural domain and meanings following from later use for marketing purposes in the domain of trade. As in confusion cases, it is conceivable that the derivative literary and artistic production deliberately plays with this blend of cultural and commercial dimensions. As long as this play with the Milkmaid as an artwork and the Milkmaid as a trademark remains expressive in the sense of evoking the sign's unique, non-substitutable denotations and connotations to contribute to the artistic discourse, the cultural setting of the use inhibits the trademark owner from rebutting the presumption of non-actionable use.

In consequence, the proposed gatekeeper criterion of use as a mark can put an end to anti-dilution claims at an early stage. In the above-described German case *Lila Postkarte* (section 6.2.1), for instance, the German Federal Court of Justice could have stopped the infringement action at an early stage by holding that, in light of the unique mix of associations triggered by Milka's trademarks, the Milka insignia used on the postcards constituted rhetorically unique tools for an artistic comment on the intact Milka world with mountains and happy cows.[1839] Milka may have argued that the parody interfered with its own communication and the idyllic brand image which was the fruit of long-standing, substantial investment in marketing. Milka may also have asserted that the postcards received considerable extra attention because they played with well-known badges of origin. These counterarguments, however, would have been in vain because the case did not offer starting points to suspect that the postcard producers had selected the Milka trademarks in bad faith to damage and unfairly exploit the idyllic Milka brand image. The Milka signs simply constituted a rhetorically unique means of making an ironic statement in the cultural domain. Given the public interest in this type of free expression and the public's contribution to the making of the brand image,[1840] Milka was thus bound to tolerate an interference with its own trademark communication and additional attention

1839. Cf. German Federal Court of Justice, 3 February 2005, case I ZR 159/02, Lila Postkarte, *GRUR* 2005, 584-585.

1840. Cf. Peukert 2019, 1181-1182; Gangjee 2013, 51-56; Tan 2013, 225; Gerhardt 2010, 101; Ramsey 2010b, 851; Heymann 2009, 651; Litman 1999, 15-16; Wilf 1999, 4-5; Kozinski 1993, 960; Dreyfuss 1990, 415 and 424.

for the parody that might have been attributable to the widespread recognition of Milka's marks. Under the trademark use standard developed above, these inevitable side effects are not sufficient to neutralize the legal presumption of non-actionable use (other than as a mark) because the postcard producers did not deliberately blur, tarnish or take advantage of the well-known Milka insignia.

This does not mean that trademark proprietors will no longer have success with trademark enforcement actions whenever the alleged infringer argues that the unauthorized use of a well-known trademark offers a rhetorically unique opportunity for a specific statement in the cultural domain. In *Styriagra* (section 6.2.3), for instance, the proposed threshold requirement of use as a mark would have left room for the Austrian Supreme Court to accept the trademark owner's argument that the free expression arguments advanced by the alleged infringer only formed a pretext for masking a use that intentionally sought to exploit, in an unfair manner, the magnetism of the VIAGRA trademark and the blue colour of Viagra pills.[1841] As the primary purpose of the use was the sale of pumpkin products and the subtle references to Viagra only served this commercial objective (rather than enriching the cultural landscape), Pfizer would have been in a position to overcome the legal presumption of non-actionable use and prohibit the exploitation of her marks in the guise of parody.

9.2.1.6 Extension to Iconic Trade Symbols

The latter examples already indicate that it is only a small step from establishing an upfront test of 'use as a trademark' in respect of artistic use of a trademarked cultural sign (sections 5.2.1 and 5.2.3), to the adoption of similar measures to permit the use of the expressive meanings and connotations of iconic trade symbols (section 5.2.5). Both case scenarios used to illustrate the practical impact of the legal presumption of non-actionable use – the German *Lila Postkarte* case and the Austrian *Styriagra* case – concerned iconic trade symbols (see the case analyses in sections 6.2.1 and 6.2.3). They did not deal with cultural signs that had been transformed into trademarks.

As discussed in section 8.3.2, it is desirable from the perspective of the cultural imperative to introduce a new set of rules in trademark law that allow the remix and reuse of trade symbols in a cultural context. In fact, it is not too difficult to draw a parallel with the scenario that occupied centre stage in the preceding sections – the use of a trademarked cultural sign in a cultural setting. While the foregoing discussion of artistic use of trademarked cultural signs concerned the freedom of using the rich spectrum of expressive meanings that stem from a sign's evolution in the cultural domain, the

1841. Cf. Austrian Supreme Court, 22 September 2009, case 17Ob15/09v, 'Styriagra', para. 3.4.

scenario relating to iconic trade symbols concerns the freedom of using the rich spectrum of expressive meanings that stem from the capacity of strong brands to symbolize a particular lifestyle or attitude. These expressive meanings may be the result of investments made by the trademark proprietor.[1842] As already pointed out in section 8.3.1, however, the richness of associations and meanings attached to a trademark may also follow from consumer activity. The consuming public frequently imbues trademarks with connotations distinct from and sometimes unrelated to the advertising messages conveyed by the trademark owner.[1843] Against this background, Rochelle Dreyfuss identified a need to keep expressive use of the associations and meanings triggered by iconic trademarks free. Otherwise, the loss of the ability to use trademarks may impede the ability to communicate.[1844]

From this perspective, an entitlement of artists to use the expressive aspects of iconic trade symbols in the literary and artistic discourse is a corollary of the public's contribution to the creation of a trade symbol with particular cultural significance and the public's particular interest in alternative visions of society (sections 3.3.2 and 5.1). The common denominator that justifies the introduction of a similar upfront test of 'use as a mark' clearly comes to the fore: both categories of signs – trademarked cultural signs that stem from the cultural domain and iconic trade symbols that have acquired cultural connotations despite their commercial roots – offer a rich spectrum of expressive meanings that can be deemed rhetorically unique (section 9.2.1.2).[1845] They are indispensable for the artistic discourse. As Rochelle Dreyfuss observed, trademarks:

> have become products in their own right, valued as indicators of the status, preferences, and aspirations of those who use them. Some trademarks have worked their way into the English language; others provide bases for vibrant, evocative metaphors. In a sense, trademarks are the emerging lingua franca: with a sufficient command of these terms, one can make oneself understood the world over, and in the process, enjoy the comforts of home.[1846]

Trademarks have thus become focal points of communication – densely packed information units 'infused with sets of denotations and associated connotations'.[1847] Use in the cultural domain is likely to focus on this

1842. Cf. Ginsburg 2018b, 254-255, and Ginsburg 2016, 73-75, who describes a further step in the transformation of trademarks into cultural artefacts: 'the development of trademarks into copyrightable characters and other visual goods'.
1843. Litman 1999, 15-16. Cf. Peukert 2019, 1181-1182; Gangjee 2013, 51-56; Tan 2013, 225; Gerhardt 2010, 101; Ramsey 2010b, 851; Heymann 2009, 651; Wilf 1999, 4-5; Kozinski 1993, 960; Dreyfuss 1990, 415 and 424.
1844. Dreyfuss 1990, 415-418.
1845. Aoki 1997, 542-545.
1846. Dreyfuss 1990, 397-398.
1847. Dreyfuss 1990, 415.

rhetoric uniqueness (section 9.2.1.2).[1848] Applying the above-described criteria which Dreyfuss developed to identify non-actionable, expressive use of trademarks,[1849] it can be said that, first, the connection with a literary or artistic production implies the existence of 'an expressive component'. Second, iconic trade symbols can be deemed 'rhetorically unique' because of the specific mix of core denotations and additional connotations which these signs obtain as a result of lifestyle messages stemming from advertising of the trademark proprietor and comments and nuances added by consumers. The density and richness of expressive meanings will often be similar to the amalgam of denotations and connotations arising from the transformation of a cultural sign into a trademark. Accordingly, the same presumption is justified: an artist using an iconic trade symbol in the context of a literary and artistic work is likely to rely on the expressive dimension of the sign and unlikely to interfere with its origin function.[1850] Admittedly, iconic trade symbols might have a predominant commercial meaning because of their evolution in the domain of trade. Nonetheless, the cultural setting of the use makes it plausible to presume that non-actionable use other than as a mark is the rule; actionable use as a mark is the exception. Use of iconic trade symbols in a literary and artistic work constitutes a specific form of using trademarks in a metaphorical sense: not as identifiers of commercial source but as symbols of personal or societal conditions (section 8.3.2). It concerns a metaphorical play with the associations evoked by a trademark in the minds of consumers.[1851] As a rule, use in the cultural domain remains limited to an 'expressively generic',[1852] 'non-branding'[1853] mode of use.

Given the described similarities with the scenario arising from use of a trademarked cultural sign in a cultural setting, it is appropriate to employ the same threshold requirement of use as a mark and the same legal presumption of non-actionable use in a cultural context to establish an obstacle to anti-confusion and anti-dilution claims against artistic remix activities. As in cases where trademarked cultural signs appear in literary and artistic productions, the owner of an iconic trade symbol should only be able to surmount the hurdle of a presumption of non-actionable use by producing evidence of 'individualized facts'[1854] that attest to the unusual situation where use in a cultural context explicitly misleads consumers, or deliberately damages or exploits in an unfair manner, the trade symbol's distinctiveness or repute. The criteria for identifying cases where use in the cultural domain

1848. Dreyfuss 1990, 413 and 418.
1849. Dreyfuss 1990, 413 and 418.
1850. Cf. the terminology used (and the distinction made) by Dreyfuss 1990, 400.
1851. For an example of case law recognizing this metaphorical play as a central feature of the use of trade symbols in an artistic setting, see German Federal Court of Justice, 3 February 2005, case I ZR 159/02, Lila Postkarte, *GRUR* 2005, 584-585.
1852. Dreyfuss 1990, 418.
1853. Dogan/Lemley 2008a, 542.
1854. Benkler 1999, 362-363.

occurs under these exceptional circumstances correspond to those developed in the preceding sections. As long as the iconic trade symbol is used in an expressive way – for the purpose of making a point on the basis of its rhetorically unique mix of denotations and connotations – the trademark owner cannot succeed in demonstrating actionable use as a mark. Using again the 'Rogers' test as a template (sections 9.2.1.1 and 9.2.1.3), the gatekeeper requirement for trademark infringement claims that establishes this legal presumption can be defined as follows: use of an iconic trade symbol (section 5.2.5) in a cultural context will normally not constitute actionable use as a mark unless the associations evoked by the trade symbol have no artistic relevance to the underlying work whatsoever, or, if they have some artistic relevance, unless the use of the iconic trade symbol explicitly misleads as to the source of the derivative literary and artistic work, or deliberately blurs, tarnishes or takes unfair advantage of the trade symbol's distinctiveness or repute.[1855]

9.2.1.7 Implementation of Non-Infringement Presumption in the EU

In both infringement scenarios – protection against dilution and protection against confusion – and across the broad spectrum of signs in the Mona Lisa (section 5.2.1), Mickey Mouse (section 5.2.3) and Coca Cola (section 5.2.5) category, a strict threshold requirement of use as a trademark is thus capable of shielding expressive use in the cultural domain from trademark infringement claims. In line with the public domain approach that recognizes robust freedom of use, a presumption of non-infringement in favour of users in the cultural domain deprives the trademark owner of the possibility to influence the infringement assessment in his favour by simply drawing attention to the (potentially strong) recognition of the sign as a trademark. Instead, the trademark use requirement functions as a gatekeeper that, in principle, makes it futile to assert trademark rights against decorative use in the expressive context of a literary and artistic production – unless the trademark owner manages to furnish proof of artistic use that explicitly misleads consumers as to the commercial source of the artwork or deliberately damages or exploits in an unfair manner the trademark's magnetism.

This distribution of the burden of proof can hardly be deemed an outlier in EU trademark law. Article 9(3)(f) EUTMR and Article 10(3)(f) TMD already provide for this solution with regard to comparative advertising. Stipulating that unauthorized use in comparative advertising is only actionable if it is contrary to MCAD rules, Article 9(3)(f) EUTMR and Article 10(3)(f) TMD impose the burden of proving non-compliance with one of the

1855. Cf. the 'Rogers' formula developed by the U.S. Court of Appeals for the Second Circuit, 5 May 1989, Rogers/Grimaldi, 875 F.2d 994 (2nd Cir. 1989), 999.

advertising requirements on the trademark proprietor.[1856] This can be seen as a corollary of the freedom of lawful comparative advertising which the CJEU recognized in *O2/Hutchison* and *L'Oréal/Bellure*.[1857] Use in comparative advertising fulfilling the MCAD requirements is exempted from the control of the trademark proprietor. If, however, EU trademark law achieves this result by reversing the burden of proof in respect of freedom of commercial expression, there is substantial reason to take the same measures with regard to freedom of artistic expression. In the human rights analysis following from ECtHR jurisprudence,[1858] freedom of commercial expression carries less weight than freedom of artistic or political expression.[1859] Therefore, measures to safeguard artistic remix activities should be at least as effective as those adopted to offer room for commercial freedom of speech.[1860] As the burden of proof rests on the trademark owner in the case of comparative advertising, it is consistent to take the same step with regard to artistic remix activities.

The trademark use requirement with the conceptual contours described in the preceding sections achieves this result. It establishes a bias in favour of users in the artistic domain and places the burden on the trademark proprietor to prove specific circumstances that justify a trademark infringement claim. Interestingly, EU trademark law already contains a starting point for the practical implementation of this solution. Recital 21 EUTMR and Recital 27 TMD read as follows:

> Use of a trade mark by third parties for the purpose of artistic expression should be considered as being fair as long as it is at the same time in accordance with honest practices in industrial and commercial matters.

Arguably, the trademark use concept developed above fits in this statutory framework. As it focuses on use of trademarked cultural signs in the context of new literary and artistic creations, it concerns use 'for the purpose of artistic expression'. Moreover, the rhetoric uniqueness of affected signs – coming originally from the cultural domain or having acquired a cultural

1856. Kur/Senftleben 2017, para. 5.308-5.309.

1857. CJEU, 12 June 2008, case C-533/06, O2/Hutchison, para. 45; CJEU, 18 June 2009, case C-487/07, L'Oréal/Bellure, para. 54. Cf. Kur/Senftleben 2017, para. 5.308.

1858. For an overview of criteria and the interplay between CJEU en ECtHR jurisprudence, see Geiger/Izyumenko 2020, 292-302.

1859. As to the recognition of the fundamental freedom of expression with regard to commercial speech, see ECtHR, 22 May 1990, app. no. 12726/87, Autronic/Switzerland, para. 47. With regard to the wider margin of appreciation in cases concerning commercial freedom of expression, see ECtHR, 20 November 1989, app. no. 10572/83, Markt Intern Verlag GmbH and Klaus Beermann/Germany, para. 26 and 32-38.

1860. As to the elevated status of freedom of artistic expression, see Geiger/Izyumenko 2020, 293-294. Cf. ECtHR, 24 May 1988, app. no. 10737/84, Müller and Others/Switzerland, para. 27; ECtHR, 8 July 1999, app. no. 23168/94, Karataş/Turkey, paras 49-52; CJEU, 29 July 2019, case C-476/17, Pelham and Others, para. 34.

dimension because of marketing and lifestyle messages – makes it plausible that the unauthorized use concerns the sign's expressive function and not its trademark function of identifying the commercial source of goods and services. As a rule, the use can thus be deemed 'fair' in the sense of the Recitals.

The proviso of compliance with 'honest practices in industrial and commercial matters', however, poses particular problems. As already pointed out in section 6.2.4, artists can hardly be expected to be aware of behavioural standards in the area of industry and commerce. Accordingly, they can hardly be expected to align their creative work with these behavioural norms. Moreover, it is undesirable that industrial and commercial standards of honesty reign supreme over creative processes in the literary and artistic domain. The use of industrial and commercial standards as prevailing assessment factors undermines the autonomy of the field of literary and artistic production in society. A legal framework following the norms of industry and commerce can hardly offer an environment that supports and encourages free artistic expression (section 3.3.1.1). From a legal-doctrinal perspective, it can be added that the CJEU tends to determine compliance with honesty in industrial and commercial matters on the basis of the same criteria that inform the infringement analysis in confusion and dilution cases (section 6.2.4).[1861] This entails the risk of a circular line of reasoning that renders the trademark use requirement incapable of shielding artistic remix activities against the corrosive effect of trademark infringement claims. The gatekeeper requirement of use as a mark can hardly be effective in practice if its application depends on the same criteria that are employed to find infringement.[1862]

Interestingly, the configuration of the trademark use requirement developed in the preceding sections may alleviate the problems arising from this flaw in current EU legislation and CJEU jurisprudence. In connection with the 'Recommendation on Measures to Safeguard Freedom of Expression and Undistorted Competition in EU Trade Mark Law'[1863] which sought to provide guidance for the 2015 reform of EU trademark law,[1864] the

1861. CJEU, 8 July 2010, C-558/08, Portakabin, para. 69; CJEU, 17 March 2005, case C-228/03, Gillette/LA-Laboratories, para. 49. Cf. Kur/Senftleben 2017, para. 6.73; Senftleben/Bently/Dinwoodie et al. 2015, 339; Senftleben 2013b, 168-169; Simon Fhima/Jacob 2014, 274; Simon Fhima 2012, 501-502.

1862. For an analysis leading to the same conclusion with regard to limitations of trademark rights that provide defence arguments after the establishment of prima facie infringement, see Senftleben/Bently/Dinwoodie et al. 2015, 339. Cf. Schovsbo 2018, 565-566; Ramsey/Schovsbo 2013, 676. See also Lemley/McKenna 2010, 416 and 447, who argue for 'proof of materiality' in the sense of an impact on consumer purchasing decisions.

1863. Senftleben/Bently/Dinwoodie et al. 2015, 341-343.

1864. At the end of 2015, the reform led to the current texts of the EUTMR and the TMD. As to the underlying preparatory work in the area of limitations of trademark rights, see Knaak/Kur/von Mühlendahl 2011, 117-124.

contours of a potential way out of the dilemma of circular reasoning were drawn as follows:

> The only way to make sense of the wording would be to clarify that although the basic concepts (likelihood of confusion, abuse of reputation) informing the evaluation of honest business practices are the same as those governing infringement, their application is different in that the leeway for using a basically conflicting mark is much broader where applications or limitations apply, thereby confining the proprietor's right to oppose such use to cases of disproportionate harm.[1865]

As explained above, the proposed trademark use requirement raises the bar for a finding of actionable confusion or dilution. It establishes a bias in favour of users in the artistic domain that provides much broader leeway than regular confusion and dilution tests. Use of trademarked cultural signs and iconic trade symbols is presumably fair in artistic contexts unless the trademark proprietor presents 'individualized facts'[1866] that overcome the legal presumption. More specifically, the trademark owner must demonstrate that, despite the cultural setting, the use explicitly misleads consumers as to the commercial origin of the derivative work. In the case of a cultural sign or trade symbol with a reputation, the trademark owner must show that the use deliberately damages or exploits in an unfair manner the distinctiveness or repute of the protected sign (sections 9.2.1.3 and 9.2.1.6). As the words 'explicitly' and 'deliberately' indicate, this threshold is higher than in regular anti-confusion or anti-dilution cases. Because of the cultural context that requires deference to freedom of expression,[1867] the unauthorized user in the artistic domain enjoys more breathing space. In consequence, the proposed trademark use requirement can help to reduce the risk of a circular line of reasoning that merely copies standard infringement criteria in confusion or dilution cases.

Following the configuration of the proposed test of use as a mark, it is not decisive whether some consumers may wonder about an economic link with the trademark owner and it is not decisive whether the artwork may receive some extra attention because it incorporates a sign that has become a well-known trademark. Instead, the primary question is whether the trademarked cultural sign or iconic trade symbol has artistic relevance to the

1865. Senftleben/Bently/Dinwoodie et al. 2015, 339.

1866. Benkler 1999, 362-363.

1867. For an in-depth analysis, see Sakulin 2010. Cf. Bohaczewski 2020, 856; Żelechowski 2018, 115-135; Senftleben 2015, 354; Ramsey/Schovsbo 2013, 671; Simon Fhima 2013, 293; Geiger 2010a, 163; Burrell/Gangjee 2010, 544; Nasser 2009, 188; Bently 2008, 1205; Dreyfuss 2008, 261; Geiger 2007, 317; Ramsey 2010a, 405; Weckström 2007, 671; Gulasekaram 2005, 887; Leval 2004, 187; Timbers/Huston 2003, 1278; Aoki 1997, 523; Dreyfuss 1990, 415-418.

allegedly infringing cultural production.[1868] If the answer is in the affirmative, the confusion and dilution criteria are qualified: *explicitly* confusing or *deliberately* diluting use is necessary to arrive at a finding of use as a mark that has sufficient trademark relevance to allow the trademark owner to bring his claim. Hence, the proposed test of use as a mark offers an enriched and modified set of assessment factors that differs from the infringement criteria in standard confusion and dilution cases.

Therefore, it is possible to avoid the described risk of a circular line of reasoning by aligning the honest practices enquiry with the modified confusion and dilution criteria that form part of the proposed trademark use requirement. Following this approach, the trademark owner must demonstrate a higher degree of harm. If the unauthorized use of trademarked material is artistically relevant to the allegedly infringing cultural production, the use complies with honest practices in industrial and commercial matters as long as it does not explicitly mislead consumers as to the commercial source of the literary and artistic work, and as long as it does not deliberately damage or derive unfair advantage from the distinctiveness or repute of the trademark at issue. Bringing the honest practices proviso in line with the test of explicitly confusing or deliberately diluting use (the criteria for rebutting the legal presumption of permissible use in the artistic domain that follows from the proposed trademark use requirement), the leeway for users in the artistic domain becomes broader and the rights of the trademark owner remain limited to cases of disproportionate harm.[1869]

To some extent, this alignment of the honest practices proviso with the qualified confusion and dilution criteria of the proposed trademark use requirement also takes care of the concern that behavioural standards in the sector of industry and commerce may prevail over creative processes in the cultural domain and erode the autonomy of the field of literary and artistic production. Under the proposed trademark use requirement, the first question is whether the unauthorized use of a trademarked cultural sign or an iconic trade symbol has artistic relevance to the allegedly infringing cultural production. Hence, the trademark use requirement introduces an assessment factor that reflects standards of the literary and artistic domain. Instead of allowing trademark categories of infringement to dominate the analysis, the question of artistic relevance enters the picture and raises the bar for a finding of actionable use as a mark. In cases where the protected sign is artistically relevant to the cultural production at issue, the trademark proprietor can establish use as a mark only if the allegedly infringing use explicitly misleads

1868. U.S. Court of Appeals for the Ninth Circuit, 5 November 2008, E.S.S. Entertainment 2000/Rock Star Videos, 547 F.3d 1095 (9th Cir. 2008), 1100.

1869. Cf. the above-cited recommendation by Senftleben/Bently/Dinwoodie et al. 2015, 339. Cf. the analysis by Schovsbo 2018, 578-579, who raises the question of whether 'the courts should begin their analysis from the perspective of the artist or from the perspective of what is fair as seen from a commercial point of view', and recommends an interpretation that supports artistic freedom of expression.

the public or deliberately dilutes the mark. As a result, an assessment criterion from the cultural domain – artistic relevance – reduces the impact of trademark rights. Instead of allowing any form of confusion or dilution to tip the scales against the user in the artistic domain, only forms of use are actionable that are clearly harmful from a trademark perspective. The supremacy of behavioural standards known from the field of industry and commerce is confined to cases of evidently disproportionate harm which the trademark owner can hardly be expected to tolerate. As stated above, however, the trademark owner need not yield to the societal interest in free artistic expression, if the literary and artistic context is only a pretext for blatant trademark infringement.

In sum, a circular repetition of standard confusion or dilution criteria in the honest practices analysis can be prevented by aligning the honest practices proviso with the test of explicitly confusing or deliberately diluting use. Under the trademark use concept developed in sections 9.2.1.3 and 9.2.1.6, this qualified test of confusion or dilution constitutes the threshold for rebutting the legal presumption of non-actionable use in an artistic context. When the higher threshold of explicitly misleading or deliberately diluting use is applied to identify dishonest practices in connection with the use of trademarked cultural signs or iconic trade symbols in a cultural production, the honest practices test can be applied without depriving the proposed trademark use requirement of its function to reduce the deterrent effect of trademark protection on cultural follow-on innovation (section 6.3). Instead, the honest practices test is equated with the question of whether the trademark owner can rebut the legal presumption of fair use that follows from the finding of artistic relevance.

This implementation strategy finds support in Recital 21 EUTMR and Recital 27 TMD. As discussed, these Recitals stipulate that unauthorized use for the purpose of artistic expression should be deemed fair as long as it is in accordance with honest practices in industrial and commercial matters. In addition, however, Recital 21 EUTMR and Recital 27 recall the necessity to safeguard freedom of expression:

> Furthermore, this Regulation [this Directive] should be applied in a way that ensures full respect for fundamental rights and freedoms, and in particular the freedom of expression (addition within brackets added).

As Jens Schovsbo explains, this additional reference to freedom of expression impacts the application of all individual norms of EU trademark law, including the honest practices proviso itself:

> The first part of the Recital provides for limitations but only to the extent that the use by third parties is fair and in accordance with honest practices in industrial and commercial matters. The application of fundamental rights and freedoms is not, however, made subject to the

> 'fair and honest practices' test. Instead, this part constitutes a freestanding test (cf. the use of the word 'furthermore'). This is also the effect of the use of the opening word – 'furthermore' – and by the adjective 'full respect.' It thus follows from the wording of the Recital itself that these interests should be taken into account when applying any rule or principle of trademark law […] including the definition of which uses are 'fair' and in conformity with 'honest practices'[1870] (emphasis in the original text).

Therefore, it is important to recognize that the honest practices proviso itself is subject to more thorough scrutiny in the light of freedom of expression. In cases where trademarked cultural signs or iconic trade symbols appear in a literary and artistic context, the second part of Recital 21 EUTMR and Recital 27 TMD (the sentence starting with 'furthermore') makes it necessary to give the honest practices proviso a meaning which 'fully' respects freedom of expression. To achieve this goal, it is consistent to weave a bias in favour of users in the artistic domain into the honest practices test. Instead of the standard confusion or dilution analysis, a higher threshold for demonstrating dishonest use must be applied. The proposed higher bar of *explicitly* misleading or *deliberately* diluting use is in line with this approach. As explained, this qualification of the confusion and dilution test prevents the honest practices proviso from depriving the trademark use requirement of its function to serve as a shield against trademark infringement claims. Only if use in the artistic domain is evidently disproportionate and harmful, the trademark owner can successfully invoke trademark rights. Only then, it is justified to allow behavioural standards of industry and commerce to inform the analysis because the literary and artistic context proves to be a mere disguise for obvious trademark infringement. This configuration of the honest practices test in cases concerning artistic use is not only an appropriate strategy for implementing the proposed trademark use requirement but also a legal obligation that follows from the second part of Recital 21 EUTMR and Recital 27 TMD.

Taking Schovsbo's statement as a starting point, it may even be argued that the test of honest practices has no impact on the proposed trademark use requirement at all. As Schovsbo rightly points out, the 'furthermore' sentence in the second part of Recital 21 EUTMR and Recital 27 TMD establishes a 'freestanding' legal obligation to fully respect fundamental rights and, in particular, freedom of expression.[1871] Arguably, the introduction of a gatekeeper requirement of use as a mark is indispensable to reduce the deterrent effect which trademark rights to cultural signs and iconic trade symbols may have on cultural follow-on innovation (section 6.3). From this perspective, the proposed trademark use requirement (sections 9.2.1.3 and

1870. Schovsbo 2018, 568.
1871. Schovsbo 2018, 568.

9.2.1.6) can be regarded as a necessary modification of the infringement analysis in cases involving the use of trademarked cultural signs and iconic trade symbols in literary and artistic productions – a modification that follows directly from the obligation to fully respect freedom of expression, as stated in Recital 21 EUTMR and Recital 27 TMD.[1872] This alternative approach places the trademark use requirement outside the scope of the honest practices proviso altogether. It finds support in the legislative text itself. The substantive provisions of the EUTMR and the TMD only contain the honest practices test in Article 14(2) dealing with the limitations of trademark rights listed in Article 14(1). These limitations can serve as defences for artists using trademarked material in their work (section 6.2.4).[1873] Apparently, the legislator intended the test of honest practices to enter the picture only *after* the trademark proprietor has managed to establish prima facie infringement. The proposed trademark use requirement, however, serves the purpose of identifying situations where use in the artistic domain has trademark relevance at all. It is a gatekeeper requirement to be satisfied *before* the trademark owner can establish a valid infringement claim. Arguably, the honest practices proviso does not cover this early stage of the infringement analysis but only the appreciation of defence arguments after the establishment of prima facie infringement. The upfront test of use as a mark is an inherent limit of trademark rights. It need not be characterized as a limitation in the sense of Article 14(1) EUTMR and Article 14(1) TMD.

Following this line of reasoning, a clear distinction between the two parts of Recital 21 EUTMR and Recital 27 TMD comes to the fore: the first part of the Recitals – referring to honest practices in connection with artistic expression – only concerns the regulation of the limitations of trademark rights laid down in Article 14 EUTMR and Article 14 TMD. These provisions explicitly set forth the obligation to ensure compliance with honest practices in industrial and commercial matters.[1874] In respect of this specific reference to honest practices, the first part of Recital 21 EUTMR and Recital 27 TMD offers guidance when artistic expression is at stake. By contrast, the second part of the Recitals – the freestanding 'furthermore' obligation to fully respect freedom of expression – applies across all substantive provisions of EU trademark law and supports measures to give full weight to fundamental rights and freedoms, such as the adoption of a trademark use requirement with the described conceptual contours and functions (sections 9.2.1.3 and 9.2.1.6). As this second part of the Recitals applies universally to all EU trademark law provisions, it covers the entire infringement analysis and offers a solid basis for the adoption of a test of use

1872. For a confirmation of the impact of freedom of expression on the application of trademark norms, see CJEU, 27 February 2020, case C-240/18P, Constantin Film/EUIPO ('Fack Ju Göhte'), para. 56.

1873. Article 14(1)(b) and (c) EUTMR; Article 14(1)(b) and (c) TMD.

1874. Article 14(2) EUTMR; Article 14(2) TMD.

as a mark that poses an additional obstacle to infringement claims against artistic use of trademarked material (cultural signs and iconic trade symbols). In this way, the second part of the Recitals enhances the breathing space for freedom of expression in the cultural domain.

A survey of implementation options, thus, sheds light on two avenues that would lead to the inclusion of an effective trademark use requirement in EU trademark law. Both approaches would prevent a circular repetition of standard infringement criteria in the context of the honest practices proviso. On the one hand, the honest practices test can be aligned with the criteria for rebutting the legal presumption of fair, permissible use in an artistic setting. This first approach equates the honest practices enquiry with the question of whether the allegedly infringing use in an artistic context explicitly misleads consumers as to the source of the artwork, or deliberately damages or derives unfair advantage from the distinctiveness or the repute of the trademark. Only if the trademark owner succeeds in demonstrating this evidently disproportionate harm, she can rebut the legal presumption of permissible fair use with artistic relevance and, at the same time, substantiate that the use was not in compliance with honest practices in industrial and commercial matters. In consequence, the use can be qualified as actionable use with trademark relevance: actionable use 'as a mark'.

On the other hand, the honest practices proviso can be declared inapplicable to the trademark use requirement altogether. This second approach attaches importance to the fact that, in the substantive provisions of the EUTMR and the TMD, the honest practices test only appears in Article 14(2) as an additional requirement to be satisfied when the specific limitations of trademark rights set forth in Article 14(1) are applied. Accordingly, the first part of Recital 21 EUTMR and Recital 27 TMD (which refers to the honest practices proviso in the context of artistic expression) can be understood as a guideline for the honest practices enquiry in the specific context of these statutory limitations. As the proposed trademark use requirement is an inherent limit of trademark rights and not a limitation listed in Article 14(1), there is no need to apply the honest practices test to the requirement of use as a mark. By contrast, the second part of Recital 21 EUTMR and Recital 27 TMD is decisive which requires full respect for freedom of expression and supports a legal presumption of fair, permissible use when a trademarked cultural sign or iconic trade symbol is artistically relevant to a derivative literary and artistic work. Again, the trademark owner can only overcome this legal presumption by demonstrating explicitly confusing or deliberately diluting use. This rebuttal option follows directly from the configuration of the proposed trademark use requirement (sections 9.2.1.3 and 9.2.1.6). It is not the result of an honest practices test that focuses on behavioural standards in industry and commerce which, by definition, are inappropriate for the appreciation of use in a cultural setting.

As both approaches raise the bar for a finding of actionable use as a mark (both require evidently confusing or deliberately diluting use to rebut the legal presumption of fair, permissible use), they would both ensure that the honest practices proviso does not neutralize the gatekeeper function of the trademark use requirement. They would allow the test of use as a mark to serve as a bulwark against trademark infringement claims when the allegedly infringing use takes place in the cultural domain. Owners of trademark rights to cultural signs or iconic trade symbols could only prevail if they demonstrate evidently disproportionate harm – a degree of harm which they need not tolerate because the cultural context surrounding the unauthorized use is merely a pretext for blatant trademark infringement.

Seeking to implement this approach in the EU, the decision of the Benelux Court of Justice in *Moët Hennessy/Cedric Art* can serve as a compass. As explained in section 6.2.4, the Court held in this case that 'artistic expression that is the original result of a creative shaping process'[1875] does not amount to trademark infringement unless the artistic expression aims at harming the trademark or the proprietor of the trademark.[1876] The Court thus brought the question into focus whether the artist deliberately aims at causing damage. This decision resembles the 'Rogers' test in the U.S. (section 9.2.1.1). It rests on the assumption that breathing space for creative processes is the rule and infringing use is an exception. Accordingly, the Benelux Court of Justice required evidence of an intention to harm the trademark or the trademark owner. As the 'Rogers' test, the decision points in the direction of a legal presumption of non-infringement that can only be rebutted when exceptional circumstances arise. Interestingly, the Benelux Court of Justice explicitly relied on Article 10(1) ECHR to undergird the artist's right to include trademarks in artistic expression without prior authorization. Instead of referring to trademark norms, such as the honest practices proviso, the Benelux Court of Justice based the exception of deliberately damaging use on Article 10(2) ECHR which allows limitations of freedom of expression that are 'necessary in a democratic society […] for the protection of the reputation or rights of others … '.[1877] Hence, the Court viewed the trademark infringement claim through the prism of fundamental rights and refrained from presuming any superiority of trademark protection that could have led to an assessment on the basis of confusion or dilution standards. Quite clearly, freedom of artistic expression is the rule in this decision and infringing use is the exception. Instead of scrutinizing the artistic use in the light of trademark infringement categories, the Court aligned its ruling with the guarantee of freedom of expression in the ECHR and required use that specifically aims at causing damage.

The decision in *Moët Hennessy*, thus, reflects several components of the proposed approach to the question of honest practices: the bias in favour of

1875. Benelux Court of Justice, 14 October 2019, case A2018/1/8, Moët Hennessy/Cedric Art, para. 9.

1876. Benelux Court of Justice, *ibid.*, para. 9.

1877. Benelux Court of Justice, *ibid.*, para. 9.

the artist (instead of the trademark owner) that makes it possible to assume compliance with honest practices unless the use deliberately aims at causing harm; the invocation of freedom of expression that allows judges to set aside the question of honest practices and solve the case on the basis of constitutional assessment standards. Nonetheless, the decision failed to directly introduce the legal presumption of non-infringement that is proposed here. Instead of recalibrating the requirements for establishing prima facie infringement, it concerned the due cause defence in Article 2.20(2)(d) of the Benelux Convention on Intellectual Property which the artist can assert after the trademark owner has developed a valid infringement argument (section 6.2.4). It is thus necessary to apply the reasoning of the Benelux Court of Justice mutatis mutandis to the gatekeeper requirement of use as a mark that has been developed above. Once this additional step is taken, the *Moët Hennessy* decision can lead to the described legal presumption of non-infringement and pave the way for introducing the intended bias in favour of artistic use in EU trademark law.

9.2.1.8 Counterargument of False Symmetry and Missing Contours

The proposal of a trademark use requirement with the described conceptual contours (sections 9.2.1.3 and 9.2.1.6) would be incomplete without a discussion of arguments that have been advanced against the adoption of the upfront gatekeeper criterion of 'use as a mark'. The vivid debate on the trademark use requirement in the U.S. offers important reference points in this respect.[1878] Criticizing recourse to the trademark use concept as a remedy against overbroad trademark rights,[1879] Graeme Dinwoodie and Mark Janis expressed the concern that the requirement of use as a mark lacked sufficient clarity to allow the consistent development of trademark policy:

> the range of unauthorized third-party conduct that proponents purport to bring under the umbrella of non-trademark use is both vast and diverse. Much of this conduct should indeed be deemed noninfringing but for many different reasons. To subsume all of this conduct under a single (remarkably opaque) doctrine, such as trademark use, would mask the

1878. Cf. Barrett 2006, 371; Dogan/Lemley 2008a, 542; Dinwoodie/Janis 2007a, 1657-1658; Davison/Di Giantomasso 2009, 443; McKenna 2009, 773. As to the debate about an adequate trademark use concept in the EU, see Kur/Senftleben 2017, para. 5.14-5.15 and 5.49-5.56; Yap 2009, 86-87; Kur 2008, 11; Simon Fhima 2005, 401; Loughlan 2000, 328.

1879. Cf. Dinwoodie/Janis 2007a, 1654: '[r]ather, we believe that trademark use theorists seek to curtail what they regard as the unwarranted expansion of trademark rights. Yet, to prune trademark rights back to their core may require a more effective cutting tool'.

> real reasons for confining the scope of trademark rights in an expansionist era. It would thus impoverish the transparent development of trademark policy, deciding hard cases for unstated reasons.[1880]

They also warned of an erroneous alignment of the infringement analysis with use criteria informing the decision on a sufficient degree of distinctiveness at the registration stage:

> [o]nce consumer understanding, and hence a trademark right, is established, the primary goal of trademark law is to protect the integrity of that understanding by minimizing consumer confusion. Although consumer understanding will likely only develop when a sign is used 'as a mark,' a range of uses by a third party may interfere with that understanding. Thus, a teleological analysis of trademark law would suggest that the concept of use sufficient to establish rights might differ radically from the type of use by a defendant that might give rise to infringement.[1881]

Hence, their discussion of use as a mark as a threshold requirement yields two central counterarguments: the risk of a false symmetry between registration and infringement criteria[1882] and the risk of introducing a formalistic obstacle to infringement claims that fails to provide a proper basis for a consistent and appropriate assessment of the wide variety of infringement scenarios in which the trademark use test would become relevant. In their view, the requirement of 'use as a mark' fails to make an autonomous analytical contribution. It is likely to serve merely as a proxy that judges will use as a backdoor to consider – potentially in truncated and disfigured form[1883] – more specific infringement criteria, such as a likelihood of confusion and consumer association concepts.[1884]

However, Dinwoodie and Janis also explain which approach should be taken instead to arrive at an appropriate infringement analysis in trademark law. This additional point of their analysis shows that their primary concern is reliance on an overly formalistic,[1885] simplistic[1886] threshold requirement that deprives courts hearing trademark cases of the opportunity to give weight to all relevant circumstances and the entire spectrum of interests, including the trademark proprietor's interest in preserving a trademark's

1880. Dinwoodie/Janis 2007a, 1608.
1881. Dinwoodie/Janis 2007a, 1613.
1882. For a more detailed discussion of this point, see Dinwoodie/Janis, 1642.
1883. See the example given by Dinwoodie/Janis 2007a, 1649.
1884. Dinwoodie/Janis 2007a, 1644-1646.
1885. See Dinwoodie/Janis 2007a, 1658, characterizing the trademark use concept as a 'formalistic monolith'.
1886. Dinwoodie/Janis 2007a, 1621.

brand and merchandising value.[1887] Instead of focusing on the source-identifying nature of allegedly infringing use – 'the supposedly binary switch between trademark use/non-trademark use'[1888] – Dinwoodie and Janis, accordingly, propose to broaden the frame of assessment factors and devote attention to the individual context in which allegedly infringing use takes place:

> However, legitimate debates over the role of trademark law in regulating contextual advertising, parody, merchandising, and product design simulation, to mention but a few examples, implicate a number of different values and considerations far too extensive to be captured adequately by the single concept of trademark use. Trademark use is simply too blunt a concept, no matter how defined, to capture the full range of values at play in these debates. Contextualism is a better alternative than the formalism of trademark use and has always been important in trademark law. Context is the means by which courts have traditionally constrained the scope of trademark law and trademark rights.[1889]

With contextualism as an overarching principle, Dinwoodie and Janis seek to establish a legal framework that is capable of capturing the 'multivalence'[1890] of modern trademark law – the need to integrate values and considerations ranging from personal identity and free speech interests to the enhancement of consumer information and consumer choice, the prevention of distortions of competition, and the furtherance of e-commerce and new business models that evolve rapidly in the digital environment.[1891]

In the light of this critique of the trademark use concept, it is important to point out that the proposal to adopt 'use as a mark' as a strict gatekeeper criterion in the preceding sections does not intend to establish a general symmetry between the enquiry into genuine trademark use at the registration stage and the test of use as a mark as an element of the infringement analysis. The concept developed above is far from aligning an examination of the nature of use across the wide range of potential infringement scenarios with use standards applied to ascertain sufficient distinctive character in the context of trademark registrations. Furthermore, it does not aim at collapsing the multifaceted spectrum of values, interests and considerations in modern trademark law into one archaic, binary test of trademark use/non-trademark use. In the last decennia, new ways of using trademarks on the Internet, such as keyword advertising, sparked the debate on introducing or reinforcing the

1887. Dinwoodie/Janis 2007a, 1654.
1888. Dinwoodie/Janis 2007a, 1659 and 1662.
1889. Dinwoodie/Janis 2007a, 1657.
1890. Dinwoodie/Janis 2007a, 1659.
1891. Dinwoodie/Janis 2007a, 1659 and 1667.

threshold requirement of trademark use.[1892] The current analysis, however, is not part of the quest for a magical formula capable of reacting adequately to all challenges arising from the architecture of the world wide web and new online business models. By contrast, it deals with the specific question of interferences of trademark protection with follow-on innovation in the literary and artistic domain. Given this focus on a specific context, the current proposal to adopt a strict threshold requirement of use as a mark may even be regarded as an exponent of the contextualism advocated by Dinwoodie and Janis. The current proposal is confined to remixing and reusing trademarked signs with cultural significance for the purpose of creating new literary and artistic productions. It only covers signs that stem from the cultural domain (section 9.2.1.3) and, as an extension, iconic trade symbols that have acquired cultural significance (section 9.2.1.6).

The important nuance resulting from this focus is this: while Dinwoodie and Janis use their plea for contextualism as a basis to categorically reject the trademark use concept, the current analysis has shown that, in artistic contexts, the values competing with the trademark owner's legal position are typically so strong that they outplay the trademark protection interest and should prevent the establishment of prima facie infringement from the outset to avoid an unnecessary exposure of artists to trademark infringement claims. The above analysis rests on the assumption that it is possible to identify specific contexts in which the upfront preclusion of trademark claims is an adequate response, namely the specific context arising from trademark rights to signs with cultural significance and the specific context of use in the literary and artistic domain. In other words: a focus on specific contexts can lead to the insight that the adoption of a strict threshold requirement of use as a mark is the most adequate solution. More specifically, the above discussion of trademark use as a gatekeeper requirement brought to light two central contextual factors: first, the appearance of a trademarked cultural sign or iconic trade symbol in a literary or artistic production (sections 9.2.1.1 and 9.2.1.2). This implies use with an undeniable 'expressive component'.[1893] Second, the sign's cultural significance: the capability to evoke an individual mix of core denotations and additional connotations which makes the sign 'rhetorically unique':[1894] a unique vehicle for contributing to the discourse in the artistic domain (sections 9.2.1.2 and 9.2.1.6).

Given these specific characteristics, there can be little doubt that the trademark use concept developed above is not intended to sacrifice sophisticated infringement criteria in trademark law in favour of an unsophisticated, monolithic[1895] test of use as a trademark. Considering the outlined

---

1892. Cf. Dogan/Lemley 2004, 777; Barrett 2006, 371; Dinwoodie/Janis 2007b, 1703.
1893. Cf. Dreyfuss 1990, 418.
1894. Cf. Dreyfuss 1990, 413 and 418.
1895. Cf. Dinwoodie/Janis 2007a, 1658.

conceptual contours, the counterargument of 'too blunt a concept'[1896] loses its power of persuasion. Dinwoodie and Janis stress that, even in the area of trademark parodies, it is necessary to walk the fine line between undesirable restrictions of free speech and an appropriate scope of protection for the trademark owner:

> In such cases, courts often refer to free speech concerns that might counsel in favor of the defendant's speech not being enjoined, but the conclusion of a court rarely depends upon free speech values trumping concerns about confusion. Yet some parodies are less likely to confuse consumers, suggesting a lesser need to be concerned about the affirmative goals of trademark law. And some parodies might be less justified by our principles of free speech than others, thus warranting lesser solicitude to effectuate those values. But those calculations cannot be made simply by calling the activity parody (say, as opposed to satire), and the relevant policy considerations that guide courts cannot fully be assessed by characterizing the entire use by defendant as protected speech.[1897]

As explained above, the trademark use concept proposed here focuses on those instances of artistic remix where a sign's expressive function – and not its source-identifying function[1898] – occupies centre stage. Reliance on trademark use as an upfront filter requires an expressive component stemming from the inclusion of the sign at issue in a literary and artistic production. Moreover, it requires an affected sign to have artistic relevance in the cultural discourse due to its rhetoric uniqueness. Hence, the proposed trademark use requirement is unlikely to permit consumer confusion in the guise of cultural remix. In addition, it offers an important safety valve. If the trademark owner identifies a case of use in the cultural domain that explicitly causes confusion or deliberately damages or derives unfair advantage from the trademark, the trademark use concept, as developed above, does not offer full immunity from trademark claims. It only provides for a legal presumption of non-actionable use. The trademark owner can rebut this presumption by providing evidence of 'individualized facts'[1899] showing that the artist used the cultural setting as a pretext for blatant trademark infringement.

On balance, the counterarguments asserted by Dinwoodie and Janis do not carry sufficient weight in the light of the specific context and limited ambit of operation of the trademark use concept developed above. The risk of a false symmetry between trademark use considerations at the registration and infringement stage, and the risk of a simplistic, formalistic trademark use test swallowing more sophisticated infringement criteria, are unlikely to

1896. Dinwoodie/Janis 2007a, 1657.
1897. Dinwoodie/Janis 2007a, 1661.
1898. Cf. the terminology used (and the distinction made) by Dreyfuss 1990, 400.
1899. Cf. Benkler 1999, 362.

materialize when use as a mark is introduced as an upfront filter to allow the expressive use of trademarked cultural signs and iconic trade symbols in remix and reuse activities in the artistic domain. Dinwoodie's and Janis' arguments against trademark use as a gatekeeper requirement impacting all types of infringement claims do not offer a basis for condemning more specific trademark use concepts, such as the highly contextual concept developed in the preceding sections.

9.2.1.9 Comparison with Defences and Restrictions of Remedies

As a final point in the discussion of trademark use as a gatekeeper requirement, it is important to draw attention to the particular merits of the approach. Dinwoodie and Janis aptly describe the practical effect of trademark use as an upfront filter as follows:

> According to this argument, sometimes called the trademark use theory, the nature of the defendant's use serves as a threshold filter, requiring courts to engage in a preliminary inquiry regarding the nature of that use, thereby downgrading any analysis of its effects on consumer understanding. Indeed, courts following this new theory would not even reach the question of confusion absent the defendant's use being a 'trademark use.' A defendant engaged in non-trademark use would ipso facto be immune from liability.[1900]

While Dinwoodie and Janis are critical about the immunizing effect of the trademark use requirement (see preceding section), the described 'ipso facto' immunity is desirable from the perspective of the cultural imperative. Seeking to create safeguards against impediments of cultural follow-on innovation in trademark law, the immunity following from trademark use as a threshold requirement appears as a particularly attractive tool to reduce the deterrent effect on artistic activities which trademark rights to cultural signs and iconic trade symbols may have (section 6.3). Because of its immunizing effect, the test of trademark use is the most effective instrument for securing breathing space for artistic use, if trademark rights to cultural signs (sections 5.2.1 and 5.2.3) are not denied from the outset. The same is true when a trademark acquires the status of an iconic trade symbol with cultural significance (section 5.2.5). Again, the upfront trademark use filter is the most effective tool to satisfy the enhanced need for freedom of artistic remix and reuse that arises from the cultural importance of the trade symbols.

The difference between the gatekeeper requirement of trademark use and traditional defences against infringement claims clearly comes to the fore when considering the distribution of the burden of proof. In a trademark

---

1900. Dinwoodie/Janis 2007a, 1599-1600. For examples of immunity that can follow from the application of trademark use as an upfront filter, see Dogan/Lemley 2004, 809-811.

system with a threshold requirement of trademark use, the trademark proprietor must argue and demonstrate that the allegedly infringing use constitutes actionable 'use as a mark' before judges lend weight to more specific infringement arguments based on a likelihood of confusion or dilution. Hence, the burden of proving that artistic use has relevance under trademark law – and allows the invocation of trademark rights – rests on the trademark proprietor.[1901] Ideally, this leads to a situation where legal counsels, from the outset, advise against claims targeting remix and reuse in the cultural domain. If the upfront refusal of trademark claims because of missing trademark relevance becomes established case law, attempts to assert trademark rights against artists using trademarked cultural signs or iconic trade symbols appear futile indeed. In addition, the imposition of the burden of proof on the trademark owner leads to a situation where the latter must make the trademark claim plausible. It may be said that the trademark owner must justify the invocation of trademark rights against use in the artistic domain. This situation corresponds with the public domain concept that includes robust user freedoms – use that any person is 'privileged to make absent individualized facts that make a particular use by a particular person unprivileged' (section 8.2.1).[1902] The adoption of trademark use as an upfront filter implies that, even if the artist remains silent and does not submit counterarguments, the trademark claim will still be dismissed unless the trademark owner manages to provide convincing proof of use with trademark relevance: explicitly misleading or deliberately diluting use that constitutes actionable use as a mark despite the artistic context (sections 9.2.1.3 and 9.2.1.6).

In comparison with this *ipso facto* immunity,[1903] a mere defence against infringement claims is less effective.[1904] A trademark system relying on defences in favour of artistic remix and reuse gives the trademark proprietor the opportunity to establish prima facie infringement and send cease-and-desist letters without any need to justify these enforcement measures. In principle, the infringement action is legitimate despite the specific artistic context in which the allegedly infringing use takes place. In consequence, the artist must bear the burden of proving that the use falls within the scope of a valid defence against the trademark infringement claim. She carries the burden of demonstrating exceptional circumstances that neutralize the infringement action which, prima facie, appears legitimate.[1905] The burden of proof is thus reversed to the detriment of users in the cultural domain: while the trademark use test obliges the trademark owner to produce evidence of specific circumstances justifying the infringement claim, an approach relying

1901. Kur 2009, 293.
1902. Benkler 1999, 362.
1903. Dinwoodie/Janis 2007a, 1600.
1904. Cf. Ginsburg 2016, 70.
1905. Kur 2009, 293.

on defences obliges the artist to give evidence of specific circumstances justifying the unauthorized use. As a result, the artist is less privileged and enjoys a less robust freedom of use. Even critics of upfront filtering on the basis of a trademark use requirement concede that the defence scenario is less favourable and enhances the risk of a deterrent effect of trademark protection:

> At the same time, it is surely true that our approach is subject to one drawback that is characteristic of standards-based approaches: it achieves flexibility at the cost of trading away some certainty, and it therefore has the potential to chill some valuable social and commercial activity.[1906]

In the light of the objective to support cultural follow-on innovation, the adoption of a strict test of trademark use is thus preferable. The establishment of defences is the second-best option. It preserves the public domain of cultural expressions in a less effective way than the proposed gatekeeper requirement of use as a mark (section 9.2.1.3).[1907]

Making comparisons between different strategies to reduce the corrosive effect of cumulative copyright and trademark protection, it can finally be added that a remedies-based approach would be the least satisfactory solution. The imposition of limits on remedies would be even less effective than the development of robust defences. In literature, Laura Heymann proposed to curb benefits accruing from cumulative intellectual property protection 'by calibrating remedies to the nature of the harm incurred'[1908] (section 7.3.2). Instead of providing remedies in accordance with the various labels which owners of cumulative rights may apply to their infringement claims, judges should consider the underlying nature of the harm at issue and strictly limit the grant of remedies to those 'best designed to ameliorate that harm'.[1909] Obviously, however, this approach is incapable of limiting the deterrent effect of trademark rights in cultural signs (section 6.3). In a remedies-based system, the trademark proprietor is not confronted with specific obstacles that make it difficult to establish prima facie infringement. Moreover, in a system placing its primary reliance on remedies, artists are not necessarily equipped with particularly strong defences. Instead, an artist facing infringement claims would have to seek refuge in arguments that seek to limit the spectrum of remedies in the light of the asserted harm.[1910] Even

1906. Dinwoodie/Janis 2007a, 1663. As to the underlying plea for the development of 'defenses and limitations on trademark rights' as an alternative solution, see Dinwoodie/Janis, *ibid.*, 1662.

1907. For a discussion of the interplay between the gatekeeper requirement of use as a mark and defences exempting specific types of use, such as descriptive or decorative use, in trademark systems providing for both elements, see Barrett 2010, 61-63.

1908. Heymann 2013, 273.

1909. Heymann 2013, 275.

1910. Heymann 2013, 275.

then, however, the artist cannot prevent the grant of the remedy that appears most appropriate. The infringement claim would only vanish if the asserted harm proves to be completely untenable and, accordingly, incapable of supporting any remedy.

Considering these practical consequences, a remedy-based approach must be rejected.[1911] Evidently, it is the least artist-friendly approach. A remedy-based solution is insufficient to safeguard cultural follow-on innovation. Even Joseph Liu's proposal to confine remedies to 'a disclaimer, which would address the confusion without limiting the ability of a third party to use the underlying work' misses the point in the case of artistic remix activities.[1912] While relief in the form of clear labelling obligations may appear as a light burden,[1913] it fails to strike at the root of the problem. As the solution is remedy based, it does not prevent the trademark owner from establishing prima facie infringement. Hence, the deterrent effect of trademark rights remains (section 6.3). In comparison with a strict gatekeeper requirement of use as a mark and the development of particularly robust defences, the limitation of trademark claims at the level of remedies is the least effective and least desirable solution. Therefore, a remedy-based approach must be rejected.

9.2.2 *Robust Defences Against Infringement Claims*

The discussion in the preceding section has shown that the development of defences against infringement claims offers less effective support for remix and reuse in the cultural domain than a strict gatekeeper requirement of use as a mark. While the upfront test of use as a mark would put an end to infringement claims at an early stage – even before prima facie infringement can be established – defences are only capable of preventing the final verdict of infringement. They do not inhibit the trademark proprietor from developing a valid infringement argument. Moreover, the party invoking a defence – the artist in cases involving remix and reuse of trademarked signs – must prove that all requirements for applying the invoked defence provision are fulfilled. In contrast to a solution based on a gatekeeper requirement of trademark use, a defence-based approach, thus, imposes the burden on the artist to convince the judge of exceptional circumstances that permit the allegedly infringing use without authorization. Reliance on defences leads to a scenario where, aside from the specific mode of use covered by a limitation of exclusive trademark rights, infringement claims are valid. Hence, a defence-based approach only offers certain safety valves to avoid an erosion

1911. For an opposite view recommending the exploration of remedy-based solutions, see Dinwoodie 2020, 34.

1912. Liu 2013, 1433.

1913. See the support for this solution expressed by Ginsburg 2018b, 264.

of artistic freedom of use. It does not introduce a general bias in favour of artistic remix and reuse in the trademark system.

Nonetheless, it is important to devote attention to defences as second-best safeguards of breathing space for cultural follow-on innovation. In copyright law, exemptions enabling the transformative use of existing, copyrighted works play a crucial role. Copyright limitations for the purposes of making quotations and creating parodies can serve as examples. They offer later authors the opportunity to use the individual, protected expression of their predecessors to express themselves. Allowing the productive reuse of protected material, they are central to cultural innovation processes (section 3.1).[1914]

Therefore, a first question in the field of defences concerns legal mechansims that allow the application of copyright limitations for transformative use, such as the right of quotation and the exemption of parody, in the trademark arena. If trademark rights to cultural signs are not denied from the outset and infringement claims are not stopped at an early stage by applying a strict test of use as a mark, the trademark system should offer, as a last resort, the same limitations of exclusive rights that support remix and reuse in the copyright system. In this way, it can be ensured that use privileges for cultural follow-on innovation remain intact when trademark protection is granted on top of copyright protection. Obviously, it is possible to achieve this goal by incorporating copies of relevant copyright limitations into the trademark system. The moment trademark rights are limited in the same way as copyright, an artist can invoke the right of quotation and the exemption of parody as a defence against both the copyright claim and the trademark claim alike. This, in turn, allows a judge hearing a case about cumulative copyright and trademark infringement to let the quotation or parody defence prevail over both arguments of infringement. It is thus important to explore avenues to arrive at an effective system of horizontal defences that are applicable across copyright and trademark law. To shield cultural follow-on innovation against trademark infringement claims that would undermine use privileges in copyright law, it is conceivable to establish a network of corresponding defences for artistic remix in both domains of intellectual property (following section 9.2.2.1), introduce a rule of universal, direct applicability of pertinent limitations, such as the right of quotation and the exemption of parody, not only in copyright law but also in trademark law (section 9.2.2.2), or apply relevant copyright limitations by analogy (section 9.2.2.3). Moreover, the constitutional guarantee of freedom of expression – as a higher-ranking norm – may serve as a horizontal safeguard of breathing space for artistic remix and reuse that impacts both copyright and trademark law alike (section 9.2.2.4).

A closer look at these approaches, however, reveals that it is not sufficient to ensure the applicability of specific limitations, such as the right

1914. Cf. Buccafusco/Bechtold/Sprigman 2017, 44-45.

of quotation and the exemption of parody, in both copyright and trademark law. While horizontal applicability of copyright limitation prototypes may be sufficient in the Mickey Mouse scenario where trademark rights relate to a creation that still enjoys copyright protection, and where copyright law itself still reduces the breathing space for remix and reuse activities (section 5.2.3), a more ambitious approach is necessary in the Mona Lisa scenario where trademark rights are acquired with regard to a cultural heritage sign that was in the public domain (section 5.2.1). Prior to the reappropriation via trademark law, signs in this category have been unencumbered by any intellectual property right. Accordingly, users in the artistic domain enjoyed unlimited freedom of remix and reuse. To avoid the erosion of this absolute freedom, trademark law must develop defences that emulate, to the greatest extent possible, the public domain status which affected cultural heritage signs had prior to the acquisition of trademark rights. This requires stronger efforts than the mere copying of specific copyright limitations (section 9.2.2.5).

Hence, it is necessary to ascertain the extent to which trademark limitations are capable of emulating the public domain status of cultural heritage signs. In EU trademark law, the defences for referential use and non-distinctive use laid down in Article 14(1)(b) and (c) EUTMR and Article 14(1)(b) and (c) TMD are important in this respect. If these limitations are applied flexibly in the light of freedom of expression, they can serve as vehicles to offer robust freedom of use (sections 9.2.2.6 and 9.2.2.7). Following this strategy, it is also possible to fill the gap of missing counterparts of quotation and parody rules in EU trademark law. Rightly understood, the referential use defence and the non-distinctive use defence cover use scenarios that would fall within the scope of the right of quotation or the exemption of parody from a copyright perspective. Within the inherent limits of any defence-based approach (no absolute freedom of use; mere exemption of specific use modalities), the exemption of referential use and the exemption of non-distinctive use in EU trademark law can thus absorb some negative repercussions caused by the loss of absolute freedom of use that existed prior to the grant of trademark rights to a cultural heritage sign (section 9.2.2.8). Moreover, the analysis leads to the insight that the line of argument supporting the application of the referential use defence and the non-distinctive use defence to cultural heritage signs (Mona Lisa scenario, section 5.2.1) is also valid with regard to symbols of contemporary mainstream culture (Mickey Mouse scenario, section 5.2.3) and iconic trade symbols (Coca Cola scenario, section 5.2.5). International trademark law permits the introduction of defences for artistic remix and reuse with these proportions (section 9.2.2.9).

9.2.2.1 Network of Corresponding Use Privileges

Cumulative copyright and trademark protection entails the risk of eroding use privileges for artistic remix and reuse that are available in copyright law. If trademark law does not provide for the same use privileges, the freedom of remix and reuse that should exist from a copyright perspective will inevitably be diminished.[1915] To avoid this loss of freedom for cultural follow-on innovation, it is advisable to establish a network of corresponding use privileges: in principle, the same limitations of exclusive rights that safeguard freedom of transformative remix and reuse in copyright law should be available in trademark law when a literary and artistic work is transformed into a trademark and the problem of cumulative copyright and trademark protection arises.

One way to achieve this result is the adoption of congruent defences in both copyright and trademark law.[1916] Current EU law, however, does not offer a network of corresponding limitations of protection that could give artists confidence in the validity and success of defence arguments across copyright and trademark law. The limitation infrastructure in the two fields differs markedly. EU copyright law provides for limitation prototypes that address specific use scenarios. Article 5(3)(d) ISD exempts 'quotations for purposes such as criticism or review'.[1917] Article 5(3)(k) ISD contains a use privilege for 'caricature, parody or pastiche'.[1918] These limitation categories are sought in vain in EU trademark law which, instead, provides for an open-ended defence of 'due cause' that is capable of covering artistic forms of expression. The ambit of operation of this flexible, open-ended limitation is confined to infringement claims based on the dilution of trademarks with a reputation (section 6.2.4).[1919] EU copyright law, however, does not contain any flexible, open-ended limitation rule. As already indicated, it sets forth a closed list of specific limitation prototypes which Member States are free to adopt at the national level.[1920] Hence, not only a congruent set of specific

---

1915. Cf. Jacques 2016, 471; Derclaye/Leistner 2011, 244-245; Kur 2002, 604-608.

1916. For a proposal to establish such a congruent limitation infrastructure, see Jacques 2016, 480-481; Senftleben 2013b, 170-175.

1917. As to the freedom of expression underpinning of this limitation, see CJEU, 1 December 2011, case C-145/10, Painer, para. 132-134. As to its conceptual contours, see CJEU, 29 July 2019, case C-476/17, Pelham and Others, paras 69-71. Cf. Aplin/Bently 2020, 156-222; Bently/Aplin 2019, 28-31; Senftleben 2012a, 351-360.

1918. As to the scope of this limitation, see CJEU, 3 September 2014, case C-201/13, Deckmyn, para. 20. As to its interpretation in the light of freedom of expression, see CJEU, *ibid.*, paras 25-27. Cf. the in-depth analysis by Jacques 2019, 91-133, and the statements by Pötzlberger 2018, 681; Hudson 2017, 348-352; Senftleben 2012a, 360-367.

1919. Article 9(2)(c) EUTMR; Article 10(2)(c) TMD. Cf. Senftleben 2017c, 256-265.

1920. For a more detailed discussion and critique of this copyright limitation infrastructure, see Senftleben 2013d, 37-39; Leistner 2011, 417; Guibault 2010, 55.

limitations in copyright and trademark law but also a system of corresponding elastic due cause (or fair use) provisions is missing.[1921]

Current EU law, thus, fails to offer artists a safe harbour network of corresponding copyright and trademark limitations to support transformative remix activities.[1922] Developments in other areas of intellectual property show that the harmonization of limitations across different protection regimes is possible. Article 27(k) UPCA exempts 'the acts and the use of the obtained information as allowed under Articles 5 and 6 of [the Computer Programs] Directive 2009/24/EC, in particular, by its provisions on decompilation and interoperability'. This direct reference to EU copyright legislation incorporates limitations relating to computer programs into patent law. It covers the use of software for the intended purpose, including error correction, the making of backup copies, reverse engineering and code decompilation to achieve interoperability. As a result, copyright limitations that serve as defences for users can survive when software patents are granted.[1923] The reference technique in Article 27(k) UPCA ensures an identical limitation infrastructure and the validity of defence arguments in both copyright and patent law. With corresponding use privileges, the patent system has less difficulty to cope with potential impediments of follow-on innovation that may arise from cumulative copyright and patent protection in the field of computer software. As innovation in the software sector is known to occur in small incremental steps, it is important to preserve breathing space for follow-on innovation in the software sector when a computer program is additionally patented. Otherwise, overlapping patent protection may become too heavy a burden, in particular for small and medium-sized enterprises not involved in the patenting of software and unable to pool patent portfolios to obtain use permissions for patented algorithms and interfaces.[1924]

1921. For proposals to introduce such a system of corresponding, open-ended norms, see Senftleben 2011c, 180-181; Senftleben 2017c, 249-284; Kur 2002, 612-613. With regard to the proposal to introduce an open norm in copyright law but not in the field of industrial property rights, see Geier 2015, 137-144 and 146-148.

1922. Cf. Kur 2002, 608, who recommends the insertion of 'an express limitation in favour of parodies' in trademark law. For examples of parody cases that could not be solved consistently in the absence of a corresponding limitation infrastructure, see Voorhoof 2002, 646-647.

1923. For a discussion of this protection overlap and the need for limitations supporting derivative innovation in this area, see Samuelson 2019, 291-301; Li 2019, 823-859; Dane 2018a, 1-16; Dane 2018b, 5-15; Sterckx/Cockbain 2010, 366-402; Ballardini 2008, 563-575; Leistner 2008, 188; Ghidini/Arezzo 2005, 166; Hilty/Geiger 2005, 615; Burk/Lemley 2005, 81-100; Weyand/Haase 2005, 647; Cohen/Lemley 2001, 41-42; Caron 2000, 3. As to the denial of copyright protection for functional elements of software, see CJEU, 2 May 2012, case C-406/10, SAS Institute, paras 39-41.

1924. Cf. Leistner 2008, 188; Ghidini/Arezzo 2005, 166; Hilty/Geiger 2005, 615; Weyand/Haase 2005, 647; Cohen/Lemley 2001, 41-42; Caron 2000, 3.

With regard to overlapping copyright and trademark protection, a tendency of approximating defences can be observed on the other side of the Atlantic.[1925] U.S. legislation in the field of well-known marks recognized the need for specific fair use limitations covering transformative use. After the U.S. Supreme Court had required 'a showing of actual dilution, rather than a likelihood of dilution' in *Moseley/V Secret Catalogue*,[1926] the 2006 Trademark Dilution Revision Act amended the anti-dilution provisions in the U.S. Lanham Act.[1927] The adoption of new anti-dilution legislation was accompanied by the introduction of a statutory, open-ended fair use provision that created breathing space for commercial as well as cultural freedom of speech. Section 43(c)(3) of the Lanham Act, as amended, reads as follows:

> (3) EXCLUSIONS – The following shall not be actionable as dilution by blurring or dilution by tarnishment under this subsection:
> (A) Any fair use, including a nominative or descriptive fair use, or facilitation of such fair use, of a famous mark by another person other than as a designation of source for the person's own goods or services, including use in connection with –
> (i) advertising or promotion that permits consumers to compare goods or services; or
> (ii) identifying and parodying, criticizing, or commenting upon the famous mark owner or the goods or services of the famous mark owner.
> (B) All forms of news reporting and news commentary.
> (C) Any noncommercial use of a mark.

Hence, a statutory provision was enacted that sets limits to trademark rights to support the use of trademarked material for transformative purposes, such as use in quotations and parody.[1928] The purposes of 'identifying and parodying, criticizing or commenting upon the famous mark' are explicitly exempted from the control of the trademark owner. The enumeration of these privileged purposes in trademark legislation recalls Section 107 of the U.S. Copyright Act: the copyright fair use doctrine which, based on a case-by-case

1925. Ginsburg 2018b, 248-252 and 269-270.
1926. U.S. Supreme Court of the United States of America, 4 March 2003, Moseley/V Secret Catalogue, Inc., 537 U.S. 418 (2003). Moskin 2004, 842-859.
1927. Trademark Dilution Revision Act of 2006 (H.R. 683) amending the U.S. Trademark Act of 1946 (15 U.S.C. 1125). With regard to the required proof of dilution, this new legislation clarifies that protection against dilution is to be granted 'regardless of the presence or absence of actual or likely confusion, of competition, or of actual economic injury'. Cf. Beebe 2006, 1143.
1928. For a description of the situation under the former U.S. Federal Trademark Dilution Act, see Cantwell 2004, 549. With regard to common law fair use defences in the U.S., see Moskin 2005, 848.

analysis in the light of abstract assessment factors,[1929] permits the unauthorized use of copyrighted material for purposes 'such as criticism, comment, news reporting, teaching […], scholarship, or research'.[1930] As a guiding principle, the notion of transformative use has evolved in U.S. court decisions (section 3.1). The transformative nature of allegedly infringing use constitutes an important factor capable of tipping the scales to a finding of fair use, for example, in parody cases.[1931] In the light of this established case law, the direct reference to 'identifying and parodying' in the trademark provision can be regarded as an additional link with the copyright doctrine. If a cultural creation enjoys cumulative copyright and trademark protection, the network of fair use provisions in U.S. law, thus, seems capable of ensuring that the freedom of transformative use – breathing space for cultural follow-on innovation – offered in copyright law can also prevail under applicable trademark standards.[1932] As explained, EU copyright and trademark law do not provide for a comparable network of corresponding use privileges. Hence, the question arises whether other principles of horizontal applicability could fill the gap in the EU.

9.2.2.2 Rule of Universal, Direct Application

In the absence of a well-functioning network of corresponding use privileges in copyright and trademark law, it is necessary to explore alternative legal mechanisms that could lead to an obligation to lend weight to copyright provisions that support artistic remix and reuse in a trademark context. In literature, David Lange outlined the following strategy for universalizing copyright limitations:

> Consider copyright's fair use doctrine. Under the proposal I have advanced here, that doctrine should now be seen as an affirmative aspect of the public domain at large, rather than as a mere affirmative defense to an allegation of copyright infringement. So viewed, fair use would not be limited in the protection it confers merely to those instances in which copyright infringement is alleged. It would extend as well, and as fully, to species of infringement recognized under other doctrines, including

1929. Cf. U.S. Supreme Court, 17 January 1984, Sony Corporation of America/Universal City Studios, Inc., 464 U.S. 417 (1984), section IV.B. As to the application of the fair use doctrine in practice, see Sag 2012, 47; Samuelson 2009, 2537; Beebe 2008, 156; Leval 1990, 1105; Litman 1997, 588. For critical comments on the predictability and consistency of U.S. fair use decisions, see Nimmer 2003, 263; Förster 2008, 197-201.
1930. Section 107 U.S. Copyright Act. As to the open-ended nature of the list of privileged purposes, see Seltzer 1978, 19-20.
1931. Cf. U.S. Supreme Court, 7 March 1994, Campbell/Acuff-Rose, 510 U.S. 569, 579 (1994); Sag 2012, 55-58, 76-77, 79-81; Beebe 2008, 603-606.
1932. Cf. the examples given by Ginsburg 2018b, 248-252 and 269-270.

the right of publicity, trademarks, misappropriation in unfair competition, trade secrets, ideas, and even patent.[1933]

To ensure the applicability of limitations for transformative use across different domains of intellectual property protection (and beyond), Lange thus seeks to redefine relevant copyright provisions, such as the U.S. fair use doctrine (see the description in section 3.1), as manifestations of a horizontal public domain principle to be observed in all branches of intellectual property. In a nutshell, Lange's approach would make it possible to detach copyright limitations from the copyright context in which they evolved, and let them prevail in other environments, such as trademark law, as well. However, Lange himself concedes that an 'agenda of this sort would require years to realize'.[1934] While the proposed elevated form of public domain recognition is fascinating, Lange's pessimism with regard to its practical implementation does not come as a surprise. The proposal is based on a fundamental status change. First, it would be necessary to recognize the public domain as a legal position capable of outperforming the interest in protecting intellectual property rights. Second, it would be necessary to derive, from this elevated legal status of the public domain, the further rule that a robust defence to infringement claims, such as a well-established fair use doctrine, constitutes a universal use privilege that can function as a horizontal shield against infringement claims across different domains of intellectual property law, including trademark law.

As discussed above, the first step – the recognition of the public domain as a protected legal position and element of *ordre public* – is already controversial. Court decisions on both sides of the Atlantic have led to mixed results. Clear positions in favour of a strong legal status of the public domain are scarce (section 9.1.2.4). The second step – the direct, horizontal application of use privileges in copyright law as universal manifestations of public domain preservation – would be an even more ambitious step. It would imply that certain elements of the existing canon of intellectual property norms – setting limits to protection and creating areas of freedom – serve the overarching purpose of public domain preservation and are applicable universally for this reason. Obviously, this additional step goes beyond the mere recognition of the public domain within an individual intellectual property system. It would culminate in the redefinition of copyright limitations, such as the right of quotation and the exemption of parody, as superior public domain norms with repercussions on other protection regimes, such as trademark law.[1935]

Undoubtedly, Lange's rule of universal, direct application of use privileges for artistic remix and reuse would minimize the risk of an erosion

1933. Lange 2003, 478-479.

1934. Lange 2003, 479.

1935. As to the recognition of copyright limitations, such as the right of quotation, as user rights in the context of copyright law, see CJEU, 29 July 2019, case C-516/17, Spiegel

of relevant copyright limitations when it comes to overlapping copyright and trademark protection. It would ensure that the same user freedoms that are available in copyright law can directly be invoked in trademark law as well. Given the described steps of public domain recognition to be taken, however, this solution is a long shot.[1936] It would require not only the recognition of the public domain as a protected legal position but also the recognition of copyright limitations for transformative use as universal, superior manifestations of the public domain that prevail over infringement claims not only in copyright law but also in trademark law. While Lange's proposal of universal, direct application may be the most satisfactory solution in the absence of congruent use privileges in copyright and trademark law, the substantial legal-doctrinal hurdles to be surmounted make it necessary to also explore alternative, less radical (and potentially even equally effective) solutions. The option to declare copyright limitations, such as the right of quotation and the exemption of parody, applicable by analogy in trademark cases involving the remix and reuse of trademarked cultural signs appears as such a promising alternative solution that should be taken into consideration.

9.2.2.3 Rule of Analogous Application

The starting point for a discussion of analogous application is the same as in the case of a rule of universal, direct application of use privileges: in the absence of a network of congruent limitations of exclusive rights in copyright and trademark law, it is indispensable to survey legal mechanisms that may allow the horizontal application of limitations for creative remix and reuse in both copyright and trademark law.[1937] If a rule of universal, direct application is beyond reach because of the legal-doctrinal obstacles described in the preceding section, it makes sense to examine whether similar results could be achieved by permitting – or even requiring – the application of pertinent copyright limitations by analogy in trademark law. As Bernt Hugenholtz has pointed out, each protection regime in the field of intellectual property reflects a specific balance between the grant of exclusive rights and limitations that offer room for unauthorized use supporting countervailing values, such as freedom of expression and freedom of competition. When protection overlaps arise, it should be possible, according to Hugenholtz, to safeguard the public interest underlying limitations of exclusive rights even if the legislator has not explicitly provided for corresponding legal instruments in all protection regimes involved. Depending on the rationale of the

Online, para. 54; CJEU, 29 July 2019, case C-469/17, Funke Medien NRW, para. 70. For a more detailed discussion of this point, see Aplin/Bently 2020, 75-84; Geiger/Izyumenko 2020, 292-298.

1936. Cf. Peukert 2019, 1195. As to the lack of a coherent and sufficiently potent underpinning of the public domain principle, see Peukert 2019, 1189-1190 and 1198; Boyle 2003b, 53 and 69; Boyle 1997, 115.

1937. Cf. Dinwoodie 2020, 35-36; Vaver 2011, 38.

limitation at issue, this goal could be achieved by applying limitations by analogy – *a fortiori* when fundamental rights are at stake.[1938]

Without establishing a general rule of analogous application, the CJEU adopted this approach in *Dior/Evora*. The case concerned the advertising of parallel imports of Dior perfumes sold in Kruidvat drugstores owned by Evora. Given the presentation of the luxury perfumes in regular Kruidvat advertising brochures, Dior was concerned about potential negative effects on its prestigious brand image. It asserted cumulative copyright and trademark protection relating to the perfume packaging and bottles to stop the advertising and shield its exclusive distribution network of official Dior dealers. Seeking to safeguard freedom of competition, the CJEU underlined the need to reconcile the fundamental interest in the protection of trademark rights with the fundamental interest in the free movement of goods within the internal market.[1939] Weighing these fundamental interests, the Court arrived at the conclusion that the trademark proprietor was not entitled to oppose the use of the trademark by a reseller who habitually marketed articles of the same kind, but not necessarily of the same quality, as long as the reseller used ways of advertising that were customary in his sector of trade. A reseller was free to use the trademark in advertising to inform the public about the further commercialization of branded goods, unless it was established that, given specific circumstances, the use for this purpose seriously damaged the reputation of the mark.[1940]

As Dior had also relied on copyright protection, the case posed the additional question whether the fundamental interest in free competition would prevail in copyright law as well. In this respect, the CJEU contented itself with a reference to earlier case law, according to which an exhausted copyright could not be invoked to prevent or restrict the importation of protected works which had been lawfully marketed in another EU Member State.[1941] The Court held that the protection conferred by copyright as regards the reproduction of protected works in a reseller's advertising may not, in any event, be broader than that which was conferred on a trademark owner in the same circumstances.[1942] Hence, the Court limited copyright protection in the same way as it had limited trademark protection. Holding that the copyright claim could not be stronger than the trademark claim, the CJEU de facto aligned the limits of copyright protection with the limits of trademark protection.

This 1997 *Dior/Evora* decision predated the adoption of a catalogue of permissible copyright limitations in Article 5 ISD which occurred in 2001.

1938. Hugenholtz 2000b, 242.
1939. CJEU, 4 November 1997, case C-337/95, Dior/Evora, paras 42-44.
1940. CJEU, *ibid.*, para. 48 and 54.
1941. CJEU, 20 January 1981, joined cases 55/80 and 57/80, Musik-Vertrieb Membran GmbH/GEMA, para. 15.
1942. CJEU, 4 November 1997, case C-337/95, Dior/Evora, para. 58.

Against this background, it does not come as a surprise that the CJEU did not embark on a more detailed discussion of room for the limitation of exclusive rights within the copyright system. The Supreme Court of the Netherlands, by contrast, took the *Dior/Evora* case as a starting point to open up the closed catalogue of exceptions in the Dutch Copyright Act and pave the way for more flexibility that would allow the adequate balancing of the fundamental interests at stake.[1943] In the national *Dior/Evora* decision that preceded the described CJEU judgment,[1944] the Supreme Court of the Netherlands identified the following room for the creation of additional breathing space within the Dutch system of copyright limitations:

> In § 6 of Chapter 1 of the Dutch Copyright Act, several exceptions to copyright are enumerated which, as a general rule, are based on a balancing of the interests of copyright owners against social or economic interests of third parties or against the public interest. However, these explicit exceptions do not exclude the possibility that the limits of copyright must also be determined more closely in other cases on the basis of a comparable balancing of interests, in particular when the lawmaker was not aware of the need for the limitation concerned and the latter fits in the system of the law – this in the light of the development of copyright as a means of protecting commercial interests. For the required balancing of interests, one or more of the exceptions enumerated in the law can be used as a reference point.[1945]

Recalling that the copyright on Dior packaging and bottles was exhausted after the first sale of perfume under Dior's control, the Supreme Court of the Netherlands expressed the view that Dior's interest in copyright as a weapon against further reproduction and distribution in the context of advertising did not have much weight.[1946] The Court drew a parallel between this situation and the exception in Article 23 of the Dutch Copyright Act which allows the owner of a work of (applied) art to include the work in a catalogue necessary for a public exhibition or sale. Considering the preference given to the interest in the unauthorized inclusion of an artistic work in an exhibition or sale catalogue, the Court concluded that in principle, Evora's interest in the advertising of the resale of Dior perfume in the Netherlands also had to prevail. However, Evora had to observe Dior's moral rights. Moreover, the advertising of parallel imports would be unacceptable if it took place under circumstances that could be detrimental to the copyright owner.

1943. With regard to the general need for enhanced flexibility, cf. Geiger 2008a, 178.
1944. ECJ, 4 November 1997, case C-337/95, Dior/Evora, available at www.curia.eu.
1945. Supreme Court of the Netherlands, 20 October 1995, *NJ* 1996, no. 682, Dior/Evora, para. 3.6.2 (translation by the author).
1946. Supreme Court of the Netherlands, *ibid.*, para. 3.6.2.

Harm could flow, for instance, from the way in which Evora advertised the sale of Dior products.[1947]

On the basis of national copyright rules, the Dutch Supreme Court thus arrived at a solution that corresponded with the later decision of the CJEU. In the Netherlands, the decision was predominantly understood as a step to open up the closed catalogue of specific exceptions in the Dutch Copyright Act, as in force at that time.[1948] Several commentators placed the decision in the context of the open-ended fair use doctrine in the U.S.[1949] Instead of relying on abstract factors as guidelines for the identification of a fair use, the Supreme Court of the Netherlands acknowledged that there was a possibility of using existing exceptions in the Dutch Copyright Act as a model for the creation of new exceptions. On the basis of a comparable balancing of interests, gaps in the limitation infrastructure could be filled as long as the envisaged new use privilege was in line with the Dutch system of copyright limitations.[1950] Because of the use of an existing exception as a model provision for a new use privilege, Herman Cohen Jehoram saw the *Dior/Evora* decision of the Dutch Supreme Court as an example of the application of legal norms by analogy. He expressed the view that such an analogous application of the law 'was always permitted' – even in the case of an exception to copyright.[1951]

Obviously, the approach in the described *Dior/Evora* decisions is different: the CJEU developed a solution that may be qualified as a 'true', cross-cutting analogy. After concluding that the allegedly infringing use did not amount to trademark infringement, the CJEU stated that the outcome could not be different in copyright law. Hence, the Court automatically converted the protection limit identified in trademark law into a limit of copyright protection. In consequence, the decision led to a full congruence of copyright and trademark limitations with regard to the use at issue. The Dutch Supreme Court, by contrast, sought to create room for the allegedly infringing use by applying existing copyright limitations by analogy.[1952] Hence, the Dutch Supreme Court did not impose a limitation on copyright owners that had come to the fore in a trademark context. Instead, it used a rule of internal analogous application of copyright limitations. This solution stays within the existing canon of copyright rules and enhances the chances of corresponding results by adding flexibility to the existing system of copyright limitations.

1947. Supreme Court of the Netherlands, *ibid.*, para. 3.6.2.
1948. Cf. Grosheide 1996, 43.
1949. See Section 107 of the U.S. Copyright Act and the case comments by J.H. Spoor, *NJ* 1996, no. 682, para. 2; P. Steinhauser, *BIE* 1998, p. 195 (212).
1950. Supreme Court of the Netherlands, 20 October 1995, *NJ* 1996, no. 682, Dior/Evora, para. 3.6.2.
1951. See the case comment by H. Cohen Jehoram, *AA* 46 (1997), p. 640 (644).
1952. For the discussion of a similar, 'internal' copyright solution developed by the German Federal Court of Justice, see Derclaye/Leistner 2011, 245-246.

The forms of analogous application are thus markedly different. Following in the footsteps of the Dutch Supreme Court, the establishment of a corresponding use privilege in another domain of intellectual property depends on whether this intellectual property domain provides for limitations that are broad enough to create the same breathing space. In this context, the application of limitations by analogy serves as a tool to widen the spectrum of privileged uses that are available for realizing this objective. The approach adopted by the CJEU, by contrast, does not depend on the existing canon of limitations of exclusive rights in a given intellectual property regime. The CJEU simply posited that, in the *Dior/Evora* scenario, it was necessary to set the same limits to copyright and trademark protection.

To attain the goal of congruent use privileges for artistic remix and reuse in copyright and trademark law, the latter approach is preferable. As it allows the importation of limitations of protection stemming from one protection regime into another protection system by analogy, it makes it possible to ensure that cumulative trademark protection does not erode copyright limitations, such as the right of quotation and the exemption of parody. Following the rule of cross-cutting analogy which the CJEU adopted in *Dior/Evora*, the right of quotation and the exemption of parody known from copyright law can be applied – in analogous form – as a defence against a trademark infringement claim. As Hugenholtz rightly points out, the application by analogy depends on the rationale underlying the limitations at issue.[1953] In light of the societal importance of room for cultural follow-on innovation (section 3.3) and the strong freedom of expression underpinning of copyright limitations supporting transformative use (section 3.1),[1954] this precondition does not pose much difficulty in cases concerning trademarked cultural signs. There can be little doubt that a rule of analogous application is not a mere option but a necessity when trademark rights to cultural signs are asserted against artistic remix and reuse of protected signs in the cultural domain.

The rule of cross-cutting analogy, however, has not become established case law in CJEU jurisprudence yet. In *Ford Motor Company*, the car manufacturer Ford brought a lawsuit against Wheeltrims, a supplier of replacement parts for various motor vehicles, including Ford cars. Wheeltrims marketed wheel covers showing a faithful reproduction of the Ford trademark without authorization.[1955] Seeking to defend its unauthorized use of the Ford trademark, Wheeltrims invoked the 'repair clause'[1956] in EU industrial designs law which permits the use of a protected design for the

1953. Hugenholtz 2000b, 242.
1954. Cf. CJEU, 1 December 2011, case C-145/10, Painer, para. 132-134; CJEU, 3 September 2014, case C-201/13, Deckmyn, paras 25-27.
1955. CJEU, 6 October 2015, case C-500/14, *Ford Motor Company*, paras 21-22.
1956. Article 14 DD and Article 110 CDR.

purpose of repairing a complex product and restoring its original appearance.[1957] The crucial question, therefore, was whether the repair clause known from industrial designs law could serve as a cross-cutting defence capable of shielding Wheeltrims not only against a finding of industrial design infringement but also against Ford's trademark rights. Raising this issue in its prejudicial questions, the Turin District Court wondered whether the repair clause involved only a derogation from the protection afforded to a design and not from any other industrial property right, particularly a registered trademark. The Turin Court also outlined an alternative approach, according to which the repair clause constituted a general clause applicable across all domains of industrial property law. The Turin District Court indicated that such a broad understanding may be necessary to enable a manufacturer of replacement parts to operate on the market on an equal footing with the original producer – irrespective of the type of protection invoked by the latter. Evidently, a repair clause capable of shielding Wheeltrims against industrial design and trademark rights alike would allow the reproduction of the original part with all its aesthetic and functional features, including elements enjoying trademark protection.[1958]

In the context of discussing different rules of analogous interpretation, the decision in *Ford Motor Company* is of particular importance because the CJEU, in this case, refrained from confirming the cross-cutting approach taken earlier in *Dior/Evora*. The Court was reluctant to hold that Ford's trademark rights could not have a broader scope than industrial design rights and that, accordingly, the same limits – in this case the repair clause – had to be observed not only in industrial designs law but also in trademark law. Instead, the CJEU pointed out that the repair clause imposed certain limitations 'only on protection as designs, without any reference to protection as trade marks'.[1959] The Court also emphasized that the repair clause in EU industrial designs law did not contain any derogation from the provisions in harmonized EU trademark law.[1960]

As to the underlying objective of undistorted competition, the CJEU was satisfied that EU legislation in the field of trademark law already took this concern into account by providing for certain limitations of exclusive rights that prevented impediments of the free movement of goods and services while, at the same time, allowing trademarks to fulfil their essential role in a system of undistorted competition.[1961] The provisions on exclusive rights and limitations in EU trademark law had the effect of a complete harmonization of the scope of trademark protection which left no room for

1957. CJEU, *ibid.*, para. 24.
1958. CJEU, *ibid.*, paras 27-28.
1959. CJEU, *ibid.*, para. 39.
1960. CJEU, *ibid.*, para. 42.
1961. CJEU, *ibid.*, para. 43. See the provisions in Article 14 EUTMR and Article 14 TMD. Cf. CJEU, 23 February 1999, case C-63/97, BMW/Deenik, para. 62; CJEU, 17 March 2005, case C-228/03, Gillette/LA-Laboratories, para. 29.

the importation of additional limitations from other fields of intellectual property, such as EU industrial designs law.[1962] Wheeltrims was thus prevented from relying on the repair clause stemming from EU industrial designs law as a defence against the trademark rights which Ford had asserted. As a rule of industrial designs law, the repair clause did not provide a basis for Wheeltrims to make unauthorized use of the Ford trademark to restore the original appearance of Ford cars.[1963]

On balance, a survey of CJEU case law, thus, yields mixed results. While the Court adopted a cross-cutting approach and aligned the limits of copyright protection with those of trademark protection in *Dior/Evora*,[1964] it did not follow the same approach in *Ford Motor Company*. Instead, the CJEU declared the repair clause known from industrial designs law inapplicable in trademark law. As EU trademark law contained a complete and closed system of exclusive rights and limitations, the Court saw no room in *Ford Motor Company* for the analogous application of the repair privilege stemming from industrial designs law.[1965] Seeking to explain the difference between the *Dior/Evora* decision and the outcome of *Ford Motor Company*, two factors seem important. First, the *Dior/Evora* case concerned a situation where both trademark rights and copyright had been exhausted. The CJEU could thus rely on the exhaustion principle as common ground – in the sense of a principle to be observed in both copyright and trademark law[1966] – for establishing corresponding rules on advertising that sought to bring the further commercialization of genuine products to the attention of the public. Second, the 1997 *Dior/Evora* decision predated the adoption of a closed list of permissible copyright limitations in the 2001 Information Society Directive.[1967] Hence, the Court was not bound by a set of harmonized rules that could be understood as a complete and closed system of copyright limitations.

Against this background, the more recent decision in *Ford Motor Company* reflects the Court's preference for staying within a particular regime of intellectual property protection – at least when the legislator has taken account of the general objective underlying the use privilege at stake. As harmonized EU trademark law contains provisions that seek to reconcile trademark protection with the need to ensure the free movement of goods and services, the CJEU saw no room to add the repair clause as a further measure to ensure undistorted competition.[1968] With regard to potential interferences with cultural follow-on innovation, this status quo of CJEU jurisprudence is

---

1962. CJEU, 6 October 2015, case C-500/14, *Ford Motor Company*, para. 44.
1963. CJEU, *ibid.*, para. 45.
1964. CJEU, 4 November 1997, case C-337/95, Dior/Evora, para. 58.
1965. CJEU, 6 October 2015, case C-500/14, *Ford Motor Company*, paras 43-44.
1966. CJEU, 4 November 1997, case C-337/95, Dior/Evora, paras 54-57.
1967. See the enumeration of permissible limitation prototypes in Article 5 ISD.
1968. CJEU, 6 October 2015, case C-500/14, *Ford Motor Company*, paras 43-44.

worrisome.[1969] As pointed out above (section 6.2.4), Recital 27 TMD and Recital 21 EUTMR stipulate that unauthorized use of a trademark for the purpose of artistic expression should be considered fair as long as it is in accordance with honest practices in industrial and commercial matters. Furthermore, these provisions make it clear that EU trademark law 'should be applied in a way that ensures full respect for fundamental rights and freedoms, and in particular the freedom of expression'. Following in the footsteps of *Ford Motor Company*, the CJEU could thus be tempted to refrain from any analogous application of use privileges stemming from other intellectual property regimes, such as the right of quotation and the exemption of parody known from copyright law, by arguing that the EU trademark legislator has factored into the equation the need to reconcile trademark protection with artistic freedom of expression when adopting the current EU trademark legislation.

Accordingly, room for artistic remix and reuse would have to be found within the framework of existing EU trademark legislation – understood as a complete and closed regulation of exclusive trademark rights and limitations. The breathing space for artistic remix and reuse, however, could not be enhanced by applying use privileges stemming from copyright law by analogy. In light of Recital 27 TMD and Recital 21 EUTMR, the CJEU could arrive at the conclusion that a gap in the regulation of EU trademark protection – offering room for the application of copyright norms by analogy – is missing. A closer look at the Court's line of reasoning in *Ford Motor Company* reveals that this risk of categorically excluding any analogy is quite high. Drawing the conclusion that EU trademark law provided a complete and closed system of exclusive rights and limitations,[1970] the CJEU referred back to earlier case law, in particular its decision in *Martin Y Paz Diffusion*, where it had already made the same point.[1971]

The assumption of a complete and closed system of trademark rights and limitations is highly doubtful. In *Martin Y Paz Diffusion*, this mantra of complete harmonization already precluded the application of national doctrines reflecting general principles of fairness and equity, such as abuse of right and the prohibition of unfair competition, even though alternative legal mechanisms are sought in vain at EU level.[1972] The assumption of a complete and closed system of exclusive trademark rights and limitations may also pose an obstacle to the analogous application of use privileges for transformative use, such as the copyright rules concerning quotations and parody. Nonetheless, the fact remains that, instead of confirming the cross-cutting approach taken in *Dior/Evora*, more recent CJEU jurisprudence, such as the

1969. Cf. Dinwoodie 2020, 35, who recommends approaches 'making defences portable'.
1970. CJEU, *ibid.*, para. 44.
1971. CJEU, 19 September 2013, case C-661/11, *Martin Y Paz Diffusion*, paras 54-55.
1972. For a more detailed explanation of this critique, see Senftleben 2016, 350-357; Kur 2014, 450-453.

decision in *Ford Motor Company*, supports the problematic mantra of complete harmonization and a closed system of trademark rights and limitations.[1973]

In sum, the analysis confirms that a rule of analogous application of copyright limitations, such as the right of quotation and the exemption of parody, could prevent trademark rights to cultural signs from stifling breathing space for artistic remix and reuse that would be available in the absence of trademark rights. Following the guidelines provided by Bernt Hugenholtz, such a rule of analogous application could be based on the strong rationales underlying relevant use privileges, in particular the objective to support freedom of expression and the need to safeguard important societal functions of cultural follow-on innovation. While the CJEU decision in *Dior/Evora* offers a promising starting point for the establishment of a rule of analogous application of use privileges across copyright and trademark law, more recent CJEU jurisprudence points in the opposite direction, precluding the application of copyright limitations by analogy on the ground that EU trademark law sets forth a complete and closed system of trademark rights and limitations.

To arrive at a satisfactory solution on the basis of a rule of analogous application, the CJEU would thus have to change course and create room for the application of use privileges known from copyright law by analogy. Instead of repeating the mantra of complete harmonization, the Court would have to establish that, in respect of unauthorized use of trademarked cultural signs for the purposes of artistic remix and reuse, EU trademark law is incomplete and has gaps to be filled with the transformative use provisions laid down in copyright law. Until this turnaround occurs, recourse to higher-ranking, constitutional norms seems the only remaining option to minimize the risk of an erosion of copyright limitations when overlapping trademark rights offer an alternative basis for infringement claims against transformative use in the cultural domain.

9.2.2.4 Freedom of Expression as Horizontal Defence

As indicated in the preceding section (see also section 6.2.4), EU trademark law offers a solid starting point for reliance on the constitutional guarantee of freedom of expression as a compass for the interpretation of trademark provisions. In line with Recital 27 TMD and Recital 21 EUTMR, EU trademark law 'should be applied in a way that ensures full respect for fundamental rights and freedoms, and in particular the freedom of expression'. Rightly understood, this reference to freedom of expression as an overarching norm impacts the application of each and every rule and

---

1973. CJEU, 6 October 2015, case C-500/14, *Ford Motor Company*, para. 44; CJEU, 19 September 2013, case C-661/11, *Martin Y Paz Diffusion*, para. 55.

principle in EU trademark law (see the discussion in section 9.2.1.7).[1974] Prior to the codification in Recital 27 TMD and Recital 21 EUTMR, the need to strike a balance between trademark protection and freedom of expression already had become a recurring theme in opinions of Advocates General at EU level.[1975] In *Google France and Google*, AG Miguel Poiares Maduro underlined the importance of appropriate counterbalances in the light of brand value protection:

> Nevertheless, whatever the protection afforded to innovation and investment, it is never absolute. It must always be balanced against other interests, in the same way as trade mark protection itself is balanced against them. I believe that the present cases call for such a balance as regards freedom of expression and freedom of commerce.[1976]

Similarly, AG Niilo Jääskinen urged the CJEU in his opinion in *L'Oréal/eBay* not to forget:

> that the listings uploaded by users to eBay's marketplace are communications protected by the fundamental rights of freedom of expression and information provided by Article 11 of [the] Charter of Fundamental Rights of the EU and Article 10 of the European Convention on Human Rights.[1977]

In the area of copyright, a corresponding obligation to safeguard freedom of expression has been recognized in case law. In *Ashby Donald/France*, the ECtHR held that even if the online dissemination of literary and artistic works (in this case fashion photographs) amounts to copyright infringement, it may still be necessary in the light of freedom of expression to offer room for sharing information and refrain from prohibiting the communication to the public.[1978] As Christophe Geiger points out, the decision demonstrates that:

> even in a situation in which there has been clear copyright infringement, it is always necessary to evaluate whether the resulting restriction to freedom of expression is 'necessary in a democratic society' so as to strike a fair balance between the different rights at issue... The [ECtHR] thus made it clear that intellectual property rights must be interpreted as exceptions to freedom of expression and that, given the great importance of that freedom within the framework of a democratic

1974. Schovsbo 2018, 568.
1975. Senftleben 2013b, 157-158.
1976. AG Poiares Maduro, Opinion of 22 September 2009, cases C-236/08-238/08, Google France and Google, para. 102. Cf. Senftleben/Bently/Dinwoodie et al. 2015, 338.
1977. AG Jääskinen, Opinion of 9 December 2010, case C-324/09, L'Oréal/eBay, para. 49.
1978. ECtHR, 10 January 2013, app. no. 36769/08, Ashby Donald/France, para. 38; ECtHR, 19 February 2013, app. no. 40397/12, Neij and Sunde Kolmisoppi/Sweden ('Pirate Bay'), section A. Cf. Geiger/Izyumenko 2014, 316.

society, judges need to be very careful indeed in the presence of a restriction, particularly when it comes to political and artistic speech.[1979]

With regard to use privileges supporting transformative use of protected source material, the CJEU already recognized in this vein that it was indispensable to ensure the effectiveness of statutory copyright limitations, such as the right of quotation and the exemption of parody,[1980] as vehicles to maintain a 'fair balance' between the rights of copyright holders and the rights of users relying on freedom of expression.[1981] In *Funke Medien* and *Spiegel Online*, the CJEU explicitly confirmed the status of user rights by pointing out that 'although Article 5 [ISD] is expressly entitled "Exceptions and limitations", it should be noted that those exceptions or limitations do themselves confer rights on the users of works or of other subject matter'.[1982] The crucial question, however, is whether the CJEU is also willing to invoke the fundamental guarantee of freedom of expression as an overarching, *external* limitation of copyright – a limitation outside EU copyright legislation that is capable of justifying unauthorized use and preventing the verdict of infringement even when no statutory defence for remix activities, such as the quotation or parody argument, is applicable within the copyright system.[1983] The ECtHR decision in *Ashby Donald/France* clearly points in the direction of this external effect of the constitutional guarantee of freedom of expression and its application to override findings of infringement in copyright law.[1984]

In the discussion about horizontal safeguards of remix and reuse activities that can serve as universal shields against infringement claims in copyright and trademark law, it is of particular importance to explore this external limitation effect: the invocation of freedom of expression as an alternative avenue to arrive at a use privilege that is not reflected in copyright and trademark legislation itself. If the constitutional guarantee of freedom of expression can prevail over a finding of infringement and set external limits to copyright, it can have the same limiting effect in the realm of trademark

---

1979. Geiger 2018a, 11-12. Cf. Geiger 2004b, 268.

1980. Article 5(3)(d) and (k) ISD.

1981. CJEU, 1 December 2011, case C-145/10, Painer, para. 132-134; CJEU, 3 September 2014, case C-201/13, Deckmyn, paras 25-27. Cf. Jongsma 2019, 126-135.

1982. CJEU, 29 July 2019, case C-516/17, Spiegel Online, para. 54; CJEU, 29 July 2019, case C-469/17, Funke Medien NRW, para. 70. For a more detailed discussion of this point, see Aplin/Bently 2020, 75-84; Geiger/Izyumenko 2020, 292-298.

1983. As to the debate on this question, see Geiger/Izyumenko 2019, 131; Schovsbo 2018, 571-573; Voorhoof 2002, 639-645; Dreier 2001a, 295.

1984. ECtHR, 10 January 2013, app. no. 36769/08, Ashby Donald/France, para. 38. For a confirmation of this understanding and impact of the decision at the national level, see Dutch Supreme Court, 3 April 2015, case ECLI:NL:HR:2015:841, GeenStijl Media/Sanoma, *NJ* 2015, no. 183, para. 5.2.5. Cf. Geiger 2018a, 11-12; Schovsbo 2018, 560-561.

law due to its higher rank in the norm hierarchy.[1985] As an external balancing tool, it can ensure that the same breathing space for artistic remix remains available when copyright and trademark protection overlap, and limitations of protection do not have the same scope in the two domains of intellectual property.

National case law offers several examples of copyright and trademark decisions in which courts employed freedom of expression as a means to broaden or go beyond the statutory set of limitations of protection. In the field of copyright, the decisions of the German Federal Constitutional Court in *Metall auf Metall* (section 6.3)[1986] and *Germania 3* (section 3.1)[1987] fall in this category. In both cases, the Court overruled previous findings of infringement and stated that at least when the economic harm flowing from an artistic remix activity could not be perceived as significant, freedom of expression had to prevail over the right holder's interest in the exploitation of protected source material.[1988] An even clearer example of the creation of breathing space outside the internal copyright limitation infrastructure can be found in the Netherlands. The right of quotation, as delineated in Article 15a of the Dutch Copyright Act, only permits the unauthorized use of sources that have already been lawfully made available to the public.[1989] Nonetheless, the Court of Appeal of The Hague ruled in favour of the journalist Karin Spaink in *Scientology/Spaink*. On an XS4All webpage, Spaink had posted parts of the so-called Fishman Affidavit – a semi-secret written declaration that had been submitted in other court proceedings initiated by Scientology against Steven Fishman. Spaink used quotations from confidential parts of the Fishman Affidavit reflecting the teachings and organization of Scientology to undergird her critique of Scientology.[1990] As the document had never been published lawfully, the statutory right of quotation was unavailable as a defence.[1991] However, Spaink successfully argued for direct application of the fundamental guarantee of freedom of expression and information in Article 10 ECHR. The Court of Appeal of The Hague agreed that the quotations contributed to a legitimate form of criticizing Scientology's questionable ideas and behaviour. In the opinion of the Court, Spaink's use

1985. Cf. Derclaye/Leistner 2011, 320; Geiger 2004b, 268.

1986. German Federal Constitutional Court, 31 May 2016, case 1 BvR 1585/13, 'Sampling', para. 100.

1987. German Federal Constitutional Court, 29 June 2000, case 1 BvR 825/98, 'Germania 3', *Zeitschrift für Urheber- und Medienrecht* 2000, 868 (869).

1988. German Federal Constitutional Court, 31 May 2016, case 1 BvR 1585/13, 'Sampling', para. 101-107; German Federal Constitutional Court, 29 June 2000, case 1 BvR 825/98, 'Germania 3', *Zeitschrift für Urheber- und Medienrecht* 2000, 868 (869).

1989. For a more detailed discussion of the conceptual contours of the Dutch regulation of quotations, see Senftleben 2012a, 359. The requirement of lawful prior publication can also be found at the international level. See Article 10(1) BC.

1990. Court of Appeal of The Hague, 4 September 2003, case 99/1040, ECLI:NL:GHSGR :2003:AI5638, Scientology/Spaink, *AMI* 2003, 217, para. 2.

1991. Court of Appeal of The Hague, *ibid.*, para. 7.11.

of the documents did not amount to copyright infringement against this background.[1992]

The decision of the French Supreme Court in *Klasen/Malka* confirms the impact of freedom of expression on the assessment of copyright infringement. This case concerned the inclusion of three photographs taken from an Italian fashion magazine in paintings. The photographs showed the face of a young model. The appropriation artist, Peter Klasen, had reproduced the photographs in blue to create a contrast with the original works.[1993] Using the photographs as symbols of consumerism, he sought to provoke reflection on excessive consumption.[1994] As statutory copyright limitations, such as the right of quotation and the exemption of parody, were declared inapplicable,[1995] Klasen finally had recourse to the guarantee of freedom of expression in Article 10 ECHR.[1996] The French Supreme Court agreed that this external defence argument – outside the canon of use privileges laid down in French copyright legislation itself – was valid. Rejecting the view that a second author's freedom of artistic expression could not constitute a higher-ranking interest capable of trumping the copyright of the author of the original work,[1997] the French Supreme Court made it clear that the case required the establishment of a fair balance between the competing property and free expression rights at issue. The invocation of artistic freedom of expression could not be dismissed without 'explaining in a concrete manner' why the quest for a right equilibrium culminated in a finding of infringement in the specific case.[1998]

As to the process of weighing copyright protection against artistic freedom of expression, another supreme court decision is of particular interest which arose from a similar fact pattern: the integration of a photograph (showing the alleged murderer of Olof Palme) in a painting. In *Swedish Scapegoats*, the Supreme Court of Sweden discussed whether the derivative work was characterized by the second author's individuality and possessed such a degree of originality that there was a new creation with independent copyright protection.[1999] The Court deemed it decisive whether the original work used as a model had been transformed to such an extent

1992. Court of Appeal of The Hague, *ibid.*, para. 8.2 and 13. Cf. Senftleben 2012a, 372-373.
1993. French Supreme Court, 15 May 2015, case 13-27391, ECLI:FR:CCASS:2015:C100 519, Klasen/Malka. Cf. Geiger 2018a, 6.
1994. French Supreme Court, *ibid.* Cf. Geiger 2018a, 7.
1995. Court of Appeals of Paris, 18 September 2013, Pole 5, 1st Chamber, case 12/02480, Klasen/Malka.
1996. Cf. Geiger, *ibid.*, 7-8.
1997. Court of Appeals of Paris, *ibid.*
1998. French Supreme Court, *ibid*: 'Qu'en se déterminant ainsi, sans expliquer de façon concrète en quoi la recherche d'un juste équilibre entre les droits en présence commandait la condamnation qu'elle prononçait, la cour d'appel a privé sa décision de base légale au regard du texte susvisé.'
1999. Supreme Court of Sweden, 21 February 2017, case T 1963-15, 'Swedish Scapegoats', *GRUR Int.* 2019, 93, para. 12.

that a new and independent work had been created.[2000] The analysis led to the result that – despite copying from a pre-existing photographic work – the painting at issue did not amount to copyright infringement:

> Overall, in such a transformation of the photographic work, M[arkus] A[ndersson] has achieved a new and independent work of art that expresses his individuality. Therefore, MA's use of his artwork does not infringe J[onas] L[emberg]'s copyright in the photographic work.[2001]

In the field of trademark law, national courts in the EU applied the open-ended defence of 'due cause'[2002] as a vehicle to offer room for artistic and political freedom of expression.[2003] As explained in section 6.2.1, the German Federal Court of Justice let freedom of art prevail over the trademark owner's interest in the protection of a well-known mark in the *Lila Postkarte* decision. Milka's concerns about harm flowing from an ironic play with its brand insignia did not have sufficient weight to justify inroads into free artistic expression. Instead, the Court found the parody to constitute legitimate use with due cause.[2004] In the light of freedom of expression, the German Federal Court of Justice also permitted the use of the expression 'gene-milk' in connection with products bearing the trademarks MÜLLER, WEIHENSTEPHAN, SACHSENMILCH and LOOSE to make consumers aware of the risks of genetically modified milk in milk products.[2005] The French Supreme Court allowed the use of the trademark ESSO for the purposes of an environmental campaign which Greenpeace had organized to criticize environmental policies of the company on the basis of the trademark caricature 'E$$O' – insinuating that the company was only caring for money but not for the environment.[2006] In the Dutch case *Mercis and Bruna/Punt* (section 6.2.3), the due cause defence served as a safe harbour for biting Miffy parodies. Emphasizing the parodist's humorous and ironical intention, the Court of Appeals of Amsterdam was satisfied that the depiction of Miffy as a 9/11 terrorist could be deemed permissible.[2007]

However, the due cause defence is only available in the area of trademark protection against dilution.[2008] With regard to other types of

2000. Supreme Court of Sweden, *ibid.*, para. 12.
2001. Supreme Court of Sweden, *ibid.*, paras 18-19.
2002. Article 9(2)(c) EUTMR; Article 10(2)(c) TMD.
2003. For an overview, see Kur/Senftleben 2017, para. 5.267 and 6.59– 6.70.
2004. German Federal Court of Justice, 3 February 2005, case I ZR 159/02, 'Lila Postkarte', *GRUR* 2005, 583 (585).
2005. German Federal Court of Justice, 11 March 2008, case VI ZR 7/07, 'Gen-Milch', *NJW* 2008, 2110.
2006. French Supreme Court, 8 April 2008, case 06-10961, Greenpeace/Esso. See also French Supreme Court, 8 April 2008, case 07-11251, Greenpeace/Areva. Cf. Schovsbo 2018, 562-563.
2007. Court of Appeals of Amsterdam, 13 September 2011, case ECLI:NL:GHAMS:2011:BS7825, Mercis and Bruna/Punt, *AMI* 2012, 28, para. 4.19.
2008. Article 9(2)(c) EUTMR and Article 10(2)(c) TMD.

trademark protection in the EU,[2009] a comparable safeguard against encroachments upon artistic remix activities is sought in vain. The limitation infrastructure is wanting (section 6.2.4). In particular, an open-ended balancing tool, such as the defence of 'due cause', is missing in the area of protection against confusion[2010] – despite the extension of the confusion concept to harm flowing from wrong assumptions about affiliation and sponsorship (section 6.2.3). The lack of robust defences in this area makes the integration of free expression values in the infringement analysis difficult, if not impossible. Prior to the 2015 EU trademark law reform, the need for external balancing mechanisms already became apparent in the context of the double identity rule which, nowadays, is laid down in Article 9(2)(a) EUTMR and Article 10(2)(a) TMD. In the comparative advertising case *O2/Hutchison*, the CJEU was unable to find sufficient room for commercial freedom of expression inside trademark law. Therefore, the Court relied on harmonized comparative advertising rules as external balancing instruments:

> Consequently, in order to reconcile the protection of registered marks and the use of comparative advertising, Article 5(1) and (2) of Directive 89/104 and Article 3a(1) of Directive 84/450 must be interpreted to the effect that the proprietor of a registered trade mark is not entitled to prevent the use, by a third party, of a sign identical with, or similar to, his mark, in a comparative advertisement which satisfies all the conditions, laid down in Article 3a(1) of Directive 84/450, under which comparative advertising is permitted.[2011]

The CJEU confirmed this exemption of permissible comparative advertising from trademark infringement claims in *L'Oréal/Bellure*.[2012] In the course of the 2015 law reform, this new limitation made its way into the text of EU trademark legislation.[2013]

With regard to artistic forms of use, the constitutional guarantee of freedom of expression could set a similar process in motion.[2014] As an external impact factor, it could safeguard artistic freedom of expression ad hoc. At the same time, it could play the role of a catalyst which, ultimately,

2009. More specifically, the double identity rule in Article 9(2)(a) EUTMR and Article 10(2)(a) TMD and the anti-confusion protection offered in Article 9(2)(b) EUTMR and Article 10(2)(b) TMD.
2010. Article 9(2)(b) EUTMR; Article 10(2)(b) TMD.
2011. CJEU, 12 June 2008, case C-533/06, O2/Hutchison, para. 45.
2012. CJEU, 18 June 2009, case C-487/07, L'Oréal/Bellure, para. 54.
2013. Articles 9(3)(f) and 14(1)(c) EUTMR; Articles 10(3)(f) and 14(1)(c) TMD. Cf. Kur/Senftleben 2017, para. 6.08 and 6.42-6.54; Knaak/Kur/von Mühlendahl 2011, para. 2.260-2.262.
2014. Cf. Schovsbo 2018, 577-578. As to the elevated status of freedom of artistic expression in the human rights analysis, see Geiger/Izyumenko 2020, 293-294. Cf. ECtHR, 24 May 1988, app. no. 10737/84, Müller and Others/Switzerland, para. 27; ECtHR, 8 July 1999, app. no. 23168/94, Karataş/Turkey, paras 49-52; CJEU, 29 July 2019, case C-476/17, Pelham and Others, para. 34.

leads to the introduction of more specific defences in trademark law, such as a quotation right and a parody rule which unequivocally seek to offer breathing space for use that places pre-existing, protected signs in new contexts. Recital 21 EUTMR and Recital 27 TMD encourage this development. Underlining the obligation to apply the provisions of EU trademark law 'in a way that ensures full respect for fundamental rights and freedoms, and in particular the freedom of expression', they support an approach that recalibrates, interprets and gives meaning to existing trademark norms in the light of freedom of expression.

Quite clearly, however, Recital 21 EUTMR and Recital 27 TMD refer to an approach that aims at the integration of freedom of expression values in the trademark analysis and makes freedom of expression a guiding principle for the *internal* interpretation and application of trademark norms (within trademark law). Recital 21 EUTMR and Recital 27 TMD do not encourage courts to override trademark norms and suppress a finding of infringement in the light of trademark standards where this is necessary to safeguard freedom of expression. The Recitals concern internal balancing (interpretations of trademark norms that support free expression within the trademark system) rather than endorsing external balancing (forcing trademark norms onto the sidelines to allow freedom of expression to prevail).

CJEU jurisprudence addressing the internal/external balancing dichotomy[2015] points in the same direction. In the sound sampling case *Pelham and Others* (see section 6.3 for a description of the underlying facts), the Court was confident that the EU copyright framework laid down in the Information Society Directive offered sufficient flexibility to safeguard a fair balance between the interest of right holders in the protection of copyright and related rights, and the interests and fundamental rights of users of protected subject matter as well as of the public interest.[2016] The Court stated that:

> [t]he mechanisms allowing those different rights and interests to be balanced are contained in Directive 2001/29 itself, in that it provides inter alia, first, in Articles 2 to 4 thereof, rightholders with exclusive rights and, second, in Article 5 thereof, for exceptions and limitations to those rights which may, or even must, be transposed by the Member States ...[2017]

Assuming that the harmonized EU system of rights and limitations constituted a complete and closed universe, the CJEU rejected the national free adaptation rule which had evolved in Germany.[2018] In the national

2015. Cf. Geiger 2006, 371; Voorhoof 2002, 639-640; Dreier 2001a, 295.
2016. CJEU, 29 July 2019, case C-476/17, Pelham and Others, para. 59.
2017. CJEU, *ibid.*, para. 60. Cf. CJEU, 29 July 2019, case C-469/17, Funke Medien NRW, para. 58, where the Court uses the same formula.
2018. CJEU, 29 July 2019, case C-476/17, Pelham and Others, paras 56-57 and 65.

decisions that gave rise to the prejudicial questions in *Pelham and Others*, German courts had applied the traditional domestic copyright rule that a derivative work could be deemed permissible if it had new features of its own that made the individual features of the incorporated source material fade away.[2019] The CJEU, however, saw no basis for this national doctrine within the harmonized EU copyright system. Instead of creating additional breathing space in the light of freedom of expression, it declared the German free adaptation rule incompatible with EU law.[2020] Sound sampling could be deemed permissible only if the remix artist included the sample in her derivative creation 'in a modified form unrecognizable to the ear'.[2021] Quite clearly, the CJEU sought to avoid the application of freedom of expression as an external balancing tool capable of supplementing the norms of EU copyright law with an additional use privilege. As explained in section 9.2.2.3, the trademark decision in *Martin Y Paz Diffusion* also attests to the Court's conviction that harmonized EU systems of intellectual property rights and limitations must be regarded as complete and closed legal frameworks for striking a proper balance – as closed systems that preclude the application of national doctrines reflecting general principles of fairness and equity.[2022]

It remains to be seen whether the Court will depart from this mantra in cases which require a degree of flexibility that is unavailable within the harmonized canon of rights and limitations. In the aforementioned case *Scientology/Spaink*, for instance, the Dutch right of quotation was inapplicable because the source material had never been published lawfully.[2023] At EU level, Article 5(3)(d) ISD also confines the right of quotation to source material that has 'already been lawfully made available to the public'. If the CJEU upholds the mantra of complete and closed regulation of copyright and limitations in a *Scientology/Spaink* scenario, inroads into freedom of expression and freedom of the press seem inescapable. Takings from unpublished sources will inevitably fall outside the scope of Article 5(3)(d)

2019. CJEU, ibis., para. 22. Cf. German Federal Court of Justice, 16 April 2015, case I ZR 225/12, 'Goldrapper', *GRUR* 2015, 1189 (1198); German Federal Court of Justice, 1 December 2010, case I ZR 12/08, 'Perlentaucher', *GRUR* 2011, 134 (137-138); German Federal Court of Justice, 20 March 2003, case I ZR 117/00, 'Gies-Adler', *GRUR* 2003, 956 (958). For a more detailed discussion of this German free adaptation rule, see Bently/Dusollier/Geiger et al. 2019, 486-487; Hilty/Senftleben 2015, 321-324; Hugenholtz/Senftleben 2011, 26-27; Geller 2010, 901. As to the application of a corresponding free adaptation rule in the light of freedom of expression, see Austrian Supreme Court, 13 July 2010, case 4 Ob 66/10z, 'Lieblingshauptfrau'.
2020. CJEU, *ibid.*, paras 56-57 and 65.
2021. CJEU, *ibid.*, para. 39.
2022. CJEU, 19 September 2013, case C-661/11, *Martin Y Paz Diffusion*, paras 54-55. Cf. Senftleben 2016, 350-357; Kur 2014, 450-453.
2023. Court of Appeal of The Hague, 4 September 2003, case 99/1040, ECLI:NL:GHSGR:2003:AI5638, Scientology/Spaink, *AMI* 2003, 217, para. 2 and 7.11.

ISD – regardless of their importance to the debate and the need to inform the public. In *Funke Medien NRW*, the Court already came within a hair's breadth of this dilemma. The case concerned the 'Afghanistan papers': military status reports on the deployment of German armed forces.[2024] Given the confidentiality of these documents, German courts had denied the right of quotation because the requirement of prior lawful publication was not fulfilled.[2025] Not surprisingly, the prejudicial questions raised the issue of an extensive interpretation of the right of quotation in the light of freedom of expression and freedom of the press. The CJEU managed to bypass this delicate issue by following an alternative path and adopting a flexible interpretation of the concept of 'reporting of current events' which is central to one of the press privileges laid down in Article 5(3)(c) ISD. As Funke Medien had presented the Afghanistan papers on its website 'in a structured form in conjunction with an introductory note, further links and a space for comments',[2026] the Court was satisfied that the online publication could be qualified as a privileged form of 'use of works […] in connection with […] reporting'.[2027] In this way, the Court paved the way for the application of Article 5(3)(d) ISD and concealed the dilemma arising from the lawful publication requirement in Article 5(3)(d) ISD.[2028] Moreover, this strategy allowed the Court to maintain the rule that copyright had to be reconciled with freedom of expression and freedom of the press within the system of rights and limitations in EU copyright law.[2029]

Nevertheless, this confirmation of the internal balancing approach need not be the last word on the issue. As the Court of Appeals of The Hague in *Scientology/Spaink*,[2030] the CJEU may have to embark on external corrections of the scope of copyright in future cases of takings from secret documents.[2031] Admittedly, there is a crucial difference between the external balancing tools which the Court already rejected in *Pelham and Others* and *Martin Y Paz* on the one hand and the external norms which the CJEU could invoke in a *Scientology/Spaink* scenario on the other hand. In *Pelham and Others* and *Martin Y Paz*, the national courts sought clarity about the applicability of domestic doctrines of fairness and equity.[2032] Given the

2024. CJEU, 29 July 2019, case C-469/17, Funke Medien NRW, para. 9.
2025. German Federal Court of Justice, 1 June 2017, case I ZR 139/15, 'Afghanistan Papiere', *GRUR* 2017, 901, paras 27-30.
2026. CJEU, 29 July 2019, case C-469/17, Funke Medien NRW, para. 75.
2027. CJEU, *ibid.*, para. 75.
2028. CJEU, *ibid.*, para. 75.
2029. CJEU, *ibid.*, para. 58.
2030. Court of Appeal of The Hague, 4 September 2003, case 99/1040, ECLI:NL:GHSGR:2003:AI5638, Scientology/Spaink, *AMI* 2003, 217, para. 7.11.
2031. With regard to the general problem of insufficient breathing space within the system of copyright limitations in the EU, see Leistner 2011, 417; Guibault 2010, 55; Senftleben 2010b, 528-529.
2032. CJEU, 29 July 2019, case C-476/17, Pelham and Others, paras 56-57; CJEU, 19 September 2013, case C-661/11, *Martin Y Paz Diffusion*, paras 54-55.

national roots and anchorage of these doctrines, the CJEU may have feared that green light for their application would endanger the harmonization objective at EU level. In a *Scientology/Spaink* scenario, by contrast, the CJEU could rely on the guarantee of freedom of expression and freedom of the press in the EU Charter of Fundamental Rights.[2033] Hence, the Court has a balancing tool outside of copyright law at its disposal that stems from primary EU law and allows a decision that does not go beyond the harmonized legal framework. This may reduce the Court's reluctance to override the system of rights and limitations in secondary EU copyright and trademark legislation. On the basis of Article 11 CFR, the Court could stay within the realm of EU law and still offer room for quotations from documents that have not been published previously with authorization.

Although harmonized EU law provides the legal instruments necessary to use freedom of expression as an external, overriding balancing tool in copyright/trademark remix cases, however, the fact remains that current EU legislation and CJEU jurisprudence reflect a preference for internal balancing within the existing framework of harmonized copyright and trademark law. Inevitably, future decisions in which the CJEU invokes Article 11 CFR to override secondary EU copyright and trademark law will remain outliers: exceptions to the general rule of complete and closed harmonization which the Court established in *Pelham and Others* and *Martin Y Paz*.[2034] As exceptional deviations from the standard rule of internal balancing, these potential future decisions can hardly be expected to offer much legal certainty outside the specific blend of facts that may give rise to an extraordinary future decision to open up the system of rights and limitations in EU copyright and trademark law. In addition, it remains to be seen whether lower courts arrive at an appropriate and consistent set of assessment factors when they turn to the balancing exercise following from supreme court decisions. As Christophe Geiger's analysis of pertinent French decisions shows, lower instance judges may be tempted to question the legitimacy and merit of unauthorized remix activities in the artistic domain. They may impose the burden on second authors to prove a clear necessity to use the selected original work. They may also introduce doubtful assessment factors which the artist can hardly influence, such as the capacity of the audience to understand the critical comment which the artist is trying to make on the basis of the reproduced original work.[2035]

Hence, reliance on freedom of expression as a horizontal guarantee of breathing space for artistic remix in cases of overlapping copyright and trademark protection is problematic. Unless the balancing of intellectual property protection against freedom of expression becomes a standard

2033. Article 11 CFR.

2034. CJEU, 29 July 2019, case C-476/17, Pelham and Others, para. 65; CJEU, 19 September 2013, case C-661/11, *Martin Y Paz Diffusion*, paras 54-55.

2035. Geiger 2018a, 18-24. Cf. Rosati 2018, 525.

exercise that is carried out routinely and rests on a robust body of case law and supreme court guidelines, an open-ended assessment of infringement in the light of freedom of expression as an external, countervailing value is unlikely to offer sufficient legal certainty for artists who are risk-averse (section 6.3). The constitutional guarantee of freedom of expression can serve as a safety valve in extraordinary cases. However, it has not yet attained the status of a well-established defence with clear conceptual contours. The mere possibility of future CJEU decisions using freedom of expression as a last resort in legal disputes about artistic remix activities is not sufficient to qualify external balancing on the basis of freedom of expression as a robust use privilege capable of dispelling concerns about interferences of cumulative copyright and trademark protection with cultural follow-on innovation. It is far from constituting a clear-cut case of privileged use that routinely and reliably provides shelter for artists seeking to use trademarked cultural signs as building blocks of new literary and artistic works (sections 8.1.2 and 8.2.2).[2036]

9.2.2.5 Need to Emulate Public Domain Status

The discussion in the preceding sections has shown that, under current EU trademark law and practice, the analogous application of copyright limitations, such as the right of quotation and the exemption of parody, is unlikely. Instead, the constitutional guarantee of freedom of expression – as an external, higher-ranking norm – may function as a horizontal safeguard capable of preventing impediments of cultural follow-on innovation. While the invocation of freedom of expression as an external balancing tool affords judges the opportunity to override the restrictive limitation infrastructure of EU trademark law (section 6.2.4), this solution can hardly be deemed sufficiently well established, well developed and reliable to dispel concerns about an erosion of use privileges for artistic remix when trademark rights to cultural signs are obtained.

In addition, it is important to bear in mind that, if trademark rights affect cultural heritage material in the public domain (Mona Lisa scenario, section 5.2.1), the task of ensuring the survival of user freedoms for artistic remix and reuse goes far beyond the maintenance of specific use privileges, such as the right of quotation and the exemption of parody laid down in EU copyright law.[2037] The public domain status – in the sense of an absence of any intellectual property right (section 8.1.1) – bestows on users in the cultural domain unlimited freedom to use the cultural sign at issue as a basis for new literary and artistic productions. Against this background, the application of specific copyright limitations by analogy is only a first step in the right direction. The horizontal application of an open-ended, flexible

2036. Cf. Benkler 1999, 362-363.

2037. Article 5(3)(d) and (k) ISD.

limitation, such as the U.S. fair use doctrine, may lead to considerable breathing space for transformative use across different domains of intellectual property law (section 9.2.2.1).[2038] It may bring the degree of freedom close to the unlimited freedom of using public domain works (section 8.1.2).[2039] EU copyright law, however, does not contain an open-ended, flexible copyright limitation that could be compared with the U.S. fair use doctrine.[2040] Instead, the EU system provides for narrowly circumscribed use privileges, such as the right of quotation and the exemption of parody.[2041] Even if these use privileges were applied in trademark law by analogy, they would only create breathing space within their specific field of application. From the outset, the analogous application of narrowly defined EU copyright limitations will thus never lead to a degree of freedom that could come close to the unlimited freedom resulting from the public domain status.

Hence, a second, more ambitious step is necessary to emulate the public domain status in Mona Lisa scenarios. To approximate the situation in trademark law to the unlimited freedom of artistic remix and reuse following from the expiry (or absence) of copyright protection, it is indispensable to introduce a carte blanche for transformative use: a general exemption of use of trademarked cultural signs in the cultural domain. On its merits, this *en bloc* exemption of transformative use would have to fulfil the same role in the field of limitations of trademark rights which a strict gatekeeper requirement of 'use as a mark' (section 9.2.1.3) would play at the earlier stage of ascertaining prima facie infringement. It would have to reliably immunize cultural remix and reuse activities against trademark infringement claims. While the trademark use requirement would achieve this goal *ex ante* – before the trademark owner can establish prima facie infringement (section 9.2.1.9) – an effective defence for remix and reuse in the cultural domain would shield artists against the verdict of infringement *ex post* – after the trademark owner has successfully built his prima facie infringement argument.[2042]

From the perspective of the cultural imperative, this difference makes a defence-based solution less attractive than an upfront test of use as a mark (section 9.2.1.9). Nonetheless, the functional symmetry allows the application of similar criteria. As in the discussion of the gatekeeper requirement of use as a mark, it can be posited that a general, *en bloc* exemption of cultural remix and reuse activities should be available in trademark law when the use has 'artistic relevance' to the derivative literary and artistic production (section 9.2.1.1) and the cultural sign concerned is used in an expressive

2038. Lange 2003, 478-479.
2039. Benkler 1999, 362-363.
2040. For a critique of this unsatisfactory situation, see Senftleben 2013d, 37-39.
2041. As to the conceptual contours of these use privileges, see CJEU, 1 December 2011, case C-145/10, Painer, para. 132-134; CJEU, 3 September 2014, case C-201/13, Deckmyn, paras 25-27.
2042. Kur 2009, 293.

sense because it constitutes a 'rhetorically unique' communication tool.[2043] When a trademarked cultural sign is used in a cultural context, these criteria will routinely be satisfied (section 9.2.1.2). Accordingly, it can be presumed that the use does not amount to infringement unless it proves to cause evidently disproportionate harm by explicitly misleading consumers as to the commercial source of the cultural production or deliberately damaging, or deriving unfair advantage from, the highly distinctive character or repute of the trademark aspect of the sign at issue (section 9.2.1.3).

Hence, the crucial question is whether the criteria for invoking EU limitations of trademark protection can be aligned with these criteria. To arrive at a satisfactory solution, it would be necessary to interpret an existing limitation of trademark rights in such a way that it becomes readily available as a defence whenever a trademarked cultural sign (= a sign that is rhetorically unique)[2044] is used in a literary or artistic context (= use to which the sign is artistically relevant).[2045] Following the guidelines that have been developed above with regard to the gatekeeper requirement of use as a mark (section 9.2.1.3), it can be said that, as a rule, use of a trademarked cultural sign in a cultural context should fall within the scope of a limitation of trademark rights (which artists can invoke as a defence against infringement claims) unless the cultural sign or iconic trade symbol has no artistic relevance to the artist's derivative work whatsoever, or, if it has some artistic relevance, unless the use of the cultural sign explicitly misleads as to the source of the derivative work, or deliberately blurs, tarnishes or takes unfair advantage of the distinctiveness or repute of the trademark aspect of the cultural sign.[2046] As the foregoing discussion of the impact of fundamental rights has shown, the most promising strategy for achieving this result in EU trademark law is a flexible, broad interpretation of an existing, statutory limitation of trademark rights in the light of freedom of expression. Recital 21 EUTMR and Recital 27 TMD support this approach. They underline the necessity to offer sufficient room when applying the provisions of EU trademark law:

> Furthermore, this Regulation [this Directive] should be applied in a way that ensures full respect for fundamental rights and freedoms, and in particular the freedom of expression.

2043. Dreyfuss 1990, 413, 418 and 421.
2044. Section 9.2.1.2. Cf. Dreyfuss 1990, 413, 418 and 421.
2045. Section 9.2.1.1. Cf. U.S. Court of Appeals for the Second Circuit, 5 May 1989, Rogers/Grimaldi, 875 F.2d 994 (2nd Cir. 1989), 999; U.S. Court of Appeals for the Ninth Circuit, 5 November 2008, E.S.S. Entertainment 2000/Rock Star Videos, 547 F.3d 1095 (9th Cir. 2008), 1100.
2046. Cf. the 'Rogers' formula developed by the U.S. Court of Appeals for the Second Circuit, 5 May 1989, Rogers/Grimaldi, 875 F.2d 994 (2nd Cir. 1989), 999.

This horizontal obligation to safeguard freedom of expression concerns each individual norm of EU trademark law.[2047] It is of particular importance in the context of limitations that serve as defences and safety valves to prevent overbroad protection. Hence, the time has come to revisit the referential use defence (following section 9.2.2.6) and raise the question whether an interpretation in the light of freedom of expression can remedy the shortcomings discussed above (section 6.2.4). Moreover, it is important to devote attention to a new element of the EU limitation infrastructure. As a result of the 2015 trademark law reform, the current texts of Article 14(1)(b) EUTMR and Article 14(1)(b) TMD contain not only the traditional descriptive use defence (which is unsatisfactory, as discussed in section 6.2.4) but also a defence covering non-distinctive use in a more general sense.[2048] This non-distinctive use defence may offer substantial breathing space for artistic remix and reuse (section 9.2.2.7).

9.2.2.6 Referential Use Defence Revisited

As discussed in section 6.2.4, artists may seek to justify their unauthorized use of trademarked cultural signs by invoking the referential use defence laid down in Article 14(1)(c) EUTMR and Article 14(1)(c) TMD. These provisions describe referential use as use 'for the purpose of identifying or referring to goods or services as those of the proprietor of that trade mark'. However, it is an open question whether this referential use concept is broad enough to encompass the inclusion of trademarked cultural signs, such as signs stemming from the public domain of literary and artistic expressions (Mona Lisa scenario, section 5.2.1), in a derivative literary and artistic production. If the artistic remix addresses the cultural dimension of the trademarked sign, it is doubtful whether it concerns use 'for the purpose of identifying or referring to goods or services as those of the proprietor of that trade mark'.[2049] The artist may have no intention to refer to the sign as an identifier of commercial source. Instead, the artist seeks to contribute to the artistic discourse by referring to the sign as a cultural artefact. In this scenario, the referential use defence may fail to cover the artistic play because the use of the sign does not concern the identification of goods or services as those of the trademark owner but the identification of a work of art that offers an important reference point for cultural follow-on innovation (section 6.2.4).

To eliminate the legal uncertainty arising from an artist's focus on the cultural dimension of a trademarked cultural sign, it is necessary to adopt a more flexible approach. Arguably, use addressing the cultural meaning of a

2047. Schovsbo 2018, 568.

2048. As to the considerations underlying this legislative change, see Kur/Senftleben 2017, para. 6.27-6.29.

2049. Article 14(1)(c) EUTMR; Article 14(1)(c) TMD.

sign is less detrimental to the trademark proprietor than use that concerns the sign's trademark function. Hence, there is room for an argument *a maiore ad minus*. If the referential use defence in Article 14(1)(c) EUTMR and Article 14(1)(c) TMD is capable of exempting use that concerns the sign as a trademark, there is even more reason to apply the referential use defence when the use does not even focus on this trademark aspect. If the use addresses the sign as a cultural artefact, it has less trademark relevance than the referential use scenario described in Article 14(1)(c) EUTMR and Article 14(1)(c) TMD. If, for instance, a French parody of Vermeer's 'Milkmaid' refers to the painting as an element of mankind's universal cultural heritage and does not allude to the fact that the Milkmaid is used intensively as a trademark for dairy products in France,[2050] the potential harm to the trademark owner is more limited than in the case of a clear reference to the sign's trademark function. Some consumers may recognize the sign as a trademark despite the focus on the sign's cultural meaning. Nonetheless, the cultural setting will reduce the degree of trademark recognition and minimize the impact on the trademark owner's legitimate interests. As the statutory referential use defence focuses on use that clearly identifies the sign as the owner's trademark, it can be said that Article 14(1)(c) EUTMR and Article 14(1)(c) TMD cover use which refers entirely (100%) to the trademark aspect of the sign. Given this scope of the provision, it is plausible that the defence is also capable of covering forms of use which less than 100% of the relevant public perceive as a reference to the trademark function because the use focuses attention on the cultural dimension of the sign.

In CJEU jurisprudence, reliance on a line of argument *a maiore ad minus* is not unusual. In *Davidoff/Gofkid*, the CJEU applied this argumentation scheme to extend the scope of protection against dilution to identical and similar goods or services. At the time of the decision, EU trademark law only provided for protection against dilution when the allegedly infringing use concerned dissimilar goods or services.[2051] Davidoff, however, had brought an action against Gofkid's use of a sign similar to its well-known DAVIDOFF mark for identical and similar goods.[2052] Against this background, the case gave rise to the question whether the explicit reference to dissimilar goods and services in statutory law prevented the grant of anti-dilution protection. Considering the 'overall scheme and objectives'[2053] of the system of EU trademark protection, the CJEU held that it would be inappropriate to adopt a strict, literal interpretation which would lead to marks with a reputation having less protection where a sign was used for identical or

2050. Cf. Bianchi 2017.

2051. See Article 5(2) TMD 2008 which, on this point, left the earlier Trade Mark Directive 89/104/EEC of the Council of December 21, 1988 (*OJ* 1989, L 40, p. 1), unchanged. This latter legislative text governed the decision in *Davidoff/Gofkid*. See CJEU, 9 January 2003, case 292/00, Davidoff/Gofkid, para. 5.

2052. CJEU, *ibid.*, para. 12.

2053. CJEU, *ibid.*, para. 24.

similar goods than where a sign was used for non-similar goods. The Court concluded that, where a sign was used for identical or similar goods or services, a mark with a reputation had to enjoy protection which was 'at least as extensive' as where a sign was used for non-similar goods and services.[2054]

If such an argument *a fortiori* can serve as a tool to enhance the scope of exclusive trademark rights, it is consistent to take similar steps in the field of limitations of protection. This is even indispensable where freedom of expression is at stake. As explained in section 9.2.1.7, Recital 21 EUTMR and Recital 27 TMD explicitly provide that EU trademark law 'should be applied in a way that ensures full respect for fundamental rights and freedoms, and in particular the freedom of expression'. This guarantee of sufficient room for free expression impacts the application of all individual norms of EU trademark law.[2055] With regard to the referential use defence laid down in Article 14(1)(c) EUTMR and Article 14(1)(c) TMD, it offers strong support for the described extension of the referential use defence to scenarios where an artist refers to a trademarked cultural sign as a cultural artefact. Rightly understood, the referential use defence covers this scenario because an artist's use of a trademarked cultural sign as an artwork has less trademark relevance than use for the sole purpose of identifying the sign as a trademark. As the referential use defence covers direct references to the sign as a trademark, there is even more reason to apply the defence when the use concerns the cultural dimension of the sign. The artist must enjoy a degree of freedom which is 'at least as extensive' as where a trademarked cultural sign is used in commerce to identify goods or services as those of the trademark owner.

9.2.2.7 Non-distinctive Use Defence

The described recalibration of the referential use defence on the basis of an argument *a maiore ad minus* is not the only strategy to develop appropriate defences in EU trademark law for artistic remix of trademarked cultural signs. A closer inspection of the non-distinctive use defence in Article 14(1)(b) EUTMR and Article 14(1)(b) TMD sheds light on additional breathing space. The provisions stipulate that the grant of trademark rights shall not entitle the proprietor to prohibit a third party from using, in the course of trade:

> signs or indications which are not distinctive or which concern the kind, quality, quantity, intended purpose, value, geographical origin, the time of production of goods or of rendering of the service, or other characteristics of goods or services (emphasis added).

2054. CJEU, *ibid.*, paras 25-26.
2055. Schovsbo 2018, 568.

Evidently, this limitation of trademark rights has two branches. First, Article 14(1)(b) EUTMR and Article 14(1)(b) TMD set forth the traditional descriptive use defence which has already been criticized above (section 6.2.4). The decorative inclusion of a pre-existing cultural sign in a derivative literary and artistic production is unlikely to qualify as a permissible form of descriptive use under current CJEU assessment standards. The Court is reluctant to regard purely decorative use as an indication of product characteristics.[2056] According to the Court, this type of use leads to the incorporation of the cultural sign into the product and makes the sign an element of the product itself (section 6.2.4). Prior to the 2015 EU trademark law reform, this discouraging result may have been the final word on the issue. After the reform, however, a different picture can be drawn:[2057] second, Article 14(1)(b) EUTMR and Article 14(1)(b) TMD exempt use of 'signs or indications which are not distinctive'. Discussing this new feature of the provisions, Annette Kur draws the following line between descriptive use and non-distinctive use:

> Similar to descriptive signs which, even when they are registered after having acquired distinctiveness, still contain residues of their original descriptive character that others are free to make use of, inherently indistinctive signs as well will never become the 'sole property' of the trademark holder, but must leave room for use by others that only relates to the sign in its original, non-distinctive capacity.[2058]

This explanation offers a template for the extension of the defence argument to trademarked cultural signs. In its primary state, a cultural sign, such as the Mona Lisa or the Night Watch, lacks the inherent distinctive character necessary to serve as an identifier of commercial source – at least in respect of literary and artistic productions.[2059] The trademark owner must

2056. CJEU, 10 April 2008, case C-102/07, Adidas/Marca, para. 48.
2057. Kur/Senftleben 2017, para. 6.27.
2058. Kur 2018, 101.
2059. In German Federal Patent Court, 25 November 1997, case 24 W (pat) 188/96, Mona Lisa, *GRUR* 1998, 1021 and 1023, and Court of Appeals of The Hague, 29 August 2017, case 200.205.771/01, ECLI:NL:GHDHA:2017:2446, Chiever/Benelux-Organisatie voor de Intellectuele Eigendom ('Nachtwacht'), para. 12, the Mona Lisa and the Night Watch were declared indistinctive with regard to an even broader range of goods and services. The decisions of the Court of Appeals of Brussels, 3 October 2013, cases 2013/7132 and 2013/7133, Anne Frank Foundation/Benelux Office for Intellectual Property, para. 6 and 10, and German Federal Court of Justice, 24 April 2008, case I ZB 21/06, Marlene-Dietrich-Bildnis, paras 12-15, focused on the descriptive character of cultural signs vis-à-vis goods and services relating to the literary and artistic domain. This descriptive character in respect of literary and artistic productions implies that the sign is also devoid of distinctive character with regard to goods and services in this category. See CJEU, 12 February 2004, case C-363/99, Koninklijke KPN/Benelux-Merkenbureau ('Postkantoor'), para. 86: 'In particular, a word mark which is descriptive of characteristics of goods or services for the purposes of Article 3(1)(c) of the Directive is, on that account, necessarily devoid of any

actively transform the sign into a badge of origin. Regardless of the acquisition of distinctive character through use, however, a non-distinctive 'residue' in the sense of Kur's explanation, namely the sign's original cultural meaning, always remains. As other types of non-distinctive and descriptive signs,[2060] a cultural sign thus never becomes the sole property of the trademark owner. The sign's literary and artistic character – the residue stemming from the sign's evolution in the cultural domain – is beyond reach for the trademark owner.[2061] As this cultural residue is non-distinctive in the context of literary and artistic productions, it falls outside the scope of trademark rights which, by definition, only relate to the secondary, source-identifying meaning added by the trademark owner. Exempting use of non-distinctive signs or indications, Article 14(1)(b) EUTMR and Article 14(1)(b) TMD, thus, offer room for artistic use that only relates to the sign in its original, cultural (and non-distinctive) capacity.[2062] As use of a cultural sign to indicate a specific artistic position is use of the sign as a non-distinctive, cultural reference point, the non-distinctive use defence can be deemed applicable. Rightly understood, Article 14(1)(b) EUTMR and Article 14(1)(b) TMD cover use of a trademarked cultural sign in an artistic way – as an indication of a cultural meaning that does not concern the sign's trademark function of indicating commercial source.

The described distinction between a sign's non-distinctive, primary meaning (which remains outside the scope of trademark rights) and its secondary, acquired trademark connotation (which falls within the scope of trademark rights) also comes to the fore in other illustrative examples of the field of application of the non-distinctive use defence. With regard to abstract colour marks, Annette Kur explains:

> The starting point must be that using a color in advertisements, websites, or other elements accompanying market appearance is neutral as such. Even if the same or a similar color is protected as a mark, this does not change the fact that the color retains its basic capacity of 'simply coloring,' without conveying any meaning besides the conceptual and emotional message inherent in the color itself. This is not different from a descriptive word which, after acquiring distinctiveness, still has the

---

distinctive character with regard to the same goods or services within the meaning of Article 3(1)(b) of the Directive.'

2060. Kur 2018, 103, gives the example of a shape which, as such, is non-distinctive but may acquire distinctive character through use. Notwithstanding the acquisition of distinctive character, the non-distinctive use defence may allow use of a similar product shape in packages clearly indicating the defendant's own word mark. Arguably, this use only relates to the non-distinctive properties of the shape and the function of indicating commercial source is left to the defendant's own word mark on the packages.

2061. For an aesthetic functionality concept reflecting these residues of 'widely shared cognitive, psychological, or aesthetic propensities', see Hughes 2015, 1231.

2062. Cf. Ohly 2019, 337-338, who also sees room for the cultivation of this defence argument in cases of remix in the artistic domain.

> capacity to describe, and can be used for that purpose. That double role is aptly expressed in the term 'secondary meaning.' While a new meaning is acquired, the original, 'primary' meaning is retained and justifies use by others.[2063]

However, the distinction between a primary, non-distinctive meaning (which remains freely available) and a secondary, distinctive meaning (which falls within the scope of trademark protection) inevitably introduces a contextual factor in the equation. Even if the mark as such has the requisite level of distinctiveness because of the secondary trademark meaning, the sign used by the alleged infringer may appear indistinctive because it relates to the primary, non-distinctive meaning. This depends on the circumstances surrounding the presentation of the sign in the setting chosen by the defendant. It is therefore necessary to ask whether, given the individual parameters of the unauthorized use, it can be concluded that the defendant's activity relates to the primary, non-distinctive meaning of the sign. If, for instance, trademark protection is vested in the shape of a product that is regularly sold in packages, the use of a highly similar shape by a competitor, with a clearly different mark being displayed on the packages, may be found permissible on the ground that, under the concrete circumstances qualifying the use made by the competitor, the allegedly infringing sign is indistinctive.[2064]

As already pointed out, a trademarked cultural sign is likely to appear indistinctive in a cultural setting because the artist uses the sign as an indication of a specific artistic position and the audience perceives the sign as an expressive element of the derivative work (section 9.2.1.2). The specific circumstances surrounding the presentation of the sign militate against a finding of use for the purpose of indicating commercial origin. Instead, an artist is likely to use a trademarked cultural sign in an indistinctive sense to evoke the primary, cultural meaning which the sign already had prior to the acquisition of trademark rights. Given these specific use parameters, the non-distinctive use defence in Article 14(1)(b) EUTMR and Article 14(1)(b) TMD is applicable. Artists can invoke the defence to shield their remix activities from allegations of trademark infringement. The obligation to interpret the norms of EU trademark law in a way that safeguards freedom of expression[2065] supports this cultivation of the non-distinctive use defence as a tool to immunize cultural follow-on innovation against potential trademark claims.

2063. Kur 2018, 104.
2064. Kur 2018, 103; Kur/Senftleben 2017, para. 6.33.
2065. Recital 21 EUTMR; Recital 27 TMD. Cf. Schovsbo 2018, 568.

9.2.2.8 Maximum Scope and Honest Practices

In sum, a survey of existing limitations of exclusive rights in EU trademark law sheds light on two promising strategies to equip artists with effective defences against infringement claims relating to the remix and reuse of trademarked cultural signs. First, the scope of the referential use defence laid down in Article 14(1)(c) EUTMR and Article 14(1)(c) TMD can be broadened on the basis of an argument *a maiore ad minus* (section 9.2.2.6). Second, the non-distinctive use defence in Article 14(1)(b) EUTMR and Article 14(1)(b) TMD can be understood to exempt use of cultural residues – original, cultural meanings – of a trademarked cultural sign from the control of the trademark proprietor (section 9.2.2.7). However, the focus on cultural heritage signs in the preceding sections (Mona Lisa scenario, section 5.2.1) raises the additional question of whether a defence strategy based on referential use and non-distinctive use may also have success in cases that concern the artistic remix of trademarked cultural signs stemming from contemporary mainstream productions (Mickey Mouse scenario, section 5.2.3) or iconic trade symbols (Coca Cola scenario, section 5.2.5).

The referential use argument seems fully applicable in respect of these additional categories of signs.[2066] In the case of Mickey Mouse and comparable symbols of contemporary mainstream culture, the degree of trademark recognition may be higher than in the case of cultural heritage signs, such as the Mona Lisa and the Night Watch. As explained in section 9.2.2.6, however, the referential use defence laid down in Article 14(1)(c) EUTMR and Article 14(1)(c) TMD covers even a full (100%) reference to the sign as a trademark. Arguing *a maiore ad minus*, it can be stated against this background that the defence also covers any reference which less than 100% of the relevant public would perceive as a reference to Mickey Mouse as a Disney trademark. If, for instance, 70% of consumers perceive use of Mickey Mouse in a derivative literary and artistic production as a reference to a Disney trademark and 30% of consumers regard the use as a reference to Mickey Mouse as a literary and artistic work, the impact of the use on the legitimate interests of the trademark owner would still be less than in cases of an unequivocal, 100% reference to the trademark aspect of the sign. Hence, the referential use defence is capable of covering not only artistic remix and reuse of trademarked cultural heritage signs, such as the Mona Lisa, but also the cultural remix of trademarked symbols of contemporary mainstream culture, such as Mickey Mouse.

As to Coca Cola and comparable trade symbols, the invocation of the referential use argument is even more straightforward. Well-established trade symbols, such as the logos of Coca Cola and Louis Vuitton, have a primary, source-identifying meaning. Their appearance in an artistic context is unusual. Accordingly, consumers are likely to perceive the inclusion of an

2066. Cf. Żelechowski 2018, 127-128.

iconic trade symbol in a literary and artistic work as a full (100%) reference to the sign as a trademark. Even without any argument *a maiore ad minus*, this use scenario falls directly within the scope of the referential use defence laid down in Article 14(1)(c) EUTMR and Article 14(1)(c) TMD. It constitutes use for the purpose of identifying the sign as the badge of origin adopted by the trademark owner. The referential use defence is thus also applicable to artistic use of iconic trade symbols, such as Coca Cola.[2067]

However, a more nuanced picture arises when the non-distinctive use argument is placed in the context of trademarked cultural signs derived from contemporary mainstream culture and iconic trade symbols. A sign that evolved in the domain of commerce and trade, such as COCA COLA, can hardly be deemed to have a primary, cultural meaning – a cultural residue that remains unprotected even after the acquisition of trademark rights. By contrast, the cultural significance which the sign has acquired over time appears as a secondary meaning. Similarly, it may be said that modern merchandising strategies lead to an almost inseparable amalgam of cultural and commercial connotations of iconic symbols of contemporary mainstream culture, such as Mickey Mouse. In consequence, it is more difficult, also in this case, to base the invocation of the non-distinctive use defence on the argument that artistic remix relates to unprotected, cultural residues of the sign and does not concern the sign's trademark aspect.

These differences, however, need not preclude the successful invocation of the non-distinctive use defence. As pointed out in the preceding section 9.2.2.7, the distinction between a non-distinctive, cultural meaning (which remains freely available) and a distinctive, source-identifying meaning (which falls within the scope of trademark protection) inevitably introduces a contextual assessment factor. Even if the affected sign has always been a trademark or has been impregnated with trademark messages from the very beginning, use in the artistic domain may still appear indistinctive because it employs the sign in a non-distinctive, metaphorical sense. Rochelle Dreyfuss' distinction between the expressive and the source-identifying function of trademarked signs sheds light on this important nuance (sections 8.3.2 and 9.2.1.2). The non-actionable, expressive mode of use – employing the trademark as a metaphor for a particular societal or personal condition[2068] – will regularly come to the fore in cases where an artist includes a symbol of contemporary mainstream culture (Mickey Mouse) or an iconic trade symbol (Coca Cola) in a derivative literary and artistic work. As concluded in section 9.2.2.7, a trademarked sign is likely to appear indistinctive in a cultural setting because the artist uses the sign as a tool to make a specific artistic statement and the audience perceives the sign as an expressive element of the

2067. Cf. Benelux Court of Justice, 14 October 2019, case A2018/1/8, Moët Hennessy/Cedric Art, para. 9, for a similar line of argument in the context of the open-ended defence of 'due cause'.

2068. Dreyfuss 1990, 400.

derivative work (and not as indication of commercial source). The specific circumstances surrounding the presentation of the sign militate against a finding of use for the purpose of indicating commercial origin. Given the specific parameters of expressive use in the artistic domain, the non-distinctive use defence in Article 14(1)(b) EUTMR and Article 14(1)(b) TMD can be deemed applicable even though the affected sign does not have a primary cultural residue comparable to the original meaning of cultural heritage signs in the Mona Lisa category. As long as the remix in the cultural domain employs a trademarked sign as an expressive tool to make an artistic statement, the use can be classified as an indistinctive form of use that falls within the scope of the non-distinctive use defence (cf. section 8.3.2).

Therefore, both defence arguments – referential use[2069] and non-distinctive use[2070] – are fully applicable not only to cultural heritage signs that have been reappropriated via trademark law (Mona Lisa scenario) but also to cultural signs stemming from mainstream literary and artistic productions (Mickey Mouse scenario) and iconic trade symbols (Coca Cola scenario). A final question, however, arises from the honest practices proviso in Article 14(2) EUTMR and Article 14(2) TMD which delineates the field of application of both defence arguments. Article 14(2) provides that the defences for referential use and non-distinctive use apply only if the unauthorized use is 'in accordance with honest practices in industrial or commercial matters'. As discussed in section 9.2.1.7, this general requirement is:

- inadequate because artists can hardly be expected to be aware of behavioural norms in the industrial and commercial sector;
- inappropriate because the obligation to align the creation of derivative artistic works with behavioural norms stemming from the industrial and commercial sector cements the undesirable supremacy of the societal field of commerce and trade over the societal field of literary and artistic production; and
- circular because the CJEU tends to apply the same criteria for the identification of dishonest practices which have already supported the foregoing finding of prima facie infringement.

As one way out of the dilemma, the discussion of a general gatekeeper requirement of use as a mark in section 9.2.1.7 has led to the insight that it is possible to set a higher standard for a finding of dishonest practices in cases of artistic remix and reuse.[2071] This approach equates the honest practices enquiry with the question of whether the allegedly infringing use in

2069. Article 14(1)(c) EUTMR; Article 14(1)(c) TMD.

2070. Article 14(1)(b) EUTMR; Article 14(1)(b) TMD.

2071. U.S. Court of Appeals for the Second Circuit, 5 May 1989, Rogers/Grimaldi, 875 F.2d 994 (2nd Cir. 1989), 999. Cf. sections 9.2.1.1 (as to confusion claims) and 9.2.1.2 (as to dilution claims).

an artistic context explicitly misleads consumers as to the source of the artwork, or deliberately damages or derives unfair advantage from the distinctiveness or the repute of the trademark. Only if the trademark owner succeeds in satisfying this higher threshold requirement of evidently disproportionate harm, she can demonstrate that the cultural setting was mere pretence and the unauthorized use was not in compliance with honest practices in industrial and commercial matters. Applying this approach mutatis mutandis, referential use in the sense of Article 14(1)(c) EUTMR and Article 14(1)(c) TMD, and non-distinctive use in the sense of Article 14(1)(b) EUTMR and Article 14(1)(b) TMD, should be deemed incompatible with honest practices in industrial and commercial matters only if the artistic use at issue explicitly misleads consumers as to the source of the artwork, or deliberately damages or derives unfair advantage from the distinctiveness or the repute of the trademark. In this way, the beneficial effect of the EU defence infrastructure can be approximated to the immunizing effect which a general gatekeeper requirement of use as a mark would have (sections 9.2.1.3 and 9.2.1.6). As already pointed out in section 9.2.1.9, however, a solution based on the development of defences for artists will always remain the second-best solution. In comparison with an upfront test of use as a mark, it fails to prevent the trademark owner from establishing prima facie infringement. Moreover, the burden of proving referential use or non-distinctive use rests on the artist. The threshold requirement of use as a mark, by contrast, imposes the burden on the trademark proprietor to establish that the allegedly infringing use in the artistic domain has trademark relevance at all (section 9.2.1.7).

With regard to the question of corresponding use privileges for transformative use (sections 9.2.2.1 to 9.2.2.3), the cultivation of the referential use defence and the non-distinctive use defence has positive effects. It reduces the need for fully congruent limitations in copyright and trademark law, or a rule of direct or analogous application of copyright limitations in trademark law. With the proposed conceptual contours and the introduction of a dishonest practices test requiring evidently disproportionate harm, the referential use defence and the non-distinctive use defence become capable of covering forms of use that fall within the scope of the right of quotation and the exemption of parody in EU copyright law. As a result, cumulative copyright and trademark protection no longer erode use privileges which copyright law makes available to support cultural follow-on innovation. Instead, artists can reframe their quotation and parody arguments in a trademark dispute, asserting that a permissible quotation or parody in the sense of EU copyright law constitutes a permissible form of referential or non-distinctive use in EU trademark law. Following the guidelines given above, the trademark categories of referential use and non-distinctive use can be developed into counterparts of the copyright categories of quotation and parody. In this way, it is possible to avoid a loss of breathing space for cultural follow-on innovation in the field of limitations of exclusive rights when copyright and trademark protection overlap.

In the preceding sections, the starting point for an enquiry into the scope of the referential use defence and the non-distinctive use defence was the question of whether trademark law is capable of emulating the public domain status which cultural heritage signs have prior to their reappropriation on the basis of trademark law. Surveying the results of the analysis, the answer to this question is twofold: on the one hand, the grant of trademark rights in a cultural heritage sign, by definition, entails a loss of freedom of use. With the trademark registration, absolute freedom of use (section 8.1.1) is sacrificed in favour of a scenario in which trademark rights can serve as a basis for an infringement action.[2072] Moreover, the trademark owner obtains exclusive rights that allow him to impregnate an affected cultural sign with commercial connotations that may devalue the sign as a reference point for the artistic discourse (section 8.2.3.3). While this damage cannot be undone once trademark rights have been awarded, the transformation of referential use and non-distinctive use into robust defences, on the other hand, can alleviate the burden resulting from the registration of a cultural heritage sign as a trademark (section 8.1.2). To achieve this goal, use of the sign in an artistic context must constitute an 'easy case': a form of use commonly perceived as permissible absent special circumstances, such as individualized facts that make a particular use by a particular artist unprivileged (section 8.2.1).[2073]

To emulate the public domain status to the largest extent possible, the application of the referential use defence and the non-distinctive use defence in cases involving artistic remix of trademarked cultural signs must therefore become a well-established court practice. Judges would have to routinely accept the defence argument unless the trademark proprietor manages to produce evidence of individualized facts that unmask the artistic setting as a mere pretence for blatant trademark infringement. Relying on the insights derived from the discussion of the threshold requirement of use as a mark (section 9.2.1.3), it can be stated that courts in the EU would have to create a legal environment which offers a degree of legal certainty and reassurance for artists that is comparable with the legal certainty and reassurance following from the 'Rogers' test in the U.S.[2074] However, this environment will not arise until the successful invocation of referential use and non-distinctive use as defence arguments has become established case law that shields artists effectively against trademark infringement claims – until artistic use of trademarked cultural signs has become an 'easy case' of permissible use that routinely survives scrutiny in the light of trademark rights.

2072. Cf. Senftleben 2017b, 688.
2073. Cf. Benkler 1999, 362-363.
2074. U.S. Court of Appeals for the Second Circuit, 5 May 1989, Rogers/Grimaldi, 875 F.2d 994 (2nd Cir. 1989), 999.

9.2.2.9 Compliance with International Law

Finally, it is important to point out that international trademark law does not pose obstacles to the cultivation of the referential use defence and the non-distinctive use defence, as proposed in the preceding sections 9.2.2.6 to 9.2.2.8. Article 17 TRIPS allows WTO Members to:

> provide limited exceptions to the rights conferred by a trademark, such as fair use of descriptive terms, provided that such exceptions take account of the legitimate interests of the owner of the trademark and of third parties.

This international basis for the introduction of defences at the national level has been interpreted in the framework of WTO dispute settlement in *European Communities – Protection of Trademarks and Geographical Indications for Agricultural Products and Foodstuffs*.[2075] In this dispute, Australia and the U.S. asserted that Council Regulation (EEC) No. 2081/92 of 14 July 1992 on the Protection of Geographical Indications and Designations of Origin for Agricultural Products and Foodstuffs violated the TRIPS Agreement because it established a regime of geographical indication/trademark coexistence.[2076] Article 14(2) of the Regulation, as in force at the time,[2077] provided that trademark owners, on certain further conditions, could continue to use geographically descriptive trademarks notwithstanding the registration of a conflicting geographical indication,[2078] if they had applied for, registered, or established their trademarks by use, prior to either the date of protection of the geographical indication in the country of origin or the date of filing an application for registration with the European Commission. A prior trademark, therefore, did not necessarily prevail over a later geographical indication. By contrast, the Regulation

2075. WTO Panel, 15 March 2005, WTO Document WT/DS174/R, European Communities – Protection of Trademarks and Geographical Indications for Agricultural Products and Foodstuffs, para. 7.650-7.651, based on a complaint by the U.S. and the twin report WTO Document WT/DS290/R dealing with a parallel complaint by Australia. As to the interpretation of Article 17 TRIPS, the reports are identical in substance. Following references concern the report on the U.S. complaint. For comments on the WTO Panel reports in the area of exceptions to intellectual property rights, see Senftleben 2006, 407; Ficsor 2002, 111; Oliver 2002, 119; Brennan 2002, 213; Ginsburg 2001, 13; Hugenholtz 2000c, 197.

2076. As to the underlying heated debate on the protection of geographical indications, see O'Connor 2004, 35; Goebel 2004, 964; Bullbrook 2004, 501; Cortés Martín 2004, 287; Staten 2005, 221; Torsen 2005, 31; Grazioli 2005, 902.

2077. With regard to current EU legislation in this area, see Regulation (EU) No. 1151/2012 of the European Parliament and of the Council of 21 November 2012 on quality schemes for agricultural products and foodstuffs, *OJ* 2012 L 343, p. 14. Cf. Gangjee 2012.

2078. The term is to be understood here to comprise both 'geographical indications' and 'designations of origin' in the sense of the Council Regulation (EEC) No. 2081/92, as amended.

envisaged that both coexist.[2079] Australia and the U.S. asserted that the Regulation thus failed to ensure that trademark proprietors could prevent uses of geographical indications that were likely to cause confusion with a prior trademark.[2080] To defend its coexistence regime, the EC pointed towards several safeguards in the Regulation itself, such as Article 14(3) which provided that a geographical indication should not be registered where, in the light of a trademark's reputation and renown and the length of time it had been used, the registration was liable to mislead the consumer as to the true identity of the product. It also referred to EC directives on labelling, presentation and advertising of foodstuffs, and on misleading advertising.[2081] Given these safeguards, the EC was confident that its coexistence regime could be justified as a limited exception under Article 17 TRIPS.

Turning to this Article 17 argument and, more specifically, the first requirement of 'limited exceptions', the WTO Panel embarked on the measurement of the extent to which a curtailment of exclusive trademark rights resulted from the EC Regulation requiring prior trademarks, in specific circumstances, to coexist with later geographical indications. Referring to the fair use example given in Article 17 TRIPS itself, the Panel noted that fair use of descriptive terms was not limited in terms of the number of third parties who may benefit from the limited exception, nor in terms of the quantity of exempted goods or services.[2082] Against this background, the Panel held that the EC coexistence regime kept within these conceptual contours and could pass the limited exceptions test.[2083]

With regard to the remaining 'legitimate interests' test, the Panel lent weight to the fact that the prohibition of an unreasonable prejudice to be found in corresponding tests[2084] in Articles 13 and 30 TRIPS had been omitted in Article 17 TRIPS. The Panel inferred from this omission 'a lesser standard of regard for the legitimate interests of the owner of the trademark'.[2085] Nonetheless, every trademark owner had a legitimate interest in preserving the distinctiveness, or capacity to distinguish, of her trademark.[2086] In addition, consumers had a legitimate interest in being able to distinguish the goods or services of one undertaking from those of another, and to avoid confusion.[2087] The EC coexistence regime allowed the refusal

2079. As to the current configuration of the relationship between geographical indications and trademarks in the EU, see Knaak 2015, 843-867; Evans 2010, 645-674.
2080. WTO Panel, *ibid.*, para. 7.512 and 7.532 – 7.539.
2081. WTO Panel, *ibid.*, para. 7.540 – 7.549.
2082. WTO Panel, *ibid.*, para. 7.654.
2083. WTO Panel, *ibid.*, para. 7.659.
2084. For a discussion of the different TRIPS provisions derived from the so-called three-step test in international copyright law, see Senftleben 2006, 411-412.
2085. WTO Panel, *ibid.*, para. 7.671.
2086. WTO Panel, *ibid.*, para. 7.664.
2087. WTO Panel, *ibid.*, para. 7.676.

of the registration of a geographical indication in the light of the reputation and renown of a prior trademark, and the length of time that a prior trademark had been used. Moreover, it addressed consumers by providing for the refusal of the registration of a geographical indication where the registration was liable to mislead consumers as to the true identity of the product. For these reasons, the Panel was satisfied that the legitimate interests of the trademark owner and consumers had been taken into account.[2088]

International trademark law, therefore, offers considerable breathing space for the limitation of trademark rights. Comparing the proposed defences for artistic remix and reuse (sections 9.2.2.6 to 9.2.2.8) with the EC coexistence regime and the example of fair use of descriptive terms addressed in the WTO Panel decision, there can be little doubt that international law offers sufficient room to develop the proposed referential use and non-distinctive use defences in EU trademark law. On the one hand, the conceptual contours of the proposed defences are more specific than the general descriptive use defence mentioned in Article 17 TRIPS or a coexistence regime for geographical indications and trademarks. The group of beneficiaries of use privileges for artistic remix and reuse is confined to artists. The circle of affected signs is limited to trademarks with cultural significance. The proposed defences only concern the inclusion of trademarked cultural signs in a derivative literary and artistic work. The purpose underlying the use privilege is cultural follow-on innovation and the prevention of a corrosive effect on free artistic expression. Given this specific framework, the proposed referential use and non-distinctive use defences only make small inroads into trademark rights and constitute 'limited exceptions' in the sense of Article 17 TRIPS.

As to the further obligation to take account of 'legitimate interests', it is to be noted from the outset that consumers are unlikely to perceive use of a trademarked cultural sign in an artistic setting as an indication of commercial source. Instead of affecting the source-identifying function of trademarks, referential use and non-distinctive use for the purpose of creating a derivative literary and artistic work concerns the expressive, cultural aspect of the protected sign (section 8.3.2). Use to indicate a specific artistic position and use in a metaphorical sense to evoke a certain lifestyle or attitude can serve as examples (sections 9.2.1.2 and 9.2.2.6).[2089] Hence, the proposed defences for artistic use are unlikely to jeopardize the trademark owner's interest in preserving the trademark as a badge of origin, or consumers' interest in a transparent market without confusing indications of commercial source. If the cultural context of unauthorized use is only a pretext for encroachments upon these legitimate interests, the configuration of the proposed defences, moreover, offers safety valves. If the artistic use

2088. WTO Panel, *ibid.*, para. 7.666 and 7.677.
2089. Dreyfuss 1990, 400.

explicitly aims at consumer confusion or trademark dilution, the trademark owner can rebut the argument of permissible use in the cultural domain, for instance by demonstrating incompliance with honest practices in industrial and commercial matters (sections 9.2.1.7 and 9.2.2.8). As U.S. courts pointed out in the context of the 'Rogers' test (section 9.2.1.1), it is also important to consider that consumers have a dual interest when it comes to artistic remix and reuse of trademarked cultural signs: not only an interest in not being misled but also an interest in enjoying the results of an artist's freedom of expression (section 9.2.1.1).[2090] In light of the guarantee of freedom of expression at the national and international level,[2091] this latter interest must also be factored into the equation. It constitutes a legitimate interest that functions as an important counterweight to trademark protection interests.[2092] On balance, the proposed referential use and non-distinctive use defences, thus, pass the 'legitimate interests' test of Article 17 TRIPS. There is no compelling reason to cast doubt upon compliance of the proposed referential and non-distinctive use defences for artistic remix activities with international trademark law.

9.2.3 Conclusion

If it is not possible to avoid the grant of trademark rights to a cultural sign on the basis of cultural grounds for refusal, in particular considerations based on public order or morality (section 9.1.2.2), legislators and judges seeking to offer breathing space for cultural follow-on innovation within the trademark system can pursue two different strategies:

(1) they can either implement a strict test of 'use as a mark' that functions as a gatekeeper requirement and prevents trademark owners from establishing prima facie trademark infringement; or

---

2090. U.S. Court of Appeals for the Second Circuit, 5 May 1989, Rogers/Grimaldi, 875 F.2d 994 (2nd Cir. 1989), 999.

2091. The Universal Declaration of Human Rights enunciates in Article 19 that 'everyone has the right to freedom of opinion and expression' and recognizes that 'this right includes freedom to hold opinions without interference and to seek, receive and impart information and ideas through any media and regardless of frontiers'. See also Article 19 of the International Covenant on Civil and Political Rights. Cf. Geiger/Gervais/Senftleben 2014, 602-603; Geiger 2008b, 111; Helfer 2007, 977; Yu 2007a, 1041; Yu 2007b, 711; Marceau 2002, 756. As to the situation in Europe, see Article 10 EVRM; Article 11 CFR.

2092. Benelux Court of Justice, 14 October 2019, case A2018/1/8, Moët Hennessy/Cedric Art, para. 9. Cf. Bohaczewski 2020, 856; Żelechowski 2018, 115-135; Senftleben 2015, 354; Ramsey/Schovsbo 2013, 671; Simon Fhima 2013, 293; Sakulin 2010; Geiger 2010a, 163; Burrell/Gangjee 2010, 544; Nasser 2009, 188; Bently 2008, 1205; Dreyfuss 2008, 261; Geiger 2007, 317; Ramsey 2010a, 405; Weckström 2007, 671; Gulasekaram 2005, 887; Leval 2004, 187; Timbers/Huston 2003, 1278; Aoki 1997, 523; Dreyfuss 1990, 415-418.

(2) develop robust limitations of trademark rights that can serve as defences for users in the cultural domain.

In both scenarios, the overarching goal is the creation of a bias in favour of users who embark on the remix and reuse of cultural signs in the artistic domain. When a trademarked cultural sign is used in connection with a literary or artistic production, the artist should be able to rely on a well-established legal presumption that the use does not amount to actionable use as a trademark.

To achieve this goal with the first strategy – the implementation of a gatekeeper requirement of 'use as a mark' – it is advisable to combine the approach underlying the U.S. 'Rogers' test[2093] with the insight that use in a cultural setting normally concerns the cultural, expressive meaning of a sign with cultural significance.[2094] This type of use is unlikely to confuse consumers, damage the trademark reputation, or exploit trademark magnetism in an unfair manner. By contrast, use in the cultural domain will address the rhetoric uniqueness of cultural signs: the specific set of meanings and connotations which these signs evoke as a result of their evolution in the cultural domain and which makes them indispensable communication tools for cultural follow-on innovation. Only if the trademark owner succeeds in demonstrating that – despite the cultural setting – an artist specifically aims at causing consumer confusion or damaging and unfairly exploiting the sign's trademark distinctiveness or repute, he should be able to rebut the legal presumption of use in an expressively generic,[2095] non-branding,[2096] way. Only then, the trademark owner should be able to save a trademark claim from being dismissed as unfounded from the outset. The corresponding gatekeeper requirement of use as a mark can be defined as follows: use of a trademarked cultural sign in a cultural context will normally not constitute actionable use as a mark unless the cultural sign has no artistic relevance to the underlying work whatsoever, or, if it has some artistic relevance, unless the use of the cultural sign explicitly misleads as to the source of the derivative literary and artistic work, or deliberately blurs, tarnishes or takes unfair advantage of the distinctiveness or repute which the cultural sign has acquired as a trademark.[2097]

Given the focus on rhetoric uniqueness stemming from a sign's cultural past, it is obvious that this upfront test of trademark use is applicable to cultural heritage signs (Mona Lisa scenario, section 5.2.1) and symbols of contemporary mainstream culture (Mickey Mouse scenario, section 5.2.3).

2093. U.S. Court of Appeals for the Second Circuit, 5 May 1989, Rogers/Grimaldi, 875 F.2d 994 (2nd Cir. 1989), 999.
2094. Dreyfuss 1990, 418.
2095. Dreyfuss 1990, 418.
2096. Dogan/Lemley 2008a, 542.
2097. Cf. the 'Rogers' formula developed by the U.S. Court of Appeals for the Second Circuit, 5 May 1989, Rogers/Grimaldi, 875 F.2d 994 (2nd Cir. 1989), 999.

However, similar measures can be adopted with regard to the expressive dimension of iconic trade symbols (Coca Cola scenario, section 5.2.5). While the Mona Lisa and Mickey Mouse scenarios concern the freedom of using the rich spectrum of expressive meanings that stem from a sign's evolution in the cultural domain, the Coca Cola scenario relating to iconic trade symbols concerns the freedom of using the rich spectrum of expressive meanings that stem from the capacity of iconic trademarks to symbolize a particular lifestyle or attitude. The common denominator that justifies the introduction of a similar upfront test of use as a mark lies in the rich spectrum of expressive meanings that makes it possible to presume that use in the cultural domain will focus on the sign's rhetoric uniqueness.[2098] As in the case of trademarked cultural signs, it can be posited that use of iconic trade symbols for the purpose of explicitly misleading consumers or deliberately damaging or exploiting the mark's distinctiveness or repute is exceptional in artistic contexts even if the sign at issue has acquired the status of a mark with a reputation.

To effectively implement the threshold criterion of use as a mark, it is necessary to overcome additional obstacles, such as the EU requirement of 'honest practices' in industrial and commercial matters which is mentioned in connection with artistic use in Recital 21 EUTMR and Recital 27 TMD. In this respect, two strategies are available. On the one hand, the honest practices enquiry can be equated with the question of whether the allegedly infringing use in an artistic context explicitly misleads consumers as to the source of the artwork, or deliberately damages or derives unfair advantage from the distinctiveness or the repute of the trademark. If the trademark owner succeeds in demonstrating this evidently disproportionate harm, she can rebut the legal presumption of permissible use with artistic relevance and, at the same time, substantiate that the use was not in compliance with honest practices in industrial and commercial matters. On the other hand, the honest practices proviso can be declared inapplicable to the trademark use requirement altogether. This second approach focuses on the fact that, in the substantive provisions of the EUTMR and the TMD, the honest practices test only appears in Article 14(2) as an additional requirement to be met when specific limitations of trademark rights set forth in Article 14(1) are applied. As the proposed trademark use requirement is an inherent limit of trademark rights and not a specific limitation in the sense of Article 14(1), the honest practices test, arguably, does not affect the gatekeeper requirement of use as a mark.

The proposed upfront test of use as a mark imposes the burden of proving trademark relevance on trademark owners. Hence, it prevents the establishment of prima facie infringement in the absence of convincing evidence that rebuts the legal presumption of non-actionable use in an artistic context. This strategy to shield artists against trademark claims has clear

2098. Dreyfuss 1990, 413 and 418.

advantages over an approach relying on mere defences, such as descriptive or referential use.[2099] Defences only offer an immunity at a later stage of the infringement analysis. They fail to inhibit trademark owners from building a prima facie infringement case and confronting artists with claims that are valid at first glance. In addition, a defence-based approach imposes the burden on artists to prove the facts supporting the invocation of a defence.

From this perspective, the development of robust defences against infringement claims – the second strategy to safeguard cultural follow-on innovation when trademark rights are granted to cultural signs – offers less effective support for artistic remix. A defence-based approach only provides certain safety valves to avoid an erosion of artistic freedom of use. It does not introduce a general bias in favour of artists in the trademark system. A closer look at the spectrum of solutions in this area reveals that it is not sufficient to ensure the applicability of specific limitations, such as the right of quotation and the exemption of parody, in both copyright and trademark law. While horizontal applicability of copyright defence prototypes may be sufficient in the Mickey Mouse scenario (section 5.2.3) where trademark rights relate to a creation that still enjoys copyright protection, a more ambitious approach is necessary in the Mona Lisa scenario (section 5.2.1) where trademark rights are acquired with regard to a cultural heritage sign that was in the public domain. Prior to the reappropriation via trademark law, signs in the Mona Lisa category have been unencumbered by any intellectual property right. Accordingly, users in the artistic domain enjoyed unlimited freedom of remix and reuse. To avoid the erosion of this absolute freedom, trademark law must develop defences that emulate, to the greatest extent possible, the public domain status which affected cultural heritage signs had prior to the acquisition of trademark rights. This requires stronger efforts than the mere copying of specific copyright limitations. In the EUTMR and the TMD, the defences for referential use and non-distinctive use laid down in Article 14(1)(b) and (c) play a crucial role in this respect. Within the inherent limits of any defence-based approach, these limitations of trademark rights can absorb some negative repercussions caused by the loss of absolute freedom of use that existed prior to the grant of trademark rights to cultural heritage signs in the public domain. Moreover, referential use and non-distinctive use arguments can fill the gap of missing counterparts of quotation and parody rules in EU trademark law.

The scope of the referential use defence can be broadened by applying an argument *a maiore ad minus*. As the referential use defence exempts use that identifies the protected sign as a trademark, there is even more reason to apply the defence when the use does not even focus on this trademark aspect but refers to the sign as a cultural artefact. This artistic use does not aim at trademark-related messages which the trademark owner attached to the sign. It has less trademark relevance than the standard referential use scenario

2099. Article 14(1)(b) and (c) EUTMR; Article 14(1)(b) and (c) TMD.

which clearly falls within the scope of the defence. In addition, the non-distinctive use defence is capable of exempting the use of primary, cultural meanings which a sign already had prior to the acquisition of trademark rights. Arguably, these pre-existing cultural connotations remain unprotected residues of the sign's evolution in the cultural domain even after the trademark proprietor attached secondary marketing messages. However, the application of the referential use defence and the non-distinctive use defence in cases of artistic remix would have to become a well-established court practice to emulate the lost public domain status of these signs to the largest extent possible. Judges would have to routinely accept the defence argument unless the trademark proprietor produces evidence of individualized facts that unmask the artistic setting as a mere pretence for blatant trademark infringement. They would have to create a legal environment which offers a high degree of legal certainty and reassurance for artists that trademark infringement claims targeting artistic remix activities will have no success.[2100]

Both defence arguments – referential use and non-distinctive use – are fully applicable not only to cultural heritage signs that have been reappropriated via trademark law (Mona Lisa scenario, section 5.2.1) but also to the unauthorized use, in an artistic context, of trademarked cultural signs stemming from mainstream literary and artistic productions (Mickey Mouse scenario, section 5.2.3) and iconic trade symbols (Coca Cola scenario, section 5.2.5). As to the honest practices proviso in Article 14(2) EUTMR and Article 14(2) TMD, the discussion in the context of the general gatekeeper requirement of use as a mark has already led to the insight that it is possible to set a higher standard for a finding of dishonest practices in cases of artistic remix. Applying this insight mutatis mutandis, referential use and non-distinctive use should be deemed incompatible with honest practices in industrial and commercial matters only if the artistic use at issue explicitly misleads consumers as to the source of the artwork, or deliberately damages or derives unfair advantage from the distinctiveness or the repute of the trademark.

In this way, the beneficial effect of defences, such as referential use and non-distinctive use, can be approximated to the immunizing effect which a gatekeeper requirement of trademark use would have.[2101] In comparison with an upfront test of use as a mark, however, a defence-based approach only offers correction tools after the trademark proprietor established prima facie infringement and confronted artists with a trademark claim that appears valid when viewed in isolation (not factoring defences into the equation).[2102]

2100. As to the lack of legal certainty under current assessment standards, see Assaf 2008, 70-71.

2101. As to the immunizing effect of a threshold requirement of trademark use, see Dinwoodie/Janis 2007a, 1599-1600; Dogan/Lemley 2004, 809-811.

2102. Kur 2009, 293.

Moreover, a defence-based approach imposes the burden of proving privileged referential or non-distinctive use on the artist. As the party benefitting from the defence, the artist must invoke and substantiate the defence argument.[2103] Room for cultural follow-on innovation may thus follow from the development of robust defences. The configuration of these defences may even rest on the same considerations and criteria that support the introduction of a gatekeeper requirement of use as a mark. As to the establishment of prima facie infringement and the burden of proof, however, a defence-based approach remains less favourable to artists. It is the inverse (no prevention of prima facie infringement; artist carries burden of proof) of a strategy seeking to implement an effective upfront test of use as a mark (prevention of prima facie infringement; trademark owner carries burden of proof). Hence, a strategy based on the development of defences will always remain the second-best solution.

2103. Kur/Senftleben 2017, para. 6.78-6.79.

Chapter 10
Overlap Dilemma Revisited

The following summary (section 10.1) provides an overview of the main findings and insights that result from the foregoing analysis. Drawing conclusions (section 10.2), the broader dimension of the research will come to light: the approach that has been applied to copyright/trademark overlaps in the preceding chapters offers a universal formula for activating the self-healing forces of the intellectual property system and curing the disease of an increasingly inconsistent amalgamation of rights stemming from different protection regimes (section 2.1). Arguably, the same approach can be put to good use with regard to other areas of cumulative protection, such as copyright/patent and copyright/industrial design overlaps. Reflecting on the cumulative protection theme at this higher level of abstraction, the contours of a systems theory and protection regime typology in intellectual property law become discernible – a systems theory that may offer starting points for further research endeavours (section 10.3).

10.1 SUMMARY

The cumulation of intellectual property rights thwarts the conceptual differences between individual protection regimes and endangers the delicate balance that is inherent in the configuration of copyright, patent and trademark law. Where it becomes possible to invoke coexisting protection under different intellectual property regimes, the individual balance between rights and freedoms in one protection regime is in danger of being eroded by parallel protection in another regime. As the delicate balance in copyright, patent and trademark law is tailored to specific needs in the domains of culture, technology and trade (section 2.1), overlapping protection constitutes a serious threat to the inner consistency of the intellectual property system and its efficient functioning in different sectors. Copyright law has been particularly vulnerable to the continuous extension of overlapping intellectual property protection in recent years. Due to the elastic originality test and the absence of registration requirements, copyright law has become a melting pot of the continuous growth of intellectual property overlaps. Cumulative copyright and trademark protection for elements of contemporary literary and artistic productions, such as fictional characters, and the possibility of acquiring trademark rights in cultural expressions in the public domain, attests to this trend (section 2.2). As copyright law lies at the core of the currently inflated system of overlapping rights, guidelines for preventing protection overlaps from impeding the proper functioning of the copyright system have the potential to yield more general insights into appropriate reactions to the overlap dilemma. An in-depth examination of the copyright/trademark interface is an important case study from this broader perspective (section 2.3).

To derive overarching insights from a discussion of copyright/trademark overlaps, it is indispensable to have clarity about inalienable, constituent elements of the copyright system: preconditions for the proper functioning of the protection system in the literary and artistic domain. In the foregoing analysis, these constituent parts have been described as 'cultural imperative': essential features of copyright law that allow the protection system to ensure the constant evolution of fresh cultural expressions on the basis of pre-existing source material, and the constant enrichment of the public domain as a provider of intellectual resources for the continuation of the ongoing process of cyclic cultural innovation. The cultural imperative has two main elements. On the one hand, it is imperative to guarantee intergenerational equity. Later authors should be free to learn of the history of their art and ground their own creative activities in the creations of their predecessors. On the other hand, it is imperative to preserve and cultivate the public domain of cultural expressions as a reservoir of source material for new literary and artistic productions. From a functional perspective, these two aspects of the cultural imperative shed light on the primary task of the copyright system to safeguard cyclic cultural innovation by awarding authors protection who succeed in creating a new literary or artistic work on the basis of pre-existing source material. This protection, however, must expire after a limited period of time to make the protected work freely available for future generations of authors who also wish to build upon pre-existing cultural expressions. With the guarantee of intergenerational equity and the recognition of the public domain, the cultural imperative in copyright law safeguards an ongoing remix process in the literary and artistic domain and ensures the incessant evolution of new literary and artistic productions (section 3.1).

A closer analysis of the cultural imperative in the light of theoretical foundations of copyright law has shown that the guarantee of intergenerational equity and the recognition of the public domain are central to the proper functioning of the copyright system from the perspective of both legal traditions of copyright law. Taking a utilitarian approach, intergenerational equity is indispensable to prevent the grant of copyright protection from becoming an obstacle to the creation of new works inspired by, or based upon, pre-existing protected material. The recognition of the public domain is necessary to preserve an area of freedom that makes cultural expressions available for future creativity and cultural follow-on innovation (section 3.2.1). Following the natural law approach, the recognition of the public domain constitutes a precondition for the acquisition of copyright. Without a rich public domain of freely available cultural expressions, there would be no world of abundance in which an author could acquire copyright through the mere act of creation. Moreover, acceptance of intergenerational equity is the price to be paid for the acquisition of copyright. An author can only fulfil her obligation to leave the abundant world of cultural expressions intact by offering later generations of authors freedom to use protected works as a source of inspiration and basis for the creation of new works (section 3.2.2).

In addition, the foregoing analysis demonstrated that the cultural imperative has societal relevance that goes far beyond the objective to secure the proper functioning of copyright law. In the field of literary and artistic production, the guarantee of intergenerational equity ensures that the copyright system remains neutral in the ongoing struggle between different groups of authors for power to set quality standards and dictate the internal discourse. Based on Pierre Bourdieu's sociological analysis, it can be said that the autonomy of the field of literary and artistic production requires independence from economic and political powers (section 3.3.1.1). Instead of striving for commercial success, an autonomous literary or artistic production aims at internal recognition within the field. As a result, the consecration mechanisms in the literary and artistic domain – the power to set quality standards and dominate the internal discourse – become self-referential: *l'art pour l'art*. Viewed from this perspective, the grant of exploitation rights and the focus on pecuniary incentives in copyright law is problematic. The prospect of monetary rewards may entice autonomous artists away from the independent *l'art pour l'art* logic of the literary and artistic field (section 3.3.1.2). At the same time, the constant evolution of fresh, autonomous avant-garde productions depends on mechanisms that allow new generations of autonomous artists to legitimize their unorthodox, new rules by criticizing the dogmata of the presently predominant school of thought. Copyright law can support this constant process of renewal within the group of autonomous artists by guaranteeing user freedoms. It can enable a new generation of artists to destruct an established order and erect a new one by exempting the use of protected, pre-existing works for the formulation of new aesthetic positions. The guarantee of intergenerational equity ensures this freedom. It ensures that copyright law does support not only the creative efforts of profit-oriented authors but also the work of independent, autonomous authors (section 3.3.1.3).

The second aspect of the cultural imperative – the recognition of the public domain – has particular societal relevance as well. It ensures that artworks remain freely available resources for dialogic communication in the literary and artistic domain. In the light of aesthetic theory (sections 3.3.2.1 to 3.3.2.3), it becomes apparent that this contribution to an open artistic discourse supports literary and artistic productions that can offer important impulses for the improvement of societal conditions by identifying defects in social and political systems and providing alternative visions of a better society. To safeguard this important societal function, it is important to preserve the 'artistic discourse potential' of public domain material: after copyright expiry, works of art must constitute free sources of inspiration that are made available as building blocks for new acts of creation in an open communication process that is not dominated by an individual speaker, such as the owner of exclusive trademark rights. As trademark law offers the trademark owner an exclusive position, the definition power is higher than the degree of control resulting from other forms of commercial use, such as mere use in advertising without trademark rights. The grant of stable, indefinitely renewable trademark rights substantially enhances the risk of impregnating the artwork with commercial messages that may devalue the sign as a reference point in the artistic discourse. The debate about the artwork is no longer as open and free as it was before. If the trademark right is acquired after the artwork entered the public domain, the resulting imbalance is self-evident. Unlimited freedom of use is sacrificed in favour of a scenario where all speakers, including artists in the cultural domain, must ensure that their contributions to the debate do not amount to trademark infringement. Intentionally or unintentionally, the trademark proprietor will bring trademark claims against those forms of artistic use which, from her point of view, interfere with her own strategy for the development of the message and meaning of the sign (section 3.3.2.4).

Considering this problem scenario, it is of particular interest that, developing his aesthetic theory, Theodor Adorno explicitly warned of the risk of artworks losing their subversive character through efforts to submerge their critical meaning and popularize them in commercial products. Once art is consumed and enjoyed, it inevitably loses its value as a mirror of defects in society and a provocation that is capable of triggering necessary changes. Instead, it becomes a means of pretending that the present situation is sufficient and acceptable. From this perspective, it is indispensable to shield artworks from the corrosive effect of use in product marketing to safeguard the potential of art to expose flaws in society. Therefore, the recognition of the need to preserve a rich and robust public domain of cultural expression – understood in the sense of efforts to preserve an artwork's potential for dialogic communication in the artistic domain – is of particular importance to society. It ensures that alternative visions of society that are evoked in literary and artistic works remain intact – visions that may provide impulses for artistic follow-on innovation and societal reforms (section 3.3.2.4).

After the identification of inalienable core elements of the copyright system, the analysis turned to the question of whether overlapping trademark protection may erode these essential, constituent parts of copyright law: the cultural imperative with its two components intergenerational equity and public domain recognition. Embarking on a comparison of the functional configuration of copyright law with other types of intellectual property rights, several functional parallels came to light in respect of patent law (section 4.1.1). As copyright law, patent law can be understood to support a process of cyclic innovation. While copyright law seeks to safeguard cyclic cultural innovation, patent law seeks to stimulate cyclic technical innovation. It confers exclusive rights to provide an incentive for the development of new technical solutions on the basis of pre-existing technical knowledge. As copyright protection, patent protection expires after a limited period of time. In this way, the protection system makes protected know-how freely available for future generations of inventors. As in copyright law, the guarantee of intergenerational equity (between inventors in the case of patent law) and the recognition of a need to preserve the public domain are of crucial importance. Hence, a convergence of principles comes to the fore: both copyright and patent law aim to foster an incessant process of follow-on innovation. Protection under copyright and patent law is cyclic in the sense that it is awarded whenever a new creation evolves in the constant process of innovation in the respective field, and it is taken away after a limited period of time to prevent an impediment of the cyclic innovation process that lies at the core of both protection systems (section 4.1.1).

A discussion of trademark law, however, revealed that the core ingredients of copyright law – the guarantee of intergenerational equity and the recognition of the public domain – do not have much weight. By contrast, the objective to ensure market transparency occupies centre stage. To achieve this goal, trademark law must offer static protection that guarantees a stable distribution of available intellectual resources. Instead of seeking to support the productive reuse of distinctive signs, trademark law aims at stability once a certain sign is linked with a particular trader. Protection is not a reward for the creation of something new on the basis of pre-existing source and inspiration material. By contrast, it is a means of solidifying the ownership situation with regard to a particular intellectual resource that plays a central role in the distinction of the commercial origin of goods and services in the marketplace. Accordingly, trademark protection must continue as long as this is necessary to secure market transparency. If the trademark owner does not cease making genuine use of the protected sign in the marketplace, she can renew trademark protection indefinitely. Comparing this imperative of market transparency with the cultural imperative inherent in copyright law, the conclusion is inescapable that there is a divergence of principles (section

4.2.1). Certain traces of intergenerational equity and public domain recognition may be found in trademark law. The possibility to exclude signs from protection because of a need to keep them free for other traders and the requirement of genuine use play an important role in this regard. However, a closer inspection of these elements of the protection system leads to the insight that they are subordinated to the overarching objective to ensure market transparency (section 4.2.2). In contrast to copyright law, intergenerational equity and public domain recognition are not central, constituent parts of trademark law.

When protection overlaps arise, the incompatibility between the cultural imperative in copyright law and the trademark imperative of market transparency will inevitably pose major difficulties, including the risk of an impediment of the cultural innovation cycle which copyright law seeks to support (section 4.2.3). While copyright protection is limited in time, trademark protection is not. While copyright law stimulates the creative remix of pre-existing intellectual resources, trademark law does not. The problems arising from this incompatibility must not be underestimated. In the domain of technology (where a similar impediment of cyclic technical innovation may occur), it is possible to rely on objective criteria to identify non-substitutable technical solutions which must be kept free to safeguard the technical innovation cycle. At least theoretically, efforts to keep technical know-how available in the case of protection overlaps can be confined to these indispensable solutions (section 4.1.2). In the domain of culture, by contrast, it is impossible to identify non-substitutable literary and artistic works on the basis of objective criteria. Cultural creativity depends on how an artist embarking on the creation of a new work assesses the relevance of pre-existing literary and artistic resources for the envisaged creative work. The assessment criteria are subjective. They are likely to differ from artist to artist. Accordingly, it is not foreseeable which literary and artistic works will be indispensable for future generations of artists to arrive at new cultural productions and keep the cultural innovation cycle intact. The subjectivity of the assessment of source material in the cultural domain, however, is no reason to assume that the cultural innovation cycle is less vulnerable than the technical innovation cycle when it comes to coexisting trademark protection. While literary and artistic works may be substitutable at the consumption level, they are not substitutable at the production level (section 4.1.3). If trademark protection leads to a situation where artists refrain from use of a given piece of art as a building block for new artistic works, the spectrum of derivative works that could have followed from this piece of art will be lost and the cultural innovation cycle will be impoverished in this respect. Therefore, efforts to prevent potential encroachments of coexisting trademark protection upon the cultural innovation cycle should cover a wide range of cultural signs that may become relevant to the evolution of new literary and artistic works in the cultural domain. A distinction between substitutable and non-substitutable cultural material is not possible (section 4.1.4).

In the subsequent analysis, the finding that a wide range of cultural signs should be kept available for cultural follow-on innovation gave rise to the further question how trademark examiners and judges could identify relevant cultural signs in practice. To trace the contours of the concept of 'cultural sign', the aesthetic and sociological theories employed to substantiate the societal need to safeguard cyclic cultural innovation served as signposts (section 5.1). Viewed through this lens, the concept of 'cultural sign' must cover not only signs derived from works of fine art, ranging from cultural heritage material to modern creations that still enjoy copyright protection (Mona Lisa scenario, section 5.2.1), but also signs derived from cultural mainstream productions (Mickey Mouse scenario, section 5.2.3). Contemporary mainstream works, such as fictional characters, enter the picture because they may constitute important reference points for artists seeking to mirror current societal conditions. Moreover, the concept of 'cultural sign' should encompass the titles of works in the fine art and the cultural mainstream category. Viewed in isolation, these titles often fail to meet the originality test in copyright law. Strictly speaking, trademark protection of work titles is not an issue of copyright/trademark overlaps. Nonetheless, the close connection with literary and artistic works and the need to enable artists to clearly identify their source materials justifies their inclusion in the concept of 'cultural sign' (section 5.2.4). Insofar as measures to safeguard cyclic cultural innovation are compatible with the use protocols of indigenous communities, the concept of 'cultural sign' may also include traditional cultural expressions. However, the ultimate goal of the enquiry into copyright/trademark overlaps – the preservation of unrestricted freedom to use cultural signs for the purpose of follow-on innovation in the literary and artistic field – should not be extended to traditional cultural expressions without considering potential use restrictions that may follow from the customary law of indigenous peoples (section 5.2.2).

To identify signs belonging to this spectrum of cultural signs in practice, trademark offices and courts can use a multifactor test (section 5.3) raising the following questions:

- does the sign feature in a fine art creation or a cultural mainstream production? Can it be found in an online library or collection of a cultural institution, ranging from museums to movie theatres? (factor one);
- does an online search reveal that the sign has already served as a basis for parodies, remixes or other forms of mash-up? (factor two);
- does the sign display typical style features known from other literary or artistic creations which the trademark office has included in reference material for the identification of signs with cultural significance? (factor three);

- does the sign fall under one of the work categories listed in Article 2(1) BC? Does it clearly meet copyright's originality test because it reflects a high degree of free, creative choices? (factor four);
- could the sign theoretically serve as an embellishment to improve the outward appearance of a product, or would it describe the contents of a product when it was applied to goods or services in the cultural domain? Would consumers perceive the sign as a descriptive or decorative element in a hypothetical scenario where the sign features prominently on a product or where it is used in relation to goods or services in the cultural domain? (factor five).

In the assessment based on these factors, the status of 'cultural sign' must not exclusively depend on whether a given sign currently serves as a reference point for remix and reuse in the cultural domain. If it does, this is a clear indication that it is relevant to cultural follow-on innovation. In addition, however, a prospective analysis is necessary that asks whether a sign can reasonably be expected to serve as source material for the creation of new literary and artistic works in the future. Hence, the assessment should not be confined to use necessities that have already materialized. Otherwise, measures seeking to minimize the corrosive effect of trademark protection on cultural remix would only focus on current building blocks of derivative works and lose sight of potential future sources of inspiration. These future sources, however, are particularly relevant. They may pave the way for new, currently underexplored artistic positions (section 5.1).

Examining the conceptual contours of 'cultural sign', the analysis finally pointed out that genuine trademarks and other trade symbols should not be qualified as cultural signs even if these commercial symbols acquire cultural significance as symbols of a particular lifestyle or attitude. Iconic product design or trademarks may provide important reference points for a critique of societal conditions, such as consumerism and materialism. The contrast between artworks and commercial trade symbols may serve as a means to comment on the societal role and function of art itself. Nonetheless, the appearance of trademarks and other trade symbols in works of art does not make them 'cultural signs'. The contrast arising from the use of an iconic trademark in an artistic context can only be produced as long as the sign constitutes a well-functioning trade symbol that is used in a commercial marketing context. Declaring a famous trademark a cultural sign would miss the point. As an antipode of cultural signs, trademarks and other trade symbols must be kept separate. This separate status, however, does not imply that initiatives to safeguard the cultural innovation cycle will never affect trademarks and other trade symbols. Even though they constitute commercial – and not cultural – signs, it may be advisable to take measures to support their use in artworks seeking to comment on societal conditions (section 5.2.5).

The circumscription of the concept of 'cultural signs' completed the process of laying groundwork for the more detailed legal analysis of incompatibilities between copyright and trademark protection. The mere fact that copyright and trademark protection are incompatible from an abstract, functional perspective (contrast between a cyclic and a static intellectual property system) does not make it possible to jump to the conclusion that, by definition, trademark rights to cultural signs thwart cultural follow-on innovation. The nature and scope of trademark rights may differ from the exclusive rights granted in copyright law to such an extent that, in practice, the impact of trademark protection remains limited. Hence, it was necessary to examine whether trademark rights are so different in nature and scope that their potential corrosive effect on future creativity in the cultural domain may remain negligible (section 6.1). The analysis of this question showed that at least advanced trademark systems, such as EU trademark law, offer trademark proprietors various starting points for infringement claims against remix and reuse of trademarked cultural signs in a literary and artistic context (sections 6.1.2 and 6.2.1). Use in the artistic domain may be deemed to cause confusion as to affiliation or sponsorship (section 6.2.2). Even if it does not cause confusion, a trademark action need not fail. If a trademark has acquired the status of a mark with a reputation, the trademark proprietor can still argue that use in the cultural domain damages, or takes unfair advantage of, the economic and communication value of the trademark (section 6.2.3). In cases where the allegedly infringing use concerns use of a sign identical to a trademarked cultural sign for identical goods or services, EU trademark law even offers protection of communication, advertising and investment functions without making it a prerequisite that the registered cultural sign has a reputation (section 6.2.3). General limitations of trademark protection, such as the exemption of descriptive and referential use, do not equip artists with sufficiently robust defences to dispel concerns about an impediment of cyclic cultural innovation. The open-ended defence of 'due cause' could fill this gap. However, this defence is not applicable across all types of EU trademark rights (section 6.2.4).

Given the broad spectrum of infringement arguments which trademark proprietors have at their disposal, the proportions of trademark protection in the EU entail a serious risk of inroads into artistic freedom of expression. In particular, it is no longer accurate to describe trademark rights as defensive instruments that merely preserve a sign's function of indicating the commercial origin of goods or services. The nature of trademark rights has changed considerably during the last decades. Although a sound justificatory basis for this expansion is missing (section 6.1.2), trademark rights have become exploitation instruments that come close to the exclusive rights awarded in copyright law (section 6.1.1). As they cover the economic and communication value of protected signs, interferences with use in the artistic discourse seem inevitable. As copyright, trademark rights offer the opportunity to exert considerable control over the communication surrounding a protected sign (section 6.1.2). Against this background, the deterrent effect of exposure of artists to a trademark infringement action must not be underestimated once trademark rights in a cultural sign are granted. If the trademark proprietor sends a cease-and-desist letter stating that use of a trademarked cultural sign amounts to infringement, this will often suffice to put an end to use of the affected cultural sign in a literary and artistic context. Growing fears of artists to be sued for intellectual property infringement reflect the dimension of this problem (section 6.3).

The scope of trademark rights in cultural signs, thus, proved to be far from unproblematic in advanced trademark systems that no longer confine protection to the traditional origin function of trademarks. Against this background, the time had come for a more detailed exploration of encroachments upon cyclic cultural innovation. This exploration of potential interferences with cultural follow-on innovation took place in two steps. Focusing first on the need to ensure that, after copyright expiry, cultural signs enter the public domain in line with the guarantee of intergenerational equity, it could be demonstrated that trademark law fails to offer adequate safeguards against an artificial perpetuation of copyright exclusivity after the expiry of copyright protection. While the functionality doctrine in trademark law may prevent overlaps between patent and trademark protection (section 7.1.5) and lead to a far-reaching separation of industrial design and trademark protection (section 7.2.5), a comparably strong mechanism for policing the border between copyright and trademark protection has not evolved yet (section 7.3.4). When it comes to cultural signs stemming from books, paintings, drawings, musical compositions and films, the cumulation of copyright and trademark protection is often possible. As these signs need not define product characteristics (but may be attached to goods as mere labels), the functionality doctrine is incapable of banning trademark rights (section 7.3.1).

The remaining obstacle – the basic requirement of distinctive character – is a hurdle which trademark applicants can surmount in many cases (section 7.3.4). While the test of distinctiveness may restrict trademark rights to merchandising articles that are not directly related to the primary information products embodying the cultural sign concerned, even this remaining safeguard against broad protection overlaps is lost in the case of cultural signs that are consistently used as indicators of commercial origin, such as fictional characters and work titles. In this case, the goods and services covered by a trademark registration may encompass the exploitation of the books, films and music containing the cultural expression at stake. The corrosive effect on cultural follow-on innovation is self-evident. In practice, the acceptance of overlapping copyright and trademark protection for literary and artistic works often rests on the assumption that trademark rights do not offer protection for a cultural creation as such, but only for certain functions which the cultural creation fulfils as a distinctive sign in respect of goods and services to which it is attached (section 7.3.3). However, this argument is only valid as long as differences in the configuration of copyright and trademark protection really lead to different outcomes in practice. Considering the metamorphosis of trademark rights into exploitation instruments that are comparable with the copyright monopoly, it is not convincing to justify copyright/trademark overlaps any longer by emphasizing differences in the configuration of the respective protection regimes (sections 7.3.2 and 7.3.5.1).

Moreover, it was recalled in the analysis that cultural follow-on innovation is as vulnerable as innovation processes in the area of technology and product design. It would be wrong to assume that, in contrast to technical solutions, literary and artistic works are substitutable when it comes to processes of cultural follow-on innovation. In the context of inventions and industrial designs, an outright exclusion of trademark protection does not even depend on the existence of alternatives for competitors (sections 7.1.2 and 7.2.2). Against this background, the grant of trademark rights to cultural signs cannot be justified by assuming that artists seeking to base new creations on pre-existing cultural expressions can easily find alternatives for unavailable source material (section 7.3.5.2). Admittedly, the mark/product dichotomy which offers an additional reason for the categorical exclusion of inventions and industrial designs from trademark protection (sections 7.1.3 and 7.2.3) is unavailable in the field of literary and artistic works. While technical solutions and industrial designs typically define product characteristics, a literary and artistic work may be attached to goods as a mere label (section 7.1.3). This formal difference, however, does not change the equation with regard to the risk of an artificial perpetuation of copyright exclusivity and the risk of an encroachment upon artistic freedom of expression. Considering these fundamental concerns, arguments based on the formal distinction between the mark and the product in trademark law do not offer a sufficient basis for granting trademark rights to cultural signs (section 7.3.5.3).

It is to be conceded, however, that an exclusion of literary and artistic works from trademark protection may temporarily give rise to incidents of consumer confusion when, in fact, a cultural creation has acquired distinctive character as a result of use in trade. However, this risk of consumer confusion is willingly accepted to safeguard the freedom of innovation in the domains of inventions and industrial designs (sections 7.1.4 and 7.2.4). There is no compelling reason to decide otherwise in respect of literary and artistic works, cultural follow-on innovation and freedom of expression (section 7.3.5.4). Moreover, it is not convincing to assert that indefinitely renewable trademark rights offer ongoing economic incentives for continued investment in literary and artistic works. As the copyright owner enjoys a long period of copyright protection, she can be expected to be well prepared for the rigours of free competition after copyright expiry. Instead of killing investment, the end of copyright will strengthen efforts of the former copyright owner to preserve her market dominance by investing in new and improved versions of the cultural expression at stake (section 7.3.5.5). Seeking trademark protection, the copyright owner only tries to escape the obligation to provide public domain material for second authors. The enrichment of the public domain, however, is the price to be paid for the enjoyment of copyright protection. As the long monopoly period following from copyright protection allows the copyright owner to use market exclusivity strategically to impregnate a literary and artistic work with the source-identifying function necessary to obtain trademark rights, the acquisition of trademark rights even appears as a dysfunctional, unfair advantage that is derived from the monopoly position awarded in copyright law (section 7.3.5.6).

In sum, the analysis of copyright/trademark overlaps from the perspective of intergenerational equity confirmed that a limited term of protection is crucial not only to innovation in the areas of technology and product design but also to the continuous evolution of literary and artistic works. As the cyclic innovation imperatives in patent and industrial designs law, the cultural imperative in copyright law should prevail over the commercial imperative of market transparency and the grant of indefinitely renewable trademark rights. To remedy the current imbalance within the intellectual property system, it would be necessary to introduce a categorical exclusion of literary and artistic works from trademark protection that is as effective as the functionality doctrine in the area of inventions and industrial designs. In this way, intellectual property law could arrive at an equal treatment of cyclic innovation systems and shield processes of cultural follow-on innovation adequately from the corrosive effect of static trademark protection (section 7.4).

Turning to the need to ensure that cultural expressions are not removed from the public domain, the analysis showed that trademark law poses a particular threat to the objective to recognize and preserve a rich and robust public domain as a central element of the cultural imperative in copyright law. Inevitably, the reappropriation of cultural heritage signs via trademark law erodes the absolute freedom of use following from the public domain status. The prospect of acquiring trademark rights may encourage freeriding on the particularly rich spectrum of connotations which cultural signs offer as a result of their evolution in the artistic domain (section 8.2.3.1). Moreover, the use of cultural material for marketing purposes is likely to interfere with open, dialogic communication in the artistic domain, erode the artistic discourse potential of affected signs (section 8.2.3.2) and devalue them as sources of inspiration and building blocks of new artistic works (section 8.2.3.3).

As to the arsenal of countermeasures that may be taken into consideration, the discussion about the concept of 'public domain' in literature has shed light on a broad spectrum of preservation mechanisms that differ with regard to the degree of effectiveness. An outright, categorical exclusion of cultural heritage signs from trademark protection is the most effective public domain preservation tool. It ensures that cultural heritage signs cannot be removed from the public domain through the acquisition of trademark rights.

The adoption of this measure is in line with the legal status definition of the public domain which makes absence of any intellectual property right a precondition for awarding public domain status (section 8.1.1). Less far-reaching preservation tools enter the picture when the public domain is understood to encompass robust user freedoms that remain after the acquisition of trademark protection (section 8.1.2). User freedoms may result from inherent limits of trademark rights and play an important role in the preservation of artistic freedom of use (section 8.2.1). Forms of using protected signs may also be exempted from the control of trademark owners by adopting limitations of exclusive rights that provide defences in infringement cases (section 8.2.2). However, the closer inspection of these regulatory tools has shown that inherent limits of exclusive rights become less reliable safeguards with every expansion of trademark protection. The weaker the inherent limits of exclusive trademark rights become in advanced trademark systems, such as the EU system, the stronger the need for the adoption of limitations of protection that explicitly exempt culturally relevant forms of use from the scope of trademark rights. Specific defences against trademark infringement claims, however, only constitute appropriate preservation tools in the sense of public domain concepts that take account of freedom of use, if they are reliable and robust. Artistic use must become an 'easy case' in which infringement arguments are regularly doomed to fail (section 8.1.2).

Moreover, it is to be considered that both – inherent limits of exclusive rights and explicit exceptions that serve as defences – do not preclude the acquisition of trademark rights. As a result of the grant of protection, the trademark owner will be able to influence or even dictate the communication process surrounding the protected sign (section 8.2.3.2). Commercial connotations may be added to the sign that reduce its value for cultural forms of use or even suppress its potential for open, dialogic communication in the literary and artistic domain (section 8.2.3.3). Given the predominance of the trademark proprietor, the communication concerning affected cultural expressions is no longer as open and free as it would have been in the absence of the grant of exclusive trademark rights. Hence, there is a qualitative difference between inherent limits of exclusive rights and specific defences on the one hand and the categorical exclusion of trademark protection on the other. An effective exclusion of trademark rights keeps signs free from trademark protection and does not provide an incentive for the attachment of marketing messages. This incentive is offered, however, when trademark protection is granted. Inherent limits of, and limited exceptions to, the exclusive rights of trademark owners are thus incapable of preserving signs as part of an information commons that can freely be shaped and defined in the course of an open communication process (section 3.3.2.4). The contribution of these legal mechanisms to the preservation of the public domain is limited in comparison with an effective exclusion from trademark protection.

In the light of these results, a clear hierarchy of preservation tools comes to the fore. From the perspective of the cultural imperative in copyright law, it is preferable to exclude cultural heritage signs categorically from trademark protection (section 8.2.3). This is the most effective strategy to preserve the public domain of cultural expressions and ensure the openness of the communication process surrounding literary and artistic public domain material. A solution based on implicit (section 8.2.1) or explicit (section 8.2.2) limitations of exclusive rights only constitutes the second-best option. Even if a trademark system succeeds in setting robust and reliable limits to exclusive rights, the fact remains that the trademark proprietor obtains the opportunity to remove cultural signs from the public domain and embark on the attachment of commercial marketing messages. The trademark proprietor is a privileged speaker in the communication arena. He has more impact on the communication process than other speakers because he can avail himself of exclusive rights to influence the perception of the affected sign. In the case of cultural signs, the adoption of limitations is thus less effective than the categorical denial of trademark rights.

This is different when it comes to famous trademarks and other iconic trade symbols that have acquired cultural significance. Once a trade symbol has acquired cultural significance, it may be argued from the perspective of public domain enrichment that trademark protection should be revoked to broaden the reservoir of freely available source material for cultural follow-on innovation and allow unrestricted remix activities in the literary and artistic domain (section 8.3.1). Practically speaking, however, the termination of trademark rights because of cultural significance is beyond reach in the light of international protection standards. Moreover, the end of trademark protection would deprive the trade symbol of its *raison d'être*. After the sign has fallen into the public domain, its commercial meaning is likely to vanish because the trademark proprietor loses his dominant position in the communication process and the opportunity to maintain a specific brand image with specific lifestyle messages. As trade symbols are commercial creations, the ultimate loss of trademark meaning entails the risk of losing important reference points for cultural follow-on innovation as well. Once the sign is no longer perceived as a commercial symbol, artists can no longer employ the sign to create a contrast between the world of art and the world of commerce. Hence, a peculiar situation arises where the loss of commercial meaning reduces the possibilities for artists to comment on societal conditions. Given this specific result, it is preferable not to revoke trademark protection in the case of iconic trade symbols. Instead, the cultural significance of the sign should be made available for artistic remix activities by adopting reliable and robust limitations of trademark rights that support unauthorized metaphorical use of the expressive meaning of iconic trade symbols in literary and artistic productions (section 8.3.2).

After the abstract assessment of existing legal instruments in the light of the objective to safeguard cultural follow-on innovation, the analysis finally addressed the question how the different regulatory tools – ranging from an outright exclusion of trademark rights to the development of tailor-made defences for artists – could be implemented in practice. With regard to the categorical exclusion of trademark protection, this final step in the analysis confirmed that the current reliance of trademark examiners and judges on the basic trademark requirement of distinctive character is problematic. In the pantheon of absolute grounds for refusal, a lack of distinctiveness is a particularly weak exclusion argument because it often remains limited to specific goods and services, such as goods and services that are directly connected with the literary and artistic production at issue. Moreover, trademark applicants can overcome the registration obstacle through continuous use of a cultural sign in trade. As the requirement of distinctiveness constitutes a genuine category of trademark law, it is also incapable of providing an appropriate forum for discussing concerns about an impediment of follow-on innovation in the cultural domain (section 9.1.2.1). Instead of permitting the direct articulation of cultural concerns about the acquisition of trademark rights, the test of distinctiveness only gives trademark offices and courts the chance to let these concerns prevail in the guise of an argument based on market transparency. They must hide the central point – concerns about an impediment of cultural follow-on innovation – behind a rhetoric of lacking distinctiveness. To force the trademark system to process cultural concerns more appropriately, a ground for refusal is needed that allows offices and courts to clearly express a cultural argument against the grant of trademark rights without being obliged to repackage that argument as a concern about distinctive character. For example, offices and courts should be able to base a refusal on the argument that the grant of trademark rights to cultural signs entails an inacceptable risk of blurring and finally erasing the sign's cultural meaning as a result of the attachment of marketing messages, interfering with open, dialogic communication in the artistic domain, encouraging freeriding on favourable connotations which the sign has a result of its evolution in the cultural domain, obtaining unfair competitive advantages because of this freeriding and, ultimately, artificially perpetuating copyright after the expiry of the limited term of copyright protection and impeding the cultural innovation cycle.

As the analysis has shown, a refusal based on a conflict with morality or public order offers much more room for the articulation of these cultural concerns in a trademark context. The cultivation of morality and public order as reference points for the assessment is an important step in the right direction. If the refusal decision rests on a conflict with morality or *ordre public*, it can apply across the whole spectrum of goods and services. Moreover, it is robust in the sense that continuous use in trade does not enable the trademark applicant to surmount the registration obstacle (section 9.1.2.2). Following in the footsteps of the EFTA Court decision in *Vigeland*, four central exclusion arguments can be distinguished in this area:

- the relevant public may perceive the registration as a trademark as offensive because certain pieces of art enjoy a 'particular status as prominent parts of a nation's cultural heritage, an emblem of sovereignty or of the nation's foundations and values'[2104] (morality ground 1);
- the relevant public may perceive the registration as a trademark as offensive because it would lead to a 'misappropriation or a desecration of the artist's work, in particular if it is granted for goods or services that contradict values of the artist or the message communicated through the artwork in question'[2105] (morality ground 2);
- the registration as a trademark would pose a genuine and sufficiently serious threat to 'certain fundamental values',[2106] 'a fundamental interest of society'[2107] or 'a fundamental concern to the State and the whole of society'[2108] (public order ground 1);
- the registration as a trademark would run counter to the need to safeguard the public domain which amounts to a genuine and serious threat if this need 'itself, is considered a fundamental interest of society'[2109] (public order ground 2).

These exclusion arguments make it possible to state candidly that trademark law is not intended to serve as a basis for freeriding on the reputation and positive image of cultural symbols, the reduction of a sign's artistic discourse potential as a result of exposure to commercial marketing strategies, and the impairment of the unhindered, open communication process surrounding the sign in the cultural domain. The attachment of commercial meanings in the course of marketing campaigns, for example, may be qualified as a desecration of the artist's work in the sense of morality ground 2. In the case of signs with a particular status in society – the status of important cultural heritage, an emblem of sovereignty or a symbol of a nation's foundations and values – morality ground 1 allows a refusal based on the social and political dimension of cultural signs (section 9.1.2.3). Unfair freeriding on positive connotations of cultural signs may be seen as an interference with society's fundamental interest in undistorted competition that justifies the invocation of public order ground 1. The use of trademark rights to prevent the remix and reuse of cultural signs in the artistic domain may be deemed inacceptable from the perspective of freedom of expression: a fundamental interest of society that may be defended on the basis of public order ground 1 as well. Finally, public order ground 2 applies in legal systems where the cultivation of the public domain – in and of itself – is

2104. EFTA Court, 6 April 2017, case E-5/16, Municipality of Oslo ('Vigeland'), para. 92.
2105. EFTA Court, *ibid.*, para. 92.
2106. EFTA Court, *ibid.*, para. 96.
2107. EFTA Court, *ibid.*, para. 95.
2108. EFTA Court, *ibid.*, para. 94.
2109. EFTA Court, *ibid.*, para. 96.

qualified as a fundamental interest of society, for instance, to preserve alternative visions of society that are evoked in literary and artistic works and should remain intact to provide impulses for societal change (section 9.1.2.4).

Public order and morality, thus, offer various starting points for trademark examiners and judges to arrive at a categorical exclusion of cultural signs from trademark protection. In comparison with the broad spectrum of exclusion arguments provided by public order and morality considerations, other grounds for refusal have a rather limited potential to keep cultural signs free. From a legal-doctrinal perspective, aesthetic functionality can be qualified as a special case of public order and morality considerations. The ambit of operation of aesthetic functionality, however, is unsatisfactory because it is confined to situations where a cultural sign defines product characteristics (section 9.1.3.2). Specific grounds for refusal that focus on a particular status of cultural signs, such as high symbolic value, have a rather limited scope as well: by definition, these grounds for refusal only cover cultural signs that meet the specific status requirement set forth in relevant provisions. While a status-based ground for refusal, such as the denial of protection in the case of signs with high symbolic value, may be effective within its limited field of application, it must not be regarded as a *lex specialis* precluding the invocation of more general public order and morality considerations. Otherwise, the introduction of a specific, status-based ground for refusal would be a Trojan Horse thwarting the objective to arrive at a robust exclusion of various types of cultural signs instead of furthering the attainment of this goal (section 9.1.3.3).

Finally, bad faith may pose an obstacle to the acquisition of trademark rights in cases of cultural heritage grabbing. However, this exclusion mechanism is largely rendered ineffective in many trademark systems, including the trademark regimes in the EU, because of the grace period of permissible non-use that follows the trademark registration. Until the end of this grace period, the cultural heritage grabber can maintain the trademark registration without developing genuine use activities in the marketplace. For this reason, it can be particularly difficult for trademark offices and courts to establish bad faith at the moment where the trademark application is received. As trademark proprietors can wait several years before finally embarking on genuine use in the marketplace, it is not sufficient that, at the time of applying for a trademark registration, the applicant has not already made preparations for product marketing based on the cultural sign (section 9.1.3.4).

While a refusal of trademark rights based on aesthetic functionality, high symbolic value or bad faith adds little to public order and morality considerations, the communication of emblems of states and international intergovernmental organizations under Article 6*ter* PC sheds light on an important complementary feature of sign exclusion mechanisms in the field of trademark law: the prospect of using notifications of cultural signs to establish a ‘white list’ of cultural expressions to be kept free across Paris Union and WTO Members (section 9.1.4.2). The closer inspection of this communication avenue, however, yields the insight that the employment of the existing 6*ter* system for the purpose of preventing trademark rights in cultural signs is undesirable. The communication under Article 6*ter* PC leads not only to the exclusion of notified signs but also to the exertion of state control. It cannot be ruled out that a state uses 6*ter* communications strategically to claim the right of authorizing and regulating the use of notified cultural signs. Ultimately, the qualification of cultural signs as ‘state emblems’ may culminate in nation branding campaigns with a corrosive effect on the sign’s potential to serve as a basis for open, dialogic communication in the artistic domain (section 9.1.4.3).

In sum, considerations of public order and morality, by far, are the most promising vehicles to achieve an outright exclusion of cultural signs from trademark protection under existing trademark legislation. The public order and morality criteria that can be distilled from the *Vigeland* decision of the EFTA Court offer trademark offices and courts considerable room for the application and further development of this ground for refusal in cases involving cultural signs. It is thus advisable to explore the full potential of public order and morality as grounds for refusing trademark rights to cultural signs. As also pointed out in the foregoing analysis, public order and morality decisions should aim at preventing the acquisition of trademark rights and the evolution of overlapping copyright/trademark protection *ex ante*. Ideally, public order and morality criteria fulfil a gatekeeper function that is comparable with the role of utilitarian and aesthetic functionality in the field of technical solutions and industrial designs (section 9.1.1.7).

Considering the risk of copyright protection coming into being accidentally with regard to logos and other signs that are specifically made to serve as identifiers of commercial source, however, an additional rule is necessary to refine the application of public order and morality. When it comes to these hybrid signs, trademark applicants should have the opportunity to formally declare that the sign will not be used in a cultural context. This declaration of non-use in a cultural context should be registered together with the sign itself. If copyright protection is later invoked in respect of a sign registered under these circumstances, this enforcement step should automatically qualify as use in a cultural context. As the trademark proprietor avails herself of protection stemming from the cultural aspect of the sign, the trademark should become liable to be declared invalid and the defendant facing the copyright claim should be able to bring a counterclaim demanding this invalidation. Hence, the implementation of cultural grounds for refusal on the basis of public order or morality should not only provide for the *ex ante* exclusion of trademark protection but also for a later invalidation in cases where a declaration of non-use in a cultural context has been made (section 9.1.2.5).

In the U.S., the Supreme Court decisions in *Matal/Tam* and *Iancu/Brunetti* do not pose lasting obstacles to the cultivation of public order and morality as grounds for refusal when trademark applicants seek to register cultural signs as trademarks. The fact pattern underlying these decisions favoured an approach focusing on speech constraints which the trademark applicant may experience. When public order and morality are invoked to deny the registration of a cultural sign as a trademark, however, the use of these grounds for refusal furthers freedom of speech. It safeguards and enhances the freedom of speech of other participants in the debate, in particular artists. The free speech equation is different. Denying trademark rights, the communication process concerning the cultural sign remains open. No individual trademark owner obtains a position that is stronger than the position of other speakers. Therefore, neither *Matal/Tam* nor *Iancu/Brunetti* prevent the U.S. Supreme Court from embracing public order and morality as grounds for refusal in a future decision that concerns the freedom of speech of third parties (in particular artists). For a change of course, a fact pattern is necessary that offers the Court the opportunity to consider the corrosive effect of positive discrimination in favour of commercial speech (following from the grant of exclusive rights) instead of simply addressing negative discrimination against the trademark applicant (section 9.1.2.6).

If it is not possible to avoid the grant of trademark rights to a cultural sign on the basis of cultural grounds for refusal, legislators and judges seeking to offer breathing space for cultural follow-on innovation within the trademark system can pursue two different strategies:

(1) they can either implement a strict test of 'use as a mark' that functions as a gatekeeper requirement and prevents trademark owners from establishing prima facie trademark infringement (section 9.2.1); or
(2) develop reliable and robust limitations of trademark rights that can serve as defences for users in the cultural domain (section 9.2.2).

In both scenarios, the overarching goal is the creation of a bias in favour of users who embark on the remix and reuse of cultural signs in the artistic domain. Where a trademarked cultural sign is used in connection with a literary or artistic production, it is important to establish a legal presumption that the use does not amount to actionable use as a trademark.

To achieve this goal with the first strategy – the implementation of a gatekeeper requirement of 'use as a mark' – it is advisable to combine the approach underlying the U.S. 'Rogers' test (section 9.2.1.1) with the insight that use in a cultural setting normally concerns the cultural, expressive meaning of a sign with cultural significance (section 9.2.1.2). This type of use is unlikely to confuse consumers, damage the trademark reputation, or exploit trademark magnetism in an unfair manner. By contrast, use in the cultural domain will address the rhetoric uniqueness of cultural signs: the specific set of meanings and connotations which these signs evoke as a result of their evolution in the cultural domain and which makes them indispensable communication tools for cultural follow-on innovation.

Against this background, it is appropriate to adopt a legal presumption of non-actionable use – in both confusion (section 9.2.1.4) and dilution (section 9.2.1.5) contexts – to pose a hurdle which the trademark owner must surmount before he can establish prima facie infringement and bring a claim. Only if the trademark owner succeeds in demonstrating that – despite the cultural setting – an artist specifically aims at causing consumer confusion or damaging and unfairly exploiting the sign's trademark distinctiveness or repute, he can rebut the legal presumption of use in an expressively generic, non-branding, way. Only then, the trademark owner can save a trademark claim from being dismissed as unfounded from the outset. The corresponding gatekeeper requirement of use as a mark can be defined as follows: use of a trademarked cultural sign in a cultural context will normally not constitute actionable use as a mark unless the cultural sign has no artistic relevance to the underlying work whatsoever, or, if it has some artistic relevance, unless the use of the cultural sign *explicitly* misleads as to the source of the derivative literary and artistic work, or *deliberately* blurs, tarnishes or takes unfair advantage of the distinctiveness or repute which the cultural sign has acquired as a trademark (section 9.2.1.3).

Given the focus on rhetoric uniqueness stemming from a sign's evolution in the cultural domain, it is obvious that this upfront test of use as a mark is applicable to cultural heritage signs and symbols of contemporary mainstream culture alike. However, similar measures can be adopted with regard to the expressive dimension of iconic trade symbols – the capacity of these signs to symbolize a particular lifestyle or attitude. The common denominator that justifies the introduction of a similar upfront test of use as a mark lies in the rich spectrum of expressive meanings that makes it possible to presume that metaphorical use in the cultural domain will focus on the sign's rhetoric uniqueness. As in the case of trademarked cultural signs, it can be posited that use of iconic trade symbols for the purpose of explicitly misleading consumers, or deliberately damaging or exploiting the mark's distinctiveness or repute, is exceptional in artistic contexts even if the sign at issue has acquired the status of a mark with a reputation (section 9.2.1.6).

To effectively implement the threshold criterion of use as a mark, it may be necessary to overcome additional obstacles, such as the EU requirement of 'honest practices' in industrial and commercial matters which is mentioned in connection with artistic use in Recital 21 EUTMR and Recital 27 TMD. In this respect, a survey of implementation options brought two solutions to light. On the one hand, the honest practices enquiry can be equated with the question of whether the allegedly infringing use in an artistic context explicitly misleads consumers as to the source of the artwork, or deliberately damages or derives unfair advantage from the distinctiveness or the repute of the trademark. If the trademark owner succeeds in demonstrating this evidently disproportionate harm, she can rebut the legal presumption of permissible use with artistic relevance and, at the same time, substantiate that the use was not in compliance with honest practices in industrial and commercial matters. On the other hand, the honest practices proviso can be declared inapplicable in the context of the trademark use requirement altogether. This second approach rests on the consideration that, in the substantive provisions of the EUTMR and the TMD, the honest practices test only appears in Article 14(2) as an additional requirement to be met when specific limitations of trademark rights set forth in Article 14(1) are applied. As the proposed trademark use requirement is an inherent limit of trademark rights and not a specific limitation in the sense of Article 14(1), the honest practices test, arguably, does not affect the gatekeeper requirement of use as a mark from the outset (section 9.2.1.7).

Given the focus on use of protected signs for expressive purposes in the cultural domain, the gatekeeper requirement of use as a mark is not exposed to the same criticism which more ambitious plans to introduce a general test of trademark use have raised. The proposed trademark use requirement is not grounded in a false symmetry with registration requirements and does not lack sufficiently clear conceptual contours (section 9.2.1.8). As the proposed upfront test of use as a mark imposes the burden of proving trademark relevance on trademark owners, it prevents the establishment of prima facie infringement in the absence of convincing evidence that rebuts the legal presumption of non-actionable use in an artistic context. This strategy to shield artists against trademark claims has clear advantages over an approach relying on mere defences, such as descriptive or referential use. Defences only offer an immunity at a later stage of the infringement analysis. They fail to inhibit trademark owners from building a prima facie infringement case and confronting artists with claims that are valid at first glance. In addition, a defence-based approach imposes the burden on artists to prove the facts supporting the invocation of a defence (section 9.2.1.9).

From this perspective, the development of robust defences against infringement claims – the second strategy to safeguard cultural follow-on innovation when trademark rights are granted to cultural signs – offers less effective support for artistic remix. A defence-based approach only provides certain safety valves to avoid an erosion of artistic freedom of use. It does not introduce a general bias in favour of artists in the trademark system. To defend artistic remix activities against trademark infringement claims that would undermine use privileges in copyright law, it is conceivable to establish a network of corresponding defences for artistic remix and reuse in both domains of intellectual property (section 9.2.2.1), introduce a rule of universal, direct applicability of pertinent limitations (section 9.2.2.2), or apply relevant copyright limitations by analogy (section 9.2.2.3). Moreover, the constitutional guarantee of freedom of expression – as a higher-ranking norm – can serve as a horizontal safeguard of breathing space for artistic remix and reuse that impacts both copyright and trademark law alike (section 9.2.2.4).

A closer look at this spectrum of solutions, however, reveals that it is not sufficient to ensure the applicability of specific limitations, such as the right of quotation and the exemption of parody, in both copyright and trademark law. While horizontal applicability of copyright defence prototypes may be sufficient in the field of contemporary mainstream productions where trademark rights relate to a cultural creation that still enjoys copyright protection, and where copyright law itself still reduces the breathing space for remix and reuse activities, a more ambitious approach is necessary in a cultural heritage scenario where trademark rights are acquired with regard to public domain material. Prior to the reappropriation via trademark law, signs in this category have been unencumbered by any intellectual property right. Accordingly, users in the artistic domain enjoyed unlimited freedom of remix and reuse. To avoid the erosion of this absolute freedom, trademark law must develop defences that emulate, to the greatest extent possible, the public domain status which affected cultural heritage signs had prior to the acquisition of trademark rights (section 9.2.2.5). This requires stronger efforts than the mere copying of specific copyright limitations. In the EUTMR and the TMD, the defences for referential use and non-distinctive use laid down in Article 14(1)(b) and (c) play a crucial role in this respect. Within the inherent limits of any defence-based approach, these limitations of trademark rights can absorb some negative repercussions caused by the loss of absolute freedom of use that existed prior to the grant of trademark rights to cultural heritage signs in the public domain. Moreover, referential use and non-distinctive use arguments can fill the gap of missing counterparts of quotation and parody rules in EU trademark law.

The scope of the referential use defence can be broadened by applying an argument *a maiore ad minus* (section 9.2.2.6). As the referential use defence exempts use that identifies the protected sign as a trademark, there is even more reason to apply the defence when the use does not even focus on this trademark aspect but refers to the sign as a cultural artefact. This artistic use does not aim at trademark-related messages which the trademark owner attached to the sign. It has less trademark relevance than the standard referential use scenario which clearly falls within the scope of the defence. In addition, the non-distinctive use defence covers the use of primary, cultural meanings which a sign already had prior to the acquisition of trademark rights. Arguably, these pre-existing cultural connotations remain unprotected residues of the sign's evolution in the cultural domain even after the trademark proprietor attached secondary marketing messages. The non-distinctive use defence is thus capable of exempting use of a trademarked cultural sign that relates to the sign's unprotected cultural residues: its primary cultural connotations (section 9.2.2.7). However, the application of the referential use defence and the non-distinctive use defence in cases involving artistic remix of trademarked cultural heritage signs would have to become a well-established court practice to emulate the lost public domain status of these signs to the largest extent possible. Judges would have to routinely accept the defence argument unless the trademark proprietor produces evidence of individualized facts that unmask the artistic setting as a mere pretence for blatant trademark infringement. Drawing a parallel with the discussion of the gatekeeper requirement of use as a mark, it can be posited that courts would have to create a legal environment which, at least, offers a degree of legal certainty and reassurance for artists that is comparable with the legal certainty and reassurance following from the 'Rogers' test in the U.S. (section 9.2.2.8).[2110]

Both defence arguments – referential use and non-distinctive use – are fully applicable not only to cultural heritage signs that have been reappropriated via trademark law but also to the unauthorized use, in an artistic context, of trademarked cultural signs stemming from mainstream literary and artistic productions, such as fictional characters. Moreover, the referential use defence and the non-distinctive use defence cover the cultural remix of iconic trade symbols. As to the honest practices proviso in Article 14(2) EUTMR and Article 14(2) TMD, the discussion in the context of the general gatekeeper requirement of use as a mark had already led to the insight that it is possible to set a higher standard for a finding of dishonest practices in cases of artistic remix. Applying this insight mutatis mutandis, referential use and non-distinctive use should be deemed incompatible with honest practices in industrial and commercial matters only if the artistic use at issue explicitly misleads consumers as to the source of the artwork, or deliberately damages or derives unfair advantage from the distinctiveness or the repute of the trademark (section 9.2.2.8).

In this way, the beneficial effect of defences, such as referential use and non-distinctive use, can be approximated to the immunizing effect which a gatekeeper requirement of trademark use would have. In comparison with an upfront test of use as a mark, however, a defence-based approach only offers correction tools after the trademark proprietor established prima facie infringement and confronted artists with a trademark claim that appears valid when viewed in isolation (not factoring defences into the equation). Moreover, a defence-based approach imposes the burden of proving privileged referential or non-distinctive use on the artist. As the party benefitting from the defence, the artist must invoke and substantiate the defence argument. A defence-based approach, thus, remains less favourable to artists. It is the inverse (no prevention of prima facie infringement; artist carries burden of proof) of a strategy seeking to implement an effective upfront test of use as a mark (prevention of prima facie infringement; trademark owner carries burden of proof). Hence, a strategy based on the development of

2110. U.S. Court of Appeals for the Second Circuit, 5 May 1989, Rogers/Grimaldi, 875 F.2d 994 (2nd Cir. 1989), 999.

defences will always remain the second-best solution in comparison with the adoption of a gatekeeper criterion of use as a mark.

10.2 CONCLUSION

The detailed analysis of the cultural imperative in copyright law and potential encroachments of overlapping trademark protection on the proper functioning of the copyright system culminates in a simple, universal insight: *the cumulation of intellectual property rights ought to imply the cumulation of obligations to ensure the proper functioning of all affected protection regimes*. The intellectual property system must not become a self-service machine that affords owners of creations of the mind the opportunity to conquer as much territory as they wish in the field of intellectual property protection. It is indispensable to impose the responsibility on intellectual property owners to keep intact the intellectual property system in general, and each individual protection regime in particular. Intellectual property owners must acquiesce in the quid pro quo – the checks and balances – underlying the system as a whole and each individual branch of protection. In particular, intellectual property owners must refrain from combinations of rights that would render individual protection regimes dysfunctional or cause imbalances in the intellectual property system as a whole.

To achieve this goal and put an end to the insatiable appetite for cumulative protection under as many individual intellectual property regimes as possible, owners of intellectual creations must have to bear the burden of protection overlaps themselves. It is not sufficient to leave the task of policing the borders of individual protection regimes and preserving the balance of the system as a whole to intellectual property offices and courts. By contrast, intellectual property owners themselves must develop a desire to focus on one individual protection regime and confine protection to one individual protection title. This reorientation, however, will only take place when the cumulation of rights no longer constitutes a vehicle to maximize protection by reaping the benefits of all individual regimes in a diversified intellectual property portfolio. Instead of paving the way for a *maximization of benefits*, the cumulation of intellectual property rights must lead to a *minimization of protection* that is readily available.

In principle, cumulative protection must have the result that only the common denominator of protection tools – those rights and interests that are compatible with the configuration of all intellectual property systems involved – remains available to the intellectual property owner. The more individual protection regimes are included in an intellectual property portfolio, the smaller the common ground of shared rights and interests, and the lower the resulting common denominator. The more divergent the configuration of the protection regimes involved, the higher the risk of minimizing rights and interests from the outset. In particular, the combination of a cyclic protection regime, such as copyright or patent law, with a static regime, such as trademark law, must have this minimizing effect when considering the incongruence of the rationales of protection and the divergent configuration of the protection regimes involved (section 4.2).

Hence, the regulation of intellectual property overlaps must aim at rendering cumulative protection unattractive. To activate the self-healing forces of the intellectual property system (section 2.3), it is not sufficient to erect legal-doctrinal bulwarks against the cumulation of intellectual property rights. As long as rights owners who manage to surmount these hurdles obtain enhanced protection as a reward, the system will still provide wrong incentives that lead to investment in intellectual property accumulation strategies. Only if the cumulation of rights reduces the scope of protection and makes the enforcement of rights more difficult, right holders will stop striving for mixed intellectual property portfolios and develop a preference for protection under one individual protection regime instead. In this way, the intellectual property system can heal itself: not by seeking to reduce the corrosive effect of protection overlaps *ex post*, but by preventing the emergence of protection overlaps *ex ante*. To achieve this recalibration of the system, the cumulation of intellectual property rights should not constitute a desirable legal position from the outset. As a result of the minimization of rights and enforcement options surviving the combination of different forms of intellectual property protection, the cumulation of rights must become so costly that owners of creations of the mind no longer seek to acquire several protection titles and, instead, focus on one specific protection regime that best meets their protection needs: copyright protection for a creation that is intended to feature in a literary and artistic production; trademark protection for a creation that is intended to serve as an identifier of commercial source. Even if a literary and artistic production has the potential to fulfil the role of an indication of commercial origin as well, the minimization of protection and enforcement options must render cumulative copyright and trademark protection so unattractive that the rights owner prefers the development of a separate identifier of commercial source over the transformation of the literary and artistic work into a trademark.

Shedding light on a fraction of this considerable recalibration task, the foregoing analysis of copyright/trademark overlaps may serve as a compass for first steps in the right direction. Due to its limited scope, however, the analysis of copyright/trademark overlaps is incapable of providing an overview of all challenges and potential solutions in the rights cumulation arena. Nonetheless, it offers important general guidelines – universal insights into available regulatory tools that may be put to good use when regulating cumulative protection in other galaxies of the intellectual property universe. To minimize the corrosive effect of protection overlaps and render rights accumulation strategies less attractive, it is advisable to:

- cultivate legal mechanisms that allow the categorical exclusion of protection in a given intellectual property system, such as the outright exclusion of trademark protection for literary and artistic works, inventions and industrial designs that follows from a denial of protection because of a conflict with public order or morality (section 9.1.2) or a finding of functionality (sections 7.1 and 7.2). To develop these categorical exclusion tools in a way that effectively bans rights accumulation, evergreening and resurrection strategies, it is important to weave values of one protection regime, such as intergenerational equity and public domain recognition in copyright law (section 3.1), into the fabric of the other protection regime, such as grounds for refusal in trademark law (sections 9.1.2.3 and 9.1.2.4). Hence, it is necessary to enrich the spectrum of assessment factors. Values stemming from other protection regimes must enter the picture. Instead of obliging trademark examiners and judges to rely on standard assessment categories of trademark law, such as a lack of distinctive character (section 9.1.2.1), it is important to create categorical exclusion tools that allow them to articulate clearly their concerns about the corrosive effect of cumulative protection and include arguments for denying the grant of rights that stem from another protection regime, such as the public domain principle in copyright law;
- if it is not possible to categorically exclude protection under a given intellectual property regime altogether, the second-best regulatory response to overlap scenarios is the development of a bias in favour of users in the domain where the creation of the mind evolved (artists in the cultural domain when rights cumulation strategies concern literary and artistic works). This bias can follow from additional infringement criteria that make it difficult for the owner of cumulative or resurrected protection to establish prima facie infringement. As a result of these additional criteria, the burden of producing evidence of infringement – a burden of proof that rests on the owner of a mixed intellectual property portfolio – should be particularly high. In particular, the owner of a creation of the mind enjoying double protection should be obliged to demonstrate that the allegedly infringing use falls within the province and meaning of the asserted type of intellectual property right. In the case of copyright/trademark overlaps, for instance, the trademark proprietor should be bound to establish that – despite use in a cultural setting – an artist specifically aims at causing consumer confusion or damaging and unfairly exploiting the trademark distinctiveness or repute of the affected cultural sign (and not its cultural value). Based on this requirement of 'use as a mark', a finding of prima facie infringement should only be possible if the cultural sign has no artistic relevance to the allegedly infringing use whatsoever, or, in case of artistic relevance, if the use

explicitly misleads as to the source of the allegedly infringing literary and artistic work, or deliberately blurs, tarnishes or takes unfair advantage of the distinctiveness or repute which the cultural sign has acquired as a trademark – and not as a cultural symbol (section 9.2.1);
- if neither the categorical exclusion of cumulative or resurrected protection nor the establishment of a strict gatekeeper requirement of use in the sense of the asserted type of intellectual property right is possible, the attractiveness of rights cumulation strategies can still be reduced by developing particularly robust defences that apply horizontally and limit intellectual property protection across all protection regimes involved. This regulatory response has the disadvantage of imposing the burden of proof on the alleged infringer. In the case of copyright/trademark overlaps, this disadvantage weighs heavily because artists are likely to be risk-averse. They may shy away from the intended, culturally valuable use once the trademark owner manages to substantiate prima facie infringement (section 6.3). Hence, the defence argument must constitute an 'easy case' – a case that is commonly deemed non-actionable unless the holder of cumulative intellectual property rights succeeds in proving individualized facts that make a particular use by a particular artist unprivileged.[2111] Moreover, it is necessary to develop an appropriate strategy for universalizing defences that are available in a given intellectual property system. It is conceivable to establish a network of corresponding defences in different fields of intellectual property, introduce a rule of universal, direct applicability of limitations across all fields of intellectual property, or apply limitations by analogy (section 9.2.2). Whatever avenue is chosen, the final result should be an accumulation of obligations to tolerate privileged unauthorized use. If an intellectual property owner acquires double rights, she should also have to carry the double burden of exposure to all limitations of protection in the intellectual property regimes involved. Instead of escaping a limitation in protection regime A by invoking exclusive rights under protection regime B, the holder of cumulative rights should have to face a minimization of the scope of protection due to horizontal applicability of all limitations (A+B) in both intellectual property systems involved. Hence, only the smallest common denominator of exclusive rights – the scope of protection after subtraction of all forms of permissible unauthorized use – should remain available.

As an overarching insight, these regulatory options reflect the need to intersperse one intellectual property system with values from another protection system when it comes to overlapping or resurrected intellectual

2111. Benkler 1999, 362.

property rights. The preconditions for the proper functioning of any affected protection regime (intergenerational equity and public domain recognition in the case of copyright law, section 3.1) must be factored into the equation when taking decisions on the grant and enforcement of protection in the other protection system involved (trademark law in the case of an amalgam of copyright and trademark protection). The development of legal instruments to:

- refuse the grant of rights from the outset (such as a categorical exclusion of trademark rights on the basis of public order or morality, section 9.1.2);
- make the establishment of prima facie infringement particularly difficult for the rights owner (for instance, by requiring evidence of use as a mark, section 9.2.1); and
- support unauthorized use with robust defences (such as defences based on referential use and non-distinctive use, section 9.2.2)

are regulatory responses that seek to open doors in protection system B (trademark law) to allow values from protection system A (copyright law) to enter the assessment process and impact decisions on the grant and enforcement of protection. In the case of copyright/trademark overlaps, this means that the imperative of market transparency in trademark law must not prevail without lending sufficient weight to the copyright imperative of intergenerational equity and public domain recognition. To give sufficient deference to copyright values, a legal solution is necessary that keeps the cultural innovation cycle intact that follows from the configuration of copyright law. As explained in the foregoing analysis, considerations from the cultural domain must therefore inform decision-making in trademark law to such an extent that the market transparency logic of trademark law no longer undermines the copyright logic of cyclic cultural innovation.

10.3 TOWARDS A SYSTEMS THEORY

Arguably, these insights – derived from the analysis of copyright/trademark overlaps – can be put to good use whenever an overlap scenario arises in intellectual property law. The problems that featured prominently in the foregoing analysis of copyright/trademark overlaps are prototypes of regulatory challenges. Variations of these challenges are likely to come to the fore whenever right holders form conglomerates of different intellectual property rights:

- with regard to logos which, from the outset, have been designed to serve as trademarks and attract copyright protection only accidentally due to the absence of a registration requirement in copyright law (trademark/copyright overlap, section 9.1.2.5),[2112] it may be asked whether copyright protection undermines preconditions for the proper functioning of trademark protection by neutralizing grounds for refusal in trademark law,[2113] artificially extending the scope of protection to all market segments (instead of confining protection to the goods or services for which the logo has been registered as a trademark), broadening exclusive rights by suppressing specific infringement criteria, such as a likelihood of confusion,[2114] and eroding limitations of trademark protection in the absence of a congruent set of limitations in copyright law;[2115]

- with regard to product design that enjoys sui generis protection under specific industrial design legislation and protection as a work of applied art under copyright law (industrial design/copyright overlap),[2116] the question arises whether copyright interferes with the proper functioning of specific industrial design legislation by prolonging the shorter term of industrial design protection (section 9.1.1.4),[2117] offering the opportunity to circumvent registration requirements,[2118] overriding specific industrial design infringement criteria,[2119] and providing for a different set of limitations of protection;[2120]

2112. Cf. EFTA Court, 6 April 2017, case E-5/16, Municipality of Oslo ('Vigeland'), para. 97.

2113. Article 6quinquies(B) PC. As to the impact of this rule of *telle quelle* protection on national systems, see Ng-Loy 2018, 147-164; Kunz-Hallstein 2006, 487; Beier 1992, 243; Ladas 1975, 1211-1240; Bodenhausen 1969, 113-119. As to the EU catalogue of grounds for refusal, see Article 4 TMD; Article 7 EUTMR.

2114. Article 16(1) TRIPS.

2115. For instance, see the limitation infrastructure in Article 14 TMD and Article 14 EUTMR on the one hand and Article 5 ISD on the other. Cf. Senftleben 2013b, 172. As to the risk of compromising trademark values, in particular the objective to prevent consumer confusion, see Dinwoodie 2020, 33.

2116. For an overview of the different approaches to the regulation of cumulative copyright and industrial design protection, see the various contributions to Derclaye 2018. As to the position in the EU, see CJEU, 12 September 2019, case C-683/17, Cofemel, para. 31 and 35-48 and 52-55.

2117. Article 26(3) TRIPS; Article 12 CDR and Article 10 DD. Cf. Article 7(4) BC.

2118. As to the absence of registration requirements in copyright law, see Article 5(2) BC. As to the configuration of this prohibition of formalities, see Van Gompel 2011, 18-20, 175-176 and 194-195.

2119. For example, see the discussion on the application of 'overall impression' criteria in industrial designs and copyright law. As to the approximation of infringement criteria, compare Article 9(1) DD with Dutch Supreme Court, 29 December 1995, case LJN ZC1942, Decaux/Mediamax, *NJ* 1996, no. 546; Dutch Supreme Court 29 November 2002, case LJN AE8456, 'Una Voce Particolare', *AMI* 2003, 21, para. 3.5; Dutch Supreme Court, 12 April 2013, case LJN BY1532, Stokke/Fikszo, *NJ* 2013, no. 502, para. 4.2. Cf. Spoor/Verkade/Visser 2019, 190-194; De Zwaan, 2016, 117-119.

2120. In District Court of The Hague, 4 May 2011, case LJN BQ3525, Nadia Plesner/Louis Vuitton, para. 2.1-2.8, for instance, it became obvious that industrial designs law does not offer limitations supporting transformative use, whereas copyright law provides for

– cumulative copyright and patent protection for software (copyright/patent overlap),[2121] begs the question of whether patent protection thwarts the objectives of the copyright system by eroding the freedom of ideas, concepts and methods in copyright law,[2122] neutralizing the exemption of decompilation for achieving interoperability,[2123] and interfering with the rules of open-source software.[2124] Vice versa, the question arises whether copyright protection leads to an artificial extension of the shorter term of patent protection and undermines limitations of patent rights, in particular the freedom of experimental use.[2125]

In these and other overlap scenarios, the same recipe that helps to avoid an encroachment of trademark protection upon cyclic cultural innovation in the case of copyright/trademark overlaps can activate the self-healing forces of the intellectual property system: the development of a function-based typology of intellectual property protection regimes (cyclic versus static protection systems, Chapter 4), the identification of core requirements for the proper functioning of intellectual property protection within each individual system (Chapter 3) and the exploration of checks and balances that can serve as tools to avoid interferences with other protection regimes that are part of an amalgam of intellectual property rights stemming from different domains (Chapter 9).

Viewed from this bird's-eye perspective, the current analysis offers an agenda for further research that takes similar steps with regard to other overlap scenarios and focuses attention on self-healing forces in other areas of intellectual property law: self-healing forces in the sense of measures that render cumulative protection unattractive to such an extent that owners of creations of the mind no longer strive for an amalgam of different protection titles from the outset. The research reflected in this book brings to light several common themes of overlapping and resurrected intellectual property rights. It also raises overarching questions that concern the characteristics of individual protection regimes in intellectual property law and the degree of incompatibility with regimes that have a different functional configuration.

a right of quotation and an exemption of parody, caricature and pastiche. See Article 5(3)(d) and (k) ISD. Cf. Visser 2011, 740-742.

2121. For a discussion of this protection overlap, see Samuelson 2019, 291-301; Li 2019, 823; Dane 2018a, 1; Dane 2018b, 5; Sterckx/Cockbain 2010, 366; Ballardini 2008, 563; Leistner 2008, 188; Ghidini/Arezzo 2005, 166; Hilty/Geiger 2005, 615; Burk/Lemley 2005, 81; Weyand/Haase 2005, 647; Cohen/Lemley 2001, 41; Caron 2000, 3.

2122. Article 9(2) TRIPS; Article 2 WCT. Cf. Dutch Supreme Court, 29 March 2013, case LJN BY8661, Broeren/Duijsens, para. 3.5.

2123. For instance, see Articles 5 and 6 of the Computer Programs Directive 2009/24/EC. As to countermeasures seeking to preserve this use privilege in the case of copyright/patent overlaps, see Article 27(k) UPCA.

2124. Cf. Evans/Layne-Farrar 2004, 9-28; Schultz/Urban 2012, 10-14.

2125. Cf. Metzger 2020, 389-391.

Are cyclic protection systems, such as copyright and patent law, more vulnerable than static protection systems, such as trademark law? If so, is it possible to assume that, as a rule, the constitutive features of cyclic systems must prevail over the market transparency imperative that lies at the core of trademark law? Does the preference for a stable distribution of intellectual resources in static systems, such as trademark law (section 4.2), always have a strong corrosive effect on cyclic systems (section 4.1)? A corrosive effect strong enough to posit that the remix rationale of cyclic systems must reign supreme not only in copyright/trademark overlap scenarios but also in other cases of overlaps with trademark protection? The broad application of the doctrine of functionality in patent cases (section 7.1) and industrial design cases (section 7.2) points in this direction. May static protection systems (such as trademark law), therefore, be regarded as weaker systems that, as a rule, have to show deference to the rules of cyclic systems?[2126]

These questions pave the way for a more holistic, dynamic view of the intellectual property universe. They focus attention on the relationship between different protection systems instead of analysing individual protection mechanisms in isolation. In this way, the outlined research agenda can enhance the understanding of intellectual property law as a system of interdependent parts. In all areas of overlap, the impact of the cumulation of rights on all affected protection regimes must occupy centre stage. Moreover, the need to preserve an appropriate balance between individual protection regimes in the intellectual property system as a whole must be factored into the equation. The more bridges and submarine tunnel systems connect the islands of copyright, patent and trademark protection with each other and allow the creation of protection overlaps (section 2.1),[2127] the more bridges and submarine tunnel systems are necessary at a legal-doctrinal level to allow the values of one protection system to inform the process of granting rights and delineating the scope of protection in another system that forms part of an amalgamation of protection titles.

In a nutshell, *double rights entail double obligations*. Once the need to ensure the proper functioning of all affected protection systems is taken seriously in an overlap scenario, the cumulation of intellectual property rights no longer maximizes protection. Instead, it comes at the price of less protection.

2126. Cf. Köklü/Nérisson 2016, 573; Dinwoodie 2020, 29-32, who arrives at the conclusion that, already at this point, there is a 'relegation of trade marks below copyright, patent and design in the European intellectual property firmament'. See also Geier 2015, 149-151, who rejects the introduction of a hierarchy at an abstract level but sees room for prevalence of one individual protection regime at the concrete level of individual decision-making.

2127. Heymann 2013, 242-247; Ohly 2008, 203; Dinwoodie 2002, 499-501; Kur 2002, 594-595; Spoor 1990, 41-60; Lange 1981, 147.

Bibliography

Abegg 2018

B. Abegg, 'The Geographical Trade Mark: A Swiss Innovation Worth Copying?', *IIC* 49 (2018), 565

Adler 2016

A. Adler, 'Fair Use and the Future of Art', *New York University Law Review* 91 (2016), 559

Adorno 1970

T.W. Adorno, *Ästhetische Theorie*, edited by G. Adorno/R. Tiedemann, Frankfurt am Main: Suhrkamp 1970

Amabile 1996

T.M. Amabile, *Creativity in Context*, Boulder: Westview Press 1996

Anemaet 2016

L. Anemaet, 'The Public Domain is Under Pressure: Why We Should Not Rely on Empirical Data When Assessing Trademark Distinctiveness', *IIC* 47 (2016), 303

Anemaet 2020

L. Anemaet, 'The Many Faces of the Average Consumer: Is It Really So Difficult to Assess Whether Two Stripes Are Similar to Three?', *IIC* 51 (2020), 187

Aoki 1997

K. Aoki, 'How the World Dreams Itself to be American: Reflections on the Relationship Between the Expanding Scope of Trademark Protection and Free Speech Norms', *Loyola of Los Angeles Entertainment Law Journal* 17 (1997), 523

Aplin/Bently 2020

T. Aplin/L. Bently, *Global Mandatory Fair Use: The Nature and Scope of the Right to Quote Copyright Works*, Cambridge: Cambridge University Press 2020

Arnet 2004

R. Arnet, 'Markenschutz für Formen', *sic!* 2004, 829

Assaf 2008

K. Assaf, 'The Dilution of Culture and the Law of Trademarks', *IDEA: The Intellectual Property Law Review* 1 (2008), 49

Assaf 2009

K. Assaf, 'Der Markenschutz und seine kulturelle Bedeutung: Ein Vergleich des deutschen mit dem US-amerikanischen Recht', *GRUR Int.* 2009, 1

Aufderheide/Jaszi 2004

P. Aufderheide/P. Jaszi, *Untold Stories: Creative Consequences of the Rights Clearance Culture for Documentary Filmmakers*, Washington D.C.: American University 2004

Aufderheide/Jaszi/Bello et al. 2014

P. Aufderheide/P. Jaszi/B. Bello/T. Milosevic, *Copyright, Permissions, and Fair Use in the Visual Arts Communities: An Issues Report*, Washington D.C.: American University 2014, available at: https://cmsimpact.org/wp-content/uploads/2016/01/fair_use_for_visual_arts_ communities.pdf

Austin 2003

G.W. Austin, 'Copyright's Modest Ontology – Theory and Pragmatism in Eldred v. Ashcroft', *Canadian Journal of Law and Jurisprudence* 16 (2003), 163

Ballardini 2008

R.M. Ballardini, 'Software Patents in Europe: the Technical Requirement Dilemma', *Journal of Intellectual Property Law and Practice* 3 (2008), 563-575

Banerjee 2012

A. Banerjee, 'Non-Origin Infringement – Has Trade Mark Law Gone Too Far?', *IIC* 43 (2012), 555

Barrett 2006

M. Barrett, 'Internet Trademark Suits and the Demis of "Trademark Use"', *UC Davis Law Review* 39 (2006), 371

Barrett 2010

M. Barrett, 'Reconciling Fair Use and Trademark Use', *Cardozo Arts and Entertainment Law Journal* 28 (2010), 1

Basire 2014

Y. Basire, *Les fonctions de la marque, Essai sur la cohérence du régime juridique d'un signe distinctif*, Paris: Litec 2014

Basire 2018

Y. Basire, 'Public Domain Versus Trade Mark Protection: The Vigeland Case', *Journal of Intellectual Property Law and Practice* 13 (2018), 434

Beckerman-Rodau 2011

A. Beckerman-Rodau, 'The Problem with Intellectual Property Rights: Subject Matter Expansion', *Yale Journal of Law and Technology* 13 (2011), 36

Bercovitz 2001

A. Bercovitz, 'Marken und Urheberrecht', *GRUR Int.* 2001, 611

Beebe 2005

B. Beebe, 'Search and Persuasion in Trademark Law', *Michigan Law Review* 103 (2005), 2020

Beebe 2006, 1143

B. Beebe, 'A Defense of the New Federal Trademark Antidilution Law', *Fordham Intellectual Property, Media & Entertainment Law Journal* 16 (2006), 1143

Beebe 2008

B. Beebe, 'An Empirical Study of U.S. Copyright Fair Use Opinions, 1978-2005', *University of Pennsylvania Law Review* 156 (2008), 549

Beebe 2012

B. Beebe, 'Report on Canada and the United States of America', in: M.R.F. Senftleben (ed.), *Study on Misappropriation of Signs*, WIPO Document CDIP/9/INF/5, Geneva: WIPO 2012, 69

Beebe 2017

B. Beebe, 'Bleistein, the Problem of Aesthetic Progress, and the Making of American Copyright Law', *Columbia Law Review* 117 (2017), 319

Beebe/Fromer 2019

B. Beebe/J.C. Fromer, 'Immoral or Scandalous Marks: An Empirical Analysis', *NYU Journal of Intellectual Property and Entertainment Law* 8 (2019), 169

Beier 1992

F.K. Beier, 'Unterscheidungskraft und Freihaltebedürfnis – Zur Markenschutzfähigkeit individueller Herkunftsangaben nach § 4 WZG und Art. 6quinquies PVÜ', *GRUR Int.* 1992, 243

Benkler 1999

Y. Benkler, 'Free as the Air to Common Use: First Amendment Constraints on Enclosure of the Public Domain', *New York University Law Review* 74 (1999), 354

Benkler 2003

Y. Benkler, 'Through the Looking Glass: Alice and the Constitutional Foundations of the Public Domain', *Law and Contemporary Problems* 66 (2003), 173

Bently 2008a

L. Bently, 'The Making of Modern Trade Mark Law: the Construction of the Legal Concept of Trade Mark (1860-1880)', in: L. Bently, J. Davis/J.C. Ginsburg (eds), *Trade Marks and Brands—An Interdisciplinary Critique*, Cambridge: Cambridge University Press 2008, 3

Bently 2008b

L. Bently, 'From Communication to Thing: Historical Aspects of the Conceptualisation of Trade Marks as Property', in: G.B. Dinwoodie/M.D. Janis (eds), *Trademark Law and Theory: A Handbook of Contemporary Research*, Cheltenham: Edward Elgar 2008, 3

Bently 2018

L. Bently, 'The Design/Copyright Conflict in the United Kingdom: A History', in: E. Derclaye (ed.), *The Copyright/Design Interface: Past, Present and Future*, Cambridge: Cambridge University Press 2018, 171

Bently/Aplin 2019

L. Bently/T. Aplin, 'Whatever Became of Global Mandatory Fair Use? A Case Study in Dysfunctional Pluralism', in: S. Frankel (ed.), *Is Intellectual Property Pluralism Functional?*, Cheltenham: Edward Elgar 2019, 8

Bently/Dusollier/Geiger et al. 2019

L. Bently/S. Dusollier/C. Geiger/J. Griffiths/A. Metzger/A. Peukert/M.R.F. Senftleben, 'Sound Sampling, a Permitted Use Under EU Copyright Law? Opinion of the European Copyright Society in Relation to the Pending Reference Before the CJEU in Case C-476/17, Pelham GmbH v. Hütter', *IIC* 50 (2019), 467-490

Bently/Sherman/Gangjee/Johnson 2018

L. Bently/B. Sherman/D. Gangjee/P. Johnson, *Intellectual Property Law*, 5th ed., Oxford: Oxford University Press 2018

Van den Bergh/Lehmann 1992

R. van den Bergh/M. Lehmann, 'Informationsökonomie und Verbraucherschutz im Wettbewerbs- und Warenzeichenrecht', *GRUR Int.* 1992, 588

Bernitz 1990

U. Bernitz, 'Logo Licensing of Tobacco Products—Can it be Prohibited?', *EIPR* 12 (1990), 137

Bianchi 2017

F. Bianchi, 'La Laitière: comment un tableau de Vermeer a fini sur un pot de yaourt', *BFM Business*, posted 20 February 2017, available at: https://bfmbusiness.bfmtv.com/entreprise/la-laitiere-comment-un-tableau-de-vermeer-a-fini-sur-un-pot-de-yaourt-1106560.html (last visited on 14 October 2020)

Bingener 2004

S. Bingener, 'Das Wesen der Positionsmarke oder Wo die Positionsmarke hingehört', *Markenrecht* 2004, 377

BIRPI 1925

United International Bureaux for the Protection of Intellectual Property (BIRPI), *Actes de la conférence réunie à La Haye du 8 octobre au 6 novembre 1925*, Bern: BIRPI 1925

Bodenhausen 1969

G.H.C. Bodenhausen, *Guide to the Application of the Paris Convention for the Protection of Industrial Property*, Geneva: BIRPI 1969, reprinted in: WIPO publication No. 611, Geneva: WIPO 2004

Bölling 2004

M. Bölling, 'Der EuGH und die abstrakte Farbmarke – Von der bewussten Entwertung einer Markenform', *Markenrecht* 2004, 384

Bohaczewski 2020

M. Bohaczewski, 'Conflicts Between Trade Mark Rights and Freedom of Expression Under EU Trade Mark Law: Reality or Illusion?', *IIC* 51 (2020), 856

Bonadio 2012

E. Bonadio, 'Plain Packaging of Tobacco Products Under EU Intellectual Property Law', *EIPR* 2012, 599

Bone 2006

R.G. Bone, 'Hunting Goodwill: A History of the Concept of Goodwill in Trademark Law', *Boston University Law Review* 86 (2006), 547

Bone 2015

R.G. Bone, 'Trademark Functionality Reexamined', Journal of Legal Analysis 7 (2015), 183

Born 2006

C. Born, 'Zur Zulässigkeit einer humorvollen Markenparodie – Anmerkungen zum Urteil des BGH "Lila Postkarte"', *GRUR* 2006, 192

Bourdieu/Chartier/Darnton 1985

P. Bourdieu/R. Chartier/R. Darnton, 'Dialog über die Kulturgeschichte', *Freibeuter – Vierteljahreszeitschrift für Kultur und Politik* 26 (1985), 22

Bourdieu 1992/1999

P. Bourdieu, *Die Regeln der Kunst. Genese und Struktur des literarischen Feldes*, Frankfurt/Main: Suhrkamp 1999 (French original: P. Bourdieu, *Les règles de l'art. Genèse et structure du champ littéraire*, Paris: Éditions du Seuil 1992)

Bourdieu 1996

P. Bourdieu, 'Die Logik der Felder', in: P. Bourdieu/L.J.D. Wacquant (eds) *Reflexive Anthropologie*, Frankfurt/Main: Suhrkamp, 124

Bouvel 2004

A. Bouvel, 'Qu'importe le flacon... Le droit des marques malmené par les emballages', *Propriétés Intellectuelles* 2004, 863

Bouvel 2008

A. Bouvel, 'Marques et renommée: À propos de l'arrêt "Intel" rendu par la Cour de justice des communautés européennes le 27 novembre 2008 (aff. C-252/07)', in: C.

Geiger/J. Schmidt-Szalewski (eds), *Les défis du droit des marques au 21e siècle/ Challenges for Trademark Law in the 21st Century*, Paris: Litec 2010, 123

Boyle 1997

J. Boyle, 'A Politics of Intellectual Property: Environmentalism for the Net?', *Duke Law Journal* 47 (1997), 87

Boyle 2003a

J. Boyle, 'Foreword: the Opposite of Property?', *Law and Contemporary Problems* 66 (2003), 1

Boyle 2003b

J. Boyle, 'The Second Enclosure Movement and the Construction of the Public Domain', *Law and Contemporary Problems* 66 (2003), 33

Bracha 2008

O. Bracha, 'The Ideology of Authorship Revisited: Authors, Markets, and Liberal Values in Early American Copyright', *Yale Law Journal 118* (2008), 186

Van den Braembussche 1996

A. van den Braembussche, 'The Value of Art: A Philosophical Perspective', in: A. Klamer (ed.), *The Value of Culture – On the Relationship Between Economics and Arts*, Amsterdam: Amsterdam University Press 1996, 31

Breitschaft 2009

A. Breitschaft, 'Intel, Adidas & Co – Is the Jurisprudence of the European Court of Justice on Dilution Law in Compliance with the Underlying Rationales and Fit for the Future?', *EIPR* 2009, 497

Brennan 2002

D.J. Brennan, 'The Three-Step Test Frenzy – Why the TRIPS Panel Decision might be considered Per Incuriam', *Intellectual Property Quarterly* 2002, 213

Bresler 2003

J. Bresler, 'Begged, Borrowed or Stolen: Whose Art is it Anyway? An Alternative Solution of Fine Art Licensing', *Journal of the Copyright Society of the U.S.A.* 50 (2003), 15

Brown 1999

R.S. Brown, 'Advertising and the Public Interest: Legal Protection of Trade Symbols', *Yale Law Journal* 108 (1999), 1619

Buccafusco/Bechtold/Sprigman 2017

C. Buccafusco/S. Bechtold/C.J. Sprigman, 'The Nature of Sequential Innovation', *William & Mary Law Review* 59 (2017), 1

Buccafusco/Heald 2013

C. Buccafusco/P.J. Heald, 'Do Bad Things Happen When Works Enter the Public Domain? Empirical Tests of Copyright Term Extension', *Berkeley Technology Law Journal* 28 (2013), 2

Bürger 1974

P. Bürger, *Theorie der Avantgarde*, Frankfurt/Main: Suhrkamp 1974

Bugdahl 2010

V. Bugdahl, 'Marken und Kunst – Kunst und Marken', *Markenrecht* 2010, 369

Bullbrook 2004

J. Bullbrook, 'Geographical Indications Within GATT', *Journal of World Intellectual Property* 2004, 501

Burk/Lemley 2005

D.L. Burk/M.A. Lemley, 'Designing Optimal Software Patents', in: R.W. Hahn (ed.), *Intellectual Property Rights in Frontier Industries: Software and Biotechnology*, Washington: AEI Press 2005, 81-100

Burrell/Gangjee 2010

R. Burrell/D. Gangjee, 'Trade Marks and Freedom of Expression: A Call for Caution', *IIC* 41 (2010), 544

Buydens 2011

M. Buydens, 'Pouvoir distinctif de la marque et risque de confusion: larvatus prodeo?', in: Benelux Office for Intellectual Property (ed.), *In Varietate Concordia? National and European Trademarks Living Apart Together*, The Hague: Benelux Office for Intellectual Property 2011, 33

Calandrillo 1998

S.P. Calandrillo, 'An Economic Analysis of Property Rights in Information: Justifications and Problems of Exclusive Rights, Incentives to Generate Information, and the Alternative of a Government-Run Reward System', *Fordham Intellectual Property Media & Entertainment Law Journal* 9 (1998), 301

Calboli 2014a

I. Calboli, 'Overlapping Trademark and Copyright Protection: A Call for Concern and Action', *Illinois Law Review Slip Opinion* 2014, No. 1, 25

Calboli 2014b

I. Calboli, 'Overlapping Rights: The Negative Effects of Trademarking Creative Works', in: S. Frankel/D.J. Gervais (eds), *The Evolution and Equilibrium of Copyright in the Digital Age*, Cambridge: Cambridge University Press 2014, 52

Calboli 2018

I. Calboli, 'Hands Off "My" Colors, Patterns, and Shapes! How Non-Traditional Trademarks Promote Standardization and May Negatively Impact Creativity and Innovation', in: I. Calboli/M.R.F. Senftleben (eds), *The Protection of Non-Traditional Trademarks – Critical Perspectives*, Oxford: Oxford University Press 2018, 287

Calboli/Senftleben 2018

I. Calboli/M.R.F. Senftleben (eds), *The Protection of Non-Traditional Trademarks – Critical Perspectives*, Oxford: Oxford University Press 2018

Calvert 2019

C. Calvert, 'Iancu v. Brunetti's Impact on First Amendment Law: Viewpoint Discrimination, Modes of Offensive Expression, Proportionality and Profanity', *Columbia Journal of Law and the Arts* 43 (2019), 37

Cantwell 2004

M.K. Cantwell, 'Confusion, Dilution and Speech: First Amendment Limitations on the Trademark Estate: An Update', *The Trademark Reporter* 94 (2004), 549

Caron 2000

C. Caron, 'Réflexions sur la coexistence du droit d'auteur et du droit des brevets sur un même logiciel', *RIDA* 184 (2000), 3

Casparie-Kerdel 2001

S. Casparie-Kerdel, 'Dilution Disguised: Has the Concept of Trade Mark Dilution Made its Way into the Laws of Europe?', *EIPR* 2001, 185

Castren 1995

M. Castren, 'Tobacco Advertising and Trade Mark Law in Finland', *EIPR* 17 (1995), 87

Cheng 2013

T. Cheng, 'Putting Innovation Incentives Back in the Patent-Antitrust Interface', *Northwestern Journal of Technology and Intellectual Property* 11 (2013), 385

Cherpillod 1985

I. Cherpillod, *L'objet du droit d'auteur*, Lausanne: Centre du droit de l'entreprise de l'Université de Lausanne (CEDIDAC) 1985

Cohen 2006

J.E. Cohen, 'Copyright, Commodification, and Culture: Locating the Public Domain', in: L.M.C.R. Guibault/P.B. Hugenholtz (eds), *The Future of the Public Domain – Identifying the Commons in Information Law*, The Hague/London/New York: Kluwer Law International 2006, 121

Cohen 2007

J.E. Cohen, 'Creativity and Culture in Copyright Theory', *University of California, Davis Law Review* 40 (2007), 1151

Cohen Jehoram 2012

T. Cohen Jehoram, 'The Function Theory in European Trade Mark Law and the Holistic Approach of the CJEU', *The Trademark Reporter* 102 (2012), 1243

Cohen Jehoram/Van Helden 2011

T. Cohen Jehoram/H. Van Helden, 'Bekend, bekender, bekendst: Goodwill-bescherming van merken', in: Benelux Office for Intellectual Property (ed.), *In Varietate Concordia? National and European Trademarks Living Apart Together*, The Hague: Benelux Office for Intellectual Property 2011, 111

Cohen Jehoram/Van Nispen/Huydecoper 2008

T. Cohen Jehoram/C.J.J.C. van Nispen/J.L.R.A. Huydecoper, *Industriële eigendom – Deel 2: Merkenrecht*, Deventer: Kluwer 2008

Cohen Jehoram/Van Nispen/Huydecoper 2010

T. Cohen Jehoram/C.J.J.C. van Nispen/J.L.R.A. Huydecoper, *European Trademark Law*, Alphen aan den Rijn: Kluwer Law International 2010

Cohen/Lemley 2001

J.E. Cohen/M.A. Lemley, 'Patent Scope and Innovation in the Software Industry', *California Law Review* 89 (2001), 1

Conde Gallego 2006

B. Conde Gallego, 'Die Anwendung des kartellrechtlichen Missbrauchsverbots auf "unerlässliche" Immaterialgüterrechte im Lichte der IMS Health- und Standard-Spundfass-Urteile', *GRUR Int.* 2006, 16

Conley/Braegelmann 2009

N. Conley/T. Braegelmann, 'Metall auf Metall: the Importance of the Kraftwerk Decision for the Sampling of Music in Germany', *Journal of the Copyright Society of the U.S.A.* 56 (2009), 1017

Coombe 1998

R.J. Coombe, *The Cultural Life of Intellectual Properties: Authorship, Appropriation, and the Law*, Durham: Duke University Press 1998

Coombe 2003

Rosemary J. Coombe, 'Fear, Hope, and Longing for the Fututre of Authorship and a Revitalized Public Domain in Global Regimes of Intellectual Property', *DePaul Law Review* 52 (2003), 1171

Coombe 2005

R.J. Coombe, 'Legal Claims to Culture in and Against the Market: Neoliberalism and the Global Proliferation of Meaningful Difference', *Law, Culture and the Humanities* 1 (2005), 35

Coombe/Cohen 1999

R.J. Coombe/J. Cohen, 'The Law and Late Modern Culture: Reflections on Between Facts and Norms From the Perspective of Cultural Legal Studies', *Denver University Law Review* 76 (1999), 1029

Coombe/Herman 2001

R.J. Coombe/A. Herman, 'Culture Wars on the Net: Trademarks, Consumer Politics, and Corporate Accountability on the World Wide Web', *South Atlantic Quarterly* 100 (2001), 919

Cooper 2018

E. Cooper, *Art and Modern Copyright – The Contested Image*, Cambridge: Cambridge University Press 2018

Cornish 1998

W.R. Cornish, 'Experimental Use of Patented Inventions in European Community States', *IIC* 29 (1998), 735

Correa 2007

C.M. Correa, *Trade-Related Aspects of Intellectual Property Rights: A Commentary on the TRIPS Agreement,* Oxford: Oxford University Press 2007, 179-180

Cortés Martín 2004

J.M. Cortés Martín, 'The WTO TRIPS Agreement – The Battle Between the Old and the New World over the Protection of Geographical Indications', *Journal of World Intellectual Property* 7 (2004), 287**Craig 2011**

C.J. Craig, *Copyright, Communication and Culture – Towards a Relational Theory of Copyright Law*, Cheltenham: Edward Elgar 2011

Cramer 2015

F. Cramer, 'Geef iedereen het recht op parodie', *NRC Handelsblad*, posted 15 April 2015, available at: https://www.nrc.nl/nieuws/2015/04/15/geef-iedereen-het-recht-op-parodie-1484558-a197827 (last visited on 26 August 2020)

Cramer 2019

F. Cramer, 'Crapularity-Ästhetik. Dystopien zeitgenössischer Kunst – und das unterschiedliche Erbe von kritischer Theorie und Konzeptualismus in der Bildenden Kunst und Neuen Musik', *Neue Zeitschrift für Musik* 180, No. 4 (2019), 12

Curtin 2018

R.S. Curtin, 'Zombie Cinderella and the Undead Public Domain', *Tennessee Law Review* 85 (2018), 961

Dane 2018a

T.G. Dane, 'Part I: Are the Federal Circuit's Recent Section 101 Decisions a "Specific Improvement" in Patent Eligibility Law?', *Computer and Internet Lawyer* 35, No. 3 (2018), 1-16

Dane 2018b

T.G. Dane, 'Part II: Are the Federal Circuit's Recent Section 101 Decisions a "Specific Improvement" in Patent Eligibility Law?', *Computer and Internet Lawyer* 35, No. 4 (2018), 5-15

Davis 2015

J. Davis, 'Revisiting the Average Consumer: An Uncertain Presence in European Trade Mark Law', *Intellectual Property Quarterly* (2015), 15

Davison 2012

M. Davison, 'The Legitimacy of Plain Packaging Under International Intellectual Property Law: Why There is No Right to Use a Trademark Under Either the Paris

Convention or the TRIPS Agreement', in A. Mitchell, T. Voon, and J. Liberman (eds), *Public Health and Plain Packaging of Cigarettes: Legal Issues*, Cheltenham: Edward Elgar, 2012, 81

Davison/Di Giantomasso 2009

M. Davison/F. Di Giantomasso, 'Use as a Trade Mark: Avoiding Confusion When Considering Dilution', *EIPR* 2009, 443

Davison/Emerton 2014

M. Davison/P. Emerton, 'Rights, Privileges, Legitimate Interests, and Justifiability: Article 20 of TRIPS and Plain Packaging of Tobacco', *American University International Law Review* 29 (2014), 505

De Carvalho 2014

N.P. de Carvalho, *The TRIPS Regime of Trademarks and Designs*, 3rd ed., Austin/Boston/Chicago/New York: Kluwer Law International 2014

De Cock Buning/Van Lingen 2014

M. de Cock Buning/N. van Lingen, 'Tien jaar verder – De parodie-exceptie in de rechtspraktijk', *AMI* 38 (2014), 190

De Haas 2003

C. de Haas, 'La « contrefaçon » de la marque notoire en droit comparé américain, européen et français : une leçon américaine encore mal comprise', *Propriétés intellectuelles* 2003, 137

Derclaye 2018

E. Derclaye, *The Copyright/Design Interface: Past, Present and Future*, Cambridge: Cambridge University Press 2018

Derclaye/Leistner 2011

E. Derclaye/M. Leistner, *Intellectual Property Overlaps – A European Perspective*, Oxford and Portland (Oregon): Hart Publishing 2011

Denicola 1982

R.C. Denicola, 'Trademarks as Speech: Constitutional Implications of the Emerging Rationales for the Protection of Trade Symbols', *Wisconsin Law Review* 158 (1982), 158

Depoorter 2004

B. Depoorter, 'The Several Lives of Mickey Mouse: The Expanding Boundaries of Intellectual Property Law', *Virginia Journal of Law and Technology* 9 (2004), 1

Desbois 1978

H. Desbois, *Le droit d'auteur en France*, 2nd edn. – mise a jour 1973, Paris: Dalloz 1978

Devlin 2009

A. Devlin, 'Restricting Experimental Use', *Harvard Journal of Law & Public Policy* 32 (2009), 599

Dewey 1934

J. Dewey, *Art as Experience*, New York: Perigee 1934

Di Cataldo 2011

V. Di Cataldo, 'The Trade Mark with a Reputation in EU Law – Some Remarks on the Negative Condition "Without Due Cause"', *IIC* 42 (2011), 833

Dietz 1978

A. Dietz, *Das Urheberrecht in der Europäischen Gemeinschaft*, Baden-Baden: Nomos 1978

Dietz 1985

A. Dietz, 'Copyright Protection for Computer Programs: Trojan Horse or Stimulus for the Future Copyright System', *Archiv für Urheber-, Film- und Theaterrecht* 110 (1985), 57

Dietz 1995

A. Dietz, 'The Moral Right of the Author: Moral Rights and the Civil Law Countries', *Columbia-VLA Journal of Law & Arts* 19 (1995), 199

Dinwoodie 1999

G.B. Dinwoodie, 'The Death of Ontology: A Teleological Approach to Trademark Law', *Iowa Law Review* 84 (1999), 611

Dinwoodie 2002

G.B. Dinwoodie, 'Trademark and Copyright: Complements or Competitors?', in: J.C. Ginsburg/J.M. Besek (eds), *Adjuncts and Alternatives to Copyright – Proceedings of the ALAI Congress June 13-17, 2001*, New York: Kernochan Center for Law, Media and the Arts, Columbia University School of Law 2002, 498

Dinwoodie 2009

G.B. Dinwoodie, 'Lewis & Clark Law School Ninth Distinguished IP Lecture: Developing Defenses in Trademark Law', *Lewis and Clark Law Review* 13/1 (2009), 99

Dinwoodie 2020

G.B. Dinwoodie, 'Overlap and Redundancy in the Intellectual Property System – Trade Mark Always Loses', in: G.W. Austin/A.F. Christie/A.T. Kenyon/M. Richardson (eds), *Across Intellectual Property – Essays in Honour of Sam Ricketson*, Cambridge: Cambridge University Press 2020, 26

Dinwoodie 2021

G.B. Dinwoodie, '*Rogers* and the Structure of Trademark Defenses', in: B. Beebe/H. Sun (eds), *Charting Limitations on Trademark Rights*, Oxford: Oxford University Press 2021, forthcoming

Dinwoodie/Dreyfuss 2006

G.B. Dinwoodie/R. Cooper Dreyfuss, 'Patenting Science: Protecting the Domain of Accessible Knowledge', in: L.M.C.R. Guibault/P.B. Hugenholtz (eds), *The Future of the Public Domain – Identifying the Commons in Information Law*, The Hague/London/New York: Kluwer Law International 2006, 191

Dinwoodie/Gangjee 2016

G.B. Dinwoodie/D.S. Gangjee, 'The Image of the Consumer in European Trade Mark Law', in: D. Leczykiewicz/S. Weatherill (eds), *The Images of the Consumer in EU Law: Legislation, Free Movement and Competition Law*, Oxford and Portland, Oregon: Hart Publishing 2016, 339

Dinwoodie/Janis 2006

G.B. Dinwoodie/M.D. Janis, 'Dilution's (Still) Uncertain Future', *Michigan Law Review First Impressions* 105 (2006)

Dinwoodie/Janis 2007a

G.B. Dinwoodie/M.D. Janis, 'Confusion Over Use: Contextualism in Trademark Law', *Iowa Law Review* 92 (2007), 1597

Dinwoodie/Janis 2007b

G.B. Dinwoodie/M.D. Janis, 'Lessons from the Trademark Use Debate', *Iowa Law Review* 92 (2007), 1703

Dogan 2016

S.L. Dogan, 'Bullying and Opportunism in Trademark and Right-of-Publicity Law', *Boston University Law Review* 96 (2016), 1293

Dogan/Lemley 2004

S.L. Dogan/M.A. Lemley, 'Trademarks and Consumer Search Costs on the Internet', *Houston Law Review* 41 (2004), 777

Dogan/Lemley 2008a

S.L. Dogan/M.A. Lemley, 'The Trademark Use Requirement in Dilution Cases', *Santa Clara Computer & High Technology Law Journal* 24 (2008), 541

Dogan/Lemley 2008b

S.L. Dogan/M.A. Lemley, 'Grounding Trademark Law Through Trademark Use', *The Trademark Reporter* 98 (2008), 1345

Dogan/Lemley 2015

S.L. Dogan/M.A. Lemley, 'Parody as Brand', *The Trademark Reporter* 105 (2015), 1177

Dommering 2000

E. Dommering e.a., *Informatierecht – Fundamentele rechten voor de informatiesamenleving*, Amsterdam: Otto Cramwinckel 2000

Dougherty 2007

F.J. Dougherty, 'RIP, MIX and BURN: Bemerkungen zu aktuellen Entwicklungen im Bereich des digitalen Sampling nach US-amerikanischem und internationalen Recht', *GRUR Int.* 2007, 481

Dreier 2001a

T. Dreier, 'Balancing Proprietary and Public Domain Interests: Inside or Outside of Proprietary Rights?', in: R.C. Dreyfuss, D. Leenheer-Zimmerman, H. First (eds), *Expanding the Boundaries of Intellectual Property. Innovation Policy for the Knowledge Economy*, Oxford: Oxford University Press 2001, 295

Dreier 2001b

T. Dreier, 'Primär- und Folgemärkte', in: G. Schricker/T. Dreier/A. Kur (eds), *Geistiges Eigentum im Dienste der Innovation*, Baden-Baden: Nomos 2001, 51

Dreier/Schulze 2018

T. Dreier/G. Schulze, *Urheberrechtsgesetz – Kommentar*, 6th ed., Munich: C.H. Beck 2018

Dreyfuss 1990

R.C. Dreyfuss, 'Expressive Genericity: Trademarks as Language in the Pepsi Generation', *Notre Dame Law Review* 65 (1990), 397

Dreyfuss 1996

R.C. Dreyfuss, 'We Are Symbols and Inhabit Symbols, so Should we be Paying Rent? Deconstructing the Lanham Act and Rights of Publicity', *Columbia-VLA Journal of Law & Arts* 20 (1996), 123

Dreyfuss 2004

R.C. Dreyfuss, 'Protecting the Public Domain of Science: Has the Time for an Experimental Use Defense Arrived?', *Arizona Law Review* 46 (2004), 457

Dreyfuss 2008

R.C. Dreyfuss, 'Reconciling Trademark Rights and Expressive Values: How to Stop Worrying and Learn to Love Ambiguity', in: G.B. Dinwoodie/M.D. Janis (eds), *Trademark Law and Theory: A Handbook of Contemporary Research*, Cheltenham: Edward Elgar Publishing 2008, 261

Dreyfuss 2020

R.C. Dreyfuss, 'Cultural Heritage and the Public Domain: What the US's Myriad and Mayo can Teach Oslo's Angry Boy', in: N. Bruun/G.B. Dinwoodie/M. Levin/A. Ohly (eds), *Transition and Coherence in Intellectual Property Law: Essays in Honour of Annette Kur*, Cambridge: Cambridge University Press 2020, 322

Drexl 2004

J. Drexl, 'Intellectual Property and Antitrust Law: IMS Health and Trinko – Antitrust Placebo for Consumers Instead of Sound Economics in Refusal-To-Deal Cases', *IIC* 35 (2004), 788

Drexl 2008

J. Drexl (ed.), *Research Handbook on Intellectual Property and Competition Law*, Cheltenham: Edward Elgar 2008

Drexl 2013

J. Drexl, *Copyright, Competition and Development – Report by the Max Planck Institute for Intellectual Property and Competition Law*, Munich: Max Planck Institute 2013

Du Mont/Janis 2018

J.J. Du Mont/M.D. Janis, 'US Design Patent Law: A Historical Look at the Design Patent/Copyright Interface', in: E. Derclaye (ed.), *The Copyright/Design Interface: Past, Present and Future*, Cambridge: Cambridge University Press 2018, 341

Dusollier 2015

S. Dusollier, 'A Positive Status for the Public Domain', in: D. Beldiman (ed.), *Innovation, Competition and Collaboration*, Cheltenham: Edward Elgar 2015, 135

Dusollier 2018

S. Dusollier, 'Realigning Economic Rights with Exploitation of Works: The Control of Authors over the Circulation of Works in the Public Sphere', in: P.B. Hugenholtz (ed.), *Copyright Reconstructed – Rethinking Copyright's Economic Rights in a Time of Highly Dynamic Technological and Economic Change*, Alphen aan den Rijn: Kluwer Law International 2018, 163

Dworkin 1995

G. Dworkin, 'The Moral Right of the Author: Moral Rights and the Common Law Countries', *Columbia-VLA Journal of Law&Arts* 19 (1995), 229

Economides 1988

N. Economides, 'The Economics of Trademarks', *The Trademark Reporter* 78 (1988), 523

ECS 2017

European Copyright Society, 'Trade Mark Protection of Public Domain Works: A Comment on the Request for an Advisory Opinion of the EFTA Court: Case E-05/16: Norwegian Board of Appeal for Industrial Property Rights – Appeal from the Municipality of Oslo', *EIPR* 39 (2017), 457

ECS 2020

European Copyright Society, 'Comment of the European Copyright Society on the Implementation of Art.14 of the Directive (EU) 2019/790 on Copyright in the Digital Single Market', *Journal of Intellectual Property, Information Technology and E-Commerce Law* 2020, forthcoming, available at: https://europeancopyrightsociety.org/opinions/ (last visited on 14 October 2020)

Edelman 1994

B. Edelman, 'The Law's Eye: Nature and Copyright', in: B. Sherman/A. Strowel (eds), *Of Authors and Origins*, Oxford: Clarendon Press 1994, 79

Elkin-Koren 1996

N. Elkin-Koren, 'Cyberlaw and Social Change: A Democratic Approach to Copyright in Cyberspace', *Cardozo Arts & Entertainment Law Journal* 14 (1996), 215

Elkin-Koren 1997

N. Elkin-Koren, 'Copyright Policy and the Limits of Freedom of Contract', *Berkeley Technology Law Journal* 12 (1997), 93

Epstein/Kuhlik 2004

R.A. Epstein/B. Kuhlik, 'Is There a Biomedical Anticommons?', *Regulation* 27 (2004), 54

Evans 2010

G. Evans, 'The Comparative Advantages of Geographical Indications and Community Trade Marks for the Marketing of Agricultural Products in the European Union', *IIC* 41(2010), 645

Evans/Layne-Farrar 2004

D.S. Evans/A. Layne-Farrar, 'Software Patents and Open Source: The Battle Over Intellectual Property Rights', *Virginia Journal of Law and Technology* 9 (2004), 1

Farley 2015

C. Haight Farley, 'No Comment: Will *Cariou v. Prince* Alter Copyright Judges' Taste in Art?', *IP Theory* 5/1 (2015), 19

Farrar 2014

A.L. Farrar, 'Proactive or Reactive? An Empirical Assessment of IPR Policy Revisions in the Wake of Antitrust Actions', *The Antitrust Bulletin* 2014, 373

Fezer 2003

K.H. Fezer, 'Entwicklungslinien und Prinzipien des Markenrechts in Europa – Auf dem Weg zur Marke als einem immaterialgüterrechtlichen Kommunikationszeichen', *GRUR* 2003, 457

Fezer 2009

K.H. Fezer, *Markenrecht*, 4th ed., Munich: C.H. Beck 2009

Ficsor 2002

M. Ficsor, 'How Much of What? The Three-Step Test and Its Application in Two Recent WTO Dispute Settlement Cases', *RIDA* 192 (2002), 111

Firth/Gredley/Maniatis 2001

A. Firth/E. Gredley/S.M. Maniatis, 'Shapes as Trade Marks: Public Policy, Functional Considerations and Consumer Perception', *EIPR* 2001, 86

Fisher 1988

W.W. Fisher, 'Reconstructing the Fair Use Doctrine', *Harvard Law Review* 101 (1988), 1659

Förster 2008

A. Förster, *Fair Use*, Tübingen: Mohr Siebeck 2008

Frankel 2005

S.R. Frankel, 'Third-Party Trade Marks as a Violation of Indigenous Cultural Property – A New Statutory Safeguard', *Journal of World Intellectual Property* 2005, 83

Frankel 2008

S.R. Frankel, 'Trademarks and Traditional Knowledge and Cultural Intellectual Property', in: G.B. Dinwoodie/M.D. Janis (eds), *Trademark Law and Theory: a Handbook of Contemporary Research*, Cheltenham: Edward Elgar Publishing 2008, 433

Frankel 2012

S. Frankel, 'Branding Indigenous Peoples' Traditional Knowledge', in: A.T. Kenyon/M. Richardson/W.L. Ng-Loy (eds), *The Law of Reputation and Brands in the Asia Pacific*, Cambridge: Cambridge University Press 2012, 253

Frankel/Gervais 2013

S. Frankel/D. Gervais, 'Plain Packaging and the Interpretation of the TRIPS Agreement', *Vanderbilt Journal of Transnational Law* 46 (2013), 1149

Fromer 2010

J.C. Fromer, 'A Psychology of Intellectual Property', *Northwestern University Law Review* 104 (2010), 1441

Fromer 2012

J.C. Fromer, 'Expressive Incentives in Intellectual Property', *Virginia Law Review* 98 (2012), 1745

Fromer/McKenna 2018

J.C. Fromer/M.P. McKenna, 'Claiming Design', *University of Pennsylvania Law Review* 167 (2018), 123

Frosio 2014

G.F. Frosio, 'Rediscovering Cumulative Creativity From the Oral Formulaic Tradition to Digital Remix: Can I Get a Witness?', *John Marshall Review of Intellectual Property Law* 13 (2014), 341

Frosio 2018

G.F. Frosio, *Cumulative Creativity: From the Oral-Formulaic Tradition to Digital Remix*, Cheltenham: Edward Elgar 2018

Gangjee 2012

D.S. Gangjee, *Relocating the Law of Geographical Indications*, Cambridge: Cambridge University Press 2012

Gangjee 2013

D.S. Gangjee, 'Property in Brands: the Commodification of Conversation', in: H.R. Howe/J. Griffiths (eds), *Concepts of Property in Intellectual Property Law*, Cambridge: Cambridge University Press 2013, 29

Garde 2004

T.V. Garde, 'The Effect of Disparate Treatment of the Experimental Use Exemption on the Balancing Act of 35 U.S.C. § 104', *IIC* 35 (2004), 241

Gaubiac 1982

Y. Gaubiac, 'La théorie de l'unité de l'art', *RIDA* 111 (1982), 3

Geier 2015

A. Geier, *Schutzkumulationen*, Tübingen: Mohr Siebeck 2015

Geiger 2004a

C. Geiger, *Droit d'auteur et droit du public à l'information*, Paris: Litec 2004

Geiger 2004b

C. Geiger, 'Fundamental Rights, a Safeguard for the Coherence of Intellectual Property?', *IIC* 35 (2004), 268

Geiger 2006

C. Geiger, '"Constitutionalising" Intellectual Property Law? The Influence of Fundamental Rights on Intellectual Property in the European Union', *IIC* 37 (2006), 371

Geiger 2007

C. Geiger, 'Trade Marks and Freedom of Expression – the Proportionality of Criticism', *IIC* 38 (2007), 317

Geiger 2008a

C. Geiger, 'Flexibilising Copyright – Remedies to the Privatisation of Information by Copyright Law', *IIC* 39 (2008), 178

Geiger 2008b

C. Geiger, 'The Constitutional Dimension of Intellectual Property', in: P.L.C. Torremans (ed.), *Intellectual Property and Human Rights*, The Hague/London/New York: Kluwer Law International 2008, 101

Geiger 2009

C. Geiger, 'Intellectual Property Shall be Protected!? Article 17(2) of the Charter of Fundamental Rights of the European Union: A Mysterious Provision With an Unclear Scope', *EIPR* 31 (2009), 113

Geiger 2010a

C. Geiger, 'Marques et droits fondamentaux', in: C. Geiger/J. Schmidt-Szalewski (eds), *Les défis du droit des marques au 21e siècle/Challenges for Trademark Law in the 21st Century*, Paris: Litec 2010, 163

Geiger 2010b

C. Geiger, 'Promoting Creativity through Copyright Limitations, Reflections on the Concept of Exclusivity in Copyright Law', *Vanderbilt Journal of Entertainment and Technology Law* 12 (2010), 515

Geiger 2015

C. Geiger 2015, 354; (ed.), *Research Handbook on Human Rights and Intellectual Property*, Cheltenham: Edward Elgar 2015, 354

Geiger 2017

C. Geiger, 'Statutory Licenses as Enabler of Creative Uses', in: K.-C. Liu/R.M. Hilty (eds), *Remuneration of Copyright Owners – Regulatory Challenges of New Business Models*, Berlin: Springer 2017, 305

Geiger 2018a

C. Geiger, '"Fair Use" Through Fundamental Rights in Europe – When Freedom of Artistic Expression Allows Creative Appropriations and Opens Up Statutory Copyright Limitations', *Center for International Intellectual Property Studies Research Paper Series,* paper no. 2018-09, Strasbourg: CEIPI 2018

Geiger 2018b

C. Geiger, 'Freedom of Artistic Creativity and Copyright Law: A Compatible Combination?', *U.C. Irvine Law Review* 8 (2018), 413

Geiger/Gervais/Senftleben 2014

C. Geiger/D. Gervais/M.R.F. Senftleben, 'The Three-Step Test Revisited: How to Use the Test's Flexibility in National Copyright Law', *American University International Law Review* 29 (2014), 581

Geiger/Izyumenko 2014

C. Geiger/E. Izyumenko, 'Copyright on the Human Rights' Trial: Redefining the Boundaries of Exclusivity Through Freedom of Expression', *IIC* 45 (2014), 316

Geiger/Izyumenko 2016

C. Geiger/E. Izyumenko, 'The Role of Human Rights in Copyright Enforcement Online: Elaborating a Legal Framework for Website Blocking', *American University International Law Review* 32 (2016), 43

Geiger/Izyumenko 2019

C. Geiger/E. Izyumenko, 'Freedom of Expression as an External Limitation to Copyright Law in the EU: The Advocate General of the CJEU Shows the Way', *EIPR* 41 (2019), 131

Geiger/Izyumenko 2020

C. Geiger/E. Izyumenko, 'The Constitutionalization of Intellectual Property Law in the EU and the Funke Medien, Pelham and Spiegel Online Decisions of the CJEU: Progress, but Still Some Way to Go!', *IIC* 51 (2020), 282

Geiger/Machado Pontes 2017

C. Geiger/L. Machado Pontes, *Trade Mark Registration, Public Policy, Morality and Fundamental Rights*, Centre for International Intellectual Property Studies Research Paper No. 2017-01, Strasbourg: CEIPI 2017

Geller 1994

P.E. Geller, 'Must Copyright Be For Ever Caught Between Marketplace and Authorship Norms?', in: B. Sherman/A. Strowel (eds), *Of Authors and Origins*, Oxford: Clarendon Press 1994, 159

Geller 2010

P.E. Geller, 'A German Approach to Fair Use: Test Cases for TRIPS Criteria for Copyright Limitations?', *Journal of the Copyright Society of the U.S.A.* 57 (2010), 901

Gerhardt 2010

D.R. Gerhardt, 'Consumer Investment in Trademarks', *North Carolina Law Review* 88 (2010), 101

Gervais 2019

D. Gervais, *The Law of Human Progress*, Amsterdam: deLex 2019

Ghidini 2018

G. Ghidini, *Rethinking Intellectual Property – Balancing Conflicts of Interest in the Constitutional Paradigm*, Cheltenham: Edward Elgar 2018

Ghidini/Arezzo 2005

G. Ghidini/E. Arezzo, 'Patent and Copyright Paradigms vis-à-vis Derivative Innovation: The Case of Computer Programs', *IIC* 36 (2005), 166

Gibson 2007

J. Gibson, 'Risk Aversion and Rights Accretion in Intellectual Property Law', *Yale Law Journal* 116 (2007), 882

Ginsburg 1994

J.C. Ginsburg, 'A Tale of Two Copyrights: Literary Property in Revolutionary France and America', in: B. Sherman/A. Strowel (eds), *Of Authors and Origins*, Oxford: Clarendon Press 1994, 131

Ginsburg 1995

J.C. Ginsburg, 'Putting Cars on the "Information Superhighway": Authors, Exploiters, and Copyright in Cyberspace', *Columbia Law Review* 95 (1995), 1466

Ginsburg 1997

J.C. Ginsburg, 'Authors and Users in Copyright', *Journal of the Copyright Society of the USA* 45 (1997), 1

Ginsburg 2001

J.C. Ginsburg, 'Toward Supranational Copyright Law? The WTO Panel Decision and the "Three-Step Test" for Copyright Exceptions', *RIDA* 2001, 13

Ginsburg 2008

J.C. Ginsburg, 'Of Mutant Copyrights, Mangled Trademarks, and Barbie's Beneficence: the Influence of Copyright on Trademark Law', in: G.B. Dinwoodie/M.D. Janis (eds), *Trademark Law and Theory: A Handbook of Contemporary Research*, Cheltenham: Edward Elgar 2008, 481

Ginsburg 2016

J.C. Ginsburg, 'Licensing Commercial Value: from Copyright to Trademarks and Back', in: I. Calboli/J. de Werra (eds), *The Law and Practice of Trademark Transactions – A Global and Local Outlook*, Cheltenham: Edward Elgar 2016, 53

Ginsburg 2018a

J.C. Ginsburg, '"Courts Have Twisted Themselves into Knots" (and the Twisted Knots Remain to Untangle): US Copyright Protection for Applied Art after *Star Athletica*', in: E. Derclaye (ed.), *The Copyright/Design Interface: Past, Present and Future*, Cambridge: Cambridge University Press 2018, 297

Ginsburg 2018b

J.C Ginsburg, 'Intellectual Property As Seen by Barbie and Mickey: The Reciprocal Relationship of Copyright and Trademark Law', *Journal of the Copyright Society of the U.S.A.* 65 (2018), 245

Goebel 2004

B. Goebel, 'Geographical Indications and Trademarks – The Road from Doha', *The Trademark Reporter* 93 (2004), 964

Götting 2001

H.-P. Götting, 'Persönlichkeitsmerkmale von verstorbenen Personen der Zeitgeschichte als Marke', *GRUR* 2001, 615

Van Gompel 2007

S. van Gompel, 'Unlocking the Potential of Pre-Existing Content: How to Address the Issue of Orphan Works in Europe?', *IIC* 38 (2007), 669

Van Gompel 2011

S. van Gompel, *Formalities in Copyright Law – An Analysis of Their History, Rationales and Possible Future*, The Hague/London/New York: Kluwer Law International 2011

Van Gompel 2017

S. van Gompel, 'Niet zomaar een slapstick: Charly & Chaplin en het verval van auteursrecht op modellen', *AMI* 2017, 69

Van Gompel 2019

S. van Gompel, 'Smaak, auteursrecht en objectafbakening: over perceptie en bepaalbaarheid', *AMI* 2019, 9

Gordon 1982

W.J. Gordon, 'Fair Use as Market Failure: A Structural and Economic Analysis of the Betamax Case and its Predecessors', *Columbia Law Review* 82 (1982), 1600

Gordon 1993

W.J. Gordon, 'A Property Right in Self-Expression: Equality and Individualism in the Natural Law of Intellectual Property', *Yale Law Journal* 102 (1993), 1533

Grazioli 2005

A. Grazioli, 'OMC – La protection des indications géographiques et des marques', *Zeitschrift für Immaterialgüter-, Informations- und Wettbewerbsrecht* 2005, 902

Greenburg 1992

L.A. Greenberg, 'The Art of Appropriation: Puppies, Piracy and Post-Modernism', *Cardozo Arts and Entertainment Law Journal* 11 (1992), 1

Gulasekaram 2005

P. Gulasekaram, 'Policing the Border Between Trademarks and Free Speech: Protecting Unauthorized Trademark Use in Expressive Works', *Washington Law Review* 80 (2005), 887

Greener 2015

J. Greener, 'If You Give a Mouse a Trademark: Disney's Monopoly on Trademarks in the Entertainment Industry', *Wake Forest Journal of Business and Intellectual Property Law* 15 (2015), 598

A. Griffiths 2008

A. Griffiths, 'A Law-and-Economic Perspective on Trade Marks', in: L. Bently, J. Davis/J.C. Ginsburg (eds), *Trade Marks and Brands—An Interdisciplinary Critique*, Cambridge: Cambridge University Press 2008, 241

A. Griffiths 2012

A. Griffiths, 'Trade Marks and Responsible Capitalism', *IIC* 43 (2012), 798

A. Griffiths 2013

A. Griffiths, 'Quality in European Trade Mark Law', *Northwestern Journal of Technology and Intellectual Property* 11 (2013), 621

J. Griffiths 2015

J. Griffiths, '"On the Back of a Cigarette Packet"—Standardised Packaging Legislation and the Tobacco Industry's Fundamental Right to (Intellectual) Property', *Intellectual Property Quarterly* 2015, 343

J. Griffiths/Geiger/Senftleben/Xalabarder/Bently 2015

J. Griffiths/C. Geiger/M.R.F. Senftleben/R. Xalabarder/L. Bently, 'The European Copyright Society's 'Opinion on the Judgment of the CJEU in Case C-201/13 Deckmyn', *EIPR* 37, No. 3 (2015), 127

J. Griffiths/McDonagh 2013

J. Griffiths/L. McDonagh, 'Fundamental Rights and European IP Law – the Case of Art 17(2) of the EU Charter', in: C. Geiger (ed.), *Constructing European Intellectual Property Achievements and New Perspectives*, Cheltenham: Edward Elgar 2013, 75

Grosheide 1986

F.W. Grosheide, *Auteursrecht op Maat*, Deventer: Kluwer 1986

Grosheide 1994

F.W. Grosheide, 'Paradigms in Copyright Law', in: B. Sherman/A. Strowel (eds), *Of Authors and Origins*, Oxford: Clarendon Press 1994, 203

Grosheide 1996

F.W. Grosheide, 'De commercialisering van het auteureursrecht', *Informatierecht/AMI* 1996, 43

Grosheide 1998

F.W. Grosheide, 'Zwakke werken. Een pleidooi voor een merkenrechtelijke benadering van de inbreukvraag in het auteursrecht', in: D.W.F. Verkade/D.J.G. Visser (eds), *Intellectuele eigenaardigheden – Opstellen aangeboden aan mr Theo R. Bremer*, Kluwer: Deventer 1998, 121

Grosheide 2015

F.W. Grosheide, 'Heksentoer', *Intellectuele eigendom en reclamerecht* 2015, 207

Guibault 2002

L.M.C.R. Guibault, *Copyright Limitations and Contracts – An Analysis of the Contractual Overridability of Limitations on Copyright*, The Hague/London/Boston: Kluwer Law International 2002

Guibault 2010

L.M.C.R. Guibault, 'Why Cherry-Picking Never Leads to Harmonisation', *Journal of Intellectual Property, Information Technology and E-Commerce Law* 1 (2010), 55

Guibault/Hugenholtz 2006

L.M.C.R. Guibault/P.B. Hugenholtz (eds), *The Future of the Public Domain – Identifying the Commons in Information Law*, The Hague/London/New York: Kluwer Law International 2006

Hacker 2009

F. Hacker, 'Funktionenlehre und Benutzungsbegriff nach "L'Oréal"', *Markenrecht* 2009, 333

Hamme Ramirez 2004

H. Hamme Ramirez, 'Defending the Privatization of Research Tools: An Examination of the "Tragedy of the Anticommons" in Biotechnology Research and Development', *Emory Law Journal* 53 (2004), 359

Handler 2007

M. Handler, 'Trade Mark Dilution in Australia?', *EIPR* 29 (2007), 307

Handler 2012

M. Handler, 'Australia and the South Pacific', in: M.R.F. Senftleben (ed.), *Study on Misappropriation of Signs*, WIPO Document CDIP/9/INF/5, Geneva: World Intellectual Property Organization 2012, 232

Handler 2018

M. Handler, 'What Should Constitute Infringement of a Non-Traditional Mark? The Role of "Trademark Use"', in: I. Calboli/M.R.F. Senftleben (eds), *The Protection of Non-Traditional Trademarks – Critical Perspectives*, Oxford: Oxford University Press 2018, 165

Hauck 2005

F. Hauck, 'Aktuelle Entwicklungen bei der Eintragung von Farbmarken', *GRUR* 2005, 363

Heald/Erickson/Kretschmer 2015

P. Heald/K. Erickson/M. Kretschmer, 'The Valuation of Unprotected Works: A Case Study of Public Domain Images on Wikipedia', *Harvard Journal of Law and Technology* 29 (2015), 1

Heinemann 2006

A. Heinemann, 'Gefährdung von Rechten des geistigen Eigentums durch Kartellrecht? Der Fall "Microsoft" und die Rechtsprechung des EuGH', *GRUR* 2006, 705

Helfer 2007

L.R. Helfer, 'Toward a Human Rights Framework for Intellectual Property', *U.C. Davis Law Review* 40 (2007), 971

Heller/Eisenberg 1998

M.A. Heller/R.S. Eisenberg, 'Can Patents Deter Innovation? The Anticommons in Biomedical Research', *Science* 280 (1998), 698

Helm 1996

H. Helm, 'Die bösgläubige Markenanmeldung', *GRUR* 1996, 593

Henning-Bodewig 2005

F. Henning-Bodewig, 'A New Act Against Unfair Competition in Germany', *IIC* 36 (2005), 421

Henning-Bodewig 2008

F. Henning-Bodewig, 'Nicht markenmäßiger Gebrauch und Art. 5 Abs. 5 Markenrichtlinie', *GRUR Int.* 2008, 301

Heymann 2013

L.A. Heymann, 'Overlapping Intellectual Property Doctrines: Election of Rights versus Selection of Remedies', *Stanford Technology Law Review* 17 (2013), 239

Hick 2013

D.H. Hick, 'Appropriation and Transformation', *Fordham Intellectual Property, Media and Entertainment Law Journal* 23 (2013), 1155

Hieber 1996

T. Hieber, 'Die Zulässigkeit von Versuchen an patentierten Erfindungen nach § 11 Nr. 2 PatG 1981', *GRUR* 1996, 439

Hilty 2009a

R.M. Hilty, 'Renaissance der Zwangslizenzen im Urheberrecht? – Gedanken zu Ungereimtheiten auf der urheberrechtlichen Wertschöpfungskette', *GRUR* 2009, 633

Hilty 2009b

R.M. Hilty, 'Rationales for the Legal Protection of Intangible Goods and Cultural Heritage', *IIC* 40 (2009), 883

Hilty/Geiger 2005

R.M. Hilty/C. Geiger, 'Patenting Software? A Judicial and Socio-Economic Analysis', *IIC* 36 (2005), 615

Hilty/Senftleben 2015

R.M. Hilty/M.R.F. Senftleben, 'Rückschnitt durch Differenzierung? – Wege zur Reduktion dysfunktionaler Effekte des Urheberrechts auf Kreativ- und Angebotsmärkte', in: T. Dreier/R.M. Hilty (eds), *Vom Magnettonband zu Social Media – Festschrift 50 Jahre Urheberrechtsgesetz (UrhG)*, Munich: C.H. Beck 2015, 317-338

Höpperger/Senftleben 2007

M. Höpperger/M.R.F. Senftleben, 'Protection Against Unfair Competition at the International Level – The Paris Convention, the 1996 Model Provisions and the Current Work of the World Intellectual Property Organization', in: R.M. Hilty/F. Henning-Bodewig (eds), *Law Against Unfair Competition – Towards a New Paradigm in Europe?*, MPI Studies on Intellectual Property, Competition and Tax Law, Vol. 1, Berlin/Heidelberg: Springer 2007, 61

Hofrichter 2007

Jesse A. Hofrichter, 'Tool of the Trademark: Brand Criticism and Free Speech Problems with the Federal Dilution Revision Act of 2006', *Cardozo Law Review* 28 (2007), 1923

Holthuis/Van den Eijnde 2019

J.D. Holthuis/V.F.R.M. van den Eijnde, 'Artikel 14 DSM-richtlijn: Werken van beeldende kunst in het publieke domein', *AMI* 2019, 133

Hou 2012

L. Hou, 'The Essential Facilities Doctrine – What Was Wrong in Microsoft?', *IIC* 43 (2012), 251

Hovenkamp 2012

H.J. Hovenkamp, 'Markets in IP and Antitrust', *Georgetown Law Journal* 100 (2012), 2133

Hubmann 1988

H. Hubmann, 'Die Idee vom geistigen Eigentum, die Rechtsprechung des Bundesverfassungsgerichts und die Urheberrechtsnovelle von 1985', *Zeitschrift für Urheber- und Medienrecht* 1988, 4

Hudson 2017

E. Hudson, 'The Pastiche Exception in Copyright Law: a Case of Mashed-Up Drafting?', *Intellectual Property Quarterly* 2017, 346

Hudson Hick 2013

D. Hudson Hick, 'Appropriation and Transformation', *Fordham Intellectual Property and Entertainment Law Journal* 23 (2013), 1155

Hugenholtz 1989

P.B. Hugenholtz, *Auteursrecht op informatie*, Deventer: Kluwer 1989

Hugenholtz 2000a

P.B. Hugenholtz, 'Copyright, Contract and Code: What Will Remain of the Public Domain?', *Brooklyn Journal of International Law* 26 (2000), 77

Hugenholtz 2000b

P.B. Hugenholtz, 'Over cumulatie gesproken', *Bijblad bij de industriële eigendom* 2000, 240

Hugenholtz 2000c

P.B. Hugenholtz, 'De wettelijke beperkingen beperkt. De WTO geeft de driestappentoets tanden', *AMI* 2000, 197

Hugenholtz 2002

P.B. Hugenholtz, 'Copyright and Freedom of Expression in Europe', in: N. Elkin-Koren/N.W. Netanel (eds), *The Commodification of Information*, The Hague/London/Boston: Kluwer 2002, 239

Hugenholtz 2006

P.B. Hugenholtz, Case comment: Dutch Supreme Court, 16 June 2006, case LJN AU8940, Kecofa/Lancôme, *Ars Aequi* 2006, 822

Hugenholtz 2016

P.B. Hugenholtz, 'Flexible Copyright, Can EU Author's Right Accommodate Fair Use?', in: R. Okediji (ed.), *Copyright Law in an Age of Limitations and Exceptions*, Cambridge: Cambridge University Press 2016, 242

Hugenholtz/Senftleben 2011

P.B. Hugenholtz/M.R.F. Senftleben, *Fair Use in Europe. In Search of Flexibilities*, Amsterdam: Institute for Information Law/VU Centre for Law and Governance 2011

Hughes 1999

J. Hughes, '"Recoding" Intellectual Property and Overlooked Audience Interests', *Texas Law Review* 77 (1999), 923

Hughes 2015

J. Hughes, 'Cognitive and Aesthetic Functionality in Trademark Law', *Cardozo Law Review* 36 (2015), 1227

Jacques 2016

S. Jacques, 'A Parody Exception : Why Trade Mark Owners Should Get the Joke', *EIPR* 38 (2016), 471

Jacques 2019

S. Jacques, *The Parody Exception in Copyright Law*, Oxford: Oxford University Press 2019

Jaszi 2009

P. Jaszi, 'Is There Such A Thing As Postmodern Copyright?', *Tulane Journal of Technology and Intellectual Property* 12 (2009), 105

Jurt 2008

J. Jurt, *Bourdieu*, Stuttgart: Reclam 2008

Jongsma 2019

D.J.W. Jongsma, *Creating EU Copyright Law – Striking a Fair Balance*, Helsinki: Hanken School of Economics 2019

Kabel/Quaedvlieg 2012

J.J.C. Kabel/A.A. Quaedvlieg, 'Moral Rights', in: P.B. Hugenholtz/A.A. Quaedvlieg/ D.J.G. Visser (eds), *A Century of Dutch Copyright Law – Auteurswet 1912-2012*, Amstelveen: deLex 2012, 307

Kehrli 1989

T. Kehrli, *Der urheberrechtliche Werkbegriff im Bereich der bildenden Kunst*, Bern: Stämpfli 1989

Keim 2009

R. Keim, *Der markenrechtliche Tatbestand der Verwechslungsgefahr*, Baden-Baden: Nomos 2009

Keller 2019

P. Keller, 'Over artikel 14 DSM-richtlijn: Das Kunstwerk im Zeitalter seiner digitalen Reproduzierbarkeit', *AMI* 2019, 172

Kirchhof 1988

P. Kirchhof, *Der Gesetzgebungsauftrag zum Schutz des geistigen Eigentums gegenüber modernen Vervielfältigungstechniken*, Heidelberg: R. v. Decker & C.F. Müller 1988

Klamer 1996

A. Klamer, 'Introduction to the Conversation', in: A. Klamer (ed.), *The Value of Culture – On the Relationship Between Economics and Arts*, Amsterdam: Amsterdam University Press 1996, 7

Klinkert/Schwab 1999

F. Klinkert/F. Schwab, 'Markenrechtlicher Raubbau an gemeinfreien Werken – ein richtungsweisendes "Machtwort" durch den Mona Lisa-Beschluss des Bundespatentgerichts?', *GRUR* 101 (1999), 1067

Knaak/Kur/von Mühlendahl 2011

R. Knaak/A. Kur/A. von Mühlendahl, *Study on the Functioning of the European Trade Mark System, Max Planck Institute for Intellectual Property & Competition Law Research Paper No. 12-13*, Munich: Max Planck Institute 2011, available at http://ec.europa.eu/ internal_market/indprop/tm/index_en.htm

Knaak 2015

R. Knaak, 'Geographical Indications and Their Relationship with Trade Marks in EU Law', *IIC* 46 (2015)

Köklü/Nérisson 2016

K. Köklü/S. Nérisson, 'How Public Is the Public Domain? The Perpetual Protection of Inventions, Designs and Works by Trademarks', in: H. Ullrich/R.M. Hilty/M. Lamping/J. Drexl (eds), *TRIPS plus 20 – From Trade Rules to Market Principles*, Berlin/Heidelberg: Springer 2016, 561

Koschtial 2005

U. Koschtial, 'Design Law: Individual Character, Visibility and Functionality', *IIC* 36 (2005), 297

Koselleck 1985

R. Koselleck, *Futures Past. On the Semantics of Historical Time*, translated by K. Tribe, Cambridge, MA: MIT Press 1985 (originally published in German: *Vergangene Zukunft. Zur Semantik geschichtlicher Zeiten*, Frankfurt/Main: Suhrkamp 1979)

Kozinski 1993

A. Kozinski, 'Trademarks Unplugged', *New York University Law Review* 68 (1993), 960

Kreile 1993

R. Kreile, 'Die Sozialbindung des geistigen Eigentums', in: P. Badura/R. Scholz, *Festschrift für Peter Lerche zum 65. Geburtstag*, München 1993, 251

Kummer 1968

M. Kummer, *Das urheberrechtlich schützbare Werk*, Bern: Stämpfli 1968

Kunz-Hallstein 2006

H.P. Kunz-Hallstein, 'Art. 6quinquies PVÜ – Grundlage einer einheitlichen Eintragungspraxis von Marken in der Gemeinschaft?', *Markenrecht* 2006, 487

Kur 1994

A. Kur, 'Formalschutz dreidimensionaler Marken – neue Aufgaben für die Markenabteilung des Deutschen Patentamts', in: Deutsches Patentamt, Deutsche Vereinigung für gewerblichen Rechtsschutz und Urheberrecht e.a. (eds), *Festschrift 100 Jahre Deutsches Marken-Amt*, München: Thomson Reuters 1994, 175

Kur 1996a

A. Kur, 'TRIPs and Design Protection', in: F.-K. Beier/G. Schricker (eds), *From GATT to TRIPs*, Weinheim/New York: VCH Publishers 1996, 151

Kur 1996b

A. Kur, 'The Right to Use One's Own Trade Mark: A Self-Evident Issue or a New Concept in German, European and International Trade Mark Law?', *EIPR* 16 (1996), 198

Kur 2000

A. Kur, 'The WIPO Recommendations for the Protection of Well-Known Marks', *IIC* 31 (2000), 824

Kur 2001

A. Kur, 'Funktionswandel von Schutzrechten: Ursachen und Konsequenzen der inhaltlichen Annäherung und Überlagerung von Schutzrechtstypen', in: G. Schricker/T.

Dreier/A. Kur (eds), *Geistiges Eigentum im Dienst der Innovation*, Baden-Baden: Nomos 2001, 23

Kur 2002

A. Kur, 'Does/Should Trademark Law Prohibit Conduct to which Copyright Exceptions Apply?', in: J.C. Ginsburg/J.M. Besek (eds), *Adjuncts and Alternatives to Copyright – Proceedings of the ALAI Congress June 13-17, 2001*, New York: Kernochan Center for Law, Media and the Arts, Columbia University School of Law 2002, 594

Kur 2004

A. Kur, 'Alles oder Nichts im Formmarkenschutz?', *GRUR Int.* 2004, 755

Kur 2008

A. Kur, 'Confusion over Use? – Die Benutzung "als Marke" im Lichte der EuGH-Rechtsprechung', *GRUR Int.* 2008, 1

Kur 2009

A. Kur, 'Of Oceans, Islands, and Inland Water – How Much Room for Exceptinos and Limitations Under the Three-Step Test?', *Richmond Journal of Global Law and Business* 8 (2009), 287

Kur 2011

A. Kur, *Too pretty to protect? Trade Mark Law and the Enigma of Aesthetic Functionality*, Max Planck Institute for Intellectual Property & Competition Law Research Paper No. 11-16, Munich: Max Planck Institute 2011

Kur 2014

A. Kur, 'Trademarks Function, Don't they?', *IIC* 45 (2014), 434

Kur 2017

A. Kur, 'Gemeinfreiheit und Markenschutz – Bemerkungen zur Entscheidung des EFTA-Gerichtshofs im Vigeland-Fall', *GRUR* 2017, 1082

Kur 2018

A. Kur, 'Yellow Dictionaries, Red Banking Services, Some Candies, and a Sitting Bunny: Protection of Color and Shape Marks from a German and European Perspective', in: I. Calboli/M.R.F. Senftleben (eds), *The Protection of Non-Traditional Trademarks – Critical Perspectives*, Oxford: Oxford University Press 2018, 89

Kur/Bently/Ohly 2009

A. Kur/L. Bently/A. Ohly, 'Sweet Smells and a Sour Taste – the ECJ's L'Oréal Decision', *Max Planck Institute for Intellectual Property, Competition and Tax Law Research*

Paper Series No. 09-12, Munich: Max Planck Institute 2009, online available at http://ssrn.com/abstract=1492032

Kur/Senftleben 2017

A. Kur/M.R.F. Senftleben, *European Trade Mark Law – A Commentary*, Oxford: Oxford University Press 2017

Kurtz 1986

L.A. Kurtz, 'The Independent Legal Lives of Fictional Characters', *Wisconsin Law Review* 1986 (1986), 429

Ladas 1975

S.P. Ladas, *Patents, Trademarks, and Related Rights – National and International Protection*, Vol. II, Cambridge, Massachusetts: Harvard University Press 1975

Lamping 2015

M. Lamping, 'Refusal to Licence as an Abuse of Market Dominance – From Commercial Solvents to Microsoft', in: R.M. Hilty/K.-C. Liu (eds), *Compulsory Licensing – Practical Experiences and Ways Forward*, Berlin/Heidelberg: Springer 2015, 121

Landes 2000

W.M. Landes, 'Copyright, Borrowed Images, and Appropriation Art: An Economic Approach', *George Mason Law Review* 9 (2000), 1

Landes/Posner 1988

W.M. Landes/R.A. Posner, 'The Economics of Trademark Law', *The Trademark Reporter* 78 (1988), 267

Landes/Posner 1989

W.M. Landes/R.A. Posner, 'An Economic Analysis of Copyright Law', *Journal of Legal Studies* 18 (1989), 325

Landes/Posner 2003a

W.M. Landes/R.A. Posner, *The Economic Structure of Intellectual Property Law*, Harvard: Harvard University Press 2003

Landes/Posner 2003b

W.M. Landes/R.A. Posner, 'Indefinitely Renewable Copyright', *University of Chicago Law Review* 70 (2003), 471

Lange 1981

D. Lange, 'Recognizing the Public Domain', *Law and Contemporary Problems* 44 (1981), 147

Lange 2003

D. Lange, 'Reimagining the Public Domain', *Law and Contemporary Problems* 66 (2003), 463

Van Leeuwen 2013

R. van Leeuwen, 'Sherrie Levine: Re-photographed Photographs of Reproductions of Photographs', in: *Fans in a Flashbulb*, International Center of Photography, posted on 29 October 2013, available at https://fansinaflashbulb.wordpress.com/2013/10/29/sherrie-levine-re-photographed-photographs-of-reproductions-of-photographs/ (last visited on 14 October 2020)

Lehmann 1986

M. Lehmann, 'Die wettbewerbswidrige Ausnutzung und Beeinträchtigung des guten Rufs bekannter Marken, Namen und Herkunftsangaben—Die Rechtslage in der Bundesrepublik Deutschland', *GRUR Int.* 1986, 6

Leistner 2008

M. Leistner, 'Computerimplementierte Erfindungen im System des "Geistigen Eigentums"', in: O. Depenheuer/K.N. Peifer (eds), *Geistiges Eigentum: Schutzrecht oder Ausbeutungstitel*, Berlin/Heidelberg: Springer 2008, 187

Leistner 2011

M. Leistner, 'The German Federal Supreme Court's Judgment on Google's Image Search – A Topical Example of the "Limitations" of the European Approach to Exceptions and Limitations', *IIC* 42 (2011), 417

Leistner 2016

M. Leistner, 'Die "Metall auf Metall"-Entscheidung des BVerfG – Oder: Warum das Urheberrecht in Karlsruhe in guten Händen ist', *GRUR* 2016, 772

Lemley 1997

M.A. Lemley, 'The Economics of Improvement in Intellectual Property Law', *Texas Law Review* 75 (1997), 989

Lemley 1999

M.A. Lemley, 'The Modern Lanham Act and the Death of Common Sense', *Yale Law Journal* 108 (1999), 1687

Lemley/McKenna 2010

M.A. Lemley/M.P. McKenna, 'Irrelevant Confusion', *Stanford Law Review* 62 (2010), 413

Lemley/McKenna 2012

M.A. Lemley/M.P. McKenna, 'Is Pepsi Really a Good Substitute for Coke? Market Definition in Antitrust and IP', *Georgetown Law Journal* 100 (2012), 2055

Lerach 2018

M. Lerach, '"Der neue Stein des Schwans" – Markenschutz für Sehenswürdigkeiten', *GRUR – Praxis im Immaterialgüter und Wettbewerbsrecht* 2018, 461

Lessig 2004

L. Lessig, *Free Culture: How Big Media Uses Technology and the Law to Lock Down Culture and Control Creativity*, New York: Penguin Press 2004

Leval 1990

P.N. Leval, 'Toward a Fair Use Standard', *Harvard Law Review* 103 (1990), 1105

Leval 2004

P.N. Leval, 'Trademark: Champion of Free Speech', *Columbia Journal of Law and the Arts* 27 (2004), 187

Levy 2006

R.S. Levy, 'The Lego Case: The Supreme Court of Canada Makes it Harder to Protect Product Shapes as Trademarks', *The Trademark Reporter* 96 (2006), 596

Lewalter/Schrader 2005

I. Lewalter/P.T. Schrader, 'Die Fühlmarke', *GRUR* 2005, 476

Li 2019

Y. Li, 'The Current Dilemma and Future of Software Patenting', *IIC* 50 (2019), 823-859

Litman 1990

J. Litman, 'The Public Domain', *Emory Law Journal* 39 (1990), 965

Litman 1997

J. Litman, 'Reforming Information Law in Copyright's Image', *University of Dayton Law Review* 22 (1997), 588

Litman 1999

J. Litman, 'Breakfast with Batman: The Public Interest in the Advertising Age', *Yale Law Journal* 108 (1999), 1717

Liu 2013

J.P. Liu, 'The New Public Domain', *University of Illinois Law Review* 2013 (2013), 1395

Locke 1698

J. Locke, *Two Treatises of Government*, 3rd ed., London: Awnsham and John Churchill 1698

Loughlan 2000

P.L. Loughlan, 'Protecting Culturally Significant Uses of Trade Marks (Without a First Amendment)', *EIPR* 22 (2000), 328

Lucas/Ginsburg 2016

A. Lucas/J.C. Ginsburg, 'Copyright, Freedom of Expression and Free Access to Information (Comparative Study of American and European Law)', *RIDA* 249 (2016), 5

Luhmann 1984

N. Luhmann, *Soziale Systeme: Grundriß einer allgemeinen Theorie*, Frankfurt/Main: Suhrkamp 1984

Lunney 1999

G.S. Lunney, Jr, 'Trademark Monopolies', *Emory Law Journal* 48 (1999), 367

Lunney 2018

G.S. Lunney, Jr, *Copyright's Excess – Money and Music in the US Recording Industry*, Cambridge: Cambridge University Press 2018

Macciacchini 2000

S. Macciacchini, *Urheberrecht und Meinungsfreiheit*, Bern: Stämpfli 2000

Macfarlane/Pallotta 2006

R.H.C. MacFarlanc/C.M. Pallotta, 'Kirkbi Ag and Lego Canada Inc v. Ritvik Holdings Inc.: A Review of the Canadian Decisions', *The Trademark Reporter* 96 (2006), 575

Machnicka 2012

A. Machnicka, 'The Perfume Industry and Intellectual Property Law in the Jurisprudence of the Court of Justice of the European Union and of National Courts', *IIC* 43 (2012), 123

Maggiolino 2011

M.T. Maggiolino, *Intellectual Property and Antitrust: A Comparative Economic Analysis of US and EU Law*, Cheltenham: Edward Elgar 2011

Maier/Mattson 2001

G.J. Maier/R.C. Mattson, 'State Street Bank ist kein Ausreißer: Die Geschichte der Softwarepatentierung im US-amerikanischen Recht', *GRUR Int.* 2001, 677

Maniatis/Kamperman Sanders 1997

S. Maniatis/A. Kamperman Sanders, 'A Quixotic Raid Against the Tobacco Mill', *EIPR* 19 (1997), 237

Marceau 2002

G. Marceau, 'WTO Dispute Settlement and Human Rights', *European Journal of International Law* 13 (2002), 753

Margoni 2014

T. Margoni, *The Digitization of Cultural Heritage: Originality, Derivative Works and (Non) Original Photographs*, Amsterdam: Institute for Information Law 2014

McCarthy 2004

J.T. McCarthy, 'Dilution of a Trademark: European and United States Law Compared', *The Trademark Reporter* 94 (2004), 1163

McGeveran 2008

W. McGeveran, 'Four Free Speech Goals for Trademark Law', *Fordham Intellectual Property, Media and Entertainment Law Journal* 18 (2008), 1205

McGeveran 2015

W. McGeveran, 'The Imaginary Trademark Parody Crisis (and the Real One)', *Washington Law Review* 90 (2015), 713

McGuire 2011

M.-R. McGuire, 'Kumulation und Doppelschutz – Ursachen und Folgen des Schutzes einer Leistung durch mehrere Schutzrechte', *GRUR* 2011, 767

McKenna 2007

M.P. McKenna, 'The Normative Foundations of Trademark Law', *Notre Dame Law Review* 82 (2007), 1839

McKenna 2009a

M.P. McKenna, 'An Alternate Approach to Channeling?', *William and Mary Law Review* 51 (2009), 873

McKenna 2009b

M.P. McKenna, 'Trademark Use and the Problem of Source', *University of Illinois Law Review* 2009 (2009), 773

McKenna 2011

M.P. McKenna, '(Dys)Functionality', *Houston Law Review* 48 (2011), 823

Mende/Isaac 2012

C.S. Mende/B. Isaac, 'When Copyright and Trademark Rights Overlap', in: N. Wilkof/S. Basheer (eds), *Overlapping Intellectual Property Rights*, Oxford: Oxford University Press 2012, 137

Merges 2004

R.P. Merges, 'A New Dynamism in the Public Domain', *University of Chicago Law Review* 71 (2004), 183

Merwe 2000

A. Van der Merwe, 'Experimental Use and Submission of Data for Regulatory Approval', *IIC* 31 (2000), 380

Metzger 2000

A. Metzger, 'Germania 3 Gespenster am toten Mann oder Welchen Zweck darf ein Zitat gemäß § 51 Nr. 2 UrhG verfolgen?', *Zeitschrift für Urheber- und Medienrecht* 2000, 924

Metzger 2020

A. Metzger, 'Copyright and Patents on Software: the UPC's Answer to an Old Problem of Intellectual Property Overlaps', in: N. Bruun/G.B. Dinwoodie/M. Levin/A. Ohly (eds), *Transition and Coherence in Intellectual Property Law: Essays in Honour of Annette Kur*, Cambridge: Cambridge University Press 2020, 382

Michelman 1967

F. I. Michelman, 'Property, Utility, and Fairness: Comments on the Ethical Foundations of "Just Compensation" Law', *Harvard Law Review* 80 (1967), 1165

Midlemiss/Warner 2009

S. Middlemiss/S. Warner, 'The Protection of Marks with a Reputation: Intel v CPM', *EIPR* 2009, 326

Moffat 2004

V.R. Moffat, 'Mutant Copyrights and Backdoor Patents: The Problem of Overlapping Intellectual Property Protection', *Berkeley Technology Law Journal* 19 (2004), 1473

Mohr 2004

J. Mohr, 'Unshackle Academia and Allow it to Exemplify the Purpose of Patent Law: "To Promote the Progress of Science and the Useful Arts"', *Marquette Law Review* 88 (2004), 671

Morcom 2009

C. Morcom, 'L'Oréal v Bellure – Who Has Won?', *EIPR* 2009, 627

Morgan 2004

O. Morgan, 'Protecting Indigenous Signs and Trade Marks – The New Zealand Experiment', *Intellectual Property Quarterly* 2004, 58

Morley 2015

J. Morley, 'The Unfettered Expansion of Appropriation Art Protection by the Fair Use Doctrine: Searching for Transformativeness in Cariou v. Prince and Beyond', *IDEA: The Intellectual Property Law Review* 55 (2015), 385

Morrison 2008

D.M. Morrison, 'Bridgeport Redux: Digital Sampling and Audience Recoding', *Fordham Intellectual Property, Media and Entertainment Law Journal* 19 (2008), 75

Moskin 2004

J. Moskin, 'Victoria's Big Secret: Wither Dilution Under the Federal Dilution Act', *The Trademark Reporter* 93 (2004), 842

Moskin 2005

J. Moskin, 'Frankenlaw: The Supreme Court's Fair and Balanced Look at Fair Use', *The Trademark Reporter* 95 (2005), 848

Mueller 2001

J.M. Mueller, 'No "Dilettante Affair": Rethinking the Experimental Use Exception to Patent Infringement for Biomedical Research Tools', *Washington Law Review* 76 (2001), 1

Mueller 2004

J.M. Mueller, 'The Evanescent Experimental Use Exemption From United States Patent Infringement Liability: Implications for University and Nonprofit Research and Development', *Baylor Law Review* 56 (2004), 917

Mues 1974

G.R. Mues, 'Dual Copyright and Design Patent Protection: Works of Art and Ornamental Designs', *St. John's Law Review* 49 (1974), 543

Nasser 2009

M. Nasser, 'Trade Marks and Freedom of Expression', *IIC* 40 (2009), 188

Netanel 1996

N.W. Netanel, 'Copyright and a Democratic Civil Society', *Yale Law Journal* 106 (1996), 283

Netanel 2008

N.W. Netanel, *Copyright's Paradox*, New York: Oxford University Press 2008

Ng-Loy 2018

W.L. Ng-Loy, 'Absolute Bans on the Registration of Product Shape Marks – A Breach of International Law?', in: I. Calboli/M.R.F. Senftleben (eds), *The Protection of Non-Traditional Trademarks – Critical Perspectives*, Oxford: Oxford University Press 2018, 147

Nimmer 2003

D. Nimmer, '"Fairest of Them All" and Other Fairy Tales of Fair Use', *Law and Contemporary Problems* 66 (2003), 263

Nordemann 1997

W. Nordemann, 'Mona Lisa als Marke', *Wettbewerb in Recht und Praxis* 1997, 389

O'Connor 2004

B. O'Connor, 'The Legal Protection of Geographical Indications', *Intellectual Property Quarterly* 2004, 35

Van Oerle/Hagemans 2000

R.C.K. van Oerle/N. Hagemans, 'Tekeningen en Modellen', in: L. Wichers Hoeth/C. Gielen/N. Hagemans (eds), *Kort begrip van het intellectuele eigendomsrecht*, 8th ed., Zwolle: W.E.J. Tjeenk Willink 2000

Oguamanam 2004

C. Oguamanam, 'Localizing Intellectual Property in the Globalization Epoch: The Integration of Indigenous Knowledge', *Indiana Journal of Global Legal Studies* 11 (2004), 135

Ohly 2004

A. Ohly, 'Das neue UWG – Mehr Freiheit für den Wettbewerb?', *GRUR* 2004, 889

Ohly 2008

A. Ohly, 'Von einem Indianerhäuptling, einer Himmelsscheibe, einer Jeans und dem Lächeln der Mona Lisa – Überlegungen zum Verhältnis zwischen Urheber- und Kennzeichenrecht', in: L. Pahlow/J. Eisfeld (eds), *Grundlagen und Grundfragen des Geistigen Eigentums, Festgabe für Diethelm Klippel zum 65. Geburtstag*, Tübingen: Mohr Siebeck 2008, 203

Ohly 2019

A. Ohly, 'Schutz von Kulturgütern durch das Markenrecht?', in: F. Hacker/F. Thiering (eds), *Festschrift für Paul Ströbele zum 75. Geburtstag*, Cologne: Carl Heymanns 2019, 325

Oliver 2002

J. Oliver, 'Copyright in the WTO: The Panel Decision on the Three-Step Test', *Columbia Journal of Law & the Arts* 25 (2002), 119

O'Rourke 2000

M.A. O'Rourke, 'Toward a Doctrine of Fair Use in Patent Law', *Columbia Law Review* 100 (2000), 1177

Osborne 2013

P. Osborne, *Anywhere or Not at All – Philosophy of Contemporary Art*, London/New York: Verso 2013

Osei-Tutu 2017

J.J. Osei-Tutu, 'Harmonizing Cultural IP Across Borders: Fashionable Bags & Ghanaian Adinkra Symbols', *Akron Law Review* 51 (2017), 1051

Osenberg 1996

R. Osenberg, 'Markenschutz für urheberrechtlich gemeinfreie Werkteile', *GRUR* 98 (1996), 101

Owens 2005

J.L. Owens, '"Not Quite Dead Yet": The Near Fatal Wounding of the Experimental Use Exception and its Impact on Public Universities', *Journal of Telecommunication and High Tech Law* 3 (2005), 453

Pacek 2009

G. Pacek, 'Marks as Imitations of State Emblems "From a Heraldic Point of View"', *Journal of Intellectual Property Law & Practice* 2009, 673

Pagenberg 2004

J. Pagenberg, 'Trade Dress and the Three-Dimensional Marks – The Neglected Children of Trademark Law?', *IIC* 35 (2004), 831

Pager 2011

S.A. Pager, 'Beyond Culture vs. Commerce: Decentralizing Cultural Protection to Promote Diversity Through Trade', *Northwestern Journal of International Law and Business* 31 (2011), 63

Parchomovsky/Siegelman 2002

G. Parchomovsky/P. Siegelman, 'Towards an Integrated Theory of Intellectual Property', *Vanderbilt Law Review* 88 (2002), 1455

Pessach 2003

G. Pessach, 'Copyright Law as a Silencing Restriction on Noninfringing Materials: Unveiling the Scope of Copyright's Diversity Externalities', *Southern California Law Review* 76 (2003), 1067

Pessers 2016

L.W.P. Pessers, *The Inventiveness Requirement in Patent Law – An Exploration of Its Foundations and Functioning*, Alphen aan den Rijn: Kluwer Law International 2016

Peukert 2012

A. Peukert, *Die Gemeinfreiheit*, Tübingen: Mohr Siebeck 2012

Peukert 2016

Peukert, 'Vom Warenzeichen zum Markeneigentum. Ein polanyischer Erklärungsversuch', in: W. Büscher/J. Glöckner/A. Nordemann/C. Osterrieth/R. Rengier (eds),

Marktkommunikation zwischen Geistigem Eigentum und Verbraucherschutz. Festschrift für Karl-Heinz Fezer zum 70. Geburtstag, Munich: C.H. Beck 2016, 405

Peukert 2019

A. Peukert, 'Fictitious Commodities: A Theory of Intellectual Property Inspired by Karl Polanyi's Great Transformation', *Fordham Intellectual Property, Media and Entertainment Law Journal* 29 (2019), 1151

Pflüger 2011

M. Pflüger, 'PC, Article 6quinquies', in: T. Cottier/P. Véron (eds), *Concise International and European IP Law*, 2nd ed, Alphen aan den Rijn: Kluwer Law International 2011, 235

Phillips 2005

J. Phillips, 'Trade Mark Law and the Need to Keep Free – Intellectual Property Monopolies Have Their Limits', *IIC* 36 (2005), 389

Phillips/Simon Fhima 2004

J. Phillips/I. Simon Fhima, 'No Marks for Hitler. A Radical Reappraisal of Trade Mark Use and Political Sensitivity', *EIPR* 2004, 327

Pinckaers 2013

J.C.S. Pinckaers, Case comment: Dutch Supreme Court, 29 March 2013, case LJN BY8661, Broeren/Duijsens, *AMI* 2013, 114

Podszun 2010

R. Podszun, 'Lizenzverweigerung – Ernstfall im Verhältnis von Kartell- und Immaterialgüterrecht', in: P. Matousek/E. Müller/T. Thanner (eds), *Jahrbuch Kartell- und Wettbewerbsrecht*, Wien/Graz: Neuer Wissenschaftlicher Verlag 2010, 57

Podszun 2016

R. Podszun, 'Postmoderne Kreativität im Konflikt mit dem Urheberrechtsgesetz und die Annäherung an "fair use"', *Zeitschrift für Urheber- und Medienrecht* 2016, 606

Podszun 2017

R. Podszun, 'SEP Litigation and Huawei: Negotiations in the Shadow of Competition Law', *The Antitrust Bulletin* 62 (2017), 786

Podszun 2019

R. Podszun, 'Standard Essential Patents and Antitrust Law in the Age of Standardisation and the Internet of Things: Shifting Paradigms', *IIC* 50 (2019), 720

Pötzlberger 2018

Florian Pötzlberger, 'Pastiche 2.0: Remixing im Lichte des Unionsrechts', *GRUR* 2018, 675

Pollaud-Dulian 2001

F. Pollaud-Dulian 2001, 'Marques de renommée – Histoire de la dénaturation d'un concept', *Propriétés intellectuelles* 2001, 43

Poort/Theeuwes 2010

J.P. Poort/J.J.M. Theeuwes, 'Prova d'Orchestra – Een economische analyse van het voorontwerp Auteurscontractenrecht', *AMI* 2010, 137

Posner 2005

R.A. Posner, 'Intellectual Property: The Law and Economics Approach', *Journal of Economic Perspectives* 19 (2005), 57

Pulsinelli 2006

G. Pulsinelli, 'Share and Share Alike: Increasing Access to Government-Funded Inventions Under the Bayh-Dole Act', *Minnisota Journal of Law, Science and Technology* 7 (2006), 393

Quaedvlieg 1987

A.A. Quaedvlieg, *Auteursrecht op techniek – De auteursrechtelijke bescherming van het technisch aspect van industriële vormgeving en computerprogrammatuur*, Zwolle: W.E.J. Tjeenk Willink 1987

Quaedvlieg 1998

A.A. Quaedvlieg, 'Three Times a Hybrid – Typecasting Hybrids Between Copyright and Industrial Property', in: J.J.C. Kabel/G.J.H.M. Mom (eds), *Intellectual Property and Information Law – Essays in Honour of Herman Cohen Jehoram*, Den Haag/London/Boston: Kluwer 1998, 47

Quaedvlieg 2004

A.A. Quaedvlieg, 'Concurrence and Convergence in Industrial Design: Three-Dimensional Shapes Excluded by Trade Mark Law', in: W. Grosheide/J. Brinkhof (eds), *Intellectual Property Law: Articles on Crossing Borders Between Traditional and Actual*, Antwerpen: Intersentia 2004, 23

Quaedvlieg 2006

A.A. Quaedvlieg, 'Overlap/Relationships Between Copyright and Other Intellectual Property Rights', in: E. Derclaye (ed.), *Research Handbook on the Future of EU Copyright*, Cheltenham: Edward Elgar 2006, 479

Quaedvlieg 2007

A.A. Quaedvlieg, 'Verwaterd of verward, een kwestie van bekendheid?', in: D.J.G. Visser/D.W.F. Verkade (eds), *Een eigen, oorspronkelijk karakter – Opstellen aangeboden aan prof. mr. Jaap H. Spoor*, Amsterdam: DeLex 2007, 275

Quaedvlieg 2009a

A.A Quaedvlieg, 'INTEL en verwatering: Economisch gedrag en juridisch bewijs', *Bijblad bij de industriële eigendom* 2009, 253

Quaedvlieg 2009b

A.A. Quaedvlieg, 'Herkomst- en goodwillinbreuk in het merkenrecht na INTEL en l'Oréal', *Ars Aequi* 2009, 799

Quaedvlieg 2013

A.A. Quaedvlieg, 'De techniek, het Hof en de duivel – De technische uitsluiting bij merken, modellen en de slaafse nabootsingsleer', *Berichten industriële eigendom* 2013, 231

Quanjel-Schreurs 2005

R.A.M. Quanjel-Schreurs, 'Dastar Corp. v. Twentieth Century Fox – Een Amerikaanse uitspraak over een poging tot verkapte verlenging van het auteursrecht met behulp van merkenrecht', *Bijblad industriële eigendom* 73 (2005), 133

Quanjel-Schreurs 2007

R.A.M. Quanjel-Schreurs, 'Enkele procesrechtelijke aspecten van cumulatie van auteurs- en merkenrecht, naar aanleiding van het Benetton/G-Star-arrest', *AMI* 2007, 76

Ramsey 2003

L.P. Ramsey, 'Descriptive Trademarks and the First Amendment', *Tennessee Law Review* 70 (2003), 1095

Ramsey 2010a

L.P. Ramsey, 'Free Speech and International Obligations to Protect Trademarks', *Yale Journal of International Law* 35 (2010), 405

Ramsey 2010b

L.P Ramsey, 'Brandjacking on Social Networks: Trademark Infringement by Impersonation of Markholders', *Buffalo Law Review* 58 (2010), 851

Ramsey 2018

L.P. Ramsey, 'Free Speech Challenges to Trademark Law after Matal v. Tam', *Houston Law Review* 56 (2018), 401

Ramsey/Schovsbo 2013

L.P. Ramsey/J. Schovsbo, 'Mechanisms for Limiting Trade Mark Rights to Further Competition and Free Speech', *IIC* 44 (2013), 671

Raue 2010

B. Raue, *Nachahmungsfreiheit nach Ablauf des Immaterialgüterrechtsschutzes?*, Göttingen: V&R unipress 2010

Reeskamp 2010

P. Reeskamp, 'Dr No in Trade Mark Country: A Dutch Point of View', *Journal of Intellectual Property Law and Practice* 2010, 29

Richardson 2004

M. Richardson, 'Trade Marks and Language', *Sydney Law Review* 26 (2004), 193

Ricketson 1987

S. Ricketson, *The Berne Convention for the Protection of Literary and Artistic Works*, London: Kluwer 1987

Ricketson/Ginsburg 2006

S. Ricketson/J. Ginsburg, *International Copyright and Neighbouring Rights: the Berne Convention and Beyond*, 2nd ed., Oxford: Oxford University Press 2006

Ronga 1966

G. Ronga, 'Der Schutz von Kennzeichen zwischenstaatlicher Organisationen nach der Pariser Verbandsübereinkunft', *GRUR Int.* 1966, 148

Rosati 2018

E. Rosati, 'Not Sufficiently "Transformative" Appropriation of a Photograph Held Infringing by French Court', *Journal of Intellectual Property Law and Practice* 13 (2018), 525

Rosenblatt 2015

E.L. Rosenblatt, 'The Adventure of the Shrinking Public Domain', *University of Colorado Law Review* 86 (2015), 561

Rubenfeld 2002

J. Rubenfeld, 'The Freedom of the Imagination: Copyright's Constitutionality', *Yale Law Journal* 112 (2002), 1

Ruess 2018

P. Ruess, 'Anmerkung zu EuGH, 6. September 2018, Rechtssache C-488/16 P, Bundesverband Souvenir – Geschenke – Ehrenpreise („Neuschwanstein")', *GRUR* 2018, 1150

Ruijsenaars 1997

H.E. Ruijsenaars, *Character Merchandising – eine rechtsvergleichende Untersuchung zum Schutz der Vermarktung fiktiver Figuren*, Leiden/Munich 1997

Sag 2012

M. Sag, 'Predicting Fair Use', *Ohio State Law Journal* 73 (2012), 47

Sakulin 2010

W. Sakulin, *Trademark Protection and Freedom of Expression – An Inquiry into the Conflict between Trademark Rights and Freedom of Expression under European Law*, The Hague/London/New York: Kluwer Law International 2010

Salzberger 2006

E.M. Salzberger, 'Economic Analysis of the Public Domain', in: L.M.C.R. Guibault/P.B. Hugenholtz (eds), *The Future of the Public Domain – Identifying the Commons in Information Law*, The Hague/London/New York: Kluwer Law International 2006, 27

Sambuc 1997

T. Sambuc, 'Das Freihaltebedürfnis an beschreibenden Angaben und der Ware selbst nach dem Markengesetz', *GRUR* 1997, 403

Samuelson 2006a

P. Samuelson, 'Enriching Discourse on Public Domains', *Duke Law Journal* 55 (2006), 101

Samuelson 2006b

P. Samuelson, 'Challenges in Mapping the Public Domain', in: L.M.C.R. Guibault/P.B. Hugenholtz (eds), *The Future of the Public Domain – Identifying the Commons in Information Law*, The Hague/London/New York: Kluwer Law International 2006, 7

Samuelson 2009

P. Samuelson, 'Unbundling Fair Uses', *Fordham Law Review* 77 (2009), 2537

Samuelson 2017

P. Samuelson, 'Strategies for Discerning the Boundaries of Copyright and Patent Protections', *Notre Dame Law Review* 92 (2017), 1493

Samuelson 2019

P. Samuelson, 'Staking the Boundaries of Software Copyrights in the Shadow of Patents', *Florida Law Review* 71 (2019), 243

Schechter 1927

F.I. Schechter, 'The Rational Basis of Trademark Protection', *Harvard Law Review* 40 (1927), 813

Schiller 1794-1795

F. Schiller, *Über die ästhetische Erziehung des Menschen*, edited by K.L. Berghahn, Stuttgart: Reclam 2000

Schippers 2014

B.H.M. Schippers, 'Het chilling effect van Kraftwerk I/II op sound sampling: pleidooi voor zelfregulering ter bevordering van samplegebruik', *AMI* 2014, 105

Schovsbo 2018

J. Schovsbo, '"Mark My Words" – Trademarks and Fundamental Rights in the EU', *UC Irvine Law Review* 8 (2018), 555

Schroeder 2008

J.E. Schroeder, 'Brand Culture: Trade marks, Marketing and Consumption', in: L. Bently, J. Davis/J.C. Ginsburg (eds), *Trade Marks and Brands – An Interdisciplinary Critique*, Cambridge: Cambridge University Press 2008, 161

Schultz/Urban 2012

J. Schultz/J.M. Urban, 'Protecting Open Innovation: The Defensive Patent License as a New Approach to Patent Threats, Transaction Costs, and Tactical Disarmament', *Harvard Journal of Law and Technology* 26 (2012), 1

Schulze 1983

G. Schulze, *Die kleine Münze und ihre Abgrenzungsproblematik bei den Werkarten des Urbeberrechts*, Freiburg: Schriftenreihe Archiv für Urheber-, Film- und Theaterrecht, no. 66, 1983

Scott/Oliver/Ley-Pineda 2008

D. Scott/A. Oliver/M. Ley-Pineda, 'Trade Marks as Property: a Philosophical Perspective', in: L. Bently, J. Davis/J.C. Ginsburg (eds), *Trade Marks and Brands – An Interdisciplinary Critique*, Cambridge: Cambridge University Press 2008, 285

Seifert 2000

F. Seifert, 'Markenschutz und urheberrechtliche Gemeinfreiheit', *Wettbewerb in Recht und Praxis* 2000, 1014

Seltzer 1978

L.E. Seltzer, *Exemptions and Fair Use in Copyright: The Exclusive Rights Tensions in the 1976 Copyright Act*, Cambridge (Massachusetts)/London: Harvard University Press 1978

Senftleben 2004

M.R.F. Senftleben, *Copyright, Limitations and the Three-Step Test – An Analysis of the Three-Step Test in International and EC Copyright Law*, The Hague/London/New York: Kluwer Law International 2004

Senftleben 2006

M.R.F. Senftleben, 'Towards a Horizontal Standard for Limiting Intellectual Property Rights? – WTO Panel Reports Shed Light on the Three-Step Test in Copyright Law and Related Tests in Patent and Trademark Law', *IIC* 37 (2006), 407

Senftleben 2009a

M.R.F. Senftleben, 'The Trademark Tower of Babel – Dilution Concepts in International, US and EC Trademark Law', *IIC* 40 (2009), 45

Senftleben 2010a

M.R.F. Senftleben, 'Der kulturelle Imperativ des Urheberrechts', in: M. Weller/N.B. Kemle/T. Dreier (eds), *Kunst im Markt – Kunst im Recht*, Baden-Baden: Nomos 2010, 75

Senftleben 2010b

M.R.F. Senftleben, 'Bridging the Differences between Copyright's Legal Traditions – The Emerging EC Fair Use Doctrine', *Journal of the Copyright Society of the U.S.A.* 57, No. 3 (2010), 521

Senftleben 2010c

M.R.F. Senftleben, 'The International Three-Step Test – A Model Provision for EC Fair Use Legislation', *Journal of Intellectual Property, Information Technology and E-Commerce Law* 1 (2010), 67

Senftleben 2011a

M.R.F. Senftleben, 'Keyword Advertising in Europe – How the Internet Challenges Recent Expansions of EU Trademark Protection', *Connecticut Journal of International Law* 27 (2011), 39

Senftleben 2011b

M.R.F. Senftleben, 'Trade Mark Protection – A Black Hole in the Intellectual Property Galaxy?', *IIC* 42 (2011), 383

Senftleben 2011c

M.R.F. Senftleben, 'Overprotection and Protection Overlaps in Intellectual Property Law – the Need for Horizontal Fair Use Defences', in: Kur, A./Mizaras, V. (eds), *The Structure of Intellectual Property Law: Can One Size Fit All?*, Cheltenham: Edward Elgar 2011, 136

Senftleben 2012a

M.R.F. Senftleben, 'Quotations, Parody and Fair Use', in: P.B. Hugenholtz/A.A. Quaedvlieg/D.J.G. Visser (eds), *A Century of Dutch Copyright Law – Auteurswet 1912-2012*, Amstelveen: deLex 2012, 359

Senftleben 2012b

M.R.F. Senftleben (ed.), *Study on Misappropriation of Signs*, WIPO Document CDIP/9/INF/5, dated 14 March 2012, Geneva: World Intellectual Property Organization 2012, available at http://www.wipo.int/meetings/en/doc_details.jsp?doc_id=216882

Senftleben 2012b

M.R.F. Senftleben, 'Keyword Advertising in Europe – How the Internet Challenges Recent Expansions of EU Trademark Protection', *Connecticut Journal of International Law* 27 (2012), 39

Senftleben 2013a

M.R.F. Senftleben, 'Public Domain Preservation in EU Trademark Law – A Model for Other Regions?', *The Trademark Reporter* 103 (2013), 775

Senftleben 2013b

M.R.F. Senftleben, 'Adapting EU Trademark Law to New Technologies – Back to Basics?', in: C. Geiger (ed.), *Constructing European Intellectual Property*, Cheltenham: Edward Elgar 2013, 137

Senftleben 2013c

M.R.F. Senftleben, 'Trademark Law and the Public Domain', in: D. Beldiman (ed.), *Access to Information and Knowledge: 21st Century Challenges in Intellectual Property and Knowledge Governance*, Cheltenham: Edward Elgar 2013, 112

Senftleben 2013d

M.R.F. Senftleben, 'Comparative Approaches to Fair Use: An Important Impulse for Reforms in EU Copyright Law', in: G.B. Dinwoodie (ed.), *Methods and Perspectives in Intellectual Property*, Cheltenham: Edward Elgar 2013, 30

Senftleben 2014a

M.R.F. Senftleben, 'Function Theory and International Exhaustion: Why it is Wise to Confine the Double Identity Rule in EU Trade Mark Law to Cases Affecting the Origin Function', *EIPR* 2014, 518

Senftleben 2015

M.R.F. Senftleben, 'Free Signs and Free Use - How to Offer Room for Freedom of Expression within the Trademark System', in C. Geiger (ed.), *Research Handbook on Human Rights and Intellectual Property*, Cheltenham: Edward Elgar 2015, 354

Senftleben 2016

M.R.F. Senftleben, 'Trademark Transactions in EU Law: Refining the Approach to Selective Distribution Networks and National Unfair Competition Law', in: J. de Werra/I. Calboli (eds), *The Law and Practice of Trademark Transactions – A Global and Local Outlook*, Cheltenham: Edward Elgar 2016, 327

Senftleben 2017a

M.R.F. Senftleben, 'Copyright, Creators and Society's Need for Autonomous Art – The Blessing and Curse of Monetary Incentives', in: R. Giblin/K. Weatherall (eds), *What if We Could Reimagine Copyright?*, Canberra: ANU Press 2017, 25

Senftleben 2017b

M.R.F. Senftleben, '*Vigeland* and the Status of Cultural Concerns in Trade Mark Law – The EFTA Court Develops More Effective Tools for the Preservation of the Public Domain', *IIC* 48 (2017), 683

Senftleben 2017c

M.R.F. Senftleben, 'The Perfect Match – Civil Law Judges and Open-Ended Fair Use Provisions', *American University International Law Review* 33 (2017), 231

Senftleben 2017d

M.R.F. Senftleben, 'Impacts of Competition Law: Monolithic Copyright, Market Power and Market Definition', in: K.-C. Liu & R.M. Hilty (eds), *Remuneration of Copyright Owners – Regulatory Challenges of New Business Models,* Berlin/Heidelberg: Springer 2017, 257

Senftleben 2018

M.R.F. Senftleben, 'A Clash of Culture and Commerce: Non-Traditional Marks and the Impediment of Cyclic Cultural Innovation', in: I. Calboli/M.R.F. Senftleben (eds), *The Protection of Non-Traditional Marks: Critical Perspectives*, Oxford: Oxford University Press 2018, 309

Senftleben 2019

M.R.F. Senftleben, 'Bermuda Triangle: Licensing, Filtering and Privileging User-Generated Content Under the New Directive on Copyright in the Digital Single Market', *EIPR* 41 (2019), 480

Senftleben 2020

M.R.F. Senftleben, 'Signs Eligible for Trademark Protection – Dysfunctional Incentives and a Functionality Dilemma in the EU', in: I. Calboli/J.C. Ginsburg (eds), *Cambridge Handbook on International and Comparative Trademark Law*, Cambridge: Cambridge University Press 2020, 207

Senftleben/Anemaet 2013

M.R.F. Senftleben/L. Anemaet, 'Windsurfing Chiemsee revisited – Op weg naar een normatieve toets bij inburgering?', *Berichten industriële eigendom* 2013, 245

Senftleben/Bently/Dinwoodie et al. 2015

M.R.F. Senftleben/L. Bently/G. Dinwoodie/C. Geiger/J. Griffiths/A. Kur/A. Ohly/A. Peukert/M. Ricolfi/J. Schovsbo/K. Weckström/Ł. Żelechowski, 'The Recommendation on Measures to Safeguard Freedom of Expression and Undistorted Competition: Guiding Principles for the Further Development of EU Trade Mark Law', *EIPR* 37 (2015), 337

Sewell 2005

D.G. Sewell, 'Rescuing Science From the Courts: An Appeal for Amending the Patent Code to Protect Academic Research in the Wake of Madey vs. Duke University', *Georgetown Law Journal* 93 (2005), 759

Sherman 2007

D.B. Sherman, 'Cost and Resource Allocation Under the Orphan Works Act of 2006: Would the Act Reduce Transaction Costs, Allocate Orphan Works Efficiently, and

Serve the Goals of Copyright Law?', *Virginia Journal of Law & Technology* 12 (2007), 13

Sherman/Bently 1999

B. Sherman/L. Bently, *The Making of Modern Intellectual Property Law*, Cambridge: Cambridge University Press 1999

Shusterman 2000

R. Shusterman, *Pragmatist Aesthetics – Living Beauty, Rethinking Art*, 2nd ed., Lanham: Rowman and Littlefield 2000

Simon Fhima 2005

I. Simon Fhima, 'How Does "Essential Function" Doctrine Drive European Trade Mark Law?', *IIC* 36 (2005), 401

Simon Fhima 2006

I. Simon Fhima, 'Embellishment: Trademark Use Triumph or Decorative Disaster?', *EIPR* 2006, 321

Simon Fhima 2012

I. Simon Fhima, 'The Role of Legitimacy in Trade Mark Law', *Current Legal Problems* 65 (2012), 489

Simon Fhima 2013

I. Simon Fhima, 'Trade Marks and Free Speech', *IIC* 44 (2013), 293

Simon Fhima 2014

I. Simon Fhima, 'Trade Mark Law and Advertising Keywords', in: A. Savin and J. Trzaskowski (eds), *Research Handbook on EU Internet Law,* Cheltenham: Edward Elgar 2014, 143

Simon Fhima/Jacob 2014

I. Simon Fhima/R. Jacob, 'Unfair Advantage Law in the European Union', in: D. Bereskin (ed.), *International Trademark Dilution*, New York/Toronto: Thomson Reuters Westlaw 2014, 251

Spoor 1990

J.H. Spoor, *De gestage groei van merk, werk en uitvinding*, Zwolle: Tjeenk Willink 1990

Spoor 1999

J.H. Spoor, 'Beeldverhaal, Merk & Marketing – Over merkgebruik in stripverhalen', in: Beneluxvereniging voor Merken- en Modellenrecht (BMM) (ed.), *Bundel ter gelegenheid van het 25-jarig jubileum van de BMM*, The Hague: BMM 1999, 80

Spoor 2006

J.H. Spoor, Case comment: Dutch Supreme Court, 16 June 2006, case LJN AU8940, Kecofa/Lancôme, *NJ* 2006, no. 585

Spoor/Verkade/Visser 2019

J.H. Spoor/D.W.F. Verkade/D.J.G. Visser, *Auteursrecht – Auteursrecht, naburige rechten en databankenrecht*, 4th ed., Deventer: Kluwer 2019

Staten 2005

T.L. Staten, 'Geographical Indications Protection Under the TRIPS Agreement: Uniformity Not Extension', *Journal of the Patent and Trademark Office Society* 87 (2005), 221

Sterckx/Cockbain 2010

S. Sterckx/J. Cockbain, 'The Patentability of Computer Programs in Europe: An Improved Interpretation of Articles 52(2) and (3) of the European Patent Convention', *Journal of World Intellectual Property* 13 (2010), 366-402

Stieper 2012

M. Stieper, 'Geistiges Eigentum an Kulturgütern – Möglichkeiten und Grenzen der Remonopolisierung gemeinfreier Werke', *GRUR* 114 (2012), 1083

Strandburg 2004

K.J. Strandburg, 'What Does the Public Get? Experimental Use and the Patent Bargain', *Wisconsin Law Review* 2004 (2004), 81

Strandburg 2006

K.J. Strandburg, 'The Research Exemption to Patent Infringement: The Delicate Balance Between Current and Future Technical Progress', in: P.K. Yu (ed.), *Intellectual Property and Information Wealth*, Westport: Praeger Publishers 2006, 107

Stratton/Lue 2006

B.W. Stratton/H. Lue, 'Lego v. Mega Bloks in the Supreme Court of Canada: Ephemeral Rights in Toy Bricks', *The Trademark Reporter* 96 (2006), 587

Strasser 2000

M. Strasser, 'The Rational Basis of Trademark Protection Revisited: Putting the Dilution Doctrine into Context', *Fordham Intellectual Property, Media & Entertainment Law Journal* 10 (2000), 375

Strowel 1993

A. Strowel, *Droit d'auteur et Copyright*, Brussels: Bruylant 1993

Strowel 1994

A. Strowel, 'Droit d'auteur and Copyright: Between History and Nature', in: B. Sherman/A. Strowel (eds), *Of Authors and Origins*, Oxford: Clarendon Press 1994, 235

Strowel/Tulkens/Voorhoof 2006

A. Strowel/F. Tulkens/D. Voorhoof (eds), *Droit d'auteur et liberté d'expression*, Brussels: Editions Larcier 2006

Sun 2014

H. Sun, 'Reforming Anti-Dilution Protection in the Globalization of Luxury Brands', *Georgetown Journal of International Law* 45 (2014), 783

Swann 2013

J.B. Swann, 'The Evolution of Dilution in the United States from 1927 to 2013', *The Trademark Reporter* 103, No. 4 (2013), 721

Tan 2013

D. Tan, 'The Semiotics of Alpha Brands: Encoding/Decoding/Recoding/Transcoding of Louis Vuitton and Implications for Trademark Laws', *Cardozo Arts and Entertainment Law Journal* 32 (2013), 225

Taubman 2019

A. Taubman, 'New Dialogues, New Pathways: Reframing the Debate on Intellectual Property and Traditional Knowledge', *Washburn Law Journal* 58 (2019), 373

Timbers/Huston 2003

L. Timbers/J. Huston, 'The "Artistic Relevance Test" Just Became Relevant: the Increasing Strength of the First Amendment as a Defense to Trademark Infringement and Dilution', *The Trademark Reporter* 93 (2003), 1278

Torsen 2005

M. Torsen, 'Apples and Oranges (and Wine): Why the International Conversation Regarding Geographical Indications is at a Standstill', *Journal of the Patent and Trademark Office Society* 87 (2005), 31

Troller 1983

A. Troller, *Immaterialgüterrecht*, Vol. 1, 3rd ed., Basel/Frankfurt am Main: Helbing and Lichtenhahn 1983

Tsoutsanis 2005

A. Tsoutsanis, *Het merkdepot te kwader trouw*, Deventer: Kluwer 2005

Tushnet 2008

R. Tushnet, 'Gone in Sixty Milliseconds: Trademark Law and Cognitive Science', *Texas Law Review* 86 (2008), 507

Ubertazzi 2017

B. Ubertazzi, 'EU Geographical Indications and Intangible Cultural Heritage', *IIC* 48 (2017), 562

Ullmann 2003

E. Ullmann, 'Das Koordinatensystem des Rechts des unlauteren Wettbewerbs im Spannungsfeld von Europa und Deutschland', *GRUR* 2003, 817

Ullrich 2004, 401-430

H. Ullrich, 'Expansionist Intellectual Property Protection and Reductionist Competition Rules: A TRIPS Perspective', *Journal of International Economic Law* 7 (2004), 401

Ulmer 1980

E. Ulmer, *Urheber- und Verlagsrecht*, Berlin/Heidelberg/New York: Springer 1980

Vanovermeire 2009

V. Vanovermeire, 'Inschrijving als merk van een in het publiek domain gevallen werk', A. Cruquenaire/S. Dusollier (eds), *Le Cumul des droits intellectuels*, Larcier 2009, 177

Vaver 2011

D. Vaver, *Intellectual Property Law: Copyrights, Patents, Trademarks*, 2nd ed., Toronto: Irwin Law 2011

Verkade 1998

D.W.F. Verkade, 'The Cumulative Effect of Copyright Law and Trademark Law: Which Takes Precedence?', in: J.J.C. Kabel/G.J.H.M. Mom (eds), *Intellectual Property and Information Law – Essays in Honour of Herman Cohen Jehoram*, Den Haag/London/ Boston: Kluwer 1998, 69

Visser 2002

D.J.G. Visser, Case comment: Court of Appeals of Amsterdam, 26 juli 2001, ERB/ Beukenoord, *AMI* 2002, 15

Visser 2011

D.J.G. Visser, 'Darfurnica: modellenrecht versus kunstvrijheid', *Nederlands Juristenblad* 2011, 740

Voorhoof 2002

D. Voorhoof, 'Freedom of Expression, Parody, Copyright and Trademarks', in: J.C. Ginsburg/J.M. Besek (eds), *Adjuncts and Alternatives to Copyright – Proceedings of the ALAI Congress June 13-17, 2001*, New York: Kernochan Center for Law, Media and the Arts, Columbia University School of Law 2002, 636

Wallace/Euler 2020

A. Wallace/E. Euler, 'Revisiting Access to Cultural Heritage in the Public Domain: EU and International Developments', *IIC* 51 (2020), 823

Wandtke/Bullinger 1997

A. Wandtke/W. Bullinger, 'Die Marke als urheberrechtlich schutzfähiges Werk', *GRUR* 1997, 573

Weckström 2007

K. Weckström, 'The Lawfulness of Criticizing Big Business: Comparing Approaches to the Balancing of Societal Interests Behind Trademark Protection', *Lewis & Clark Law Review* 11 (2007), 671

Weinreb 1998

L.L. Weinreb, 'Copyright for Functional Expression', *Harvard Law Review* 111 (1998), 1150

Weyand/Haase 2005

J. Weyand/H. Haase, 'Patenting Computer Programs: New Challenges', *IIC* 36 (2005), 647

Wilf 1999

S. Wilf, 'Who Authors Trademarks?', *Cardozo Arts and Entertainment Law Journal* 17 (1999), 1

Wilson/Lack 2016

S. Wilson/J. Lack, *Tate Guide to Modern Art Terms*, updated and expanded edition, London: Tate Publishing 2016

WIPO 2005

World Intellectual Property Organization, *Article* 6ter *of the Paris Convention: Legal and Administrative Aspects*, Document SCT/15/3, dated 14 October 2005, WIPO: Geneva 2005

WIPO 2019

World Intellectual Property Organization, *The Protection of Traditional Cultural Expressions: Draft Articles*, Facilitators' Revision, dated 19 June 2019, WIPO: Geneva 2019, available at: https://www.wipo.int/meetings/en/doc_details.jsp?doc_id=439176 (last visited on 14 October 2020)

Van Woensel 2007

C. van Woensel, *Merk, god en verbod*, Amstelveen: deLex 2007

Van Woensel 2013

C. van Woensel, 'Anne Frank is van mij', *Ars Aequi* 2013, 372

Würtenberger 2002

G. Würtenberger, 'Risk of Confusion and Criteria to Determine the Same in European Community Trade Mark Law', *EIPR* 2002, 20

Yap 2009

P.J. Yap, 'Essential Function of a Trade Mark: From BMW to O2', *EIPR* 2009, 81

Yu 2007a

P.K. Yu, 'Reconceptualizing Intellectual Property Interests in a Human Rights Framework', *U.C. Davis Law Review* 40 (2007), 1039

Yu 2007b

P.K. Yu, 'Ten Common Questions About Intellectual Property and Human Rights', *Georgia State University Law Review* 23 (2007), 709

Yu 2009

P.K. Yu, 'The Objectives and Principles of the TRIPS Agreement', *Houston Law Review* 46 (2009), 979

Żelechowski 2018

Ł. Żelechowski, 'Invoking Freedom of Expression and Freedom of Competition in Trade Mark Infringement Disputes: Legal Mechanisms for Striking a Balance', *ERA Forum* 19 (2018), 115

Żelechowski 2020

Ł. Żelechowski, 'CJEU Rules on Absolute Ground Concerning Marks Contrary to Accepted Principles of Morality', *Journal of Intellectual Property Law and Practice* 15 (2020), 316

Zimmerman 2004

D.L. Zimmerman, 'Is There a Right to Have Something to Say? One View of the Public Domain', *Fordham Law Review* 73 (2004), 297

De Zwaan 2014

M.R. de Zwaan, 'De bevrijdende lach – Hoe het Europese Hof het keurslijf van het gesloten beperkingenstelsel minder laat knellen', *AMI* 38 (2014), 193

De Zwaan 2016

M.R. de Zwaan, 'De totaalindruk: onjuist maar niet onbruikbaar', *AMI* 2016, 113

Table of Cases

Australia

High Court of Australia

- 23 November 1961, The Shell Co. of Australia Ltd./Esso Standard Oil (Australia) Ltd., [1963] HCA 66; 109 CLR 407; 35 ALJR 355; (1962) ALR 304 (Kitto J.), **430**

Federal Court of Australia

- 5 August 1994, Musidor BV/Robert William Tansing (trading as Apple Music House), [1994] FCA 541; 52 FCR 363; 29 IPR 203, **452**
- 13 December 1994, Milpurrurru/Indofurn Pty Limited [1994] 30 IPR 209, **118**
- 3 September 1998, Bulun Bulun/R&T Textiles Pty Limited [1998] FCA 1082; 157 ALR 193; 41 IPR 513, **119**
- 30 June 2000, Koninklijke Philips Electronics NV/Remington Products Australia Pty Limited [2000] FCA 876; 100 FCR 90, **210, 216**
- 4 October 2005, Christodoulou/Disney Enterprises Inc., [2005] FCA 1401; 156 FCR 344; 66 IPR 595, **452, 453**
- 12 January 2009, Sebel Furniture Limited/Acoustic & Felts Pty Limited [2009] FCA 6; 80 IPR 244, **217**

Austria

Austrian Supreme Court (Oberster Gerichtshof)

See www.ogh.gv.at/entscheidungen/

- 13 July 2010, case 4 Ob 66/10z, 'Lieblingshauptfrau', **501**

Benelux

Benelux Court of Justice (Benelux Gerechtshof)

See www.courbeneluxhof.be/nl/arresten_lst.asp
- 1 March 1975, case A 74/1, Claeryn/Klarein, *NJ* 1975, no. 472, **228**
- 14 April 1989, case A 87/8, Superconfex/Burberrys ('Burberrys I'), *NJ* 1989, no. 834, **227, 228, 229, 237, 238**
- 16 December 1991, case A 90/4, Burberrys/Bossi ('Burberrys II'), *NJ* 1992, no. 596, **238**
- 14 October 2019, case A2018/1/8, Moët Hennessy/Cedric Art, *Berichten industriële eigendom* 2020, 25, **191, 203, 454, 468, 514, 521**

Dutch Supreme Court (Hoge Raad)

See www.rechtspraak.nl.
- 28 October 1948, Bureau I.E./Churchill's Cigars ('Winston Churchill'), *Bijblad bij de industriële eigendom* 1949, 24, **229, 338, 363**
- 29 December 1995, case LJN ZC1942, Decaux/Mediamax, *NJ* 1996, no. 546, **555**
- 16 April 1999, case LJN ZC2889, Bigott-Batco/Doucal, *NJ* 1999, no. 697, **252**
- 26 May 2000, case LJN AA5967, Cassina/Sedeti, *NJ* 2000, no. 671, **318**
- 29 November 2002, case LJN AE8456, 'Una Voce Particolare', *AMI* 2003, 21, **555**
- 8 September 2006, case LJN AV3384, Benetton/G-Star, *NJ* 2006, no. 492, **252**
- 3 April 2009, case LJN BH1225, Benetton/G-Star II, *NJ* 2010, no. 41, **228**
- 29 March 2013, case LJN BY8661, Broeren/Duijsens, *AMI* 2013, 108, **12, 27, 28, 89, 556**
- 12 April 2013, case LJN BY1532, Stokke/Fikszo, *NJ* 2013, no. 502, **555**
- 3 April 2015, ECLI:NL:HR:2015:841, GeenStijl Media/Sanoma, *NJ* 2015, no. 183, **495**

Court of Appeals of Amsterdam (Hof Amsterdam)

See www.rechtspraak.nl.
- 26 juli 2001, ERB/Beukenoord, *AMI* 2002, 12, **122, 152, 189, 426**
- 30 januari 2003, Van Toor/Phanta Vision, *AMI* 2003, 94, **123, 153**
- 6 November 2003, ECLI:NL:GHAMS:2003:AN7646, Rowling/Byblos, *Intellectuele eigendom en reclamerecht* 2004, 20, **121, 123, 176**
- 13 September 2011, ECLI:NL:GHAMS:2011:BS7825, Mercis and Bruna/Punt, *AMI* 2012, 28, **172, 178, 184, 191, 203, 431, 498**

Court of Appeals of Brussels (Hof van Beroep Brussel)

- 3 October 2013, case 2013/7132, Anne Frank Foundation/Benelux Office for Intellectual Property ('Het dagboek van Anne Frank'), **6, 106, 125, 256, 257, 258, 260, 261, 263, 276, 332, 350, 510**
- 3 October 2013, case 2013/7133, Anne Frank Foundation/Benelux Office for Intellectual Property ('Het Achterhuis'), **6, 106, 125, 256, 257, 258, 260, 261, 263, 276, 332, 350, 510**

European Union

Court of Justice of the European Union (CJEU), former European Court of Justice (ECJ)
See www.curia.eu.

General Court of the European Union (GCEU)

See www.curia.eu.

German Federal Court of Justice (Bundesgerichtshof)

See www.bundesgerichtshof.de.

German Federal Patent Court (Bundespatentgericht)

See www.bundespatentgericht.de

England and Wales Court of Appeal

See www.bailii.org

United States

U.S. Supreme Court

U.S. Courts of Appeal

U.S. District Courts

World Trade Organization

WTO Appellate Body

See www.wto.org

WTO Panel

See www.wto.org.

Index

INFORMATION LAW SERIES

1. Egbert J. Dommering & P. Bernt Hugenholtz, *Protecting Works of Fact: Copyright, Freedom of Expression and Information Law,* 1991 (ISBN 90-654-4567-6).
2. Willem F. Korthals Altes, Egbert J. Dommering, P. Bernt Hugenholtz & Jan J.C. Kabel, *Information Law Towards the 21st Century,* 1992 (ISBN 90-654-4627-3).
3. Jacqueline M.B. Seignette, *Challenges to the Creator Doctrine: Authorship, Copyright Ownership and the Exploitation of Creative Works in the Netherlands, Germany and The United States,* 1994 (ISBN 90-654-4876-4).
4. P. Bernt Hugenholtz, *The Future of Copyright in a Digital Environment, Proceedings of the Royal Academy Colloquium,* 1996 (ISBN 90-411-0267-1).
5. Julius C.S. Pinckaers, *From Privacy Toward a New Intellectual Property Right in Persona,* 1996 (ISBN 90-411-0355-4).
6. Jan J.C. Kabel & Gerard J.H.M. Mom, *Intellectual Property and Information Law: Essays in Honour of Herman Cohen Jehoram,* 1998 (ISBN 90-411-9702-8).
7. Ysolde Gendreau, Axel Nordemann & Rainer Oesch, *Copyright and Photographs: An International Survey,* 1999 (ISBN 90-411-9722-2).
8. P. Bernt Hugenholtz, *Copyright and Electronic Commerce: Legal Aspects of Electronic Copyright Management,* 2000 (ISBN 90-411-9785-0).
9. Lucie M.C.R. Guibault, *Copyright Limitations and Contracts: An Analysis of the Contractual Overridability of Limitations on Copyright,* 2002 (ISBN 90-411-9867-9).
10. Lee A. Bygrave, *Data Protection Law: Approaching its Rationale, Logic and Limits,* 2002 (ISBN 90-411-9870-9).
11. Niva Elkin-Koren & Neil Weinstock Netanel, *The Commodification of Information,* 2002 (ISBN 90-411-9876-8).
12. Mireille M.M. van Eechoud, *Choice of Law in Copyright and Related Rights: Alternatives to the Lex Protectionis,* 2003 (ISBN 90-411-2071-8).
13. Martin Senftleben, *Copyright, Limitations and the Three-Step Test: An Analysis of the Three-Step Test in International and EC Copyright Law,* 2004 (ISBN 90-411-2267-2).
14. Paul L.C. Torremans, *Copyright and Human Rights: Freedom of Expression – Intellectual Property – Privacy,* 2004 (ISBN 90-411-2278-8).
15. Natali Helberger, *Controlling Access to Content: Regulating Conditional Access in Digital Broadcasting,* 2005 (ISBN 90-411-2345-8).
16. Lucie M.C.R. Guibault & P. Bernt Hugenholtz, *The Future of the Public Domain: Identifying the Commons in Information Law,* 2006 (ISBN 978-90-411-2435-7).

17. Irini Katsirea, *Public Broadcasting and European Law: A Comparative Examination of Public Service Obligations in Six Member States,* 2008 (ISBN 978-90-411-2500-2).
18. Paul L.C. Torremans, *Intellectual Property and Human Rights: Enhanced Edition of Copyright and Human Rights,* 2008 (ISBN 978-90-411-2653-5).
19. Mireille van Eechoud, P. Bernt Hugenholtz, Stef van Gompel, Lucie Guibault & Natali Helberger, *Harmonizing European Copyright Law: The Challenges of Better Lawmaking,* 2009 (ISBN 978-90-411-3130-0).
20. Ashwin van Rooijen, *The Software Interface between Copyright and Competition Law: A Legal Analysis of Interoperability in Computer Programs,* 2010 (ISBN 978-90-411-3193-5).
21. Irini A. Stamatoudi, *Copyright Enforcement and the Internet,* 2010 (ISBN 978-90-411-3346-5).
22. Wolfgang Sakulin, *Trademark Protection and Freedom of Expression: An Inquiry into the Conflict between Trademark Rights and Freedom of Expression under European Law,* 2011 (ISBN 978-90-411-3415-8).
23. Stef van Gompel, *Formalities in Copyright Law: An Analysis of their History, Rationales and Possible Future,* 2011 (ISBN 978-90-411-3418-9).
24. Nadezhda Purtova, *Property Rights in Personal Data: A European Perspective,* 2012 (ISBN 978-90-411-3802-6).
25. Brad Sherman & Leanne Wiseman, *Copyright and the Challenge of the New,* 2012 (ISBN 978-90-411-3669-5).
26. Ewa Komorek, *Media Pluralism and European Law*, 2012 (ISBN 978-90-411-3894-1).
27. Joris van Hoboken, *Search Engine Freedom: On the Implications of the Right to Freedom of Expression for the Legal Governance of Web Search Engines,* 2012 (ISBN 978-90-411-4128-6).
28. Natali Helberger, Lucie Guibault, Marco Loos, Chantal Mak, Lodewijk Pessers & Bart van der Sloot, *Digital Consumers and the Law: Towards a Cohesive European Framework*, 2012 (ISBN 978-90-411-4049-4).
29. Tatiana-Eleni Synodinou, *Codification of European Copyright Law: Challenges and Perspectives,* 2012 (ISBN 978-90-411-4145-3).
30. Heather Ann Forrest, *Protection of Geographic Names in International Law and Domain Name System Policy*, Second Edition, 2017 (ISBN 978-90-411-8839-7).
31. Sari Depreeuw, *The Variable Scope of the Exclusive Economic Rights in Copyright*, 2014 (ISBN 978-90-411-4915-2).
32. Vikrant Narayan Vasudeva, *Open Source Software and Intellectual Property Rights*, 2014 (ISBN 978-90-411-5228-2).
33. Frederik J. Zuiderveen Borgesius, *Improving Privacy Protection in the Area of Behavioural Targeting*, 2015 (ISBN 978-90-411-5990-8).
34. Paul L.C. Torremans, *Intellectual Property Law and Human Rights*, Fourth Edition, 2020 (ISBN 978-94-035-1304-1).

35. Irini A. Stamatoudi, *New Developments in EU and International Copyright Law*, 2016 (ISBN 978-90-411-5991-5).
36. Lodewijk W.P. Pessers, *The Inventiveness Requirement in Patent Law: An Exploration of Its Foundations and Functioning*, 2016 (ISBN 978-90-411-6731-6).
37. Susy Frankel & Daniel Gervais, *The Internet and the Emerging Importance of New Forms of Intellectual Property*, 2016 (ISBN 978-90-411-6789-7).
38. Axel M. Arnbak, *Securing Private Communications: Protecting Private Communications Security in EU Law – Fundamental Rights, Functional Value Chains, and Market Incentives*, 2016 (ISBN 978-90-411-6737-8).
39. Christina Angelopoulos, *European Intermediary Liability in Copyright: A Tort-Based Analysis*, 2017 (ISBN 978-90-411-6835-1).
40. João Pedro Quintais, *Copyright in the Age of Online Access: Alternative Compensation Systems in EU Law*, 2017 (ISBN 978-90-411-8667-6).
41. P. Bernt Hugenholtz, *Copyright Reconstructed: Rethinking Copyright's Economic Rights in a Time of Highly Dynamic Technological and Economic Change*, 2018 (ISBN 978-90-411-9103-8).
42. Manon Oostveen, *Protecting Individuals Against the Negative Impact of Big Data: Potential and Limitations of the Privacy and Data Protection Law Approach*, 2018 (ISBN 978-94-035-0131-4).
43. Tatiana Eleni Synodinou (ed.), *Pluralism or Universalism in International Copyright Law*, 2019 (ISBN 978-94-035-0355-4).
44. Martin Senftleben, *The Copyright/Trademark Interface: How the Expansion of Trademark Protection Is Stifling Cultural Creativity*, 2021 (ISBN 978-94-035-2370-5).

www.ingramcontent.com/pod-product-compliance
Lightning Source LLC
Chambersburg PA
CBHW070250260926
51849CB00001BA/104
* 9 7 8 9 4 0 3 5 2 3 7 0 5 *